U.S. Presidential Candidates and the Elections

U.S. Presidential Candidates and the Elections

A Biographical and Historical Guide

JAMES T. HAVEL

VOLUME 2
THE ELECTIONS, 1789–1992

MACMILLAN LIBRARY REFERENCE USA
Simon & Schuster Macmillan
NEW YORK

Prentice Hall International
LONDON MEXICO CITY NEW DELHI SINGAPORE SYDNEY TORONTO

To Roberta,
Who brings grace and delight to my
life, and to Julie, Emily, Jay, and
Lianna, who together represent the
best legacy I have to offer the future.
They are the sum of my joy, a part of
my tears, most of my hopes, none of my
fears—but always the source and
recipients of all of my love.

Macmillan Library Reference USA
Simon & Schuster Macmillan
1633 Broadway
New York, NY 10019

Library of Congress Catalog Card Number: 96–12074

Printed in the United States of America

Printing Number

1 2 3 4 5 6 7 8 9 10

Library of Congress Cataloging-in-Publication Data

Havel, James T.
    U.S. presidential elections and the candidates : a biographical
and historical guide / James T. Havel.
    2 v.
    Contents: v. 1. The candidates--v. 2. The elections, 1789-1992.
    ISBN 0–02–864622–1 (v. 1)--ISBN 0–02–864623–1 (v. 2)
    1. Elections--United States --History.   2. Presidential candidates--
United States --Biography.   3. Presidents --Unites States --Election.
I. Title.
JK528.H38   1996
324.6'3'0973 --dc20

Ref. v. 2

This paper meets the requirements of ANSI/NISO Z39.48–1992 (Permanence of Paper).

CONTENTS

PREFACE

U.S. Presidential Candidates and the Elections: A Biographical and Historical Guide is the culmination of more than 30 years of work identifying and gathering data on the vast array of men and women who have sought to hold the highest office in the land. The guide grew out of the author's lifelong fascination with American presidential elections and particularly the role of third parties in our nation's electoral history.

As students of electoral politics know, there is a dearth of coverage of third party and less famous candidates in historical reference works, while biographical information on major contenders for the presidency abounds. Yet, third parties and their leaders often altered the political landscape significantly, out of all proportion to the number of votes they garnered. For example, the Prohibition Party was the first to suggest the direct election of United States Senators. Victoria Claflin Woodhull, the first woman to seek the presidency, ran on an obscure Equal Rights Party platform in 1872. And many of the innovations of the New Deal were articulated first in the platforms of the Socialist and Socialist Labor parties.

Quite apart from the substantive contributions of minor party candidates, the relatively unknown presidential contenders often added color, zest, and humor to our national election contests. People such as Lar Daly, in his unforgettable Uncle Sam suit; George Francis Train and his egocentric oratory; and Henry Krajewski, who strolled the campaign trail with a pig on a leash—all added to the quadrennial celebration of presidential election campaigns and our enjoyment of this unique theater of history. With the exception of a line or two in some election histories, however, these people and events are mere footnotes that have passed into oblivion.

The guide is divided into two volumes: *The Candidates* and *The Elections. Volume 1: The Candidates* is an alphabetically arranged biographical directory whose purpose is to preserve basic information on the lives of the great, the infamous, and the ludicrous who have sought to become president or vice president, without passing judgment on their aspirations or achievements. The casual reader or ardent scholar can find here a simple, unvarnished recitation of biographical details—often supplied by the candidates themselves through biographical questionnaires, but frequently obtained through consulting myriad resources and archival materials.

Volume 2 of this work, *The Elections, 1789–1992*, provides a brief but detailed summary of each presidential election, including information on the parties and their platforms, conventions, and primary and election results. A bibliography of key works consulted in the preparation of this work concludes this volume.

ACKNOWLEDGMENTS

In compiling the essential information about candidates and elections for this work, the author relied upon the kind assistance of candidates and their families, librarians, election officials, newspaper staff, and numerous other individuals. It would be an egregious error to fail to acknowledge with gratitude the time and energy they devoted to bringing this project to fruition. Similarly, the suggestions of the editors at Macmillan—particularly Catherine Carter, Sabrina Bowers, and Andy Ambraziejus, who assisted in the final preparation of the manuscript—helped improve the format of this work. Their valuable support is sincerely appreciated.

INTRODUCTION

The Declaration of Independence articulated a belief that "all men are created equal," but neither the Articles of Confederation nor the original federal Constitution fully embraced the concept. Even after adoption of the Bill of Rights, the newly independent American Republic still tolerated slavery and counted those in bondage as less than fully human. It permitted property and religious qualifications for suffrage and denied women the right to vote. Indeed, access to the ballot was reserved for the privileged few, and both the national presidency and the Senate were separated from the direct control of the people. The members of the U.S. Senate were elected by state legislatures and the presidency was determined by ballot of an electoral college.

Article II, Section 1, of the Constitution initially provided that the president and vice president would be chosen by presidential electors who would gather in their respective states' capitols on a common date—statutorily the first Monday after the second Wednesday in December. Electors were chosen in accordance with state law and equaled in number the congressional representation in the House of Representatives and Senate. Each elector was permitted to cast two votes for president, one of which had to be cast for someone outside the elector's state. The candidate with the highest number of votes would become president and the candidate with the second highest number of votes would become vice president. In the event of a tie or lack of a majority of electoral votes, the election was decided by the House of Representatives, with the Senate deciding when the election of a vice president was in doubt.

This scheme was based on the theory that the process would enable both the first and second choices of the nation to serve in executive office. Unfortunately, it did not anticipate the rise of the political factions or the divisive nature of personal ambition. From the start, however, broad philosophical differences between nationalists (i.e., the Federalists who supported a strong central government) and proponents of states' rights could be detected in informal legislative groups in Congress and among segments of the general public. Nascent political alliances were often ephemeral but developed greater stability with the passage of time.

As John Adams assumed the presidency, the inadequacies in the constitutional method of choosing the country's leaders were becoming apparent. Thomas Jefferson and Adams were rivals—the one an acknowledged leader of advocates for decentralization of power, the other a staunch Federalist. Yet Adams was yoked to Jefferson by a selection process that almost guaranteed a discordant administration. Jefferson had the second highest number of votes in the electoral college, so Adams was forced to tolerate his opponent as vice president in the Adams administration. While this unhappy situation was endured until the next presidential election in 1800, it highlighted the need for a constitutional amendment to avoid such an occurrence in the future.

By 1800, partisan cleavages were clearer than ever. Jefferson again challenged Adams for the presidency but this time the electors of the Democratic-Republicans (as Jefferson's followers were known) achieved a majority. They had their votes lined up and victory was assured, but they failed to recognize the possibility of a tie vote if each victorious elector cast his two votes for the same individuals as all other electors sharing a common partisan outlook. That is exactly what happened. Jefferson was running on a ticket with Aaron Burr, who was considered his vice-presidential running mate, even though he would actually obtain votes for president under the existing system. When the ballots of the electoral college were counted in January 1801, Jefferson and Burr tied and the election was thrown to the House of Representatives for resolution.

In the House, each state was accorded one vote, which was cast in favor of the candidate with the greatest support in that state's delegation. Personally ambitious, Burr sensed an opportunity to become president and began to lobby support among the members of the House.

While Jefferson was ultimately elected, the episode resulted in ratification of the Twelfth Amendment to the Constitution, which changed the method of voting in the electoral college. Under the amendment, which was ratified on June 15, 1804, electors were required to cast separate ballots for president and vice president, eliminating the possibility of repeating the fiasco of 1800.

The Twelfth Amendment fixed a flaw in the electoral college but it did not extend the franchise to those who were denied its exercise. Yet, while the fledgling Republic may not have been as broadly democratic as its aspirations, it did contain the seeds that would eventually flower into universal suffrage. The egalitarian notion expressed in the Declaration was left to unfold in an evolutionary course through other constitutional amendments, internal conflagration, and the gradual political maturation of the American people.

By the election of 1828, the loosely organized factions of the eighteenth century had taken on a more substantial form as political parties. The Federalists had given way to the Whigs, while Jefferson's Democratic-Republicans had shifted to a base among the "common man." The broad outlines of a two-party system were evident, although third parties like the Anti-Masons contributed creative new ideas such as platforms and nominating conventions to the political landscape. The convention system, in particular, increased public participation in the process of selecting a presidential candidate, although still retaining an indirect and representational flavor.

Initially, the major political parties nominated candidates in a variety of ways. On occasion, party leaders would convene a meeting of their members in Congress—called a caucus—to decide on candidates. At other times, state legislatures or state party conventions would advance candidates, so that different regions might have different candidates running under the same party banner.

The Anti-Masons, however, had a better idea. They called a national convention in 1828 to present a single party candidate for consideration. While their candidate was not successful, their idea was. From that point on, most significant political parties have held national nominating conventions to select their candidates.

There are some exceptions to this general rule, though. For example, the modern Greenback Party and the Socialists have experimented with a mail referendum of their membership to nominate candidates. In other instances, candidates have emerged first, with supporting parties created solely to advance their candidacies (e.g., Teddy Roosevelt, Robert La Folette, and Henry Wallace and their respective Progressive Parties; John Anderson and the National Unity Party; and Ross Perot and United We Stand, America).

Delegates to national conventions are selected in accordance with party rules and state laws. Because selection as a delegate is an honor for party faithful, competition is sometimes keen for a seat in a state delegation. To reduce rivalry and accommodate as many people as possible, parties have frequently permitted the designation of alternates with convention privileges and the right to vote in the absence of a regular delegate. They have also provided for more than one person to share a convention vote allotted to a particular state, through a system of fractional voting. Under this arrangement, two people might each serve as a delegate, each casting a half vote at the convention. Any number of "delegates" could be seated in this manner by splitting votes into whatever fraction was necessary to meet the demand for seats. This device accounts for the sometimes bizarre fractional vote totals recorded in convention proceedings.

The convention system has yielded another strange phenomenon. Since the vice presidency has a reputation as an afterthought both in the governmental structure of our nation and in our political life, conventions have tended to downplay the importance of the vice-presidential nomination. As a result, in conventions characterized by protracted conflict—like the Democratic conventions of 1924 and 1968—resolution of the presidential nomination has tended to leave exhausted delegates unwilling to submit to party discipline in the vice-presidential nomination. In consequence, these conventions have frequently witnessed a huge number of "candidates" receiving votes for the vice-presidential nomination—including nonpolitical contenders such as Will Rogers, Roger Mudd, or the spouse of the weary candidate.

Usually, the presidential candidate of a major party is selected first and his or her choice for vice president is presented to a convention for ratification after the presidential balloting. Under normal circumstances, this frequently produces a motion to nominate the vice-presidential candidate by acclamation. Occasionally, a presidential candidate may not declare a preference and a spirited contest for vice president may develop. This happened in 1956 when Estes Kefauver defeated John F. Kennedy to become Adlai Stevenson's running mate.

Only rarely does the choice of a vice-presidential running mate make a critical difference in an election. But Ronald Reagan apparently thought it might make a difference in his ability to obtain the 1976 Republican nomination, during his unsuccessful challenge to President Gerald R. Ford. Reagan announced that he wanted Senator Richard Schweiker on the ticket with him if he were nominated. He hoped his early declaration would win him the support of party moderates. Instead, his 1976 effort and Schweiker's place in it became another footnote of history.

Conventions have not always run smoothly, particularly among third parties. Parties of both the extreme right and the extreme left have experienced periodic schisms that have produced "rump" conventions and rival candidates. Conventions have been forced to adjourn and reconvene after a factional tumult has died down. Individuals have declared themselves as contenders for the nominations of more than one third party at a time. Not infrequently, they have declined nominations of third parties aligned with the wrong faction from their perspective. Sometimes, parties have "nominated" candidates to hold ballot positions before a convention has been held. These "stand-in" candidates may then relinquish their nominations after a convention has taken action. But they also may be forced to remain on a state ballot, even though a party has officially nominated someone else to head its ticket. Following the twists and turns of third party conventions is a challenge for professional historians no less than for casual students.

In addition to providing innovations such as the convention system, early third party efforts also reflected stress points in American society—chief among which was the growing controversy over slavery in the first half of the nineteenth century. The Liberty and Free Soil parties, with their abolitionist agendas, and the States Rights Party of 1832, with its pro-slavery posture, helped crystallize the dichotomy that threatened to, and eventually did, tear the nation apart.

Out of the tragedy of the American Civil War came a major expansion of the democratic ideal. The Thirteenth (1865) and Fifteenth (1870) Amendments to the Constitution abolished slavery and granted freedmen the right to vote. Unfortunately, over time the right to vote was eroded by de facto electoral restrictions that included literacy tests, poll taxes, or exclusionary primaries. By the mid-twentieth century, however, the Supreme Court had abolished these discriminatory subterfuges, which had been relied upon by many former Confederate states to deny African Americans the ballot, and had restored the forward momentum toward universal suffrage. The poll tax was officially abolished in federal elections by constitutional prohibition when the Twenty-fourth Amendment was adopted January 23, 1964.

Property qualifications and religious tests for voting also fell as the nation forsook its elitist roots under the leveling influence of westward expansion and frontier equality. With the demise of these voting barriers, the significance of the electoral college began to wane—a trend further strengthened by the populist sentiments of the late nineteenth century.

Democratic reforms were also accelerated by the prohibition movement, which argued that entrenched liquor interests were protected by a male-dominated political establishment. The movement sought to circumvent the existing power structure through a broadened electorate. The Prohibition Party grew out of that crusade and was the first to advocate the direct election of Senators and women's suffrage. While the genealogy is not strictly linear, one can also see a ready relationship between the Prohibitionists and the later Progressives of 1912–1924. While World War I significantly altered the role of women who were left to care for the home front and gave impetus to the demand for political equality between the sexes, it was largely the Progressives (whether within a third party or as part of the Democratic and Republican parties) who found common cause with the suffragists, making adoption of the Seventeenth Amendment (providing for the direct election of Senators) in 1913 and the Nineteenth Amendment (granting women the right to vote) in 1920 possible after years of agitation for these electoral changes. Not incidentally, the Eighteenth Amendment (outlawing the liquor trade) was sandwiched between these two monumental reforms, being ratified in 1919 and repealed in 1933.

The Progressives made other contributions to our electoral process that added to the democratic evolution of our nation. At the state and local levels, the initiative and referendum were made features of many voting laws, while the development of the primary election to select party candidates for public office (including selection of delegates to national presidential nominating conventions) gained in popularity throughout the first half of the twentieth century.

The most recent constitutional developments to affect presidential elections were the adoption of the Twenty-third and Twenty-sixth Amendments, which respectively granted residents of the District of Columbia the right to vote for president and vice president and prohibited discrimination in presidential elections against otherwise qualified electors over the age of 18 solely on the basis of age. The 18–year-old voting amendment embodies a right previously granted under the laws of several states, recognizing the stake of young adults in our political system. The Twenty-third Amendment was adopted in 1961, the Twenty-sixth in 1971.

A notable consequence of the presidential primary system and the continuing expansion of the franchise has been an almost complete eclipse of the electoral college as an important factor in presidential elections. The electoral college had been in decline with each advance of democracy in the voting process but it could occasionally reassert its importance in a negative way through the election of a president who received a majority of the electoral vote but only a minority of the popular vote. Or through near disasters such as the 1876 election, when a special electoral commission had to decide the outcome because electoral votes were in dispute. But it was really the primary system—that allowed the people to vote directly for their preferences for presidential nominations or to select delegates to nominating conventions—that made the archaic electoral college a moribund institution which could no longer shield the selection of the president from the direct influence of the people.

Today, the electoral college still exists. Its defenders point to a limited utility in legitimizing the outcome of close elections. Its detractors argue its obsolescence and antidemocratic character. Yet it remains testament of the distance we have come as a nation from the days when only white, male aristocrats had a direct voice in governance to our present circumstance when, under the flag of this Republic, all men and women are truly "created equal." In this sense, the history of presidential elections not only parallels the myriad of great issues that have confronted the United States since its birth, but also traces and articulates the noble ideals of the Declaration of Independence in their journey from a promise to a reality.

DEFINITIONS OF SELECTED TERMS AND PHRASES USED IN VOLUME 2

Volume 2 of U.S. Presidential Candidates and the Elections: A Biographical and Historical Guide provides a quadrennial summary of presidential nominations and elections. Each election year contains a capsule narrative highlighting important features of the election; lists of candidates; details about parties, conventions, and platforms; and the results of primary, general, and electoral college balloting. Most of the materials should be self-evident but a few terms merit special explanation, especially those that relate to vote tabulations and convention procedures.

blank and void votes	Ballots that have been cast in an election but which are unmarked in terms of candidate preference or are declared void because they are improperly cast, unreadable, or otherwise successfully challenged.
independent candidates	Persons who have declared as candidates or been advanced as candidates without a known party designation. Since the creation of the Federal Election Commission, the number of persons who have filed with the commission as candidates for president without indicating a partisan affiliation has increased with each election cycle. In this work, party information has been obtained from a variety of sources, but where it is not available the candidate has been identified as an "independent" candidate. In addition, candidates who identify themselves as "independent" are included in this category.
informal ballot	Prior to the commencement of official balloting for a nomination, some conventions have resorted to an informal ballot as a way to measure a candidate's strength. An informal ballot is not subject to the rules applied to a regular ballot. This device may save time by encouraging minor candidates to drop out of the contest or placing pressure on an undeclared candidate to accept nomination. It can also be used to avoid embarrassment in situations where a popular candidate may decline nomination on an informal ballot and therefore not be considered in the formal proceedings.
none of the above	Some states now permit voters to reject all candidates listed for a particular office by marking a line labeled "None of the above." The action is largely symbolic because it does not help elect or nominate anyone. Nonetheless, the ballot line is counted and conveys some measure of voter dissatisfaction with the field of candidates.
others	Votes cast on behalf of unspecified candidates. These are generally scattered votes (see below), but on occasion election officials will simply not differentiate between votes cast for candidates other than those representing the major parties. Instead, they will simply report all minor candidates in an aggregate category of "other" votes.
rising vote	A parliamentary device in which people indicate their preference by standing up in support of a particular question before an assembly. Sometimes a rising vote is counted, but if the majority position is visually apparent a count may not be taken or recorded.
scattering	Votes cast for miscellaneous candidates. Such votes are frequently not tabulated by individual name but are simply lumped together by election officials as "scattered" votes.

self-selected/ self-declared	It is increasingly common for minor candidates to simply identify themselves as presidential contenders without any party backing or formal campaign organization. This may take the form of a filing with the Federal Election Commission, an announcement of candidacy in a newspaper, or any other public notice of their intent. On occasion, these candidates will create ephemeral "parties" that exist solely to advance their campaigns. As used in this work, "self-selected" and "self-declared" are synonymous.
shift	During the balloting for nomination of a candidate, convention rules usually allow delegates to change their votes at any time prior to the announcement of the total count of votes being cast. It has become common practice for delegates to "shift" their votes to a candidate who is about to receive the nomination in order to be on the winning side. As long as this happens before the roll call is completed, the official record records the votes as they were cast after the shift.
unanimous nomination	Theoretically, a nomination made without opposition. It involves a motion to cast a single unanimous ballot for a candidate and is usually carried by a voice vote rather than a recorded roll call. It has become common for such a motion to be made immediately after a candidate has received a nomination, in order to demonstrate party solidarity behind its standard-bearer.
unpledged delegate	Convention delegates may "pledge" to support the candidate for whom they have declared (or under whose banner they were elected in the primary) until released by the candidate. They also may be free to vote for someone else after the initial ballot. In some cases, delegates may be sent to a convention without a declared preference for a candidate. These delegates are free to support any candidate and can be critical in a close convention vote. The procedures regulating delegate voting are governed by party rules and state law.
vacancies	Unfilled positions within the electoral college.
yes and no	In some presidential primaries, if only one candidate's name appears on the ballot, voters may be given an opportunity to vote either for or against that individual. The question is phrased so that a "yes" vote is for the nomination of the listed candidate and a "no" vote is against such nomination.

Because election reporting is subject to individual state regulation and human foibles, the anomalies in reported results are many. Votes totals may vary among sources and between states. The totals used in this work represent the author's best judgment for states in which conflicting totals are sometimes given in different sources.

Where candidates who have qualified to have their votes tabulated have no recorded votes in a particular state, blank spaces or the use of an "unreported" designation are used to indicate the absence of reported votes. For convention voting, however, the situation may be different. A delegate may be absent or may choose not to vote on a roll call, and thus may be recorded as "not voting." If a person receives convention votes on one ballot, but not on others, the absence of previous or subsequent votes is indicated by a "—" entry in the column listing the results of a particular roll call.

In all cases, question marks after an entry indicate that the information provided remains subject to validation.

ABBREVIATIONS FOR VOLUME 2

A	American
AIL	Anti-Imperialist League
A (K-N)	American (Know-Nothing)
A-M	Anti-Masonic
AM FIR	America First
AM VEG	American Vegetarian
ANP	American National
BTR	Black and Tan Republican
CHR	Christian
CHR NAT	Christian Nationalist
CL	Commonwealth Land
COM	Communist
CON	Continental Party
CU (A)	Constitutional Union (American)
CW	Clay Whig
D	Democratic
D-R	Democratic-Republican
F	Federalist
FL or FAR	Farmer Labor
FS (D)	Free Soil (Democratic)
FSD	Free Soil Democratic
FS (L)	Free Soil (Liberty)
GRE LAB	Greenback Labor (National)
I	Independent
I-D	Independent-Democratic
ID	Independent Democrat
ILR	Independent Liberal Republican (Revenue Reform)
IND NAT	Independent National (Greenback)
INS REF	Insurgent Referendum
IP	Independence Party
I-R	Independent-Republican
JOB	Jobless
L or LIB	Liberty

MS IND REP	Mississippi Independent Republican
MS REG DEM	Mississippi Reular Democrats
NA	Native American
NAT	National
NAT DEM	National Democratic (Sound Money Democratic) [1896]
NAT GRE	National Greenback (Greenback Labor)
ND	National Democratic
(N) D	(Northern) Democratic
NL	National Liberty
NR	National Republican
PEO	People's (Populist, Middle-of-the-Road)
PEO-ANTI	People's (Populist, Middle-of-the-Road, Anti-Fusionist)
PROG	Progressive
PROH	Prohibition
PROHIB	National Prohibition Reform
R	Republican
S or SOC	Socialist
SC SOUTH DEM	South Carolina Southern Democrats
SD	Southern Democratic
SL	Socialist Labor
SOC DEM	Social Democratic
SOC LAB	Socialist Labor
SR	Southern Rights
ST	Single Tax
TAP	Straight-Out (Taproot) Democratic
UNI	Union
UNI CHR	United Christian
UNI LAB	Union Labor
UNIT LAB	United Labor
UNI REF	Union Reform
W	Whig
W (C)	Workers' (Communist)

The Elections

1789–1992

ELECTION OF JANUARY 7, 1789

President
GEORGE WASHINGTON

Vice President
JOHN ADAMS

HIGHLIGHTS

No political parties or conventions were involved in the first presidential election under the U.S. Constitution. Only ten states voted, for New York, North Carolina, and Rhode Island did not participate. After George Washington received one electoral vote from each presidential elector, he was unanimously declared elected as president. John Adams, with the second highest number of electoral votes, was declared elected as vice president.

CANDIDATES FOR PRESIDENT:

John Adams (MA)
James Armstrong (GA)
George Clinton (NY)
John Hancock (MA)
Robert Hanson Harrison (MD)
Samuel Huntington (CT)
John Jay (NY)
Benjamin Lincoln (MA)
John Milton (GA)
John Rutledge (SC)
Edward Telfair (GA)
George Washington (VA)

GENERAL ELECTION SUMMARY FOR 1789		
Candidate	*Electoral Votes*	*States*
Washington	69	10
Adams	34	6
Jay	9	3
Harrison	6	1
Rutledge	6	1
Hancock	4	3
Clinton	3	1
Huntington	2	1
Milton	2	1
Armstrong	1	1
Lincoln	1	1
Telfair	1	1
vacancies	4	

ELECTION OF NOVEMBER 6, 1792

President
GEORGE WASHINGTON
Vice President
JOHN ADAMS

HIGHLIGHTS

Formal political parties had not yet organized, although George Washington and John Adams were known as Federalists and their critics were known as Democratic-Republicans. Washington essentially faced no opposition. After Washington received one electoral vote from each presidential elector, he again was unanimously declared elected as president. Adams was declared elected as vice president.

CANDIDATES FOR PRESIDENT:
John Adams (MA)
Aaron Burr (NY)
George Clinton (NY)
Thomas Jefferson (VA)
George Washington (VA)

GENERAL ELECTION SUMMARY FOR 1792		
Candidate	Electoral Votes	States
Washington	132	15
Adams	77	10
Clinton	50	5
Jefferson	4	1
Burr	1	1
vacancies	3	

ELECTION OF NOVEMBER 8, 1796

President
JOHN ADAMS
Vice President
THOMAS JEFFERSON

HIGHLIGHTS

The third presidential election resulted in a partisan split between the president and vice president. John Adams, as George Washington's successor, was a Federalist, while Thomas Jefferson, with the second highest number of votes, was chosen vice president as a Democratic-Republican.

DEMOCRATIC–REPUBLICAN PARTY
CANDIDATES FOR PRESIDENT:
Samuel Adams (MA)
Aaron Burr (NY)
George Clinton (NY)
John Henry (MD)
James Iredell (NC)
Thomas Jefferson (VA)
Samuel Johnson (NC)
Charles Cotesworth Pinckney (SC)
George Washington (VA)

FEDERALIST PARTY
CANDIDATES FOR PRESIDENT:
John Adams (MA)
Oliver Ellsworth (CT)
John Jay (NY)
Thomas Pinckney (SC)

GENERAL ELECTION SUMMARY FOR 1796		
Candidate	*Electoral Votes*	*States*
Adams (F)	71	12
Jefferson (D-R)	68	8
Pinckney (F)	59	11
Burr (D-R)	30	6
Adams (D-R)	15	1
Ellsworth (F)	11	3
Clinton (D-R)	7	2
Jay (F)	5	1
Iredell (D-R)	3	1
Washington (D-R)	2	2
Henry (D-R)	2	1
Johnson (D-R)	2	1
Pinckney (D-R)	1	1

ELECTION OF NOVEMBER 4, 1800

President
THOMAS JEFFERSON
Vice President
AARON BURR

HIGHLIGHTS

Thomas Jefferson and Aaron Burr each received seventy-three electoral votes and tied for president. The election then devolved to the U.S. House of Representatives, where each state was entitled to cast a single vote. The voting took place from February 11 to February 17, 1801. On the thirty-sixth ballot, Jefferson received a majority, with ten states choosing him, four favoring Burr, and two abstaining. Thus, Jefferson became president and Burr became vice president.

DEMOCRATIC-REPUBLICAN PARTY

CANDIDATES FOR PRESIDENT:
Aaron Burr (NY)
Thomas Jefferson (VA)

CONGRESSIONAL CAUCUS:
May 11, 1800, Marache's Boarding House, Philadelphia (PA)

The congressional leadership of the Democratic-Republican Party adopted the first national statement of partisan principles at this caucus. They advocated states' rights and denounced the Federalist administration.

DEMOCRATIC-REPUBLICAN PARTY
VOTE FOR PRESIDENTIAL AND
VICE-PRESIDENTIAL NOMINATIONS:

Jefferson was selected as the presidential nominee, and Burr was selected as the vice-presidential nominee.

FEDERALIST PARTY

CANDIDATES FOR PRESIDENT:
John Adams (MA)
John Jay (NY)
Charles Cotesworth Pinckney (SC)

CONGRESSIONAL CAUCUS:
May 3, 1800, Senate chamber, U.S. Capitol, Washington, DC

The Federalists met in congressional caucus, the first regular caucus for the nomination of presidential candidates.

FEDERALIST PARTY
VOTE FOR PRESIDENTIAL AND
VICE-PRESIDENTIAL NOMINATIONS:

Adams was selected as the presidential nominee, and Pinckney was selected as the vice-presidential nominee.

GENERAL ELECTION SUMMARY FOR 1800

Candidate	Electoral Votes	States
Jefferson (D-R)	73	9
Burr (D-R)	73	9
Adams (F)	65	10
Pinckney (F)	64	10
Jay (F)	1	1

ELECTION OF NOVEMBER 6, 1804

President
THOMAS JEFFERSON
Vice President
GEORGE CLINTON

HIGHLIGHTS

The presidential election of 1804 was the first one held under the Twelfth Amendment to the U.S. Constitution, which requires electors to cast separate ballots for the president and the vice president. Bitterness over Burr's political intrigues foreclosed his renomination by the Democratic-Republicans; but nonetheless, the party's nominees, Thomas Jefferson and George Clinton, won in electoral vote landslides.

DEMOCRATIC-REPUBLICAN PARTY

CANDIDATE FOR PRESIDENT:
Thomas Jefferson (VA)

CANDIDATE FOR VICE PRESIDENT:
George Clinton

CANDIDATES FOR VICE-PRESIDENTIAL NOMINATION:
John Breckinridge (KY)
George Clinton (NY)

CONGRESSIONAL CAUCUS:
February 25, 1804, U.S. Capitol, Washington, DC

The party held a congressional caucus.

FEDERALIST PARTY

CANDIDATE FOR PRESIDENT:
Charles Cotesworth Pinckney (SC)

CANDIDATE FOR VICE PRESIDENT:
Rufus King (NY)

CONVENTION:
February 22, 1804, Washington, DC

The Federalists held a public dinner at which they selected their candidates.

DEMOCRATIC-REPUBLICAN PARTY VOTE FOR PRESIDENTIAL NOMINATION: JEFFERSON WAS UNANIMOUSLY NOMINATED FOR PRESIDENT, ALTHOUGH NO FORMAL VOTE WAS TAKEN.	
VOTE FOR VICE-PRESIDENTIAL NOMINATION:	
Candidate	Ballot: 1
Clinton	67
Breckinridge	41

GENERAL ELECTION SUMMARY FOR 1804		
Candidate	Electoral Votes	States
Jefferson (D-R)	162	15
Cotesworth Pinckney (F)	14	3

ELECTION OF NOVEMBER 8, 1808

President
JAMES MADISON
Vice President
GEORGE CLINTON

HIGHLIGHTS

James Madison, a strict constructionist, was elected over his Federalist rival, Charles Cotesworth Pinckney. Thomas Jefferson had defeated Pinckney four years earlier.

DEMOCRATIC–REPUBLICAN PARTY
CANDIDATE FOR PRESIDENT:
James Madison

CANDIDATE FOR VICE PRESIDENT:
George Clinton

DEMOCRATIC-REPUBLICAN PARTY VOTE FOR PRESIDENTIAL NOMINATION:	
Candidate	Ballot: 1
Madison	83
Clinton	3
Monroe	3
VOTE FOR VICE-PRESIDENTIAL NOMINATION:	
Candidate	Ballot: 1
Clinton	79
Langdon	5

CANDIDATES FOR PRESIDENTIAL NOMINATION:
George Clinton (NY)
James Madison (VA)
James Monroe (VA)

CANDIDATES FOR VICE-PRESIDENTIAL NOMINATION:
George Clinton (NY)
John Langdon (NH)

CONGRESSIONAL CAUCUS:
January 23, 1808, the Senate chambers of the U.S. Capitol, Washington, DC

FEDERALIST PARTY
CANDIDATE FOR PRESIDENT:
Charles Cotesworth Pinckney (SC)

CANDIDATE FOR VICE PRESIDENT:
Rufus King (NY)

MEETING:
Third week of August 1808, New York (NY)

FEDERALIST PARTY VOTE FOR PRESIDENTIAL AND VICE-PRESIDENTIAL NOMINATIONS: PINCKNEY WAS UNANIMOUSLY NOMINATED FOR PRESIDENT AND KING FOR VICE PRESIDENT.

GENERAL ELECTION SUMMARY FOR 1808		
Candidate	Electoral Votes	States
Madison (D-R)	122	12
Pinckney (F)	47	7
Clinton (D-R)	6	1
vacancies	1	

ELECTION OF NOVEMBER 3, 1812

President
JAMES MADISON
Vice President
ELBRIDGE GERRY

HIGHLIGHTS

This election was held during the turmoil of the War of 1812, which Congress had declared on June 18, 1812. James Madison was elected with the votes of the agrarian South and the new western states, which favored the war.

DEMOCRATIC–REPUBLICAN PARTY

CANDIDATE FOR PRESIDENT:
James Madison (VA)

CANDIDATE FOR VICE PRESIDENT:
Elbridge Gerry

DEMOCRATIC-REPUBLICAN PARTY
VOTE FOR PRESIDENTIAL NOMINATION: MADISON
WAS THE UNANIMOUS CHOICE OF THE CAUCUS,
RECEIVING EIGHTY-TWO VOTES.

VOTE FOR VICE-PRESIDENTIAL NOMINATION:

Candidate	Ballot: 1[1]	2[2]
Gerry	16	74
Langdon	64	0
other	2	3

[1]first caucus
[2]second caucus

Langdon was nominated for vice president over Gerry, but Langdon declined. A second caucus was held on June 8, 1812, and Gerry was nominated for vice president.

CANDIDATES FOR VICE-PRESIDENTIAL NOMINATION:
Elbridge Gerry (MA)
John Langdon (NH)

CONGRESSIONAL CAUCUS:
May 18, 1812, the Senate chamber of the U.S.
Capitol, Washington, DC

The Democratic-Republicans held a congressional caucus.

FEDERALIST PARTY

CANDIDATE FOR PRESIDENT:
De Witt Clinton (NY)

CANDIDATE FOR VICE PRESIDENT:
Jared Ingersoll (PA)

CONGRESSIONAL CAUCUS:
September 15–17, 1812, New York (NY)

Clinton was not actually nominated at this convention, although the general consensus was that he was the top contender. Ingersoll was selected as Clinton's running mate at a meeting in Lancaster (PA) on August 26, 1812. No formal nomination was made, but a consensus developed. Ingersoll was nominated prior to the emergence of Clinton as the consensus candidate.

GENERAL ELECTION SUMMARY FOR 1812

Candidate	Electoral Votes	States
Madison (D-R)	128	11
Clinton (F)	89	8
vacancies	1	

ELECTION OF NOVEMBER 5, 1816

President
JAMES MONROE
Vice President
DANIEL D. TOMPKINS

HIGHLIGHTS

The election of 1816 witnessed the decline of the Federalist Party, which failed to select candidates formally. In fact, in several states, the Federalists did not even present slates of presidential electors.

DEMOCRATIC–REPUBLICAN PARTY

CANDIDATE FOR PRESIDENT:
James Monroe

CANDIDATE FOR VICE PRESIDENT:
Daniel D. Tompkins

CANDIDATES FOR PRESIDENTIAL NOMINATION:
William H. Crawford (GA)
James Monroe (VA)

DEMOCRATIC-REPUBLICAN PARTY VOTE FOR PRESIDENTIAL NOMINATION: MARCH 16, 1816	
Candidate	*Ballot: 1*
Monroe	65
Crawford	54
VOTE FOR VICE-PRESIDENTIAL NOMINATION:	
Candidate	*Ballot: 1*
Tompkins	85
Snyder	30

CANDIDATES FOR VICE-PRESIDENTIAL NOMINATION:
Simon Snyder (PA)
Daniel D. Tompkins (NY)

CONGRESSIONAL CAUCUS:
March 10, 1816, the House Chamber of the U.S. Capitol, Washington, DC

Only fifty-seven senators and representatives attended the congressional caucus. Therefore, another caucus was held in the Capitol on March 16, 1816, with 119 members attending.

FEDERALIST PARTY

CANDIDATE FOR PRESIDENT:
Rufus King (NY)

CANDIDATES FOR VICE PRESIDENT:
Robert Goodloe Harper (MD)
John Eager Howard (MD)
John Marshall (VA)
James Ross (PA)

GENERAL ELECTION SUMMARY FOR 1816		
Candidate	*Electoral Votes*	*States*
Monroe (D-R)	183	16
King (F)	34	3
vacancies	4	

ELECTION OF NOVEMBER 13, 1820

President
JAMES MONROE
Vice President
DANIEL D. TOMPKINS

HIGHLIGHTS

No conventions were held. Instead, candidates were selected by congressional caucus in Washington, DC, on April 5, 1820, and electors were chosen by state legislatures. President James Monroe was so popular that he had practically no opposition, thus giving rise to the phrase "Era of Good Feeling" to describe this period. One elector, William Plumer, Sr. (NH), voted for John Quincy Adams for president to preserve the honor of a unanimous election exclusively for George Washington.

CANDIDATES FOR PRESIDENT:
John Quincy Adams (MA)
James Monroe (VA)

CANDIDATES FOR VICE PRESIDENT:
Robert Goodloe Harper (MD)
Daniel Rodney (DE)
Richard Rush (PA)
Richard Stockton (NJ)
Daniel D. Tompkins (NY)

GENERAL ELECTION SUMMARY FOR 1820		
Candidate	Electoral Votes	States
Monroe	231	24
Adams	1	1
vacancies	3	

ELECTION OF NOVEMBER 2, 1824

President
JOHN QUINCY ADAMS
Vice President
JOHN CALDWELL CALHOUN

HIGHLIGHTS

Nominated by state legislatures were four candidates for president, representing different factions of the Democratic-Republican Party, and six candidates for vice president. A congressional caucus, held February 14, 1824, in the House chamber of the U.S. Capitol, resulted in the nominations of William H. Crawford for president and Albert Gallatin for vice president. Gallatin resigned his nomination on October 24, 1824, and the caucus action played little role in the election. After no candidate received a majority of the electoral votes, for the second time in U.S. history the election devolved to the U.S. House of Representatives. Each state had one vote in selecting the president from the three leading contenders. Henry Clay's supporters helped to elect John Quincy Adams, with a vote of thirteen for Adams, seven for Andrew Jackson, and four for William Harris Crawford.

CANDIDATES FOR PRESIDENT:
John Quincy Adams (MA)
Henry Clay (KY)
William Harris Crawford (GA)
Andrew Jackson (TN)
William Lowndes (SC)

CANDIDATES FOR VICE PRESIDENT:
John Caldwell Calhoun (SC)
Henry Clay (KY)
Andrew Jackson (TN)
Nathaniel Macon (NC)
Nathan Sanford (NY)
Martin Van Buren (NY)

GENERAL ELECTION SUMMARY FOR 1824			
Candidate	Electoral Votes	States	Popular Votes[1]
Jackson	99	7	153,544
Adams	84	7	108,740
Crawford	41	3	47,136
Clay	37	3	46,618
Lowndes	0	0	unknown

[1] There were 6,616 unpledged Republican popular votes from Massachusetts. There were also 6,437 popular votes for which the candidates were unknown, 4,753 of which were from Massachusetts, 1,188 from Connecticut, 256 from North Carolina, 200 from Rhode Island, 33 from Missouri, and 7 from Indiana.

ELECTION OF NOVEMBER 4, 1828

President
ANDREW JACKSON
Vice President
JOHN CALDWELL CALHOUN

HIGHLIGHTS

The election of 1828 witnessed the triumph of Jacksonian democracy and the growing influence of the newly admitted states from the western frontier.

DEMOCRATIC PARTY

CANDIDATE FOR PRESIDENT:
Andrew Jackson (TN)

CANDIDATE FOR VICE PRESIDENT:
John Caldwell Calhoun (SC)

CONVENTION:
Jackson was nominated by the Tennessee legislature in October 1825. No conventions or congressional caucuses were held.

NATIONAL REPUBLICAN PARTY

CANDIDATE FOR PRESIDENT:
John Quincy Adams (MA)

CANDIDATE FOR VICE PRESIDENT:
Richard Rush

CANDIDATES FOR VICE-PRESIDENTIAL NOMINATION:
Richard Rush (PA)
John Andrew Shulze (PA)

CONVENTION:
Adams was nominated for president by several state conventions. Rush was similarly nominated for vice president, although Shulze was also nominated by at least one state convention.

GENERAL ELECTION SUMMARY FOR 1828			
Candidate	Electoral Votes	States	Popular Votes
Jackson (D)	178	17	647,231
Adams (NR)	83	10	509,097
unknown	0	0	4,568

ELECTION OF NOVEMBER 6, 1832

President
ANDREW JACKSON
Vice President
MARTIN VAN BUREN

HIGHLIGHTS

The election of 1832 was the first election in which all political parties formally held national nominating conventions. At the National Republican Convention in Baltimore (MD) on December 12, 1831, the party adopted the first formal platform of a political party.

ANTI-MASONIC PARTY

CANDIDATE FOR PRESIDENT:
William Wirt

CANDIDATE FOR VICE PRESIDENT:
Amos Ellmaker (PA)

CANDIDATES FOR PRESIDENTIAL NOMINATION:
John McLean (OH)
Richard Rush (PA)
William Wirt (MD)

CONVENTION:
September 26–28, 1831, The Athenaeum, Baltimore (MD)
John C. Spencer (NY), permanent chairman

The Anti-Masonic Party was created in New York in 1827. A national organizing convention was held in Philadelphia (PA) from September 11 to September 18, 1830. The 1831 convention was the first national nominating convention of any political party. In all, 112 delegates from thirteen states attended the convention.

ANTI-MASONIC PARTY VOTE FOR PRESIDENTIAL NOMINATION:	
Candidate	Ballot: 1
Wirt	108
Rush	1
not voting	2
Wirt's nomination was made unanimous.	

DEMOCRATIC PARTY

CANDIDATE FOR PRESIDENT:
Andrew Jackson (TN)

CANDIDATE FOR VICE PRESIDENT:
Martin Van Buren

CANDIDATES FOR VICE-PRESIDENTIAL NOMINATION:
Philip Pendleton Barbour (VA)
Richard Mentor Johnson (KY)
Martin Van Buren (NY)

CONVENTION:
May 21–23, 1832, The Athenaeum, Baltimore (MD)
Robert Lucas (OH), permanent chairman

Every state except Missouri sent delegates to this convention. John C. Calhoun, having served two terms as vice president, did not seek renomination. He was elected to the Senate on December 12, 1832, and resigned as vice president sixteen days later.

DEMOCRATIC PARTY VOTE FOR PRESIDENTIAL NOMINATION: JACKSON WAS UNANIMOUSLY RENOMINATED FOR PRESIDENT BY ACCLAMATION.	
VOTE FOR VICE-PRESIDENTIAL NOMINATION:	
Candidate	Ballot: 1
Van Buren	208
Barbour	49
Johnson	26

INDEPENDENT PARTY

CANDIDATE FOR PRESIDENT:
John Floyd (VA)

CANDIDATE FOR VICE PRESIDENT:
Henry Lee (MA)

CONVENTION:
November 20, 1832, Charleston (SC)

This party represented the nullification faction within the Democratic Party. It believed that states' rights and the ability of states to veto the effect of federal legislation were essential features of the Union.

NATIONAL REPUBLICAN PARTY

CANDIDATE FOR PRESIDENT:
Henry Clay (KY)

CANDIDATE FOR VICE PRESIDENT:
John Sergeant (PA)

CONVENTION:
December 12–15, 1831, The Athenaeum, Baltimore (MD)
Abner Lacock (PA), temporary chairman
James Barbour (VA), permanent chairman

This anti-Jackson faction eventually formed the nucleus of the Whig Party. Attending this convention were 157 delegates from seventeen states. The National Republican platform supported a uniform system of internal improvements and opposed the "spoils system." Clay was nominated for president on the first ballot.

GENERAL ELECTION SUMMARY FOR 1832			
Candidate	Electoral Votes	States	Popular Votes
Jackson (D)	219	16	687,507
Clay (NR)	49	6	530,189
Floyd (I)	11	1	unknown
Wirt (A-M)	7	1	101,712
unknown	0	0	7,273

ELECTION OF NOVEMBER 1, 1836

President
MARTIN VAN BUREN
Vice President
RICHARD MENTOR JOHNSON

HIGHLIGHTS

The election of 1836 saw the rise of the Whig Party, which entered this election with a series of regional candidates. Martin Van Buren, Andrew Jackson's vice president, defeated William Henry Harrison and inaugurated an independent treasury system. Richard Mentor Johnson received 147 electoral votes for vice president, an insufficient number to secure election. Accordingly, the duty of electing the vice president devolved upon the Senate, which elected Johnson by a vote of 33 to 16.

DEMOCRATIC PARTY

CANDIDATE FOR PRESIDENT:
Martin Van Buren (NY)

CANDIDATE FOR VICE PRESIDENT:
Richard Mentor Johnson

CANDIDATES FOR VICE-PRESIDENTIAL NOMINATION:
Richard Mentor Johnson (KY)
William Cabell Rives (VA)

CONVENTION:
May 20–22, 1835, First Presbyterian Church, Baltimore (MD)
Andrew Stevenson (VA), temporary and permanent chairman

More than six hundred delegates, representing twenty-two states and two territories, attended the Democratic Party convention.

DEMOCRATIC PARTY
VOTE FOR PRESIDENTIAL NOMINATION: VAN BUREN WAS NOMINATED FOR PRESIDENT ON THE FIRST BALLOT, WITH 265 VOTES. HIS NOMINATION WAS MADE UNANIMOUS.

VOTE FOR VICE-PRESIDENTIAL NOMINATION:

Candidate	Ballot: 1
Johnson	178
Rives	87

WHIG PARTY

CANDIDATES FOR PRESIDENT:
William Henry Harrison (OH)
Willie Person Mangum (NC)
Daniel Webster (MA)
Hugh Lawson White (TN)

CANDIDATES FOR VICE PRESIDENT:
Francis Granger (NY)
William Smith (AL)
John Tyler (VA)

CONVENTION:
December 14, 1835, Harrisburg (PA)

A state convention, it was similar to conventions held in New York, Ohio, and elsewhere that confirmed the nominations of Harrison for president and Granger for vice president. A number of states, however, selected other candidates. For example, the Maryland Whig Convention nominated Harrison for president and Tyler for vice president, White was nominated by the legislatures of Alabama and Tennessee, and other states nominated a Webster and Mangum ticket. As a result, four different Whig tickets were fielded, for no national nominating convention was held to determine a single ticket.

GENERAL ELECTION SUMMARY FOR 1836

Candidate	Electoral Votes	States	Popular Votes
Van Buren (D)	170	15	762,678
Harrison (W)	73	7	550,816
White (W)	26	2	146,107
Webster (W)	14	1	41,201
Mangum (W)	11	1	unknown
unknown	0	0	1,234

ELECTION OF NOVEMBER 3, 1840

President
WILLIAM HENRY HARRISON
Vice President
JOHN TYLER

HIGHLIGHTS

The election of 1840 witnessed growing opposition to the Bank of the United States and concern over the activities of abolitionists. The Liberty Party, opposed to the institution of slavery, entered the political arena for the first time. In the middle of a depression, incumbent president Martin Van Buren refused to spend land revenues, which made him quite unpopular.

William Henry Harrison, the victorious candidate of the Whig Party, died on April 4, 1841, only thirty-one days after his inauguration as the ninth president of the United States. He was succeeded by his vice president, John Tyler.

DEMOCRATIC PARTY

CANDIDATE FOR PRESIDENT:
Martin Van Buren (NY)

CANDIDATES FOR VICE PRESIDENT:
Richard Mentor Johnson (KY)
James Knox Polk (TN)
Littleton Waller Tazewell (VA)

3D CONVENTION:
May 5–6, 1840, Hall of the Musical Association, Baltimore (MD)
Isaac Hill (NH), temporary chairman
William Carroll (TN), permanent chairman

Delegates from twenty-one states attended this convention. Connecticut, Delaware, Illinois, South Carolina, and Virginia were not represented. The convention officially designated the party as the Democratic Party for the first time, thus recognizing popular usage.

DEMOCRATIC PARTY
VOTE FOR PRESIDENTIAL NOMINATION: VAN BUREN WAS UNANIMOUSLY NOMINATED FOR PRESIDENT ON THE FIRST BALLOT.

VOTE FOR VICE-PRESIDENTIAL NOMINATION: THE NOMINATION FOR VICE PRESIDENT WAS LEFT TO THE DISCRETION OF INDIVIDUAL STATES.

LIBERTY (ABOLITIONIST) PARTY

CANDIDATE FOR PRESIDENT:
none (James Gillespie Birney [NY] declined)

CANDIDATES FOR VICE PRESIDENT:
none (Thomas Earle [PA] and Francis Julius Lemoyne [PA] declined)

CONVENTION:
November 13, 1839, Warsaw (NY)

Approximately five hundred delegates attended this convention. Birney and Lemoyne were nominated for president and vice president, respectively, but both declined. Consequently, a second nominating convention was held on April 1, 1840, in Albany (NY). Six states sent delegates to this convention. Birney was unanimously nominated for president, and Earle was nominated for vice president. While the new nominees of the Liberty Party also declined their nominations, more than seven thousand votes were cast for them in the general election.

WHIG PARTY

CANDIDATE FOR PRESIDENT:
William Henry Harrison

CANDIDATE FOR VICE PRESIDENT:
John Tyler (VA)

CANDIDATES FOR PRESIDENTIAL NOMINATION:
Henry Clay (KY)
William Henry Harrison (OH)
Winfield Scott (NJ)

CONVENTION:
December 4–7, 1839, Zion Lutheran Church, Harrisburg (PA)

Isaac C. Bates (MA), temporary chairman
James Barbour (VA), permanent chairman

Attending this convention were 254 delegates from twenty-two states. Arkansas, Georgia, South Carolina, and Tennessee were not represented. This national convention was the first to adopt the unit rule, which required all delegates in a state to cast a unified vote for the candidate with the most support within the state's delegation.

WHIG PARTY		
VOTE FOR PRESIDENTIAL NOMINATION:		
Candidate	Ballot: 1	2
Clay	103	90
Harrison	94	148
Scott	57	16

VOTE FOR VICE-PRESIDENTIAL NOMINATION: TYLER WAS UNANIMOUSLY NOMINATED BY COMMITTEE FOR VICE PRESIDENT.

GENERAL ELECTION SUMMARY FOR 1840			
Candidate	Electoral Votes	States	Popular Votes
Harrison (W)	234	19	1,275,016
Van Buren (D)	60	7	1,129,102
Birney (L)	0	0	7,000
unknown	0	0	767

ELECTION OF NOVEMBER 5, 1844

President
JAMES KNOX POLK

Vice President
GEORGE MIFFLIN DALLAS

HIGHLIGHTS

The election of 1844 saw the nomination of the first "dark horse" candidate for president—James Knox Polk. Since 1832, the Democrats required a ⅔ majority of delegates to nominate a candidate. In 1840, neither of the top two contenders could marshal that number. In the Democratic Convention, former President Martin Van Buren led the balloting in the first four rounds and then yielded the lead to Lewis Cass in the next three. Polk did not receive any votes until the eighth ballot, but he emerged victorious on the ninth and final ballot. He went on to win the election.

DEMOCRATIC PARTY

CANDIDATE FOR PRESIDENT:
James Knox Polk

CANDIDATE FOR VICE PRESIDENT:
George Mifflin Dallas

CANDIDATES FOR PRESIDENTIAL NOMINATION:
James Buchanan (PA)
John Caldwell Calhoun (SC)
Lewis Cass (MI)
Richard Mentor Johnson (KY)
James Knox Polk (TN)
Charles Stewart (PA)
Martin Van Buren (NY)
Levi Woodbury (NH)

CANDIDATES FOR VICE-PRESIDENTIAL NOMINATION:
Lewis Cass (MI)
George Mifflin Dallas (PA)

John Fairfield (ME)
Richard Mentor Johnson (KY)
William Learned Marcy (NY)
Charles Stewart (PA)
Levi Woodbury (NH)
Silas Wright (NY)

4TH CONVENTION:
May 27–30, 1844, Odd Fellows' Hall, Baltimore (MD)
Hendrick B. Wright (PA), temporary and permanent chairman

In attendance were 325 delegates (casting 266 votes), representing every state except South Carolina. The Democratic platform called for annexation of both Oregon and Texas and strongly denounced the Bank of the United States.

DEMOCRATIC PARTY VOTE FOR PRESIDENTIAL NOMINATION:									
Candidate	Ballot: 1	2	3	4	5	6	7	8	9
Van Buren	146	127	121	111	103	101	99	104	0
Cass	83	94	92	105	107	116	123	114	0
Johnson	24	33	38	32	29	23	21	0	0
Calhoun	6	1	2	0	0	0	0	0	0
Buchanan	4	9	11	17	26	25	22	0	0
Woodbury	2	1	2	0	0	0	0	0	0
Stewart	1	1	0	0	0	0	0	0	0
Polk	0	0	0	0	0	0	0	44	266
not voting	0	0	0	1	1	1	1	4	6

(continued)

DEMOCRATIC PARTY (cont.)
VOTE FOR VICE-PRESIDENTIAL NOMINATION:

Candidate	Ballot: 1	2	3
Wright	258	0	0
Woodbury	8	44	6
Dallas	0	13	220
Fairfield	0	107	30
Cass	0	39	0
Johnson	0	26	0
Stewart	0	23	0
Marcy	0	5	0
not voting	0	11	0

Two ballots were initially taken. Wright was nominated for the vice presidency, but he declined the nomination. No one achieved the necessary ⅔ majority on the second ballot. After a break, a third ballot was taken, and Dallas was nominated.

LIBERTY (ABOLITIONIST) PARTY
CANDIDATE FOR PRESIDENT:
James Gillespie Birney

CANDIDATE FOR VICE PRESIDENT:
Thomas Morris

CANDIDATES FOR PRESIDENTIAL NOMINATION:
James Gillespie Birney (NY)
William Jay (NY)
Thomas Morris (OH)
Gerrit Smith (NY)

CANDIDATES FOR VICE-PRESIDENTIAL NOMINATION:
Thomas Earle (PA)
Thomas Morris (OH)
Gerrit Smith (NY)
Alvan Stewart (NY)

LIBERTY (ABOLITIONIST) PARTY
VOTE FOR PRESIDENTIAL NOMINATION:

Candidate	Ballot: 1
Birney	108
Morris	2
Smith	
Jay	1

VOTE FOR VICE-PRESIDENTIAL NOMINATION:

Candidate	Ballot: 1
Morris	83
Earle	
Smith	22
Stewart	1

CONVENTION:
August 30, 1843, Buffalo (NY)
Leicester King (OH), permanent chairman

In all, 148 delegates from twelve states attended this convention. The Liberty Party's platform called for the complete abolition of slavery.

NATIONAL DEMOCRATIC (TYLER) PARTY
CANDIDATE FOR PRESIDENT:
John Tyler (VA)

CANDIDATE FOR VICE PRESIDENT:
none

CONVENTION:
May 27–28, 1844, Calvert Hall, Baltimore (MD)

This group of dissident Democrats opposed the national ticket and nominated Tyler for president. A committee was appointed to select a vice-presidential candidate.

WHIG PARTY
CANDIDATE FOR PRESIDENT:
Henry Clay (KY)

CANDIDATE FOR VICE PRESIDENT:
Theodore Frelinghuysen

CANDIDATES FOR VICE-PRESIDENTIAL NOMINATION:
    John Middleton Clayton (DE)
    John Davis (MA)
    George Evans (ME)
    Millard Fillmore (NY)
    Theodore Frelinghuysen (NJ)
    John McLean (OH)
    John Sergeant (PA)

CONVENTION:
    May 1, 1844, Universalist Church, Baltimore
        (MD)
    Arthur S. Hopkins (AL), temporary chairman
    Ambrose Spencer (NY), permanent chairman

Every state was represented at this convention. The Whig platform endorsed a protective tariff and a single term for president.

WHIG PARTY
VOTE FOR PRESIDENTIAL NOMINATION: CLAY WAS NOMINATED FOR PRESIDENT BY ACCLAMATION ON THE FIRST BALLOT.

VOTE FOR VICE-PRESIDENTIAL NOMINATION:

Candidate	Ballot: 1	2	3
Frelinghuysen	101	118	155
Davis	83	74	79
Fillmore	53	51	40
Sergeant	38	32	withdrawn

Senators John Middleton Clayton (DE) and George Evans (ME), and Supreme Court Justice John McLean all withdrew their names from consideration for the vice presidency. Frelinghuysen was nominated for vice president on the third ballot.

GENERAL ELECTION SUMMARY FOR 1844

Candidate	Electoral Votes	States	Popular Votes
Polk (D)	170	15	1,337,243
Clay (W)	105	11	1,299,062
Birney (L)	0	0	62,300
Tyler (NAT DEM [Tyler])	0	0	none recorded
unknown	0	0	2,058

ELECTION OF NOVEMBER 7, 1848

President
ZACHARY TAYLOR
Vice President
MILLARD FILLMORE

HIGHLIGHTS

Heightened antislavery sentiments led to the creation of the Free Soil Party, which entered candidates for the first time in the election of 1848. A war hero, Zachary Taylor assumed office with little political experience, but he quickly mastered the spoils system. He died on July 9, 1850, and was succeeded by his vice president, Millard Fillmore.

CLAY WHIG PARTY

CANDIDATE FOR PRESIDENT:
Henry Clay (KY)

DEMOCRATIC PARTY

CANDIDATE FOR PRESIDENT:
Lewis Cass

CANDIDATE FOR VICE PRESIDENT:
William Orlando Butler

CANDIDATES FOR PRESIDENTIAL NOMINATION:
James Buchanan (PA)
William Orlando Butler (KY)
John Caldwell Calhoun (SC)
Lewis Cass (MI)
George Mifflin Dallas (PA)
Levi Woodbury (NH)
William Jenkins Worth (NY)

CANDIDATES FOR VICE-PRESIDENTIAL NOMINATION:
William Orlando Butler (KY)
Jefferson Davis (MS)
William Rufus King (AL)
John Young Mason (NC)
James Iver McKay (NC)
John Anthony Quitman (MS)

5TH CONVENTION:
May 22–26, 1848, Universalist Church, Baltimore (MD)
J. S. Bryce (LA), temporary chairman
Andrew Stevenson (VA), permanent chairman

All states were represented at the convention. Its delegates appointed the first national committee of a political party that was organized to serve between conventions. The Democratic platform supported the institution of the presidential veto, the war with Mexico, and free trade.

DEMOCRATIC PARTY
VOTE FOR PRESIDENTIAL NOMINATION:

Candidate	Ballot: 1	2	3	4
Cass	125	133	156	179
Buchanan	55	54	40	33
Woodbury	53	56	53	38
Calhoun	9	0	0	0
Worth	6	6	5	1
Dallas	3	3	0	0
Butler	0	0	0	3

VOTE FOR VICE-PRESIDENTIAL NOMINATION:

Candidate	Ballot: 1	2
Butler	114	169
Quitman		
Mason		
King		
McKay		
Davis		

Butler's nomination came on the second ballot.

FREE SOIL (DEMOCRATIC) PARTY

CANDIDATE FOR PRESIDENT:
Martin Van Buren

CANDIDATE FOR VICE PRESIDENT:
Charles Francis Adams

CANDIDATES FOR PRESIDENTIAL NOMINATION:
John Parker Hale (NH)
Martin Van Buren (NY)

CANDIDATES FOR VICE-PRESIDENTIAL NOMINATION:
Charles Francis Adams (MA)
Henry Dodge (WI)

1ST CONVENTION:
August 9–10, 1848, Buffalo (NY)
Charles Francis Adams (MA), permanent chairman

This party combined the remnants of the Liberty Party and antislavery Democrats. An earlier convention on June 22, 1848, at Utica (NY), had nominated Van Buren for president and Dodge for vice president, but Dodge declined the nomination.

PLATFORM HIGHLIGHTS:

SUPPORTED:
- cheap postage
- improvements in rivers and harbors
- repayment of the national debt
- distribution of the public lands to actual settlers

OPPOSED:
- extension of slavery to the new states and territories

FREE SOIL (DEMOCRATIC) PARTY
VOTE FOR PRESIDENTIAL NOMINATION:

Candidate	Ballot: 1
Van Buren	154
Hale	129

VOTE FOR VICE-PRESIDENTIAL NOMINATION: ADAMS WAS NOMINATED BY ACCLAMATION TO FILL THE VACANCY FOR VICE PRESIDENT.

FREE SOIL (LIBERTY) PARTY

CANDIDATE FOR PRESIDENT:
none (John Parker Hale withdrew)

CANDIDATE FOR VICE PRESIDENT:
Leicester King

CANDIDATES FOR PRESIDENTIAL NOMINATION:
John Parker Hale (NH)
Gerrit Smith (NY)

CANDIDATES FOR VICE-PRESIDENTIAL NOMINATION:
Leicester King (OH)
Owen Lovejoy (IL)

FREE SOIL (LIBERTY) PARTY
VOTE FOR PRESIDENTIAL NOMINATION:

Candidate	Ballot: 1
Hale	103
Smith	44

VOTE FOR VICE-PRESIDENTIAL NOMINATION: KING WAS NOMINATED FOR VICE PRESIDENT OVER LOVEJOY.

CONVENTION:
October 20, 1847, Buffalo (NY)

Hale was nominated for president on the first ballot, but he later withdrew.

INDUSTRIAL CONGRESS

CANDIDATE FOR PRESIDENT:
Gerrit Smith (NY)

CANDIDATE FOR VICE PRESIDENT:
William S. Waitt (IL)

CONVENTION:
June 13, 1848, Philadelphia (PA)

LIBERTY LEAGUE

CANDIDATE FOR PRESIDENT:
Gerrit Smith

CANDIDATE FOR VICE PRESIDENT:
Charles C. Foote

CANDIDATES FOR PRESIDENTIAL NOMINATION:
Frederick Douglass (MD)
Charles C. Foote (MI)
Beriah Green (OH)
Gerrit Smith (NY)

CANDIDATES FOR VICE-PRESIDENTIAL NOMINATION:
Elihu Burritt (MA)
Charles C. Foote (MI)

CONVENTION:
June 2, 1848, Rochester (NY)
William Goodell, chairman

This abolitionist party was formed by William Goodell at Macedon Locke (NY) in June 1847.

LIBERTY LEAGUE
VOTE FOR VICE-PRESIDENTIAL NOMINATION: BURRITT WAS NOMINATED FOR VICE PRESIDENT, BUT HE DECLINED. FOOTE WAS SUBSTITUTED FOR SECOND PLACE ON THE TICKET.

NATIONAL LIBERTY PARTY

CANDIDATE FOR PRESIDENT:
Gerrit Smith

CANDIDATE FOR VICE PRESIDENT:
Charles C. Foote

CANDIDATES FOR PRESIDENTIAL NOMINATION:
Frederick Douglass (MD)
Charles C. Foote (MI)
Beriah Green (NY)
Amos A. Sampson (unknown)
Gerrit Smith (NY)

CONVENTION:
June 14–15, 1848, Buffalo (NY)

Smith was nominated for president on the first ballot. Folowing the lead of the Liberty League, the party nominated Foote for vice president.

NATIONAL LIBERTY PARTY
VOTE FOR PRESIDENTIAL NOMINATION:

Candidate	Ballot: 1
Smith	99
Green	2
Douglass	1
Sampson	1
Foote	1

NATIVE AMERICAN PARTY

CANDIDATE FOR PRESIDENT:
Zachary Taylor (LA)

CANDIDATE FOR VICE PRESIDENT:
Henry Alexander Scammell Dearborn (MA)

CONVENTION:
September 1847, Philadelphia (PA)

This was the first national campaign effort of the "Know Nothings," a nativist, anti-Catholic party.

WHIG PARTY

CANDIDATE FOR PRESIDENT:
Zachary Taylor

CANDIDATE FOR VICE PRESIDENT:
Millard Fillmore

CANDIDATES FOR PRESIDENTIAL NOMINATION:
Henry Clay (KY)
John Middleton Clayton (DE)
John McLean (OH)
Winfield Scott (NJ)
Zachary Taylor (LA)
Daniel Webster (MA)

CANDIDATES FOR VICE-PRESIDENTIAL NOMINATION:
Millard Fillmore (NY)
Abbott Lawrence (MA)

3D CONVENTION:
June 7–9, 1848, Museum Building, Philadelphia (PA)
John A. Collier (NY), temporary chairman
John M. Morehead (NC), permanent chairman

Every state except Texas was represented at the convention. The Whig platform consisted largely of praise for Taylor.

WHIG PARTY
VOTE FOR PRESIDENTIAL NOMINATION:

Candidate	Ballot: 1	2	3	4
Taylor	111	118	133	171
Clay	97	86	74	32
Scott	43	49	54	63
Webster	22	22	17	14
Clayton	4	4	1	0
McLean	2	0	0	0

VOTE FOR VICE-PRESIDENTIAL NOMINATION:

Candidate	Ballot: 1	2
Fillmore	115	173
Lawrence	109	87
scattering	51	6

GENERAL ELECTION SUMMARY FOR 1848

Candidate	Electoral Votes	States	Popular Votes
Taylor (W)	163	15	1,360,099
Cass (D)	127	15	1,220,544
Van Buren (FS [D])	0	0	291,263
Smith (NL)	0	0	2,733
Clay (CW)	0	0	89
unknown	0	0	196

ELECTION OF NOVEMBER 2, 1852

President
FRANKLIN PIERCE
Vice President
WILLIAM RUFUS KING

HIGHLIGHTS

President Millard Fillmore supported the Compromise of 1850. His policies pleased neither slaveholders nor the expansionists. As a result, he was unable to secure the nomination of his own party in 1852; but it took fifty-three ballots before the Whigs finally settled on his rival, Gen. Winfield Scott. Meanwhile, the Democrats also held a marathon convention and nominated a "dark horse," Franklin Pierce, on the forty-ninth ballot. Pierce defeated an illustrious field of James Buchanan, Lewis Cass, Stephen A. Douglas, and William L. Marcy to obtain the nomination and, ultimately, the election. The election campaign was waged without distinction, for both the Democrats and the Whigs shied away from the divisive issues of the day. As president, Pierce approved the Kansas-Nebraska Act, which left slavery to popular vote, and the Gadsden Purchase from Mexico. He failed, however, to appease the contending forces within his own party and was unable to achieve renomination in 1856.

DEMOCRATIC PARTY

CANDIDATE FOR PRESIDENT:
Franklin Pierce

CANDIDATE FOR VICE PRESIDENT:
William Rufus King

CANDIDATES FOR PRESIDENTIAL NOMINATION:
James Buchanan (PA)
William Orlando Butler (KY)
Lewis Cass (MI)
Daniel Dickinson (NY)
Henry Dodge (IA)
Stephen Arnold Douglas (IL)
Samuel Houston (TX)
Joseph Lane (OR)
William Learned Marcy (NY)
Franklin Pierce (NH)
John B. Weller (CA)

CANDIDATES FOR VICE-PRESIDENTIAL NOMINATION:
David Rice Atchison (MO)
William Orlando Butler (KY)
Howell Cobb (GA)
Jefferson Davis (MS)

DEMOCRATIC PARTY VOTE FOR PRESIDENTIAL NOMINATION:						
Candidate	Ballot: 1	10	20	30	40	49
Cass	116	111	81	33	107	2
Buchanan	93	86	92	83	27	0
Douglas	20	40	64	80	33	2
Marcy	27	27	26	26	85	0
Pierce	0	0	0	0	29	282
Lane	13	14	13	13	0	0
Houston	8	8	10	12	5	1
Weller	4	0	0	0	0	0
Dodge	3	0	0	0	0	0
Butler	2	1	1	20	1	1
Dickinson	1	1	1	1	1	0
abstentions	0	0	0	0	0	3

(continued)

DEMOCRATIC PARTY (cont.) VOTE FOR VICE-PRESIDENTIAL NOMINATION:		
Candidate	Ballot: 1	2
King	126	277
Downs	30	0
Weller	28	0
Butler	27	0
Atchison	25	0
Pillow	25	0
Strange	23	0
Rusk	12	0
Davis	2	11
Cobb	2	0
abstentions	2	14

Solomon Weathersbee Downs (LA)
William Rufus King (AL)
Gideon Johnson Pillow (TN)
Thomas Jefferson Rusk (TX)
Robert Strange (NC)
John B. Weller (CA)

6TH CONVENTION:
June 1–5, 1852, Maryland Institute Hall, Baltimore (MD)
Romulus M. Saunders (NC), temporary chairman
John W. Davis (IN), chairman

The Democratic Convention adopted a platform that re-peated the positions taken in 1848, denounced the char-tering of a national bank, and endorsed the Fugitive Slave Law and other compromises on the slavery issue.

FREE SOIL DEMOCRATIC PARTY

CANDIDATE FOR PRESIDENT:
John Parker Hale

CANDIDATE FOR VICE PRESIDENT:
George Washington Julian

CANDIDATES FOR PRESIDENTIAL NOMINATION:
Charles Francis Adams (MA)
Salmon Portland Chase (OH)
Joshua R. Giddings (OH)
John Parker Hale (NH)
John McLean (OH)
Gerrit Smith (NY)
Martin Van Buren (NY)

CANDIDATES FOR VICE-PRESIDENTIAL NOMINATION:
Charles Francis Adams (MA)
George Washington Julian (IN)
Samuel Lewis (OH)

CONVENTION:
August 11, 1852, Pittsburgh (PA)
Rufus Paine Spalding (OH), temporary chairman
Henry Wilson (MA), chairman

The Free Soiler platform urged repudiation of the Com-promise of 1850 and the Fugitive Slave Act, denounc-ing in strong terms efforts to extend slavery. It also called for public lands to be held in trust for the people, with limited quantities granted free of cost to landless settlers.

FREE SOIL DEMOCRATIC PARTY VOTE FOR PRESIDENTIAL NOMINATION: HALE WAS NOMINATED FOR PRESIDENT OVER CHASE AND SMITH. THE VOTE WAS NOT REPORTED. VOTE FOR VICE-PRESIDENTIAL NOMINATION:	
Candidate	Ballot: 1
Julian	104
Lewis	83
scattered	23

NATIVE AMERICAN PARTY

CANDIDATE FOR PRESIDENT:
Jacob Broom (PA)

CANDIDATE FOR VICE PRESIDENT:
Reynell Coates

CANDIDATES FOR VICE-PRESIDENTIAL NOMINATION:
Reynell Coates (NJ)
George Corbin Washington (DC)
Daniel Webster (MA)

The Native American (or "Know Nothing") Party advocated a nativist platform that was intolerant of foreign immigrants, Catholics, and non-Christians.

SOUTHERN RIGHTS PARTY
CANDIDATE FOR PRESIDENT:
George Michael Troup (GA)

The Southern Rights Party was a Democratic Party faction dedicated to states' rights and the preservation of slavery.

WHIG PARTY
CANDIDATE FOR PRESIDENT:
Winfield Scott
CANDIDATE FOR VICE PRESIDENT:
William Alexander Graham (NC)

CANDIDATES FOR PRESIDENTIAL NOMINATION:
Millard Fillmore (NY)
Winfield Scott (NJ)
Daniel Webster (MA)

CANDIDATES FOR VICE-PRESIDENTIAL NOMINATION:
William Alexander Graham (NC)

4TH CONVENTION:
June 16–20, 1852, Maryland Institute Hall, Baltimore (MD)
George C. Evans (ME), temporary chairman
John G. Chapman (MD), permanent chairman

All states were represented at this convention. The Whig platform supported states' rights, the improvement of rivers and harbors, and the Fugitive Slave Law.

WHIG PARTY
VOTE FOR PRESIDENTIAL NOMINATION:

Candidate	Ballot: 1	10	30	40	50	53
Fillmore	133	130	128	129	124	112
Scott	131	135	134	132	142	159
Webster	29	29	29	32	28	21

VOTE FOR VICE-PRESIDENTIAL NOMINATION: GRAHAM WAS UNANIMOUSLY NOMINATED FOR VICE PRESIDENT ON THE FIRST BALLOT, AFTER A NUMBER OF PERSONS WERE INFORMALLY OFFERED FOR CONSIDERATION AND DECLINED.

GENERAL ELECTION SUMMARY FOR 1852

Candidate	Electoral Votes	States	Popular Votes
Pierce (D)	254	27	1,601,474
Scott (W)	42	4	1,386,578
Hale (FSD)	0	0	156,149
Webster (W)	0	0	6,994
Broom (NA)	0	0	2,566
Troup (SR)	0	0	2,331
unknown	0	0	277

ELECTION OF NOVEMBER 4, 1856

President
JAMES BUCHANAN
Vice President
JOHN CABELL BRECKINRIDGE

HIGHLIGHTS

The election of 1856 witnessed the final demise of the Whig Party and the transformation of its remnants, along with the Free Soil Party, into the Republican Party. With the nation rushing toward open conflict between the slave-holding South and the industrial North, the election amplified the congressional wrangling over the issue of "bleeding Kansas" and other bitter sectional rivalries. It was an exciting contest, and the anti-Catholic fervor of the "Know-Nothing," or Native American, movement added another dimension of political excess. In the end, the relatively bland Democrat, James Buchanan, emerged victorious over the upstart Republicans, but their sizable vote portended an even more historic struggle in 1860.

AMERICAN (KNOW-NOTHING) PARTY

CANDIDATE FOR PRESIDENT:
Millard Fillmore

CANDIDATE FOR VICE PRESIDENT:
Andrew Jackson Donelson

CANDIDATES FOR PRESIDENTIAL NOMINATION:
John Bell (TN)
Erastus Brooks (NY)
Lewis Davis Campbell (OH)
Lewis Cass (MI)
John Middleton Clayton (DE)
Garrett Davis (KY)
Andrew Jackson Donelson (TN)
Millard Fillmore (NY)
Samuel Houston (TX)
George Law (NY)
John McLean (OH)
Kenneth Raynor (NC)
Richard Field Stockton (NJ)

CANDIDATES FOR VICE-PRESIDENTIAL NOMINATION:
Andrew Jackson Donelson (TN)
Henry Joseph Gardner (MA)
Kenneth Raynor (NC)
Percy Walker (AL)

CONVENTION:
February 22, 1856, National Hall, Philadelphia (PA)
Ephraim Marsh (NJ), permanent chairman

This party was originally characterized by secrecy, but the convention abolished many of the features that marked the party as a secret society. Twenty-seven states sent delegates to the convention. When a motion to nominate a candidate for president carried, 151 to 51, the delegations from Illinois, Indiana, New England Ohio, and Pennsylvania walked out. The American platform—"Americans must rule America"—supported limitations on the rights of non-native-born citizens and foreigners. Its rhetoric was a thinly disguised attack on Catholics and reflected growing resentment over Irish immigration to the United States in the wake of the potato famine.

AMERICAN (KNOW-NOTHING) PARTY VOTE FOR PRESIDENTIAL NOMINATION:	
Candidate	*Ballot: 1*
Fillmore	179
Law	24
Raynor	14
McLean	13
Davis	10
Houston	3
VOTE FOR VICE-PRESIDENTIAL NOMINATION:	
Candidate	*Ballot: 1*
Donelson	181
Gardner	12
Raynor	8
Walker	8

DEMOCRATIC PARTY

CANDIDATE FOR PRESIDENT:
James Buchanan

CANDIDATE FOR VICE PRESIDENT:
John Cabell Breckinridge

CANDIDATES FOR PRESIDENTIAL NOMINATION:
James Buchanan (PA)
Lewis Cass (MI)
Stephen Arnold Douglas (IL)
Franklin Pierce (NH)

CANDIDATES FOR VICE-PRESIDENTIAL NOMINATION:
James Asheton Bayard (DE)
Linn Boyd (KY)
John Cabell Breckinridge (KY)
Aaron Venable Brown (TN)
Benjamin Franklin Butler (MA)
James Cochrane Dobbin (NC)
Benjamin Fitzpatrick (AL)
Herschel Vespasian Johnson (GA)
Trusten Polk (MO)
John Anthony Quitman (MS)
Thomas Jefferson Rusk (TX)

7TH CONVENTION:
June 2–6, 1856, Smith and Nixon's Hall, Cincinnati
    (OH)
John E. Ward (GA), permanent chairman

PLATFORM HIGHLIGHTS:
SUPPORTED:
- presidential veto power
- free trade
- states' rights in the slavery question

OPPOSED:
- federal projects for internal improvements
- the Nativist movement

NORTH AMERICAN PARTY
CANDIDATE FOR PRESIDENT:
none (Nathaniel Sartle Prentice Banks [MA] withdrew)

CANDIDATE FOR VICE PRESIDENT:
none (William Freame Johnson [PA] withdrew)

CONVENTION:
June 12, 1856, New York (NY)

This group bolted from the American Party. Both the presidential and vice-presidential candidates later withdrew and supported the Republican candidates.

REPUBLICAN PARTY
CANDIDATE FOR PRESIDENT:
John Charles Fremont

CANDIDATE FOR VICE PRESIDENT:
William Lewis Dayton

CANDIDATES FOR PRESIDENTIAL NOMINATION::
Nathaniel Sartle Prentice Banks (MA)
John Charles Fremont (CA)
John McLean (OH)
William Henry Seward (NY)
Charles Sumner (MA)

DEMOCRATIC PARTY
VOTE FOR PRESIDENTIAL NOMINATION:

Candidate	Ballot: 1	2	3	4	5	6	7	8	9	10	11	12	13	14	15	16	17
Buchanan	135½	139	139½	141½	140	155	143½	147½	146	147½	147½	148	150	152½	168½	168	296
Pierce	122½	119½	119	119	119½	107½	89	87	87	80½	80	79	77½	75	3½	0	0
Douglas	33	31½	32	30	31	28	58	56	56	62½	63	63½	63	63	118½	122	0
Cass	5	6	5½	5½	5½	5½	5½	5½	7	5½	5½	5½	5½	5½	4½	6	0

VOTE FOR VICE-PRESIDENTIAL NOMINATION:

Candidate	Ballot: 1	2
Quitman	59	0
Breckinridge	51	296
Boyd	33	0
Bayard	31	0
Johnson	31	0
Brown	29	0
Butler	27	0
Dobbin	13	0
Fitzpatrick	11	0
Rusk	7	0
Polk	5	0

Breckinridge, Polk, Rusk, and James Alexander Seddon declined to stand for the vice-presidential nomination. Nonetheless, Breckinridge was nominated for vice president on the second ballot by unanimous vote.

REPUBLICAN PARTY
VOTE FOR PRESIDENTIAL NOMINATION:

Candidate	Ballot: Informal	1
Fremont	359	520
McLean	196	37
Sumner	2	0
Banks	1	0
Seward	1	1
abstention	1	0

Fremont was nominated unanimously for president on the first official ballot.

VOTE FOR VICE-PRESIDENTIAL NOMINATION:

Candidate	Ballot: Informal	1
Dayton	259	523
Lincoln	110	20
Banks	46	6
Wilmot	43	0
Sumner	36	3
Collamer	15	0
King	9	1
Pomeroy	8	0
Ford	7	1
Wilson	7	0
Carey	3	0
Clay	3	0
Giddings	2	0
Johnson	2	0
Pennington	1	0
abstentions	29	13

Dayton was nominated for vice president on the first official ballot.

CANDIDATES FOR VICE-PRESIDENTIAL NOMINATION:
    Nathaniel Sartle Prentice Banks (MA)
    Henry Charles Carey (PA)
    Cassius Marcellus Clay (KY)
    Jacob Collamer (VT)
    William Lewis Dayton (NJ)
    Thomas H. Ford (OH)

Joshua Reed Giddings (OH)
Whitfield Johnson (NJ)
John Alsop King (NY)
Abraham Lincoln (IL)
Aaron Pennington (NJ)
Samuel Pomeroy (KS)
Charles Sumner (MA)
David Wilmot (PA)
Henry Wilson (MA)

1ST CONVENTION:
    June 17–19, 1856, Music Fund Hall, Philadelphia (PA)
    Robert Emmet (NY), temporary chairman
    Henry Smith Lane (IN), permanent chairman

This party was formed of remnants of the Whig Party, Free Soil Party, and abolitionists. All of the northern states were represented, along with Delaware, Kentucky, Maryland, and Virginia.

PLATFORM HIGHLIGHTS:
SUPPORTED:
• admission of Kansas to the Union as a free state
• transcontinental railroad
• pursuit of other internal improvements by the national government

OPPOSED:
• extension of slavery into free territories

WHIG PARTY

CANDIDATE FOR PRESIDENT:
    Millard Fillmore (NY)

CANDIDATE FOR VICE PRESIDENT:
    Andrew Jackson Donelson (TN)

CONVENTION:
    September 17–18, 1856, Baltimore (MD)
    Edward Bates (MO), permanent chairman

This convention, with twenty-six states represented, was the Whig Party's last. Its platform condemned the sectional political parties. The convention delegates thus endorsed the American Party's nominees, urging Fillmore's election as the best means of avoiding civil war.

GENERAL ELECTION SUMMARY FOR 1856

Candidate	Electoral Votes	States	Popular Votes
Buchanan (D)	174	19	1,838,169
Fremont (R)	114	11	1,341,264
Fillmore (A [K-N])	8[1]	0	874,534[1]
unknown	0	0	3,177

[1] Totals include votes cast for the Whig ticket.

ELECTION OF NOVEMBER 6, 1860

President
ABRAHAM LINCOLN
Vice President
HANNIBAL HAMLIN

HIGHLIGHTS

Undoubtedly the most important election in U.S. history, the contest of 1860 revealed the country's deep geographical divisions as never before. The Democratic Party split into sectional factions, thus enabling the strident Republicans to capitalize on their northern base. With the nation on the brink of civil war, Abraham Lincoln's election tipped the balance toward armed conflict between North and South.

CONSTITUTIONAL UNION (AMERICAN) PARTY

CANDIDATE FOR PRESIDENT:
John Bell

CANDIDATE FOR VICE PRESIDENT:
Edward Everett (MA)

CANDIDATES FOR PRESIDENTIAL NOMINATION:
John Bell (TN)
John Minor Botts (VA)
John Jordan Crittenden (KY)
Edward Everett (MA)
William Leftwich Goggin (VA)
William Alexander Graham (NC)
Samuel Houston (TX)
John McLean (OH)
William Cabell Rives (VA)
William Lewis Sharkey (MS)

CONVENTION:
May 9–10, 1860, Presbyterian Church, Baltimore (MD)
Washington Hunt (NY), permanent chairman

This party endorsed the Union and the enforcement of the laws of the United States.

DEMOCRATIC PARTY

CANDIDATE FOR PRESIDENT:
none

CANDIDATE FOR VICE PRESIDENT:
none

CANDIDATES FOR PRESIDENTIAL NOMINATION:
Jefferson Davis (MS)
Daniel Stevens Dickinson (NY)
Stephen Arnold Douglas (IL)
James Guthrie (KY)
Robert Mercer Taliaferro Hunter (VA)
Andrew Johnson (TN)
Joseph Lane (OR)
James Alfred Pearce (MD)
Isaac Toucey (CT)

8TH CONVENTION:
April 23–28, April 30, and May 1–3, 1860, Hall of the South Carolina Institute, Charleston (SC)
Francis B. Flournoy (AR), temporary chairman
Caleb Cushing (MA), permanent chairman

The Democratic platform supported construction of the transcontinental railroad, the acquisition of Cuba, and enforcement of the Fugitive Slave Law. After fifty-seven ballots, the convention was unable to nominate candidates for president and vice president and was adjourned. The delegates reconvened on June 18, 1860, in Baltimore (MD). By the time the party reconvened, it was badly fragmented into

CONSTITUTIONAL UNION (AMERICAN) PARTY
VOTE FOR PRESIDENTIAL NOMINATION:

Candidate	Ballot: 1	2
Bell	68½	138
Houston	57	69
Crittenden	28	1
Everett	25	9½
Graham	24	18½
McLean	19	1
Rives	13	0
Botts	9½	5½
Sharkey	7	8½
Goggin	3	2

VOTE FOR VICE-PRESIDENTIAL NOMINATION:
EVERETT WAS UNANIMOUSLY NOMINATED
FOR VICE PRESIDENT.

southern, northern, and national factions, each of which ultimately nominated their own candidates.

DEMOCRATIC PARTY
VOTE FOR PRESIDENTIAL NOMINATION:

Candidate	Ballot: 1	57
Douglas	145½	151½
Hunter	42	16
Guthrie	35	65½
Johnson	12	0
Dickinson	7	4
Lane	6	14
Toucey	2½	0
Davis	1½	1
Pearce	1	0

NATIONAL (INDEPENDENT) DEMOCRATIC PARTY

CANDIDATE FOR PRESIDENT:
John Cabell Breckinridge

CANDIDATE FOR VICE PRESIDENT:
Joseph Lane (OR)

CANDIDATES FOR PRESIDENTIAL NOMINATION:
John Cabell Breckinridge (KY)
Daniel Stevens Dickinson (NY)

CONVENTION:
June 23, 1860, Maryland Institute Hall, Baltimore (MD)

Seceders from the Democratic Party formed this party. The nomination of the Breckinridge-Lane ticket preceded its adoption by the southern Democratic faction.

PLATFORM HIGHLIGHTS:
SUPPORTED:
• state sovereignty
• enforcement of the Fugitive Slave Law
• protection by the federal government of slave owners and their "property" in the territories
• acquisition of Cuba
• protection of the rights of naturalized citizens

NATIONAL (INDEPENDENT) DEMOCRATIC PARTY
VOTE FOR PRESIDENTIAL AND VICE-PRESIDENTIAL NOMINATIONS:

Candidate	Ballot: 1
Breckinridge	81
Dickinson	24

Breckinridge was nominated for president on the first ballot, and the nomination was made unanimous. Joseph Lane was nominated for vice president.

(NORTHERN) DEMOCRATIC PARTY

CANDIDATE FOR PRESIDENT:
Stephen Arnold Douglas

CANDIDATE FOR VICE PRESIDENT:
Herschel Vespasian Johnson

CANDIDATES FOR PRESIDENTIAL NOMINATION:
Thomas Stanhope Bocock (VA)
John Cabell Breckinridge (KY)
Daniel Stevens Dickinson (NY)
Stephen Arnold Douglas (IL)
James Guthrie (KY)
Horatio Seymour (NY)
Henry Alexander Wise (VA)

CANDIDATES FOR VICE-PRESIDENTIAL NOMINATION:
Benjamin Fitzpatrick (AL)
Herschel Vespasian Johnson (GA)

CONVENTION:
June 18–23, 1860, Front Street Theatre, Baltimore (MD)
Caleb Cushing (MA), temporary chairman
David Tod (OH), permanent chairman

(NORTHERN) DEMOCRATIC PARTY
VOTE FOR PRESIDENTIAL NOMINATION:

Candidate	Ballot: 1	2
Douglas	173½	181½
Guthrie	9	5½
Breckinridge	5	7½
Seymour	1	0
Bocock	1	0
Dickinson	½	0
Wise	½	0
abstentions	112½	99½

The nomination of Douglas was made unanimous.

VOTE FOR VICE-PRESIDENTIAL NOMINATION: FITZPATRICK WAS NOMINATED FOR VICE PRESIDENT ON THE FIRST BALLOT, RECEIVED 198½ VOTES (WITH 103½ VOTES NOT CAST AND 1 BLANK VOTE) BUT DECLINED THE NOMINATION. JOHNSON WAS SUBSTITUTED BY VOTE OF THE DEMOCRATIC NATIONAL COMMITTEE, WHICH WAS CONTROLLED BY THE NORTHERN DEMOCRATIC FACTION.

REPUBLICAN PARTY

CANDIDATE FOR PRESIDENT:
Abraham Lincoln

CANDIDATE FOR VICE PRESIDENT:
Hannibal Hamlin

CANDIDATES FOR PRESIDENTIAL NOMINATION:
Edward Bates (MO)
Simon Cameron (PA)
Salmon Portland Chase (OH)
Cassius Marcellus Clay (KY)
Jacob Collamer (VT)
William Lewis Dayton (NJ)
John Charles Fremont (CA)
Abraham Lincoln (IL)
John McLean (OH)
John Meredith Read (PA)
William Henry Seward (NY)
Charles Sumner (MA)
Benjamin Franklin Wade (OH)

CANDIDATES FOR VICE-PRESIDENTIAL NOMINATION:
Nathaniel Sartle Prentice Banks (MA)
Cassius Marcellus Clay (KY)

REPUBLICAN PARTY
VOTE FOR PRESIDENTIAL NOMINATION:

Candidate	Ballot: 1	2	3
Seward	173½	184½	180
Lincoln	102	181	231½
Cameron	50½	2	0
Chase	49	42½	24½
Bates	48	35	22
Dayton	14	10	1
McLean	12	8	5
Collamer	10	0	0
Wade	3	0	0
Fremont	1	0	0
Read	1	0	0
Sumner	1	0	0
Clay	0	2	1
abstentions	1	1	1

Before the third ballot was completed, delegates began shifting votes, and Lincoln obtained a total of 364. The votes were entered on the roll call as indicated in the table above, however.

VOTE FOR VICE-PRESIDENTIAL NOMINATION:

Candidate	Ballot: 1	2
Hamlin	194	367
Clay	101½	86
Hickman	58	13
Reeder	51	0
Banks	38	0
Davis	8	0
Houston	6	0
Dayton	3	0
Read	1	0
abstentions	7	0

Henry Winter Davis (MD)
William Lewis Dayton (NJ)
Hannibal Hamlin (ME)
John Hickman (PA)
Samuel Houston (TX)
John Meredith Read (PA)
Andrew Horatio Reeder (PA)

2D CONVENTION:
May 16–18, 1860, The Wigwam, Chicago (IL)
David Wilmot (PA), temporary chairman
George Ashmun (MA), permanent chairman

All of the free states sent delegates to the 2d Republican Convention, as did Delaware, the District of Columbia, the Kansas and Nebraska territories, Kentucky, Maryland, Missouri, Texas, and Virginia.

PLATFORM HIGHLIGHTS:
SUPPORTED:
- admission of Kansas as a free state
- construction of the transcontinental railroad

OPPOSED:
- destruction of the Union
- restrictions on the rights of immigrants who become citizens

SOUTHERN DEMOCRATIC PARTY
CANDIDATE FOR PRESIDENT:
John Cabell Breckinridge (KY)

CANDIDATE FOR VICE PRESIDENT:
Joseph Lane (OR)

CONVENTION:
June 18–28, 1860, Market Hall, Baltimore (MD)
Caleb Cushing (MA), permanent chairman

This faction of the Democratic Party demanded strict enforcement of the Fugitive Slave Law.

SOUTHERN DEMOCRATIC PARTY
VOTE FOR PRESIDENTIAL AND VICE-PRESIDENTIAL NOMINATIONS: BRECKINRIDGE AND LANE WERE UNANIMOUSLY NOMINATED FOR PRESIDENT AND VICE PRESIDENT, RESPECTIVELY.

UNION PARTY

CANDIDATE FOR PRESIDENT:
Gerrit Smith (NY)

The Union Party, a remnant of the Liberty Party, promoted abolition and preservation of the Union in opposition to secession.

GENERAL ELECTION SUMMARY FOR 1860			
Candidate	Electoral Votes	States	Popular Votes
Lincoln (R)	180	18	1,866,452
Breckinridge (SD)	72[1]	11[1]	847,953[1]
Bell (CU [A])	39	3	590,631
Douglas ([N] D)	12	2	1,375,157
Smith (U)	0	0	171
unknown	0	0	360

[1]includes votes cast for the National (Independent) Democratic ticket

ELECTION OF NOVEMBER 8, 1864

President
ABRAHAM LINCOLN
Vice President
ANDREW JOHNSON

HIGHLIGHTS

In the middle of the Civil War, Lincoln's fortunes seemed to hinge on the North's progress toward victory. A strong antiwar sentiment existed in New York City and other urban areas with significant Irish populations, and radical abolitionists within the Republican Party were disappointed by the president's refusal to enlist fully in their ranks. The Democrats, with Gen. George McClellan heading their ticket, held high hopes of winning the election. But Gen. William T. Sherman's triumphant march into Atlanta in early September gave Lincoln's reelection campaign the boost it needed to achieve victory in November.

CITIZENS PARTY

CANDIDATE FOR PRESIDENT:
George Francis Train (NE)

George Francis Train's "party" was a collection of personal admirers of his eccentricity. His campaign was largely a self-promotional effort.

DEMOCRATIC PARTY

CANDIDATE FOR PRESIDENT:
George Brinton McClellan

CANDIDATE FOR VICE PRESIDENT:
George Hunt Pendleton

CANDIDATES FOR PRESIDENTIAL NOMINATION:
George Brinton McClellan (NJ)
Charles O'Conor (NY)
Horatio Seymour (NY)
Thomas Hart Seymour (CT)
George Francis Train (NE)

CANDIDATES FOR VICE-PRESIDENTIAL NOMINATION:
George Washington Cass (PA)
John Dean Caton (IL)
Augustus Caesar Dodge (IA)
James Guthrie (KY)
George Hunt Pendleton (OH)
John Smith Phelps (MO)
Lazarus Whitehead Powell (KY)
Daniel Wolsey Voorhees (IN)

9TH CONVENTION:
August 29–31, 1864, Amphitheatre, Chicago (IL)
William Bigler (PA), temporary chairman
Horatio Seymour (NY), permanent chairman

Twenty-three states participated in this convention. The Democratic Party's platform supported ceasing hostilities between the North and South, proposed better treatment

DEMOCRATIC PARTY
VOTE FOR PRESIDENTIAL NOMINATION:

Candidate	Ballot: 1a[1]	1b[2]
McClellan	174	202½
Seymour, T.	38	23½
Seymour, H.	12	0
O'Conor	½	0
abstentions	1½	0

[1]ballot one, before the shift
[2]ballot one, after the shift

McClellan's nomination was made unanimous.

VOTE FOR VICE-PRESIDENTIAL NOMINATION:

Candidate	Ballot: 1
Guthrie	65
Pendleton	55
Powell	32
Cass	26
Caton	16
Voorhees	13
Dodge	9
Phelps	8

A second ballot was held and Pendleton received the unanimous vote of the delegates for the vice-presidential nomination.

for prisoners of war, and called for respect for civil laws in all states not in insurrection.

INDEPENDENT

CANDIDATE FOR PRESIDENT:
E. Cheeseborough (KS)

INDEPENDENT-DEMOCRATIC PARTY

CANDIDATE FOR PRESIDENT:
none (Alexander Long [OH] declined)

At a meeting in Columbus (OH), peace Democrats expressed their disappointment with General McClellan's "unconditional surrender" approach to the war. Delegates nominated Representative Long for president, but he promptly declined.

INDEPENDENT REPUBLICAN PARTY

CANDIDATE FOR PRESIDENT:
none (John Charles Fremont [CA] withdrew)

CANDIDATE FOR VICE PRESIDENT:
none (John Cochrane [NY] withdrew)

CONVENTION:
May 31, 1864, Cleveland (OH)
John Cochrane (NY), permanent chairman

This group bolted from the Republican Party on the issue of limiting the president to one term. About 350 delegates attended the convention. The candidates withdrew on September 21, 1864, and the party supported the Republican ticket in the general election.

PLATFORM HIGHLIGHTS:
SUPPORTED:
- suppression of the rebellion without compromise
- confiscation of the lands of the rebels for distribution to Union soldiers and actual settlers
- the Monroe Doctrine
- a constitutional amendment to abolish slavery
- a constitutional amendment to limit the president to a single term

---

INDEPENDENT REPUBLICAN PARTY
VOTE FOR PRESIDENTIAL AND VICE-PRESIDENTIAL NOMINATIONS: FREMONT AND COCHRANE WERE NOMINATED BY ACCLAMATION FOR PRESIDENT AND VICE PRESIDENT, RESPECTIVELY.

REPUBLICAN (NATIONAL UNION) PARTY

CANDIDATE FOR PRESIDENT:
Abraham Lincoln

CANDIDATE FOR VICE PRESIDENT:
Andrew Johnson

CANDIDATES FOR PRESIDENTIAL NOMINATION:
Ulysses Simpson Grant (IL)
Abraham Lincoln (IL)

CANDIDATES FOR VICE-PRESIDENTIAL NOMINATION:
Ambrose Everett Burnside (RI)
Benjamin Franklin Butler (MA)
Schuyler Colfax (IN)
Daniel Stevens Dickinson (NY)
Hannibal Hamlin (ME)
Joseph Holt (KY)
Andrew Johnson (TN)
John Alsop King (NY)
Lovell Harrison Rousseau (LA)
David Tod (OH)

3D CONVENTION:
June 7–8, 1864, Front Street Theatre, Baltimore (MD)
Rev. Dr. Robert J. Breckinridge (KY), temporary chairman
William Dennison (OH), permanent chairman

Thirty-one states, including eight southern states, attended this convention.

REPUBLICAN (NATIONAL UNION) PARTY
VOTE FOR PRESIDENTIAL NOMINATION:

Candidate	Ballot: 1
Lincoln	484
Grant	22

Lincoln's nomination was made unanimous.

VOTE FOR VICE-PRESIDENTIAL NOMINATION:

Candidate	Ballot: 1	2
Johnson	200	492
Hamlin	150	9
Dickinson	108	17
Butler	28	0
Rousseau	21	0
Colfax	6	0
Burnside	2	0
Holt	2	0
King	1	0
Tod	1	1

PLATFORM HIGHLIGHTS:

SUPPORTED:

- the need to quell the southern rebellion
- the unconditional surrender of Confederate forces
- a constitutional amendment to abolish slavery

- the speedy construction of the transcontinental railroad

ALSO:

- praised both Abraham Lincoln and the soldiers and sailors of the Union forces

GENERAL ELECTION SUMMARY FOR 1864			
Candidate	Electoral Votes[1]	States	Popular Votes
Lincoln (R)	212	22	2,213,635
McClellan (D)	21	3	1,805,237
Cheeseborough (I)	0	0	543
Train (C)	0	0	0
unknown	0	0	149

[1]Eleven Confederate states with eighty votes did not vote in this election.

ELECTION OF NOVEMBER 3, 1868

President
ULYSSES SIMPSON GRANT

Vice President
SCHUYLER COLFAX

HIGHLIGHTS

By 1868, the radical Republicans' support for Andrew Johnson had eroded to the point of outright hostility. On February 24, 1868, the House adopted articles of impeachment against the president, asserting that his removal of Secretary of War Edwin Stanton had violated the Tenure in Office Act. The Senate vote, however, was one short of the two-thirds majority necessary to convict the president of the charges brought by the House. Thus, while Johnson remained in office for the balance of his term, clearly he could not win renomination. Instead, the Republicans turned to the great hero of the War Between the States, Ulysses S. Grant. In a hotly contested convention race, the Democrats chose Horatio Seymour. President Johnson endorsed Seymour late in the campaign, but Grant still overwhelmed his opponent.

DEMOCRATIC PARTY

CANDIDATE FOR PRESIDENT:
Horatio Seymour

CANDIDATE FOR VICE PRESIDENT:
Francis Preston Blair, Jr.

CANDIDATES FOR PRESIDENTIAL NOMINATION:
Charles Francis Adams (MA)
John Quincy Adams II (MA)
Francis Preston Blair, Jr. (MO)
Salmon Portland Chase (OH)
Sanford Elias Church (NY)
James Rood Doolittle (WI)
James Edward English (CT)
Stephen Johnson Field (NY)
Winfield Scott Hancock (PA)
Thomas Andrews Hendricks (IN)
John T. Hoffman (NY)
Andrew Johnson (TN)
Reverdy Johnson (MD)
George Brinton McClellan (NJ)
Asa Packer (PA)
Joel Parker (NJ)
George Hunt Pendleton (OH)
Horatio Seymour (NY)
Thomas Hart Seymour (CT)
George Francis Train (NE)

CANDIDATES FOR VICE-PRESIDENTIAL NOMINATION:
Francis Preston Blair, Jr. (MO)
Augustus Caesar Dodge (IA)
Thomas Ewing, Jr. (KY)
John Alexander McClernand (IL)

10TH CONVENTION:
July 4–9, 1868, Tammany Hall, New York (NY)
Henry L. Palmer (WI), temporary chairman
Horatio Seymour (NY), permanent chairman

PLATFORM HIGHLIGHTS:

SUPPORTED:
- amnesty for persons formerly in rebellion against the United States
- return of civil government in the defeated areas of the Confederacy
- payment of public debts in paper money ("greenbacks") where payment in coin was not required

ALSO:
- criticized radical Republicans for their oppression and tyranny in the South
- characterized the Reconstruction Acts as unconstitutional usurpations
- praised President Johnson for his "patriotic efforts" in resisting Congress

INDEPENDENT

CANDIDATES FOR PRESIDENT:
Samuel J. Crawford (KS)
C. B. Lines (KS)
Walter Ross (KS)

REPUBLICAN PARTY

CANDIDATE FOR PRESIDENT:
Ulysses Simpson Grant

CANDIDATE FOR VICE PRESIDENT:
Schuyler Colfax

DEMOCRATIC PARTY
Vote for Presidential Nomination:

Candidate	Ballot: 1	5	8	16	18	20	21	22
Pendleton	105	122	156½	107½	56½	0	0	0\0
A. Johnson	65	24	6	5½	10	0	0	0\0
Church	34	33	0	0	0	0	0	0\0
Hancock	33½	46	28	113½	142½	144½	135½	103½\0
Packer	26	27	26	0	0	0	0	0\0
English	16	7	6	0	0	16	19	7\0
Doolittle	13	15	12	12	12	12	12½	4\0
Parker	13	13	7	7	3½	0	0	0\0
R. Johnson	8½	0	0	0	0	0	0	4\0
Hendricks	2½	19½	75	70½	87	121	132	145½\0
Blair	½	9½	0	0	0	13	0	0\0
Chase	0	0	0	0	½	0	½	0\0
H. Seymour	0	0	0	0	0	0	0	22\317
J. Q. Adams II	0	1	0	0	0	0	0	0\0
Field	0	0	6	0	0	9	8	0\0
T. H. Seymour	0	0	0	0	0	½	0	0
McClellan	0	0	0	0	0	0	½	0\0
Hoffman	0	0	0	0	0	0	½	0\0
not voting	0	0	0	1	0	2	0	31\0

The nomination was declared unanimous before the final vote could be recorded.

Vote for Vice-Presidential Nomination: Dodge, Ewing, and McClernand were placed in nomination for vice president, but all withdrew. Thereupon, Blair was unanimously nominated for vice president on the first ballot.

CANDIDATES FOR PRESIDENTIAL NOMINATION:
Dan Rice (NJ)
Ulysses Simpson Grant (IL)

CANDIDATES FOR VICE-PRESIDENTIAL NOMINATION:
Schuyler Colfax (IN)
John Angel James Creswell (MD)
Andrew Gregg Curtin (PA)
Reuben Eaton Fenton (NY)
Hannibal Hamlin (ME)
James Harlan (IA)
William Darrah Kelley (PA)
Samuel Clarke Pomeroy (KS)
James Speed (KY)
Benjamin Franklin Wade (OH)
Henry Wilson (MA)

4TH CONVENTION:
May 20–21, 1868, Crosby's Opera House, Chicago (IL)
Carl Schurz (MO), temporary chairman
Joseph Roswell Hawley (CT), permanent chairman

Six hundred fifty delegates attended the convention. The Republicans' platform supported the program of the radicals, denouncing President Johnson for "treacherous" acts, and the selective removal of disqualification from holding office for former "rebels" who cooperated with Reconstruction efforts. It also opposed any efforts to repudiate the national debt.

REPUBLICAN PARTY

VOTE FOR PRESIDENTIAL NOMINATION: GRANT WAS NOMINATED FOR PRESIDENT BY UNANIMOUS VOTE ON THE FIRST BALLOT. A RELATIVE UNKNOWN, DAN RICE (NEE DANIEL MCCLAREN), ALSO SOUGHT THE NOMINATION PRIOR TO THE CONVENTION.

VOTE FOR VICE-PRESIDENTIAL NOMINATION:

Candidate Ballot: 1	2	3	4	5
Wade	147	170	178	206	38
Fenton	126	144	139	144	69
Wilson	119	114	101	87	0
Colfax	115	145	165	186	541
Curtin	51	45	40	0	0
Hamlin	28	30	25	25	0
Speed	22	0	0	0	0
Harlan	16	0	0	0	0
Creswell	14	0	0	0	0
Pomeroy	6	0	0	0	0
Kelley	4	0	0	0	0
not voting	0	0	0	2	2

GENERAL ELECTION SUMMARY FOR 1868

Candidate	Electoral Votes	States	Popular Votes
Grant (R)	214	26	3,012,833
Seymour (D	80	8	2,703,249
Crawford (I)	0	0	1
Lines (I)	0	0	1
Ross (I)	0	0	1
uncounted	0	0	26[1]
unknown	0	0	43

[1]Three unreconstructed states with twenty-six votes—Mississippi with ten, Texas with six, and Virginia with ten—were not permitted to select electors and therefore were not included in the count of the electoral college.

ELECTION OF NOVEMBER 5, 1872

President
ULYSSES SIMPSON GRANT
Vice President
HENRY WILSON

HIGHLIGHTS

In the election of 1872, the Democratic Party desperately sought a workable coalition to unseat the ruling party of the Union—the Republican Party—but Democrats could not call on the vanquished southern states, which were still disenfranchised under Reconstruction. Despite the rampant corruption of his administration, the incumbent president, Ulysses S. Grant, remained quite popular. When the Democrats, Liberal Republicans, and others combined to offer the redoubtable Horace Greeley as a candidate for president, their hopes momentarily brightened. Greeley, however, died before the electoral college could meet, leaving his electors to vote for a variety of alternative candidates. Despite the predictable outcome, the unique election offered the electorate many "firsts": a female candidate for president, Victoria Woodhull; the nomination of a biracial ticket, with Woodhull at the head of the ticket and Frederick Douglass—the great African-American abolitionist, as her running mate; a Roman Catholic presidential candidate, Charles O'Conor, the standard-bearer of the Straight-Out Democrats; and finally, candidates nominated by the Prohibition Party.

ANTI-MASONIC PARTY

CANDIDATE FOR PRESIDENT:
None (Charles Francis Adams [MA] withdrawn)

CANDIDATE FOR VICE PRESIDENT:
Joseph Lorenzo Barlow (IL) (Charles Henry Howard [IL] declined)

CONVENTION:
May 21, 1872, Oberlin (OH)

Adams was nominated for president while he was out of the country. Upon his return, the party discovered that he was a Royal Arch Mason, and withdrew his nomination. Howard was nominated for vice president, but he declined with a statement of support for President Grant. Barlow of Illinois was then substituted for second place on the ticket. The Anti-Masonic Party withdrew from the canvass with the collapse of its national ticket.

CHEESE PARTY

CANDIDATE FOR PRESIDENT:
Sidney S. Warner (OH)

CONVENTION:
May 25, 1872, Wellington (OH)

The convention did not make a nomination for vice president, suggesting that the second place on the ticket be filled by a nominee from the fishing interests "on the lake shore."

CITIZENS PARTY

CANDIDATE FOR PRESIDENT:
George Francis Train (NE)

CONVENTION:
September 3, 1872, Louisville Opera House, Louisville (KY)

At this "nominating convention," Train charged admission.

DEMOCRATIC PARTY

CANDIDATE FOR PRESIDENT:
Horace Greeley

CANDIDATE FOR VICE PRESIDENT:
Benjamin Gratz Brown

CANDIDATES FOR PRESIDENTIAL NOMINATION:
James Asheton Bayard (DE)
Jeremiah Sullivan Black (PA)
Horace Greeley (NY)
William Slocum Groesbeck (OH)
George Francis Train (NE)

CANDIDATES FOR VICE-PRESIDENTIAL NOMINATION:
Benjamin Gratz Brown (MO)
John White Stevenson (KY)

11TH CONVENTION:
July 9–10, 1872, Ford's Opera House, Baltimore (MD)

Thomas J. Randolph (VA), chairman pro tempore
James Rood Doolittle (WI), permanent chairman

PLATFORM HIGHLIGHTS:
The Democrats adopted the Liberal Republican platform as their own.

DEMOCRATIC PARTY
VOTE FOR PRESIDENTIAL NOMINATION:

Candidate	Ballot: 1
Greeley	686
Black	21
Bayard	16
Groesbeck	2
blank votes	7

Greeley's nomination was made unanimous.

VOTE FOR VICE-PRESIDENTIAL NOMINATION:

Candidate	Ballot: 1
Brown	713
Stevenson	6
blank votes	13

INDEPENDENT
CANDIDATES FOR PRESIDENT:
Daniel Pratt (MA)[1]
George Washington Frost Mellen (MA)[2]
George W. Slocum (IA)
James Baird Weaver (IA)
William Palmer (KS)

INDEPENDENT LIBERAL REPUBLICAN (REVENUE REFORM) PARTY
CANDIDATE FOR PRESIDENT:
William Slocum Groesbeck

CANDIDATE FOR VICE PRESIDENT:
Frederick Law Olmsted (NY)

CANDIDATES FOR PRESIDENTIAL NOMINATION:
William Cullen Bryant (NY)
William Slocum Groesbeck (OH)

CONVENTION:
June 21, 1872, Fifth Avenue Hotel, New York (NY)
Thomas T. Gaunt (MO), chairman

[1] The views of eccentric Daniel Pratt combined astronomical, biblical, political, social, and moral "misinformation," according to one commentator of the time.
[2] A rival and friend of Pratt, Mellen apparently ran for president to oppose Pratt.

This convention was held by Liberal Republicans opposed to the nominations of Horace Greeley and Benjamin Gratz Brown.

PLATFORM HIGHLIGHTS:
SUPPORTED:
• complete amnesty for Confederate war veterans
• return to civil government in the South
• civil service reform
• free trade
• redemption of greenbacks

LABOR REFORM PARTY
CANDIDATE FOR PRESIDENT:
Charles O'Conor

CANDIDATE FOR VICE PRESIDENT:
None

CANDIDATES FOR PRESIDENTIAL NOMINATION:
Benjamin Gratz Brown (MO)
David Davis (IL)
Horace H. Day (NY)
John White Geary (PA)
Horace Greeley (NY)
George Washington Julian (IN)
Charles O'Conor (NY)
John McCauley Palmer (IL)
Joel Parker (NJ)
Wendell Phillips (MA)
George Francis Train (NE)

CANDIDATES FOR VICE-PRESIDENTIAL NOMINATION:
William Given Brien (TN)
Edwin Martin Chamberlin (MA)
Thomas Ewing (OH)
Joel Parker (NJ)
Absolom Madden West (MS)

CONVENTION:
February 21–22, 1872, Columbus (OH)
Edwin Martin Chamberlin (MA), chairman

This convention boasted delegates—mostly trade union representatives—from seventeen states.

PLATFORM HIGHLIGHTS:
SUPPORTED:
• a "purely national circulating medium" (greenbacks)
• repayment of the national debt
• elimination of the exemption from taxation of high-yield government bonds
• restrictions on the disposal of public lands
• modification of the tariff
• prohibition of imported Chinese labor
• the eight-hour workday
• abolition of contract labor in prisons
• regulation of railroads and telegraph corporations
• civil service reform

- limits of one term for the presidency
- general amnesty for Confederate veterans

LABOR REFORM PARTY
VOTE FOR PRESIDENTIAL NOMINATION:

Candidate	Ballot: Inf*	1	2	3
Davis	47	88	93	201
Day	59	21	59	3
Geary	60	0	0	0
Phillips	13	12	0	0
Palmer	8	0	0	0
Parker	7	7	7	0
Julian	6	5	0	0
Brown	0	14	0	0
Greeley	0	11	0	0

VOTE FOR VICE-PRESIDENTIAL NOMINATION:

Candidate	Ballot: 1	2
Parker	70	112
Chamberlin	72	57
Ewing	31	22
West	18	0
Brien	10	0

Both Davis and Parker declined. The convention was reconvened, but only a small number of delegates attended. Charles O'Conor was then nominated for president, but no candidate was named for vice president.

*Informal

LIBERAL REPUBLICAN PARTY
CANDIDATE FOR PRESIDENT:
Horace Greeley
CANDIDATE FOR VICE PRESIDENT:
Benjamin Gratz Brown
CANDIDATES FOR PRESIDENTIAL NOMINATION:
Charles Francis Adams (MA)
Benjamin Gratz Brown (MO)
Salmon Portland Chase (OH)
Andrew Gregg Curtin (PA)
David Davis (IL)
Horace Greeley (NY)
George Francis Train (NE)
Lyman Trumbull (IL)
CANDIDATES FOR VICE-PRESIDENTIAL NOMINATION:
Benjamin Gratz Brown (MO)
Cassius Marcellus Clay (KY)
Jacob Dolson Cox (OH)
George Washington Julian (IN)
John McCauley Palmer (IL)
John M. Scovel

Thomas Weston Tipton (NE)
Lyman Trumbull (IL)
Gilbert C. Walker (VA)

CONVENTION:
May 1–3, 1872, Industrial (Music) Hall, Cincinnati (OH)
Stanley Matthews (OH), chairman pro tempore
Carl Schurz (MO), permanent chairman

The convention assembled as a mass meeting, without designated delegates.

PLATFORM HIGHLIGHTS:
SUPPORTED:
- the Thirteenth, Fourteenth, and Fifteenth Amendments to the Constitution
- the restoration of state governments in the South (in principle)
- universal amnesty for Confederate veterans
- civil service reform
- return to specie payments

OPPOSED:
- repudiation of the national debt

LIBERAL REPUBLICAN PARTY
VOTE FOR PRESIDENTIAL NOMINATION:

Candidate	Ballot: 1	2	3	4	5	6
Greeley	147	245	258	251	309	482
Adams	203	243	264	279	258	187
Trumbull	110	148	156	141	81	19
Brown	95	2	2	2	2	0
Davis	92½	75	41	51	30	6
Curtin	62	0	0	0	0	0
Chase	2½	1	0	0	24	32

VOTE FOR VICE-PRESIDENTIAL NOMINATION:

Candidate	Ballot: 1	2
Brown	237	435
Trumbull	158	175
Julian	134½	0
Walker	84½	75
Clay	34	0
Cox	25	0
Scovel	12	0
Tipton	8	3
Palmer	0	8

LIBERAL REPUBLICAN PARTY OF COLORED MEN
CANDIDATE FOR PRESIDENT:
Horace Greeley (NY)

CANDIDATE FOR VICE PRESIDENT:
Benjamin Gratz Brown (MO)

CONVENTION:
September 25, 1872, Weissiger Hall, Louisville (KY)
W. N. Saunders (MD), permanent chairman

The Liberal Republican Party of Colored Men adopted a platform endorsing the Greeley-Brown ticket and civil service reform. The platform denounced "the villainy of rulers" of the southern states and called on "colored people" of those states to rid themselves of the Reconstructionist "vampires." It accepted the tenets of the Cincinnati platform of the Liberal Republicans.

NATIONAL WORKING MEN'S PARTY

CANDIDATE FOR PRESIDENT:
Ulysses Simpson Grant (OH)

CANDIDATE FOR VICE PRESIDENT:
Henry Wilson (MA)

CONVENTION:
May 23, 1872, New York (NY)

Delegates from thirty-one states attended this convention. The platform endorsed the Republican program under Grant.

PEOPLE'S [EQUAL RIGHTS; COSMIC; FREE LOVE] PARTY

CANDIDATE FOR PRESIDENT:
Victoria C. Woodhull

CANDIDATE FOR VICE PRESIDENT:
Frederick Douglass (declined)

CANDIDATES FOR PRESIDENTIAL NOMINATION:
George Washington Julian (IN)
Victoria C. Woodhull (NY)

CANDIDATES FOR VICE-PRESIDENTIAL NOMINATION:
James Harvey Blood (MO)
Frederick Douglass (MD)
Laura De Force Gordon (CA)
Ezra H. Heywood (MA)
Robert Dale Owen (IN)
Wendell Phillips (MA)
Chief Spotted Tail (WY)
Elizabeth Cady Stanton (NY)
Theodore Tilton (NY)
Benjamin F. Wade (OH)

CONVENTION:
May 10, 1872, Apollo Hall, New York (NY)
George W. Madox (ME), temporary chairman
Judge James D. Reymart (NY), permanent chairman

This convention was attended by five hundred delegates from twenty-six states and four territories. The delegates were largely reformers and former supporters of the National Woman Suffrage Association.

PLATFORM HIGHLIGHTS:
SUPPORTED:
- a new constitution
- a uniform civil and criminal law system throughout the nation
- approval of important legislation by national referenda
- abolition of monopolies and their replacement by public ownership
- the use of greenbacks as national currency
- restrictions on the disposal of public lands
- graduated income tax
- extension of the use of international arbitration to settle disputes
- public employment programs
- uniform wage scales for labor
- abolition of capital punishment
- proportional representation and guarantees of the rights of minorities
- universal government
- public ownership of mineral and water resources
- free speech

PEOPLE'S [EQUAL RIGHTS; COSMIC; FREE LOVE] PARTY
VOTE FOR PRESIDENTIAL NOMINATION: THE RADICAL CLUB OF SAN FRANCISCO RECOMMENDED JULIAN'S NOMINATION FOR PRESIDENT, BUT IN THE EXCITEMENT OF THE CONVENTION, WOODHULL WAS NOMINATED BY ACCLAMATION.

VOTE FOR VICE-PRESIDENTIAL NOMINATION: THE RADICAL CLUB OF SAN FRANCISCO ALSO RECOMMENDED THE NOMINATION OF STANTON FOR VICE PRESIDENT, BUT DOUGLASS WAS NOMINATED BY ACCLAMATION. DOUGLASS DECLINED.

PROHIBITION PARTY

CANDIDATE FOR PRESIDENT:
James Black

CANDIDATE FOR VICE PRESIDENT:
John Russell

CANDIDATES FOR PRESIDENTIAL NOMINATION:
James Black (PA)
Benjamin F. Butler (MA)
Salmon Portland Chase (OH)
Simeon B. Chase (PA)
Jacob Dolson Cox (OH)
David Davis (IL)
Neal Dow (ME)
Horace Greeley (NY)
John Russell (MI)
Gerrit Smith (NY)

CANDIDATES FOR VICE-PRESIDENTIAL NOMINATION:
James Black (PA)

John Blackmer (NH)
Henry Fish (MI)
Stephen B. Ransom (NJ)
John Russell (MI)
Julius A. Spencer (OH)
Gideon Tabor Stewart (OH)

1ST CONVENTION:
February 22, 1872, Columbus (OH)
Henry Fish (MI), temporary chairman
Simeon B. Chase (PA), permanent chairman

One hundred ninety-four delegates from nine states attended this first nominating convention of the Prohibition Party. The Prohibition Party was formed September 1, 1869, in a convention in Chicago (IL) that was attended by five hundred delegates from nineteen states and the District of Columbia.

PLATFORM HIGHLIGHTS:
SUPPORTED:
- the full suppression of liquor traffic
- civil service reform
- direct election of the president and vice president
- bimetallism
- the rights of labor over capital
- extension of public education
- a liberal immigration policy
- woman suffrage

CANDIDATES FOR VICE-PRESIDENTIAL NOMINATION:
Joseph Carter Abbott (NC)
Charles Francis Adams (MA)
Schuyler Colfax (IN)
Edmund Jackson Davis (TX)
Joseph Roswell Hawley (CT)
John Francis Lewis (VA)
Horace Maynard (TN)
Edward Follansbee Noyes (OH)
Henry Wilson (MA)

5TH CONVENTION:
June 5–6, 1872, Academy of Music, Philadelphia
  (PA)
Morton McMichael (PA), chairman pro tempore
Thomas Settle (NC), permanent chairman

PLATFORM HIGHLIGHTS:
SUPPORTED:
- the Reconstruction amendments
- civil service reform
- cessation of land grants to corporations and monopolies
- reduction of the national debt
- extension of pensions for soldiers'
- abolition of the franking privilege
- offer of amnesty to former "rebels"

ALSO:
- recited accomplishments under Abraham Lincoln and Grant

PROHIBITION PARTY
VOTE FOR PRESIDENTIAL NOMINATION: BLACK, BUTLER, S. B. CHASE, S. P. CHASE, DAVIS, DOW, RUSSELL, AND SMITH WERE OFFERED TO THE CONVENTION FOR THE PRESIDENTIAL NOMINATION. COX AND GREELEY WERE NOT "OFFERED TO THE CONVENTION"; SOME EARLY EFFORTS WERE MADE TO SOLICIT THEIR ACCEPTANCE OF A POSSIBLE PROHIBITION NOMINATION. A NOMINATING COMMITTEE RECOMMENDED BLACK, WHO WAS UNANIMOUSLY NOMINATED FOR PRESIDENT ON THE FIRST BALLOT.

VOTE FOR VICE-PRESIDENTIAL NOMINATION: BLACK, BLACKMER, FISH, RANSOM, SPENCER, AND STEWART WERE ALL CONSIDERED FOR THE VICE-PRESIDENTIAL NOMINATION PRIOR TO THE REPORT OF THE NOMINATING COMMITTEE. THE NOMINATING COMMITTEE RECOMMENDED JOHN RUSSELL FOR THE NOMINATION, AND HE WAS UNANIMOUSLY NOMINATED FOR VICE PRESIDENT ON THE FIRST BALLOT.

REPUBLICAN PARTY
VOTE FOR PRESIDENTIAL NOMINATION: GRANT WAS NOMINATED FOR PRESIDENT ON THE FIRST BALLOT AND RECEIVED 752 VOTES. THE NOMINATION WAS MADE UNANIMOUS.

VOTE FOR VICE-PRESIDENTIAL NOMINATION:

Candidate	Ballot: 1	2
Wilson	364½	399½
Colfax	321½	308½
Maynard	26	26
Lewis	22	0
Davis	16	16
Hawley	1	1
Noyes	1	1

REPUBLICAN PARTY

CANDIDATE FOR PRESIDENT:
Ulysses Simpson Grant (OH)

CANDIDATE FOR VICE PRESIDENT:
Henry Wilson (MA)

STRAIGHT-OUT (TAPROOT) DEMOCRATIC PARTY

CANDIDATE FOR PRESIDENT:
Charles O'Conor

CANDIDATE FOR VICE PRESIDENT:
John Quincy Adams II (MA)

CANDIDATES FOR PRESIDENTIAL NOMINATION:
John Quincy Adams II (MA)
James Lyons (VA)
Charles O'Conor (NY)
George Hunt Pendleton (OH)
George Francis Train (NE)

STRAIGHT-OUT (TAPROOT) DEMOCRATIC PARTY
VOTE FOR PRESIDENTIAL NOMINATION:

Candidate	Ballot: 1
O'Conor	600
Pendleton	4

O'Conor declined the nomination. Adams was then offered the presidential nomination, but he also declined.
The convention then offered the position to Lyons, who
also declined. Finally, the convention returned to its original choice and refused to accept O'Conor's declination.

VOTE FOR VICE-PRESIDENTIAL NOMINATION: ADAMS
WAS NOMINATED FOR VICE PRESIDENT ON THE THIRD
BALLOT, OVER LYONS AND EDGERTON. ADAMS
DECLINED, BUT HIS DECLINATION WAS NOT ACCEPTED.

CANDIDATES FOR VICE-PRESIDENTIAL NOMINATION:
John Quincy Adams II (MA)
James Lyons (VA)
Alfred Peck Edgerton (IN)

CONVENTION:
September 3, 1872, Louisville (KY)
James Lyons (VA), chairman

The party's platform supported states' rights, the paramount
value of labor whenever labor and capital conflicted, and a
tariff to raise revenues, while still opposing protectionism.

VETERANS NATIONAL PARTY

CANDIDATE FOR PRESIDENT:
Ulysses Simpson Grant (OH)

CANDIDATE FOR VICE PRESIDENT:
Henry Wilson (MA)

CONVENTION:
September 17, 1872, Pittsburgh (PA)
Joseph Roswell Hawley (CT), permanent chairman

The platform endorsed the Republican ticket and programs.

GENERAL ELECTION SUMMARY FOR 1872

Candidate	Electoral Votes	States	Popular Votes
Grant (R)	286[1]	29	3,597,1326[1]
Greeley (D)	—[2]	—[2]	2,834,079[3]
O'Conor (TAP)	0	0	29,489
Liberal Republican Elector	0	0	10,447
Black (PROH)	0	0	5,608
Palmer (I)	0	0	440
Slocum (I)	0	0	424
Weaver (I)	0	0	309
Groesbeck (ILR)	0	0	???
Mellen (I)	0	0	none recorded
Pratt (I)	0	0	none recorded
Train (CIT)	0	0	none recorded
Woodhull (PEOPLE'S)	0	0	none recorded
unknown	0	0	1,090

[1]includes votes of the National Working Men's Party and the Veterans National
Party
[2]Horace Greeley died on November 29, 1872. His electoral votes were split as
follows: Thomas Andrew Hendricks (IN), 42 votes—4 states;
Benjamin Gratz Brown (MO), 18 votes—2 states; Charles Jones Jenkins (GA), 2
votes—1 state; David Davis (IL), 1 vote—1 state; Horace Greeley (NY), 3 votes (not
counted by resolution of the U.S. House of Representatives).
[3]includes votes of the Liberal Republican Party and the Liberal Republican Party of
Colored Men

ELECTION OF NOVEMBER 7, 1876

President
RUTHERFORD BIRCHARD HAYES
Vice President
WILLIAM ALMON WHEELER

HIGHLIGHTS

Following the market crash and financial panic of 1873, Democrats felt encouraged about their presidential prospects in the centennial year of 1876. Grant's final term had witnessed a succession of political scandals and Democrats carefully positioned themselves as the party of reform. The opposition party's prospects brightened still further when it won a series of important state and local elections in 1874. Even though election night saw the Democratic nominee, Samuel J. Tilden, the apparent winner, victory still eluded the Democrats. Their eventual loss resulted from a Republican challenge that initially disputed the outcome in three southern states—Florida, Louisiana, and South Carolina—and Oregon, which seemed to have gone in favor of Tilden. Under the control of Republican politicians, each of these states finally returned majorities for the Republican candidate, Rutherford B. Hayes. When the president of the Senate received the electoral vote, questions arose about the vote's validity. To resolve the issue of the disputed states, Congress appointed a special electoral commission of five senators, five representatives, and five Supreme Court justices. They began counting on February 1, 1877, and finished on March 2, with each party's representatives voting for the candidate of their party. After backroom deals were cut by political operatives of both parties, the commission decided the dispute in favor of Hayes by a one-vote margin. The quid pro quo was Hayes's agreement to end carpetbag rule in the South.

While the Hayes-Tilden electoral dispute was clearly the most significant highlight of the 1876 election, it was also the first entry of the Greenback Party into the fray. Its presence testified to a growing division within the country over economic issues such as resuming specie payments, issuing legal tender, and adhering to the gold standard.

AMERICAN ALLIANCE

CANDIDATE FOR PRESIDENT:
Rutherford Birchard Hayes (OH)

CANDIDATE FOR VICE PRESIDENT:
William Almon Wheeler (NY)

CONVENTION:
July 1876

By action of its Grand Council, the American Alliance endorsed the Republican candidates.

AMERICAN NATIONAL PARTY

CANDIDATE FOR PRESIDENT:
James B. Walker

CANDIDATE FOR VICE PRESIDENT:
Donald Kirkpatrick (NY)

CANDIDATES FOR PRESIDENTIAL NOMINATION:
Charles Francis Adams (MA)

Jonathan Blanchard (IL)
James B. Walker (IL)

CONVENTION:
June 8–10, 1875, Liberty Hall, Pittsburgh (PA)
Rev. B. T. Roberts (NY), chairman
Jonathan Blanchard (OH), keynoter

This party was formed of members of the Anti-Masonic Party, the Anti-Secret Society, and the National Christian Association.

PLATFORM HIGHLIGHTS:
SUPPORTED:
- prohibition
- the Reconstruction amendments
- international arbitration
- Bible study in public schools
- specie payment
- justice for American Indians
- abolition of the Electoral College

Opposed:
- secret societies and monopolies

Also:
- declared the United States to be a "Christian" nation
- recognized the Sabbath as day of rest

AMERICAN NATIONAL PARTY
VOTE FOR PRESIDENTIAL AND VICE-PRESIDENTIAL NOMINATIONS: ADAMS AND BLANCHARD WERE CONSIDERED FOR THE PRESIDENTIAL NOMINATION, BUT THEY DECLINED. BOTH WALKER AND KIRKPATRICK OF NEW YORK WERE UNANIMOUSLY NOMINATED FOR PRESIDENT AND VICE PRESIDENT, RESPECTIVELY, BY THE DELEGATES IN ATTENDANCE.

COMMUNIST PARTY

This election was the first in which the Communists were recorded as having received votes, predating the foundation of the American Communist Party by more than forty years. The election returns do not identify any candidates.

DEMOCRATIC PARTY

CANDIDATE FOR PRESIDENT:
Samuel Jones Tilden

CANDIDATE FOR VICE PRESIDENT:
Thomas Andrews Hendricks (IN)

CANDIDATES FOR PRESIDENTIAL NOMINATION:
William Allen (OH)
Thomas Francis Bayard (DE)
James Overton Broadhead (MO)
Winfield Scott Hancock (PA)
Thomas Andrews Hendricks (IN)
Joel Parker (NJ)
Allen Granberry Thurman (OH)
Samuel Jones Tilden (NY)

12TH CONVENTION:
June 27–29, 1876, Merchant's Exchange, St. Louis (MO)
Henry Watterson (KY), temporary chairman
John Alexander McClernand (IL), permanent chairman

PLATFORM HIGHLIGHTS:
Supported:
- a sound currency based on legal tender notes
- repeal of the Resumption Act of 1875
- an end to wasteful government spending
- disposal of public lands to railroads and others who were not "actual settlers"
- civil service reform

Opposed:
- carpetbag government in the South
- the protective tariff
- importation of Chinese labor

DEMOCRATIC PARTY
VOTE FOR PRESIDENTIAL NOMINATION:

Candidate	Ballot: 1	2
Tilden	404½	535
Hendricks	140½	85
Hancock	75	58
Allen	54	54
Bayard	33	4
Parker	18	0
Broadhead	16	0
Thurman	3	2

VOTE FOR VICE-PRESIDENTIAL NOMINATION: HENDRICKS, AS THE ONLY CANDIDATE FOR NOMINATION, WAS NOMINATED FOR VICE PRESIDENT ON THE FIRST BALLOT, ALTHOUGH EIGHT BLANK VOTES WERE ALSO CAST.

IMPERIALIST PARTY

CANDIDATE FOR EMPEROR:
William Washington (TN)

INDEPENDENT

CANDIDATE FOR PRESIDENT:
Louis Brookwater (IA)

INDEPENDENT NATIONAL (GREENBACK) PARTY

CANDIDATE FOR PRESIDENT:
Peter Cooper

CANDIDATE FOR VICE PRESIDENT:
Samuel Fenton Cary (OH)

CANDIDATES FOR PRESIDENTIAL NOMINATION:
William Allen (OH)
Newton Booth (CA)
Alexander Campbell (PA)
Peter Cooper (NY)
Andrew Gregg Curtin (PA)
David Davis (IL)
James W. Singleton (IL)
Robert F. Wingate (MO)

CANDIDATES FOR VICE-PRESIDENTIAL NOMINATION:
Newton Booth (CA)
James Buchanan (PA)
Alexander Campbell (PA)
Andrew Gregg Curtin (PA)
Moses Whelock Field (MI)
Robert F. Wingate (MO)

1ST CONVENTION:
> May 17–18, 1876, Academy of Music, Indianapolis (IN)
> Ignatius Donnelly (MN), temporary chairman
> Thomas J. Durant (DC), permanent chairman

The Greenback Party was organized November 25, 1874, in Indianapolis. There were 239 delegates from nineteen states attending this convention. The delegates chose a platform that supported repealing the Specie-Resumption Act of 1875 and the issuance of greenbacks as legal tender. It also specifically opposed the sale of government bonds to purchase gold and silver as a substitute for issuing legal tender notes.

INDEPENDENT NATIONAL (GREENBACK) PARTY
VOTE FOR PRESIDENTIAL NOMINATION:

Candidate	Ballot: 1
Cooper	352
Campbell	60
Allen	31
Curtin	58

All of the nominees had their names placed in nomination before the convention; but Campbell, Davis, and Singleton withdrew their names from consideration, although delegates still voted for Campbell. On motion, Cooper's nomination was made unanimous.

VOTE FOR VICE-PRESIDENTIAL NOMINATION:

Candidate	Ballot: 1
Booth	412
Wingate	45
Field	12

Buchanan, Campbell, and Field withdrew their names from consideration. Later, when Booth declined the nomination, Samuel Fenton Cary was substituted in his place.

PROHIBITION (NATIONAL PROHIBITION REFORM) PARTY

CANDIDATE FOR PRESIDENT:
> Green Clay Smith (KY)

CANDIDATE FOR VICE PRESIDENT:
> Gideon Tabor Stewart (OH)

2D CONVENTION:
> May 17, 1876, Halle's Hall, Cleveland (OH)
> Green Clay Smith (KY), temporary chairman
> Henry Adams Thompson (OH), permanent chairman

At this convention, the party changed its name to the National Prohibition Reform Party.

PLATFORM HIGHLIGHTS:
SUPPORTED:
- the legal prohibition of alcoholic beverages
- women's suffrage
- reduction in the cost of postage
- the suppression of lotteries and gambling
- the abolition of polygamy
- observance of the Christian Sabbath
- establishment of free public schools
- use of the Bible in public educational institutions (while supporting separation of church and state)
- the use of international arbitration
- penal reform
- the elimination of the patronage system
- the direct election of all civil officers of the United States
- a liberalized immigration policy
- protection of the right, on demand, to redeem legal notes in gold or silver
- the need for a thorough investigation into alleged abuses of the public trust

REPUBLICAN PARTY

CANDIDATE FOR PRESIDENT:
> Rutherford Birchard Hayes

CANDIDATE FOR VICE PRESIDENT:
> William Almon Wheeler

CANDIDATES FOR PRESIDENTIAL NOMINATION:
> Charles Francis Adams (MA)
> James Gillespie Blaine (ME)
> Benjamin Helm Bristow (KY)
> Roscoe Conkling (NY)
> John Frederick Hartranft (PA)
> Rutherford Birchard Hayes (OH)
> Marshall Jewell (CT)
> Oliver Hazard Perry Throck Morton (IN)
> Elihu Benjamin Washburne (IL)
> William Almon Wheeler (NY)

CANDIDATES FOR VICE-PRESIDENTIAL NOMINATION:
> Frederick Theodore Frelinghuysen (NJ)
> Joseph Roswell Hawley (CT)
> Marshall Jewell (CT)
> William Almon Wheeler (NY)
> Stewart L. Woodford (NY)

6TH CONVENTION:
> June 14–16, 1876, Exposition Hall, Cincinnati (OH)
> Theodore M. Pomeroy (NY), temporary chairman
> Edward McPherson (PA), permanent chairman

The convention wrangled over a platform plank on the resumption of specie payments. A motion to call for an immediate resumption failed.

PLATFORM HIGHLIGHTS:

SUPPORTED:

- redemption of the debt "at the earliest practicable period"
- a constitutional amendment to prohibit the use of any public funds for the benefit of schools under sectarian control
- protection of immigrants combined with an investigation of the effects of Chinese labor
- the "respectful consideration" of the demand for women's rights

ALSO:

- recited the party's accomplishments and its continuing duty to compel "pacification" of the South
- accused the Democratic Party of "being the same in character and spirit as when it sympathized with treason"

REPUBLICAN PARTY
VOTE FOR PRESIDENTIAL NOMINATION:

Candidate	Ballot: 1	2	3	4	5	6	7
Hayes	61	64	67	68	104	113	384
Blaine	285	296	293	292	286	308	351
Morton	124	120	113	108	95	85	0
Bristow	113	114	121	126	114	111	21
Conkling	99	93	90	84	82	81	0
Hartranft	58	63	68	71	69	50	0
Jewell	11	0	0	0	0	0	0
Washburne	0	1	1	3	3	4	0
Wheeler	3	3	2	2	2	2	0
not voting	2	2	1	2	1	2	0

VOTE FOR VICE-PRESIDENTIAL NOMINATION:

Candidate	Ballot: 1
Wheeler	366
Frelinghuysen	89
Jewell	86
Woodford	70
Hawley	25

By the time the roll call for vice president reached South Carolina, a motion was made to suspend the rules, and Wheeler was nominated by acclamation.

GENERAL ELECTION SUMMARY FOR 1876

Candidate	Electoral Votes	States	Popular Votes
Hayes (R)	369	38	4,036,298
Tilden (D)	184	17	4,300,590
Walker (ANP)	0	0	2,636
Cooper (IND NAT)	0	0	81,740
Smith (PROHIB)	0	0	9,522
Brookwater (I)	0	0	97
Communist	0	0	32
unknown	0	0	6,940

ELECTION OF NOVEMBER 2, 1880

President
JAMES ABRAM GARFIELD
Vice President
CHESTER ALAN ARTHUR

HIGHLIGHTS

With the exception of Ulysses Grant's attempt to secure the Republican nomination for a third term, the election of 1880 was a dull affair. The Democrats railed about the "stolen" election four years earlier, but they failed to stir any enthusiasm for their candidate, Gen. Winfield S. Hancock. In a campaign devoid of important issues, the Republican candidate also ignited few flames of passion. On election day, the Greenback Party proved pivotal, as the margin between James Garfield and Hancock was less than ten thousand out of the more than nine million votes cast. The Greenbackers had increased their strength as an independent political force with more than three hundred thousand votes.

AMERICAN PARTY

CANDIDATE FOR PRESIDENT:
John Wolcott Phelps (VT)

CANDIDATE FOR VICE PRESIDENT:
Samuel Clarke Pomeroy (KS)

The American Party was a Christian nativist party that promoted limits on immigration.

DEMOCRATIC PARTY

CANDIDATE FOR PRESIDENT:
Winfield Scott Hancock

CANDIDATE FOR VICE PRESIDENT:
William Hayden English

CANDIDATES FOR PRESIDENTIAL NOMINATION:
Thomas Francis Bayard (DE)
Jeremiah Sullivan Black (PA)
James Edward English (CT)
Thomas Ewing (OH)
Stephen Johnson Field (CA)
Winfield Scott Hancock (PA)
Thomas Andrews Hendricks (IN)
Hugh Judge Jewett (OH)
George Van Ness Lothrop (MI)
William Austin Hamilton Loveland (CO)
George Brinton McClellan (NJ)
Joseph Ewing McDonald (IN)
William Ralls Morrison (IL)
Joel Parker (NJ)
Henry B. Payne (OH)
Samuel Jackson Randall (PA)
Horatio Seymour (NY)
Allen Granbery Thurman (OH)
Samuel Jones Tilden (NY)

CANDIDATES FOR VICE-PRESIDENTIAL NOMINATION:
Richard Moore Bishop (OH)
William Hayden English (IN)

13TH CONVENTION:
June 22–24, 1880, Music Hall, Cincinnati (OH)

DEMOCRATIC PARTY VOTE FOR PRESIDENTIAL NOMINATION:			
Candidate	Ballot: 1	2a	2b
Hancock	171	320	705
Bayard	153½	112	2
Payne	81	0	0
Thurman	68½	50	0
Field	65	65½	0
Morrison	62	0	0
Hendricks	49½	31	30
Tilden	38	6	1
Ewing	10	0	0
Seymour	8	0	0
Randall	6	128½	0
Loveland	5	0	0
McDonald	2	0	0
McClellan	2	0	0
Black	1	0	0
J. E. English	1	19	0
Jewett	1	1	0
Lothrop	1	0	0
Parker	1	2	0
not voting	10½	3	0

VOTE FOR VICE-PRESIDENTIAL NOMINATION:
W. H. ENGLISH WAS NOMINATED FOR VICE PRESIDENT BY ACCLAMATION.

George Hoadly (OH), temporary chairman
John White Stevenson (KY), permanent chairman

PLATFORM HIGHLIGHTS:

SUPPORTED:

- home rule for Ireland
- honest money
- civil service reform
- amendment of the Burlingame Treaty to restrict Chinese immigration

OPPOSED:

- the protective tariff

ALSO:

- denounced the "great fraud of 1876," which denied Tilden election

GREENBACK LABOR (NATIONAL) PARTY

CANDIDATE FOR PRESIDENT:

James Baird Weaver

CANDIDATE FOR VICE PRESIDENT:

B. J. Chambers

CANDIDATES FOR PRESIDENTIAL NOMINATION:

Edward Phelps Allis (WI)
Benjamin Franklin Butler (MA)
Alexander Campbell (IL)
Solon Chase (ME)
Stephen Devalson Dillaye (NY)
James Baird Weaver (IA)
Hendrick Bradley Wright (PA)

CANDIDATES FOR VICE-PRESIDENTIAL NOMINATION:

B. J. Chambers (TX)
Absalom Madden West (MS)

CONVENTION:

June 9–11, 1880, Exposition Hall, Chicago (IL)
Rev. Gilbert De La Matyr (IN), temporary chairman
Richard F. Trevellick (MI), permanent chairman

PLATFORM HIGHLIGHTS:

SUPPORTED:

- the issuance of legal tender currency (greenbacks) as full payment for the public debt
- abolition of the national banking system
- enforcement of the eight-hour workday law
- abolition of convict and child labor
- establishment of a bureau of labor statistics
- uniform rates for passenger and freight in interstate commerce
- forfeiture of unused railroad lands
- a graduated income tax
- de-emphasis of the military
- extension of the right of suffrage to "every citizen of due age, sound mind, and not a felon"

OPPOSED:

- the Burlingame Treaty, which permitted the importation of Chinese labor
- monopolies, especially of railroads, land, and banking

GREENBACK LABOR (NATIONAL) PARTY VOTE FOR PRESIDENTIAL NOMINATION:	
Candidate	Ballot: 1
Weaver	224½
Wright	126½
Dillaye	119
Butler	95
Chase	89
Allis	41
Campbell	21

Weaver's nomination was made unanimous.

VOTE FOR VICE-PRESIDENTIAL NOMINATION:	
Candidate	Ballot: 1
Chambers	403
West	311

Chambers' nomination was made unanimous.

INDEPENDENT

CANDIDATES FOR PRESIDENT:

H. Scott Howells (IA)
W. Pitt Norris (IA)

INDEPENDENT DEMOCRAT

CANDIDATE FOR PRESIDENT:

A. C. Brewer (AR)

PROHIBITION PARTY

CANDIDATE FOR PRESIDENT:

Neal Dow (ME)

CANDIDATE FOR VICE PRESIDENT:

Henry Adams Thompson (OH)

3D CONVENTION:

June 17, 1880, Cleveland (OH)
Henry Adams Thompson (OH), temporary chairman
A. A. Miner (MA), permanent chairman

Twelve states were represented at this convention. The party's platform enumerated the evils of alcoholic beverages, demanded abolition of the "drinking system," and advocated woman suffrage. The party restored its former name.

REPUBLICAN PARTY

CANDIDATE FOR PRESIDENT:
James Abram Garfield

CANDIDATE FOR VICE PRESIDENT:
Chester Alan Arthur

CANDIDATES FOR PRESIDENTIAL NOMINATION:
James Gillespie Blaine (ME)
Roscoe Conkling (NY)
George Franklin Edmunds (VT)
James Abram Garfield (OH)
Ulysses Simpson Grant (IL)
Benjamin Harrison (IN)
John Frederick Hartranft (PA)
Rutherford Birchard Hayes (OH)
James Bennett McCreary (KY)
Philip Sheridan (MA)
John Sherman (OH)
Elihu Benjamin Washburne (IL)
William Windom (MN)

CANDIDATES FOR VICE-PRESIDENTIAL NOMINATION:
James Lusk Alcorn (MS)
Chester Alan Arthur (NY)
Blanche Kelso Bruce (MS)
Edmund Jackson Davis (TX)
Marshall Jewell (CT)
Horace Maynard (TN)
Thomas Settle (FL)
Elihu Benjamin Washburne (IL)
Stewart L. Woodford (NY)

7TH CONVENTION:
June 2–5 and 7–8, 1880, Exposition Hall, Chicago (IL)
George Frisbie Hoar (MA), temporary and permanent chairman

PLATFORM HIGHLIGHTS:
OPPOSED:
• use of public funds for parochial schools
• polygamy
• unrestrained importation of Chinese labor

REPUBLICAN PARTY
VOTE FOR PRESIDENTIAL NOMINATION:

Candidate	Ballot: 1	11	21	29	34	35	36
Garfield	0	2	1	2	17	50	399
Grant	304	305	305	305	312	313	306
Blaine	284	281	276	278	275	257	42
Sherman	93	93	96	116	107	99	3
Edmunds	34	31	31	12	11	11	0
Washburne	30	32	35	35	30	23	5
Windom	10	10	10	7	4	3	0
Hayes	0	1	0	0	0	0	0
Hartranft	0	0	1	0	0	0	0
not voting	1	1	1	1	0	0	1

VOTE FOR VICE-PRESIDENTIAL NOMINATION:

Candidate	Ballot: 1
Arthur	468
Washburne	193
Jewell	44
Maynard	30
Bruce	8
Alcorn	4
Davis	2
Settle	1
Woodford	1
not voting	5

Also:
- recited the party's accomplishments
- chastised Democrats as the party of rebellion
- gave passing acknowledgment of the need for civil service reform

GENERAL ELECTION SUMMARY FOR 1880			
Candidate	Electoral Votes	States	Popular Votes
Garfield (R)	214	19	4,454,416
Hancock (D)	155	19	4,444,952
Weaver (GRE LAB)	0	0	308,578
Dow (PROH)	0	0	10,305
Phelps (A)	0	0	700
Norris (I)	0	0	433
Brewer (ID)	0	0	322
Howells (I)	0	0	159
unknown	0	0	2,786

ELECTION OF NOVEMBER 4, 1884

President
GROVER CLEVELAND

Vice President
THOMAS ANDREWS HENDRICKS

HIGHLIGHTS

The assassination of James Garfield in 1881 brought his "Stalwart" Republican vice president, Chester A. Arthur, to the White House. Arthur surprised everyone by promoting substantial civil service reform, but in the process he alienated important elements within his own party. By 1884, he clearly could not get the party's nomination against the popular James G. Blaine. On the Democrats' side, Grover Cleveland commanded the broadest support for the nomination but was not without his enemies, particularly among party bosses like Tammany's John Kelly. In the contest between Blaine and Cleveland, mudslinging was rampant. Blaine was reminded of the 1876 scandal over several self-serving letters he had written, while Cleveland was castigated for having an illegitimate child. As Cleveland moved toward victory, the Republicans began secretly to finance the campaign of Gen. Benjamin Butler, the standard-bearer of the Greenbackers, in the hope that his candidacy would draw votes from Cleveland. In the rough-and-tumble politics of 1884, a critical miscue from a Republican Protestant leader, who denounced the Democrats as the party of "rum, Romanism, and rebellion," and Blaine's failure to disavow the remark tipped the scales in New York against him. As Irish Catholics reacted angrily to the offensive comment, Blaine lost the state and the election.

AMERICAN PROHIBITION PARTY

CANDIDATE FOR PRESIDENT:
Samuel Clarke Pomeroy

CANDIDATE FOR VICE PRESIDENT:
John A. Conant (CT)

CANDIDATES FOR PRESIDENTIAL NOMINATION:
John Charles Black (IL)
Charles Albert Blanchard (IL)
Jonathan Blanchard (IL)
Clinton Bowen Fisk (NJ)
Samuel Clarke Pomeroy (KS)
John Pierce St. John (KS)
Julius Hawley Seelye (MA)
Gideon Tabor Stewart (OH)

CONVENTION:
June 19, 1884, Chicago (IL)
Joseph Lorenzo Barlow (CT), temporary and permanent chairman

This group, a breakaway splinter party of disgruntled prohibitionists, was not a representative body but rather a mass gathering of the whole party.

PLATFORM HIGHLIGHTS:
SUPPORTED:
• Bible reading in educational institutions and observance of the Sabbath

• total prohibition of intoxicating beverages
• abolition of the electoral college and direct election of the president and vice president
• reduction in the tariff
• international arbitration
• women's suffrage
• patent law revision
• a sound currency
• extension of civil rights' protections to American Indians and Asians

OPPOSED:
• the use of prison and foreign labor
• secret societies

AMERICAN PROHIBITION PARTY VOTE FOR PRESIDENTIAL NOMINATION:	
Candidate	*Ballot: 1*
Pomeroy	72
J. Blanchard	7
C. A. Blanchard	3
St. John	1
Seelye	1

Black, Fisk, and Stewart had support among the delegates, but they remained loyal to the Prohibitionist Party and did not allow their names to be advanced.

- polygamy
- monopolies

ALSO:

- declared the United States to be a Christian nation

ANTI-MONOPOLY PARTY

CANDIDATE FOR PRESIDENT:
Benjamin Franklin Butler

CANDIDATE FOR VICE PRESIDENT:
Absolom Madden West (MS)

CANDIDATES FOR PRESIDENTIAL NOMINATION:
Benjamin Franklin Butler (MA)
Solon Chase (ME)
Allen Granberry Thurman (OH)

CONVENTION:
May 14, 1884, Hershey Music Hall, Chicago (IL)
Alson J. Streeter (IL), temporary chairman
John F. Henry, permanent chairman

This group was formed as the Anti-Monopoly Organization of the United States. Representatives from seventeen states and the District of Columbia attended the convention.

PLATFORM HIGHLIGHTS:
SUPPORTED:

- the use of law to control corporations
- promotion of the alliance between labor and capital "to secure justice for both"
- a dramatic reduction in public expenses
- enforcement of the eight-hour workday law
- prohibitions against the use of foreign contract labor
- the breakup of monopolies
- passage of an interstate commerce bill
- repayment of the public debt
- direct election of U.S. senators
- a graduated income tax
- an end to land grants for corporations
- a special appeal to farmers to join the antimonopoly effort

ANTI-MONOPOLY PARTY
VOTE FOR PRESIDENTIAL NOMINATION:

Candidate	Ballot: 1
Butler	124
Thurman	2
Chase	1

VOTE FOR VICE-PRESIDENTIAL NOMINATION: WEST, THE VICE-PRESIDENTIAL CANDIDATE, WAS CHOSEN BY A COMMITTEE NEGOTIATING WITH OTHER POLITICAL PARTIES.

DEMOCRATIC PARTY

CANDIDATE FOR PRESIDENT:
Grover Cleveland

CANDIDATE FOR VICE PRESIDENT:
Thomas Andrews Hendricks

CANDIDATES FOR PRESIDENTIAL NOMINATION:
Thomas Francis Bayard (DE)
John Griffin Carlisle (KY)
Grover Cleveland (NY)
Roswell Pettibone Flower (NY)
Thomas Andrews Hendricks (IN)
George Hoadly (OH)
Joseph Ewing McDonald (IN)
Samuel Jackson Randall (PA)
Allen Granberry Thurman (OH)
Samuel Jones Tilden (NY)

CANDIDATES FOR VICE-PRESIDENTIAL NOMINATION:
John Charles Black (IL)
George Washington Glick (KS)
Thomas Andrews Hendricks (IN)
William Starke Rosecrans (CA)

14TH CONVENTION:
July 8–11, 1884, Exposition Hall, Chicago (IL)
Richard B. Hubbard (TX), temporary chairman
William Freeman Vilas (WI), permanent chairman

When the Democrats met in convention, the Republican Party was enjoying its twenty-third consecutive year in control of the White House. Thus, the Democratic platform complained that "it is indispensable . . . that the government should not always be controlled by one political party . . . [and] hence a change is demanded."

DEMOCRATIC PARTY
VOTE FOR PRESIDENTIAL NOMINATION:

Candidate	Ballot: 1	2
Cleveland	392	683
Bayard	170	81½
Thurman	88	4
Randall	78	4
McDonald	56	2
Carlisle	27	0
Flower	4	0
Hoadly	3	0
Hendricks	1	45½
Tilden	1	0

VOTE FOR VICE-PRESIDENTIAL NOMINATION: HENDRICKS WAS UNANIMOUSLY NOMINATED FOR VICE PRESIDENT ON THE FIRST BALLOT. FOUR DELEGATES DID NOT VOTE.

PLATFORM HIGHLIGHTS:

SUPPORTED:

- "honest" money
- correction of monopoly abuses but reaffirmed support for the right of property
- abolition of Chinese contract labor
- rebuilding the merchant marine
- internal improvements on the Mississippi River and other waterways

ALSO:

- recited a long litany of failures by the Republicans
- pledged to reduce the tariff, calling for the equivalent of a "balanced budget" that would restrict the raising of revenues to those taxes necessary to meet the limited purposes of government

EQUAL RIGHTS PARTY

CANDIDATE FOR PRESIDENT:

Belva Ann Bennett Lockwood (DC)

CANDIDATE FOR VICE PRESIDENT:

Marietta Lizzie Bell Stow (CA)

CONVENTION:

September 20, 1884, San Francisco (CA)
Marietta Lizzie Bell Stow, permanent chairman

This convention was held by the Women's Rights Party and other reformist groups.

PLATFORM HIGHLIGHTS:

SUPPORTED:

- women's suffrage
- abolition of distinctions in property rights between men and women
- prohibition
- a "moderate" tariff
- trade with Central and South America
- reenactment of the Arrears Act and prompt payment of pensions for veterans
- abolition of American Indian tribal areas and bestowal of full citizenship for American Indians
- uniform state laws governing marriage and divorce, descent of property, and the limitation of contracts
- civil service reform
- broad public education
- restrictions on distributing the public lands solely to actual settlers

OPPOSED:

- monopolies
- war as an instrument of public policy
- sectionalism within the United States

NATIONAL GREENBACK (GREENBACK LABOR) PARTY

CANDIDATE FOR PRESIDENT:

Benjamin Franklin Butler

CANDIDATE FOR VICE PRESIDENT:

Absolom Madden West (MS)

CANDIDATES FOR PRESIDENTIAL NOMINATION:

Edward Phelps Allis (WI)
Benjamin Franklin Butler (MA)
Solon Chase (ME)
David Davis (IL)
Jesse Harper (IL)

CONVENTION:

May 28–29, 1884, English's Opera House, Indianapolis (IN)
John Tyler (FL), temporary chairman
James Baird Weaver (IA), permanent chairman

PLATFORM HIGHLIGHTS:

SUPPORTED:

- the right of Congress to issue legal tender notes and demanded the issuance of "greenbacks" in sufficient quantities to meet the needs of commerce and repay the public debt
- reclamation of public lands granted to corporations
- establishment of a government postal-telegraph system
- prohibitions against discriminatory rates, "pooling," stock-watering, and other abuses of the business and financial communities
- a graduated income tax
- abolition of convict and child labor
- government safety and sanitation inspections of mines and factories
- prompt payment of pensions for "deserving soldiers"
- congressional reforms, including a constitutional amendment to reduce the term of office of U.S. senators
- a referendum on the issues of prohibition and women's suffrage

OPPOSED:

- railroad, banking, and other monopolies
- foreign contract labor

NATIONAL GREENBACK (GREENBACK LABOR) PARTY
VOTE FOR PRESIDENTIAL NOMINATION:

Candidate	Ballot: 1
Butler	323
Harper	98
Chase	2
Allis	1
Davis	0

VOTE FOR VICE-PRESIDENTIAL NOMINATION: WEST OF MISSISSIPPI WAS NOMINATED FOR VICE PRESIDENT BY ACCLAMATION.

PROHIBITION HOME PROTECTION (PROHIBITION) PARTY

CANDIDATE FOR PRESIDENT:
John Pierce St. John

CANDIDATE FOR VICE PRESIDENT:
William Daniel (MD)

CANDIDATES FOR PRESIDENTIAL NOMINATION:
James Black (PA)
Clinton Bowen Fisk (NJ)
Richard Hayes McDonald (CA)
John Pierce St. John (KS)
Gideon Tabor Stewart (OH)

CANDIDATES FOR VICE-PRESIDENTIAL NOMINATION:
William Daniel (MD)
Clinton Bowen Fisk (NJ)
George P. Rodgers (CT)

CONVENTION:
July 23–24, 1884, Lafayette Hall, Pittsburgh (PA)
William Daniel (MD), temporary chairman
Samuel Dickie (MI), permanent chairman

More than seven hundred delegates and alternates from thirty-one states and territories attended this convention. At this convention the party changed its name from the Prohibition Home Protection Party (adopted after the 1880 election) back to its original designation as the Prohibition Party.

PLATFORM HIGHLIGHTS:

SUPPORTED:

- total prohibition of the importation, manufacture, sale, or consumption of intoxicating drinks
- civil service reforms (including election of postmasters)
- pension support for veterans
- government issuance of legal tender
- limitations on the distribution of public lands
- civil and political equality between the sexes, including women's suffrage

---

PROHIBITION HOME PROTECTION (PROHIBITION) PARTY

VOTE FOR PRESIDENTIAL NOMINATION: BLACK, FISK, MCDONALD, AND STEWART WERE OFFERED TO THE CONVENTION FOR THE PRESIDENTIAL NOMINATION, BUT ALL DECLINED. ST. JOHN WAS UNANIMOUSLY NOMINATED FOR PRESIDENT ON THE FIRST BALLOT.

VOTE FOR VICE-PRESIDENTIAL NOMINATION: DANIEL WAS UNANIMOUSLY NOMINATED FOR VICE PRESIDENT ON THE FIRST BALLOT.

REPUBLICAN PARTY

CANDIDATE FOR PRESIDENT:
James Gillespie Blaine

CANDIDATE FOR VICE PRESIDENT:
John Alexander Logan

CANDIDATES FOR PRESIDENTIAL NOMINATION:
Chester Alan Arthur (NY)
James Gillespie Blaine (ME)
George Franklin Edmunds (VT)
Joseph Roswell Hawley (CT)
Robert Todd Lincoln (IL)
John Alexander Logan (IL)
John Sherman (OH)
William Tecumseh Sherman (MO)

CANDIDATES FOR VICE-PRESIDENTIAL NOMINATION:
Lucius Fairchild (WI)
Joseph Benson Foraker (OH)
Walter Quintin Gresham (IN)
John Alexander Logan (IL)

8TH CONVENTION:
June 3–6, 1884, Exposition Hall, Chicago (IL)
John Roy Lynch (MS), temporary chairman
John Brooks Henderson (MO), permanent chairman

This convention is notable for the selection of John R. Lynch, a prominent African-American, as temporary chairman, and for its rejection of the incumbent president, Chester A. Arthur, for the presidential nomination. The platform was largely self-congratulatory, reciting past successes, and, the delegates mourned the death of President Garfield.

REPUBLICAN PARTY
VOTE FOR PRESIDENTIAL NOMINATION:

Candidate	Ballot: 1	2	3	4
Blaine	334½	349	375	541
Arthur	278	276	274	207
Edmunds	93	85	69	41
Logan	63½	61	53	7
J. Sherman	30	28	25	0
Hawley	13	13	13	15
Lincoln	4	4	8	2
W. T. Sherman	2	3	2	0
not voting	2	1	1	7

VOTE FOR VICE-PRESIDENTIAL NOMINATION:

Candidate	Ballot: 1
Logan	779
Fairchild	7
Gresham	6
Foraker	1
not voting	34

PLATFORM HIGHLIGHTS:

SUPPORTED:

- the concept of the "protective tariff" and urged relief for the sheep industry through a readjustment of the duties on foreign wool
- establishment of an international monetary standard
- regulation of the railroads to prevent discriminatory rates
- establishment of a bureau of labor
- promotion of international arbitration
- restriction of the importation of Chinese labor
- civil service reform
- suppression of polygamy
- restrictions on the appointment power of the president
- full payment of soldiers' claims

GENERAL ELECTION SUMMARY FOR 1884			
Candidate	Electoral Votes	States	Popular Votes
Cleveland (D)	219	20	4,874,986
Blaine (R)	182	18	4,851,981
Butler (NAT GRE)	0	0	175,096[1]
St. John (PROH)	0	0	147,482
Lockwood (ER)	0	0	0
Pomeroy (AM PROH)	0	0	0
unknown	0	0	3,619

[1]includes votes for the Anti-Monopoly Party

ELECTION OF NOVEMBER 6, 1888

President
BENJAMIN HARRISON
Vice President
LEVI PARSONS MORTON

HIGHLIGHTS

By 1888, the question of protective tariffs had taken center stage on the U.S. political scene, with the Democrats lining up on the side of freetrade and the Republicans squarely in favor of protectionism. Proponents of Henry George's "single-tax" philosophy emerged during the 1888 campaign, as did the Socialist Laborites, who preached abolition of the presidency. At the Republican Convention, Frederick Douglass became the first African-American to receive a vote for the presidential nomination of a major party.

The Democratic incumbent, Grover Cleveland, was hamstrung during the campaign by his preoccupation with Congress. Nonetheless, when the popular votes were counted, he had more than one hundred thousand votes over his chief rival, Republican Benjamin Harrison. Unfortunately for Cleveland, his popular strength was not reflected in his 168 electoral votes, and Harrison won with 233 electoral votes.

AMERICAN PARTY

CANDIDATE FOR PRESIDENT:
James Langdon Curtis

CANDIDATE FOR VICE PRESIDENT:
Peter Dinwiddie Wigginton (CA)

CANDIDATES FOR PRESIDENTIAL NOMINATION:
James Langdon Curtis (NY)
Abram Stevens Hewitt (NY)
James Scott Negley (PA)

CONVENTION:
August 14–15, 1888, Grand Army Hall, Washington, DC

The convention had 126 delegates, of whom 65 were from New York and 15 from California. On the second day of the convention, all delegates except those from New York and California seceded and held a convention of their own. The secessionists did not make nominations.

PLATFORM HIGHLIGHTS:
SUPPORTED:
- a constitutional amendment to prohibit alien voting
- restrictions on foreign immigration
- denial of the right of nonresident aliens to own land and limitations on the ownership of land by resident aliens
- exclusion of the use of any flags beyond municipal, state, and national flags on public buildings
- taxation of church property

DEMOCRATIC PARTY

CANDIDATE FOR PRESIDENT:
Grover Cleveland (NY)

CANDIDATE FOR VICE PRESIDENT:
Allen Granberry Thurman

CANDIDATES FOR VICE-PRESIDENTIAL NOMINATION:
John Charles Black (IL)
Isaac P. Gray (IN)
Allen Granberry Thurman (OH)

15TH CONVENTION:
June 5–7, 1888, Exposition Building, St. Louis (MO)
Stephen Mallory White (CA), temporary chairman
Patrick Andrew Collins (MA), chairman

PLATFORM HIGHLIGHTS:
SUPPORTED:
- tariff reform consistent with greater free trade

AMERICAN PARTY
VOTE FOR PRESIDENTIAL NOMINATION:

Candidate	Ballot: 1
Curtis	45
Hewitt	15
Negley	4

The nomination of Curtis was made unanimous.

VOTE FOR VICE-PRESIDENTIAL NOMINATION:
JAMES R. GREER OF TENNESSEE WAS NOMINATED FOR VICE PRESIDENT BUT DECLINED. THEN WIGGINTON WAS SUBSTITUTED.

- revenue reduction
- admission of the territories of Dakota (Montana), New Mexico, and Washington as states
- home rule for Ireland

ALSO:

- recited the achievements of the Cleveland administration

DEMOCRATIC PARTY
VOTE FOR PRESIDENTIAL NOMINATION:
CLEVELAND WAS NOMINATED BY ACCLAMATION,
RECEIVING 822 VOTES.

VOTE FOR VICE-PRESIDENTIAL NOMINATION:

Candidate	Ballot: 1
Thurman	690
Gray	105
Black	25

EQUAL RIGHTS PARTY

CANDIDATE FOR PRESIDENT:
Belva Ann Bennett Lockwood (DC)

CANDIDATE FOR VICE PRESIDENT:
Charles Stuart Wells (NY)

CONVENTION:
May 15, 1888, Des Moines (IA)
Nettie Sandford Chapin (IA), chairman

This convention was sparsely attended, and proxy ballots were used.

PLATFORM HIGHLIGHTS:
SUPPORTED:

- women's suffrage
- soldiers' pension relief
- repeal of the tax on whiskey and tobacco
- repeal of immigration restrictions
- a protective tariff, except for sugar and lumber, which were not to be subject to a tariff

A ticket with Lockwood and Alfred Henry Love of Pennsylvania was nominated on the first ballot. The nominees received 310 votes apiece. Love subsequently declined the vice-presidential nomination, and Wells was substituted for second place on the ticket.

NATIONAL GREENBACK PARTY

Eight delegates convened in Cincinnati (OH) on September 12, 1888, in an effort to revive the National Greenback Party. A statement of principles was adopted, but no nominations were made.

INDEPENDENT LABOR PARTY

The Grand Council of the Independent Labor Party met in Detroit (MI) on July 16, 1888. Rather than enter its own ticket, the party endorsed the Republican candidates.

INDUSTRIAL (INDUSTRIAL REFORM) PARTY

CANDIDATE FOR PRESIDENT:
Albert E. Redstone (CA)

CANDIDATE FOR VICE PRESIDENT:
John A. Colvin (KS)

CONVENTION:
February 22–23, 1888, Grand Army Hall, Washington, DC
J. W. Ethridge (NC), temporary chairman
Charles Pelham (AL), president
Miss A. E. Jacobs, secretary

About forty-nine delegates participated in this convention, which was a continuation of an earlier convention of the Industrial Reform Conference in Springfield (IL). The convention was convened to express opposition to national banks but ended up with a broader perspective through resolutions representative of the views of the Knights of Labor, Prohibitionists, former American Party followers, and women's suffragists in attendance.

The original platform endorsed the use of greenbacks as legal tender, urged immediate redemption of all interest-bearing public debt, and called for the abolition of all banks of issue. Following its adoption, a series of resolutions were offered. According to a news account of the day, "just exactly what was adopted and what rejected, even the secretary could not possibly tell."

PLATFORM HIGHLIGHTS:
SUPPORTED:

- women's suffrage
- retention of the war tariff until the obligation to veterans was paid
- forfeiture of unearned railroad land grants
- prohibition of Chinese and convict labor
- enforcement of the eight-hour workday
- nationalization of the railroads and telegraph system
- subsidies for Negro emigration to Liberia
- graduated income tax

ALSO:

- considered prohibition

INDEPENDENT

CANDIDATE FOR PRESIDENT:
E. W. Perry

PROHIBITION PARTY

CANDIDATE FOR PRESIDENT:
Clinton Bowen Fisk

CANDIDATE FOR VICE PRESIDENT:
John Anderson Brooks

CANDIDATES FOR PRESIDENTIAL NOMINATION:
Clinton Bowen Fisk (NJ)
Green Clay Smith (KY)

CANDIDATES FOR VICE-PRESIDENTIAL NOMINATION:
George W. Bain (KY)
John Anderson Brooks (MO)
E. L. Dohoney (TX)
Joshua Levering (MD)
Samuel W. Small (GA)
John T. Tanner (AL)

5TH CONVENTION:
May 30–31, 1888, Tomlinson Hall, Indianapolis (IN)
Rev. H. A. Delano (CT), temporary chairman
John Pierce St. John (KS), chairman

One thousand twenty-nine delegates were present, representing nearly every state.

PLATFORM HIGHLIGHTS:
SUPPORTED:
- suppression of the liquor trade through complete prohibition and repeal of the tax on alcohol
- a protective tariff
- universal suffrage
- civil service reform
- abolition of polygamy
- establishment of uniform marriage and divorce laws
- Sunday observance laws
- promotion of international arbitration
- labor reforms
- prohibition of monopolies
- prohibition of voting by noncitizens

PROHIBITION PARTY
VOTE FOR PRESIDENTIAL AND VICE-PRESIDENTIAL NOMINATIONS: FISK AND BROOKS WERE NOMINATED FOR PRESIDENT AND VICE PRESIDENT, RESPECTIVELY, BY ACCLAMATION.

REPUBLICAN PARTY

CANDIDATE FOR PRESIDENT:
Benjamin Harrison

CANDIDATE FOR VICE PRESIDENT:
Levi Parsons Morton

CANDIDATES FOR PRESIDENTIAL NOMINATION:
Russell Alexander Alger (MI)
William Boyd Allison (IA)
James Gillespie Blaine (ME)
Chauncey Mitchell Depew (NY)
Frederick Douglass (DC)
E. H. Fitler (PA)
Joseph Benson Foraker (OH)
Frederick Dent Grant (NY)
Walter Quintin Gresham (IN)
Benjamin Harrison (IN)
Joseph Roswell Hawley (CT)
Creed Haymond (CA)
John James Ingalls (KS)
Robert Todd Lincoln (IL)
William McKinley, Jr. (OH)
Samuel Freeman Miller (IA)
William Walter Phelps (NJ)
Jeremiah McLain Rusk (WI)
John Sherman (OH)

CANDIDATES FOR VICE-PRESIDENTIAL NOMINATION:
William O'Connell Bradley (KY)
Blanche Kelso Bruce (MS)
Levi Parsons Morton (NY)
William Walter Phelps (NJ)
Walter F. Thomas (TX)

9TH CONVENTION:
June 19–23, 25, 1888, Civic Auditorium, Chicago (IL)
John M. Thurston (NE), temporary chairman
Morris M. Estee (CA), chairman

This convention lasted six days. Its delegates adopted a platform that endorsed protectionism for U.S. industries and maintaining the duty on imported wool.

PLATFORM HIGHLIGHTS:
SUPPORTED:
- prohibitions against foreign contract labor
- promotion of homesteads on public lands
- home rule in the territories
- bimetallism
- reduction in postage costs
- free schools
- statehood for South Dakota
- the rebuilding of the navy and merchant marine
- construction of a canal through Nicaragua
- protection of U.S. fisheries
- civil service reform

OPPOSED:
- monopolies and the exploitive use of combinations of capital
- polygamy

SOCIALIST LABOR PARTY
The party had no candidates. Electors for the Socialist Labor Party were instructed to vote "no president" if elected.

				REPUBLICAN PARTY				
				VOTE FOR PRESIDENTIAL NOMINATION:				
Candidate	Ballot: 1	2	3	4	5	6	7	8
Sherman	229	249	244	235	224	244	231	118
Gresham	111	108	123	98	87	91	91	59
Depew	99	99	91	0	0	0	0	0
Alger	84	116	122	135	142	137	120	100
Harrison	80	91	94	217	213	231	278	544
Allison	72	75	88	88	99	73	76	0
Blaine	35	33	35	42	48	40	15	5
Ingalls	28	16	0	0	0	0	0	0
Rusk	25	20	16	0	0	0	0	0
Phelps	25	18	5	0	0	0	0	0
Fitler	24	0	0	0	0	0	0	0
Hawley	13	0	0	0	0	0	0	0
Lincoln	3	2	2	1	0	0	2	0
McKinley	2	3	8	11	14	12	16	4
Miller	0	0	2	0	0	0	0	0
Douglass	0	0	0	1	0	0	0	0
Foraker	0	0	0	1	0	1	1	0
Grant	0	0	0	0	0	1	0	0
Haymond	0	0	0	0	0	0	1	0

VOTE FOR VICE-PRESIDENTIAL NOMINATION:	
Candidate	Ballot: 1
Morton	591
Phelps	119
Bradley	103
Bruce	11
Thomas	1

UNION LABOR PARTY

CANDIDATE FOR PRESIDENT:
Alson Jenness Streeter (IL)

CANDIDATE FOR VICE PRESIDENT:
Charles Edward Cunningham

CANDIDATES FOR VICE-PRESIDENTIAL NOMINATION:
Charles Edward Cunningham (AR)
Theodore P. Rynder (PA)
Samuel Evans (TX)

CONVENTION:
May 15–17, 1888, Cincinnati (OH)
Seymour Frank Norton (IL), temporary
chairman
John Seitz, chairman

The Union Labor Party was organized February 24, 1887, in Cincinnati. Delegates to the convention came from the Knights of Labor, Agricultural Wheelers, Corngrowers, Homesteadry, Farmers, Alliances, Greenbackers, and Grangers. Two hundred twenty delegates attended the convention from twenty states.

PLATFORM HIGHLIGHTS:

SUPPORTED:
- homestead exemptions
- public ownership of communications and transportation systems
- a graduated income tax
- benefits for veterans
- labor arbitration
- abolition of foreign contract, convict, and child labor
- enactment of industrial safety laws
- equal pay for equal work regardless of gender
- reduction of work hours
- free coinage of silver
- issuance of greenbacks as legal tender
- redemption of the national debt
- direct election of U.S. senators
- Chinese exclusion from immigration and expulsion of contract laborers
- woman suffrage

OPPOSED:
- land monopolies and demanded forfeiture of unearned land grants

UNION LABOR PARTY
VOTE FOR PRESIDENTIAL NOMINATION: STREETER
WAS NOMINATED FOR PRESIDENT BY ACCLAMATION.

VOTE FOR VICE-PRESIDENTIAL
NOMINATION:

Candidate	Ballot: 1
Evans	124
Rynder	44
Cunningham	32

Evans declined, so Cunningham was substituted.

UNITED LABOR PARTY

CANDIDATE FOR PRESIDENT:
Robert Hall Cowdrey (IL)

CANDIDATE FOR VICE PRESIDENT:
William H. T. Wakefield (KS)

CONVENTION:
May 16, 1888, Grand Opera House, Cincinnati (OH)
William B. Ogden (KY), chairman

This party, an outgrowth of the Henry George single-tax movement of 1886, met in Cincinnati one day after the Union Labor Party. Attendance at the convention was sparse, with approximately ninety delegates. The platform called for a single national tax to be imposed on land values "to give all men an interest in their country." In accordance with Henry George's views, all other taxes would be abolished. Greenbacks would be established as a legal tender circulating medium under control of the government.

PLATFORM HIGHLIGHTS:
SUPPORTED:
- government ownership of both railroads and telegraphs
- reduction in work hours
- abolition of child and convict labor
- sanitation inspections of tenements, factories, and mines
- simplification of the legal system and a reduction in the expense of legal proceedings
- adoption of Australia's secret ballot system
- renunciation of the "corruption" of the two major parties

GENERAL ELECTION SUMMARY FOR 1888

Candidate	Electoral Votes	States	Popular Votes
Harrison (R)	233	20	5,444,337
Cleveland(D)	168	18	5,540,309
Fisk (PROH)	0	0	249,506
Streeter (UNI LAB)	0	0	146,935
Cowdrey (UNIT LAB)	0	0	2,818
Socialist Labor	0	0	2,068
Curtis (AP)	0	0	1,612
Perry (I)	0	0	399
Lockwood (ER)	0	0	not on ballot
Redstone (IN REF)	0	0	not on ballot
unknown	0	0	3,597

ELECTION OF NOVEMBER 8, 1892

President
GROVER CLEVELAND
Vice President
ADLAI EWING STEVENSON

HIGHLIGHTS

The election of 1892 saw the emergence of a third force in U.S. politics, one that had its roots in radicalism and the antimonopoly and Greenback movements. The People's Party brought together disgruntled farmers, workers, and reformers. It inherited the mantle of the Greenback and Anti-Monopoly parties and gathered under its fold Agricultural Wheelers (members of an early farm organization called the Agricultural Wheel), equal rights advocates, Unionists, and industrial reformers. It had enough strength to breach the two-party control of the electoral college, the first time a party had done so since 1860. But despite its growing appeal, the populist revolt could not turn an otherwise dull campaign into an exciting election contest. This election, however, was still unique: for the first time a former president who had four years earlier been defeated in his reelection bid, Grover Cleveland, won. He was able to make the most of the tariff issue, condemning the Republicans and the incumbent Benjamin Harrison, while maintaining an ambiguous position himself. Playing to his strength, Cleveland largely ignored the agrarian revolt in the West and South and instead focused on the conservative interests of the East. The People's Party, with its strength centered in areas normally solidly in the Republican ranks, helped ensure a Democratic victory.

DEMOCRATIC PARTY

CANDIDATE FOR PRESIDENT:
Grover Cleveland

CANDIDATE FOR VICE PRESIDENT:
Adlai Ewing Stevenson

CANDIDATES FOR PRESIDENTIAL NOMINATION:
Horace Boies (IA)
James Edwin Campbell (OH)
John Griffin Carlisle (KY)
Grover Cleveland (NY)
Arthur Pue Gorman (MD)
David Bennett Hill (NY)
William Ralls Morrison (IL)
Robert Emory Pattison (PA)
William Eustis Russell (MA)
Adlai Ewing Stevenson (IL)
William Collins Whitney (NY)

CANDIDATES FOR VICE-PRESIDENTIAL NOMINATION:
Horace Boies (IA)
Bourke Cockran (NY)
Isaac P. Gray (IN)
John L. Mitchell (WI)
Allen B. Morse (MI)
Adlai Ewing Stevenson (IL)
Lambert Tree (IL)
Henry Watterson (KY)

16TH CONVENTION:
June 21–23, 1892, Special Building, Chicago (IL)
William C. Owens (KY), temporary chairman
William Lyne Wilson (WV), chairman

PLATFORM HIGHLIGHTS:
SUPPORTED:
- regulation of trusts and combinations
- trade reciprocity
- repeal of the tax on state bank issues
- civil service reform
- federal intervention to oppose the pogroms in Russia
- Irish home rule
- liberal pensions for veterans
- limitations on immigration and the importation of cheap labor
- internal improvements in waterways
- the construction of a canal through Nicaragua and financial support for the Columbian World's Fair (i.e., World's Columbian Exposition held in Chicago in 1893)
- admission of New Mexico and Arizona as states
- protection of railroad employees
- abolition of sweat shops, convict labor, and child labor

OPPOSED:
- sumptuary laws
- Republican protectionism, the McKinley Act, and the Sherman Act

Also:

- evaded specifics on the monetary question, supporting coinage in both gold and silver with parity between the two metals
- lauded the Democrats' efforts to reclaim public lands given away to corporate interests

DEMOCRATIC PARTY
VOTE FOR PRESIDENTIAL NOMINATION:

Candidate	Ballot: 1
Cleveland	617⅓
Hill	114
Boies	103
Gorman	36½
Stevenson	16⅔
Carlisle	14
Morrison	3
Campbell	2
Pattison	1
Russell	1
Whitney	1

Cleveland's nomination was made unanimous.

VOTE FOR VICE-PRESIDENTIAL NOMINATION:

Candidate	Ballot: 1
Stevenson	402
Gray	343
Morse	86
Mitchell	45
Watterson	26
Cockran	5
Tree	1
Boies	1

The nomination of Stevenson was made unanimous.

NATIONAL SCHOOL HOUSE PARTY
CANDIDATE FOR PRESIDENT:
John Bidwell (CA)

CANDIDATE FOR VICE PRESIDENT:
Sylvester M. Douglas (IL)

This party was an offshoot of the Prohibition Party and advocated a temperance platform.

PEOPLE'S PARTY (POPULIST PARTY)
CANDIDATE FOR PRESIDENT:
James Baird Weaver

CANDIDATE FOR VICE PRESIDENT:
James Gaven Field

CANDIDATES FOR PRESIDENTIAL NOMINATION:
Ignatius Donnelly (MN)
Walter Quintin Gresham (IN)
James Henderson Kyle (SD)
Seymour Frank Norton (IL)
Mann Page (VA)
Leonidas Lafayette Polk (NC)
Leland Stanford (CA)
James Baird Weaver (IA)

CANDIDATES FOR VICE-PRESIDENTIAL NOMINATION:
James Gaven Field (VA)
Ben S. Terrell (TX)

The People's Party was organized May 19, 1891, at a national convention in Cincinnati (OH). It was composed of members of the Farmers' Alliance and various industrial unions.

1ST CONVENTION:
July 2–5, 1892, Convention Hall Coliseum, Omaha (NE)
C. H. Ellington (GA), temporary chairman
Henry Langford Loucks (SD), chairman

PLATFORM HIGHLIGHTS:
SUPPORTED:
- government ownership of the railroads and telephone and telegraph systems
- enactment of the subtreasury plan of the Farmers' Alliance
- free and unlimited coinage of silver and gold at the ratio of 16 to 1
- an increase in the circulating medium of exchange by not less than fifty dollars per capita
- enactment of a graduated income tax
- creation of postal savings banks
- prohibitions against speculative and alien ownership of land
- adoption of Australia's secret ballot system
- federal funding for the pensions of ex-Union soldiers and sailors
- restrictions on contract labor and "undesirable immigration"
- enforcement of the eight-hour workday law
- abolition of the "Pinkerton system" of private industrial armies
- adoption of the initiative and referendum and constitutional amendments providing for the direct election of senators and a one-term limitation for president and vice president

OPPOSED:
- all public subsidies to private corporations

ALSO:
- denounced the "robber barons" of U.S. industry, the demonetization of silver, and the generally depressed circumstances of workers and farmers
- asserted that the tariff issue was a "sham battle" to distract voters from the real evils facing the nation

---

PEOPLE'S PARTY (POPULIST PARTY)
VOTE FOR PRESIDENTIAL NOMINATION:

Candidate	Ballot: 1
Weaver	995
Kyle	265
Norton	1
Page	1
Stanford	1

Weaver's nomination was made unanimous. Polk died before the convention.

VOTE FOR VICE-PRESIDENTIAL NOMINATION:

Candidate	Ballot: 1
Field	733
Terrell	554

PROHIBITION PARTY

CANDIDATE FOR PRESIDENT:
John Bidwell

CANDIDATE FOR VICE PRESIDENT:
James Britton Cranfill (TX)

CANDIDATES FOR PRESIDENTIAL NOMINATION:
George Washington Bain (KY)
Henry Clay Bascom (NY)
John Bidwell (CA)
Amos Briggs (PA)
Volney Byron Cushing (ME)
William Jennings Demorest (NY)
Edward Hazard East (TN)
Walter Barnard Hill (GA)
David Campbell Kelley (TN)
Adna Bradway Leonard (OH)
Eli Foster Ritter (IN)
Gideon Tabor Stewart (OH)
William Thomas Wardwell (NY)
Andrew Givens Wolfenbarger (NE)

CANDIDATES FOR VICE-PRESIDENTIAL NOMINATION:
Thomas Rosabaum Carskadon (WV)
James Britton Cranfill (TX)
Joshua Levering (MD)
William Wilson Satterly (MN)

6TH CONVENTION:
June 29–30, 1892, Music Hall, Cincinnati (OH)

John Pierce St. John (KS), temporary chairman
Eli Foster Ritter (IN), chairman

Four thousand delegates and visitors attended this convention from every state but one. The Prohibition platform took a "broad-gauge" approach by addressing several issues beyond its normal demand for total prohibition against alcoholic beverages.

PLATFORM HIGHLIGHTS:
SUPPORTED:
- women's suffrage and equal pay for women
- a monetary system that mixed gold, silver, and paper currencies and would grow in volume with the increase in population
- limitations on the use of the tariff to raise revenues
- government control of the railroads, telegraph, and other "public" corporations
- stiffer requirements for immigration and citizenship
- limitations on individual and corporate ownership of land and reclamation of unearned land grants
- observance of the Sabbath under law
- use of arbitration to settle national differences
- suppression of economic speculation
- the honoring of pension rights for veterans
- the teaching of English in the common schools
- a liberal appropriation for the World's Columbian Exposition, contingent on the condition that intoxicating liquors be prohibited on its grounds and that the exposition be closed on Sundays

OPPOSED:
- public aid to parochial schools

PROHIBITION PARTY
VOTE FOR PRESIDENTIAL NOMINATION:

Candidate	Ballot: 1
Bidwell	590
Stewart	179
Demorest	139
Bascom	3

Bain, Bascom, Briggs, Cushing, East, Hill, Kelley, Leonard, Ritter, Wardwell, and Wolfenbarger were asked for permission to place their names in nomination, but they refused.

VOTE FOR VICE-PRESIDENTIAL NOMINATION:

Candidate	Ballot: 1
Cranfill	417
Levering	351
Satterly	26
Carskadon	19

REPUBLICAN PARTY

CANDIDATE FOR PRESIDENT:
Benjamin Harrison

CANDIDATE FOR VICE PRESIDENT:
Whitelaw Reid (NY)

CANDIDATES FOR PRESIDENTIAL NOMINATION:
James Gillespie Blaine (ME)
Benjamin Harrison (IN)
Robert Todd Lincoln (IL)
William McKinley, Jr. (OH)
Thomas Brackett Reed (ME)

10TH CONVENTION:
June 7–10, 1892, Industrial Exposition Building,
    Minneapolis (MN)
Jacob Sloat Fassett (NY), temporary chairman
William McKinley, Jr. (OH), chairman

The Republican Party lauded its platform of 1888 and re-peated many of its themes, including the doctrine of pro-tectionism.

PLATFORM HIGHLIGHTS:
SUPPORTED:
- bimetallism at parity
- the Monroe Doctrine
- restoration of the merchant marine and a stronger navy
- stringent immigration laws
- stronger safety laws to protect workers on railroads, in mines, and in manufacturing
- home rule for Ireland
- opposition to the programs in Russia
- antitrust legislation
- lower postal fees
- construction of a canal through Nicaragua
- civil service reform
- admission into the Union of the remaining territories "at the earliest practicable day"
- the requirement that territorial officers be bona fide residents of their territories

---

REPUBLICAN PARTY
VOTE FOR PRESIDENTIAL NOMINATION:

Candidate	Ballot: 1
Harrison	535½
Blaine	182½
McKinley	182
Reed	4
Lincoln	1

VOTE FOR VICE-PRESIDENTAL NOMINATION:
REID WAS NOMINATED FOR VICE PRESIDENT
BY ACCLAMATION.

- cession of arid public lands to the states and territories
- the World's Columbian Exposition
- "all wise and legitimate efforts to lessen and prevent the evils of intemperance"

ALSO:
- acknowledged the country's obligation to honor the claims of veterans "upon a grateful people"

SOCIALIST LABOR PARTY

CANDIDATE FOR PRESIDENT:
Simon Wing (MA)

CANDIDATE FOR VICE PRESIDENT:
Charles Horatio Matchett (NY)

1ST CONVENTION:
August 28, 1892, New York (NY)

Unlike the 1888 election activity of the Socialist Laborites (that urged the election of "no president"), in 1892 the Socialist Labor Party's first formal presidential convention decided to endorse its own slate of candidates for president and vice president. Its platform, however, called for the abolition of these offices (and the Senate) in favor of an executive board elected by the House of Representatives.

PLATFORM HIGHLIGHTS:
SUPPORTED:
- reduction in working hours
- national ownership of the transportation and communications industries
- municipal ownership of various franchised utilities
- revocation of corporate land grants
- legalization of trade unions
- restriction of the right to issue money to the national government
- legislation to require scientific management of public forests and waterways
- a graduated income tax and a tax on inheritances
- compulsory education to age fourteen
- the right of labor to organize
- repeal of laws against the poor
- maintenance of statistical information on the condition of labor
- prohibition of child and convict labor and limitations on the kinds of labor required of women
- equal wages for equal work
- passage of occupational safety legislation
- the adoption of the recall, initiative, and referendum
- municipal self-government
- the use of the secret ballot and extension of the right to vote to women (with election days declared legal holidays)
- use of proportional representation in the electoral process
- abolition of capital punishment

- a uniform civil and criminal law system throughout the country
- a legal system that was publicly supported

- the scheme in which no inventions would be protected by patent, but inventors would be remunerated by the nation

GENERAL ELECTION SUMMARY FOR 1892			
Candidate	Electoral Votes	States	Popular Votes
Cleveland (D)	277	23	5,556,918
Harrison (R)	145	16	5,176,108
Weaver (PEO)	22	4[1]	1,041,028
Bidwell (PROH)	0	0	264,138
Wing (SOC LAB)	0	0	21,512
unknown	0	0	8,757

[1]plus one electoral vote each from Oregon and North Dakota

ELECTION OF NOVEMBER 3, 1896

President
WILLIAM MCKINLEY, JR.
Vice President
GARRET AUGUSTUS HOBART

HIGHLIGHTS

The election of 1896 was dominated by the money question. The Democrats and reformers pushed silver coinage in a 16 to 1 ratio in value with gold—a position popular in agricultural and western mining areas but considered to be anathema in the financial centers of the East—and the Republicans were entrenched behind a gold standard. The Democratic party, which had the advantage of incumbency, was split. Grover Cleveland supported the gold standard, but his second term was marred by the Panic of 1893 and the subsequent depression. William Jennings Bryan—the "boy orator of the Platte"—espoused a form of prairie radicalism that seemed a healthy alternative to the monetary conservatism of the eastern bloc of the party. Bryan's nomination caused the "gold" Democrats to break away and nominate a ticket of their own, but it also enabled the mainstream Democrats to "swallow" the Populists by substantially incorporating their Omaha platform of 1892 into the Democratic agenda. While the Populists nominated Bryan, they broke ranks to nominate a different vice-presidential candidate, one more acceptable to the "silver" partisans. This fragmentation aided the Republicans, who hid their candidate, William McKinley, behind a "back-porch campaign" (i.e., where he received visitors at home, gave speeches from his back porch, and rarely ventured out on the campaign trail). Thus, McKinley remained above the fray, while his lieutenants waged a bitter and malicious campaign against Bryan. In the end, flamboyance yielded to the appearance of stability, and McKinley emerged victorious.

DEMOCRATIC PARTY

CANDIDATE FOR PRESIDENT:
William Jennings Bryan

CANDIDATE FOR VICE PRESIDENT:
Arthur Sewall

CANDIDATES FOR PRESIDENTIAL NOMINATION:
Joseph Clay Stiles Blackburn (KY)
Richard Parks Bland (MO)
Horace Boies (IA)
William Jennings Bryan (NE)
James Edwin Campbell (PA)
David Bennett Hill (NY)
Claude Matthews (IN)
John Roll McLean (OH)
Robert Emory Pattison (PA)
Sylvester Pennoyer (OR)
William Eustis Russell (MA)
Adlai Ewing Stevenson (IL)
Henry Moore Teller (CO)
Benjamin Ryan Tillman (SC)
David Turpie (IN)

CANDIDATES FOR VICE-PRESIDENTIAL NOMINATION:
Joseph Clay Styles Blackburn (KY)
Richard Parks Bland (MO)
Horace Boies (IA)
Walter A. Clark (NC)
John Warwick Daniel (VA)
George Washington Fithian (IL)
William Francis Harrity (PA)
James Hamilton Lewis (WA)
John Roll McLean (OH)
Robert Emory Pattison (PA)
Arthur Sewall (ME)
Joseph Crocker Sibley (PA)
Henry Moore Teller (CO)
Stephen Mallory White (CA)
George Fred Williams (MA)
James Robert Williams (IL)

17TH CONVENTION:
July 7–11, 1896, Coliseum, Chicago (IL)
John Warwick Daniel (VA), temporary chairman
Stephen Mallory White (CA), chairman

There were 930 delegates present at this convention.

PLATFORM HIGHLIGHTS:
SUPPORTED:
• the unlimited coinage of silver in a 16 to 1 ratio with gold

- enlargement of the powers of the Interstate Commerce Commission and other restrictions on trusts and pools
- improvements in the public waterways
- the refusal of Congress to pass the Pacific Railroad funding bill
- tariffs for revenue purposes only
- a merit system for civil service
- the integrity of veterans' pension claims
- the admission of Arizona, New Mexico, and Oklahoma as states
- the granting of a congressional delegate to Arkansas

DEMOCRATIC PARTY
VOTE FOR PRESIDENTIAL NOMINATION:

Candidate	Ballot: 1	2	3	4	5
Bryan	119	190	19	80	500
Bland	35	83	91	41	106
Pattison	95	100	97	97	95
Blackburn	83	41	7	7	0
Boies	85	41	36	33	6
McLean	54	53	54	46	0
Matthews	37	33	34	36	31
Tillman	17	0	0	0	0
Pennoyer	8	8	0	0	0
Teller	8	8	0	0	0
Stevenson	7	10	9	8	8
Russell	2	0	0	0	0
Campbell	1	0	0	0	0
Hill	1	1	1	1	1
Turpie	0	0	0	0	1
not voting	178	16	16	16	16

Bryan's nomination was made by acclamation.

VOTE FOR VICE-PRESIDENTIAL NOMINATION:

Candidate	Ballot: 1	2	3	4	5
Sewall	100	37	97	61	568
Sibley	163	113	50	0	0
McLean	111	158	10	96	3
G. F. Williams	76	16	15	9	9
Bland	6	94	55	0	0
Clark	50	[?]	[?]	46	[?]
J. R. Williams	[?]13	0	0	0	
Harrity	1	1	19	11	11
Boies	0	0	0	0	0
Blackburn	0	0	0	0	0
Daniel	11	1	6	54	36
Lewis	11	0	0	0	0
Pattison	0	1	1	1	1
Teller	1	0	0	0	0
White	1	0	0	0	0
Fithian	1	0	0	0	0
not voting	60	55	55	53	51

OPPOSED:
- the gold standard and the issuance of interest-bearing bonds in peacetime
- importation of cheap foreign labor
- national banks
- life tenure for public servants
- a third term for any presidential candidate

ALSO:
- expressed its sympathy for the people of Cuba

INDEPENDENT DEMOCRAT
CANDIDATE FOR PRESIDENT:
W. C. Douglass

NATIONAL DEMOCRATIC (SOUND MONEY DEMOCRATIC) PARTY
CANDIDATE FOR PRESIDENT:
John McAuley Palmer

CANDIDATE FOR VICE PRESIDENT:
Simon Bolivar Buckner (KY)

CANDIDATES FOR PRESIDENTIAL NOMINATION:
Edward Stuyvesant Bragg (WI)
John McAuley Palmer (IL)

CONVENTION:
September 2–3, 1896, Indianapolis (IN)
Roswell Pettibone Flower (NY), temporary chairman
Donelson Caffery (LA), chairman

Eight hundred eighty-eight delegates from forty-one states and three territories gathered at this convention in protest over the Democratic Party's abandonment of the gold standard.

PLATFORM HIGHLIGHTS:
SUPPORTED:
- a conservative monetary policy based on the gold standard
- rebuilding U.S. shipping interests
- economy in government
- arbitration in international disputes
- a liberal pension policy for veterans
- support for the Supreme Court

NATIONAL DEMOCRATIC (SOUND MONEY DEMOCRATIC) PARTY
VOTE FOR PRESIDENTIAL NOMINATION:

Candidate	Ballot: 1
Palmer	769½
Bragg	118½

VOTE FOR VICE-PRESIDENTIAL NOMINATION:
GEN. SIMON BOLIVAR BUCKNER WAS NOMINATED BY ACCLAMATION.

Also:
- condemned mainstream Democrats for subverting the right to private contract and for embracing protectionism
- applauded Cleveland's progress in civil service reform

NATIONAL PARTY

CANDIDATE FOR PRESIDENT:
Charles Eugene Bentley (NE)

CANDIDATE FOR VICE PRESIDENT:
James Haywood Southgate (NC)

CONVENTION:
May 8, 1896, Pittsburgh (PA)
A. L. Moore (MI), chairman

Two hundred ninety-nine delegates from twenty-seven states who seceded from the Prohibition Party's convention over the issue of bimetallism attended the National Party's convention. They adopted a "broad-gauge" platform that shared many Populist principles.

PLATFORM HIGHLIGHTS:
Supported:
- suppression of the manufacture and sale of intoxicants
- women's suffrage
- a bimetallic standard at a 16 to 1 ratio
- reclamation of unearned land grants
- public ownership of "natural monopolies"
- use of the protective tariff and a graduated income tax
- abolition of convict labor
- observance of a weekly "day of rest"
- direct election of the president, vice president, and Senate
- liberal pensions for veterans
- use of English in public schools
- prohibitions against the immigration of paupers and criminals
- restrictions on the electoral franchise to limit voting to citizens
- adoption of the initiative, referendum, and proportional representation

---

NATIONAL PARTY
VOTE FOR PRESIDENTIAL AND VICE-PRESIDENTIAL NOMINATIONS: BENTLEY AND SOUTHGATE WERE NOMINATED BY ACCLAMATION FOR PRESIDENT AND VICE PRESIDENT, RESPECTIVELY.

NATIONAL SILVER (BI-METALLIC LEAGUE) PARTY

CANDIDATE FOR PRESIDENT:
William Jennings Bryan (NE)

CANDIDATE FOR VICE PRESIDENT:
Arthur Sewall (ME)

CONVENTION:
July 25, 1896, Exposition Building, St. Louis (MO)
Francis Griffith Newlands (NV), temporary chairman
William P. St. John (NY), chairman

The Silver Party's platform declared the monetary question the paramount issue of 1896 and aligned itself squarely in favor of bimetallism. This stance, of course, was expected, for the party was an outgrowth of the Bi-Metallic League. Because bimetallism was "the only real issue," the convention chose not to address any other campaign issue in its platform, which was silent on everything but the need to use both gold and silver as the basis for coinage.

NATIONAL SILVER (BI-METALLIC LEAGUE) PARTY
VOTE FOR PRESIDENTIAL AND VICE-PRESIDENTIAL NOMINATIONS: ALTHOUGH JOSEPH CROCKER SIBLEY (PA) WAS CONSIDERED FOR THE PRESIDENTIAL NOMINATION, THE DEMOCRATIC CANDIDATES WERE NOMINATED BY ACCLAMATION.

PEOPLE'S (POPULIST, MIDDLE-OF-THE-ROAD) PARTY

CANDIDATE FOR PRESIDENT:
William Jennings Bryan

CANDIDATE FOR VICE PRESIDENT:
Thomas Edward Watson

CANDIDATES FOR PRESIDENTIAL NOMINATION:
William Jennings Bryan (NE)
Jacob Sechler Coxey (OH)
James Harvey Davis (TX)
Eugene Victor Debs (IN)
Ignatius Donnelly (MN)
A. L. Mims (TN)
Seymour Frank Norton (IL)
Charles Arnette Towne (MN)
Paul Vandervoort (NE)

CANDIDATES FOR VICE-PRESIDENTIAL NOMINATION:
Frank Burkitt (MS)
A. L. Mims (TN)
Mann Page (VA)
Arthur Sewall (ME)
Harry Skinner (NC)
Thomas Edward Watson (GA)

2D CONVENTION:
July 2–5, 1896, Special Auditorium, St. Louis (MO)
Marion C. Butler (NC), temporary chairman
William Vincent Allen (NE), chairman

PLATFORM HIGHLIGHTS:

SUPPORTED:

- a national currency, with unrestricted coinage of silver and gold at the 16 to 1 ratio
- an inflationary expansion of money in circulation
- a graduated income tax (in reaction to the Supreme Court decision declaring the income tax provision of the Wilson-Gorman Act unconstitutional)
- creation of postal savings banks
- government ownership of railroads and telegraphs
- prohibition of land monopolies for speculative purposes
- reclamation of unused railroad land grants
- the grant of free homes to homesteaders
- the initiative and referendum
- direct election of the president, vice president, and senators
- home rule for the territories and the District of Columbia
- a public works program to address unemployment
- freedom for Cuba
- pensions for veterans
- prohibitions against imprisonment for "indirect contempt" in labor disputes

OPPOSED:

- the sale of bonds increasing the public debt

At this convention, the nomination for the vice-presidential candidate was made before the nomination of the presidential candidate.

PEOPLE'S (POPULIST, MIDDLE-OF-THE-ROAD) PARTY
VOTE FOR PRESIDENTIAL NOMINATION:

Candidate	Ballot: 1
Bryan	104
Norton	31
Debs	8
Donnelly	3
Coxey	1

VOTE FOR VICE-PRESIDENTIAL NOMINATION:

Candidate	Ballot: 1
Watson	469½
Sewall	57½
Skinner	[0?]
Burkett	[0?]
Mims	[0?]
Page	[0?]

PROHIBITION PARTY

CANDIDATE FOR PRESIDENT:
Joshua Levering (MD)

CANDIDATE FOR VICE PRESIDENT:
Hale Johnson

CANDIDATES FOR VICE-PRESIDENTIAL NOMINATION:
Louis Cameron Hughes (AZ)
Hale Johnson (IL)

7TH CONVENTION:
May 7–8, 1896, Exhibition Hall, Pittsburgh (PA)
A. A. Stevens (PA), temporary chairman
Oliver Wayne Stewart (IL), chairman

The Prohibitionists split in 1896 over whether they should address the monetary question. "Narrow gaugers" argued the party should restrict itself to the liquor question, while "broad gaugers" wanted a fuller platform. Narrow gaugers dominated the Prohibition Party's convention, while those who seceded formed the National Party. The platform of the narrow gaugers was narrow indeed: it consisted of only four paragraphs, all of which urged the total prohibition of liquor traffic.

PROHIBITION PARTY
VOTE FOR PRESIDENTIAL NOMINATION: LEVERING WAS NOMINATED FOR PRESIDENT BY ACCLAMATION.

VOTE FOR VICE-PRESIDENTIAL NOMINATION:

Candidate	Ballot: 1
Johnson	309
Hughes	13

REPUBLICAN PARTY

CANDIDATE FOR PRESIDENT:
William McKinley, Jr.

CANDIDATE FOR VICE PRESIDENT:
Garret Augustus Hobart

CANDIDATES FOR PRESIDENTIAL NOMINATION:
William Boyd Allison (IA)
James Donald Cameron (PA)
William McKinley, Jr. (OH)
Levi Parsons Morton (NY)
Matthew Stanley Quay (PA)
Thomas Brackett Reed (ME)

CANDIDATES FOR VICE-PRESIDENTIAL NOMINATION:
Morgan Gardner Bulkeley (CT)
Chauncey Mitchell Depew (NY)
Henry Clay Evans (TN)
Frederick Dent Grant (NY)
Garret Augustus Hobart (NJ)
Charles Warren Lippitt (RI)
Levi Parsons Morton (NY)
Thomas Brackett Reed (ME)

John Mellen Thurston (NE)
James Alexander Walker (VA)

11TH CONVENTION:
June 16–18, 1896, Special Auditorium, St. Louis (MO)
Charles Warren Fairbanks (IN), temporary chairman
John Mellen Thurston (NE), chairman

Thirty-four delegates withdrew from this convention to protest the party's financial plank in the platform.

PLATFORM HIGHLIGHTS:

SUPPORTED:
- the gold standard
- protectionism and reciprocity, particularly with regard to the sugar industry and wool and woolens
- the buildup of the navy and restoration of the merchant marine
- benefits for veterans
- governance of the Hawaiian Islands by the United States
- U.S. ownership of the proposed canal through Nicaragua
- purchase of the Danish West Indies
- stronger immigration laws requiring a literacy test for entrance to the United States
- the free ballot
- free homesteads
- national arbitration

REPUBLICAN PARTY
VOTE FOR PRESIDENTIAL NOMINATION:

Candidate	Ballot: 1
McKinley	666½
Reed	84½
Quay	61½
Morton	58
Allison	35½
Cameron	1
blank votes	4

McKinley's nomination was made unanimous.

VOTE FOR VICE-PRESIDENTIAL NOMINATION

Candidate	Ballot: 1
Hobart	535½
Evans	77½
Bulkeley	39
Walker	4
Lippitt	8
Reed	3
Depew	3
Morton	1

OPPOSED:
- lynching

ALSO:
- reaffirmed the Monroe Doctrine, condemned the massacres in Armenia, and urged the federal government to use its good offices to restore peace and give independence to Cuba
- welcomed women for their opposition to the Democrats and the recognized the principles of equal pay for equal work and equal opportunities, but did not specifically endorse women's suffrage
- skirted the prohibition issue with an expression of "sympathy" for the temperance movement

SOCIALIST LABOR PARTY

CANDIDATE FOR PRESIDENT:
Charles Horatio Matchett

CANDIDATE FOR VICE-PRESIDENT:
Matthew Maguire (NJ)

CANDIDATES FOR PRESIDENTIAL NOMINATION:
Matthew Maguire (NJ)
Charles Horatio Matchett (NY)
William Watkins (OH)

2D CONVENTION:
July 4–10, 1896, Grand Central Palace, New York (NY)
William Watkins (OH), chairman

The Socialist Laborites' platform asserted that both the machinery of government and the machinery of production must be controlled by the people. It also called for an awakening of class consciousness.

PLATFORM HIGHLIGHTS:

SUPPORTED:
- a reduction of working hours
- federal ownership of national transportation and communications systems
- municipal ownership of local transportation and communications systems
- revocation of unearned land grants
- exclusive reservation of the right to issue money to the federal government
- scientific management of forests and waterways
- revisions of the patent laws
- a progressive income tax and a tax on inheritance
- compulsory public school education
- revocation of pauper laws
- prohibition of child labor and restriction of women from injurious occupations
- inauguration of a public works program for the unemployed
- equal pay for equal work for men and women
- enactment of occupational safety laws

- adoption of the initiative, referendum, and recall
- abolition of the veto
- abolition of federal and state senates
- election reforms, including universal suffrage, proportional representation, the adoption of Australia's ballot, and election holidays
- municipal self-government

SOCIALIST LABOR PARTY
VOTE FOR PRESIDENTIAL AND VICE-PRESIDENTIAL NOMINATIONS: MAGUIRE AND WATKINS WERE PLACED IN NOMINATION FOR PRESIDENT, BUT THEY DECLINED. MATCHETT AND MAGUIRE WERE THEN NOMINATED BY ACCLAMATION FOR PRESIDENT AND VICE PRESIDENT, RESPECTIVELY.

GENERAL ELECTION SUMMARY FOR 1896

Candidate	Electoral Votes	States	Popular Votes
McKinley (R)	271	23	7,104,779
Bryan (D)	176[1]	22	6,509,052
Palmer (NAT DEM)	0	0	133,148
Matchett (SOC LAB)	0	0	36,356
Benteley (NAT)	0	0	19,363
Levering (PROH)	0	0	13,007
Bryan (PEO)	0	0	2,583
Douglass (ID)	0	0	51
unknown	0	0	36,356

[1] 149 votes (for Sewall), 7 votes (for Watson) for vice president

ELECTION OF NOVEMBER 6, 1900

President
WILLIAM McKINLEY, JR.
Vice President
THEODORE ROOSEVELT

HIGHLIGHTS

U.S. imperialism was riding high after the Spanish-American War, with Hawaii, the Philippines, and Puerto Rico under U.S. ownership. Prosperity dulled the radicals' clamor for monetary reform. William McKinley's reelection seemed likely, but the Republicans had to select a new running mate after Vice President Garret Hobart's death in 1899. Their choice was not difficult—New York governor Theodore Roosevelt, the hero of San Juan Hill. The Democrats had an equally easy time of choosing their candidate for president. William Jennings Bryan was the clear favorite, although Adm. George Dewey made a futile effort to secure the nomination. The election campaign was waged between Roosevelt and Bryan, with McKinley again remaining on the sidelines. In the end, the electorate heeded the powerful capitalist Mark Hanna's advice to the country to "let well enough alone." McKinley's victory over Bryan was even greater than it had been four years earlier.

ANTI-IMPERIALIST LEAGUE

CANDIDATE FOR PRESIDENT:
William Jennings Bryan (NE)

CONVENTION:
August 16, 1900, Indianapolis (IN)

The party was also known as the Liberty Congress of the Anti-Imperialist League. Its platform condemned McKinley's foreign policy and endorsed Bryan as the best person to reverse the U.S. trend toward imperialism.

CITIZENS PARTY

CANDIDATE FOR PRESIDENT:
George Francis Train (NY) (declined)

DEMOCRATIC PARTY

CANDIDATE FOR PRESIDENT:
William Jennings Bryan (NE)

CANDIDATE FOR VICE PRESIDENT:
Adlai Ewing Stevenson

CANDIDATES FOR VICE-PRESIDENTIAL NOMINATION:
Julian Shakespeare Carr (NC)
Elliott Danforth (NY)
David Bennett Hill (NY)
James Stephen Hogg (TX)
Abram W. Patrick (OH)
John Walter Smith (MD)
Adlai Ewing Stevenson (IL)
Charles Arnette Towne (MN)

18TH CONVENTION:
July 4–6, 1900, Convention Hall, Kansas City (MO)
Charles Spalding Thomas (CO), temporary chairman
James Daniel Richardson (TN), chairman

Nine hundred thirty-six delegates attended this convention, including two women from Utah.

PLATFORM HIGHLIGHTS:
SUPPORTED:
- free coinage of silver at a ratio of 16 to 1
- the Monroe Doctrine
- the National Guard
- greater restraints on the dominant robber barons of industry
- direct election of senators
- creation of a cabinet-level Department of Labor
- liberal pensions for veterans
- the immediate construction of a canal through Nicaragua
- home rule for Alaska and Puerto Rico
- Chinese exclusion laws
- improvements in the irrigation of the arid lands of the West

OPPOSED:
- the spread of imperialism, asserting that "no nation can long endure [as] half republic and half empire"
- the taxation of Puerto Rico and demanded the prompt return of Cuba and the Philippines to full sovereignty

- militarism
- the trusts and urged that the products of the trusts be placed on a tariff free list

ALSO:

- condemned the Hay-Pauncefote Treaty, as well as the use of injunctions and the blacklist in labor disputes
- promised immediate statehood for Arizona, New Mexico, and Oklahoma
- hostile to a perceived alliance between the Republican Party and Great Britain, for the Democrats sided with the Boers in their conflict with the British

---

DEMOCRATIC PARTY
VOTE FOR PRESIDENTIAL NOMINATION:
BRYAN WAS NOMINATED ON THE FIRST BALLOT BY UNANIMOUS VOTE.

VOTE FOR VICE-PRESIDENTIAL NOMINATION:

Candidate	Ballot: 1
Stevenson	559½
Hill	200
Towne	89½
Patrick	46
Carr	23
Smith	16
Danforth	1
Hogg	1

Stevenson's nomination was made unanimous.

INDEPENDENT
CANDIDATES FOR PRESIDENT:
Silas W. Cook (WY)
William Jackson Palmer (CO)
G. W. Pape (VT)
E. W. Perrin (AR)

NATIONAL DEMOCRATIC (GOLD DEMOCRATIC) PARTY

The Gold Democrats met in Indianapolis (IN) on July 25 and condemned the candidates of the Democratic party. They adopted the platform of 1896 again, but made no nominations.

NATIONAL PARTY
CANDIDATE FOR PRESIDENT:
Donelson Caffery

CANDIDATE FOR VICE PRESIDENT:
Archibald Murray Howe (MA)

CANDIDATES FOR PRESIDENTIAL NOMINATION:
Donelson Caffery (LA)
Edward Waldo Emerson (MA)[1]

CONVENTION:
September 5, 1900, Carnegie Lyceum, New York (NY)

About on hundred volunteer delegates from several states attended this convention. The National Party's platform tried to steer a middle course.

PLATFORM HIGHLIGHTS:
SUPPORTED:

- relinquishment of foreign conquests and territories
- the gold standard and a sound banking system
- adoption of the merit system in civil service
- legislation to do away with "all corrupting special privileges" such as "subsidies, bounties, undeserved pensions, and trust-breeding tariffs"

ALSO:

- criticized "the organized forces of commercialism" while denouncing those forces promoting factionalism and class struggle

---

NATIONAL PARTY
VOTE FOR PRESIDENTIAL AND VICE-PRESIDENTIAL NOMINATIONS: BOTH CANDIDATES RECEIVING NOMINATION DECLINED.

PEOPLE'S (POPULIST, FUSIONIST FACTION) PARTY
CANDIDATE FOR PRESIDENT:
William Jennings Bryan (NE)

CANDIDATE FOR VICE PRESIDENT:
Adlai Ewing Stevenson

CANDIDATES FOR VICE-PRESIDENTIAL NOMINATION:
John William Breidenthal (KS)
Elbridge Gerry Brown (MA)
James Harvey Davis (TX)
John Jacob Lentz (OH)
Theodore P. Rynder (PA)
Adlai Ewing Stevenson (IL)
Howard Singleton Taylor (IL)
Charles Arnette Towne (MN)

3D CONVENTION:
May 9–10, 1900, Sioux Falls (SD)
P. M. Ringdale (MN), temporary chairman
Thomas MacDonald Patterson (CO), chairman

[1]Emerson was an active member of the National Party. See the General Election Summary for the popular votes he received.

The convention was attended by 856 delegates, including women. Co-opted by the Democrats in 1896, the People's Party fell into line once again in 1900, but its platform read like a paraphrase of the Democratic platform in many respects.

PLATFORM HIGHLIGHTS:

SUPPORTED:

- free coinage of silver at a 16 to 1 ratio
- adoption of a graduated income tax and inheritance tax
- creation of postal savings banks
- liberal pensions for veterans
- controls on land grants
- government ownership of railroads
- municipal ownership of public utilities
- curtailment of trusts
- use of the initiative and referendum
- restrictions on Asian immigration
- the direct election of U.S. senators "and all other officials"
- independence for the Philippines
- home rule for the territories and their early admission as states
- repeal of the tax on Puerto Rico

ALSO:

- condemned the use of soldiers in the labor disputes in Idaho
- denounced imperialism and militarism, particularly the use of a U.S. standing army abroad

---

PEOPLE'S (POPULIST, FUSIONIST FACTION) PARTY
VOTE FOR PRESIDENTIAL NOMINATION: BRYAN WAS NOMINATED BY ACCLAMATION.

VOTE FOR VICE-PRESIDENTIAL NOMINATION: TOWNE WAS NOMINATED BY ACCLAMATION AFTER BRYAN'S FORCES ATTEMPTED TO PREVENT THE NOMINATION OF A CANDIDATE. TOWNE WITHDREW ON AUGUST 7, 1900, AND THE PARTY'S NATIONAL COMMITTEE SUBSTITUTED STEVENSON ON THE FOLLOWING DAY.

PEOPLE'S (POPULIST, MIDDLE-OF-THE-ROAD, ANTI-FUSIONIST) PARTY

CANDIDATE FOR PRESIDENT:
Wharton Barker

CANDIDATE FOR VICE PRESIDENT:
Ignatius Donnelly (MN)

CANDIDATES FOR PRESIDENTIAL NOMINATION:
Wharton Barker (PA)
Frank Burkitt (MS)
Ignatius Donnelly (MN)
Milford Wriarson Howard (AL)
Seymour Frank Norton (IL)

CONVENTION:
May 9–10, 1900, Robinson's Opera House, Cincinnati (OH)
Milford Wriarson Howard (AL), temporary chairman
W. L. Peek (GA), chairman

This faction of the People's Party first bolted in 1896 and did not support fusion with the Democrats.

PLATFORM HIGHLIGHTS:

SUPPORTED:

- the initiative, recall, and referendum
- public ownership of railroads and telegraphs
- restrictions on land speculation
- free coinage of silver at the legal ratio of 16 to 1
- imposition of a graduated income tax
- direct election of the president, vice president, federal judges, and U.S. senators
- efforts to curb monopolies through public ownership of utilities

---

PEOPLE'S (POPULIST, MIDDLE-OF-THE-ROAD, ANTI-FUSIONIST) PARTY
VOTE FOR PRESIDENTIAL NOMINATION:

Candidate	Ballot: 1	2
Barker	323 ⁴⁄₁₀	370
Howard	326 ⁶⁄₁₀	336
Donnelly	70	7
Norton	3	2

Barker's nomination was made unanimous.

VOTE FOR VICE-PRESIDENTIAL NOMINATION: DONNELLY WAS UNANIMOUSLY NOMINATED FOR VICE PRESIDENT.

PROHIBITION PARTY

CANDIDATE FOR PRESIDENT:
John Granville Woolley

CANDIDATE FOR VICE PRESIDENT:
Henry Brewer Metcalf

CANDIDATES FOR PRESIDENTIAL NOMINATION:
Hale Johnson (IL)
Silas Comfort Swallow (PA)
John Granville Woolley (IL)

CANDIDATES FOR VICE-PRESIDENTIAL NOMINATION:
Thomas Rosabaum Carskadon (WV)
Ephraim Llewellyn Eaton (IA)
Henry Brewer Metcalf (RI)
Silas Comfort Swallow (PA)
James A. Tate (TN)

8TH CONVENTION:
June 27–28, 1900, First Regiment Armory, Chicago (IL)

Samuel Dickie (MI), temporary and permanent chairman

Seven hundred thirty-five delegates from thirty-seven states attended this convention.

PLATFORM HIGHLIGHTS:
The Prohibition Party's platform returned to a narrow-gauge approach in 1900 and tied all issues to the liquor question. For example, it noted an increase in the liquor exports to Cuba and the Philippines and declared the alcoholic beverage industry the most dangerous trust and monopoly of them all. Nonetheless, three resolutions addressing other issues were adopted outside of the platform. One called for women's suffrage, and the second and third urged party support for the Young People's Prohibition Leagues.

PROHIBITION PARTY
VOTE FOR PRESIDENTIAL NOMINATON:

Candidate	Ballot: 1
Woolley	380
Swallow	329
Johnson	withdrew

An effort was made to persuade Swallow to accept the vice-presidential nomination but he declined.

VOTE FOR VICE-PRESIDENTIAL NOMINATION:

Candidate	Ballot: 1
Metcalf	380
Carskadon	130
Eaton	113

Tate declined the nomination.

REPUBLICAN PARTY
CANDIDATE FOR PRESIDENT:
William McKinley, Jr. (OH)

CANDIDATE FOR VICE PRESIDENT:
Theodore Roosevelt (NY)

12TH CONVENTION:
June 19–21, 1900, Exposition Auditorium, Philadelphia (PA)
Edward Oliver Wolcott (CO), temporary chairman
Henry Cabot Lodge (MA), chairman

Nine hundred twenty-four delegates attended this convention. The Republican platform recited the achievements of the preceding four years under McKinley, noting the prosperity of the country, the growth of exports, and the U.S. victory in the Spanish-American War.

PLATFORM HIGHLIGHTS:
SUPPORTED:
- the gold standard
- a protectionist trade policy based on reciprocity
- further restrictions on the immigration of cheap labor
- raising the age limit for child labor
- the extension of education for working children
- prohibition of convict labor under contract
- an effective system of labor insurance
- liberal pension for soldiers
- extension of the rural free delivery system
- reduction in the war tax
- construction of an isthmian canal by the United States
- creation of a cabinet-level Department of Commerce
- annexation of Hawaii

OPPOSED:
- the free coinage of silver
- trusts

ALSO:
- recognized the overdependence of the nation on foreign shipping
- lauded the Republican administration of the civil service in the territories
- condemned state violations of the Fifteenth Amendment
- promised early statehood for Arizona, New Mexico, and Oklahoma and independence for Cuba
- commended McKinley for taking part in the Peace Conference at The Hague and lending his good offices to help resolve the Boer dispute with Great Britain

REPUBLICAN PARTY
VOTE FOR PRESIDENTIAL NOMINATION: THE INCUMBENT, MCKINLEY, WAS RENOMINATED ON THE FIRST BALLOT BY UNANIMOUS VOTE.

VOTE FOR VICE-PRESIDENTIAL NOMINATION: ROOSEVELT WAS NOMINATED FOR VICE PRESIDENT ON THE FIRST BALLOT. HE RECEIVED THE VOTE OF EVERY DELEGATE EXCEPT HIMSELF.

SILVER REPUBLICAN PARTY
CANDIDATE FOR PRESIDENT:
William Jennings Bryan (NE)

CANDIDATE FOR VICE PRESIDENT:
Adlai Ewing Stevenson (IL)

CONVENTION:
July 4–6, 1900, Auditorium, Kansas City (MO)

Henry Moore Teller (CO), temporary chairman
L. W. Brown (OH), chairman

Including delegates and visitors, about twelve hundred persons representing twenty-four states and territories attended this convention.

PLATFORM HIGHLIGHTS:

SUPPORTED:
- bimetallism
- a graduated income tax
- direct election of senators
- adoption of the merit system in the civil service
- liberal pensions for veterans
- the Monroe Doctrine
- construction of a canal through Nicaragua
- implementation of the principles of direct legislation
- public ownership of utilities
- federal assistance to reclaim the arid lands of the West
- statehood for Arizona, New Mexico, and Oklahoma

OPPOSED:
- trusts and monopolies
- Asian laborers
- alien ownership of land and franchises

ALSO:
- took an anti-imperialist perspective on foreign policy, expressing sympathy for the Boers, supporting freedom for Cuba and repeal of the Puerto Rico tariff law, urging self-government for the Philippines, and demanding repeal of the war taxes levied to carry on the war with Spain

This party was later known as the Socialist Party. The Social Democratic platform condemned capitalism as being responsible for the misery of workers and the disappearance of the middle class.

PLATFORM HIGHLIGHTS:

SUPPORTED:
- establishment of a national system of cooperative industry, based on the social or common ownership of the means of production and distribution through revision of the Federal Constitution
- public ownership of all industries controlled by monopolies, trusts, and combines
- public ownership of railroads, telegraphs and telephones, waterworks, gas and electric plants, and other public utilities
- public ownership of various mines and fossil fuel resources
- a reduction in working hours
- initiation of a system of public works to counteract unemployment
- revision of patent laws
- nationalization of labor legislation
- enactment of industrial insurance programs and social security
- equal rights for men and women
- adoption of the initiative, referendum, and proportional representation
- the abolition of war and the introduction of international arbitration

---

SILVER REPUBLICAN PARTY

VOTE FOR PRESIDENTIAL NOMINATION: BRYAN WAS NOMINATED FOR PRESIDENT BY ACCLAMATION.

VOTE FOR VICE-PRESIDENTIAL NOMINATION: NO NOMINATION WAS MADE FOR VICE PRESIDENT. ON JULY 7, THE PARTY'S NATIONAL COMMITTEE MET IN KANSAS CITY (MO) AND SELECTED STEVENSON AS ITS VICE-PRESIDENTIAL CANDIDATE.

SOCIAL DEMOCRATIC PARTY

CANDIDATE FOR PRESIDENT:
Eugene Victor Debs

CANDIDATE FOR VICE PRESIDENT:
Job Harriman (CA)

CANDIDATES FOR PRESIDENTIAL NOMINATION:
Eugene Victor Debs (IN)
Job Harriman (CA)

CONVENTION:
March 6–7, 1900, Indianapolis (IN)

SOCIAL DEMOCRATIC PARTY

VOTE FOR PRESIDENTIAL AND VICE-PRESIDENTIAL NOMINATIONS: DEBS AND TWO OTHERS WERE OFFERED THE NOMINATION FOR PRESIDENT, BUT THEY DECLINED. HARRIMAN WAS THEN NOMINATED WITH MAX S. HAYES OF OHIO AS HIS RUNNING MATE, WHEREUPON DEBS INDICATED THAT HE WOULD ACCEPT THE NOMINATION. ACCORDINGLY, THE CONVENTION NOMINATED DEBS FOR PRESIDENT AND HARRIMAN FOR VICE PRESIDENT.

SOCIALIST LABOR PARTY

CANDIDATE FOR PRESIDENT:
Joseph Francis Malloney

CANDIDATE FOR VICE PRESIDENT:
Valentine Remmel

CANDIDATES FOR PRESIDENTIAL NOMINATION:
Willard B. Hammond (MN)
Joseph Francis Malloney (MA)
John Raymond Pepin (IL)
Valentine Remmel (PA)

CANDIDATES FOR VICE-PRESIDENTIAL NOMINATION:
Willard B. Hammond (MN)

John Raymond Pepin (IL)
Valentine Remmel (PA)

10TH CONVENTION:
June 2–8, 1900, Palm Garden, Grand Central
Palace, New York (NY)
Thomas Curran (RI), temporary chairman
Daniel De Leon (NY), chairman

This convention was attended by eighty-three delegates from nineteen states. It readopted its 1896 platform, with the exception of a portion known as "general demands."

SOCIALIST LABOR PARTY
VOTE FOR PRESIDENTIAL NOMINATION:

Candidate	Ballot: 1
Malloney	60
Remmel	17
Hammond	1
Pepin	0
absent	7

Malloney's nomination was made unanimous.

VOTE FOR VICE-PRESIDENTIAL NOMINATION:

Candidate	Ballot: 1
Remmel	69
Hammond	7
Pepin	2
absent	7

UNION REFORM PARTY

CANDIDATE FOR PRESIDENT:
Seth Hockett Ellis (OH)

CANDIDATE FOR VICE PRESIDENT:
Samuel Thorne Nicholson (PA)

CONVENTION:
September 3, 1900, Baltimore (MD)

This party was organized March 1, 1899, in Cincinnati (OH) by Silver Republicans, Populists, Socialist La-

---

UNION REFORM PARTY
VOTE FOR PRESIDENTIAL AND VICE-PRESIDENTIAL NOMINATIONS: IN JANUARY 1900, THE UNION REFORM PARTY'S NATIONAL COMMITTEE SENT OUT BALLOTS TO MEMBERS OF THE PARTY. IN APRIL, THE CANVASSING BOARD ANNOUNCED ELLIS'S NOMINATION FOR PRESIDENT AND NICHOLSON'S FOR VICE PRESIDENT.

---

borites, Liberty Party members, and others. At its convention, the Union Reform Party reaffirmed the platform it adopted in 1899. It called for direct legislation through the initiative and referendum, and condemned corruption in politics caused by political bosses and corporate influences.

UNITED CHRISTIAN PARTY

CANDIDATE FOR PRESIDENT:
Jonah Fitz Randolph Leonard

CANDIDATE FOR VICE PRESIDENT:
David Herron Martin

CANDIDATES FOR PRESIDENTIAL NOMINATION:
William Rudolph Benkert (IA)
Jonah Fitz Randolph Leonard (IA)
Charles Monroe Sheldon (KS)
Wallace R. Struble (IL)
Silas Comfort Swallow (PA)

CANDIDATES FOR VICE-PRESIDENTIAL NOMINATION:
David Herron Martin (PA)
John Granville Woolley (IL)

CONVENTION:
May 1–2, 1900, Rock Island (IL)

The United Christian Party was organized July 4, 1898, under the guidance of William Rudolph Benkert. Its platform acknowledged Jesus Christ as the sovereign ruler of nations and the Bible as the standard for moral conduct in political life.

PLATFORM HIGHLIGHTS:
SUPPORTED:
- prohibition
- the system of direct legislation and proportional representation
- international arbitration to settle disputes
- supported equal rights for men and women
- daily Bible reading in the public schools
- government ownership of public utilities
- direct election of the president, vice president, and U.S. senators

OPPOSED:
- secular marriage and divorce laws
- desecration of the Sabbath
- the sale of tobacco products to minors

UNITED CHRISTIAN PARTY
VOTE FOR PRESIDENTIAL AND VICE-PRESIDENTIAL NOMINATIONS: BOTH SWALLOW AND WOOLLEY DECLINED THE NOMINATIONS, SO LEONARD AND MARTIN WERE SUBSTITUTED ON THE TICKET.

GENERAL ELECTION SUMMARY FOR 1900			
Candidate	Electoral Votes	States	Popular Votes
McKinley (R)	292	28	7,207,923
Bryan (D)[1]	155	17	6,358,138
Woolley (PROH)	0	0	208,914
Debs (SOC DEM)	0	0	87,814
Barker (PEO-ANTI)	0	0	50,373
Malloney (SOC LAB)	0	0	39,739
Ellis (UNI REF)	0	0	5,700
Leonard (UNI CHR)	0	0	5,500
Emerson (NAT)	0	0	342
Bryan (AIL)	0	0	45
Perrin	0	0	27
Palmer (I)	0	0	26
Cook (I)	0	0	21
Pape (I)	0	0	1
unknown	0	0	234

[1]includes Silver Party votes and People's Party votes

ELECTION OF NOVEMBER 8, 1904

President
THEODORE ROOSEVELT
Vice President
CHARLES WARREN FAIRBANKS

HIGHLIGHTS

William McKinley's assassination thrust the young Theodore Roosevelt into the presidency in 1901. Roosevelt was vigorous and brought a new excitement to the White House. Despite enemies in his party, his renomination was assured. Having twice unsuccessfully flirted with its radical wing, the Democrats in 1904 looked for a more conservative alternative. They found it in the colorless Alton B. Parker, but he failed to win the enthusiastic support of Bryan and his legions. The Democrats added to their problems by nominating for vice president the oldest candidate for national office on a major party ticket—eighty-year-old Sen. Henry Gassaway Davis. The 1904 election was notable for featuring only the second African-American ever nominated for president—William T. Scott, the presidential candidate of the National Liberty Party. (F. Douglass was a candidate for nomination for president in 1848 and 1888, but Scott was the first to receive the nomination.) Nonetheless, the 1904 campaign was relatively boring. Roosevelt sailed to an easy victory, setting a record-breaking margin in the popular vote.

CONTINENTAL PARTY

CANDIDATE FOR PRESIDENT:
Austin Holcomb

CANDIDATE FOR VICE PRESIDENT:
A. A. King

CANDIDATES FOR PRESIDENTIAL NOMINATION:
Austin Holcomb (GA)
Charles Henry Howard (IL)

CANDIDATES FOR VICE-PRESIDENTIAL NOMINATION:
A. A. King (MO)
George Henry Shibley (DC)

CONVENTION:
August 31, 1904, Chicago (IL)

Howard and Shibley were nominated, respectively, for president and vice president, but both declined. Holcomb and King were then substituted by the national committee.

DEMOCRATIC PARTY

CANDIDATE FOR PRESIDENT:
Alton Brooks Parker

CANDIDATE FOR VICE PRESIDENT
Henry Gassaway Davis

CANDIDATES FOR PRESIDENTIAL NOMINATION:
Francis Marion Cockrell (MO)
Bird Sim Coler (NY)
Arthur Pue Gorman (PA)
George Gray (DE)
William Randolph Hearst (NY)
George Brinton McClellan (NJ)
Nelson Appleton Miles (MA)
Richard Olney (MA)
Alton Brooks Parker (NY)
Robert Emory Pattison (PA)
Charles Arnette Towne (MN)
Edward Clarence Wall (WI)
John Sharp Williams (MS)

CANDIDATES FOR VICE-PRESIDENTIAL NOMINATION:
Charles Brantley Aycock (NC)
John Crepps Wickliffe Beckham (KY)
Edward Ward Carmack (TN)
Henry Gassaway Davis (WV)
Alexander Monroe Dockery (MO)
William Alexander Harris, Jr. (KS)
Clark Howell (GA)
George Turner (WA)
Robert Williams (IL)

19TH CONVENTION:
July 6–9, 1904, Coliseum, St. Louis (MO)
John Sharp Williams (MS), temporary chairman
Champ Clark (MO), chairman

The two-time failure of "Bryanism" created an opportunity for the conservative wing of the Democratic Party, but without a strong candidate, it was unable to capitalize on it. Nonetheless, the platform reflected the party's right-ward tilt, despite some concessions made to Bryan to keep him from disrupting the convention.

PLATFORM HIGHLIGHTS:

SUPPORTED:

- Philippine independence
- tariff reduction
- reciprocity with Canada
- liberal pensions for veterans
- civil service reform
- efforts to strengthen the Interstate Commerce Commission
- enforcement of the eight-hour workday law
- use of arbitration between employers and employees in labor disputes
- liberal appropriations to improve inland waterways, reclamation of arid lands, and construction of an isthmian canal
- the direct election of senators
- restrictions on judicial authorities
- stronger antitrust laws

OPPOSED:

- sectional and race agitation
- imperialism

DEMOCRATIC PARTY
VOTE FOR PRESIDENTIAL NOMINATION:

Candidate	Ballot: 1a	1b
Parker	658	679
Hearst	200	181
Cockrell	42	42
Olney	38	38
Wall	27	27
Gray	12	12
Williams	8	8
Pattison	4	4
Miles	3	3
McClellan	3	3
Towne	2	2
Coler	1	1
Gorman	2	0

Parker's nomination was made unanimous.

VOTE FOR VICE-PRESIDENTIAL NOMINATION:

Candidate	Ballot: 1
Davis	654
Williams	165
Turner	100
Harris	58
not voting	23

The nomination of Davis was made unanimous.

- the protective tariff
- polygamy

ALSO:

- condemned Roosevelt indirectly by asserting the need for a chief executive who would not be guilty of "executive usurpation"

INDEPENDENT

CANDIDATE FOR PRESIDENT:
Thomas Ogle Clark (MD)

LINCOLN PARTY

CANDIDATE FOR PRESIDENT:
John J. Jones (IL)

CANDIDATE FOR VICE PRESIDENT:
E. P. Penn (WV)

NATIONAL LIBERTY (NATIONAL CIVIL LIBERTY) PARTY

CANDIDATE FOR PRESIDENT:
George Edwin Taylor

CANDIDATE FOR VICE PRESIDENT:
William C. Payne (VA)

CANDIDATES FOR PRESIDENTIAL NOMINATION:
Pinckney Benton Stewart Pinchback (LA)
William T. Scott (IL)
George Edwin Taylor (AR)
James Milton Turner (MO)

CONVENTION:
July 5–6, 1904, Douglas Hotel, St. Louis (MO)
Stanley P. Mitchell (TN), temporary chairman
William T. Scott (IL), chairman
I. L. Walton (DC), secretary

This convention was attended by twenty-eight delegates representing thirty-six states. The party was associated with the Civil and Personal Liberty League, the National Democratic League, and the Negro Jefferson Association.

PLATFORM HIGHLIGHTS:

SUPPORTED:

- universal suffrage
- liberal pensions for veterans
- creation of a National Arbitration Board
- elimination of commercial subsidies by the government
- nullification and repeal of all class legislation
- abolition of trusts and combines
- reduction of the tariff
- pensions for ex-slaves

OPPOSED:

- polygamy

ALSO:
- protested the disenfranchisement of two million African-American citizens through discriminatory devices like the poll tax and made common cause between African-Americans and the general working class

---

NATIONAL LIBERTY (NATIONAL CIVIL LIBERTY) PARTY
VOTE FOR PRESIDENTIAL NOMINATION: MITCHELL WAS OFFERED FOR NOMINATION, BUT HE DECLINED. SCOTT WAS THEN NOMINATED BUT WAS SUBSEQUENTLY CONVICTED OF KEEPING A "DISORDERLY HOUSE" (I.E., A HOUSE OF PROSTITUTION) AND WITHDREW AS THE PARTY'S CANDIDATE. ON JULY 20, 1904, TAYLOR WAS NAMED TO REPLACE SCOTT AS THE PRESIDENTIAL CANDIDATE.

NATIONAL VETERANS ASSOCIATION
CANDIDATE FOR PRESIDENT:
Nelson Appleton Miles (MA)

CANDIDATE FOR VICE PRESIDENT:
John Charles Black (IL)

PEOPLE'S (POPULIST) PARTY
CANDIDATE FOR PRESIDENT:
Thomas Edward Watson

CANDIDATE FOR VICE PRESIDENT:
Thomas Henry Tibbles (NE)

CANDIDATES FOR PRESIDENTIAL NOMINATION:
William Vincent Allen (NE)
Thomas Edward Watson (GA)
Frank W. Williams (IN)

4TH CONVENTION:
July 4–6, 1904, Springfield (IL)

A demoralized People's Party met to nominate candidates for president and vice president. Clearly, the party representing the Populist movement had lost its political clout.

PLATFORM HIGHLIGHTS:
SUPPORTED:
- government ownership of the railroads and public utilities
- sufficient money in circulation to stabilize prices and reserved the right to print money to Congress alone
- the creation of postal savings banks
- the right of labor to organize
- abolition of child labor, sweat shops, competitive use of convict labor, and exclusion of foreign pauper labor
- a shorter work day
- the initiative, referendum, recall, proportional representation, and direct election of all public officers
- government regulation and taxation of trusts and corporate monopolies

- enactment of a general law uniformly regulating companies engaged in interstate commerce

OPPOSED:
- militarism
- land monopolies and alien ownership of land

PROHIBITION PARTY
CANDIDATE FOR PRESIDENT:
Silas Comfort Swallow

CANDIDATE FOR VICE PRESIDENT:
George Washington Carroll

CANDIDATES FOR PRESIDENTIAL NOMINATION:
Nelson Appleton Miles (MA)
Silas Comfort Swallow (PA)

CANDIDATES FOR VICE-PRESIDENTIAL NOMINATION:
Isaiah H. Amos (OR)
George Washington Carroll (TX)
A. U. Coates (IA)

9TH CONVENTION:
June 29-July 1, 1904, Indianapolis (IN)
Homer L. Castle (PA), temporary chairman
Andrew Givens Wolfenbarger (NE), permanent chairman

The Prohibition Party's platform reflected the single issue associated with the party—complete prohibition of the liquor trade.

PLATFORM HIGHLIGHTS:
SUPPORTED:
- the initiative and referendum
- direct election of senators
- civil service reform
- use of international arbitration to settle disputes between nations
- impartial enforcement of laws and the "rigid application of the principles of justice" to combinations and organizations of capital and labor
- settlement of tariff questions by an omnipartisan commission
- the notion that the right to vote be based on the mental and moral qualifications of the citizen

---

PROHIBITION PARTY
VOTE FOR PRESIDENTIAL NOMINATION: THE NOMINATION WAS OFFERED TO MILES, WHO DECLINED THE HONOR. ACCORDINGLY, SWALLOW WAS NOMINATED BY ACCLAMATION.

VOTE FOR VICE-PRESIDENTIAL NOMINATION: COATES WAS PLACED IN NOMINATION, BUT HE DECLINED. CARROLL WAS THEN NOMINATED FOR VICE PRESIDENT OVER AMOS.

OPPOSED:

- polygamy
- prostitution

REPUBLICAN PARTY

CANDIDATE FOR PRESIDENT:
Theodore Roosevelt (NY)

CANDIDATE FOR VICE PRESIDENT:
Charles Warren Fairbanks (IN)

13TH CONVENTION:
June 21–23, 1904, Coliseum, Chicago (IL)
Elihu Root (NY), temporary chairman
Joseph Gurney Cannon (IL), chairman

The Republican platform recounted the Republicans' recent successes and described the misdeeds of the Democrats, boasting "we have every right to congratulate ourselves."

PLATFORM HIGHLIGHTS:

SUPPORTED:

- the protective tariff and reciprocity in foreign trade
- the gold standard
- a strong merchant marine and navy
- enforcement of antitrust laws
- liberal pensions for soldiers and sailors
- international arbitration
- investigation of voting discrimination and possible reduction in a guilty state's congressional and electoral college representation

ALSO:

- acknowledged both combinations of capital and labor unions to be subject to the law
- lauded Roosevelt

REPUBLICAN PARTY

VOTE FOR PRESIDENTIAL NOMINATION: INCUMBENT PRESIDENT ROOSEVELT WAS UNANIMOUSLY NOMINATED ON THE FIRST BALLOT.

VOTE FOR VICE-PRESIDENTIAL NOMINATION: FAIRBANKS WAS NOMINATED BY ACCLAMATION.

SOCIALIST LABOR PARTY

CANDIDATE FOR PRESIDENT:
Charles Hunter Corregan (NY)

CANDIDATE FOR VICE PRESIDENT:
William Wesley Cox (IL)

11TH CONVENTION:
July 2–8, 1904, Grand Central Palace, New York (NY)
William Wesley Cox (IL), temporary chairman
August Gilhaus (NY), chairman for July 3, 1904
John D. Goerke (OH), chairman for July 5, 1904

Forty-one delegates and four alternates from eighteen states, plus three fraternal delegates attended this convention. The Socialist Labor Party's platform stressed the need for class consciousness and demanded that the means of production be publicly owned. It called for the "unconditional surrender of the Capitalist Class" but contained no planks addressing individual issues confronting the electorate.

SOCIALIST PARTY

CANDIDATE FOR PRESIDENT:
Eugene Victor Debs (IN)

CANDIDATE FOR VICE PRESIDENT:
Benjamin Hanford (NY)

1ST CONVENTION:
May 1–6, 1904, Brand's Hall, Chicago (IL)
Frank Sieverman (NY), session chairman

This gathering was the first nominating convention of the Socialist Party, which was formed March 25, 1900, in Indianapolis (IN). Attending were 183 delegates from thirty-six states. The party was an offshoot of the Socialist Labor Party and the Social Democratic Party of 1900. After reciting the evils of capitalism, the Socialist platform pledged fidelity to the principles of international socialism and declared socialism and the establishment of a cooperative commonwealth as, "sooner or later," inevitable.

PLATFORM HIGHLIGHTS:

SUPPORTED:

- a shorter workday
- increased wages
- insurance programs to protect workers from accident, sickness, and unemployment
- old age pensions
- public ownership of transportation and communications systems
- imposition of a graduated income tax and inheritance tax
- abolition of child labor and complete education for children
- prohibitions against the use of the military to break strikes
- the free administration of justice
- equal suffrage
- use of the initiative, recall, referendum, and proportional representation
- municipal home rule

SOCIALIST PARTY

VOTE FOR PRESIDENTIAL NOMINATION: DEBS WAS NOMINATED BY ACCLAMATION.

VOTE FOR VICE-PRESIDENTIAL NOMINATION: HANFORD WAS NOMINATED UNANIMOUSLY.

UNITED CHRISTIAN PARTY

2D CONVENTION:
May 2, 1904, St. Louis (MO)

The delegates adopted a platform but did not make any nominations. The United Christian Party's document reiterated its opposition to liquor traffic and urged the electorate to embrace the tenets of Christian morality in public life. If elected, the United Christians promised "Golden Rule Government."

PLATFORM HIGHLIGHTS:

SUPPORTED:

- observance of the Christian Sabbath
- direct elections and use of the initiative, referendum, and recall
- government ownership of mines, wells, and public utilities
- uniform marriage and divorce laws
- suppression of prostitution
- elimination of capital punishment

GENERAL ELECTION SUMMARY FOR 1904

Candidate	Electoral Votes	States	Popular Votes
Roosevelt (R)	336	32	7,623,486
Parker (D)	140	13	5,077,911
Debs (SOC)	0	0	402,283
Swallow (PROH)	0	0	258,536
Watson (PEO)	0	0	117,183
Corregan (SOC LAB)	0	0	31,249
Holcomb (CON)	0	0	1,000
Clark (I)	0	0	4
Jones (LINC)	0	0	none recorded
Miles (NAT VET)	0	0	none recorded
Taylor (NL)	0	0	none recorded
unknown	0	0	351

ELECTION OF NOVEMBER 3, 1908

President
WILLIAM HOWARD TAFT
Vice President
JAMES SCHOOLCRAFT SHERMAN

HIGHLIGHTS

The dismal showing of Alton B. Parker in 1904 combined with a continuing popular affection for the "boy orator of the Platte" helped to resurrect the political fortunes of William Jennings Bryan. He easily captured the Democratic nomination in 1908 to square off against William Howard Taft, who had inherited the Republican mantle of Theodore Roosevelt. While the nascent Progressive movement was growing in the West, the Populists were waning as a political power. The Socialists appeared to be gaining in strength, and a new party, the Independence Party, made its brief appearance on the political stage as a vehicle for spreading the interests of William Randolph Hearst. All in all, the campaign was a dull affair, even with Roosevelt's energetic attacks on Bryan on Taft's behalf. In the end, Bryan lost his third try for the presidency with a smaller percentage of the vote than he had received in either 1896 or 1900.

DEMOCRATIC PARTY

CANDIDATE FOR PRESIDENT:
William Jennings Bryan

CANDIDATE FOR VICE PRESIDENT:
John Worth Kern

CANDIDATES FOR PRESIDENTIAL NOMINATION:
William Jennings Bryan (NE)
George Gray (DE)
John Albert Johnson (MN)

CANDIDATES FOR VICE-PRESIDENTIAL NOMINATION:
Clark Howell (GA)
John Worth Kern (IN)
Archibald McNeil (CT)
Charles Arnette Towne (NY)

20TH CONVENTION:
July 8–10, 1908, Civic Auditorium, Denver (CO)
Theodore A. Bell (CA), temporary chairman
Henry De Lamar Clayton (AL), chairman

The Democratic platform of 1908 reflected the style of William Jennings Bryan. It denounced the Republicans, the increase in officeholders, the misuse of patronage, and the arbitrary power of House Speaker Joe Cannon. The Democrats asked, "Shall the people rule?"

PLATFORM HIGHLIGHTS:
SUPPORTED:
- campaign finance reform (to curb corporate abuses)
- immediate reduction in the tariff
- prohibition of private monopolies and interlocking directorates

- enlargement of the authority of the Interstate Commerce Commission to regulate railroads
- rate regulation and banking reforms
- a constitutional amendment to authorize an income tax
- the eight-hour day on government work and recognition of the legitimacy of unions
- a general employer's liability act to protect workers injured on the job
- creation of a Department of Labor and a National Bureau of Public Health
- civil service reform
- pension for veterans
- restrictions on the importation of Asian labor
- the establishment of agricultural experiment stations and secondary agricultural and mechanical colleges in the states
- endorsement of the Panama Canal

DEMOCRATIC PARTY VOTE FOR PRESIDENTIAL NOMINATION:	
Candidate	Ballot: 1
Bryan	888½
Gray	59½
Johnson	46

VOTE FOR VICE-PRESIDENTIAL NOMINATION:
KERN WAS NOMINATED UNANIMOUSLY FOR VICE PRESIDENT ON THE FIRST BALLOT.

- statehood for Arizona and New Mexico
- various internal improvements in waterways and post roads
- regulation of telegraph and telephone systems
- direct election of senators
- conservation of natural resources

ALSO:

- striking a muted anti-imperialist chord, sought certain rights for Alaska, Hawaii, and Puerto Rico and independence for the Philippines

INDEPENDENCE PARTY

CANDIDATE FOR PRESIDENT:

Thomas Louis Hisgen

CANDIDATE FOR VICE-PRESIDENT:

John Temple Graves

CANDIDATES FOR PRESIDENTIAL NOMINATION:

John Temple Graves (GA)
William Randolph Hearst (NY)
Thomas Louis Hisgen (MA)
Milford Wriarson Howard (AL)
Reuben Robie Lyon (NY)

CONVENTION:

July 27–29, 1908, Chicago (IL)

Financed by William Randolph Hearst, the Independence Party adopted a lengthy platform with many progressive features, while disavowing any intent "to effect a radical change in the American system of government." The party painted itself as a conservative force against the tyranny of "selfish interests, political tricksters, and corrupt bosses."

PLATFORM HIGHLIGHTS:

SUPPORTED:

- direct nominations, direct elections of senators and judges, and adoption of the initiative, referendum, and recall
- legislation against corrupt election practices and a requirement that campaign contributions be publicly disclosed
- frugality in government
- the formation of unions and farmers' organizations
- the eight-hour workday law
- cleaner and safer factories, mines, and other places of employment
- prohibition of child and convict labor
- creation of a Department of Labor and National Department of Public Health
- enactment of legislation for employers' liability
- creation of a central government bank to control issuance of currency
- reduction in the tariff
- elimination of rebates and other forms of discrimination by railroads

- regulation of business to prevent trusts and combinations in restraint of trade
- establishment of an Interstate Commerce Court
- government ownership of the telegraphs and other public utilities
- creation of government postal savings banks
- development of a national system of roads
- statehood for Arizona and New Mexico
- a strong navy
- international arbitration
- restrictions on the importation of cheap Asian labor
- internal improvements to waterways and arid lands
- initiation of a strong conservation program
- a graduated income tax
- protection of the rights of U.S. citizens abroad

OPPOSED:

- overcapitalization in corporations
- the use of the writ of injunction and contempt proceedings in labor disputes
- the "bucket shop" and fictitious sale of commodity futures
- blacklisting

INDEPENDENCE PARTY
VOTE FOR PRESIDENTIAL NOMINATION:

Candidate	Ballot: 3
Hisgen	83
Howard	38
Graves	7
Hearst	2

INDEPENDENT

CANDIDATES FOR PRESIDENT:

Edward Thorne Clark (NC)
S. H. Lasiter (CO)
Edwin H. Lentz (NH)
B. J. McGrue (CO)

PEOPLE'S (POPULIST) PARTY

CANDIDATE FOR PRESIDENT:

Thomas Edward Watson (GA)

CANDIDATE FOR VICE PRESIDENT:

Samuel Williams (IN)

5TH CONVENTION:

April 2–3, 1908, St. Louis (MO)

This election saw the dying thrust of the People's Party, which had degenerated into a small party of minor importance. Its platform reaffirmed the principles of the Omaha platform of 1892.

PLATFORM HIGHLIGHTS:

SUPPORTED:

- sought creation of postal savings banks
- reclamation of public lands purchased or granted to aliens or corporations
- government ownership or control of railroads and public utilities (including the general telegraph and telephone systems)
- elimination of special privileges for trusts and monopolies
- uniform regulation of companies in interstate commerce and taxing monopoly privileges through a general law enacted by Congress
- the initiative, referendum, proportional representation, and direct election and recall for public officers
- the right to form unions
- enactment of health and safety protections for workers
- passage of laws to establish employers' liability for the benefit of employees
- creation of a public works program to counteract unemployment

OPPOSED:

- the use of union-busting techniques like the injunction
- sweat shops, child and convict labor, and the use of foreign pauper labor
- corruption and the influence of corporate money in government

ALSO:

- called for Congress to assume responsibility for the issuance of legal tender money directly to the people

---

> ### PEOPLE'S (POPULIST) PARTY
> VOTE FOR PRESIDENTIAL NOMINATION: WATSON WAS NOMINATED FOR PRESIDENT ON THE FIRST BALLOT.
>
> VOTE FOR VICE-PRESIDENTIAL NOMINATION: WILLIAMS WAS NOMINATED, BUT NO VOTE TOTAL WAS RECORDED.

PROHIBITION PARTY

CANDIDATE FOR PRESIDENT:
Eugene Wilder Chafin

CANDIDATE FOR VICE PRESIDENT:
Aaron Sherman Watkins (OH)

CANDIDATES FOR PRESIDENTIAL NOMINATION:
Eugene Wilder Chafin (IL)
James Britton Cranfill (TX)
Alfred Lee Manierre (NY)
William Beverly Palmore (MO)
Robert Howard Patton (IL)
Charles Scanlon (MN)
Daniel Robinson Sheen (IL)
Oliver Wayne Stewart (IL)
George Rutledge Stuart (TN)

Joseph Platt Tracy (MI)
Frederick Freeman Wheeler (CA)
Seaborn Wright (GA)

10TH CONVENTION:
July 15–16, 1908, Columbus (OH)
Robert Howard Patton (IL), temporary chairman
Charles Scanlon (MN), permanent chairman

Attending this convention were 1,126 delegates.

PLATFORM HIGHLIGHTS:

SUPPORTED:

- a constitutional amendment to prohibit the manufacture, sale, importation, exportation, and transportation of alcoholic beverages
- the direct election of senators
- enactment of a graduate income tax and inheritance tax
- establishment of postal savings banks and a guaranteed bank deposit program
- regulation of corporations engaged in interstate commerce
- creation of a permanent tariff commission
- the suppression of prostitution
- uniform marriage and divorce laws
- an equitable employers' liability act
- court review of post office decisions
- prohibition of child labor
- preservation of the nation's mineral and forest resources
- improvements in highways and waterways
- universal suffrage limited only by intelligence and the ability to read and write the English language

---

> ### PROHIBITION PARTY
> VOTE FOR PRESIDENTIAL NOMINATION:
>
> | Candidate | Ballot: 1 | 2 | 3 |
> |---|---|---|---|
> | Chafin | — | — | 636 |
> | Palmore | — | — | 451 |
> | Wheeler | | | |
> | Cranfill | | | |
> | Sheen | | | |
> | Tracy | | | |
> | Manierre | | | |
> | Stewart | 61 | 0 | 0 |
> | Stuart | 7 | 0 | 0 |
>
> The above table is based on an incomplete convention record.

REPUBLICAN PARTY

CANDIDATE FOR PRESIDENT:
William Howard Taft

CANDIDATE FOR VICE PRESIDENT:
James Schoolcraft Sherman

CANDIDATES FOR PRESIDENTIAL NOMINATION:
Joseph Gurney Cannon (IL)
Charles Warren Fairbanks (IN)
Joseph Benson Foraker (OH)
Charles Evans Hughes (NY)
Philander Chase Knox (PA)
Robert Marion La Follette (WI)
Theodore Roosevelt (NY)
William Howard Taft (OH)

CANDIDATES FOR VICE-PRESIDENTIAL NOMINATION:
Charles Warren Fairbanks (IN)
Curtis Guild (MA)
Edward Franklin Murphy (NJ)
George Lawson Sheldon (NE)
James Schoolcraft Sherman (NY)

14TH CONVENTION:
June 16–19, 1908, Coliseum, Chicago (IL)
Julius Caesar Burrows (MI), temporary chairman
Henry Cabot Lodge (MA), chairman

Having declared against a "third term," President Theodore Roosevelt endorsed his secretary of War, William Howard Taft, for the Republican nomination. A coalition of favorite-son candidates from the North, known as the "Allies," tried unsuccessfully to block the nomination. The platform, too, reflected the personal views of both Roosevelt and Taft, despite unsuccessful efforts to amend it to include more progressive planks. It was a lengthy document of limited substance.

PLATFORM HIGHLIGHTS:
SUPPORTED:
• tariff revision "immediately following the inauguration of the next president
• creation of a National Monetary Commission and a postal savings bank system
• strengthening of the Sherman Anti-Trust Act
• reasonable railroad regulation
• enactment of health and safety laws to protect workers
• creation of a Bureau of Mines and Mining
• immediate admission of Arizona and New Mexico as states

OPPOSED:
• the use without notice of the injunction in labor disputes, "except where irreparable injury would result from delay"

ALSO:
• praised what the party had accomplished for farmers, Negroes, the army and navy, protection of natural resources, the extension of foreign commerce, veterans' pensions, civil service reform, international relations through the use of arbitration, and the strengthening of the merchant marine

• described Cuba Panama, the Philippines, and Puerto Rico as "happy" examples of U.S. influence and enlightenment
• noted the centenary of Lincoln's birth
• castigated the Democrats
• asserted that the "trend of the Democracy is toward socialism"

REPUBLICAN PARTY
VOTE FOR PRESIDENTIAL NOMINATION:

Candidate	Ballot: 1
Taft	702
Knox	68
Hughes	67
Cannon	58
Fairbanks	40
La Follette	25
Foraker	16
Roosevelt	3
not voting	1

Taft's nomination was made unanimous.

VOTE FOR VICE-PRESIDENTIAL NOMINATION:

Candidate	Ballot: 1
Sherman	816
Murphy	77
Guild	75
Sheldon	10
Fairbanks	1
not voting	1

SOCIALIST LABOR PARTY
CANDIDATE FOR PRESIDENT:
Morris R. Preston (NV) (ineligible; replaced by August Gillhaus of New York)

CANDIDATE FOR VICE PRESIDENT:
Donald L. Munro (VA)

SOCIALIST LABOR PARTY
VOTE FOR PRESIDENTIAL NOMINATION: PRESTON WAS UNANIMOUSLY NOMINATED FOR PRESIDENT ON THE FIRST BALLOT, BUT HE WAS INELIGIBLE TO SERVE BECAUSE HE WAS UNDER THE CONSTITUTIONAL AGE REQUIREMENT. IN ADDITION, PRESTON WAS SERVING A TWENTY-FIVE-YEAR TERM IN THE NEVADA STATE PENITENTIARY FOR HAVING KILLED A MAN IN 1905. GILLHAUS WAS LATER SELECTED TO REPLACE PRESTON.

CONVENTION:
  July 2–5, 1908, New York (NY)

The Socialist Labor Party platform was identical to that adopted in 1904.

SOCIALIST PARTY

CANDIDATE FOR PRESIDENT:
  Eugene Victor Debs

CANDIDATE FOR VICE PRESIDENT:
  Benjamin Hanford

CANDIDATES FOR PRESIDENTIAL NOMINATION:
  James F. Carey (MA)
  Eugene Victor Debs (IN)
  William Dudley Haywood (CO)
  Carl Algie Martin Simons (IL)
  Dean Thompson (WI)

CANDIDATES FOR VICE-PRESIDENTIAL NOMINATION:
  Benjamin Hanford (NY)
  George Washington Woodbey (CA)
  four others

2D CONVENTION:
  May 10–17, 1908, Brand's Hall, Chicago (IL)

The Socialist Party's platform contained a lengthy preamble of principles, before declaring itself the party of the working class. It noted the recent assault on organized labor, particularly the attempt to destroy the Western Federation of Miners, and demanded the immediate relief of unemployment through a government public works program.

PLATFORM HIGHLIGHTS:
SUPPORTED:
- collective ownership of transportation and communications systems, land, and national industries in which competition was non-existent
- extension of the public domain to mines, quarries, oil wells, forests, and waterpower
- the scientific reforestation of timberlands and the reclamation of swamps
- freedom of speech, press, and assembly
- improvements in the lot of industrial workers through shorter hours, a mandatory day of rest, and safety inspections in the work site
- prohibition of child labor
- the institution of compulsory insurance programs covering unemployment, illness, accidents, old age, and death
- a graduated income tax and an inheritance tax
- equal suffrage
- adoption of the initiative, referendum, proportional representation, and the recall
- abolition of the Senate and creation of separate cabinet-level Departments of Education, Labor, and Public Health

- limitations on the power of the Supreme Court to rule on the constitutionality of laws
- direct election of judges
- free administration of justice
- curbs on the power to issue injunctions
- provision for amending the Constitution by simple majority vote of the people

SOCIALIST PARTY
VOTE FOR PRESIDENTIAL NOMINATION:

Candidate	Ballot: 1
Debs	159
Carey	16
Thompson	14
Simons	9

The nomination of Debs was made unanimous.

VOTE FOR VICE-PRESIDENTIAL NOMINATION:

Candidate	Ballot: 1
Hanford	106
Woodbey	1
others	78

UNITED CHRISTIAN PARTY

CANDIDATE FOR PRESIDENT:
  Daniel Braxton Turney (IL)

CANDIDATE FOR VICE PRESIDENT:
  Lorenzo Sweet Coffin (S. P. Carter, declined)

CANDIDATES FOR VICE-PRESIDENTIAL NOMINATION:
  S. P. Carter
  Lorenzo Sweet Coffin (IA)
  H. A. Simpson (IL)

3D CONVENTION:
  May 1, 1908, Rock Island (IL)
  William Rudolph Benkert (IA), temporary chairman
  Laura Fixen (IL), permanent chairman
  Kitty M. Benkert, secretary

The United Christian Party platform consisted of the Ten Commandments plus an eleventh that enjoined people to "love one another." Appended to the platform were a series of principles that recognized Jesus Christ as "King of all nations" and declared the United States to be a Christian nation.

PLATFORM HIGHLIGHTS:
SUPPORTED:
- observance of the Christian Sabbath
- abolition of capital punishment
- government ownership of public utilities, coal mines, and oil wells

- adoption of the initiative, referendum, and recall
- direct election of public officials
- equal rights and women's suffrage
- adoption of uniform marriage and divorce laws
- suppression of prostitution

OPPOSED:

- the liquor trade
- war
- "all trusts and combines contrary to the welfare of the common people"

> **UNITED CHRISTIAN PARTY**
> VOTE FOR PRESIDENTIAL AND VICE-PRESIDENTIAL NOMINATIONS: TURNEY WAS UNANIMOUSLY NOMINATED FOR PRESIDENT. COFFIN WAS CHOSEN AS THE CANDIDATE FOR VICE PRESIDENT OVER SIMPSON.

GENERAL ELECTION SUMMARY FOR 1908			
Candidate	*Electoral Votes*	*States*	*Popular Votes*
Taft (R)	321	29	7,678,908
Bryan (D)	162	17	6,409,104
Debs (SOC)	0	0	420,793
Chafin (PROH)	0	0	253,840
Hisgen (IP)	0	0	82,872
Watson (PEO)	0	0	29,100
Gillhaus (SOC LAB)	0	0	14,021
Davidson Faction (R)	0	0	987
Turney (UNI CHR)	0	0	400
Clark (I)	0	0	13
Lentz (I)	0	0	8
Lasiter (I)	0	0	1
McGrue (I)	0	0	1
unknown	0	0	72

ELECTION OF NOVEMBER 5, 1912

President
THOMAS WOODROW WILSON
Vice President
THOMAS RILEY MARSHALL

HIGHLIGHTS

The election of 1912 saw the advent of the presidential primary system and the entrance of the Progressive movement as an independent political force in U.S. politics. Theodore Roosevelt's split with his protege, the incumbent Republican president William Howard Taft, arose in large measure because of Taft's drift toward the conservative wing of the party. When Roosevelt lost the Republican nomination to Taft in a tightly controlled convention, he "threw his hat in the ring" as a third-party candidate against Taft, opening up a serious three-way race. The Democratic Convention featured a prolonged contest among several favorite sons: James Beauchamp "Champ" Clark of Missouri, Judson Harmon of Ohio, and Governor Woodrow Wilson of New Jersey. After numerous ballots, Clark received a majority of the votes but failed to obtain the two-thirds required under party rules. A well-regarded reformer, Wilson pulled ahead on the twenty-eighth ballot and finally obtained the required number of votes on the forty-sixth ballot.

In the general election campaign among candidates Roosevelt, Taft, and Wilson, Wilson held on to his base of Democratic strength and won. Surprisingly, however, the Bull Moose campaign surpassed the electoral strength of the Republicans, and Roosevelt came in second in both popular and electoral votes. One notable event of the campaign was the attempted assassination of Roosevelt, who was shot by a deranged man on October 14, while stumping in Milwaukee. The candidate was not seriously wounded; the bullet lodged in his ribs.

Two long-standing issues were essentially resolved by the time of the 1912 elections. The Sixteenth and Seventeenth Amendments to the Constitution—the first authorizing an income tax and the second providing for the direct election of senators—were in the final stages of ratification and would be officially incorporated into the Constitution early in 1913.

DEMOCRATIC PARTY

CANDIDATE FOR PRESIDENT:
Thomas Woodrow Wilson

CANDIDATE FOR VICE PRESIDENT:
Thomas Riley Marshall

CANDIDATES FOR PRESIDENTIAL NOMINATION:
Simeon Eben Baldwin (CT)
John Burke (ND) (declined)
William Jennings Bryan (NE)
James Beauchamp "Champ" Clark (MO)
Eugene Noble Foss (MA)
William Jay Gaynor (NY)
Judson Harmon (OH)
Ollie Murray James (KY)
John Worth Kern (IN)
James Hamilton Lewis (IL)
Thomas Riley Marshall (IN)

William Sulzer (NJ)
Oscar Wilder Underwood (AL)
Thomas Woodrow Wilson (NJ)

CANDIDATES FOR VICE-PRESIDENTIAL NOMINATION:
John Burke (ND)
George Earle Chamberlain (OR)
James Beauchamp "Champ" Clark (MO) (withdrew)
Elmore W. Hurst (IL)
Thomas Riley Marshall (IN)
William Frank McCombs (NY)
John Eugene Osborne (WY)
James Harry Preston (MD)
William Sulzer (NJ)
Martin Joseph Wade (IA)

PRIMARIES:
MARCH 19, 1912 (ND):
Burke 9,357

DEMOCRATIC PARTY
VOTE FOR PRESIDENTIAL NOMINATION:

Candidate	Ballot: 1	5	20	42	46
Clark	440½	443	512	430	84
Wilson	324	351	388½	494	990
Harmon	148	141½	29	27	0
Underwood	117½	119½	121½	104	12
Marshall	31	31	30	0	0
Baldwin	22	0	0	0	0
Sulzer	2	0	0	0	0
Bryan	1	0	1	½	0
Foss	0	0	2	28	0
Gaynor	0	0	0	1	0
James	0	0	3	1	0
Kern	0	2	1	1	0
Lewis	0	0	0	1	0
not voting	8	6	6	6½	8

VOTE FOR VICE-PRESIDENTIAL NOMINATION:

Candidate	Ballot: 1	2
Marshall	389	644½
Burke	304⅔	386⅓
Chamberlain	157	12½
Hurst	78	0
Preston	58	0
Wade	26	0
McCombs	18	0
Osborne	8	0
Sulzer	3	0
not voting	46⅓	44⅔

APRIL 2, 1912 (WI):
Wilson 45,945
Clark 36,464
others 148

APRIL 9, 1912 (IL):
Clark 218,483
Wilson 75,527

APRIL 13, 1912 (PA):
Wilson 98,000

APRIL 19, 1912 (NE):
Clark 21,027
Wilson 14,289
Harmon 12,454
others 3,499

APRIL 19, 1912 (OR):
Wilson 9,588
Clark 7,857
Harmon 606
others 49

APRIL 30, 1912 (MA):
Clark 34,575

Wilson 15,002
others 627

MAY 6, 1912 (MD):
Clark 34,021
Wilson 21,490
Harmon 7,070

MAY 14, 1912 (CA):
Clark 43,163
Wilson 17,214

MAY 21, 1912 (OH):
Harmon 96,164
Wilson 85,084
Clark 2,428
others 2,440

MAY 28, 1912 (NJ):
Wilson 48,336
Clark 522

JUNE 4, 1912 (SD):
Wilson 4,694
Clark 4,275

Clark . . . .
2,722 (rival ticket[1])
others. . . . .
1,655

21ST CONVENTION:
June 25–29 and July 1–2, 1912, Fifth Maryland Regiment Armory, Baltimore (MD)
Alton Brooks Parker (NY), temporary chairman
Ollie Murray James (KY), chairman

There were 1,088 delegates at this convention.

PLATFORM HIGHLIGHTS:

SUPPORTED:

- reforms in the antitrust laws
- use of the presidential primary
- legislation prohibiting corporate campaign contributions
- a constitutional amendment to limit the president to a single term
- accomplishments of the Democratic House of Representatives
- efficient supervision and rate regulation for the railroads, express companies, and telegraph and telephone systems
- banking reforms
- exploration of the value of instituting a system of rural credits
- construction of new bank and levee controls to improve internal waterways and the initiation of flood-control projects
- development of waterpower
- aid to develop post roads
- enactment of a workers' compensation law
- an aggressive conservation program
- prohibitions against gambling in agricultural products by organized exchanges
- development of the merchant marine
- enactment of pure food and public health laws
- legal reforms and further refinements in the civil service laws
- independence for the Philippines
- extension of parcel post and rural free delivery
- pensions for veterans
- Panama Canal Exposition (to be held in 1915)

OPPOSED:

- the high tariff imposed under Taft
- Republican extravagance

PROGRESSIVE (BULL MOOSE) PARTY
CANDIDATE FOR PRESIDENT:
Theodore Roosevelt (NY)

[1]Two slates favorable to Clark were on the ballot, each led by a local politician representing a faction within the state party.

CANDIDATE FOR VICE PRESIDENT:
Hiram Warren Johnson (CA)

CONVENTION:
August 5–7, 1912, Coliseum, Chicago (IL)

The Progressive Party was organized on June 19, 1912, by disgruntled Roosevelt supporters who seceded from the Republican Party. The lengthy party platform was drafted to conform to Roosevelt's perspective.

PLATFORM HIGHLIGHTS:

SUPPORTED:

- rule by the people through direct elections
- nationwide preferential primaries for president
- the initiative, referendum, and recall
- use of the short ballot
- easier amendment of the federal Constitution and flexibility in interpreting states' rights in relation to national problems
- women's suffrage
- registration of lobbyists
- limitations on the political activities of federal employees
- limitations on campaign contributions
- application of the referendum to state court decisions
- prohibitions against injunctions in labor disputes
- creation of a department of labor
- occupational health and safety laws
- prohibition of convict and child labor and night work for women
- minimum wage standards
- eight-hour workday and one day's rest per seven days
- collection of vital labor statistics
- social insurance programs to compensate workers for death, retirement, injury, and unemployment
- an end to illiteracy
- organized labor
- establishment of industrial research laboratories
- development of agricultural credit and co-operation
- restoration of the Country Life Commission
- promotion of agricultural extension services and the teaching of agriculture in the schools
- constructive regulation of interstate corporations
- reform of the patent laws
- strengthening of the Interstate Commerce Commission
- placement of currency exclusively in the hands of the federal government
- a strong conservation program
- early construction of national highways
- development of Alaskan and inland waterways
- reduction of the protective tariff
- graduated inheritance and income taxes
- international limitation of naval forces
- dispersal of immigrants congregated in certain cities
- pensions for veterans
- creation of a parcel post
- further civil service reform

- application of improved business methods to the operation of government
- government supervision over investments

> **PROGRESSIVE (BULL MOOSE) PARTY**
> VOTE FOR PRESIDENTIAL NOMINATION:
> ROOSEVELT WAS NOMINATED BY ACCLAMATION ON THE FIRST BALLOT.

PROHIBITION PARTY

CANDIDATE FOR PRESIDENT:
Eugene Wilder Chafin

CANDIDATE FOR VICE PRESIDENT:
Aaron Sherman Watkins (OH)

CANDIDATES FOR PRESIDENTIAL NOMINATION:
Eugene Wilder Chafin (IL)
F. W. Emerson (WI)
Finley C. Hendrickson (MD)
Andrew Jackson Houston (TX)
Oliver Wayne Stewart (IL)
Aaron Sherman Watkins (OH)

11TH CONVENTION:
July 10–12, 1912, Atlantic City (NJ)
Clinton Norman Howard (NY), temporary chairman
Charles H. Mead (NJ), permanent chairman

Delegates from forty-two states attended this convention.

PLATFORM HIGHLIGHTS:
SUPPORTED:
- complete prohibition of alcoholic beverages
- women's suffrage
- uniform marriage and divorce laws and banning of polygamy and prostitution
- international arbitration
- protection of the rights of labor and the abolition of child labor
- direct election of senators
- a single-term limit of six years for the president
- adoption of an equitable graduated income and inheritance tax
- the initiative, referendum and recall
- creation of an efficient parcel post and postal savings banks, along with extension of rural free delivery
- creation of a permanent omnipartisan tariff commission
- conservation of forest and mineral resources and the reclamation of wastelands

> **PROHIBITION PARTY**
> VOTE FOR PRESIDENTIAL NOMINATION:
> CHAFIN WAS NOMINATED BY ACCLAMATION ON THE FIRST BALLOT.

- regulation of interstate corporations
- greater efficiency and economy in government
- protection of one day in seven as a day of rest

REPUBLICAN PARTY

CANDIDATE FOR PRESIDENT:
William Howard Taft

CANDIDATE FOR VICE PRESIDENT:
James Schoolcraft Sherman (NY)[1]

CANDIDATES FOR PRESIDENTIAL NOMINATION:
Albert Baird Cummins (IA)
Charles Evans Hughes (NY)
Robert Marion La Follette (WI)
Theodore Roosevelt (NY)
William Howard Taft (OH)

CANDIDATES FOR VICE-PRESIDENTIAL NOMINATION:
Albert Jeremiah Beveridge (IN)
William Edgar Borah (ID)
Nicholas Murray Butler (NY)
Howard Frank Gillette (IL)
Herbert Spencer Hadley (MO)
Charles Edward Merriam (IL)
James Schoolcraft Sherman (NY)

PRIMARIES:
MARCH 19, 1912 (ND):
La Follette 34,123
Roosevelt 23,669
Taft 1,876

MARCH 26, 1912 (NY):
unpledged delegates . . . . (figures not available)

APRIL 2, 1912 (WI):
La Follette 133,354
Taft 47,514
Roosevelt 628
others 643

APRIL 9, 1912 (IL):
Roosevelt 266,917
Taft 127,481
La Follette 42,692

APRIL 13, 1912 (PA):
Roosevelt 282,853
Taft 191,179

APRIL 19, 1912 (NE):
Roosevelt 45,795
La Follette 16,785
Taft 13,341
others 2,036

---

[1] James Schoolcraft Sherman, the Republican vice-presidential nominee, died on October 30, 1912. The Republican National Committee nominated Nicholas Murray Butler (NY) as his replacement, and Republican electors accordingly transferred their eight electoral votes for vice president from Sherman to Butler.

APRIL 19, 1912 (OR):

Roosevelt 28,905
La Follette. 22,491
Taft 20,517
others 14

APRIL 30, 1912 (MA):

Taft 86,722
Roosevelt 83,099
La Follette. 2,058
others 99

MAY 6, 1912 (MD):

Roosevelt 29,124
Taft 25,995

MAY 14, 1912 (CA):

Roosevelt 138,563
Taft 69,345
La Follette. 45,876

MAY 21, 1912 (OH):

Roosevelt 165,809
Taft 118,362
La Follette. 15,570

MAY 28, 1912 (NJ):

Roosevelt 61,297
Taft. 44,034
La Follette. 3,464

JUNE 4, 1912 (SD):

Roosevelt 38,106
Taft 19,960
La Follette. 10,944

15TH CONVENTION:

June 18–22, 1912, Coliseum, Chicago (IL)
Elihu Root (NY), temporary chairman and chairman

There were 1,078 delegates at this convention.

PLATFORM HIGHLIGHTS:

SUPPORTED:

- recent achievements of the party
- previous Republican administrations, including those of both Roosevelt and Taft
- creation of a Federal Trade Commission
- both readjustment of certain tariffs and protectionism
- revision of the banking system
- the need for a sound currency
- easy credit for farmers
- refinements in the civil service law
- disclosure of campaign contributions
- prohibitions against corporate contributions to national political campaigns
- development of a parcel post
- protection of U.S. citizens abroad
- construction of new ships for the navy
- development of the merchant marine
- flood prevention in the Mississippi Valley

- reclamation of arid lands
- improvement of rivers and harbors
- development of Alaska's resources
- restrictions on foreign immigration
- protection of U.S. seamen

OPPOSED:

- monopolies and special privileges
- accepting responsibility for the high cost of living

REPUBLICAN PARTY
VOTE FOR PRESIDENTIAL NOMINATION:

Candidate	Ballot: 1
Taft	556
Roosevelt	107
La Follette	41
Cummins	17
Hughes	2
not voting	348
absent	7

VOTE FOR VICE-PRESIDENTIAL NOMINATION:

Candidate	Ballot: 1
Sherman	596
Borah	21
Merriam	20
Hadley	14
Beveridge	2
Gillette	1
not voting	352
absent	72

SOCIALIST LABOR PARTY

CANDIDATE FOR PRESIDENT:

Arthur Elmer Reimer

CANDIDATE FOR VICE PRESIDENT:

August Gillhaus (NY)

CANDIDATES FOR PRESIDENTIAL NOMINATION:

John M. Francis (IL)
Arthur Elmer Reimer (MA)

CONVENTION:

April 7–10, 1912, New York (NY)

The Socialist Labor Party's platform expressed the view that conditions had become so bad that "the Republic of Capital is at the end of its tether."

PLATFORM HIGHLIGHTS:

SUPPORTED:

- defending socialist gains through force, if necessary
- establishment of an Industrial or Socialist Republic, in which private ownership is unknown and "the shackles of wage slavery are no more"

OPPOSED:
- the notion that the party "capture the Trust of the people by ballot only"
- the idea that force alone could capture the trust of the masses, because the task was simply too big to accomplish under revolutionary conditions

SOCIALIST PARTY

CANDIDATE FOR PRESIDENT:
Eugene Victor Debs

CANDIDATE FOR VICE PRESIDENT:
Emil Seidel

CANDIDATES FOR PRESIDENTIAL NOMINATION:
Eugene Victor Debs (IN)
Charles Edward Russell (NY)
Emil Seidel (WI)

CANDIDATES FOR VICE-PRESIDENTIAL NOMINATION:
Daniel Hogan (AR)
John W. Slayton (PA)
Emil Seidel (WI)

3D CONVENTION:
May 12–18, 1912, Tomlinson Hall, Indianapolis (IN)
Lewis J. Duncan (MT), chairman of the day

PLATFORM HIGHLIGHTS:

SUPPORTED:
- establishment of a cooperative commonwealth
- collective ownership of banks, the currency system, railroads, wire and wireless telegraphs and telephones, express service, steamboat lines, large-scale industries, grain elevators, stockyards, storage warehouses, and other distribution agencies
- extension of the public domain to include mines, quarries, oil wells, forests, and waterpower
- a conservation program
- collective ownership of land "wherever practicable"
- a public works program to aid the unemployed
- shorter workdays and a mandatory weekly day and a half of rest
- occupational health and safety inspections
- prohibition of child labor
- the cooperative organization of prison industries for the benefit of convicts and their dependents
- establishment of a minimum wage
- the creation of old age and social insurance programs for workers and their families
- freedom of press, speech, and assembly
- adoption of a graduated income tax and the extension of inheritance taxes
- patent reforms
- universal suffrage
- use of the initiative, referendum, proportional representation, and the recall at all levels of government
- abolition of the Senate and the president's veto power
- direct election of the president and vice president
- restrictions on the power of the Supreme Court
- granting suffrage and congressional representation for the District of Columbia
- creation of a Department of Education and an independent Bureau of Health
- separation of the Bureau of Labor from the Department of Commerce and Labor and its elevation to cabinet status
- abolition of all federal district courts and U.S. circuit courts and the direct election of judges
- free administration of the law
- restrictions on the use of injunctions
- the convening of a federal constitutional convention

SOCIALIST PARTY
VOTE FOR PRESIDENTIAL NOMINATION:

Candidate	Ballot: 1
Debs	163
Seidel	56
Russell	54

Debs's nomination was made unanimous.

GENERAL ELECTION SUMMARY FOR 1912

Candidate	Electoral Votes	States	Popular Votes
Wilson (D)	435	40	6,293,454
Roosevelt (PROG)	88	6	4,119,538
Taft (R)	8	2	3,484,980
Debs (SOC)	0	0	900,672
Chafin (PROH)	0	0	206,275
Reimer (SOC LAB)	0	0	28,750

ELECTION OF NOVEMBER 7, 1916

President
THOMAS WOODROW WILSON
Vice President
THOMAS RILEY MARSHALL

HIGHLIGHTS

War was raging across Europe. President Wilson, who was easily renominated, campaigned on the slogan that "he kept us out of war"; but World War I was to involve the Americans only months after the election (April 6, 1917). Gen. John Pershing's invasion of Mexico was an inflammatory issue, although most U.S. citizens felt that the border bandits could not be permitted to make incursions on U.S. soil. Labor unrest was also attacked as "subversive," with some pointing to the bomb explosion at San Francisco's Preparedness Day parade in July (creating the cause celebre of the Mooney-Billings trial) as proof of the dangers of radicalism. The political mood of the country was clearly moving toward the Right; however, the turmoil at both the domestic and international levels did not translate into an exciting election campaign. Instead, it was a rather boring affair, chiefly notable for causing a split in the Socialist Party over the war issue and for the Progressive Party's collapse during its second campaign. Charles Evans Hughes looked like the possible winner, even up to the last hours of the election, but when California fell into the Democratic column, it finally carried the day for Wilson.

AMERICAN PARTY

CANDIDATE FOR PRESIDENT:
none (William Sulzer [NY] declined)

CANDIDATE FOR VICE PRESIDENT:
none (John Milliken Parker [LA] declined)

CONVENTION:
July 25, 1916, Minneapolis (MN)

This party was an outgrowth of the American Federation of Patriotic Societies. Sulzer was nominated for president and Parker was nominated for vice president, but both candidates declined. After the candidates refused to run together, the American Party endorsed the Republican ticket.

DEMOCRATIC PARTY

CANDIDATE FOR PRESIDENT:
Thomas Woodrow Wilson (NJ)

CANDIDATE FOR VICE PRESIDENT:
Thomas Riley Marshall (IN)

PRIMARIES:

MARCH 7, 1916 (IN):
Wilson.................................160,423

MARCH 14, 1916 (MN):
Wilson..................................45,136

MARCH 14, 1916 (NH):
Wilson...................................5,684

MARCH 21, 1916 (ND):
Wilson..................................12,341

APRIL 3, 1916 (MI):
Wilson..................................84,972

APRIL 4, 1916 (NY):
Wilson.................................112,538

APRIL 4, 1916 (WI):
Wilson.................................109,462
others......................................231

APRIL 11, 1916 (IL):
Wilson.................................136,839
others......................................219

APRIL 18, 1916 (NE):
Wilson..................................69,506
others....................................9,744

APRIL 21, 1916 (MT):
Wilson..................................17,960

APRIL 25, 1916 (IA):
Wilson..................................31,447

APRIL 25, 1916 (MA):
Wilson..................................19,580

APRIL 25, 1916 (NJ):
Wilson25,407

APRIL 25, 1916 (OH):
Wilson..................................82,688
others....................................2,415

MAY 2, 1916 (CA):
Wilson 75,085

MAY 16, 1916 (PA):
Wilson 142,202
others 1,839

MAY 16, 1916 (VT):
Wilson 3,711
others 23

MAY 19, 1916 (OR):
Wilson 27,898

MAY 23, 1916 (SD):
Wilson 10,341

JUNE 6, 1916 (WV):
figures not available

22D CONVENTION:
June 14–16, 1916, Coliseum, St. Louis (MO)
Martin Henry Glynn (NY), temporary chairman
Ollie Murray James (KY), chairman

PLATFORM HIGHLIGHTS:
SUPPORTED:
- the achievements of President Woodrow Wilson's first term
- a limited tariff
- an activist role for the United States in protecting the peace and in ensuring security of international borders (particularly those of the smaller states)
- efforts to strength U.S. ties with other nations in the Western Hemisphere
- the merchant marine
- promotion of conservation
- development of rural agricultural communities
- national aid for the construction of public highways
- just employment in the public sector
- prison work that would rehabilitate prisoners
- prison pay that could offset the expenses of dependents
- creation of a federal bureau of safety in the Department of Labor
- creation of a federal employment service and federal assistance in job training
- enforcement of civil service laws
- establishment of tuberculosis sanitariums by the federal government
- reforms in Senate rules and further reforms in the budget process in the House of Representatives
- independence for the Philippines
- state action to extend the right to vote to women rather than a constitutional amendment to guarantee women's suffrage
- a comprehensive plan for the control and improvement of the Mississippi River and other inland waterways and harbors
- traditional territorial governments under U.S. law for Alaska, Hawaii, and Puerto Rico

OPPOSED:
- divisive domestic activities on behalf of a foreign power and called for military preparedness
- child and convict labor

ALSO:
- bemoaned the necessity for "intervention" in Mexico.

DEMOCRATIC PARTY
VOTE FOR PRESIDENTIAL NOMINATION: WILSON WAS
RENOMINATED FOR PRESIDENT ON THE FIRST BALLOT,
RECEIVING 1,093 VOTES. NOMINATION WAS MADE
UNANIMOUS BY ACCLAMATION. MARSHALL WAS ALSO
RENOMINATED FOR A SECOND TERM.

PROGRESSIVE PARTY

CANDIDATE FOR PRESIDENT:
Charles Evans Hughes (NY)

CANDIDATE FOR VICE PRESIDENT:
none (John Milliken Parker [LA] withdrew)

CONVENTION:
June 7–10, 1916, Auditorium, Chicago (IL)
George W. Perkins, chairman

Former President Theodore Roosevelt was nominated for president but declined. At his recommendation, the national committee endorsed the Republican Hughes. Parker was nominated for vice president. After Roosevelt's withdrawal, he remained in the race even though the Progressive National Committee voted 32 to 15 against a separate ticket. Eventually, he withdrew and supported Wilson for reelection. The party dissolved before the end of the election.

PROGRESSIVE PARTY OF MINNESOTA

CANDIDATE FOR PRESIDENT:
Edward J. Meier (MN)

PROHIBITION PARTY

CANDIDATE FOR PRESIDENT:
James Frank Hanly

CANDIDATE FOR VICE PRESIDENT:
Ira David Landrith

CANDIDATES FOR PRESIDENTIAL NOMINATION:
Willis Greenleaf Calderwood (MN)
Miriam Ferguson (TX)
William Porter Frisbee Ferguson (PA)
Henry Ford (MI)
Eugene Noble Foss (MA)
James Frank Hanly (IN)
Myron Wilbur Haynes (IN)
Finley C. Hendrickson (MD)

James Gilbert Mason (NJ)
William Sulzer (NJ)

CANDIDATES FOR VICE-PRESIDENTIAL NOMINATION:
Marie Caroline Brehm (CA)
William Lloyd Clark (IL)
Finley C. Hendrickson (MD)
Ira David Landrith (TN)
Harold King Rockhill (WA)

12TH CONVENTION:
July 19–21, 1916, St. Paul (MN)
Daniel Alfred Poling (PA), temporary chairman
Robert Howard Patton (IL), permanent chairman

PLATFORM HIGHLIGHTS:

SUPPORTED:

• total prohibition of alcoholic beverages, by an amendment to the Constitution, if necessary
• women's suffrage, by an amendment to the Constitution, if necessary
• disarmament and reliance on a world court to settle international differences
• seeking ways to take profit out of the business of war
• engagement of the military in useful domestic works in peacetime
• transition of the navy to nonmilitary uses, such as to a merchant marine or passenger vessels and crews
• international trade through incentives to businesses and transportation services
• restoration of law and order in Mexico
• protection of U.S. interests
• disengagement from any militaristic adventures
• conservation
• judicial review of federal agency decisions
• the role of the federal government as a model employer
• enactment of old age and disability pensions for workers and relief for needy mothers
• extension of the merit system
• uniform marriage and divorce laws
• labor arbitration, abolition of child labor, adoption of an eight-hour workday, and passage of occupational health and safety laws
• efforts to ensure economy and efficiency in government, such as a line-item veto for the president
• a single six-year term for the president
• public ownership or control of "natural monopolies"
• separation of church and state
• adoption of the initiative, referendum, and recall
• construction of cotton warehouses and federally owned terminal elevators
• grain inspections
• abolition of trading in options, futures, or other speculative devices

OPPOSED:

• militarism and universal conscription for military duty
• immediate self-government for the Philippines, but favored granting independence "as soon as they are prepared"

PROHIBITION PARTY
VOTE FOR PRESIDENTIAL NOMINATION:

Candidate	Ballot: 1
Hanly	440
Sulzer	188
Hendrickson	68
Calderwood	22
Mason	14
Ferguson, W. P.	2
Ford	1

VOTE FOR VICE-PRESIDENTIAL NOMINATION:
AN EFFORT WAS MADE TO NOMINATE HENDRICKSON FOR VICE PRESIDENT BY ACCLAMATION, BUT THE MOTION FAILED. BREHM, CLARK, HENDRICKSON, LANDRITH, AND ROCKHILL WERE THEN PLACED IN NOMINATION FOR VICE PRESIDENT. BREHM, CLARK, AND HENDRICKSON WITHDREW. A MOTION WAS MADE TO NOMINATE LANDRITH FOR VICE PRESIDENT BY ACCLAMATION, AND THE MOTION CARRIED.

REPUBLICAN PARTY

CANDIDATE FOR PRESIDENT:
Charles Evans Hughes

CANDIDATE FOR VICE PRESIDENT:
Charles Warren Fairbanks

CANDIDATES FOR PRESIDENTIAL NOMINATION:
William Edgar Borah (ID)
Martin Grove Brumbaugh (PA)
Theodore Elijah Burton (OH)
Albert Baird Cummins (IA)
Thomas Coleman du Pont (DE)
Henry Dodge Estabrook (NY)
Charles Warren Fairbanks (IN)
Henry Ford (MI)
Warren Gamaliel Harding (OH)
Charles Evans Hughes (NY)
Philander Chase Knox (PA)
Robert Marion La Follette (WI)
Henry Cabot Lodge (MA)
Samuel Walker McCall (MA)
Theodore Roosevelt (NY)
Elihu Root (NY)
Robert G. Ross (NE)
Lawrence Yates Sherman (IL)
William Gerald Simpson (MI)
William Alden Smith (MI)
William Howard Taft (OH)

John Wanamaker (PA)
John Wingate Weeks (MA)
Frank Bartlett Willis (OH)
Leonard Wood (MA)

CANDIDATES FOR VICE-PRESIDENTIAL NOMINATION:
William Edgar Borah (ID)
Elmer Burkett (NE)
Theodore Elijah Burton (OH)
Charles Warren Fairbanks (IN)
Hiram Warren Johnson (CA)
William Grant Webster (IL)

PRIMARIES:
MARCH 7, 1916 (IN):
Fairbanks.................................176,078

MARCH 14, 1916 (MN):
Cummins...............................54,214
others...................................16,403

MARCH 14, 1916 (NH):
unpledged delegates......................9,687

MARCH 21, 1916 (ND):
La Follette..............................23,374
Estabrook................................9,851

APRIL 3, 1916 (MI):
Ford.....................................83,057
Smith....................................77,872
Simpson..................................14,365

APRIL 4, 1916 (NY):
unpledged delegates.....................147,038

APRIL 4, 1916 (WI):
La Follette.............................110,052
others...................................1,347

APRIL 11, 1916 (IL):
Sherman.................................155,945
Roosevelt...............................15,348
others...................................1,689

APRIL 18, 1916 (NE):
Cummins...............................29,850
Ford....................................26,884
Hughes..................................15,837
Estabrook................................8,132
Ross.....................................5,506
Roosevelt................................2,256
others.....................................142

APRIL 21, 1916 (MT):
Cummins...............................10,415
others...................................1,173

APRIL 25, 1916 (IA):
Cummins...............................40,257

APRIL 25, 1916 (MA):
unpledged delegates.....................60,462
Roosevelt...............................45,117

APRIL 25, 1916 (NJ)[1]:
Roosevelt...............................1,076
Hughes....................................383

APRIL 25, 1916 (OH):
Burton.................................122,165
Roosevelt...............................1,932
Ford....................................1,683
Hughes....................................469
others..................................14,428

MAY 2, 1916 (CA):
unpledged delegates....................236,277

MAY 16, 1916 (PA):
Brumbaugh..............................233,095
Ford....................................20,265
Roosevelt...............................12,359
Hughes..................................1,804
others...................................2,682

MAY 16, 1916 (VT):
Hughes...................................5,480
Roosevelt................................1,931
others.....................................423

MAY 19, 1916 (OR):
Hughes..................................56,764
Cummins...............................27,558
others..................................10,593

MAY 23, 1916 (SD):
Cummins...............................29,656

JUNE 6, 1916 (WV):
Burton....................no figures are available

16TH CONVENTION:
June 7–10, 1916, Coliseum, Chicago (IL)
Warren Gamaliel Harding (OH), temporary chairman and chairman

PLATFORM HIGHLIGHTS:
SUPPORTED:
• a "strict and honest neutrality" in Europe and the use of arbitration to settle international disputes
• closer ties with Latin America
• the right of expatriation and expressed the hope that peace would return to Europe
• the buildup of the nation's army and navy to protect the country
• protective tariff
• regulation of transportation and other industries
• rural credits and rural free delivery
• a strong merchant marine, bolstered by liberal payments for delivering the mails
• federal control of interstate and intrastate transportation, through constitutional amendment, if necessary

[1]A variety of approaches were tried when primaries were first used. New Jersey's low vote may be an artifact of its peculiar system and/or a result of the presumption that Teddy Roosevelt would receive New Jersey support.

- a businesslike national budget to promote economy in government, along with a "careful husbandry" of the nation's natural resources
- civil service reform
- the appoint of only bona fide residents of territories to administer territorial governments
- vocational education
- popular labor reforms
- individual states enacting measures favoring women's suffrage

OPPOSED:
- the Wilsonian policy of recognizing one of the belligerents in Mexico and pledged the Republican administration to firmness in restoring order and peace in that country
- the Democrats' efforts to "abandon the Philippines"

REPUBLICAN PARTY
VOTE FOR PRESIDENTIAL NOMINATION:

Candidate	Ballot: 1	2	3
Hughes	253½	328½	949½
Weeks	105	79	3
Root	103	98½	0
Cummins	85	85	0
Burton	77½	76½	0
Fairbanks	74½	88½	0
Sherman	66	65	0
Roosevelt	65	81	18½
Knox	36	36	0
Ford	32	0	0
Brumbaugh	29	0	0
La Follette	25	25	3
Taft	14	0	0
du Pont	12	13	5
Willis	4	1	0
Borah	2	0	0
McCall	1	1	0
Harding	0	1	0
Lodge	0	0	7
Wanamaker	0	5	0
Wood	0	1	0
not voting	2½	2	1

VOTE FOR VICE-PRESIDENTIAL NOMINATION:

Candidate	Ballot: 1
Fairbanks	863
Burkett	108
Borah	8
Webster	2
Burton	1
Johnson	1
not voting	4

- the Underwood Tariff Act, which the Democrats cheered
- government ownership of vessels, which was seen as a means of leaving the nation "more helpless than ever" in competition for international trade
- a constitutional amendment for women's suffrage

SOCIALIST LABOR PARTY
CANDIDATE FOR PRESIDENT:
Arthur Elmer Reimer (MA)

CANDIDATE FOR VICE PRESIDENT:
Caleb Harrison (IL)

CONVENTION:
April 29–30 and May 1–3, 1916, New York (NY)

The Socialist Labor Party Convention adopted a platform containing no specific proposals beyond its perennial call for a socialist commonwealth, guided by the principles of social ownership of the means of production. Achievement of the Socialist Laborite goal was seen as contingent on the organization of the working class and the understanding of class struggle as a dynamic of history.

SOCIALIST PARTY
CANDIDATE FOR PRESIDENT:
Allan Louis Benson

CANDIDATE FOR VICE PRESIDENT:
George Ross Kirkpatrick

CANDIDATES FOR PRESIDENTIAL NOMINATION:
Allan Louis Benson (NY)
Arthur LeSueur (ND)
James Hudson Maurer (PA)

CANDIDATES FOR VICE-PRESIDENTIAL NOMINATION:
George Ross Kirkpatrick (NJ)
Kate Richards O'Hare (KS)

4TH CONVENTION:
March 10–11, 1916, Chicago (IL)

Ballots sent to state organizations were counted at this convention. The platform adopted by the Socialists discussed the "greatest crisis and bloodiest struggle of all history," World War I, from a socialist perspective. It called for disarmament and condemned militarism, warning of the "imperialism" that lurked behind calls for U.S. "preparedness." The party strongly opposed the war in Europe and the potential for U.S. involvement—a stand that cost the party significant support when war was finally declared. It also denounced capitalists as "the parasite class" and aligned itself with workers in a "social war" of competing economic interests. Nonetheless, the Socialists found themselves in the odd position of declaring, "Socialism would not abolish private property, but greatly expand it." In the Socialist view, the capitalist oligarchy was responsible for the misery of the workers and for denying them the fruits of private property.

PLATFORM HIGHLIGHTS:

SUPPORTED:

- an end to the military buildup
- a plebiscite to declare war
- abandonment of the Monroe Doctrine
- immediate independence to the Philippines
- an international conference of neutral nations to establish a framework for peace
- the proposed women's suffrage amendment
- adoption of the initiative, referendum, proportional representation, and recall
- abolition of the U.S. Senate and the veto power of the president
- direct election of the president and vice president
- relaxation of the constitutional requirements for adopting constitutional amendments
- the convening of a federal constitutional convention
- a limit on the power of courts, particularly with reference to the use of injunctions
- free administration of the law
- equitable representation in Congress and home rule for the District of Columbia
- increases in income and inheritance tax rates
- creation of a Department of Education and a Department of Health
- patent revisions
- unrestricted exercise of freedom of the press, speech, and assembly
- expansion of collective ownership of banks, transportation, communications, and all large-scale industries

- local municipal ownership of grain elevators, stockyards, and storage warehouses
- extension of the public domain to include mines, quarries, oil wells, forests, and waterpower
- conservation of natural resources
- a soft currency
- a detailed scheme for federal government lending to local governments
- labor reform, including a requirement that the federal government pay prevailing union wages, establish employment bureaus, and participate in unemployment funds
- a shorter workday and a mandatory weekly rest period
- federal health and safety inspections at work sites
- prohibitions against child labor
- adoption of minimum wage scales
- enactment of old age and social insurance programs to protect workers and their families against diseases, accidents, and deaths, including a pension program for mothers

SOCIALIST PARTY
VOTE FOR PRESIDENTIAL NOMINATION:

Candidate	Ballot: 1
Benson	16,639
Maurer	12,264
LeSueur	3,495

VOTE FOR VICE-PRESIDENTIAL NOMINATION:
KIRKPATRICK DEFEATED O'HARE FOR
THE NOMINATION.

GENERAL ELECTION SUMMARY FOR 1916

Candidate	Electoral Votes	States	Popular Votes
Wilson (D)	277	30	9,129,606
Hughes (R)	254	18	8,538,221
Benson (S)	0	0	585,113
Hanly (PROH)	0	0	220,506
Hughes (PROG)	0	0	35,234[1]
Reimer (SL)	0	0	13,403
unknown	0	0	461

[1]includes votes of the Progressive Party of Minnesota

ELECTION OF NOVEMBER 2, 1920

President
WARREN GAMALIEL HARDING
Vice President
CALVIN COOLIDGE

HIGHLIGHTS

As Wilson's second term came to an end and the United States entered the "Roaring Twenties," Germany had been defeated in World War I; the Eighteenth Amendment had been added to the Constitution, bringing prohibition and bootlegging to the national scene; Governor Calvin Coolidge had broken the 1919 Boston police strike; and feminists were on the march, demanding the vote (the Nineteenth Amendment granted them that right just in time for the 1920 general election). The nation was becoming increasingly alarmed by the threat of communism as a result of the Bolshevik Revolution in Russia and the purported activities of "radicals" in the United States. Wilson's dream of U.S. leadership in a League of Nations was effectively crushed when the Senate refused to ratify the League's covenant on March 19, 1920. As the election approached and as the country switched to a peacetime economy, it was a time of uncertainty. The "roar" in the Twenties was still around the corner. Many of the giants of the preceding decade were either dead or retired: Roosevelt was gone and Wilson nearly so; Taft, Hughes, and Cannon wore the cloaks of elder statesmen; Bryan and La Follette were outcasts. Both major parties were essentially leaderless. In this atmosphere, the Republicans took ten ballots to nominate Warren G. Harding for president, while the Democrats needed forty-four to select finally Governor James M. Cox as their standard-bearer. In this election the young Franklin D. Roosevelt first demonstrated his charm as the Democrats' attractive vice-presidential candidate. The Socialists, on the other hand, had no difficulty once again nominating their old hero, Eugene V. Debs, for president. Debs had the unique distinction of being the first candidate to conduct his campaign from behind prison bars. He had been confined to the federal prison in Atlanta (GA) for his antiwar speeches.

AMERICAN PARTY

CANDIDATE FOR PRESIDENT:
James Edward Ferguson (TX)

CANDIDATE FOR VICE PRESIDENT:
William J. Hough (unknown)

The American Party was formed on August 14, 1919, in Fort Worth (TX), by Democrats dedicated to former Governor James Edward Ferguson. Ferguson announced his candidacy in Temple (TX) on April 21, 1920. During the campaign, he admitted that his candidacy was intended to assist Warren Gamaliel Harding, the Republican candidate, in the Texas presidential contest. In announcing his candidacy, Ferguson denounced the Democratic Party as "a blowed-up sucker." While he scathingly assailed his former party, he did not articulate a program of his own. Instead, Ferguson argued that Texans should repudiate the Democratic Party that had taken them for granted. That stance appeared to be the sum and substance of the American Party platform.

DEMOCRATIC PARTY

CANDIDATE FOR PRESIDENT:
James Middleton Cox

CANDIDATE FOR VICE PRESIDENT:
Franklin Delano Roosevelt (NY)

CANDIDATES FOR PRESIDENTIAL NOMINATION:
Annette Abbott Adams (CA)
Eugene Cleophas Bonniwell (PA)
William Jennings Bryan (NE)
James Beauchamp "Champ" Clark (MO)
Laura Clay (KY)
Irvin Shrewsbury Cobb (NY)
Bainbridge Colby (NY)
James Middleton Cox (OH)
Homer Stille Cummings (CT)
Josephus Daniels (NC)
John William Davis (WV)
Edward Irving Edwards (NJ)
James Watson Gerard (NY)

Carter Glass (VA)
Francis Burton Harrison (NY)
William Randolph Hearst (NY)
Frank Thomas Hines (VA)
Gilbert Monell Hitchcock (NE)
Jesse Holman Jones (TX)
Ringgold Wilmer "Ring" Lardner (NY)
James Hamilton Lewis (IL)
Thomas Riley Marshall (IN)
William Gibbs McAdoo (NY)
Edwin Thomas Meredith (IA)
Robert Latham Owen (OK)
Alexander Mitchell Palmer (PA)
John Joseph Pershing (DC)
Joseph Taylor Robinson (AR)
Robert G. Ross (NE)
Furnifold McLendel Simmons (NC)
Alfred Emanuel Smith (NY)
Cora Wilson Stewart (KY)
Oscar Wilder Underwood (AL)
John Sharp Williams (MS)
Thomas Woodrow Wilson (NJ)
Alfred M. Wood (PA)

PRIMARIES:
MARCH 9, 1920 (NH):
    unpledged delegates 7,103

MARCH 16, 1920 (ND):
    McAdoo 49
    others 340

MARCH 23, 1920 (SD):
    others 6,612

APRIL 5, 1920 (MI):
    McAdoo 18,665
    Edwards 16,642
    Palmer 11,187
    others 42,000

APRIL 6, 1920 (NY):
    unpledged delegates 113,300

APRIL 6, 1920 (WI):
    Cox 76
    others 3,391

APRIL 13, 1920 (IL):
    Edwards 6,933
    McAdoo 3,838
    Cox 266
    others 10,418

APRIL 20, 1920 (NE):
    Hitchcock 37,452
    Ross 13,179
    others 5,051

APRIL 23, 1920 (MT):
    others 2,994

APRIL 27, 1920 (MA):
    unpledged delegates 21,226

APRIL 27, 1920 (NJ):
    Edwards 4,163
    McAdoo 180
    others 213

APRIL 27, 1920 (OH):
    Cox 85,838
    McAdoo 292
    others 1,647

MAY 4, 1920 (CA):
    unpledged delegates 23,831

MAY 18, 1920 (PA):
    Palmer 80,356
    McAdoo 26,875
    Edwards 674
    others 1,132

MAY 18, 1920 (VT):
    McAdoo 137
    Edwards 58
    Cox 14
    others 227

MAY 21, 1920 (OR):
    McAdoo 24,951
    others 361

23D CONVENTION:
    June 28–30, July 1–3, and July 5–6, 1920, Civic Auditorium, San Francisco (CA)
    Homer Cummings (CT), temporary chairman
    Joseph Taylor Robinson (AR), permanent chairman

PLATFORM HIGHLIGHTS:
SUPPORTED:
- U.S. participation in the League of Nations
- reform in Senate rules
- applauded the actions of the newly created Federal Reserve Board
- tax revision
- economy in government
- limitations on tariff use
- governmental budget reform
- continuation of the farm loan and agricultural extension programs
- federal aid for highways
- rural, free postal delivery
- women in the work force and women's suffrage
- federal aid to education
- enactment of soldier settlements and home aid legislation to assist disabled veterans
- a fair and complete test for the Esch-Cummins Bill, which provided for the return of the railroads to private ownership and was viewed as problematic
- development of inland waterways, including construction of a Saint Lawrence Seaway

- reclamation of arid lands, flood control, and development of port facilities
- the Federal Trade Commission and federal supervision of livestock markets
- efforts to acquire additional U.S. sources of petroleum and other minerals
- self-government for Ireland
- full protection for U.S. citizens in Mexico
- territorial status for Puerto Rico
- future statehood and further development for Alaska
- independence for the Philippines
- a liberal homesteading policy in Hawaii
- the representative European governments that emerged in the wake of the war

OPPOSED:

- strikes that would "put in jeopardy the public welfare"
- application of the right of free speech and press to "enemy propaganda or the advocacy of the overthrow of the government"
- Asian immigration

DEMOCRATIC PARTY
VOTE FOR PRESIDENTIAL NOMINATION:

Candidate	Ballot: 1	44
McAdoo	266	267
Palmer	256	1
Cox	134	732½
Smith	109	0
Edwards	42	0
Marshall	37	52
Owen	33	34
Davis	32	0
Meredith	27	0
Glass	26½	1½
Cummings	25	1
Simmons	24	0
Gerard	21	0
Williams	20	0
Hitchcock	18	0
Clark	9	0
Harrison	6	0
Wood	4	0
Bryan	1	0
Colby	1	0
Daniels	1	0
Hearst	1	0
Underwood	½	0

On the forty-fourth ballot, the rules were suspended, and Cox was declared nominated unanimously.

VOTE FOR VICE-PRESIDENTIAL NOMINATION:
ROOSEVELT WAS NOMINATED FOR VICE PRESIDENT.

- the record of Republican corruption, particularly in the organization of the Senate

ALSO:

- noted that the Republican platform had failed to commend the veterans of World War I for heroic deeds
- claimed credit for creating the Department of Labor and prohibiting child labor

FARMER LABOR PARTY

CANDIDATE FOR PRESIDENT:
Parley Parker Christensen

CANDIDATE FOR VICE PRESIDENT:
Maximilian Sebastian Hayes (OH)

CANDIDATES FOR PRESIDENTIAL NOMINATION:
Jane Addams (IL)
Herbert Seely Bigelow (OH)
Parley Parker Christensen (UT)
Eugene Victor Debs (IN)
Henry Ford (MI)
Lynn Joseph Frazier (ND)
Herbert Hoover (CA)
Hiram Johnson (CA)
Robert Marion La Follette (WI)
Dudley Field Malone (NY)
Gifford Pinchot (PA)
Louis Freeland Post (IL)

CONVENTION:
July 13–15, 1920, Morrison Hotel and Carmen's Hall, Chicago (IL)
Parley Parker Christensen (UT), permanent chairman
J. A. H. Hopkins, cochairman
John Fitzpatrick (IL), keynoter

The Farmer Labor Party was formed on July 13, 1920, in Chicago and incorporated the National Labor Party.

PLATFORM HIGHLIGHTS:

SUPPORTED:

- farmers and working people "do[ing] righteous battle for democracy"
- restoration of civil liberties as "100 percent Americanism"
- amnesty for war objectors, union organizers, and religious dissenters
- repeal of the espionage, sedition, and criminal syndicalist laws used to persecute radicals
- recognition and protection of the right to strike
- an elected judiciary
- U.S. withdrawal from the Treaty of Versailles
- recognition of the Republic of Ireland and the Soviet Union
- renunciation of U.S. interests in foreign lands and colonies
- democratic control of industry and public ownership and operation of railroads, mines, and natural re-

sources, including stockyards, large abattoirs, grain elevators, waterpower, and warehouses
- creation of national and state-owned banks
- federal credit guarantees
- limitations on the use of patents
- reduction in farm tenancy
- establishment of public markets
- cheap agricultural credit
- promotion of farmers' cooperatives
- creation of a federal agency to study costs of farm and manufacturing production
- taxation of wealth accumulated in the war
- a steeply graduated income tax
- reduction in the cost of living
- federal control of the meatpacking industry
- extension of parcel post services
- pensions for veterans
- enactment of a thirteen-point Labor Bill of Rights, including a public works program, old age and unemployment benefits, equal pay for women, creation of a Department of Education, elimination of child and convict labor, and abolition of strike-breaking agencies and services

OPPOSED:
- the "financial barons" in control of the government
- the Paris Peace Conference for being a "greedy spectacle" conducted in the interests of imperial powers

---

FARMER LABOR PARTY
VOTE FOR PRESIDENTIAL NOMINATION: PRIOR TO THE CONVENTION, THE COMMITTEE OF FORTY-EIGHT SENT A QUESTIONNAIRE TO 2,100 VOTERS, ASKING THEIR PREFERENCES FOR PRESIDENT. LA FOLLETTE RECEIVED 324 VOTES; HOOVER, 191; DEBS, 172; AND JOHNSON, 157. ADDAMS WAS CONSIDERED FOR THE PRESIDENTIAL NOMINATION, BUT SHE WITHDREW. OTHERS CONSIDERED FOR THE NOMINATION INCLUDED INGERSOLL, PINCHOT, AND WALSH.

Candidate	Ballot: 1	2
Malone	166⁹⁄₁₀	174⁹⁄₁₀
Christensen	121¹⁄₁₀	193½
Debs	68	0
Ford	12⁷⁄₁₀	0
Frazier	12⁷⁄₁₀	9
Bigelow	2	0
Post	1³⁄₁₀	0

VOTE FOR VICE-PRESIDENTIAL NOMINATION: THERE WERE APPROXIMATELY TWENTY NOMINATING SPEECHES FOR THE VICE-PRESIDENTIAL SLOT, BUT MOST CONTENDERS WITHDREW. HAYES WAS NOMINATED ON THE FIRST BALLOT, WITH ALL BUT A DOZEN VOTES.

- the "invisible government" of the United States and the two major parties that did its bidding
- imposition of a sales tax

PROHIBITION PARTY

CANDIDATE FOR PRESIDENT:
Aaron Sherman Watkins

CANDIDATE FOR VICE PRESIDENT:
David Leigh Colvin

CANDIDATES FOR PRESIDENTIAL NOMINATION:
William Jennings Bryan (NE)
Robert Howard Patton (IL)
Daniel Alfred Poling (PA)
Charles Hiram Randall (CA)
Aaron Sherman Watkins (OH)

CANDIDATES FOR VICE-PRESIDENTIAL NOMINATION:
Marie Caroline Brehm (CA)
Willis Greenleaf Calderwood (MN)
David Leigh Colvin (NY)
Herman Preston Faris (MO)
Edwin J. Fithian (PA)
Henry Ford (MI)
Frank Stewart Regan (IL)
James H. Woertendyke (IL)

13TH CONVENTION:
July 21–22, 1920, Lincoln (NE)
Aaron Sherman Watkins (OH), temporary chairman
Marie Caroline Brehm (CA), permanent chairman

Attending this convention were 254 delegates.

PLATFORM HIGHLIGHTS:
SUPPORTED:
- U.S. entrance into the League of Nations
- a constitutional amendment to require peace treaties to be ratified by both houses of Congress
- disarmament
- compulsory education in the English language
- the achievement of women's suffrage
- the inclusion of the program of the National League of Women Voters with its own
- creation of a federal Department of Education
- federal support for maternity and infancy care
- vocational training in home economics
- equal opportunity for women in the civil service
- eradication of venereal disease and public education in sex hygiene
- protection for women citizens
- economy in government
- industrial peace through creation of industrial courts
- prosecution of profiteers in the marketplace
- extension of parcel post services
- development of a system of cooperative marketing in agriculture

- impartial enforcement of the law
- election of a president whose typifies the "finest and best the country can produce"

OPPOSED:
- efforts by the liquor traffic to nullify the effect of prohibition by weakening enforcement
- militarism and universal military training

PROHIBITION PARTY
VOTE FOR PRESIDENTIAL NOMINATION:

Candidate	Ballot: 1	2
Watkins	85	108
Patton	85	74
Poling	28	24
Randall	9	2

Bryan was offered the presidential nomination, but he declined. The nomination of Watkins was made unanimous.

VOTE FOR VICE-PRESIDENTIAL NOMINATION: BREHM, CALDERWOOD, COLVIN, FARIS, FITHIAN, FORD, REGAN, AND WOERTENDYKE WERE PLACED IN NOMINATION FOR VICE PRESIDENT. BREHM AND CALDERWOOD DECLINED, AND FORD'S NOMINATION WAS WITHDRAWN. COLVIN WAS NOMINATED FOR VICE PRESIDENT.

REPUBLICAN PARTY

CANDIDATE FOR PRESIDENT:
Warren Gamaliel Harding

CANDIDATE FOR VICE PRESIDENT:
Calvin Coolidge

CANDIDATES FOR PRESIDENTIAL NOMINATION:
William Edgar Borah (ID)
Nicholas Murray Butler (NY)
Calvin Coolidge (MA)
Thomas Coleman du Pont (DE)
Warren Gamaliel Harding (OH)
William Harrison Hays (IN)
Herbert Clark Hoover (CA)
Hiram Johnson (CA)
Philander Chase Knox (PA)
Robert Marion La Follette (WI)
Irving Luther Lenroot (WI)
Frank Orren Lowden (IL)
John Joseph Pershing (MO)
Emanuel Lorenz Philipp (WI)
Miles Poindexter (WA)
Peter Conley Pritchard (TN)
Robert G. Ross (NE)
William Cameron Sproul (PA)

Howard Sutherland (WV)
Charles Beecher Warren (MI)
Edward R. Wood (PA)
Leonard Wood (MA)

CANDIDATES FOR VICE-PRESIDENTIAL NOMINATION:
Samuel Ed Adams (DC)
Calvin Coolidge (MA)

PRIMARIES:
MARCH 9, 1920 (NH):
L. Wood	8,591
Johnson	2,000
unpledged delegates	5,604

MARCH 16, 1920 (ND):
Johnson	30,573
L. Wood	987
Lowden	265

MARCH 23, 1920 (SD):
L. Wood	31,265
Lowden	26,981
Johnson	26,301
others	1,144

APRIL 5, 1920 (MI):
Johnson	156,939
L. Wood	112,568
Lowden	62,418
Hoover	52,503
others	24,729

APRIL 6, 1920 (NY):
unpledged delegates 199,149

APRIL 6, 1920 (WI):
Philipp	18,350
L. Wood	4,505
Hoover	3,910
Johnson	2,413
Lowden	921

APRIL 13, 1920 (IL):
Lowden	236,802
L. Wood	156,719
Johnson	64,201
Hoover	3,401
others	2,674

APRIL 20, 1920 (NE):
Johnson	63,161
L. Wood	42,385
Pershing	27,669
Ross	1,698
others	1,734

APRIL 23, 1920 (MT):
Johnson	21,034
L. Wood	6,804
Lowden	6,503
Hoover	5,076
Harding	723

April 27, 1920 (MA):
unpledged delegates 93,356

April 27, 1920 (NJ):
L. Wood 52,909
Johnson. 51,685
Hoover 900

April 27, 1920 (OH):
Harding. 123,257
L. Wood 108,565
Johnson. 16,783
Hoover 10,467

May 3, 1920 (MD):
L. Wood 15,900
Johnson. 8,059

May 4, 1920 (CA):
Johnson. 369,853
Hoover 209,009

May 4, 1920 (IN):
L. Wood 85,708
Johnson. 79,840
Lowden 39,627
Harding. 20,782

May 18, 1920 (PA):
E. Wood 257,841
Johnson. 10,869
L. Wood 3,878
Hoover 2,825
others 4,059

May 18, 1920 (VT):
L. Wood 3,451
Hoover 564
Johnson 402
Lowden. 29
others 777

May 21, 1920 (OR):
Johnson. 46,163
L. Wood 43,770
Lowden 15,581
Hoover 14,557

May 25, 1920 (WV):
Sutherland 33,849
L. Wood 27,255

June 5, 1920 (NC):
Johnson. 15,375
L. Wood 5,603

17TH CONVENTION:
June 8–12, 1920, Coliseum, Chicago (IL)
Henry Cabot Lodge (MA), temporary and permanent chairman

PLATFORM HIGHLIGHTS:
SUPPORTED:
- an end to "executive autocracy"
- postponement of recognizing the Mexican government until U.S. interests were assured
- the Republican Congress for its opposition to Wilson and its own positive achievements
- farmers' efforts to form cooperatives and obtain cheap personal credit
- collective bargaining
- governmental reorganization in the name of greater efficiency
- retrenchment in government and a speedy return to a peacetime economy
- a reduction in the tax burden associated with the war
- the freeing of the Federal Reserve System from political influence
- banks giving credit preference to essential industries
- deflation and a means of controlling the high cost of living
- the making of a "fair return" on privately owned railroad property "reasonably sure"
- antimonopoly laws against restraint of trade
- amendments to prevent "persecution of honest business"
- development of water transportation services
- international trade (albeit subject to protective tariff)
- the merchant marine
- reclamation projects
- restriction of immigration based on the nation's ability to assimilate new arrivals
- exclusion of certain classes of undesirable aliens (including Asian laborers)
- Congress's "consider[ing] the most effective means to end lynching," but did not declare what the means should be
- conservation and "devising means" to prevent destruction of the nation's forests
- civil service reform
- the increase in postal employees' pay
- women's suffrage
- federal aid to states for vocational and agricultural training
- protections for women in industry
- equal pay for equal work
- dissemination of federal information on housing and town planning
- efforts to "Americanize" Hawaii for home rule and the "rehabilitation of the Hawaiian race"

OPPOSED:
- Wilson's desire to accept a mandate for Armenia
- participation in the League of Nations as an infringement on U.S. independence
- strikes by public employees
- public ownership of railroads
- use of child labor

ALSO:
- recited the failures of the Wilson administration, in-

cluding unpreparedness for war, huge tax burdens, and a high cost of living

- blamed Democrats for allowing profiteers to realize financial gain from the economic distress of others
- declared that aliens had no right to agitate against the government or advocate its violent overthrow
- commended the soldiers of World War I on their bravery and endurance and promised to maintain the program enacted for the care of maimed and disabled veterans

REPUBLICAN PARTY VOTE FOR PRESIDENTIAL NOMINATION:		
Candidate	Ballot: 1	10
L. Wood	287½	156
Lowden	211½	11
Johnson	133½	80⅙
Sproul	84	0
Butler	69½	2
Harding	65½	692⅕
Coolidge	34	5
La Follette	24	24
Pritchard	21	0
Poindexter	20	0
Sutherland	17	0
du Pont	7	0
Hoover	5½	9½
Borah	2	0
Warren	1	0
Hays	0	1
Lenroot	0	1
Knox	0	1
Pershing	0	0
Philipp	0	0
Ross	0	0
Wood, E.	0	0

SINGLE TAX PARTY

CANDIDATE FOR PRESIDENT:
Robert Colvin Macauley (PA)

CANDIDATE FOR VICE PRESIDENT:
Richard Clarence Barnum (OH)

CONVENTION:
July 10–14, 1920, Chicago (IL)

The Single Tax Party was organized in 1915 by followers of Henry George. By 1920, it had organizations in twenty-six states. The party believed the theory that the public collection of full ground rents on land would lead to the abolition of involuntary poverty, a just division of the products of labor, equal opportunity, and industrial justice.

PLATFORM HIGHLIGHTS:
SUPPORTED:

- the collection by the government of land's rental value
- exemption from taxation for all improvements, industry (e.g., manufacturing, mining, resource and raw materials development), and enterprise under a Single Tax administration

OPPOSED:

- the private right to own land as contrary to reason and justice

SOCIALIST LABOR PARTY

CANDIDATE FOR PRESIDENT:
William Wesley Cox (MO)

CANDIDATE FOR VICE PRESIDENT:
August Gillhaus (NY)

15TH CONVENTION:
May 5–10, 1920, New York (NY)

The party's platform supported eliminating capitalism and substituting a system of social ownership of the means of production. It also called for workers to organize themselves into a socialist industrial union, similar to the Workers' International Industrial Union (WIIU). Finally, the platform also declared World War I proof of the impending collapse of capitalism.

SOCIALIST PARTY

CANDIDATE FOR PRESIDENT:
Eugene Victor Debs (IN)

CANDIDATE FOR VICE PRESIDENT:
Seymour Stedman

CANDIDATES FOR VICE-PRESIDENTIAL NOMINATION:
Seymour Stedman (IL)
Kate Richards O'Hare (KS)

CONVENTION:
May 8–14, 1920, Finnish Socialist Hall, New York (NY)

PLATFORM HIGHLIGHTS:
SUPPORTED:

- citizens "free[ing] the country from the oppressive misrule of the old political parties"
- national ownership of vital industries and businesses, based on nonprofit principles
- development of a unified public banking system
- enactment of extensive public insurance programs for the aged, unemployed, sick, and injured
- enforcement of the federal constitution's provisions ensuring African Americans full civil, political, industrial, and educational rights
- abolition of child labor
- adoption of a minimum wage

- protections for migrant workers and unemployed individuals
- prohibitions against detective and strike-breaking agencies
- a shorter work week
- repeal of the Espionage Act and other repressive legislation
- full pardons for persons incarcerated because of their religious or political views or industrial activities
- limitations on the power of the executive branch to deport aliens
- repeal of the judicial branch's power to nullify congressional legislation
- prohibition against the use of injunctions in industrial disputes
- election of the president, vice president, and federal judges and their susceptibility to recall
- election of cabinet officers by Congress
- women's suffrage
- efforts to assist migrant workers in exercising their franchise
- an amendment to the Constitution to permit additional amendments by a majority vote of the people
- cancellation of war loans to other nations
- extension of credit in food, raw materials, and machinery to the stricken countries of Europe to aid in their rebuilding
- the replacement of the League of Nations with an elected international parliament charged with the responsibility of revising the Treaty of Peace
- immediate peace with the Central Powers (i.e., enemies of the United States during World War I)
- recognition of the Soviet Union and the Republic of Ireland

- a progressive income tax to pay for all war debts
- the income tax and a graduated inheritance tax as the major revenue sources in a Socialist government
- taxes on unearned increments of land and all unused land

OPPOSED:

- World War I
- "closed-door diplomacy"
- suppression of dissent during the war
- censorship
- antistrike laws
- unlawful deportation of aliens
- profiteering

ALSO:

- decried the failure of the United States to live up to the promise of international cooperation that was supposed to follow the war
- declared that U.S. capitalists who engaged in foreign investments should do so at their own risk
- declared that the United States should not defend the foreign property claims of U.S. capitalists

---

SOCIALIST PARTY

VOTE FOR PRESIDENTIAL NOMINATION: DEBS WAS UNANIMOUSLY NOMINATED FOR PRESIDENT ON THE FIRST BALLOT. HE WAS IN PRISON AT THE TIME.

VOTE FOR VICE-PRESIDENTIAL NOMINATION:

Candidate	Ballot: 1
Stedman	106
O'Hare	26

GENERAL ELECTION SUMMARY FOR 1920

Candidate	Electoral Votes	States	Popular Votes
Harding (R)	404	37	16,152,200
J. Cox (D)	127	11	9,147,353
Debs (S)	0	0	919,799
Christensen (FL)	0	0	265,411
Watkins (PROH)	0	0	189,408
Ferguson (A)	0	0	47,812
W. Cox (SL)	0	0	31,715
none (BTR)	0	0	27,198
Macauley (ST)	0	0	5,837
none (INS REF)	0	0	366
none (I-R)	0	0	342
unknown	0	0	1,167

ELECTION OF NOVEMBER 4, 1924

President
CALVIN COOLIDGE

Vice President
CHARLES GATES DAWES

HIGHLIGHTS

The administration of Warren Harding was largely isolationist and conservative, but it lacked both substance and style. Harding's unexpected death in August 1923 thrust Calvin Coolidge into the presidency. Amid a business boom, revelations about corruption in office under Harding barely touched Coolidge. Furthermore, he urged punishment for those found guilty in the Elk Hills and Teapot Dome scandals. His popularity made him invincible in the convention and, ultimately, in the general election. The Democrats, meanwhile, were torn apart in their convention. Delegates representing the Ku Klux Klan, prohibition, William Gibbs McAdoo, and the rural United States clashed against those favoring Alfred E. Smith, repeal of prohibition, urban areas, and ethnic minorities. After 103 exhausting ballots, Ambassador John W. Davis emerged with the tattered nomination. The vice-presidential nomination went to Governor Charles W. Bryan of Nebraska, brother of the "Great Commoner," William Jennings Bryan. Thus, it was left to the remnants of the Progressive Party, under the leadership of Robert M. La Follette, to frame the issue of corruption in government. The newly formed conference for Progressive Political Action brought together Socialists, Unionists, reformers, and radicals in one of the more notable third-party challenges in U.S. history.

The 1924 Democratic convention was also notable for: the first convention votes of a major party cast for the presidential and vice-presidential nomination on behalf of women. Emma Guffey Miller of Pennsylvania received one-half vote for president on the twenty-first ballot and a full vote on the eighty-seventh ballot. In the balloting for vice president, five women received votes.

AMERICAN PARTY

CANDIDATE FOR PRESIDENT:
Gilbert Owen Nations

CANDIDATE FOR VICE PRESIDENT:
Leander Lycurgus Pickett

CANDIDATES FOR PRESIDENTIAL NOMINATION:
Gilbert Owen Nations (DC)
Gifford Pinchot (PA)

CANDIDATES FOR VICE-PRESIDENTIAL NOMINATION:
Leander Lycurgus Pickett (KY)
Charles Hiram Randall (CA)
William David Upshaw (GA)

CONVENTION:
June 3–4, 1924, Columbus (OH)
W. M. Likins, national chairman

PLATFORM HIGHLIGHTS:
SUPPORTED:
- prohibition
- law enforcement
- immigration restrictions

- abolition of war, polygamy, white slavery, and kidnapping
- censorship of foreign-language newspapers and restrictions on the dissemination of foreign propaganda
- punishment for persons found guilty of election fraud

ALSO:
- welcomed the support of the Ku Klux Klan

AMERICAN PARTY
VOTE FOR PRESIDENTIAL NOMINATION:

Candidate	Ballot: 1
Nations	20
Pinchot	7

VOTE FOR VICE-PRESIDENTIAL NOMINATION

Candidate	Ballot: 1
Randall	16
Upshaw	10

Randall later declined the nomination, and Pickett was chosen to replace him on the ticket.

COMMONWEALTH LAND PARTY

CANDIDATE FOR PRESIDENT:
William James Wallace (NJ)

CANDIDATE FOR VICE PRESIDENT:
John Cromwell Lincoln (OH)

CONVENTION:
February 8–9, 1924, Engineering Society Building,
New York (NY)
William James Wallace (NJ), chairman

The Commonwealth Land Party was the successor of the Single Tax Party. The convention was attended by delegates from thirteen states. The party predicted that the single tax would bring about prosperity and happiness. Under the party's program, "good would take the place of evil; learning and culture would replace ignorance and crime; health would supplant disease; vice would vanish; and early and healthy marriages would make possible happy and contented homes." It also specifically supported eliminating private ownership of land and substituting land rentals, which would constitute the sole tax imposed by the government. The party opposed private ownership, believing it was the cause of the major ills of society.

DEMOCRATIC PARTY

CANDIDATE FOR PRESIDENT:
John William Davis

CANDIDATE FOR VICE PRESIDENT:
Charles Wayland Bryan

CANDIDATES FOR PRESIDENTIAL NOMINATION:
Henry Tureman Allen (DC)
Newton Diehl Baker (OH)
John Thomas Barnett (CO)
George Gordon Battle (NC)
Martin Behrman (LA)
George Leonard Berry (TN)
Fred Herbert Brown (NH)
Charles Wayland Bryan (NE)
William Jennings Bryan (NE)
John M. Callahan (WI)
John Calvin Coolidge (MA)
Royal Samuel Copeland (NY)
James Middleton Cox (OH)
William Coyne (WI)
Homer Stille Cummings
Josephus Daniels (NC)
John William Davis (WV)
Jonathan McMillan Davis (KS)
William Emmett Dever (IL)
Edward Laurence Doheny (CA)
Edward Irving Edwards (NJ)

Woodbridge Nathan Ferris (MI)
Henry Ford (MI)
William Alexander Gaston (MA)
James Watson Gerard (NY)
George Carter Glass (VA)
Byron Patrick Harrison (MS)
Gilbert Monell Hitchcock (NE)
David Franklin Houston (NY)
Cordell Hull (TN)
John Holmes Jackson (VT)
John Benjamin Kendrick (WY)
J. Richard Kevin (NY)
Roland Krebs (MI)
William H. Maloney (MT)
Thomas Riley Marshall (IN)
Frederick Collins Martin (VT)
William Gibbs McAdoo (CA)
Edwin Thomas Meredith (IA)
Belle K. Miller (OH)
Emma Guffey Miller (PA)
Albert Alexander Murphree (FL)
Robert Latham Owen (OK)
Atlee Pomerene (OH)
Samuel Moffett Ralston (IN)
Albert Cabell Ritchie (MD)
Joseph Taylor Robinson (AR)
William Penn Adair Rogers (OK)
Franklin Delano Roosevelt (NY)
Willard Saulsbury (DE)
George Sebastian Silzer (NJ)
Alfred Emanuel Smith (NY)
Thomas Joseph Spellacy (CT)
Calvin Stewart (WI)
William Ellery Sweet (CO)
Samuel Houston Thompson (CO)
Oscar Wilder Underwood (AL)
David Ignatius Walsh (MA)
Thomas James Walsh (MT)
Burton Kendall Wheeler (MT)

CANDIDATES FOR VICE-PRESIDENTIAL NOMINATION:
Newton Diehl Baker (OH)
George Leonard Berry (TN)
Martha Scarborough Bird (CT)
Charles Wayland Bryan (NE)
Margaret Chadbourne (NY)
Joel Bennett "Champ" Clark (MO)
Morton Clark
Jonathan McMillan Davis (KS)
Richard Edward Enright (NY)
Andrew C. Erwin (GA)
John J. Farrell (MN)
William Jason Fields (KY)
William Smith Flynn (RI)
Frederick Dozier Gardner (MO)
James Watson Gerard (NY)

John Campbell Greenway (AZ)
John Francis Hylan (NY)
Edwin Thomas Meredith (IA)
Belle K. Miller (OH)
Alvin Mansfield Owsley (TX)
Key H. Pittman (NV)
Maidee B. Milnor Renshaw (PA)
Albert Cabell Ritchie (MD)
George Kent Shuler (NY)
George Sebastian Silzer (NJ)
Lena Jones Springs (SC)
Samuel Houston Thompson (CO)
William David Upshaw (GA)
Thomas James Walsh (MT)
Brand Whitlock (OH)

PRIMARIES:

MARCH 11, 1924 (NH):
unpledged delegates 6,687

MARCH 18, 1924 (ND):
McAdoo 11,273

MARCH 25, 1924 (SD):
McAdoo 6,983
unpledged delegates 2,040

APRIL 1, 1924 (WI):
McAdoo 54,922
Smith 5,774
others 19,827

APRIL 7, 1924 (MI):
Ford 48,567
Ferris 42,028
others 435

APRIL 8, 1924 (IL):
McAdoo 180,544
Smith 235
others 1,724

APRIL 8, 1924 (NE):
McAdoo 9,342
Smith 700
others 6,268

APRIL 22, 1924 (NJ):
Silzer 35,601
Smith 721
McAdoo 69
others 38

APRIL 22, 1924 (PA):
McAdoo 10,376
Smith 9,029
others 4,341

APRIL 29, 1924 (MA):
unpledged delegates 30,341

APRIL 29, 1924 (OH):
Cox 4,183
McAdoo 29,267

MAY 6, 1924 (CA):
McAdoo 110,235
unpledged delegates 18,586

MAY 16, 1924 (OR):
McAdoo 33,664

MAY 28, 1924 (MT):
McAdoo 10,058

24TH CONVENTION:
June 24–28, June 30, July 1–5, and July 7–9, 1924,
  Madison Square Garden, New York (NY)
Byron Patrick Harrison (MS), temporary chairman
Thomas James Walsh (MT), permanent chairman

This meeting was the longest nominating convention of a major political party, with sixty candidates nominated for the presidency. The 1924 Democratic platform was adopted after bitter struggles over planks dealing with the Ku Klux Klan and the League of Nations—conflicts that foreshadowed the prolonged contest over the presidential nomination. The document compared the two major parties, criticized Republican corruption, and called for "honest government." The Fordney-McCumber tariff was condemned, and the Republicans were denounced for placing the greatest burden of taxation upon those financially least able to bear it.

PLATFORM HIGHLIGHTS:
SUPPORTED:
• adjustment of the tariff
• reductions in rail and water rates
• improvement of international waterway systems
• stimulation of the cooperative marketing movement
• extension of suitable credits to farmers
• institution of related measures needed to restore the agricultural export market
• development of Muscle Shoals (AL) for the production of nitrates for munitions and fertilizers
• conservation and land reclamation
• programs to promote highway improvements, mining, and the merchant marine
• federal assistance to states to improve education
• higher salaries for postal employees
• extension of the civil service
• probation as a judicial principle
• a constitutional amendment eliminating lame-duck Congresses
• the contributions of women and veterans to the nation
• campaign finance reform to limit the undue influence of wealth in the electoral process
• suppression of the narcotics trade
• enforcement of all laws relating to prohibition
• immediate independence for the Philippines
• territorial self-government for Alaska
• internal development for Hawaii and the Virgin Islands
• protection of U.S. citizens in Turkey
• Armenia and Greece

- friendship with Latin America
- arms reduction
- a national referendum on the question of U.S. membership in the League of Nations
- deep waterways and flood-control projects
- restrictions on private monopolies and fraudulent stock sales
- development of public and commercial aviation
- prohibitions against child and convict labor
- right of collective bargaining
- improved working conditions
- cooperation with states for the education, welfare, and protection of children and safeguards against exploitation of female workers

OPPOSED:
- sales taxes and other "nuisance taxes"
- "Mellon Tax Plan" as a relief act for multimillionaires

- Republican farm policy
- the tight money policies of the Coolidge administration as a primary cause of bankruptcy, depression, and unemployment
- immigration from Asia
- the perceived erosion of states' rights
- the Lausanne Treaty

FARMER LABOR PARTY

CANDIDATE FOR PRESIDENT:
none (Duncan McDonald [IL] withdrew)

CANDIDATE FOR VICE PRESIDENT:
none (William Bouck [WA] withdrew)

CONVENTION:
June 17–19, 1924, Convention Hall, St. Paul (MN)

DEMOCRATIC PARTY

VOTE FOR PRESIDENTIAL NOMINATION:			VOTE FOR VICE-PRESIDENTIAL NOMINATION:		
Candidate	*Ballot:* 1	103	*Candidate*	*Ballot:* 1a[1]	1b[1]
McAdoo	431½	11½	Berry	263½	208
Smith	241	7½	Bryan	238	740
Cox	59	0	Owsley	152	16
Harrison	43½	0	Hylan	110	6
Underwood	42½	102½	Davis	56½	4
Silzer	38	0	Springs	44	18
Davis, J. W.	31	844	Gerard	42	10
Ferris	30	0	Greenway	32	2
Ralston	30	0	Fields	26	0
Glass	25	23	Clark, J. B.	24	41
Ritchie	22½	0	Farrell	21	1
Robinson	21	20	Flynn	21	15
Davis, J. M.	20	0	Silzer	12	10
Bryan	18	0	Baker	7	7
Brown	17	0	Pittman	6	6
Sweet	12	0	Enright	5	5
Saulsbury	7	0	Shuler	4	0
Kendrick	6	0	Miller	3	3
Thompson	1	0	Renshaw	3	3
Gerard	0	7	Chadbourne	2	0
Hull	0	1	Meredith	2	0
Meredith	0	15½	Bird	1	0
Walsh, D. I.	0	58	Clark, M.	1	0
			Erwin	1	0
			Gardner	1	0
			Ritchie	1	1
			Thompson	1	0
			Upshaw	1	0
			Walsh	1	0
			Whitlock	1	1

McAdoo and Smith entered the convention with considerable delegate strength, but neither could muster the necessary two-thirds vote for nomination, particularly in a field cluttered with favorite-son candidates. Davis, a relatively obscure ambassador, was finally nominated on the record-setting 103d ballot.

[1]first ballot, before and after the shift

J. A. H. Hopkins, chairman, Committee of Forty-Eight

The Farmer Labor Party was controlled by Communists and led by William Zebulon Foster. In all, 542 delegates from twenty-nine states attended this convention.

PLATFORM HIGHLIGHTS:

SUPPORTED:

- control of the government by workers and farmers
- government ownership of forests and other natural resources
- nationalization of mines, superpower plants, railroads, banks, grain exchanges, and communications services
- worker participation in management
- interest-free loans to farmers
- control of money and credits through public and cooperative banks
- prohibition of labor injunctions and strike-breaking
- guaranteed employment with a minimum wage
- enactment of a program of unemployment insurance
- recognition of Soviet Russia
- protection of civil rights, including free exercise of speech, press and assembly

---

FARMER LABOR PARTY
VOTE FOR PRESIDENTIAL AND VICE-PRESIDENTIAL NOMINATIONS: AFTER ROBERT MARION LA FOLLETTE DENOUNCED THE PARTY'S DOMINATION BY COMMUNISTS, THE PARTY REFUSED TO ENDORSE HIS CANDIDACY. INSTEAD, MCDONALD WAS NOMINATED FOR PRESIDENT AND BOUCK WAS NOMINATED FOR VICE PRESIDENT. THE PARTY'S CANDIDATES WITHDREW ON JULY TENTH, AND THE PARTY SUPPORTED THE WORKERS' (COMMUNIST) PARTY TICKET.

INDEPENDENT PARTY

CANDIDATE FOR PRESIDENT:
none (Jane Addams [IL] withdrew)

NATIONAL INDEPENDENT (GREENBACK) PARTY

CANDIDATE FOR PRESIDENT:
John Zahnd (IN)

CANDIDATE FOR VICE PRESIDENT:
Roy M. Harrop (NE)

CONVENTION:
July 9, 1924, Indianapolis (IN)

The platform urged the printing of inflationary greenbacks to relieve unemployment and the impact of a high cost of living. The ticket fielded by the Greenback Party withdrew on July 29 in favor of the candidacy of Robert Marion La Follette (WI).

PEOPLE'S PROGRESSIVE PARTY

CANDIDATE FOR PRESIDENT:
Robert R. Pointer

CANDIDATE FOR VICE PRESIDENT:
none

CANDIDATES FOR PRESIDENTIAL NOMINATION:
Henry Ford (MI)
Robert R. Pointer (MI)

CONVENTION:
January 30–February 1, 1924, Omaha (NE)
Roy M. Harrop (NE), chairman

Twenty-seven delegates attended the convention.

PLATFORM HIGHLIGHTS:

SUPPORTED:

- currency reform with the direct issue of full legal tender currency at its face value for all debts
- immediate payment of a bonus for soldiers
- direct election of the president and vice president
- establishment of government-owned banks
- subjection of all declarations of war to popular referendum, except in the event of actual foreign invasion

OPPOSED:

- the Federal Reserve System

PEOPLE'S PROGRESSIVE PARTY
VOTE FOR PRESIDENTIAL AND VICE-PRESIDENTIAL NOMINATIONS: THE PEOPLE'S PROGRESSIVE PARTY SOUGHT UNSUCCESSFULLY TO DRAFT FORD FOR PRESIDENT. WHEN FORD DECLINED, POINTER WAS NOMINATED FOR PRESIDENT, AND ROY M. HARROP WAS NOMINATED FOR VICE PRESIDENT. HARROP LATER WITHDREW AND ENDORSED ROBERT MARION LA FOLLETTE (WI).

PROGRESSIVE PARTY

CANDIDATE FOR PRESIDENT:
Robert Marion La Follette (WI)

CANDIDATE FOR VICE PRESIDENT:
Burton Kendall Wheeler

CANDIDATES FOR VICE-PRESIDENTIAL NOMINATION:
Louis Dembitz Brandeis (DC)
Burton Kendall Wheeler (MT)

CONVENTION:
July 4, 1924, Municipal Auditorium, Cleveland (OH)

The Progressive Party was an outgrowth of the Conference on Progressive Political Action (CPPA). Two platforms were adopted: one was that of the CPPA, the other was La Follette's personal platform.

CPPA PLATFORM HIGHLIGHTS:

SUPPORTED:

- use of the federal government's power to crush private monopolies
- unqualified enforcement of the constitutional guarantees of freedom of speech, press, and assembly
- public ownership of waterpower
- conservation of natural resources
- promotion of public works in times of unemployment
- a tax policy for redistributing wealth
- revision of the Federal Reserve and Federal Farm Loan systems
- promotion of cooperative banking
- the right of collective bargaining
- creation of a government marketing corporation
- government control of the meatpacking industry
- formation of cooperative enterprises
- repeal of the Esch-Cummins railroad act
- common international action to spur economic recovery
- court reform and limitations on the use of labor injunctions
- development of deep waterways
- protections for women workers
- prohibition of child labor
- revision of the Versailles Treaty to promote peace

OPPOSED:

- war, militarism, and imperialism

LA FOLLETTE'S PLATFORM HIGHLIGHTS:

SUPPORTED:

- most of the CPPA themes
- a complete housecleaning
- protection and development of natural resources and public ownership of waterpower
- tax reduction
- adoption of a constitutional amendment to permit Congress to override a judicial veto
- reduction in the tariff and relief for farmers
- abolition of the labor injunction
- increasing salaries of postal worker
- adequate compensation for veterans
- construction of a deep waterway connecting the Great Lakes and the Atlantic
- direct nomination and election of the president
- adoption of the initiative and referendum at the federal level
- use of a popular referendum to decide questions of war
- adoption of a foreign policy free from the interests of imperialists, monopolists, and international bankers—one that would outlaw wars, abolish conscription, and reduce armaments

PROHIBITION PARTY

CANDIDATE FOR PRESIDENT:
Herman Preston Faris

CANDIDATE FOR VICE PRESIDENT:
Marie Caroline Brehm

CANDIDATES FOR PRESIDENTIAL NOMINATION:
Herman Preston Faris (MO)
Adolph Philip Gouthey (WA)
Charles Hiram Randall (CA)
William Frederick Varney (NY)

CANDIDATES FOR VICE-PRESIDENTIAL NOMINATION:
Marie Caroline Brehm (CA)
Adolph Philip Gouthey (WA)
Alfred L. Moudy (IN)

PRIMARY:
MAY 6, 1924 (CA):
Randall 7,286

14TH CONVENTION:
June 5–6, 1924, Columbus (OH)
Herman Preston Faris (MO), chairman

In all, 147 delegates attended this convention, but five delegates withdrew in disagreement over the presidential ticket.

PLATFORM HIGHLIGHTS:

SUPPORTED:

- strict enforcement of prohibition
- U.S. participation in the Court of International Justice
- legislation protecting the interests of labor, capital, and the general public
- the farmers' need for a just share of the proceeds from their toil upon the land

---

PROHIBITION PARTY
VOTE FOR PRESIDENTIAL NOMINATION:

Candidate	Ballot: 1
Faris	82
Gouthey	40
Varney	2

VOTE FOR VICE-PRESIDENTIAL NOMINATION:

Candidate	Ballot: 1
Gouthey	78½
Brehm	22½
Moudy	7

Gouthey was nominated for the vice presidency on the first ballot, but he declined. Brehm was then nominated for vice president by acclamation.

- conservation
- Bible-reading in public schools
- the "Americanization" of aliens
- the extension of the merit system
- the program of the League of Women Voters
- free institutions
- civil rights
- compulsory school attendance

OPPOSED:
- the "nullification efforts" of the two major parties to weaken prohibition
- election laws that discriminate against minor parties and efforts to use public funds for sectarian educational purposes
- violations of the separation of powers among the legislative, executive, and judicial branches

REPUBLICAN PARTY

CANDIDATE FOR PRESIDENT:
Calvin Coolidge

CANDIDATE FOR VICE PRESIDENT:
Charles Gates Dawes

CANDIDATES FOR PRESIDENTIAL NOMINATION:
Calvin Coolidge (MA)
Hiram Johnson (CA)
Robert Marion La Follette (WI)

CANDIDATES FOR VICE-PRESIDENTIAL NOMINATION:
Albert Jeremiah Beveridge (IN)
Smith Wildman Brookhart (IA)
Theodore Elijah Burton (OH)
John Lee Coulter (ND)
Charles Curtis (KS)
Charles Gates Dawes (IL)
Joseph Moore Dixon (MT)
Thomas Coleman du Pont (DE)
George Scott Graham (PA)
James Guthrie Harbord (NY)
Frank Thomas Hines (UT)
Herbert Clark Hoover (IA)
Arthur Mastick Hyde (MO)
William Purnell Jackson (MD)
William Squire Kenyon (IA)
Frank Orren Lowden (IL)
Charles Hoyt March (MN)
George William Norris (NE)
Everett Sanders (IN)
James Willis Taylor (TN)
Charles Beecher Warren (MI)
James Eli Watson (IN)
William Wrigley, Jr. (IL)

PRIMARIES:
MARCH 11, 1924 (NH):
Coolidge 17,170

MARCH 18, 1924 (ND):
Coolidge 52,815
La Follette 40,252
Johnson 32,363

MARCH 25, 1924 (SD):
Johnson 40,935
Coolidge 39,791

APRIL 1, 1924 (WI):
La Follette 40,738
Coolidge 23,324
Johnson 411
others 688

APRIL 7, 1924 (MI):
Coolidge 236,191
Johnson 103,739
others 11,312

APRIL 8, 1924 (IL):
Coolidge 533,193
Johnson 385,590
La Follette 278
others 21

APRIL 8, 1924 (NE):
Coolidge 79,676
Johnson 45,032
others 627

APRIL 22, 1924 (NJ):
Coolidge 111,739
Johnson 13,626

APRIL 22, 1924 (PA):
Coolidge 117,262
Johnson 4,345
La Follette 1,224
others 10,523

APRIL 29, 1924 (MA):
Coolidge 84,840

APRIL 29, 1924 (OH):
Coolidge 173,613
Johnson 27,578

MAY 5, 1924 (MD):
Coolidge 19,657
Johnson 3
unpledged delegates 1,326

MAY 6, 1924 (CA):
Coolidge 310,618
Johnson 261,566

MAY 6, 1924 (IN):
Coolidge 330,045
Johnson 62,603

MAY 16, 1924: (OR):
Coolidge 99,187
Johnson 30,042

MAY 27, 1924 (WV):

Coolidge 162,042

MAY 28, 1924 (MT):

Coolidge 9,200

18TH CONVENTION:

June 10–12, 1924, Municipal Auditorium, Cleveland (OH)

Theodore Elijah Burton (OH), temporary chairman

Franklin Wheeler Mondell (WY), permanent chairman

PLATFORM HIGHLIGHTS:

SUPPORTED:

- governmental economy
- reduction of the national debt and the size of the bureaucracy
- tax relief
- reorganization of the executive branch
- enforcement of the merit system
- repayment of war debts by foreign nations
- the protective tariff
- U.S. adherence to the Permanent Court of International Justice
- the Dawes Commission resolution on the question of German reparations
- the Arms Limitation Conference
- progress toward improved relations with Latin America and Mexico
- the convening of conferences to limit land and naval forces
- aid for the starving in Russia and Japan
- U.S. efforts to restrict international traffic in prostitution and child labor, drugs, and public health hazards
- reorganization of the market system to the advantage of agricultural cooperatives
- federal aid for highway construction
- development of access roads and trails in national forests
- high standards for wage, working, and living conditions for women
- a constitutional amendment dealing with child labor
- the eight-hour workday, vocational education, and free federal employment agencies
- improvement of railroad service by consolidating into a fewer number of lines
- government avoidance of competition with business
- arbitration and mediation in labor disputes
- wartime conscription of material resources
- a strong merchant marine
- flood-control projects
- liberal pensions for veterans
- conservation of natural resources
- creation of a Department of Education and Relief
- promotion of commercial aviation

- maintenance of a strong military
- enactment of a federal antilynching law
- improvement in naturalization laws

OPPOSED:

- corruption in government

ALSO:

- mourned the loss of President Harding
- recited the accomplishments of the Harding-Coolidge administration

---

REPUBLICAN PARTY
VOTE FOR PRESIDENTIAL NOMINATION:

Candidate	Ballot: 1
Coolidge	1,065
La Follette	34
Johnson	10

The nomination of Coolidge for president was made unanimous.

VOTE FOR VICE-PRESIDENTIAL NOMINATION:

Candidate	Ballot: 1	2a[1]	2b[1]	3
Lowden	222	413	766	0
Kenyon	172	95	68	75
Dawes	149	111	49	682½
Burton	139	288	94	0
Graham	81	0	0	0
Watson	79	55	7	45
Curtis	56	31	24	0
Hyde	55	36	36	0
Norris	35	2	2	29
Hines	29	15	0	0
March	28	0	0	0
Taylor	27	0	0	0
Jackson	23	0	0	0
Harbord	3	0	0	0
Beveridge	2	0	0	0
Wrigley	1	1	1	1
Brookhart	0	31	31	0
Warren, C. B.	0	23	23	0
Dixon	0	1	1	6
Coulter	0	1	1	0
Hoover	0	0	0	234½
du Pont	0	0	0	11
Sanders	0	0	0	4
absent	8	6	6	21

Lowden was unanimously nominated for vice president after the second ballot, but he declined. Dawes was then selected on the third ballot.

[1]2a was before the switch, and 2b was after the switch.

SOCIALIST LABOR PARTY

CANDIDATE FOR PRESIDENT:
Frank Teats Johns (OR)

CANDIDATE FOR VICE PRESIDENT:
Verne L. Reynolds (MD)

16TH CONVENTION:
May 10–13, 1924, New York, (NY)
Henry Kuhn (NY), temporary chairman
Henry Kuhn (NY), chairman for May 10, 1924
P. E. De Lee (NY), chairman for May 11, 1924
Theodore Gramaticoff (Bulgarian Federation), chairman for May 12, 1924
Frank Teats Johns (OR), chairman for May 13, 1924

Thirty-three delegates from ten states and four ethnic federations attended this convention. The Socialist Labor Party platform was unchanged from that adopted in 1920.

SOCIALIST LABOR PARTY
VOTE FOR PRESIDENTIAL AND VICE-PRESIDENTIAL NOMINATIONS: JOHNS AND REYNOLDS WERE UNANIMOUSLY NOMINATED FOR PRESIDENT AND VICE PRESIDENT, RESPECTIVELY. NO OTHER NAMES WERE PRESENTED BEFORE THE CONVENTION.

SOCIALIST PARTY

CANDIDATE FOR PRESIDENT:
Robert Marion La Follette (WI)

CANDIDATE FOR VICE PRESIDENT:
Burton Kendall Wheeler (MT)

CONVENTION:
July 6–8, 1924, Cleveland (OH)

The Socialist Party endorsed the Progressive candidate La Follette and his platform. The national committee was authorized at this convention to name a suitable vice-presidential candidate at a later date. Wheeler, the Progressive Party's vice-presidential candidate, was endorsed on July 22, 1924.

WORKERS' (COMMUNIST) PARTY

CANDIDATE FOR PRESIDENT:
William Zebulon Foster (IL)

CANDIDATE FOR VICE PRESIDENT:
Benjamin Gitlow (NY)

CONVENTION:
July 11, 1924, St. Paul (MN)

PLATFORM HIGHLIGHTS

SUPPORTED:
- formation of a workers' and farmers' government along Soviet lines, with a dictatorship of the proletariat
- formation of a mass farmer-labor party
- nationalization of large-scale industries and establishment of worker control over them
- unemployment compensation
- prohibitions against labor injunctions and the use of police and soldiers against workers
- release of all political prisoners
- nationalization of marketing industries for farmers
- end to militarism and imperialist wars
- recognition of the Soviet Union

OPPOSED:
- the exploiting capitalist class
- the evils of capitalism, citing such examples as the Teapot Dome scandal, tariff laws, strike-breaking, and war profiteering
- both major parties and the La Follette ticket as the tools of capitalism

---

GENERAL ELECTION SUMMARY FOR 1924

Candidate	Electoral Votes	States	Popular Votes
Coolidge (R)	382	35	15,725,016
Davis (D)	136	12	8,386,503
La Follette (PROG)	13[1]	1[1]	4,822,856[1]
Faris (PROH)	0	0	57,520
Johns (SOC LAB)	0	0	36,428
Foster (W [C])	0	0	36,386
Nations (A)	0	0	23,967
Wallace (CL)	0	0	1,582
Pointer (PEO PROG)	0	0	none recorded
Zahnd (NAT IND [G])	0	0	none recorded
unknown	0	0	4,627

[1]includes votes of the Socialist Party

ELECTION OF NOVEMBER 6, 1928

President
HERBERT CLARK HOOVER

Vice President
CHARLES CURTIS

HIGHLIGHTS

Despite the impending economic depression just around the corner (perhaps foretold by conditions in agricultural communities), many Americans in 1928 were enjoying the blush of prosperity. Business optimism reached new heights, the "Roaring Twenties" were in full swing, Charles Lindbergh was the contemporary hero, and the United States had sent Marines abroad into China and Nicaragua. When the taciturn incumbent president, Calvin Coolidge, announced that he would not seek another term in 1928, Secretary of Commerce Herbert Hoover and Governor Frank Lowden of Illinois entered the contest for the Republican nomination. By the time the convention was held, Hoover was his party's clear choice. On the Democratic side, Governor Alfred E. Smith of New York, the first Catholic to be nominated by a major party, defeated Missouri's James A. Reed and a variety of favorite sons to head his party's ticket. A Tammany protege, Smith represented the urban, immigrant, and "wet" interests of the nation, whose emerging strength was still insufficient to overcome the rural, small-town, and "dry" constituencies that supported Hoover. Despite a bitter backdrop of bigotry and anti-Catholicism, the election was relatively unexciting.

AMERICAN HOME PROGRESSIVE PARTY

CANDIDATE FOR PRESIDENT:
none (Henry Ford [MI] declined)

CANDIDATE FOR VICE PRESIDENT:
Edward Albert Filene (MA)

CONVENTION:
October 1, 1928, Springfield (MA)
Conrad Reno, chairman

DEMOCRATIC PARTY

CANDIDATE FOR PRESIDENT:
Alfred Emanuel Smith

CANDIDATE FOR VICE PRESIDENT:
Joseph Taylor Robinson (AR)

CANDIDATES FOR PRESIDENTIAL NOMINATION:
William Augustus Ayres (KS)
Theodore Gilmore Bilbo (MS)
Alvin Victor Donahey (OH)
Walter Franklin George (GA)
Byron Patton Harrison (MS)
Gilbert Monell Hitchcock (NE)
Cordell Hull (TN)
Jesse Holman Jones (TX)
William Gibbs McAdoo (CA)
Daniel Alfred Poling (PA)

Atlee Pomerene (OH)
James Alexander Reed (MO)
Alfred Emanuel Smith (NY)
Thomas James Walsh (MT)
Richard Cannon Watts (SC)
Evans Woollen (IN)
Alonzo F. Workman (MO)

CANDIDATES FOR VICE-PRESIDENTIAL NOMINATION:
Henry Tureman Allen (DC)
Alben William Barkley (KY)
George Leonard Berry (TN)
Duncan Upshaw Fletcher (FL)
Daniel J. Moody (TX)
Joseph Taylor Robinson (AR)
Nellie Tayloe Ross (WY)
Lewis Green Stevenson (IL)
John H. Taylor (NJ)
Joseph Patrick Tumulty (MD)
Evans Woollen (IN)

PRIMARIES:
MARCH 13, 1928 (NH):
unpledged delegates 9,716

MARCH 20, 1928 (ND):
Smith 10,822

APRIL 2, 1928 (MI):
Smith 77,276

Walsh 1,034
Reed 324

APRIL 3, 1928 (WI):
Reed 61,097
Smith 19,781
Walsh 541

APRIL 10, 1928 (IL):
Smith 44,212
Reed 3,786
McAdoo. 213

APRIL 10, 1928 (NE):
Hitchcock. 51,019
Smith 4,755

APRIL 24, 1928 (OH):
Smith 42,365
Pomerene 13,957
Donahey 7,935

APRIL 24, 1928 (PA):
no figures available

APRIL 28, 1928 (MA):
Smith 38,081
Walsh 254
others 478

MAY 1, 1928 (CA):
Smith 134,471
Reed 60,004
Walsh 46,770
Poling 7,263

MAY 7, 1928 (IN):
Woollen 146,934

MAY 8, 1928 (AL):
unpledged delegates 138,957

MAY 15, 1928 (NJ):
Smith 28,506

MAY 18, 1928 (OR):
Smith 17,444
Walsh 11,272
Reed 6,360
Workman. 881

MAY 22, 1928 (SD):
unpledged delegates 6,221

MAY 29, 1928 (WV):
Smith 81,739
Reed 75,796
Workman 5,789

JUNE 5, 1928 (FL):
unpledged delegates 108,167

CONVENTION
June 26–29, 1928, Sam Houston Hall, Houston (TX)
Claude G. Bowers (IN), temporary chairman
Joseph Taylor Robinson (AR), permanent chairman

PLATFORM HIGHLIGHTS:

SUPPORTED:
- states' rights
- a businesslike reorganization of government
- policy reforms in the Federal Reserve System, which worked to the advantage of stock market speculators
- reduction in taxes
- tariff reform to restrain monopolies and increase the purchasing power of wages
- farm relief
- improved management of surpluses
- encouragement of cooperatives
- credit aid and creation of a federal farm board
- civil service
- mining
- agreements to limit armaments (but found fault with the 1921 Armaments Treaty
- flood control, development of waterpower, and construction of a deep waterway between the Great Lakes and the Atlantic
- conservation, reclamation, and an efficient and economical transportation system for the country
- collective bargaining
- study of a public works program to counterbalance unemployment
- adoption of a program of accident compensation for government employees
- a "living wage" and a "fair and liberal retirement" for federal employees
- veterans, women, and children
- immigration law reform to reunite families
- government encouragement of the coal industry
- control of radio's development to prevent monopolies
- an "honest effort to enforce" prohibition
- publication of and limitations on campaign expenditures
- elimination of lame-duck Congresses
- development of the merchant marine
- limited federal assistance to state education programs
- fulfillment of U.S. commitments to Armenia
- exclusive employment of citizens in managing the Panama Canal
- development of Alaska and Hawaii through self-government
- eventual statehood for Puerto Rico
- immediate independence for the Philippines
- strict enforcement of antitrust laws
- enlargement of the Bureau of Public Health
- improved efforts to control the spread of communicable and contagious diseases

OPPOSED:
- Republican corruption
- militarism, imperialism, and war

- interference in the internal affairs of other nations (including Mexico and Nicaragua)
- executive decisions to bind the country in support of foreign governments
- convict labor and the use of labor injunctions

DEMOCRATIC PARTY
VOTE FOR PRESIDENTIAL NOMINATION:

Candidate	Ballot: 1
Smith	849⅔
George	52½
Reed	52
Hull	50⅚
Jones	43
Watts	18
Harrison	8½
Woollen	7
Donahey	5
Ayres	3
Pomerene	3
Hitchcock	2
Bilbo	1

Smith's nomination was made unanimous.

VOTE FOR VICE-PRESIDENTIAL NOMINATION:

Candidate	Ballot: 1a	1b
Robinson	914⅙	1,035
Barkley	77	9
Ross	31	2
Allen	28	21
Berry	17½	11½
Moody	9⅓	9⅓
Fletcher	7	7
Taylor	6	0
Stevenson	4	2
Woollen	2	2
Tumulty	1	0
not voting	1	1

FARMER LABOR PARTY

CANDIDATE FOR PRESIDENT:
Frank Elbridge Webb

CANDIDATE FOR VICE PRESIDENT:
none

CANDIDATES FOR PRESIDENTIAL NOMINATION:
Gale Flagman (IA)
George William Norris (NE)
Norman Thomas (NY)
Frank Elbridge Webb (CA)

CANDIDATES FOR VICE-PRESIDENTIAL NOMINATION:
James Alexander Reed (MO)
Will Vereen (GA)

CONVENTION:
July 10–11, 1928, Chicago (IL)
J. Edwin Spurr (OK), permanent chairman

Thirty delegates attended the convention.

PLATFORM HIGHLIGHTS:
SUPPORTED:
- "enforcement of all laws" governing prohibition
- abolition of labor injunctions
- farm relief with the equalization fee (a forerunner of price supports)
- government ownership of grain elevators, distribution sources, and storage agencies
- recognition of Soviet Russia
- withdrawal of U.S. Marines from Nicaragua
- independence for the Philippines
- autonomy for Puerto Rico
- a civil government for the Virgin Islands
- self-government for the District of Columbia
- abolition of lame-duck sessions of Congress
- direct election of the president and vice president
- public ownership of Boulder Dam (CO) and Muscle Shoals (AL)
- construction of a deep waterway from the Great Lakes to the Atlantic
- guaranteed public employment
- enactment of programs to aid the unemployed, elderly, widows, victims of war and industry, and the poor
- federalization of (i.e., provide federal support and protection for) overseas welfare workers
- reforestation, reclamation, irrigation, flood control, and flood relief
- ratification of the child labor amendment
- direct government issue of money and operation of the banking and exchange system

---

FARMER LABOR PARTY
VOTE FOR PRESIDENTIAL AND VICE-PRESIDENTIAL NOMINATIONS: THE PARTY HOPED FOR FUSION WITH THE PROHIBITION PARTY, WITH A TICKET HEADED BY GIFFORD PINCHOT AND WILLIAM ELLERY SWEET, BUT THE FUSION NEVER OCCURRED. NORRIS WAS NOMINATED FOR THE PRESIDENCY ON THE THIRD BALLOT, BUT HE DECLINED. WEBB WAS NAMED BY THE EXECUTIVE COMMITTEE AS THE PARTY'S STANDARD BEARER ON SEPTEMBER 6, 1928. REED WAS OFFERED THE VICE-PRESIDENTIAL NOMINATION, BUT HE DECLINED. THE EXECUTIVE COMMITTEE OF THE PARTY THEN SELECTED VEREEN, WHO ALSO DECLINED. NO EFFORT WAS MADE TO NAME OTHER CANDIDATES.

- public ownership of all natural resources, railroads, and industrial monopolies
- a "soak-the-rich" tax policy
- a constitutional convention to modernize the government
- freedom of speech, press, and assembly
- a national voter-registration process
- the use of government powers to encourage labor-saving features of trusts and corporations in the interests of the people

OPPOSED:

- bureaus, commissions, and committees exercising legislative or judicial powers

GREENBACK PARTY

CANDIDATE FOR PRESIDENT:
John Zahnd (IN)

CANDIDATE FOR VICE PRESIDENT:
Wesley Henry Bennington (OH)

INDEPENDENT

CANDIDATES FOR PRESIDENT:
Benjamin Gitlow (NY)
W. O. Ligon
H. Morgan
Z. A. Rogers

INDEPENDENT POLITICAL PARTY OF LINCOLN REPUBLICANS

CANDIDATE FOR PRESIDENT:
none

CANDIDATE FOR VICE PRESIDENT:
Simon P. W. Drew (PA)

CONVENTION:
September 3, 1928, Philadelphia (PA)

This party was an interracial group.

JEFFERSON-LINCOLN LEAGUE

CANDIDATE FOR PRESIDENT:
none (George William Norris [NE] declined)

CANDIDATE FOR VICE PRESIDENT:
none

CONVENTION:
July 10–11, 1928, Chicago (IL)

This party sought to merge with the Prohibition Party and the Farmer Labor Party.

NATIONAL PROGRESSIVE PARTY

CANDIDATE FOR PRESIDENT:
Henry Hoffman

CANDIDATE FOR VICE PRESIDENT:
John Clinton McGee (NY)

CANDIDATES FOR PRESIDENTIAL NOMINATION:
Jane Addams (IL)
Henry Hoffman (NE)

This group sought to revive the Progressive Party. It was a splinter effort with almost no popular support. Addams was offered the presidential nomination, but she declined. Hoffman then nominated himself, as did the vice-presidential candidate, McGee. The platform called for a "nonpolitical government"; adoption of the initiative, referendum, and recall; revision of the prohibition laws; and the elimination of bigotry.

PROHIBITION PARTY

CANDIDATE FOR PRESIDENT:
William Frederick Varney

CANDIDATE FOR VICE PRESIDENT:
James Arthur Edgerton (VA)

CANDIDATES FOR PRESIDENTIAL NOMINATION:
James Thomas Heflin (AL)
Herbert Clark Hoover (CA)
Daniel Alfred Poling (MA)
William Frederick Varney (NY)

PRIMARY:
MAY 1, 1928 (CA):
Poling 7,245

CONVENTION:
July 10–12, 1928, Hotel La Salle, Chicago (IL)
David Leigh Colvin (NY), keynoter
B. E. Prugh (PA), permanent chairman

In all, 152 delegates from twenty-two states attended this convention. A lengthy platform was submitted to the convention but was rejected in favor of a shorter document that was supplemented with a series of resolutions providing for the Prohibition candidates' withdrawal if the executive committee decided to endorse the Republican candidate. The shorter platform lauded the party's early espousal of prohibition and women's suffrage and condemned "nullification" of the liquor laws through their lax enforcement. Resolutions emphasized the "supreme objective" to annihilate the liquor traffic and pledged support for candidates opposing the "wet Tammany candidate."

PROHIBITION PARTY VOTE FOR PRESIDENTIAL NOMINATION:		
Candidate	*Ballot:* 1	2
Varney	52	68
Hoover	42	45

REPUBLICAN PARTY

CANDIDATE FOR PRESIDENT:

Herbert Clark Hoover

CANDIDATE FOR VICE PRESIDENT:

Charles Curtis

CANDIDATES FOR PRESIDENTIAL NOMINATION:

Calvin Coolidge (MA)
Charles Curtis (KS)
Charles Gates Dawes (IL)
Alvin Tufts Fuller (MA)
Guy Despard Goff (WV)
Herbert Clark Hoover (CA)
Charles Evans Hughes (NY)
Frank Orren Lowden (IL)
George William Norris (NE)
Robert G. Ross (NE)
James Eli Watson (IN)
Frank Bartlett Willis (OH)

CANDIDATES FOR VICE-PRESIDENTIAL NOMINATION:

Charles Curtis (KS)
Herman Lewis Ekern (WI)
Charles Gates Dawes (IL)
Hanford MacNider (IA)

PRIMARIES:

MARCH 13, 1928 (NH):
unpledged delegates 25,603

MARCH 20, 1928 (ND):
Lowden 95,857

APRIL 2, 1928 (MI):
Hoover 282,809
Lowden 5,349
Coolidge 1,666

APRIL 3, 1928 (WI):
Norris 162,822
Hoover 17,659
Lowden 3,302
Coolidge 680
Dawes 505
others 1,894

APRIL 10, 1928 (IL):
Lowden 1,172,278
Hoover 4,368
Coolidge 2,420
Dawes 756
others 946

APRIL 10, 1928 (NE):
Norris 96,726
Hoover . . . . ,815
Lowden 711
Dawes 679
Coolidge 452

APRIL 24, 1928 (OH):
Hoover 217,430

Willis 84,461
Ross 8,280
Dawes 4,311
Lowden 3,676
others 910

APRIL 24, 1928 (PA):
no figures available

APRIL 28, 1928 (MA):
Hoover 100,279
Coolidge 7,767
Fuller 1,686
Lowden 1,040
others 6,950

MAY 1, 1928 (CA):
Hoover 567,219

MAY 7, 1928 (IN):
Watson 228,795
Hoover 203,279

MAY 7, 1928 (MD):
Hoover 27,128
unpledged delegates 5,426

MAY 15, 1928 (NJ):
Hoover 382,907

MAY 18, 1928 (OR):
Hoover 01,129
Lowden 1,322

MAY 22, 1928 (SD):
unpledged delegates 34,264

MAY 29, 1928 (WV):
Goff 128,429
Hoover 109,303

CONVENTION:

June 12–15, 1928, Civic Auditorium, Kansas City
(MO)
Simeon Davison Fess (OH), temporary chairman
George Higgins Moses (NH), permanent chair-
man

PLATFORM HIGHLIGHTS:

SUPPORTED:

• Coolidge's policies of public economy, sound finance, debt retirement, and reduction of taxes
• the protective tariff as a vital element in prosperity
• a multilateral treaty to end wars in favor of pacific dispute resolution through arbitration
• the U.S. Marines' presence in Nicaragua "to maintain order and insure a fair and free election"
• international cooperation in humanitarian efforts
• the merit system in the civil service
• flood relief and control
• "wise and expert government supervision" of radio
• cheaper transportation for bulk goods from the Midwest to the sea via a deep waterway
• river and harbor improvements

- creation of a federal farm board and a federal system of organization for cooperative and orderly marketing of farm products
- expansion of the agricultural export market
- mining, highway construction, commercial aviation, and the merchant marine
- "possible" modest revision of the railroad laws
- pension, rehabilitation, and insurance programs for veterans
- state regulation of public utilities over federal regulation
- strong conservation and reclamation efforts
- "vigorous enforcement" of the Eighteenth Amendment (prohibition)
- honesty in government
- publication of campaign expenditures
- humane restriction of immigration
- loyalty limitations on naturalization
- development of Alaska and Hawaii
- maintenance of the navy at the full ratio provided [for] by the Treaty for the Limitation of Naval Armament (commonly called the London Naval Disarmament Treaty)
- conscription of material resources in event of war
- the contributions of women to public service
- an antilynching law
- rights of American Indians
- self-reliance and individual and local responsibility

OPPOSED:

- cancellation of foreign debts
- membership in the League of Nations

SOCIALIST LABOR PARTY

CANDIDATE FOR PRESIDENT:
Verne L. Reynolds

CANDIDATE FOR VICE PRESIDENT:
Jeremiah D. Crowley (NY)

CANDIDATES FOR PRESIDENTIAL NOMINATION:
Frank Teats Johns (OR)
Verne L. Reynolds (MI)

CONVENTION:
May 12–14, 1928, New York (NY)

The Socialist Labor Party platform warned of the approaching collapse of capitalism. It rejected the "iridescent theory of capturing the machinery of production for the people by the ballot only," likening this approach to firing "blank cartridges at a foe." It similarly rejected an approach that relied solely on physical force. Instead, it advocated the overthrow of the political state and the creation of an industrial government with representation based on industries and useful occupations. Craft unionism was denounced as "a harmless scarecrow upon which the capitalist birds roost at ease." Under the Socialist Labor program, the land and all means of production, transportation, and distribution would be placed in the hands of the people as a collective body—the Socialist Commonwealth.

REPUBLICAN PARTY
VOTE FOR PRESIDENTIAL NOMINATION:

Candidate	Ballot: 1
Hoover	837
Lowden	74
Curtis	64
Watson	45
Norris	24
Goff	18
Coolidge	17
Dawes	4
Hughes	1

Hoover's nomination was made unanimous.

VOTE FOR VICE-PRESIDENTIAL NOMINATION:

Candidate	Ballot: 1
Curtis	1052
Ekern	19
Dawes	13
MacNider	2
not voting	3

SOCIALIST LABOR PARTY
VOTE FOR PRESIDENTIAL NOMINATION: THE SOCIALIST LABOR PARTY "REVEALED" A SLATE THAT HAD BEEN PICKED BY THE EXECUTIVE COMMITTEE. THE SELECTIONS WERE THEN ENDORSED AT THE CONVENTION. JOHNS WAS NOMINATED FOR THE PRESIDENCY, BUT HE DIED ON MAY 20, 1928, TRYING TO SAVE A PERSON FROM DROWNING. ON MAY 22, 1928, REYNOLDS WAS NOMINATED IN HIS PLACE.

SOCIALIST PARTY

CANDIDATE FOR PRESIDENT:
Norman Mattoon Thomas (NY)

CANDIDATE FOR VICE PRESIDENT:
James Hudson Maurer

CONVENTION:
April 13–17, 1928, Finnish Socialist Hall and Manhattan Opera House, New York, (NY)

Attending the convention were 171 delegates from thirty states.

PLATFORM HIGHLIGHTS:

SUPPORTED:

- socialism as the way of winning the class struggle
- public ownership and conservation of natural resources, public power, railroads, and transportation and communications systems
- flood control and relief, reforestation, irrigation, and reclamation under federal auspices
- a public works program
- governmental relief for the unemployed, unemployment insurance, old age pensions, a shortened workday, and a five-day work week
- a constitutional amendment to abolish child labor
- elimination of convict labor under contract
- cooperative industries in penitentiaries to benefit public institutions
- an increase in taxes for the wealthy
- the appropriation by taxation of all lands held for speculation
- repeal of espionage laws and other repressive legislation
- protection of foreign-born workers
- immigration law reform to permit reunification of families
- a strong defense of civil liberties
- enactment of an antilynching law
- nationalization of the banking and currency system
- farm relief, encouragement of farmers' cooperatives, and creation of a federal crop insurance program
- a constitutional convention to provide for direct election of the president and vice president, proportional representation, and limitations on the power of the Supreme Court
- immediate withdrawal from Nicaragua
- cancellation of all war debts due the United States
- a refusal by the government to defend U.S. investments abroad
- revision of the Covenant of the League of Nations
- U.S. participation in the League of Nations
- recognition of Soviet Russia
- "aggressive activity against militarism"
- treaties outlawing war
- independence for the Philippines
- autonomy for Puerto Rico
- civil government for the Virgin Islands

OPPOSED:

- the growing poverty in the nation, attributing it to the greed of capitalists
- the oppression of the workers, citing the Mooney case and the Sacco and Vanzetti case as examples
- the war in Nicaragua
- labor injunctions and use of detective agencies to "bust" unions

WORKERS' (COMMUNIST) PARTY

CANDIDATE FOR PRESIDENT:
William Zebulon Foster (IL)

CANDIDATE FOR VICE PRESIDENT:
Benjamin Gitlow (NY)

CONVENTION:
May 25–26, 1928, Mecca Temple and Central Opera House, New York (NY)

In all, 296 delegates attended the convention. In a lengthy platform, the Workers' Party addressed the economic conditions in the nation according to Marxist analysis, citing the accumulation of wealth, the impulse toward monopoly and trusts, rampant imperialism, and the drift toward war.

PLATFORM HIGHLIGHTS:

SUPPORTED:

- enactment of old age, sickness, accident and unemployment insurance
- work-site safety inspections and health and safety standards
- a forty-hour work week (with overtime forbidden)
- establishment of public kitchens
- free legal aid
- free medical care for the unemployed
- creation of a public works program
- abolition of vagrancy laws
- workers who were fighting for high wages, striking against wage cuts, struggling against the speed-up system, organizing the unorganized, destroying company unions, amalgamating the craft unions into industrial unions, and committing to political action
- striking miners, mass resistance to antistrike tactics, and the Pennsylvania and Ohio railroad strike
- the immediate withdrawal of U.S. troops from Nicaragua
- immediate independence for all U.S. colonies and "semicolonies"
- election of military officers by soldiers and sailors
- enfranchisement of military personnel
- cancellation of all war debts
- immediate recognition of the Soviet Union
- trade relations and direct contacts between U.S. and Soviet workers
- unrestricted rights to organize, strike, and picket
- prohibitions against injunctions and the use of guards, police, and troops in labor struggles
- abolition of censorship, secret antilabor organizations, antisyndicalist laws, and the Espionage Act
- repeal of industrial court laws
- immediate release of all political prisoners
- abolition of the Senate, the Supreme Court, and the veto power of the president
- an elected judiciary
- extension of the right to vote to eighteen-year-olds and foreign-born and migratory workers

- enforcement of the voting rights of African Americans
- exemption from taxation for all wage earners and farmers, with a graduated income tax imposed on incomes above $5,000 becoming confiscatory at $25,000
- abolition of tax exemptions on bonds, stocks, and securities
- introducing a graduated inheritance tax and a gift tax
- abolition of tariffs
- a five-year moratorium on farm mortgage debts
- a farm relief fund
- forced farm foreclosures
- protection of farmers against monopoly prices and exploitation by distributing agencies
- extension of essentially the same benefits as other workers to farm laborers
- abolition of all "Jim Crow" laws
- enactment of fair housing legislation
- abolition of laws restricting voting rights and forbidding intermarriage
- equal employment opportunity and equal pay
- school integration
- antilynching legislation
- abolition of the convict lease system and chain gangs
- full integration of African Americans in public accommodations, courts and juries, trade unions, and the military
- relief from discrimination and prejudice, and equal pay for equal work for foreign-born citizens
- immediate repeal of the immigration laws and abolition of all restrictions on immigration
- a pregnancy and childbirth allowance for women

- a nine-month nursing allowance (with a half-hour's leave every three hours for nursing in on-site company-provided nurseries)
- equal pay for equal work for women
- prohibitions against night work, overtime, job work, and discrimination against women in trade unions
- child labor laws for children under sixteen
- a minimum wage for other youth
- establishment of work-schools in factories
- initiation of a school nutrition program
- free university education
- various education reforms
- rent controls
- creation of a municipal housing construction program
- abolition of the right of eviction by landlords
- compulsory repair of rental property by landlords
- development of shelters for the unemployed
- municipal aid for workers' building cooperatives
- repeal of prohibition and an energetic propaganda campaign against alcoholism

OPPOSED:
- the major parties, Progressives, and other Socialist parties as capitalist tools, with the Communists claiming for themselves the title of the "only genuine working-class party"
- John L. Lewis and other labor leaders
- the war in Nicaragua and imperialist activities in China, Latin America, and Mexico
- participation in the League of Nations
- participation in the World Court
- race discrimination

GENERAL ELECTION SUMMARY FOR 1928			
Candidate	*Electoral Votes*	*States*	*Popular Votes*
Hoover (R)	444	40	21,392,190
Smith (D)	87	8	15,016,443
Thomas (S)	0	0	267,420
Foster (W [C])	0	0	48,770
Reynolds (SOC LAB)	0	0	21,603
Varney (PROH)	0	0	20,106
Webb (FL)	0	0	6,390
Ligon (I)	0	0	524
Rogers (I)	0	0	264
Gitlow (I)	0	0	104
Morgan (I)	0	0	6
Hoffman (NAT PROG)	0	0	0
Zahnd (GRE)	0	0	0
unknown	0	0	180

ELECTION OF NOVEMBER 8, 1932

President
FRANKLIN DELANO ROOSEVELT
Vice President
JOHN NANCE GARNER

HIGHLIGHTS

With the stock market crash of October 29, 1929, the United States entered a period of disillusionment. The prosperity of the Twenties disappeared and was replaced by a harsh, severe depression worldwide. By 1932, there were 12 million persons out of work in the United States; 5.6 million in Germany; and 2.7 million in Great Britain. "Politics as usual" was discredited everywhere and the world witnessed the rising popularity of extremist agitators such as Adolf Hitler and Benito Mussolini. In the United States, protest parties arose to offer unique solutions to the Great Depression, and such older parties as the Communists and Socialists assumed new significance. Herbert Hoover was dutifully renominated by his party, but even the most stalwart Republicans seemed weary of his leadership. On the Democratic side, Governor Franklin Delano Roosevelt of New York swamped his rivals in the primaries, captured the nomination over his mentor Alfred E. Smith, and went on to win a tremendous victory in November. Roosevelt was an engaging and energetic campaigner, willing to try new things—as exemplified by his personal acceptance of the Democratic nomination at the convention. When he promised a "New Deal" to the American people, they overwhelmingly embraced his leadership and ushered in a twenty-year period of Democratic control of the White House.

COMMUNIST PARTY

CANDIDATE FOR PRESIDENT:
William Zebulon Foster (IL)

CANDIDATE FOR VICE PRESIDENT:
James William Ford (NY)

CONVENTION:
May 28–29, 1932, People's Auditorium, Chicago (IL)

The Communist platform called on workers and farmers to rally under Communist leadership "in the revolutionary struggle to overthrow capitalism." The short comings of capitalism were recited in a litany of problems associated with the Great Depression: starvation, murderous police attacks on workers, persecution of African Americans, and war in the Far East. According to the Communists, workers had to organize to win the class struggle and obtain the immediate Communist objectives:

- unemployment and social insurance
- rejection of wage cuts
- emergency relief for impoverished farmers, including exemption from taxation and no forced collection of rents or debts
- equal rights for African Americans and self-determination for the Black Belt (i.e., the portion of the south with a large African-American population)

- an end to suppression of political rights of workers
- an end to imperialist war
- support for the people of China and the Soviet Union. The Communists promised that a government of workers' and farmers' would end misery, while the old parties (including the Socialist Party) would only serve the capitalist bosses. The platform concluded with a plea for Communist and non-Communist workers to join together to establish a United States of Soviet America.

DEMOCRATIC PARTY

CANDIDATE FOR PRESIDENT:
Franklin Delano Roosevelt

CANDIDATE FOR VICE PRESIDENT:
John Nance Garner (TX)

CANDIDATES FOR PRESIDENTIAL NOMINATION:
Newton D. Baker (OH)
Harry Flood Byrd (VA)
James Middleton Cox (OH)
Leo Jeannot Chassee (WI)
John Nance Garner (TX)
Gus Hill Howard (GA)
James Hamilton Lewis (IL)
William Henry Murray (OK)
James Alexander Reed (MO)

Albert Cabell Ritchie (MD)
Franklin Delano Roosevelt (NY)
Alfred Emanuel Smith (NY)
Melvin Alvah Taylor (IL)
George White (OH)

PRIMARIES:

MARCH 8, 1932 (NH):
unpledged delegates 15,401

MARCH 15, 1932 (ND):
Roosevelt 52,000
Murray 32,000

MARCH 23, 1932 (GA):
Roosevelt 51,498
Howard 5,541

APRIL 5, 1932 (WI):
Roosevelt 241,742
Smith 3,502

APRIL 12, 1932 (NE):
Roosevelt 91,393
Garner 27,359
Murray 25,214

APRIL 13, 1932 (IL):
Lewis 590,130
Roosevelt 1,084
Smith 266
others 72

APRIL 26, 1932 (MA):
Smith 153,465
Roosevelt 56,454

APRIL 26, 1932 (PA):
Roosevelt 133,002
Smith 101,227
others 563

MAY 2, 1932 (MD):
no names entered

MAY 3, 1932 (AL):
unpledged delegates 134,781

MAY 3, 1932 (CA):
Garner 222,385
Roosevelt 175,008
Smith 141,517

MAY 3, 1932 (SD):
Roosevelt 35,370

MAY 10, 1932 (OH):
Murray 112,512
Roosevelt 1,999
Smith 951
White 834
Baker 289
Garner 72

MAY 10, 1932 (WV):
Roosevelt 219,671

Murray 19,826
Chassee 3,727

MAY 17, 1932 (NJ):
Smith 5,234
Roosevelt 3,219

MAY 20, 1932 (OR):
Roosevelt 48,554
Murray 11,993
others 1,214

JUNE 7, 1932 (FL):
Roosevelt 203,372
Murray 24,847
Chassee 3,645

26TH CONVENTION:
June 27-July 2, 1932, Chicago Stadium, Chicago (IL)
Alben William Barkley (KY), temporary chairman
Thomas James Walsh (MT), permanent chairman

The Democratic platform of 1932 was a brief, and relatively conservative, recital of the "unprecedented economic and social distress" in the nation. The Great Depression was laid squarely at the feet of the Hoover administration.

PLATFORM HIGHLIGHTS:
SUPPORTED:
• a sound currency to be preserved "at all hazards"
• a competitive tariff
• adequate flood control
• unemployment relief
• reduction in work hours
• enactment of unemployment and old age insurance under state laws
• farm mortgage loans at low interest rates
• fair prices to farmers for their commodities
• buildup of the army and navy
• antitrust laws
• laws governing holding companies, utility rates, and securities and commodity exchanges
• conservation and development of waterpower
• removal of the government from all fields of private enterprise
• bank and securities reforms
• "the full measure of justice and generosity" to war veterans
• a firm foreign policy
• adherence to the World Court (with reservations)
• consultation among the participants in the Pact of Paris as a means of avoiding war
• reductions of armaments
• cooperation in the Western Hemisphere to maintain the Monroe Doctrine
• independence for the Philippines and ultimate statehood for Puerto Rico
• cancellation of war debts owed to the United States
• employment of U.S. citizens in the operation of the Panama Canal

- a strengthening of the Corrupt Practices Act and publication of campaign contributions and expenditures
- repeal of the Eighteenth Amendment (prohibition)

OPPOSED:

- excessive influence of lobbyists and money in political and public activities
- the extravagance of the Farm Board
- the usurpation of power by the State Department in passing upon foreign securities (i.e., the State Department had to approve foreign securities before U.S. citizens could invest in them)

ALSO:

- pledged that a Democratic administration would reduce the cost of the federal government by 25 percent and balance the budget

DEMOCRATIC PARTY
VOTE FOR PRESIDENTIAL NOMINATION:

Candidate	Ballot: 1	4
Roosevelt	666¼	945
Smith	201¼	190½
Garner	90¼	0
White	52	3
Traylor	42¼	0
Byrd	25	0
Reed	24	0
Ritchie	21	3½
Baker	8½	5½
Cox	0	1

Roosevelt was nominated on the fourth ballot.

FARMER LABOR PARTY

CANDIDATE FOR PRESIDENT:
Jacob Sechler Coxey (OH)

CANDIDATE FOR VICE PRESIDENT:
Julius J. Reiter (MN)

CONVENTION:
April 26–27, 1932, Omaha (NE)

PLATFORM HIGHLIGHTS:

SUPPORTED:

- aid for the unemployed
- a bonus for soldiers
- a five-year moratorium on foreclosures of real estate mortgages and refinancing of farm mortgages
- the refinancing of small consumer debts
- flood relief
- exclusion of all immigrants until after the depression
- social insurance programs to cover unemployment, old age, maternity, poverty, sickness, and accidents
- an end to the private ownership of banks

- issuance of sound money and free coinage of silver
- repayment of German reparations
- limitations on speculation
- initiation of a public works program including projects with a six-hour workday and a minimum wage of one dollar per hour
- public ownership of railroads and communications
- state and local ownership of public utilities
- abolition of child and convict labor
- taxation of excess profits
- increased taxes on incomes over $7,500 and inheritances
- elimination of tax exemptions on real property, other than homesteads, of a certain value and personal property up to $1,000
- independence for the Philippines within ten years and an isolationist stand against U.S. participation in the League of Nations and World Court
- a gradual reduction in tariffs, with certain exceptions such as oil and farm products
- the creation of a cabinet-level Department of National Defense and a buildup of the army and navy

FARMER LABOR PARTY
VOTE FOR PRESIDENTIAL AND VICE-PRESIDENTIAL NOMINATIONS: THE EXECUTIVE COMMITTEE REPLACED FRANK ELBRIDGE WEBB OF CALIFORNIA WITH COXEY ON JULY 10, 1932. REITER WAS NAMED TO REPLACE COXEY AS THE VICE-PRESIDENTIAL CANDIDATE.

JOBLESS PARTY

CANDIDATE FOR PRESIDENT:
James Renshaw Cox (PA)

CANDIDATE FOR VICE PRESIDENT:
Victor Clifford Tisdal (OK)

CONVENTION:
August 17, 1932, Crevecoeur Speedway, St. Louis (MO)

PLATFORM HIGHLIGHTS:

SUPPORTED:

- government issuance of currency and expenditures of $5 billion to create public works projects for unemployment relief
- immediate payment in cash of a bonus for soldiers
- enactment of unemployment insurance and an old age pension program
- federal control of the banking system
- government control of all public utilities (telephone, telegraph, electric power, gas, water, and railroads)
- a five-day work week and a six-hour workday
- revision of the Volstead Act to legalize light wines and beer
- a constitutional convention to pass on (i.e., consider repeal of) the Eighteenth Amendment

---

JOBLESS PARTY

VOTE FOR PRESIDENTIAL NOMINATION: COX WAS NOMINATED BY ACCLAMATION.

LIBERTY PARTY (WEBB GROUP)

CANDIDATE FOR PRESIDENT:
Frank Elbridge Webb (CA)

CANDIDATE FOR VICE PRESIDENT:
Otis L. Spurgeon (IA) (Andrae B. Nordskog [NE] declined)

CONVENTION:
July 1–6, 1932, Kansas City (MO)

PLATFORM HIGHLIGHTS:
SUPPORTED:
- government issuance of money and placement in circulation at service cost only
- national anti-usury laws
- government banks
- expansion of the currency to pay bonuses to soldiers and permit initiation of public works projects
- government supervision of public utilities
- laws against monopoly and chain purchasing
- strict enforcement of antitrust laws and restraint of trade laws
- the six-hour workday and wages "in keeping with income of industry"
- protection of investments and capital only when invested in the United States
- "retention and observance of the entire Constitution of the United States," thus opposing the repeal of prohibition

LIBERTY PARTY (HARVEY GROUP)

CANDIDATE FOR PRESIDENT:
William Hope Harvey (AR)

CANDIDATE FOR VICE PRESIDENT:
Francis Benjamin "Frank" Hemenway (WA) (Andrae B. Nordskog [NE] declined)

CONVENTION:
August 17, 1932, Monte Ne (AR)

This party split off from the Liberty Party that nominated Frank Elbridge Webb. Its platform consisted of 103 words, expressing opposition to usury and favoring repeal of all present financial laws.

PLATFORM HIGHLIGHTS:
SUPPORTED:
- government ownership of the banking system
- a five-year moratorium staying collection of all bonds, mortgages, and other debts, except those owed to poor people
- the printing of money by government with free silver coinage coordinated with paper money. (Silver coinage

and paper money were redeemable in service rendered by the government.)
- demonetarization of gold
- public ownership of all public service, such as public utilities, relating to the common good
- an end to taxation, assessors, and tax collectors
- tax-exemption of homesteads
- a referendum before war could be declared

NATIONAL PARTY

CANDIDATE FOR PRESIDENT:
John Zahnd (IN) (Seymour E. Allen [MA], declined)

CANDIDATE FOR VICE PRESIDENT:
Florence Garvin (RI)

CONVENTION:
June 26, 1932, Indianapolis (IN)

This party has variously been known as the Greenback Party, National Party, and National Independent Party. The platform called for an investigation of the Federal Reserve System and the Treasury Department.

PROHIBITION PARTY

CANDIDATE FOR PRESIDENT:
William David Upshaw

CANDIDATE FOR VICE PRESIDENT:
Frank Stewart Regan (IL)

CANDIDATES FOR PRESIDENTIAL NOMINATION:
William Edgar Borah (ID)
Henry Clay Needham (CA)
William David Upshaw (GA)

PRIMARY:
MAY 3, 1932 (CA):
Needham 5,274

16TH CONVENTION:
July 5–7, 1932, Cadle Tabernacle, Indianapolis (IN)
Clinton Norman Howard (NY), keynoter

Approximately three hundred delegates attended this convention. The Prohibition Party's platform opposed the growing sentiment for repealing the Eighteenth Amendment, blaming its failure on the willful "nullification" of enforcement by the two major parties.

PLATFORM HIGHLIGHTS:
SUPPORTED:
- federal purchase of state and local bonds
- creation of an economic council to consider such issues as regulation of the stock exchange and boards of trade; rehabilitation of the wage schedules and hours of labor; revision of tariff schedules, the banking system, industrial stabilization, and social relief measures such as governmental unemployment and social insurance proposals, and the revaluation of utilities

- elimination of tax loopholes
- a frugal government
- agricultural aid through use of the equalization fee
- conservation
- judiciary reform
- censorship of immoral and propagandistic motion pictures
- elimination of unjust ballot laws
- membership in the World Court
- reduction in armaments
- international arbitration
- free speech and free press
- abolition of child labor
- government ownership of public utilities

OPPOSED:

- counting aliens for purposes of representation in legislative bodies and making foreign representatives subject to U.S. prohibition laws

REPUBLICAN PARTY

CANDIDATE FOR PRESIDENT:

Herbert Clark Hoover

CANDIDATE FOR VICE PRESIDENT:

Charles Curtis

CANDIDATES FOR PRESIDENTIAL NOMINATION:

John James Blaine (WI)
Alan Bogue (SD)
Calvin Coolidge (MA)
Jacob Sechler Coxey (OH)
Charles Gates Dawes (IL)
Joseph Irwin France (MD)
Herbert Clark Hoover (CA)
Hiram Warren Johnson (CA)
George William Norris (NE)
James Wolcott Wadsworth (NY)

CANDIDATES FOR VICE-PRESIDENTIAL NOMINATION:

Hiram Bingham (CT)
James Joseph Couzens, Jr. (MI)
Charles Curtis (KS)
Charles Gates Dawes (IL)
Alvan Tufts Fuller (MA)
James Guthrie Harbord (NY)
Patrick Jay Hurley (NM)
Davis Sinton Ingalls (OH)
William Squire Kenyon (IA)
Hanford MacNider (IA)
Edward Martin (PA)
Jacob Leonard Replogle (NY)
Bertrand Hollis Snell (NY)

PRIMARIES:

MARCH 8, 1932 (NH):

unpledged 22,903

MARCH 15, 1932 (ND):

France 36,000
Coxey 25,000

APRIL 5, 1932 (WI):

Norris 139,514
Hoover 6,588

APRIL 12, 1932 (NE):

France 40,481
Hoover 13,934

APRIL 13, 1932 (IL):

France 345,498
Hoover 4,368
Dawes 129

APRIL 26, 1932 (MA):

unpledged delegates 57,534

APRIL 26, 1932 (PA):

France 352,092
Hoover 20,662
others 6,126

MAY 2, 1932 (MD):

Hoover 27,324
France 17,008
unpledged delegates 1,236

MAY 3, 1932 (CA):

Hoover 657,420

MAY 3, 1932 (SD):

Johnson 64,464
Bogue 35,133

MAY 10, 1932 (OH):

Coxey 75,844
France 44,853
Hoover 8,154

MAY 10, 1932 (WV):

France 88,005

MAY 17, 1932 (NJ):

France 141,330
Hoover 10,116

MAY 20, 1932 (OR):

France 72,681
Hoover 32,599

20TH CONVENTION

June 14–16, 1932, Chicago Stadium, Chicago (IL)
Lester Jesse Dickinson (IA), temporary chairman
Bertrand Hollis Snell (NY), permanent chairman

The Republican platform pledged to assist the people in achieving economic recovery and endorsed the president's modest loan program. Unemployment and relief were seen as state and local problems.

PLATFORM HIGHLIGHTS:

SUPPORTED:

- the gold standard
- economy in government
- bank reforms
- the convening of an international monetary conference to consider the position of silver

- a home loan discount system
- high tariffs imposed to protect farmers' markets.
- cooperative marketing
- disaster relief
- the achievements of the fledgling Federal Farm Board
- minor tariff adjustments
- adequate health care and compensation for veterans
- most-favored nation principle in foreign trade
- adherence to the Kellogg-Briand Pact as the proper course in dealing with China and Japan
- withdrawal from Haiti and Nicaragua
- U.S. membership in the World Court
- the London Naval Disarmament Treaty
- high wages
- shorter workdays and work weeks
- the stimulation of home building
- limitations on immigration
- the work of the Employment Service
- further development of the merchant marine
- construction of the Saint Lawrence Seaway
- continued highway development
- state efforts to stamp out gangsters, racketeers, and kidnappers
- warfare against drug traffic
- the civil service
- submission of a constitutional amendment to give states greater control over liquor traffic

- self-government for Alaska, Hawaii, and Puerto Rico
- the White House Conference on Child Health and Protection
- American Indian rights
- reorganization of the executive branch of government

OPPOSED:

- inflationary relief measures

ALSO:

- condemned the Democrats and their obstruction in the House of Representatives
- noted achievements of the Hoover administration in the fields of labor, transportation, utility regulation, and conservation
- pledged to continue to maintain equal opportunities and the rights of African Americans
- commended the administration's welfare work

SOCIALIST LABOR PARTY

CANDIDATE FOR PRESIDENT:
Verne L. Reynolds (NY)

CANDIDATE FOR VICE PRESIDENT:
John William Aiken (MA)

CONVENTION:
April 30-May 2, 1932, Cornish Arms Hotel, New York (NY)

The Socialist Labor Party's platform declared the failure of capitalism, asserting that "the capitalist system is now creaking and breaking in every joint and cranny. It is no more 'on trial' than a horse-drawn vehicle is on trial beside a powerful motor van." It reaffirmed its earlier platforms. Reform was condemned as a way of preserving capitalism. Instead, the party called for workers to unite at the polls and bring about the "Socialist or Industrial Commonwealth of Emancipated Labor."

REPUBLICAN PARTY
VOTE FOR PRESIDENTIAL NOMINATION:

Candidate	Ballot: 1
Hoover	1,126½
Blaine	13
Coolidge	4½
France	4
Dawes	1
Wadsworth	1

VOTE FOR VICE-PRESIDENTIAL NOMINATION:

Candidate	Ballot: 1
Curtis	634¼
MacNider	182¾
Harbord	161¾
Fuller	57
Snell	56
Replogle	23⅔
Couzens	11
Dawes	9¾
Ingalls	5
Hurley	2
Kenyon	2
Bingham	1
Martin	1
not voting	6¼

SOCIALIST LABOR PARTY
VOTE FOR PRESIDENTIAL NOMINATION: ERIC HASS OF NEW YORK WAS NOMINATED FOR PRESIDENT BUT DECLINED BECAUSE HE WAS BELOW THE CONSTITUTIONAL AGE REQUIREMENT. REYNOLDS WAS THEN SUBSTITUTED AT THE HEAD OF THE TICKET.

SOCIALIST PARTY

CANDIDATE FOR PRESIDENT:
Norman Mattoon Thomas (NY)

CANDIDATE FOR VICE PRESIDENT:
James Hudson Maurer (PA)

CONVENTION:
May 20–25, 1932, Municipal Auditorium, Milwaukee (WI)

The Socialist Party's platform predicted the imminent breakdown of the capitalist system.

PLATFORM HIGHLIGHTS:

SUPPORTED:

- transference of the principal industries to social ownership and democratic control
- unemployment relief, with a call for $10 billion to be appropriated for immediate relief and public works projects
- shorter workdays and a shorter work week
- free public employment agencies
- old age, health, maternity, workers' compensation, and unemployment programs
- abolition of child labor
- an adequate minimum wage
- government aid to prevent mortgage foreclosures
- government ownership of banking, postal, and other vital services
- steeply increased inheritance and income taxes
- taxation of government securities
- weather insurance for farmers
- land utilization boards
- promotion of cooperatives
- government takeovers of grain elevators, stockyards, packing houses, and warehouses
- increased rural road construction
- a shift from property taxes to income and excess profits taxes
- constitutional changes to permit proportional representation, direct election of the president and vice president, the initiative and referendum, simplified procedures for amending the Constitution, limitations on judicial review, passage of a Workers' Rights Amendment, and repeal of the Eighteenth Amendment
- the protection of civil liberties
- the abolition of injunctions in labor disputes
- the outlawing of "yellow-dog" contracts
- repeal of the espionage law
- restoration of the rights of those unjustly convicted under wartime laws
- modification of the immigration laws to make them more humane
- enactment of an antilynching law
- full rights for African Americans
- reduction in armaments
- abolition of conscription
- recognition of the Soviet Union
- cancellation of war debts
- U.S. participation in the World Court and League of Nations
- the creation of international economic organizations (with adequate representation of labor)
- the withdrawal of the military from China, Haiti, and Nicaragua
- the complete independence of the Philippines and the prohibition of munitions sales to foreign powers

---

SOCIALIST PARTY

VOTE FOR PRESIDENTIAL NOMINATION: THOMAS WAS UNANIMOUSLY NOMINATED FOR PRESIDENT.

VOTE FOR VICE-PRESIDENTIAL NOMINATION: AFTER META SCHLICHTING BERGER OF WISCONSIN DECLINED THE NOMINATION, MAURER WAS NOMINATED FOR VICE PRESIDENT.

GENERAL ELECTION SUMMARY FOR 1932

Candidate	Electoral Votes	States	Popular Votes
Roosevelt (D)	472	42	22,821,857
Hoover (R)	59	6	15,761,845
Thomas (SOC)	0	0	881,951
Foster (COM)	0	0	102,785
Upshaw (PROH)	0	0	81,869
Harvey (LIB)	0	0	53,425
Reynolds (SOC LAB)	0	0	33,276
Coxey (FAR)	0	0	7,309
Zahnd (NAT)	0	0	1,615
Cox (JOB)	0	0	726(PA)
Independent	0	0	533
Jacksonian	0	0	152
AZ Prog Dem	0	0	9
Populist	0	0	4
Webb (LIB [WEBB])	0	0	none recorded
unknown	0	0	130

ELECTION OF NOVEMBER 3, 1936

President
FRANKLIN DELANO ROOSEVELT
Vice President
JOHN NANCE GARNER

HIGHLIGHTS

The Depression was still in full swing, Adolf Hitler was in power in Germany, and domestic social agitation continued into the 1936 election cycle. Huey Pierce Long was hawking his "share-the-wealth" program and seemed a possible presidential contender until his assassination in 1935. Father Charles Edward Coughlin and Francis Townsend sold their particular political nostrums to ready audiences, eventually joining forces to sponsor a new Union Party. The incumbent president, Franklin Delano Roosevelt, had pursued a vigorous program of reform during his first term, including passage of a Social Security Act and repeal of the Eighteenth Amendment, but he had also suffered such setbacks as the Senate's failure to approve U.S. participation in the World Court. The Republicans, still reeling from the image of "Hoovervilles," turned to Governor Alf Landon of Kansas as their standard-bearer and hoped to take advantage of the president's presumed vulnerability. They took comfort in the postcard poll of the Literary Digest, which predicted a Landon victory, but the Republicans misread the signals, badly. Roosevelt's popularity overwhelmed Landon.

CHRISTIAN PARTY

CANDIDATE FOR PRESIDENT:
William Dudley Pelley (NC)

CANDIDATE FOR VICE PRESIDENT:
Willard W. Kemp (CA)

The Christian Party was the political arm of the fascist Silver Shirt movement, which was led by William Dudley Pelley.

COMMUNIST PARTY

CANDIDATE FOR PRESIDENT:
Earl Russell Browder (KS)

CANDIDATE FOR VICE PRESIDENT:
James William Ford (NY)

CONVENTION:
June 24–28, 1936, New York (NY)

The Communist platform proclaimed the New Deal a failure, pointing to the continuation of the Depression.

PLATFORM HIGHLIGHTS:
SUPPORTED:
- the opening of closed factories under government operation
- a guaranteed annual minimum wage
- equality for women
- a thirty-hour work week without reduction in pay
- vacation pay
- provision of unemployment, old age, and social security insurance, including health and maternity benefits
- expansion of public works projects
- benefits for veterans
- programs to aid youth
- relief for farmers from debts, taxes, and foreclosures
- a "soak-the-rich" tax policy and nationalization of the banking system
- a constitutional amendment to curb the powers of the Supreme Court
- full protection of civil liberties and labor reforms to outlaw company unions and employer coercion
- release of all political prisoners
- complete equality for African Americans
- restraint of Hitler's Germany, Italian fascism, and Japanese imperialism through coordinated economic measures by the League of Nations and the United States
- adoption of a U.S. peace plan in collaboration with the Soviet Union
- nationalization of the munitions industry
- nonrecognition of Japanese conquests in China and Manchuria and the Italian invasion of Ethiopia
- independence for Puerto Rico and other "oppressed nations"
- a coalition effort to defeat fascism

OPPOSED:
- crop destruction

- the sales and poll taxes
- anti-Semitism
- efforts to deport alien workers

DEMOCRATIC PARTY

CANDIDATE FOR PRESIDENT:
Franklin Delano Roosevelt

CANDIDATE FOR VICE PRESIDENT:
John Nance Garner (TX)

CANDIDATES FOR PRESIDENTIAL NOMINATION:
Henry Breckinridge (NY)
Charles Edward Coughlin (MI)
Joseph Alphonso Coutermarsh (NH)
John Nance Garner (TX)
John Steven McGroarty (CA)
Franklin Delano Roosevelt (NY)
Upton Sinclair (CA)
Alfred Emanuel Smith (NY)

PRIMARIES:

MARCH 10, 1936 (NH):
unpledged delegates 15,752

APRIL 7, 1936 (WI):
Roosevelt 401,773
Garner 108
Smith 46

APRIL 14, 1936 (IL):
Roosevelt 1,416,411
others 411

APRIL 14, 1936 (NE):
Roosevelt 139,743

APRIL 28, 1936 (MA):
Roosevelt 51,924
Smith 2,928
Coughlin 2,854
others 2,774

APRIL 28, 1936 (PA):
Roosevelt 720,309
Breckinridge 35,351

MAY 4, 1936 (MD):
Roosevelt 100,269
Breckinridge 18,150
unpledged delegates 1,739

MAY 5, 1936 (CA):
Roosevelt 790,235
Sinclair 106,068
McGroarty 61,391

MAY 5, 1936 (SD):
Roosevelt 48,262

MAY 12, 1936 (OH):
Roosevelt 514,366
Breckinridge 32,950

MAY 12, 1936 (WV):
Roosevelt 288,799
Coutermarsh 8,162

MAY 15, 1936 (OR):
Roosevelt 88,305
others 208

MAY 19, 1936 (NJ):
Breckinridge 49,956
Roosevelt 11,676

JUNE 6, 1936 (FL):
Roosevelt 242,906
Coutermarsh 27,982

27TH CONVENTION:
June 23–27, 1936, Convention Hall, Philadelphia (PA)
Alben William Barkley (KY), temporary chairman
Joseph Taylor Robinson (AR), permanent chairman

PLATFORM HIGHLIGHTS:
The 1936 Democratic platform was a brief recital of the accomplishments of President Roosevelt's first term, including the establishment of Social Security, rural electrification, bank reform, housing programs, and veterans' benefits. Farmers, industrial workers, youth, and businessmen were reminded of the Party's efforts on their behalf.

SUPPORTED:
- strong antitrust enforcement
- disaster and unemployment relief
- constitutional amendments to correct social ills
- the merit system
- protection of civil liberties and a sound currency
- reduction in government expenses
- decreases in tariffs to open the export market
- the "Good Neighbor" policy, promising to observe neutrality in other countries' disputes
- preparations to resist aggression against the United States

OPPOSED:
- monopolies

> **DEMOCRATIC PARTY**
> VOTE FOR PRESIDENTIAL NOMINATION: ROOSEVELT WAS RENOMINATED BY ACCLAMATION, AND NO VOTE WAS TAKEN.
>
> VOTE FOR VICE-PRESIDENTIAL NOMINATION: GARNER WAS ALSO RENOMINATED BY ACCLAMATION.

FARMER-LABOR PARTY

CANDIDATE FOR PRESIDENT:
Jacob Sechler Coxey (OH) (declined)

CONVENTION:
July 8–12, 1935, Castle Hotel, Omaha (NE)
Roy M. Harrop (NE), chairman

Thirty delegates from thirty states attended the convention. The party hoped to nominate Sen. Huey Pierce Long for president, but he did not express interest in its endorsement.

PLATFORM HIGHLIGHTS:

SUPPORTED:

- a share-the-wealth program
- federally guaranteed employment
- a minimum annual wage of $2,500 and a home, radio, and automobile for everyone—all tax exempt
- an annuity of $100 per month for all qualified voters forty-five years of age and older and to those physically unfit over twenty-one years old
- full legal tender currency
- abolition of the sales tax
- government ownership of the banks, railroads, telephone and telegraph systems, electric power, and natural resources
- a reduction in government bureaucracy

NATIONAL GREENBACK PARTY

CANDIDATE FOR PRESIDENT:
John Zahnd (IN)

CANDIDATE FOR VICE PRESIDENT:
Florence Garvin (RI)

CONVENTION:
April 6, 1936, Indianapolis (IN)

This party was formerly the National Independent Party and was renamed in 1934. The Greenback Party's platform called for the inflationary printing of paper money as full legal tender for debts.

PROHIBITION PARTY

CANDIDATE FOR PRESIDENT:
David Leigh Colvin

CANDIDATE FOR VICE PRESIDENT:
Claude Alonzo Watson

CANDIDATES FOR PRESIDENTIAL NOMINATION:
Roland Casad (CA)
David Leigh Colvin (NY)
Harley Walter Kidder (VT)

CANDIDATES FOR VICE-PRESIDENTIAL NOMINATION:
Claude Alonzo Watson (CA)
Alvin Cullum York (TN)

17TH CONVENTION:
May 5–7, 1936, Niagara Falls (NY)
Harold C. Mason, permanent chairman

PLATFORM HIGHLIGHTS:

SUPPORTED:

- international arbitration to settle disputes
- tax reduction and elimination of exemptions

- diminished crime through better law enforcement, reform of the judicial system, rallying public pressure, and cutting off traffic in alcohol and narcotics
- enactment of an old age pension system
- public responsibility for aiding the unemployed
- a better system for distributing economic goods (but offered no specifics)
- a sound currency and elimination of the Federal Reserve System's right to issue money
- movie censorship

OPPOSED:

- the repeal of the Eighteenth Amendment and sought to unite the opponents of liquor traffic for its complete suppression
- gambling and lotteries
- communism and fascism

PROHIBITION PARTY
VOTE FOR PRESIDENTIAL NOMINATION:

Candidate	Ballot: 1
Colvin	unknown
Kidder	unknown
Casad	unknown

VOTE FOR VICE-PRESIDENTIAL NOMINATION: YORK WAS NOMINATED FOR VICE PRESIDENT BUT DECLINED. THE EXECUTIVE COMMITTEE THEN SUBSTITUTED WATSON FOR THE SECOND PLACE ON THE TICKET.

REPUBLICAN PARTY

CANDIDATE FOR PRESIDENT:
Alfred Mossman Landon

CANDIDATE FOR VICE PRESIDENT:
Frank Knox

CANDIDATES FOR PRESIDENTIAL NOMINATION:
William Edgar Borah (ID)
Leo Jeannot Chassee (WI)
Stephen Albion Day (OH)
Warren Everett Green (SD)
Herbert Clark Hoover (CA)
Frank Knox (IL)
Alfred Mossman Landon (KS)
Earl Warren (CA)

CANDIDATES FOR VICE-PRESIDENTIAL NOMINATION:
Walter Evans Edge (NJ)
Frank Knox (IL)
Arthur W. Little (NY)
Harry Whinna Nice (MD)

PRIMARIES:

MARCH 10, 1936 (NH):
    unpledged delegates 32,992

APRIL 7, 1936 (WI):
    Borah 187,334
    Landon 3,360

APRIL 14, 1936 (IL):
    Knox 491,575
    Borah 419,220
    Landon 3,775
    others 205

APRIL 14, 1936 (NE):
    Borah. 70,240
    Landon 23,117
    others 973

APRIL 28, 1936 (MA):
    Landon 76,862
    Hoover 7,276
    Borah. 4,259
    Knox 1,987
    others 5,032

APRIL 28, 1936 (PA):
    Borah 459,982

MAY 5, 1936 (CA):
    Warren 350,917
    Landon 260,170

MAY 5, 1936 (SD):
    Green 44,518
    Borah. 44,261

MAY 12, 1936 (OH):
    Day 155,732
    Landon 11,015

MAY 12, 1936 (WV):
    Borah 105,855
    Chassee. 18,986

MAY 15, 1936 (OR):
    Borah. 91,949
    Landon 4,467
    others 5,557

MAY 19, 1936 (NJ):
    Landon 347,142
    Borah. 91,052

21ST CONVENTION:
    June 9–12, 1936, Municipal Auditorium, Cleveland
      (OH)
    Frederick Steiwer (OR), temporary chairman
    Bertrand Hollis Snell (NY), permanent chairman

The Republicans charged the New Deal with dishonoring U.S. traditions by permitting the president to usurp congressional powers and by attacking free enterprise. It argued that states' rights and civil liberties had been violated.

PLATFORM HIGHLIGHTS:
SUPPORTED:

- maintenance of the U.S. system of constitutional and local self-government and respect for the integrity of the judiciary
- preservation of free enterprise
- removal of restrictions on production, encouragement of legitimate business, elimination of government competition with private business, and abandonment of New Deal policies that prevent reemployment
- the return of relief efforts to the local level, supported by federal grants-in-aid
- separation of public works from relief efforts and redirection of public works to those of merit
- a pay-as-you-go program of old age benefits, with matching federal and state contributions derived from a direct tax
- state laws to abolish sweatshops and child labor
- protection of women and children in the work force
- a land use program for farmers
- flood prevention, reforestation, and conservation
- experimental aid to farmers for developing new crops
- industrial use of farm products by applied science
- soil-building programs
- restrictions on competitive imports of agricultural products
- quarantine of imported livestock and other farm products when necessary to ensure health and sanitary standards
- liberalized farm credit
- cooperatives
- disaster relief
- tariff reforms
- repeal of the Reciprocal Trade Agreement Law and restoration of the principle of the flexible tariff
- restoration of the civil service
- controls on government spending, a balanced budget, and tax revision
- a sound currency without devaluation of the dollar
- disarmament but with an "adequate" national defense
- the Bill of Rights and equal opportunity extended to "our colored citizens"
- amelioration of the living conditions of American Indians
- construction of headwater storage basins to prevent floods
- adequate compensation for veterans and full collection of war debts
- government regulation of securities and interstate public utilities
- international arbitration to settle disputes

OPPOSED:

- the Social Security Trust Fund as endangering the security of the people "because the fund will contain nothing but the government's promise to pay" and not cover white-collar, agricultural, and domestic service workers.

- monopolies
- membership in the League of Nations and World Court
- legislation that discriminated against women in federal and state employment

---

REPUBLICAN PARTY
Vote for Presidential Nomination:

Candidate	Ballot: 1
Landon	984
Borah	19

Vote for Vice-Presidential Nomination: Edge, Little, and Nice were offered to the convention as potential vice-presidential candidates, but each withdrew. Accordingly, Knox was unanimously nominated for vice president.

SOCIALIST LABOR PARTY

CANDIDATE FOR PRESIDENT:
John William Aiken (MA)

CANDIDATE FOR VICE PRESIDENT:
Emil F. Teichert (NY)

CONVENTION:
April 25–28, 1936, Cornish Arms Hotel, New York (NY)

The Socialist Labor Party's platform asserted that the capitalist system has "outlived its usefulness." It called for creation of an Industrial Union government, claiming "the hour of Social Revolution has struck." It also denounced the New Deal reforms as "concealed measures of reaction." After extensive Marxist analysis of economic conditions, the platform urged all workers to organize into Socialist Revolutionary Industrial unions to bring about needed change in the social order.

SOCIALIST PARTY

CANDIDATE FOR PRESIDENT:
Norman Mattoon Thomas (NY)

CANDIDATE FOR VICE PRESIDENT:
George A. Nelson (WI)

CANDIDATES FOR VICE-PRESIDENTIAL NOMINATION:
Mary Donovan Hapgood (IN)
Powers Hapgood (IN)
Leo Krzycki (WI)
George A. Nelson (WI)

CONVENTION:
May 22–26, 1936, Municipal Auditorium, Cleveland (OH)
Leo Krzycki (WI), chairman

The Socialist Party's platform pointed to the failure of the "Old Deal" under the Republicans and the New Deal under the Democrats. It asserted that capitalism meant insecurity for workers, that it sowed the seeds of dictatorship and ultimately brought war in its wake, and that socialism provided the only solution.

PLATFORM HIGHLIGHTS:
Supported:

- constitutional limits on the Supreme Court and a constitutional amendment to streamline the amendment process itself
- social ownership and democratic control of mines, railroads, power, and other key industries
- an extensive relief program of public works at union wages
- inauguration of a public housing program
- a federal system of unemployment and old age insurance
- adequate medical care for the sick and injured
- passage of an American Youth Act to meet the immediate educational and economic needs of young people
- adequate federal support for public schools and free city colleges
- abolition of the Civilian Conservation Corps and the National Youth Administration
- a drastic increase in taxes for higher income brackets and experimentation with land-value taxation
- a thirty-hour work week
- abolition of the labor injunction
- prohibition of company unions
- an end to repressive tactics by employers
- cooperative and family farms
- agricultural price stabilization
- crop insurance and easier government credit
- civil liberties and full equality for African Americans
- enactment of an antilynching law
- neutrality
- recognition for the Soviet Union
- the consumer cooperative movement

Opposed:

- corporate and tenant farming
- all forms of militarism

SOCIALIST PARTY
Vote for Presidential Nomination: Thomas was nominated by acclamation.

UNION PARTY

CANDIDATE FOR PRESIDENT:
William Lemke (ND)

CANDIDATE FOR VICE PRESIDENT:
Thomas Charles O'Brien (MA)

CONVENTION:
June 19, 1936

The Union Party was created by the merger of several social protest movements, including remnants of the share-the-wealth effort, the Townsend Plan clubs, followers of Father Charles Edward Coughlin and Gerald Lyman Kenneth Smith, and advocates of monetary reform. The Union Party's platform espoused an isolationist perspective. It also emphasized congressional, rather than presidential, leadership.

PLATFORM HIGHLIGHTS:

SUPPORTED:

- congressional coinage and issuance of money through a central bank
- retirement of all indebtedness of the federal government and refinanced home agricultural mortgage indebtedness through an inflated currency
- an assured annual living wage
- production at profit for the farmer
- reasonable and decent security for the aged
- protection from foreign money manipulation
- an "adequate and perfect defense" while restricting the use of the military to defense of domestic shores
- the civil service
- the "ruthless eradication of bureaucracies"
- institution of federal conservation projects to create jobs and to control monopolies in the interests of small industries and private enterprise
- protection of private property from confiscation through taxation
- a confiscatory tax on net incomes above a certain amount
- the creation of opportunities for young people to earn a decent living after completing their education

GENERAL ELECTION SUMMARY FOR 1936			
Candidate	Electoral Votes	States	Popular Votes
Roosevelt (D)	523	46	27,476,673
Landon (R)	8	2	16,679,583
Lemke (UNI)	0	0	892,793
Thomas (SOC)	0	0	187,720
Browder (COM)	0	0	80,159
Colvin (PROH)	0	0	37,847
Aiken (SOC LAB)	0	0	12,777
Independent Republican	0	0	3,222
Pelley (CHR)	0	0	1,598
unknown	0	0	358

ELECTION OF NOVEMBER 5, 1940

President
FRANKLIN DELANO ROOSEVELT
Vice President
HENRY AGARD WALLACE

HIGHLIGHTS

By 1940, the war in Europe was pressing in on U.S. neutrality. As Franklin D. Roosevelt moved closer to supporting Great Britain, Republicans began charging him with "warmongering." The two-term tradition for chief executives encouraged would-be Democratic successors to the president to step forward and test the waters, including Vice President John Nance Garner and James Aloysius Farley. The president's decision to seek a third term effectively squelched other Democratic candidacies, while giving the Republicans a campaign issue. The Grand Old Party had a number of such tested aspirants as Thomas Edmund Dewey, Robert Alphonso Taft, and one surprise candidate, Wendell Lewis Willkie. A former Democrat who had never held public office, Willkie broke the convention deadlock between Dewey and Taft and surged to victory on the sixth ballot. While he was an attractive and progressive candidate, Willkie was no match for the politically skilled Roosevelt. Despite the defection of conservative and anti-third term Democrats, Roosevelt overcame a highly charged emotional campaign against him and swamped his Republican rival.

COMMUNIST (WORKERS) PARTY

CANDIDATE FOR PRESIDENT:
Earl Russell Browder (KS)

CANDIDATE FOR VICE PRESIDENT:
James William Ford (NY)

CONVENTION:
May 30 and June 1–2, 1940, Royal Windsor Hotel, New York (NY)

The Communist platform strongly opposed U.S. involvement in the European war, claiming that Wall Street favored intervention. It reflected the about-face of the Soviet Union in 1939 that aligned Adolf Hitler and Joseph Stalin in a nonaggression pact. All other parties and unions were denounced for "war-mongering." The Communists cited the failure of the New Deal and offered a "People's Program" as an alternative.

PLATFORM HIGHLIGHTS:
SUPPORTED:
- full rights for African Americans
- the defeat of imperialism
- independence for the Philippines and Puerto Rico
- a halt to anti-Soviet policies
- democratization of the military
- protection of civil rights
- elimination of the poll tax
- enactment of an antilynching bill

- abolition of the Dies Committee and repeal of anti-alien and sedition laws
- curbs on monopolies
- a thirty-hour work week and higher wages
- a federal housing program
- extension of unemployment insurance to domestic and agricultural workers
- federal health and maternity insurance
- free education for all through federal aid to schools
- prohibitions against seizure of farm land and livestock
- a homestead tax exemption and heavier taxes on large farms
- drought relief
- tenant rehabilitation
- soil conservation
- a ten-year farm debt moratorium
- expansion of the National Youth Administration and Civilian Conservation Corps
- enactment of the American Youth Act
- prosecution of trusts and monopolies
- imposition of an excess profits tax and a steeply graduated income tax
- abolition of all consumption taxes and exemptions on securities
- repeal of new tax laws hitting low-income groups

ALSO:
- urged workers to unite around a national farmer-labor party to ensure the victory of communism

DEMOCRATIC PARTY

CANDIDATE FOR PRESIDENT:
Franklin Delano Roosevelt

CANDIDATE FOR VICE PRESIDENT:
Henry Agard Wallace

CANDIDATES FOR PRESIDENTIAL NOMINATION:
Harlan C. Allen (WV)
Willis Allen (CA)
William Brockman Bankhead (AL)
James Aloysius Farley (NY)
John Nance Garner (TX)
Cordell Hull (TN)
Ellis Ellwood Patterson (CA)
Franklin Delano Roosevelt (NY)
Charles Sawyer (OH)
Millard Evelyn Tydings (MD)

CANDIDATES FOR VICE-PRESIDENTIAL NOMINATION:
Alva Blanchard Adams (CO)
William Brockman Bankhead (AL)
Alben William Barkley (KY)
Prentiss Marsh Brown (MI)
James Aloysius Farley (NY)
Louis Arthur Johnson (WV)
Jesse Holman Jones (TX)
Scott Wike Lucas (IL)
Paul Vories McNutt (IN)
Joseph Christopher O'Mahoney (WY)
Bascom Timmons (TX)
Henry Agard Wallace (IA)
David Ignatius Walsh (MA)

PRIMARIES:

MARCH 12, 1940 (NH):
unpledged delegates 10,501

APRIL 2, 1940 (WI):
Roosevelt 322,991
Garner. 105,662

APRIL 9, 1940 (IL):
Roosevelt. 1,176,531
Garner. 190,801
others 35

APRIL 9, 1940 (NE):
Roosevelt 111,902

APRIL 23, 1940 (PA):
Roosevelt 724,657

APRIL 30, 1940 (MA):
Farley 76,919

MAY 5, 1940 (SD):
unpledged delegates 27,636

MAY 7, 1940 (AL):
Bankhead 196,508

MAY 7, 1940 (CA):
Roosevelt 723,782

Garner. 114,594
Allen. 90,718
Patterson. 48,337

MAY 14, 1940 (OH):
Sawyer. 283,952

MAY 14, 1940 (WV):
Allen. 102,729

MAY 17, 1940 (OR):
Roosevelt 109,913
Garner. 15,584
others 601

MAY 21, 1940 (NJ):
Roosevelt 34,278

28TH CONVENTION:
July 15–18, 1940, Chicago Stadium, Chicago (IL)
William Brockman Bankhead (AL), temporary
    chairman
Alben William Barkley (KY), permanent chairman

The Democratic platform of 1940 enumerated the achievements of the Roosevelt administration. It lauded Roosevelt's efforts to keep the United States out of the war, while asserting that democracy must be strengthened against aggression.

PLATFORM HIGHLIGHTS:
SUPPORTED:
- destruction of antidemocratic and un-American forces in the country and preparedness in the interests of national defense
- material aid to threatened democracies
- the preservation of the "ever-normal granary" for farmers
- expansion of domestic consumption of surpluses through school lunch, food-stamp and cotton-stamp plans, and low-cost milk programs
- expansion of rural electrification
- initiatives to preserve the family farm and to ensure equitable returns on farm investment
- continued and extended pro-labor policies
- extension of Social Security to uncovered workers
- continuation of unemployment relief programs
- improvements in health care through cooperative efforts
- strong programs to enable young people to complete their education and achieve meaningful employment
- slum clearance and low-rent housing
- fair treatment for veterans
- creation of an American Indian Claims Commission
- extension of the civil service system
- protection of consumers against price increases resulting from speculation
- continued progress toward complete equality for African Americans
- self-government for Alaska, Hawaii, and Puerto Rico
- offering the right to vote for president to the District of Columbia

- policies to promote the development of western mining and other natural resources

OPPOSED:
- any effort to restore private power monopolies
- censorship of radio

DEMOCRATIC PARTY
VOTE FOR PRESIDENTIAL NOMINATION:

Candidate	Ballot: 1
Roosevelt	946$^{13}\!/_{30}$
Farley	72$^{9}\!/_{10}$
Garner	61
Tydings	9½
Hull	5⅔

Roosevelt's nomination was made by acclamation.

VOTE FOR VICE-PRESIDENTIAL NOMINATION:

Candidate	Ballot: 1
Wallace	627$^{7}\!/_{10}$
Bankhead	328⅔
McNutt	66$^{19}\!/_{30}$
Adams	11½
Farley	7⅙
Jones	5$^{9}\!/_{10}$
O'Mahoney	3
Barkley	2
Johnson	1
Brown	1
Timmons	1
Lucas	1
Walsh	½
not voting	40½

Secretary of Agriculture Wallace was the president's choice for the vice-presidential nomination, but insurgents insisted on presenting other names.

GREENBACK PARTY
CANDIDATE FOR PRESIDENT:
John Zahnd (IN) [Anna Thomsen Milburn (WA), declined]

CANDIDATE FOR VICE PRESIDENT:
James Elmer Yates (AZ)

CONVENTION:
July 4, 1940, Indianapolis (IN)

INDEPENDENT
CANDIDATE FOR PRESIDENT:
Alfred Knutson (ND)

Alfred Knutson was an organizer for the Communist Party in agricultural regions.

PROHIBITION PARTY
CANDIDATE FOR PRESIDENT:
Roger Ward Babson (MA)

CANDIDATE FOR VICE PRESIDENT:
Edgar Vaughn Moorman

CANDIDATES FOR VICE-PRESIDENTIAL NOMINATION:
Enoch Arden Holtwick (IL)
Edgar Vaughn Moorman (IL)
Sam Morris (TX)
Claude Alonzo Watson (CA)

18TH CONVENTION:
May 8–10, 1940, Chicago (IL)

The Prohibition Party's platform was a short document that emphasized the moral principles of integrity, industry, self-control, initiative, adesire to be of service, and a willingness to make sacrifices. It called for prohibition of alcoholic beverages, narcotics, gambling, indecent publications and movies, deceptive radio advertising, political graft, and "injustices of all kinds." The party pledged itself to purify government, reduce debt and taxation, conserve natural resources, aid farmers, encourage employers and workers, and limit immigration of "unfit" persons. It sought an adequate national defense, maintenance of friendly relations abroad, equitable immigration and tariff laws, aid to worthy youth and the aged, and tolerance for all. Finally, it claimed to be a coalition party and invited all church people and others who stood for righteousness to join their effort.

PROHIBITION PARTY
VOTE FOR PRESIDENTIAL NOMINATION: BABSON WAS UNANIMOUSLY CHOSEN AS THE PRESIDENTIAL CANDIDATE ON THE FIRST BALLOT.

VOTE FOR VICE-PRESIDENTIAL NOMINATION: WATSON AND HOLTWICK DECLINED THEIR NOMINATIONS, AND MORRIS'S NAME WAS WITHDRAWN. ACCORDINGLY, MOORMAN WAS NOMINATED FOR VICE PRESIDENT BY ACCLAMATION.

REPUBLICAN PARTY
CANDIDATE FOR PRESIDENT:
Wendell Lewis Willkie

CANDIDATE FOR VICE PRESIDENT:
Charles Linza McNary

CANDIDATES FOR PRESIDENTIAL NOMINATION:
John William Bricker (OH)
Henry Styles Bridges (NH)

Harlan John Bushfield (SD)
Arthur Capper (KS)
Raymond M. Davis (WV)
Thomas Edmund Dewey (NY)
Frank Ernest Gannett (NY)
Herbert Clark Hoover (CA)
Arthur Horace James (PA)
Joseph William Martin (MA)
Charles Linza McNary (OR)
Franklin Delano Roosevelt (NY)
Jerrold Lauderdale Seawell (CA)
Robert Alphonso Taft (OH)
Arthur Hendrick Vandenberg (MI)
Wendell Lewis Willkie (NY)

CANDIDATES FOR VICE-PRESIDENTIAL NOMINATION:
Henry Styles Bridges (NH)
Charles Linza McNary (OR)
Dewey Short (MO)

PRIMARIES:
MARCH 12, 1940 (NH):
unpledged delegates 34,616

APRIL 2, 1940 (WI):
Dewey 70,168
Vandenberg. 26,182
Taft 341

APRIL 9, 1940 (IL):
Dewey 977,225
others 552

APRIL 9, 1940 (NE):
Dewey 102,915
Vandenberg. 71,798

APRIL 23, 1940 (PA):
Dewey 52,661
Roosevelt 8,294
James. 8,172
Taft 5,213
Vandenberg. 2,384
Hoover 1,082
Willkie 707
others 463

APRIL 30, 1940 (MA):
unpledged delegates 98,975

MAY 5, 1940 (SD):
unpledged delegates 52,566

MAY 6, 1940 (MD):
Dewey 54,802

MAY 7, 1940 (CA):
Seawell 538,112

MAY 14, 1940 (OH):
Taft 510,025
Dewey 2,059
Bricker 188
Vandenberg 83

Willkie 53
others 69

MAY 14, 1940 (WV):
Davis. 106,123

MAY 17, 1940 (OR):
McNary. 133,488
Dewey 5,190
Taft 254
Willkie 237
Vandenberg 36

MAY 21, 1940 (NJ):
Dewey 340,734
Willkie 20,143
Roosevelt 1,202
Taft 595
Vandenberg 168

22ND CONVENTION:
June 24–28, 1940, Convention Hall, Philadelphia
   (PA)
Harold Edward Stassen (MN), temporary chairman
   and keynoter
Joseph William Martin, Jr.(MA), permanent chair-
man

The Republican platform recited the failures of the Roosevelt administration. It stressed the need for a strong national defense, claiming "the zero hour is here." At the
same time, it expressed opposition to involving the nation
in a foreign war.

PLATFORM HIGHLIGHTS:
SUPPORTED:
• efforts to put idle workers back on the job
• removal of waste and politics from relief work by turning programs over to the states
• organization of Social Security on a pay-as-you-go basis
• extension of unemployment compensation
• amendment of the National Labor Relations Act
• incentive payments and adequate credit for U.S. farmers
• protection of farm prices by tariffs and quarantines
• institution of a national land-use program reclamation
• conservation and disaster assistance
• price stabilization
• congressional control over the issuance of money
• repeal of the Thomas Inflation Amendment of 1933
  and the (foreign) Silver Purchase Act of 1934
• tax revision, regulation of securities, retirement of the
  national debt, and restraint in public spending
• submission of an Equal Rights Amendment to the
  states
• elimination of discrimination in the civil service and
  military
• enactment of laws to curb mob violence
• immigration controls to exclude undesirable aliens
  from entering the country

- adequate compensation for veterans
- settlement of American Indian claims
- statehood for Puerto Rico and the fullest home rule for Hawaii
- private enterprise through a pledge to confine government activity to essential public services
- control of monopolies, including government monopolies
- federal regulation of radio but subject to the principles of free press and free speech
- support for small businesses, regulation of stock and commodity exchanges, and government reorganization to achieve greater efficiency and restore the system of checks and balances
- a constitutional amendment to limit presidents to two terms, implicitly denouncing Roosevelt's proposed third term

Opposed:

- reciprocal trade agreements in favor of protective tariffs
- the New Deal's tolerance of subversive elements in the government, pledging to "get rid of such borers from within"
- New Deal efforts to destroy private insurance institutions

REPUBLICAN PARTY
Vote for Presidential Nomination:

Candidate	Ballot: 1	6
Dewey	360	11
Taft	189	318
Willkie	105	655
Vandenberg	76	0
James	74	0
Martin	44	0
Gannett	33	0
Bridges	28	0
Capper	18	0
Hoover	17	10
McNary	13	1
Bushfield	9	0
not voting	0	4

Vote for Vice-Presidential Nomination:

Candidate	Ballot: 1
McNary	890
Short	108
Bridges	2

SOCIALIST LABOR PARTY

CANDIDATE FOR PRESIDENT:
John William Aiken (MA)

CANDIDATE FOR VICE PRESIDENT:
Aaron M. Orange (NY)

CONVENTION:
April 27–30, 1940, Chelsea Arms Hotel, New York (NY)

The Socialist Labor Party platform reiterated its traditional claim that capitalism cannot be reformed and must be ended. It recited a litany of social ills caused by capitalism. It also argued, "The long anticipated war is now an irrevocable fact." The platform called for political and economic organization of the working class under the banners of the Socialist Labor Party and the Socialist Industrial Union. Only then, it maintained, could an Industrial Union Congress be formed and a government of the Socialist Republic be achieved.

SOCIALIST PARTY

CANDIDATE FOR PRESIDENT:
Norman Mattoon Thomas (NY)

CANDIDATE FOR VICE PRESIDENT:
Maynard Clare Krueger (IL)

CONVENTION:
April 6–8, 1940, National Press Club Auditorium, Washington, DC

Announcing that "we take our stand," the Socialist platform claimed credit for "the best of what goes by the New Deal name." But, the document pointed out, immediate reforms were not enough. Fundamental changes—social ownership and democratic control of industry—were needed to cure the problems caused by capitalism. The party steadfastly refused to endorse the impending war, even as it denounced totalitarianism. It criticized Russia for imposing a "new form of slavery" on its people and asserted that true socialism meant the extension of civil liberties and political democracy to all.

PLATFORM HIGHLIGHTS:
Supported:

- reductions in military expenditures and diversion of the funds saved into public works projects
- expansion of many of Roosevelt's programs, including the Civilian Conservation Corps (CCC), National Youth Administration (NYA), and Works Projects Administration (WPA)
- extension of unemployment and old age benefits
- new programs providing health and disability insurance
- aid for education
- soil conservation
- better management of farm surpluses
- improvements in the lives of African Americans and tenant farmers
- camp relief and resettlement for migrant workers
- abolition of absentee landlordism

- full economic and civil rights for civil service employees
- collective bargaining
- an increase in the minimum wage
- taxation of securities
- increased graduated income and inheritance taxes to finance government functions
- taxation of unimproved real estate to discourage speculation and a reduction in the assessed valuation of slum land
- a capital levy to reduce the national debt
- self-government for the District of Columbia, with its citizens granted a voice in national elections
- generous treatment of political refugees
- civil liberties
- the underground in Germany
- withdrawal of U.S. economic influence in Latin America

OPPOSED:

- the application of antitrust laws against unions
- consumption taxes
- state duties or fees that restricted free trade within the country

- the current fiscal system, which relied on gold and silver purchases
- discrimination against African Americans and Jews and other forms of bigotry

ALSO:

- endorsed the cooperative movement and invited labor, youth, and farmers to join its efforts to change the nation
- concluded with a resolution adopted on April 7, 1940, which asserted that the first demand of the American people should be "Keep America Out of War!" Despite their hostility toward Hitler, the Socialists argued that his defeat would not be a victory for democracy unless fascism and the war system were both destroyed. And, in their view, if the United States entered the war, it would become a military dictatorship, thus destroying the very democracy it sought to preserve.

SOCIALIST PARTY
VOTE FOR PRESIDENTIAL NOMINATION: THOMAS WAS NOMINATED UNANIMOUSLY ON THE FIRST BALLOT.

GENERAL ELECTION SUMMARY FOR 1940			
Candidate	Electoral Votes	States	Popular Votes
Roosevelt (D)	449	38	27,243,466
Willkie (R)	82	10	22,304,755
California Progs	0	0	166,506
Thomas (S)	0	0	99,557
Babson (PROH)	0	0	57,812
Browder (COM)	0	0	46,251
Georgia Ind Dems	0	0	22,428
Aiken (SOC LAB)	0	0	14,186
Mississippi Ind Reps	0	0	4,550
Knutson (I)	0	0	545
Independent	0	0	108
Zahnd (GRE)	0	0	not on ballot
unknown	0	0	5,701

ELECTION OF NOVEMBER 7, 1944

President
FRANKLIN DELANO ROOSEVELT
Vice President
HARRY S. TRUMAN

HIGHLIGHTS

Since the election of 1940, World War II had overtaken the United States. Even former isolationists rallied in response to the Japanese attack on Pearl Harbor and criticism of foreign policy became muted. Roosevelt was the commander in chief, and as such, he benefited politically from the nation's unified defense against Axis aggression. Nonetheless, the Republicans gained significantly in the mid-term congressional elections. Three Republican governors emerged as leading contenders for the 1944 nomination: John Bricker of Ohio, Thomas Edmund Dewey of New York, and Harold Edward Stassen of Minnesota (who had joined the navy). Wendell Willkie had faded from the scene, and Gen. Douglas MacArthur's trial balloon fizzled by April 1944. When the Republican convention assembled at the end of June 1944, only Bricker remained to challenge the favored Dewey. Dewey offered the vice-presidential nomination to Bricker, who endorsed his opponent and joined the ticket. On the Democratic side, Roosevelt's renomination was never in doubt despite a threatened bolt by southern Democrats. Vice President Henry Wallace had many enemies, however, and his fate was less certain as the Democratic convention opened. Roosevelt expressed a preference for Wallace but indicated he would accept the convention's choice for his running mate. His position was interpreted as a signal for the successful effort to recruit Harry S. Truman for the second spot. The Communist Party, which dissolved in May 1944 and reformed as the Communist Political Association, decided to sit out the 1944 contest. Indeed, there was little third-party activity of any kind in the fall campaign. And the "battle" between Dewey and Roosevelt turned out to be relatively mild. With the war taking its physical toll on the president, his legendary exuberant campaign style became more wearied in 1944, consisting largely of a few dinner addresses and three public speeches. In the end, voters decided not to "swap horses in the middle of the stream." Roosevelt was reelected to his fourth term by a landslide.

AMERICA FIRST PARTY

CANDIDATE FOR PRESIDENT:
Gerald Lyman Kenneth Smith

CANDIDATE FOR VICE PRESIDENT:
Henry A. Romer

CANDIDATES FOR PRESIDENTIAL NOMINATION:
Charles Augustus Lindbergh (MN)
Douglas MacArthur
Robert Rutherford McCormick (IL)
Gerald Prentice Nye (ND)
Robert Rice Reynolds (NC)
Gerald Lyman Kenneth Smith (MI)

CANDIDATES FOR VICE-PRESIDENTIAL NOMINATION:
Eddie Vernon Rickenbacker (OH)
Henry A. Romer (OH)

CONVENTION:
August 30, 1944, Detroit (MI)

The America First Party was created at a convention in Detroit (MI) on January 10, 1943. Composed of nationalists, isolationists, and remnants of the defunct America First Committee, it was strongly anti-Communist, anti-Semitic, and Anglophobic.

PLATFORM HIGHLIGHTS:
SUPPORTED:
• "food before whiskey"
• bonuses for veterans
• deportation of aliens
• increases in the domestic standard of living before providing foreign aid to other nations
• investigation of the Lend-Lease program
• a halt to immigration
• absorption of Canada into the United States, the purchase of Greenland, and acceptance of strategic Pacific islands as payment for war debts

- the so-called Abraham Lincoln Plan to create an African "homeland" for U.S. African Americans, with incentives for African American emigration

OPPOSED:
- entangling alliances abroad
- "bureaucratic fascism" at home

ALSO:
- singled out Henry Wallace and Bernard Baruch for criticism because of their alleged sympathies for left-wing causes

---

AMERICA FIRST PARTY

VOTE FOR THE PRESIDENTIAL NOMINATION: THE PARTY INITIALLY PROPOSED THE NOMINATION OF LINDBERGH FOR PRESIDENT AND RICKENBACKER FOR VICE PRESIDENT, BUT NEITHER MAN EXPRESSED ANY INTEREST. SMITH, THE PARTY'S FOUNDER, THEN TURNED TO NYE, WHO ALSO DECLINED. SO, TOO, DID MACARTHUR, MCCORMICK, AND REYNOLDS. FINALLY, SMITH RAN HIMSELF, AND HE WAS NOMINATED AT A PRELIMINARY NOMINATING CONVENTION IN DETROIT ON JUNE 31, 1944. SMITH WAS UNANIMOUSLY RENOMINATED AT THE SECOND "NATIONAL" CONVENTION ON AUGUST 30.

COMMUNIST PARTY

CONVENTION:
May 19–22, 1944, Riverside Plaza Hotel, New York (NY)

No candidates were nominated, though Roosevelt was favored.

DEMOCRATIC PARTY

CANDIDATE FOR PRESIDENT:
Franklin Delano Roosevelt

CANDIDATE FOR VICE PRESIDENT:
Harry S Truman (MO)

CANDIDATES FOR PRESIDENTIAL NOMINATION:
Harry Flood Byrd (VA)
James Aloysius Farley (NY)
Joseph Terence Ferguson (OH)
Fred Hildebrandt (SD)
Claude R. Linger (WV)
A. W. Powell (SD)
Franklin Delano Roosevelt (NY)
Agnes Waters (DC)

PRIMARIES:
MARCH 14, 1944 (NH):
unpledged delegates 6,772

APRIL 5, 1944 (WI):
Roosevelt 49,632
others 3,014

APRIL 11, 1944 (IL):
Roosevelt 47,561
others 343

APRIL 11, 1944 (NE):
Roosevelt 37,405
others 319

APRIL 25, 1944 (MA):
unpledged delegates 57,299

APRIL 25, 1944 (PA):
Roosevelt 322,469
others 961

MAY 2, 1944 (AL):
unpledged delegates 116,922

MAY 2, 1944 (FL):
unpledged delegates 118,518

MAY 2, 1944 (SD):
Hildebrandt 7,414
Powell 6,727

MAY 9, 1944 (OH):
Ferguson (OH) (unpledged delegates) 164,915

MAY 9, 1944 (WV):
Linger 59,282

MAY 16, 1944 (CA):
Roosevelt 770,222

MAY 16, 1944 (NJ):
Roosevelt 16,884
Dewey 60

MAY 19, 1944 (OR):
Roosevelt 79,833
others 1,057

29TH CONVENTION:
July 19–21, 1944, Chicago Stadium, Chicago (IL)
Robert Samuel Kerr (OK), temporary chairman
Samuel Dillon Jackson (IN), permanent chairman

The Democratic platform announced the party's intent to stand "on its record in peace and war." It then proceeded to outline the accomplishments of the Roosevelt administration, pledging to form a United Nations organization after the war and to adhere to an International Court of Justice.

PLATFORM HIGHLIGHTS:
SUPPORTED:
- unrestricted Jewish settlement in Palestine, with the ultimate aim of establishing a free and democratic Jewish commonwealth
- the Atlantic Charter and the Four Freedoms
- submission of an Equal Rights Amendment to the Constitution
- federal aid to education
- eventual statehood for Alaska and Hawaii
- extension of the vote for president to the District of Columbia

- full benefits for veterans
- the stability of products, employment, distribution, and prices
- agriculture's parity with industry
- small independent farms
- extension of rural electrification
- compensation of workers during demobilization
- promotion of small businesses
- elimination of wartime controls as soon as practicable
- the reopening of the gold and silver mines of the West
- encouragement of risk capital and new enterprise
- free enterprise
- social justice
- the rights of minorities
- world peace without sacrificing national sovereignty

DEMOCRATIC PARTY
VOTE FOR PRESIDENTIAL NOMINATION:

Candidate	Ballot: 1
Roosevelt	1,086
Byrd	89
Farley	1

GREENBACK PARTY

CANDIDATE FOR PRESIDENT:
Leo Charles Donnelly (MI)

CANDIDATE FOR VICE PRESIDENT:
Frank Jeffries (IN)

Candidates were chosen by mail referendum. The platform promised to reverse the "present order of things and put money into the hands of the industrious people first." It demanded conscription without compensation of property for the nation's defense. It also demanded the replacement of charity through government programs for the disabled and needy, the elimination of child labor, and payment of old age pensions. The party also sought to abolish special privilege and monopolies and to establish a "just and fair" wage law.

PROHIBITION PARTY

CANDIDATE FOR PRESIDENT:
Claude Alonzo Watson

CANDIDATE FOR VICE PRESIDENT:
Andrew Johnson

CANDIDATES FOR PRESIDENTIAL NOMINATION:
Roger Ward Babson (MA)
Earl R. Chalfant (CA)
George Barton Cutten (NY)
Clinton Norman Howard (DC)
Eli Stanley Jones (NY)
Sam Morris (TX)
Daniel Alfred Poling (PA)
Charles Hiram Randall (CA)
William David Upshaw (GA)
William Frederick Varney (NY)
Claude Alonzo Watson (CA)

CANDIDATES FOR VICE-PRESIDENTIAL NOMINATION:
J. L. R. Boyd (GA)
Floyd C. Carrier (MD)
Andrew Johnson (KY)
Sam Morris (TX) (declined)
John Raymond Schmidt (DC)

19TH CONVENTION:
November 10–12, 1943, Indianapolis (IN)

Two hundred twenty-six delegates and nine alternates, representing twenty-seven states and the District of Columbia, attended this convention. The Prohibition Party's platform began with a pledge of loyalty to the United States and an expression of concern about "the rapidly growing tendency toward totalitarian Government in the United States."

PLATFORM HIGHLIGHTS:
SUPPORTED:
- states' rights and promises to decentralize government, abolish wasteful bureaucracy, and ensure judicial review of administrative decisions
- law enforcement
- a sound currency
- reduced taxes
- government economy
- ballot law reforms
- consideration of moral and spiritual issues in the determination of national policies
- enhanced efforts against gambling, narcotics, and commercialized vice
- initiatives to prevent juvenile delinquency
- censorship of obscenity and profanity on stage and in radio, literature, and motion pictures
- extension of Social Security benefits to all persons not currently covered
- the growth of cooperatives and profit-sharing enterprises
- the opening of union books to government inspection and maintained that both labor and capital should submit to arbitration by industrial relations courts
- limits on presidents to one term in office
- elimination of monopolies
- racial justice
- uniform marriage and divorce laws
- separation of church and state
- individual ownership of farms
- stable agricultural prices
- suppression of the traffic in alcoholic beverages

- a national program to plan for postwar problems and promote world cooperation

ALSO:

- reminded voters that "of all the wrongs committed by Government none has been worse than the authorizing of the liquor traffic to degenerate our own citizenship"

PROHIBITION PARTY
VOTE FOR PRESIDENTIAL NOMINATION:

Candidate	Ballot: 1
Watson	131
Morris	31
Chalfant	0
not voting	1

Watson's nomination was made unanimous. Watson offered to decline the nomination for president if Morris would accept it, but Morris refused.

VOTE FOR VICE-PRESIDENTIAL NOMINATION:

Candidate	Ballot: 1
Carrier	130½
Johnson	17½
Schmidt	1 (withdrew)
Morris	(withdrew)

Carrier later withdrew as the nominee. Johnson was then substituted as the vice-presidential candidate.

REPUBLICAN PARTY

CANDIDATE FOR PRESIDENT:
Thomas Edmund Dewey

CANDIDATE FOR VICE PRESIDENT:
John William Bricker (OH)

CANDIDATES FOR PRESIDENTIAL NOMINATION:
Riley Alvin Bender (IL)
Joseph Henry Bottum (SD)
John William Bricker (OH)
Charles Andrew Christopherson (SD)
Thomas Edmund Dewey (NY)
Everett McKinley Dirksen (IL)
Douglas MacArthur (WI)
Edward Martin (PA)
Franklin Delano Roosevelt (NY)
Harold Edward Stassen (MN)
Earl Warren (CA)
Agnes Waters (DC)
Wendell Lewis Willkie (NY)

PRIMARIES:
MARCH 14, 1944 (NH):
unpledged delegates 16,723

APRIL 5, 1944 (WI):
MacArthur 102,421
Dewey 21,036
Stassen 7,928
Willkie 6,439
others 3,307

APRIL 11, 1944 (IL):
MacArthur 550,354
Bender 37,575
Dewey 9,192
Dirksen 581
Bricker 148
Stassen 111
Willkie 107

APRIL 11, 1944 (NE):
Stassen 51,800
Dewey 18,418
Willkie 8,249
others 432

APRIL 25, 1944 (MA):
unpledged delegates 53,511

APRIL 25, 1944 (PA):
Dewey 146,706
MacArthur 9,032
Roosevelt 8,815
Willkie 3,650
Bricker 2,936
Martin 2,406
Stassen 1,502

MAY 1, 1944 (MD):
Willkie 4,701
unpledged delegates 17,600

MAY 2, 1944 (SD):
Christopherson 33,497
Bottum 22,135

MAY 9, 1944 (OH):
unpledged delegates (Bricker) 360,139

MAY 9, 1944 (WV):
unpledged delegates 91,602

MAY 16, 1944 (CA):
Warren 594,439

MAY 16, 1944 (NJ):
Dewey 17,393
Roosevelt 1,720
Willkie 618
Bricker 203
MacArthur 129
Stassen 106

MAY 19, 1944 (OR):
Dewey 50,001
Stassen 6,061
Willkie 3,333
Bricker 3,018

MacArthur................................ 191
others 1,340

23RD CONVENTION:
  June 26–28, 1944, Chicago Stadium, Chicago (IL)
  Earl Warren (CA), temporary chairman and
    keynoter
  Joseph William Martin, Jr. (MA), permanent chair-
    man

The Republican platform pledged to prosecute the war to total victory, engaging in international cooperation but not joining a "World State." Nonetheless, it endorsed the idea of a United Nations organization and worldwide economic stability.

PLATFORM HIGHLIGHTS:
SUPPORTED:
- Pan-American solidarity based on a good neighbor philosophy
- a policy of postwar preparedness, including a strengthening of the National Guard
- extension of Social Security and unemployment insurance with a return of public employment services to the states
- strengthened programs for mothers, children, and the blind
- better health care through federal aid to the states
- decent low-cost housing
- price supports, commodity loans, and other necessary protections to ensure agricultural prosperity for farmers
- conservation, crop insurance, an orderly disposition of surplus war commodities, and intensified research to aid farmers
- cooperatives
- rural road improvements and expanded electrification
- new opportunities for small businesses with reduced tax burdens and governmental red tape
- strict regulation of insurance companies
- a strong U.S. merchant marine
- development of privately owned air transportation and communications systems, flood-control programs, and "justifiable" public works projects
- tax reduction
- restrictions on the president's control over the money supply
- use of the protective tariff
- reciprocal bilateral trade agreements approved by Congress
- immediate programs to extend relief and emergency assistance to the liberated peoples and those Allies needing humanitarian aid
- curtailment of the bureaucracy, making it more accountable
- adoption of constitutional amendments to limit the president to two terms, to outlaw the poll-tax, and to guarantee equal rights for men and women

- benefits for veterans
- creation of a permanent Fair Employment Practice Commission
- investigation into discrimination in the armed forces and its impact on morale
- enactment of an antilynching law
- "tak[ing] politics out of the administration of American Indian affairs"
- protection of the western states through reclamation and irrigation projects, prohibitions against the import of contaminated livestock and meat, and withdrawal or acquisition of lands for public uses
- giving private citizens the opportunity to own public lands
- logging on public forests on a sustained yield basis
- the reopening of mines and stockpiling minerals and metals for future emergencies
- continuation of depletion allowances on oil, gas, and minerals
- statehood for Alaska, Hawaii, and Puerto Rico
- the Balfour Declaration and the establishment of a Jewish homeland in Palestine
- protection of the free press and radio from anything but necessary wartime censorship

---

REPUBLICAN PARTY
VOTE FOR PRESIDENTIAL NOMINATION:

Candidate	Ballot: 1
Dewey	1,056
MacArthur	1
absent	2

VOTE FOR VICE-PRESIDENTIAL NOMINATION: BRICKER WAS UNANIMOUSLY NOMINATED FOR VICE PRESIDENT, ALTHOUGH THE INDIANA DELEGATION HAD EARLIER PROMOTED ITS FAVORITE SON, WILLIAM LEVI HUTCHESON. WHEN THE SECONDING SPEECHES WERE BEING MADE FOR BRICKER, REP. CHARLES ABRAHAM HALLECK OF INDIANA ENDORSED HUTCHESON FOR SECRETARY OF LABOR. BRICKER WAS THUS THE ONLY NAME PRESENTED TO THE CONVENTION.

SOCIALIST LABOR PARTY

CANDIDATE FOR PRESIDENT:
  Edward A. Teichert (PA)

CANDIDATE FOR VICE PRESIDENT:
  Arla Allen Albaugh (OH)

CONVENTION:
  April 29-May 2, 1944, Cornish Arms Hotel, New York, (NY)

The Socialist Labor Party's platform argued that society was at a crossroads. One road led to capitalism and chronic economic crisis. The other pointed to socialism, jobs and plenty for all, human brotherhood, and enduring peace. The platform asserted that, since capitalism could not solve society's problems leading up to the war, it should not be entrusted with the power to fail again after the war was over. The New Deal was a failure, it charged, and a Marxist analysis outlined other shortcomings of capitalism and its unsuitability for a postwar world. Once again, the Socialist Labor Party called for the creation of a Socialist Industrial Commonwealth of Labor through the peaceful revolution of the ballot box. In its view, industrial unionism permitted workers to carry on production and could avert chaos in the event of a capitalist reaction. According to the platform, the major parties were parties of false reform and reaction. Only the Socialist Labor Party offered a revolutionary choice to workers.

SOCIALIST PARTY

CANDIDATE FOR PRESIDENT:
Norman Mattoon Thomas (NY)

CANDIDATE FOR VICE PRESIDENT:
Darlington Hoopes (PA)

CONVENTION:
June 2–4, 1944, Berkshire Hotel, Reading (PA)

The Socialist Party's platform called for victory in the peacetime struggle against fascism on the basis of self-determination and equal rights for all peoples.

PLATFORM HIGHLIGHTS:

SUPPORTED:
- the German and Japanese peoples' replacing their governments, withdrawing their military forces from occupied territories, disarming, restoring loot, and assisting refugees

- the United Nations's freeing the European nations overrun by Germany, ending competitive armaments and military conscription, extending aid for the relief and reconstruction of devastated countries, and turning away from imperialism
- extension of social insurance programs (including coverage for farmers and other uncovered groups)
- help for returning veterans
- conversion of government-controlled war plants to peacetime uses to combat unemployment
- a "profound social and economic reorganization"
- social control over money, banking, credit, natural resources, utilities, and all monopolies and exploitive industries
- democratic rather than bureaucratic social control based on the principles of consumer involvement and cooperative organization
- sharply graduated income and inheritance taxes
- the right to bargain collectively and strike
- conservation
- family farms
- the fostering of the equality and fraternity of races
- an end to discriminatory immigration laws and restoration of the rights of Japanese-Americans interned during the war
- passage of antilynching and anti-poll tax legislation
- creation of a permanent Fair Employment Practice Committee
- the Socialist Party as the best hope for perfecting the tools of democracy and bringing justice and a better life to all

OPPOSED:
- the sales tax
- absentee landlordism
- anti-Semitism, Jim Crowism, and other forms of discrimination

GENERAL ELECTION SUMMARY FOR 1944			
Candidate	*Electoral Votes*	*States*	*Popular Votes*
Roosevelt (D)	432	36	25,602,505
Dewey (R)	99	12	22,006,278
Texas Regulars	0	0	135,439
Thomas (SOC)	0	0	80,518
Watson (PROH)	0	0	74,758
MA blank votes	0	0	49,328
Teichert (SOC LAB)	0	0	45,336
MS REG DEM	0	0	9,964
MS IND REP	0	0	7,859
SC SOUTH DEM	0	0	7,799
GA Independent Democrats	0	0	3,373
Smith (AM FIR)	0	0	1,780
Independent	0	0	69
Donnelly (GRE)	0	0	
unknown	0	0	2,527

ELECTION OF NOVEMBER 2, 1948

President
HARRY S TRUMAN
Vice President
ALBEN WILLIAM BARKLEY

HIGHLIGHTS

On April 12, 1945, the figure who had dominated U.S. politics since 1932 died. Franklin Delano Roosevelt's death brought Harry S Truman to the presidency, and it was generally conceded that he was a man of modest talents. For the 1948 elections, Republicans could taste impending victory, especially after capturing control of both the Senate and House of Representatives in the 1946 congressional elections. The Republicans only had to choose a candidate. Thomas Dewey was taking a second shot at the White House, while the conservative wing of the Grand Old Party was promoting Sen. Robert Alphonso Taft. A host of favorite sons and war heroes—Earl Warren of California, Harold Edward Stassen of Minnesota, Gen. Douglas MacArthur, Sen. Leverett Saltonstall of Massachusetts, and Sen. Arthur Hendrick Vandenberg of Michigan— were lining up as well. Gen. Dwight David Eisenhower, however, declined to enter the fray. By the time the convention opened, Dewey had a clear lead and received the nomination on the second ballot, with Governor Earl Warren as his running mate.

The Democratic Convention, meanwhile, proved a contentious affair, with its various factions in disarray. Liberals supported Eisenhower. Conservatives, led by J. Strom Thurmond of South Carolina, threatened to walk out if a strong civil rights plank was adopted. When the party's platform was brought up, Mayor Hubert H. Humphrey of Minneapolis (MN) made a stirring pitch for an unequivocal civil rights statement, which was written into the platform. Thurmond then led his walkout and ultimately headed a separate Dixiecrat ticket in the South. Once Eisenhower declined the use of his name, Truman's renomination was assured, even though Sen. Richard Russell of Georgia offered himself as a southern alternative. In an effort to quiet his southern opponents, the president selected Sen. Alben W. Barkley of Kentucky as his running mate. With one wing of the party already in revolt, Truman next confronted challenges from the Left—a Henry Wallace campaign under the Progressive banner and Norman Thomas, a perennial Socialist contender who was making his last try for the presidency. The gleeful Republicans all but anointed Dewey as the president-elect; however, they woefully underestimated the president's campaign skills. While bluntly attacking the Republican Congress, Truman launched a cross-country whistle-stop campaign. Meanwhile, Dewey glided about and played the role of dignified statesman, dull but safe. All signs pointed to a Dewey victory except the one that counted. In a squeaker outcome, Truman won a stunning upset, defying the odds and the predictions of embarrassed pollsters. The election of 1948 ranks as one of the more memorable contests in U.S. history.

AMERICAN VEGETARIAN PARTY

CANDIDATE FOR PRESIDENT:
John Albert Maxwell (IL)

CANDIDATE FOR VICE PRESIDENT:
Symon Gould (NY)

CONVENTION:
July 7, 1948, Hotel Commodore, New York (NY)

This gathering was the first convention of the American Vegetarian Party. The party's candidate for president was born in Kent, England, and was therefore constitutionally barred from becoming president.

PLATFORM HIGHLIGHTS:
SUPPORTED:
- promotion of vegetarianism
- construction of "garden cities" in underdeveloped areas
- abolition of cattle cultivation
- the printing of more money to pay off the national debt and finance a public works program, including construction of housing and a network of eight-lane highways

- alternative medicines like naturopathy, hydrotherapy, and chiropractic

OPPOSED:
- food processing and the demineralization of cereals and sugar products

CHRISTIAN NATIONALIST PARTY

CANDIDATE FOR PRESIDENT:
Gerald Lyman Kenneth Smith (MO)

CANDIDATE FOR VICE PRESIDENT:
Henry A. Romer (OH)

CONVENTION:
August 20–22, 1948, Keil Auditorium, St. Louis (MO)
Don Lohbeck (MI), chairman
Gerald Lyman Kenneth Smith (MO), keynoter

The Christian Nationalist Party was formed in 1946 as the successor to Gerald Lyman Kenneth Smith's America First Party. The Christian Nationalist platform proclaimed that the United States was a "Christian nation" and that "it is our duty to re-instate militant Christianity as a positive factor in the political, economic, and national life of our country."

PLATFORM HIGHLIGHTS:

SUPPORTED:
- "obliteration" of communism
- deportation of African Americans to a homeland in Africa and of Zionist Jews to Jerusalem
- the transfer of the homes of illegal immigrants and noncitizens to veterans
- the dissolution of the Anti-Defamation League, American Jewish Congress, Friends of Democracy, Non-Sectarian Anti-Nazi League, and otherforms of "Jewish Gestapo"
- "constructive immigration" of Christian Europeans
- an amendment to the Constitution requiring segregation
- Chiang Kai-shek's Nationalist China
- withdrawal from the United Nations
- the rebuilding of Germany to prevent the spread of communism
- a break in diplomatic relations with the Soviet Union and support for the "White Russian" opposition
- anti-Communist forces in the postwar world
- the military taking control of the atom bomb, atomic energy, safeguarding atomic secrets
- a strong national military, with a peacetime army paid wages comparable to those in private industry
- monetary reform
- adequate pensions for seniors
- reformation of citizenship laws
- private enterprise
- price stabilization for crops
- improved health care, job opportunities, decent housing, and other benefits for veterans

- unrestricted relationships between employers and employees

OPPOSED:
- bureaucratic controls over housing
- the partition of Palestine and the establishment of a new state of Israel
- secret international treaties, the Marshall Plan, the Truman Doctrine, and the UNRRA (UN Relief and Recovery Agency)
- President Franklin Roosevelt's foreign policies
- labor racketeers
- the union scale system of compensation

ALSO:
- criticized price controls and rationing
- branded Roosevelt, Secretary of the Treasury Henry Morgenthau, and other Democratic leaders as "war criminals" and advocated a congressional investigation into their activities during the war

---

CHRISTIAN NATIONALIST PARTY
VOTE FOR PRESIDENTIAL AND VICE-PRESIDENTIAL NOMINATIONS: SMITH AND ROMER WERE NOMINATED FOR PRESIDENT AND VICE PRESIDENT, RESPECTIVELY, BY ACCLAMATION. NO OTHER NOMINATIONS WERE MADE.

COMMUNIST PARTY

The Communist Party issued a platform in 1948, but it did not nominate candidates for president and vice president. The platform repeated the communist demand for housing, integration, peace, and an end to anti-Soviet foreign policy.

DEMOCRATIC PARTY

CANDIDATE FOR PRESIDENT:
Harry S Truman

CANDIDATE FOR VICE PRESIDENT:
Alben William Barkley

CANDIDATES FOR PRESIDENTIAL NOMINATION:
Wilford B. Bixler (OH)
Claude Carnot Cunningham (TX)
Dwight David Eisenhower (NY)
Lynn Fellows (SD)
Fred Hildebrandt (SD)
William Alexander Julian (OH)
Scott Wike Lucas (IL)
Douglas MacArthur (WI)
Paul Vories McNutt (IN)
Richard Brevard Russell (GA)
Harold Edward Stassen (MN)
Harry S Truman (MO)
Henry Agard Wallace (IA)

CANDIDATES FOR VICE-PRESIDENTIAL NOMINATION:
Alben William Barkley (KY)
Richard Brevard Russell (GA)

PRIMARIES:

MARCH 9, 1948 (NH):
unpledged delegates 4,409

APRIL 6, 1948 (WI):
Truman 25,415
others 4,906

APRIL 13, 1948 (IL):
Truman 16,299
Eisenhower 1,709
Lucas 427
others 1,513

APRIL 13, 1948 (NE):
Truman 67,672
others 894

APRIL 20, 1948 (NJ):
Truman 1,100
Wallace 87
others 2

APRIL 27, 1948 (MA):
unpledged delegates 51,207

APRIL 27, 1948 (PA):
Truman 328,891
Eisenhower 4,502
Wallace 4,329
Stassen 1,301
MacArthur 1,220
others 2,409

MAY 4, 1948 (AL):
unpledged delegates 161,629

MAY 4, 1948 (FL):
unpledged delegates 92,169

MAY 4, 1948 (OH):
Julian (unpledged delegates)[1] 271,146
Bixler

MAY 11, 1948 (WV):
unpledged delegates 157,102

MAY 21, 1948 (OR):
Truman 112,962
others 7,436

JUNE 1, 1948 (CA):
Truman 811,920

JUNE 1, 1948 (SD):
Fellows (Truman slate)[2] 11,193
Hildebrandt (unpledged delegates) 8,016

[1]Julian headed the ticket of electors who were unpledged, but they were
bound to follow his lead.
[2]Fellows supported Truman. He ran as an unpledged delegate, heading
a slate of delegates that were known as the "Truman slate" and publicly
committed to his support. Truman had not announced that he would run
for reelection at the time the slate was filed for election.

CONVENTION:
July 12–14, 1948, Convention Hall, Philadelphia
(PA)
Alben William Barkley (KY), temporary chairman
Samuel Taliaferro Rayburn (TX), permanent chair-
man

PLATFORM HIGHLIGHTS:
SUPPORTED:
• the accomplishments of Franklin Roosevelt and Harry
S Truman and of their administrations
• the securing of treaties of peace with former enemies of
the United States
• a strong national defense
• international control over weapons of mass destruction
(including the atomic bomb)
• implementation of the Truman Doctrine and Marshall
Plan
• the Good Neighbor Policy for Latin America
• Truman's recognition of Israel
• the eventual independence of subjugated nations
• a balanced budget and a reduction in the public debt
• tax reduction
• repeal of the Taft-Hartley Act
• a stronger Department of Labor (including the Federal
Mediation and Conciliation Service, U.S. Employment
Service, and a Labor Education Extension Service)
• adoption of a 75-cents-an-hour minimum wage
• a guarantee of equal pay for equal work regardless of
gender
• extension of Social Security and increasing benefits
• a national health program
• the Mental Health Act
• federal aid to education
• GI Bill of Rights and benefits programs for veterans
• family-size farms
• a permanent system of flexible price supports
• a school lunch program
• farm surpluses used to improve the diet of low-income
families
• an extended crop insurance program
• the repeal of discriminatory taxes on oleomargarine
• small businesses
• the fishing and mining industries
• the merchant marine
• civil service
• rural electrification
• flood control
• navigable waterways
• reclamation and conservation
• enforcement of antitrust laws
• full civil rights for all Americans
• right to political participation
• equal employment opportunity
• security of person (i.e., protection against criminal and
governmental intrusion)

- equal treatment for all races in the military
- legislation to admit a minimum of 400,000 displaced persons eligible for U.S. citizenship, primarily from Europe
- immediate statehood for Alaska and Hawaii and the right of self-determination for Puerto Rico
- submission of an equal rights amendment to the constitution
- the right to vote for the District of Columbia
- peaceful development of atomic energy
- the United Nations Commission on Human Rights
- the United Nations Economic and Social Council
- creation of a National Science Foundation
- vigorous enforcement of laws against subversive activities

OPPOSED:
- many of the domestic ills of the country, including inflation, the housing shortage, and tax inequities, for which the Republican 80th Congress was blamed
- communism

DEMOCRATIC PARTY
VOTE FOR PRESIDENTIAL NOMINATION:

Candidate	Ballot: 1
Truman	947½
Russell	263
McNutt	½

VOTE FOR VICE-PRESIDENTIAL NOMINATION: SENATORS RUSSELL AND BARKLEY WERE PLACED IN NOMINATION FOR VICE PRESIDENT. RUSSELL DECLINED, AND BARKLEY WAS NOMINATED UNDER A SUSPENSION OF THE RULES.

GREENBACK PARTY
CANDIDATE FOR PRESIDENT:
John G. Scott (NY)

CANDIDATE FOR VICE PRESIDENT:
Granville Booker Leeke (IN)

Candidates were chosen by mail referendum.

PLATFORM HIGHLIGHTS:
SUPPORTED:
- a one-term limit for presidents and abolition of the electoral college
- old age pensions and programs to support the needy and disabled
- the abolition of child labor
- printed money as the medium of exchange, with the government freely printing more as the need arose
- the right to vote regardless of race, color, or previous condition of servitude

- the reversal of the "present order of things," and putting "money into the hands of the industrious people first"

INDEPENDENT
CANDIDATES FOR PRESIDENT:
Morgan Blake (GA)
Dwight David Eisenhower (NY)
Fielding Lewis Wright (MS)

PROGRESSIVE PARTY
CANDIDATE FOR PRESIDENT:
Henry Agard Wallace (IA)

CANDIDATE FOR VICE PRESIDENT:
Glen Hearst Taylor (ID)

This newly organized party adopted the same name as the political party organized in 1912 to support Theodore Roosevelt. Wallace attracted the support of left-wing Democrats and others who favored negotiations with the U.S.S.R. to settle the Cold War. His party was accused of being dominated by Communists.

1ST CONVENTION:
July 23–25, 1948, Convention Hall, Philadelphia (PA)

PLATFORM HIGHLIGHTS:
SUPPORTED:
- peace and a negotiated settlement of differences with the Soviet Union
- an end to the peacetime draft
- the United Nations
- repeal of the National Security Act
- abandonment of military bases abroad
- the outlawing of the atomic bomb and other instruments of modern warfare and reductions in armaments
- peace treaties with Germany and Japan that would promote democratization, denazification, and the establishment of secure borders
- recognition of and strong support for the new nation of Israel
- creation of a democratic coalition government in China (excluding Chiang Kai-shek)
- reunification of Korea
- independence for Indochina, Indonesia, Malaya, and other Asian lands
- independence for Puerto Rico
- unified homelands for the Irish and Armenians
- peoples in other areas who were subjugated by colonial powers
- economic assistance to further independent economic development of Latin America
- a strong civil rights agenda ranging from adoption of an equal rights amendment to the Constitution to enactment of antilynching and anti-poll tax legislation

- amnesty for conscientious objectors imprisoned during World War II
- full political rights for Communists and other unpopular groups
- abolition of the House Un-American Activities Committee and other mechanisms for "thought control"
- foreign-born citizens and liberalization of immigration and naturalization laws
- indemnity for Japanese Americans interned during the World War II
- integration of the armed forces and revisions in the military justice system
- the direct election of the president and vice president
- home rule for the District of Columbia
- immediate admission of Alaska and Hawaii as states
- strong price and rent controls to curb inflation
- economic planning
- public ownership as an alternative to monopolies in banking, electric power, railroads, merchant marine, and the gas and other industries reliant on government funds or purchases
- repeal of the Bulwinkle Act, the Miller-Tydings law, and the Taft-Hartley Act
- the rights to organize, collectively bargain, and strike for public employees and railroad workers
- a dollar-an-hour minimum wage
- an end to blacklisting
- improved working conditions
- stronger health and safety laws
- decent pensions for all workers, including agricultural and food processing workers
- the family farm, low-cost credit and stable prices, flood control, rural electrification, crop insurance, subsidized soil conservation programs, and international commodity agreements to stabilize world markets
- a national land policy designed to discourage corporate farming, aided by a graduated land tax and a 160-acre limitation on the use of public irrigation
- a food stamp plan and school hot-lunch program were pledged
- democratically controlled programs of conservation, production, marketing, and price supports
- development loans and working capital to encourage small businesses
- a federal emergency housing program to ease the housing shortage
- elimination of discrimination and segregation in housing
- universal coverage under Social Security
- increased unemployment, disability, sickness, maternity, and pension benefits
- adequate public assistance for persons in need
- enforcement of child labor laws
- day care
- national health insurance and public health, preventive medicine, and dental care programs
- funds for health research
- employment and job security at equal wages for women

- the right to vote for eighteen-year-olds
- increased expenditures for recreational facilities for young people, particularly in rural areas
- bonuses for veterans
- expansion of the Veterans Administration
- guaranteed jobs and increased benefits to disabled veterans
- increased GI benefits, including coverage for war widows
- reforms in the tax structure to close loopholes, particularly on estates and gifts
- a graduated capital gains tax
- taxes on excess profits and undistributed profits
- elimination of excise taxes on basic necessities
- tax exemptions on personal income below a minimum standard of living
- an integrated educational system free of discrimination and supported with federal grants-in-aid
- the federal government's assistance in providing scholarships and initiating adult education programs
- creation of a cabinet-level Department of Education and a Department of Culture
- enactment of legislation to promote science, including human and social sciences
- enactment of legislation to provide public control over patents and product licenses

OPPOSED:
- the Truman Doctrine and Marshall Plan
- diplomatic relations with Francisco Franco's Spain
- the Displaced Persons Act of 1948 as anti-Catholic and anti-Semitic
- segregation and discrimination against racial and ethnic minorities
- state and local sales taxes

PROHIBITION PARTY

CANDIDATE FOR PRESIDENT:
Claude Alonzo Watson

CANDIDATE FOR VICE PRESIDENT:
Dale Harold Learn

CANDIDATES FOR PRESIDENTIAL NOMINATION:
David Leigh Colvin (NY)
Enoch Arden Holtwick (IL)
David Harold Learn (PA)
Claude Alonzo Watson (CA)

CANDIDATES FOR VICE-PRESIDENTIAL NOMINATION:
Mamie White Colvin (NY)
Ethel Hubler (CA)
Dale Harold Learn (PA)

21ST CONVENTION:
June 26–28, 1947, Winona Lake (IN)
Edward E. Blake (IL), temporary chairman

The party condemned the repeal of the Eighteenth Amendment and advised voters to join it in defeating the "liquor power." To the Prohibition Party, "no political issue confronting our citizens compares in magnitude with the necessity for suppressing the alcohol beverage traffic."

PLATFORM HIGHLIGHTS:

SUPPORTED:

- world peace and universal brotherhood
- international control of atomic energy
- opposed universal military training in peacetime
- reorganization of the government in order to reduce spending and to cut taxes
- a 1-percent property tax limitation
- constitutional government and strict enforcement of the nation's laws, without regard to spoils
- ballot law reform to eliminate discrimination against minor parties
- separation of church and state
- stronger laws against gambling, narcotics, and commercialized vice
- congressional control over the issuance of money
- an end to racial discrimination
- uniform marriage and divorce laws
- expansion of Social Security coverage
- creation of an annuity insurance system for the elderly
- initiatives to generate more housing
- cooperatives
- restoration of a balance between labor and capital for the public welfare

OPPOSED:

- denounced monopolies

PROHIBITION PARTY
VOTE FOR PRESIDENTIAL NOMINATION:

Candidate	Ballot: 1
Watson	150
Holtwick	117
Colvin	1
Learn	1

Watson's nomination was made unanimous.

VOTE FOR VICE-PRESIDENTIAL NOMINATION: HUBLER AND COLVIN WERE NOMINATED FOR VICE PRESIDENT, BUT BOTH WITHDREW. ACCORDINGLY, LEARN WAS UNANIMOUSLY NOMINATED FOR VICE PRESIDENT ON THE FIRST BALLOT.

REPUBLICAN PARTY

CANDIDATE FOR PRESIDENT:
Thomas Edmund Dewey

CANDIDATE FOR VICE PRESIDENT:
Earl Warren

CANDIDATES FOR PRESIDENTIAL NOMINATION:
Raymond Earl Baldwin (CT)
Riley Alvin Bender (IL)
Samuel Woods Byrer (WV)
Thomas Edmund Dewey (NY)
Everett McKinley Dirksen (IL)
Alfred Eastlack Driscoll (NJ)
Dwight David Eisenhower (NY)
Dwight Herbert Green (IL)
Rufus Wilbur Hitchcock (SD)
Douglas MacArthur (WI)
Edward Martin (PA)
Joseph William Martin (MA)
Brazilla Carroll Reece (TN)
Leverett Saltonstall (MA)
Harold Edward Stassen (MN)
Robert Alphonso Taft (OH)
Harry S Truman (MO)
Arthur Hendrick Vandenberg (MI)
Ellis Cutler Vander Pyl (OH)
Henry Agard Wallace (IA)
Earl Warren (CA)

CANDIDATES FOR VICE-PRESIDENTIAL NOMINATION:
Harold Edward Stassen (MN)
Earl Warren (CA)

PRIMARIES:

MARCH 9, 1948 (NH):
unpledged delegates 28,854

APRIL 6, 1948 (WI):
Stassen 64,076
MacArthur 55,302
Dewey 40,943
others 2,429

APRIL 13, 1948 (IL):
Bender 324,029
MacArthur 6,672
Stassen 1,572
Dewey 953
Taft 705
others 475

APRIL 13, 1948 (NE):
Stassen 80,979
Dewey 64,242
Taft 21,608
Vandenberg 9,590
MacArthur 6,893
Warren 1,761
Martin 910
others 24

APRIL 20, 1948 (NJ):
Dewey 3,714
Stassen 3,123
MacArthur 718
Vandenberg 516
Taft 495
Eisenhower 288
Martin 64

Driscoll. 44

Warren 14

APRIL 27, 1948 (MA):

Saltonstall (unpledged delegates) 72,191

APRIL 27, 1948 (PA):

Stassen 81,242

Dewey 76,988

Martin. 45,072

MacArthur 18,254

Taft 15,166

Vandenberg. 8,818

Truman 4,907

Eisenhower 4,726

Wallace 1,452

others 1,537

MAY 4, 1948 (OH):

unpledged delegates 426,767

MAY 11, 1948 (WV):

Stassen 110,775

Byrer 15,675

Vander Pyl 6,735

MAY 21, 1948 (OR):

Dewey 117,554

Stassen 107,946

others 1,474

JUNE 1, 1948 (CA):

Warren 769,520

JUNE 1, 1948 (SD):

Hitchcock. 45,463

24TH CONVENTION:

June 21–25, 1948, Convention Hall, Philadelphia (PA)

Dwight Herbert Green (IL), temporary chairman and keynoter

Joseph William Martin, Jr. (MA), permanent chairman

The Republican platform began with a declaration of principles, including free enterprise, a minimum dependence on law, and the interdependence of workers and employers. The record of the Republican Congress was lauded while the Truman administration was dismissed as having a "tragic lack of foresight and general inadequacy."

PLATFORM HIGHLIGHTS:

SUPPORTED:

- soil conservation
- development of the West
- the economical and more efficient administration of government
- promotion of public health, scientific research, a stable economy, and security in old age
- a strong and unified defense
- a decent standard of living

- a stronger United Nations
- an insistence on the personal dignity of the individual
- the "root[ing] out" of communism
- reduction of the public debt
- stimulation of production
- a sound currency
- a strong defense under a unified Department of National Defense
- "sustained effective action to procure sufficient manpower for the services" (i.e., conscription)
- an adequate, privately operated merchant marine
- development of waterways and harbors
- expansion of privately operated airlines and communications systems
- small businesses
- coordination of state and federal taxes
- improvements in labor-management relations
- acceleration of soil conservation programs
- protection of market prices for farmers through price supports and loans
- the family farm
- greater agricultural research
- development of water resources and flood-control programs
- use of the national forests to produce a sustained yield of timber
- reclamation of desert lands
- an adjustment in benefits for veterans
- federal aid to states for slum clearance and a limited low-rent housing program that would not compete with private enterprise
- the strengthening of the Social Security program
- federal-state programs to improve maternal and child health, the supply of hospitals, and the treatment of persons with mental illnesses
- constitutional amendments to reform the electoral college and to ensure equal rights for women
- a streamlined bureaucracy
- equal educational opportunity for all
- statehood for Alaska, Hawaii, and Puerto Rico
- self-government for the District of Columbia
- restoration of state titles to the tidal and submerged lands, tributary waters, lakes, and streams
- "steady progress toward unity in Western Europe"
- collective security arrangements within the framework of the United Nations
- creation of an international peacekeeping force
- elimination of the veto in the Security Council
- the state of Israel and its entrance to the family of nations
- continued friendship with Nationalist China
- the universal limitation and control of arms
- reciprocal trade agreements
- the "stopping [of] partisan politics at the water's edge"

OPPOSED:

- lynching and a poll tax

- "the idea of racial segregation in the armed services"
- Communists
- secret diplomatic initiatives

REPUBLICAN PARTY
VOTE FOR PRESIDENTIAL NOMINATION:

Candidate	Ballot: 1
Dewey	434
Taft	224
Stassen	157
Vandenberg	62
Warren	59
Green	56
Driscoll	35
Baldwin	19
Martin, J. W.	18
Reece	15
MacArthur	11
Dirksen	1

VOTE FOR VICE-PRESIDENTIAL NOMINATION:
ALTHOUGH ARIZONA DELEGATES WANTED TO
NOMINATE STASSEN FOR VICE PRESIDENT, WARREN
WAS NOMINATED BY ACCLAMATION WITHOUT A
FORMAL VOTE BEING TAKEN.

SOCIALIST PARTY

CANDIDATE FOR PRESIDENT:
  Norman Mattoon Thomas

CANDIDATE FOR VICE PRESIDENT:
  Tucker Powell Smith

CANDIDATES FOR PRESIDENTIAL NOMINATION:
  Maynard Clare Krueger (IL)
  Asa Philip Randolph (NY)
  Norman Mattoon Thomas (NY)

CANDIDATES FOR VICE-PRESIDENTIAL NOMINATION:
  Mary Donovan Hapgood (IN)
  Tucker Powell Smith (MI)

CONVENTION:
  May 6–9, 1948, Knights of Malta Hall and Berkshire
  Hall, Reading (PA)

More than two hundred delegates attended the convention. The Socialist platform painted a dooms day picture dominated by the atomic bomb and asserted that only socialism could prevent the coming destruction by eliminating greed, profit, and hate. Both capitalism and communism were denounced.

PLATFORM HIGHLIGHTS:
SUPPORTED:
- nationalization of all mineral, oil, electric, and atomic power, along with basic industries, public utilities, and banking and credit institutions
- joint representation of workers, management, and consumers in the management of socialized enterprises
- the need to raise the standard of living
- expansion of the nation's productive facilities through planned growth
- improvements in unemployment insurance, pensions, and Social Security
- an increase in the minimum wage
- a national health insurance program
- more research on health and mental health
- additional federal support for public education and for elimination of segregation in schools
- strengthened benefits for veterans
- creation of a home loan bank to finance home purchases
- creation of a public supply and fabricating corporation to encourage prefabricated housing
- expansion of public housing programs, imposition of rent controls, and other strategies for dealing with the housing shortage
- repeal of the Taft-Hartley Act
- abolition of the House Un-American Activities Committee and repressive legislation against the political activities of Communists
- the elimination of the poll tax
- full amnesty and restoration of civil rights for war objectors
- abolition of segregation
- creation of a fair employment practices committee
- prohibitions against lynching
- indemnity for Japanese Americans interned during the war
- family farms
- elimination of absentee ownership of land
- social ownership and cooperative farming where large-scale agricultural operations were necessary
- conservation and flood control
- an end to commodity speculation
- a progressive tax system
- reallocation of the federal budget "in the service of life and peace"
- the European Economic Recovery Program as a laudable path to peace
- outlawing of all forms of peacetime conscription by the United Nations
- universal (not unilateral) disarmament
- abolition of the veto in the Security Council
- a halt in the production of atomic bombs and internationalization of their control
- expansion of the Food and Agriculture Organization and International Trade Organization to ensure access to raw materials to all peoples of the world
- internationalization and demilitarization of strategic waterways
- an international police force under the United Nations
- "permanent liquidation" of all colonialism and an end to trade barriers

- a liberalization of U.S. refugee policy
- full self-government for the Jewish community in Palestine
- limited duration of Allied occupation of the defeated nations
- increased foreign aid to assist the economic rehabilitation of a war-ravaged world
- ultimate world government along democratic lines

OPPOSED:

- private-sector involvement in the development of atomic energy
- crop production limits

SOCIALIST PARTY
VOTE FOR PRESIDENTIAL NOMINATION:
THOMAS WAS UNANIMOUSLY CHOSEN AS THE
PRESIDENTIAL CANDIDATE.

VOTE FOR VICE-PRESIDENTIAL NOMINATION:
SMITH WAS CHOSEN ON THE FIRST BALLOT (A SECRET
BALLOT) AS THE VICE-PRESIDENTIAL NOMINEE,
DEFEATING HAPGOOD.

SOCIALIST LABOR PARTY

CANDIDATE FOR PRESIDENT:
Edward A. Teichert (PA)

CANDIDATE FOR VICE PRESIDENT:
Stephen Emery (NY)

22ND CONVENTION:
May 1–3, 1948, Cornish Arms Hotel, New York (NY)
John P. Quinn (MA), temporary chairman and chairman, May 1, 1948
Nathan Karp (NJ), chairman, May 2–3, 1948

Thirty-one delegates from sixteen states, the District of Columbia, and three ethnic federations (e.g., Slovak Federation of the United States, German-American Cultural Association) attended this convention. The Socialist Labor Party's platform painted a bleak picture of a third world war, totalitarian dictatorship, and imperialist barbarism under capitalism. It asserted that only social ownership could control the "plutocracy." Capitalism was seen as a predatory system, and its shortcomings were enumerated according to Marxist analysis. The existing unions were condemned as pro-capi-

---

SOCIALIST LABOR PARTY
VOTE FOR PRESIDENTIAL AND VICE-PRESIDENTIAL
NOMINATIONS: TEICHERT AND EMERY WERE BOTH
UNANIMOUSLY NOMINATED FOR PRESIDENT AND VICE
PRESIDENT, RESPECTIVELY, WITHOUT ANY OTHER
NAMES BEING PRESENTED TO THE CONVENTION.

---

talist, and the party urged workers to build a new union based on their class interests—"the all-embracing Socialist Industrial Union." Such a union, the party proclaimed, would bring about an Industrial Republic of Labor in which workers would manage industry democratically.

SOCIALIST WORKERS PARTY

CANDIDATE FOR PRESIDENT:
Farrell Dobbs (NY)

CANDIDATE FOR VICE PRESIDENT:
Grace Carlson (MN)

13TH ANNUAL CONVENTION:
July 2–3, 1948, Irving Plaza Hall, New York, (NY)

This Trotskyite party was founded on December 31, 1937, in Chicago, but did not offer a presidential ticket until March 3, 1948. The thirteenth annual convention ratified the selection of the candidates.

The Socialist Workers Party adopted a platform that analyzed inflation, unemployment, depression, and war in Marxian terms. The party described itself as continuing the revolutionary traditions of 1776 and 1860 and denounced the two major parties and the Progressives as representatives of "decaying capitalism." Similarly, other parties were attacked for their deficiencies, such as the Socialists' reformist tendencies and the Communists' adherence to Stalinist principles. According to the platform, only a workers and farmers government, led by the Socialist Workers Party, could prevent a third world war.

PLATFORM HIGHLIGHTS:
SUPPORTED:

- a nationwide referendum whenever war was under consideration
- withdrawal of all U.S. troops from foreign soil
- complete independence for colonial peoples
- creation of a Socialist United States of the World
- an escalator clause providing for cost-of-living adjustments in all wage and benefit plans
- price controls
- unemployment insurance equal to union wages
- a six-hour workday and a thirty-hour work week
- repeal of the Taft-Hartley Act and other antilabor laws
- end to "red-baiting and witch-hunts"
- ballot reform to encourage minority parties and to permit eighteen-year-olds to vote
- the destruction of the Jim Crow system
- enactment of laws against lynching and the poll tax
- a fair employment practices committee
- elimination of segregation
- increased efforts to combat anti-Semitism
- rural electrification
- abolition of sharecropping and absentee landlordism
- soil conservation and flood control
- a ban on commodity speculation

- an end to crop limitations
- a guarantee that working farmers would receive the cost of production on farms operated under the control of their own representatives
- the right of servicemen to participate in politics, to elect their own officers, and to be paid union wages
- nationalization of all "feeder industries" that provide building materials and creating of an emergency program to construct 25 million permanent, low-cost, low-rent housing units to resolve the housing crisis
- rent controls
- repealing payroll and sales taxes
- tax exemption for incomes under $5,000 per year and taxes on that portion of any income over $25,000 at 100 percent
- nationalization of all banks, basic industries, war plants, and natural resources
- labor's breaking its ties with the established parties and convening a united labor conference to create its own party

OPPOSED:

- the United Nations as a phony instrument of peace controlled by capitalist countries
- the draft
- the "officer caste system" in the military
- racial segregation in the armed forces

STATES' RIGHTS DEMOCRATIC (DIXIECRAT) PARTY

CANDIDATE FOR PRESIDENT:

James Strom Thurmond (SC)

CANDIDATE FOR VICE PRESIDENT:

Fielding Lewis Wright (MS)

CONVENTION:

July 17, 1948, Birmingham (AL)

The States' Rights Party was formed when southern delegates walked out of the Democratic Convention to protest its and Truman's civil rights position.

Claiming that a belief in states' rights is "the cornerstone of the Democratic Party," the Dixiecrat platform charged the Democratic leadership with abuses and usurpations of power that constituted a peril to basic rights. Denouncing the Democratic Convention's call for a civil rights law, the party reminded the Democrats of the steadfast southern support for Democratic candidates in the past. Its members reaffirmed their belief in the Constitution and promised to oppose any erosion of individual rights.

PLATFORM HIGHLIGHTS:

SUPPORTED:

- social and economic justice
- racial segregation
- home rule for cities
- local self-government
- a system of checks and balances to restrain the executive and judicial departments

OPPOSED:

- totalitarian and centralized bureaucratic government

> **STATES' RIGHTS DEMOCRATIC (DIXIECRAT) PARTY**
> VOTE FOR PRESIDENTIAL NOMINATION:
> THURMOND WAS NOMINATED BY ACCLAMATION ON THE FIRST BALLOT.

GENERAL ELECTION SUMMARY FOR 1948

Candidate	Electoral Votes	States	Popular Votes
Truman (D)	303	28	24,105,695
Dewey (R)	189	16	21,969,170
Thurmond (ST RIGHTS)	39	4	1,169,021
Wallace (PROG)	0	0	1,156,103
Thomas (SOC)	0	0	139,009
Watson (PROH)	0	0	103,216
Teichert (SOC LAB)[1]	0	0	29,061
Dobbs (SOC WOR)	0	0	13,613
Wright (I)	0	0	2,294
Smith (CHR NAT)	0	0	42
Scott (GRE)	0	0	6
Maxwell (AM VEG)	0	0	4
Blake (I)	0	0	1
Eisenhower (I)	0	0	1
unknown	0	0	10,085

[1]The Socialist Labor Party was listed as the Industrial Government Party in Minnesota, New York, and Pennsylvania.

ELECTION OF NOVEMBER 4, 1952

President
DWIGHT DAVID EISENHOWER
Vice President
RICHARD MILHOUS NIXON

HIGHLIGHTS

In April 1952, President Harry S Truman announced he would not run for reelection. His administration was under attack by such men as Sen. Joseph Raymond McCarthy of Wisconsin and Rep. Richard Milhous Nixon of California for corruption and "being soft on communism." The nation was in the midst of anti-Communist hysteria, heightened by the Chinese invasion of Korea and the resultant UN "police action" in Asia. Standing in the wings were two formidable Republicans who wanted to be president—Sen. Robert Alphonso Taft and Gen. Dwight David "Ike" Eisenhower. Taft was the darling of the conservatives, while Ike the war hero had no obvious enemies. The two met head-to-head at the Republican convention in a bitter contest, with Eisenhower gaining the honors on the first ballot. Nixon was selected for the second spot on the ticket.

The Democratic nomination appeared up for grabs, with Sen. Carey Estes Kefauver of Tennessee leading a crowded pack. Sectional and favorite-son candidates abounded, but the most acceptable candidate across factions was Governor Adlai Ewing Stevenson of Illinois. Stevenson, however, had refused to run and had to be drafted at the convention. Kefauver led on the first and second ballots, followed by Stevenson. On the third ballot, Stevenson went over the top. He chose Sen. John Jackson Sparkman of Alabama as his running mate. Sparkman was duly nominated, but only after India Moffett Edwards and Sarah Tilghman Hughes had been placed in nomination and then withdrew.

Both conventions featured extensive television coverage for the first time. The year also saw the entrance of two colorful third-party candidates onto the political scene: Bishop Homer Aubrey Tomlinson, carrying the banner of the Church of God Party, and Henry B. Krajewski, a pig farmer was the candidate of the Poor Man's Party. In the fall campaign, Stevenson presented himself as a cerebral and witty candidate while Eisenhower, who was touted as "everyone's friend," promised to end the Korean war. When Stevenson was attacked for being divorced, conservative Democrats endorsed Eisenhower. At one point, the Republicans almost dropped Nixon from the ticket when a secret campaign fund he maintained was revealed. His dramatic television defense of his humble background demonstrated his political skills and effectively killed the controversy. In the end, issues counted less than popularity, and Stevenson could not match Ike in that regard. Indeed, as the Republican slogan proclaimed, it was "time for a change." Eisenhower won in a landslide.

AMERICA FIRST PARTY

CANDIDATE FOR PRESIDENT:
Douglas MacArthur (WI)

CANDIDATE FOR VICE PRESIDENT:
Harry Flood Byrd (VA)

CONVENTION:
August 25, 1952, Kansas City (MO)

AMERICAN LABOR PARTY

CANDIDATE FOR PRESIDENT:
Vincent William Hallinan (CA)

CANDIDATE FOR VICE PRESIDENT:
Charlotta A. Spears Bass (NY)

CONVENTION:
August 28, 1952, City Center Casino, New York, (NY)

The party endorsed the candidates of the Progressive Party.

AMERICAN VEGETARIAN PARTY

CANDIDATE FOR PRESIDENT:
Daniel J. Murphy

CANDIDATE FOR VICE PRESIDENT:
Symon Gould (NY)

CANDIDATES FOR PRESIDENTIAL NOMINATION:
Herbert Charles Holdridge (CA)
Daniel J. Murphy (CA)

PLATFORM HIGHLIGHTS:
SUPPORTED:
- appointment by all governments of "ministers of peace" who would meet together on a continuous basis to promote international harmony
- a natural and healthful diet for all
- vegetarianism as a means to world peace and a higher cultural attainment by people everywhere

OPPOSED:
- "the slaughter of any living thing"

AMERICAN VEGETARIAN PARTY
VOTE FOR PRESIDENTIAL NOMINATION:
BRIGADIER GENERAL HOLDRIDGE WAS NOMINATED BUT DECLINED. MURPHY THEN BECAME THE PRESIDENTIAL CANDIDATE.

CHRISTIAN NATIONALIST PARTY
CANDIDATE FOR PRESIDENT:
Douglas MacArthur (WI)

CANDIDATE FOR VICE PRESIDENT:
Jack Breckinridge Tenney (CA)

CONVENTION:
September 8–9, 1952, Embassy Auditorium, Los Angeles (CA)

The Christian Nationalist Party's platform used only the words of Gen. Douglas MacArthur. It posed a choice between "a spiritual reawakening to overcome moral lapse or a progressive deterioration leading to ultimate national disaster." The advance of communism abroad was attributed to Truman's weak leadership as exemplified by the "blunders" in Korea.

PLATFORM HIGHLIGHTS:
SUPPORTED:
- the preservation of the religious base of the nation
- moving the country away from State Socialism and Communism
- free enterprise and states' rights
- "sound leadership" as the way out of the problems confronting the nation
- the Christian faith as "that mighty bulwark of all freedom"

OPPOSED:
- the burden of taxation
- communism as an "evil force"

CHURCH OF GOD PARTY
CANDIDATE FOR PRESIDENT:
Homer Aubrey Tomlinson (NY)

CANDIDATE FOR VICE PRESIDENT:
Willie Isaac Bass (NC)

CONVENTION:
July 2–8, 1952, Moses Tabernacle, Nashville (TN)

The Church of God Party was organized July 4, 1952, at the forty-sixth annual General Assembly of the Church of God in Nashville (TN).

CONSTITUTION PARTY
CANDIDATE FOR PRESIDENT:
Douglas MacArthur (WI)

CANDIDATE FOR VICE PRESIDENT:
Vivien Kellems (CT) (Harry Flood Byrd [VA] declined)

CONVENTION:
August 31, 1952, Philadelphia (PA)

DEMOCRATIC PARTY
CANDIDATE FOR PRESIDENT:
Adlai Ewing Stevenson

CANDIDATE FOR VICE PRESIDENT:
John Jackson Sparkman

CANDIDATES FOR PRESIDENTIAL NOMINATION:
Charles Elmer Broughton (WI)
Edmund Gerald Brown, Sr. (CA)
Robert Johns Bulkley (OH)
Charles C. Compton (CA)
Paul Howard Douglas (IL)
William Orville Douglas (WA)
Dwight David Eisenhower (NY)
James Aloysius Farley (NY)
Jerome Francis Fox (WI)
William Averell Harriman (NY)
Hubert Horatio Humphrey (MN)
Carey Estes Kefauver (TN)
Robert Samuel Kerr (OK)
Douglas MacArthur (WI)
Richard Brevard Russell (GA)
Carroll S. Shaw (FL)
Adlai Ewing Stevenson (IL)
Robert Alphonso Taft (OH)
Harry S Truman (MO)

CANDIDATES FOR VICE-PRESIDENTIAL NOMINATION:
India Moffett Edwards (MD)
Sarah Tilghman Hughes (TX)
John Jackson Sparkman (AL)

PRIMARIES:
MARCH 11, 1952 (NH):
Kefauver 19,800

Truman 15,927
MacArthur 151
Farley 77
Stevenson 40

MARCH 18, 1952 (MN):
Humphrey 102,527
Kefauver 20,182
Truman 3,634
Eisenhower 1,753

APRIL 1, 1952 (NE):
Kefauver 64,531
Kerr 42,467

APRIL 1, 1952 (WI):
Kefauver 207,520
Fox 18,322
Broughton 15,683

APRIL 8, 1952 (IL):
Kefauver 526,301
Stevenson 54,336
Truman 9,024
Eisenhower 6,655
others 23,798

APRIL 15, 1952 (NJ):
Kefauver 154,964

APRIL 22, 1952 (PA):
Kefauver 93,160
Eisenhower 28,660
Truman 26,504
Taft 8,311
Harriman 3,745
Stevenson 3,678
Russell 1,691
others 9,026

APRIL 29, 1952 (MA):
Kefauver 29,287
Eisenhower 16,007
Truman 7,256

MAY 5, 1952 (MD):
Kefauver 137,885
unpledged delegates 46,361

MAY 6, 1952 (FL):
Russell 367,980
Kefauver 285,358
Compton 11,331
Shaw 9,965

MAY 6, 1952 (OH):
Kefauver 305,992
Bulkley 184,880

MAY 13, 1952 (WV):
unpledged delegates 191,471

MAY 16, 1952 (OR):
Kefauver 142,440
Douglas 29,532

Stevenson 20,353
Eisenhower 4,690

JUNE 3, 1952 (CA):
Kefauver 1,155,839
Brown 485,578

JUNE 3, 1952 (SD):
Kefauver 22,812
others 11,741

31ST CONVENTION:
July 21–26, 1952, International Amphitheatre,
    Chicago (IL)
Paul Andrew Dever (MA), temporary chairman
Samuel Taliaferro Rayburn (TX), permanent chair-
man

The Democratic platform praised twenty years of progress under Presidents Roosevelt and Truman: ending the Depression and achieving prosperity, strengthening democracy, and building peace with honor.

PLATFORM HIGHLIGHTS:
SUPPORTED:
- the United Nations
- a fair and effective peace settlement in Korea
- a strong defense against Soviet aggression
- collective security agreements
- European unity and the North Atlantic community
- reunification of Germany under democratic control
- the victims of Soviet imperialism
- development of the Middle East and assistance for Israel
- continuation of the Good Neighbor policy in Latin America
- aid to India and Pakistan
- collective security pacts in the Pacific
- progress toward disarmament
- implementation of Point IV programs
- self-determination for small nations
- expansion of world trade
- aid for refugees from communism
- liberalization of the immigration laws
- stabilization of the economy by keeping prices down, promoting full employment, maintaining rent controls, and reducing taxes and closing tax loopholes
- restraint in government expenditures
- resource conservation
- flood prevention
- watershed protection
- farmer participation in agricultural programs
- price supports
- retention of the agricultural adjustment program
- expanded research and education programs
- reductions in trade barriers
- crop insurance
- expanded rural electrification and telephone services
- cooperatives
- liberal farm credit

- the family farm as the keystone of U.S. agriculture
- the repeal of the Taft-Hartley Act
- enforcement of fair labor standards
- employment opportunities for physically handicapped persons
- improvement in the working conditions of migratory workers
- enactment of legislation to ensure equal pay for equal work for all
- the free enterprise system
- assistance to small and independent businesses
- enforcement of antitrust laws
- protection of investors and consumers against unfair trade practices
- continued development of harbors and waterways
- the merchant marine
- expansion of the nation's road and highway network, including farm-to-market roads
- protection of natural resources
- progressive development of land and water projects
- river basin development
- the opening of the nation's phosphate rock deposits to provide commercial fertilizer
- utilization of forest and rangeland management practices
- irrigation programs
- exploration and development of mineral resources
- domestic fisheries
- improvement of recreational areas
- the use of atomic energy for peaceful purposes, eventually under international control
- the development of enough nuclear firepower to defend the nation
- benefits for veterans
- Social Security
- old age and survivors' insurance
- unemployment insurance
- public assistance programs for "our less fortunate citizens"
- private pension plans
- cooperative efforts to employ older workers
- medical research and federal aid for medical education and hospital construction
- a nonpartisan commission on health needs of the nation to study ways of reducing health care costs
- additional housing for defense workers, aged persons, migratory farm laborers, middle income families, and veterans
- federal aid to education for scholarships, new school construction, teachers' salaries, and vocational education programs
- expansion of the school lunch program
- establishment of day care programs
- improved maternal and child health and welfare services
- help for the children of migratory workers
- further reorganization of the government to promote efficiency

- improvements in the postal service
- a strengthened civil service
- legislation requiring full disclosure of campaign expenditures
- the commonwealth status of Puerto Rico
- statehood for Alaska and Hawaii
- home rule for the District of Columbia
- self-government for the Virgin Islands and other territories
- the protection of American Indians' rights as citizens and under treaty obligations
- reform of congressional procedures to prevent unreasonable obstruction of the will of the majority
- a strong civil rights program

OPPOSED:
- a federal sales tax
- special tax privileges

DEMOCRATIC PARTY
VOTE FOR PRESIDENTIAL NOMINATION:

Candidate	Ballot: 1	2	3
Kefauver	340	362½	275½
Stevenson	273	324½	617½
Russell	268	294	261
Harriman	123½	121	0
Kerr	65	5½	0
Barkley	48½	78	67½
Dever	37½	30½	½
Humphrey	26	0	0
Fulbright	22	0	0
Murray	12	0	0
Truman	6	6	0
Ewing	4	3	3
Douglas, W. O.	3	3	3
Douglas, P. H.	½	0	0
not voting	1	1½	2

Stevenson's nomination was made unanimous.

VOTE FOR VICE-PRESIDENTIAL NOMINATION:
EDWARDS, HUGHES, AND SPARKMAN WERE PLACED
IN NOMINATION FOR VICE PRESIDENT, BUT
EDWARDS AND HUGHES WITHDREW. SPARKMAN
WAS NOMINATED BY ACCLAMATION.

GREENBACK PARTY
CANDIDATE FOR PRESIDENT:
Frederick C. Proehl (WA)

CANDIDATE FOR VICE PRESIDENT:
Edward John Bedell (IN)

Candidates were chosen by mail referendum.

PLATFORM HIGHLIGHTS:

SUPPORTED:

- the reversal of the "present order of things, and put[ting] money into the hands of the industrious people first"
- conscription of property without compensation for the defense of the nation
- the replacement of charity with government programs for the disabled and needy
- the elimination of child labor
- payment of old age pensions
- abolition of special privilege and monopolies
- a "just and fair" wage law
- immediate abolition of government bonds
- the issuance of a large supply of paper money unbacked by gold or silver

INDEPENDENT

CANDIDATE FOR PRESIDENT:
Morgan Blake (GA)

LIBERTY PARTY

The Liberty Party entered a slate of presidential electors in the general election in Georgia. The slate was headed by Mrs. Jessie Jenkins.

NEW YORK BUSINESS AND PROFESSIONAL WOMEN'S FEDERATION

CANDIDATE FOR PRESIDENT:
none

CANDIDATES FOR VICE PRESIDENT:
Margaret Chase Smith (ME)

SARAH TILGHMAN HUGHES (TX)

This association endorsed women as prospective vice-presidential candidates for nomination by both major parties. Smith was recommended for the Republicans and Hughes for the Democrats.

OREGON INDEPENDENT

CANDIDATE FOR PRESIDENT:
none

CANDIDATE FOR VICE PRESIDENT:
none

PEOPLE'S PARTY OF CONNECTICUT

CANDIDATE FOR PRESIDENT:
none

CANDIDATE FOR VICE PRESIDENT:
none

POOR MAN'S PARTY

CANDIDATE FOR PRESIDENT:
Henry B. Krajewski (NJ)

CANDIDATE FOR VICE PRESIDENT:
Frank Jenkins (NJ)

PLATFORM HIGHLIGHTS:

The platform proposed an income tax moratorium on all incomes below six thousand dollars and a two-president system (because "they'd be so busy watching each other that there would be no danger of a dictatorship"). It supported a national lottery and free beer for the poor. The party's candidate opposed frequent changes in military uniforms and campaigned with a pig under his arm.

PROGRESSIVE PARTY

CANDIDATE FOR PRESIDENT:
Vincent William Hallinan (CA)

CANDIDATE FOR VICE PRESIDENT:
Charlotta A. Spears Bass (NY)

2ND CONVENTION:
July 4–6, 1952, International Amphitheatre, Chicago (IL)

PLATFORM HIGHLIGHTS:

SUPPORTED:

- an immediate cease-fire in Korea
- full and equal rights for African Americans
- restoration of the Bill of Rights
- repeal of the Taft-Hartley, Smith, and McCarran acts
- denunciation of McCarthyism
- an end to blacklisting
- promotion of U.S.-Soviet understanding and cooperation as the key to peace
- the United Nations and the convening of a conference among the five great powers (China, France, Great Britain, Soviet Union, and United States) to resolve their differences
- an international agreement to outlaw the atomic bomb
- recognition of the People's Republic of China
- discontinuation of relations with fascist Spain
- repeal of the draft
- elimination of trade barriers between East and West
- immediate independence for Puerto Rico
- self-determination around the globe
- statehood for Alaska and Hawaii
- a prompt return to a peacetime economy
- strict price ceilings and restoration of rent controls to pre-Korean War levels
- the end of the wage freeze
- the re-enactment of the Wagner Act
- a national housing program
- tax reforms favoring the poor
- strengthened federal Social Security, old age, unemployment, and disability programs
- a family allowance of three dollars per week for each child

- national health insurance
- a comprehensive farm program providing 100-percent parity prices for agricultural commodities
- an end to sharecropping
- the extension of public benefit programs to farm workers
- an increase in the minimum wage to $1.25 per hour
- federal aid for school construction, teachers' salaries, and new educational programs
- tough enforcement of mining safety laws
- creation of a national system of job training centers for young people
- the right to vote for eighteen-year-olds
- enactment of a new GI Bill of Rights for post-World War II veterans
- subsidies for the arts and theater
- enactment of antilynching and anti-poll tax legislation
- revision of Senate cloture rules
- enforcement of a federal fair employment practices law
- immediate elimination of discrimination in the armed forces and in employment involving federal contracts
- home rule for the District of Columbia
- an end to Jim Crow laws
- minority representation at all levels of government
- full citizenship for American Indians
- restoration of freedom to all U.S. citizens
- abolition of the House Un-American Activities Committee, the Senate Committee on Internal Security, the attorney general's subversive list, and other forms of government intimidation
- ratification of the United Nations Genocide Treaty
- a halt to the persecution of foreign-born U.S. citizens
- protection for lawyers who defend minority opinions and causes
- the separation of church and state
- an end to government secrecy
- the freeing of teachers from "thought control" by government

OPPOSED:
- the Korean War as the cause of the high cost of living
- the housing crisis
- the neglect of various social needs
- the rearmament of Germany
- racist and fascist regimes in South Africa and elsewhere
- segregation, calling for an end to "America's shame" of discrimination

PROHIBITION PARTY

CANDIDATE FOR PRESIDENT:
Stuart Hamblen

CANDIDATE FOR VICE PRESIDENT:
Enoch Arden Holtwick (IL)

CANDIDATES FOR PRESIDENTIAL NOMINATION:
Stuart Hamblen (CA)
Enoch Arden Holtwick (IL)

21ST CONVENTION:
November 13–15, 1951, Indianapolis (IN)

At this convention 115 delegates cast ballots.

PLATFORM HIGHLIGHTS:
SUPPORTED:
- governmental economy through reorganization
- tax reductions
- world peace and order
- religious freedom
- enforcement of all laws against gambling, narcotics, and commercialized vice
- the overthrow of liquor traffic
- free enterprise and compulsory arbitration of labor disputes
- Social Security (while deploring its use for political ends)
- enactment of uniform marriage and divorce laws
- the separation of church and state
- an end to racial discrimination
- restoration of congressional control over the issuance of money
- ballot law reform to permit independent voters and minority parties to exercise the right of free political expression

OPPOSED:
- atheistic communism
- compulsory military training

PROHIBITION PARTY
VOTE FOR PRESIDENTIAL NOMINATION:

Candidate	Ballot: 1
Hamblen	74
Holtwick	41

VOTE FOR VICE-PRESIDENTIAL NOMINATION:
HOLTWICK WAS UNANIMOUSLY NOMINATED ON THE FIRST BALLOT.

REPUBLICAN PARTY

CANDIDATE FOR PRESIDENT:
Dwight David Eisenhower

CANDIDATE FOR VICE PRESIDENT:
Richard Milhous Nixon

CANDIDATES FOR PRESIDENTIAL NOMINATION:
Riley Alvin Bender (IL)
Dwight David Eisenhower (NY)
Carey Estes Kefauver (TN)
Mary E. Jaques Kenny (NE)
Douglas MacArthur (WI)
Wayne Lyman Morse (OR)
Grant Adolph Ritter (WI)

William Richard Schneider (MO)
Edward C. Slettedahl (MN)
Harold Edward Stassen (MN)
Perry Jay Stearns (WI)
Robert Alphonso Taft (OH)
Harry S Truman (MO)
Earl Warren (CA)
Thomas Harold Werdel (CA)

CANDIDATES FOR VICE-PRESIDENTIAL NOMINATION:
Richard Milhous Nixon (CA)
Margaret Chase Smith (ME)

PRIMARIES:
MARCH 11, 1952 (NH):
Eisenhower 46,661
Taft 35,838
Stassen 6,574
MacArthur 3,227
Schneider 230

MARCH 18, 1952 (MN):
Stassen 129,706
Eisenhower 108,692
Taft 24,093
Slettedahl 22,712
Warren 5,365
MacArthur 1,369
Kefauver 386

APRIL 1, 1952 (NE):
Taft 79,357
Eisenhower 66,078
Stassen 53,238
Kenny 10,411
MacArthur 7,478
Warren 1,872
others 767

APRIL 1, 1952 (WI):
Taft 315,541
Warren 262,271
Stassen 169,679
Ritter 26,208
Stearns 2,925

APRIL 8, 1952 (IL):
Taft 935,867
Stassen 155,041
Eisenhower 147,518
Warren 22,841
Bender 22,321
MacArthur 7,504
others 1,229

APRIL 15, 1952 (NJ):
Eisenhower 390,591
Taft 228,916
Stassen 23,559

APRIL 22, 1952 (PA):
Eisenhower 863,785

Taft 178,629
Stassen 120,305
MacArthur 6,028
Warren 3,158
Truman 267
others 1,121

APRIL 29, 1952 (MA):
Eisenhower 254,898
Taft 110,188

MAY 6, 1952 (OH):
Taft 663,791
Stassen 178,739

MAY 13, 1952 (WV):
Taft 139,812
Stassen 38,251

MAY 16, 1952 (OR):
Eisenhower 172,486
Warren 44,034
MacArthur 18,603
Taft 18,009
Morse 7,105
Stassen 6,610
Schneider 350

JUNE 3, 1952 (CA):
Warren 1,029,495
Werdel 521,110

JUNE 3, 1952 (SD):
Taft 64,695
Eisenhower 63,879

25TH CONVENTION:
July 7–11, 1952, International Amphitheatre,
Chicago (IL)
Walter S. Hallanan (WV), temporary chairman
Joseph William Martin Jr. (MA), permanent chair-
man
Douglas MacArthur (WI), keynoter

The Republican platform charged the Democrats with working "unceasingly to achieve their goal of national socialism."
It blamed the Roosevelt and Truman administrations for a
variety of social ills and foreign policy blunders. It also condemned the corruption of the Truman administration and
praised the record of the Republican 80th Congress.

PLATFORM HIGHLIGHTS:
SUPPORTED:
• peace in Korea
• the elimination of loafers, incompetents, and Communists from government
• protection of U.S. interests in the Far East, Western
  Europe, and Latin America
• Israel and Arab-Israeli peace
• the United Nations
• initiation of international student exchange programs
• reciprocal trade agreements and their maintenance

- the buildup of national defense as a deterrent to Soviet aggression
- arms control
- the overhaul of loyalty and internal security programs to make them more effective
- small businesses
- elimination of federal rent controls
- slum clearance with local cooperation
- a balanced budget and a reduced national debt
- a dollar that is fully convertible on a gold basis
- a decrease in taxes and economy in government
- full parity prices for crops
- commodity loans and cheap credit for farmers
- voluntary self-supporting crop insurance
- rural electrification and communications development
- soil conservation and flood control
- decentralization and local control of many agricultural programs
- expanded agricultural research and education
- recognition of the family farm's value
- retention of the Taft-Hartley Act
- vigorous development and conservation of natural resources
- public works programs that were "economically justifiable," giving particular attention to water resource programs
- local participation in public works programs rather than "all-powerful federal socialistic valley authorities"
- restoration of the traditional Republican public land policy that promoted ownership based on the highest and best use
- increased benefits for veterans
- extension of programs to Korean War veterans
- improvements in the Veterans Administration hospitals
- Social Security, but urged "a thorough study of universal pay-as-we-go pension plans"

REPUBLICAN PARTY
VOTE FOR PRESIDENTIAL NOMINATION:

Candidate	Ballot: 1a	1b[1]
Eisenhower	595	845
Taft	500	280
Warren	81	77
Stassen	20	0
MacArthur	10	4

Eisenhower's nomination was made unanimous.

[1] first ballot, before and after the shift

VOTE FOR VICE-PRESIDENTIAL NOMINATION:
SMITH AND NIXON WERE OFFERED FOR CONSIDERATION FOR THE VICE-PRESIDENTIAL NOMINATION, BUT SMITH DECLINED. NIXON WAS THEN NOMINATED BY ACCLAMATION.

- scientific research
- state and local control of education
- state supervision of civil rights
- promotion of equal employment opportunities
- elimination of lynching
- an equal rights amendment to the U.S. Constitution
- statehood for Alaska and Hawaii and eventual statehood for Puerto Rico
- an end to segregation in the District of Columbia
- self-government and national suffrage for the District of Columbia
- full rights of citizenship for American Indians
- a personnel program for the federal career service based on merit
- more efficient and frequent mail delivery
- reorganization of the government in accordance with the Hoover Commission

OPPOSED:
- secret agreements made at Yalta
- compulsory health insurance

SOCIALIST LABOR PARTY

CANDIDATE FOR PRESIDENT:
Eric Hass (NY)

CANDIDATE FOR VICE PRESIDENT:
Stephen Emery (NY)

23RD CONVENTION:
May 3–5, 1952, Henry Hudson Hotel, New York (NY)
John P. Quinn (MA), temporary chairman
Nathan Karp (NY), permanent chairman

Twenty-nine delegates from sixteen states and the District of Columbia and three ethnic federations (e.g., Slovak Federation of the United States, German-American Cultural Association) attended this convention.

PLATFORM HIGHLIGHTS:
The platform of the Socialist Labor Party announced a revolutionary crisis and capitalism's impending collapse. The platform asserted that "the ferocious conflict that divides the world and threatens to hurl mankind into the fiery furnace of global war is an imperialist conflict." It saw both the United States and the Soviet Union as struggling to control the world's economic resources, much to the detriment of working people everywhere. To the Socialist Laborites, the class struggle was intensifying, the standard of living for workers was falling, and basic freedoms were in jeopardy.

SUPPORTED:
- the reconstruction of society based on democratic, Socialist industrial government
- collective ownership of land and all the instruments of wealth production

- worker control of industry through industrial union councils

OPPOSED:

- Soviet communism, British-type socialism, and reform movements, claiming for itself the rightful loyalty of the working class

---

SOCIALIST LABOR PARTY
VOTE FOR PRESIDENTIAL AND VICE-PRESIDENTIAL NOMINATIONS: HASS AND EMERY WERE UNANIMOUSLY NOMINATED FOR PRESIDENT VICE PRESIDENT, RESPECTIVELY, BY RISING VOTE

SOCIALIST PARTY

CANDIDATE FOR PRESIDENT:
Darlington Hoopes (PA)

CANDIDATE FOR VICE PRESIDENT:
Samuel Herman Friedman

CANDIDATES FOR VICE-PRESIDENTIAL NOMINATION:
Samuel Herman Friedman (NY)
Robin Meyers (NY)

CONVENTION:
May 30 and June 1–2, 1952, Hotel Hollenden, Cleveland (OH)

PLATFORM HIGHLIGHTS:
The Socialist Party's platform defended socialism against the misrepresentations of the McCarthyites and affirmed that socialism was the completion of political and economic democracy. The platform stressed the importance of community under democratic socialism, reminding workers that public ownership was not an end in itself and that it must include decentralized worker control.

SUPPORTED:

- social ownership and democratic management of basic industries, public utilities, and banking and credit institutions
- preservation and management of the nation's natural resources by the people rather than private interests
- planned production for use rather than for profit
- a policy of internationalism
- movement toward controlled and supervised disarmament
- organization of an international police force
- demilitarization of strategic waterways
- world planning to ensure access to food and raw materials to all peoples
- reduction of trade barriers
- establishment of a peace council
- development of regional federations of countries
- peace in Korea
- eventual evolution of the United Nations into a world government

- the end of conscription
- international control of atomic weapons
- withdrawal of U.S. troops from abroad
- the end of military involvement in civilian decisions
- the channeling of foreign aid through the United Nations to promote world development
- the fostering of international brotherhood
- denouncement of South Africa's discriminatory policies
- destruction of the Iron Curtain and of Stalinism throughout the world
- massive aid to education
- enactment of an all-inclusive health insurance plan
- expansion of medical research
- increases in maternal and child health services
- conservation of natural resources (including support for nine regional development projects)
- creation of a home loan bank to finance home purchases
- creation of a public supply corporation to set up factory units for housing production
- new housing initiatives to meet the housing shortage
- price controls as a stopgap measure to control inflation
- changes in tax policies and an expansion of production as better approaches to controlling inflation
- added benefits under Social Security
- an increase in the minimum wage to one dollar per hour
- family farms and an end to absentee ownership
- elimination of commodity speculations
- social ownership and cooperative operation of large-scale farms
- a halt to the destruction of civil liberties in the name of rooting out subversives
- limits on loyalty screening to jobs actually involving national security
- abolition of the House Un-American Activities Committee
- democratic procedures and due process when charges are levied against someone
- elimination of discrimination against the exercise of the free ballot
- repeal of the Taft-Hartley Act
- union democracy
- the rights of labor to collective action
- amnesty for conscientious objectors and restoration of their civil rights
- the banning of all forms of segregation and discrimination
- fair employment practices
- self-government for the District of Columbia
- statehood for Alaska, Hawaii, and Puerto Rico

OPPOSED:

- the aggressive imperialism of the Soviet Union
- the hostile U.S. reaction to a perceived Soviet threat
- the division between the privileged nations and the have-not nations
- capitalism

- the Smith Act and the outlawing of the Communist Party
- the poll tax
- unwarranted censorship and pressure on teachers and textbooks

SOCIALIST WORKERS PARTY

CANDIDATE FOR PRESIDENT:
Farrell Dobbs (NY)

CANDIDATE FOR VICE PRESIDENT:
Myra Tanner Weiss (NY)

CONVENTION:
July 20, 1952, New York (NY)

PLATFORM HIGHLIGHTS:
The platform of the Socialist Workers Party proclaimed impending disaster, with the military machine devouring the nation's wealth and resources. According to the party, the United States stood on the "brink of the most destructive of all wars" with "half the peoples of the world . . . ranged against us." Prosperity was reserved for the "kings of finance and industry" while "the mass of working people . . . received only the crumbs." It was not communism that threatened the United States; it was capitalism and imperialism in the form of Wall Street and the Pentagon. The party went on to denounce the Democrats and Republicans as supporters of the war program of big business.

SUPPORTED:
- the fight for a Labor Party of working people
- reorganization of the wealth of the United States on a Socialist basis, under the rule of workers and poor farmers
- withdrawal of U.S. troops from Korea and from all other overseas stations
- recognition of Communist China (i.e., the People's Republic of China)
- the right to vote for eighteen-year-olds
- a national referendum to consider war
- an end to anti-Communist witch-hunts and prosecution of political minorities
- repeal of the Smith Act and the McCarran "concentration camp" law
- an end to loyalty programs and lists of subversive activities
- repeal of the McCarran-Walters immigration law
- enactment of a fair employment practices committee
- complete abolition of segregation, restrictive covenants in housing, the poll tax, and Jim Crowism
- enactment of an antilynching law
- equal pay for equal work for all
- adequate federal nursery care and summer camps for children
- repeal of the Taft-Hartley Act and other antilabor legislation

- abolition of the wage freeze
- an end to profiteering
- compulsory cost-of-living adjustments in wages, pensions, and unemployment compensation
- imposition of price and rent controls
- taxes on the rich and not on the poor, suggesting that no taxes be required on incomes below $7,500
- national health service
- a massive public housing program
- adequate old age pensions
- a federal program to guarantee a college education for all youth
- full democratic rights and union scale wages for military personnel
- abolition of sharecropping
- expansion of rural electrification
- ending crop limits
- soil conservation and flood-control programs
- a tax exemption on savings of cooperatives
- a ban on commodity speculation
- price supports
- nationalization of basic industries, war plants, natural resources, and banks under democratically elected management of workers and technicians, resulting in a planned economy of abundance

OPPOSED:
- Stalinist rule abroad
- the evils of capitalism and militarism at home
- all sales taxes and the wage freeze
- the draft

WASHINGTON PEACE PARTY

CANDIDATE FOR PRESIDENT:
Ellen Linea W. Jensen (FL)

CANDIDATE FOR VICE PRESIDENT:
(secret candidate)

WRITE-IN

CANDIDATES FOR PRESIDENT:
Douglas MacArthur (WI)
Robert Alphonso Taft (OH)
Capt. Samuel G. Mitchell (NY)
Dwight David Eisenhower (PA)
Carey Estes Kefauver (TN)
Walter L. Hollander
William Averell Harriman (NY)

CANDIDATES FOR VICE PRESIDENT:
Earl Warren (CA)
G. Searles Aiken

GENERAL ELECTION SUMMARY FOR 1952			
Candidate	Electoral Votes	States	Popular Votes
Eisenhower (R)	442	39	33,778,964[1]
Stevenson (D)	89	9	27,314,992
SC REP	0	0	158,289
Hallinan (PROG)	0	0	135,007[2]
Hamblen (PROH)	0	0	72,769
Hass (SOC LAB)	0	0	30,376
Hoopes (SOC)	0	0	19,685
MacArthur	0	0	17,211[3]
Dobbs (SOC WOR)	0	0	10,306
Krajewski (POOR)	0	0	4,203
OR IND	0	0	3,665
PEO CT	0	0	1,466
SOC DEMS	0	0	504
Taft (WR)	0	0	2
Harriman (WR)	0	0	1
Hollander (WR)	0	0	1
Kefauver (WR)	0	0	1
Jenkins (LIB)	0	0	1
Mitchell (WR)	0	0	1
Blake (I)	0	0	
Jensen (WP)	0	0	
Murphy (AM VEG)	0	0	
Proehl (GRE)	0	0	
Tomlinson (CG)	0	0	
unknown	0	0	4,489

[1]includes one write-in vote from New York

[2]includes American Labor Party totals

[3]includes 13,883 from the Christian Nationalist Party, 3,089 from the Constitution Party, 233 from the America First Party, and 6 write-in votes from New York

ELECTION OF NOVEMBER 6, 1956

President
DWIGHT DAVID EISENHOWER
Vice President
RICHARD MILHOUS NIXON

HIGHLIGHTS

With peace and prosperity as their watchwords, the Republicans entered the fray of 1956 with great confidence. Despite his heart attack in 1955, Dwight Eisenhower's doctors had given him a clean bill of health and he remained highly popular (particularly after his Big Four summit in Geneva the same year). Richard Nixon had successfully avoided controversy and seemed a shoo-in for renomination, even though some party stalwarts had hoped for an alternative. On the Democrats' side, Adlai Stevenson was the titular leader and the likely nominee of his party, thus setting the stage for a replay of 1952. Sen. Carey Estes Kefauver of Tennessee also coveted the Democratic nomination, however, and pursued it vigorously. Harry Truman added another element to the convention suspense by announcing his support for Governor Averell Harriman of New York, but the contest was short-lived; Stevenson was nominated on the first ballot. In an unusual move, Stevenson then deferred the selection of his running mate to the convention delegates. A spirited struggle emerged among Kefauver's supporters, the backers of young Massachusetts senator John F. Kennedy, partisans of Hubert H. Humphrey, the promoters of Tennessee senator Albert A. Gore, and those endorsing New York City mayor Robert Ferdinand Wagner. The resulting Stevenson-Kefauver ticket failed to rally voter enthusiasm. It was a rather colorless and lethargic campaign, even though late-breaking news of the Soviet invasion of Hungary and the crisis in the Suez did turn some attention to foreign policy concerns. In the end, Ike was reelected in another landslide.

AMERICAN THIRD PARTY

CANDIDATE FOR PRESIDENT:
Henry B. Krajewski (NJ)

CANDIDATE FOR VICE PRESIDENT:
Anne Marie Yezo (NJ)

PLATFORM HIGHLIGHTS:
The American Third Party's platform advocated a "cold war on parents of juvenile delinquents." It also supported a national prize lottery. The party's candidate pledged that if he was elected "everybody in America will be happy."

AMERICAN VEGETARIAN PARTY

CANDIDATE FOR PRESIDENT:
Herbert MacGolphin Shelton (CA)

CANDIDATE FOR VICE PRESIDENT:
Symon Gould (NY)

CONVENTION:
July 6, 1956, Los Angeles (CA)

PLATFORM HIGHLIGHTS:
The platform of the American Vegetarian Party promoted vegetarianism.

CHRISTIAN NATIONALIST PARTY

CANDIDATE FOR PRESIDENT:
Gerald Lyman Kenneth Smith (MO)

CANDIDATE FOR VICE PRESIDENT:
Charles Franklin Robertson (AR)

PLATFORM HIGHLIGHTS:
The platform of the Christian Nationalist Party urged the outlawing of interracial marriage and the establishment of white supremacy. It sought to limit immigration, dismantle the federal bureaucracy, and withdraw the United States from the United Nations. The party called for an investigation of the Anti-Defamation League, abolition of the income tax, and support for states' rights.

CONSTITUTION PARTY

CANDIDATE FOR PRESIDENT:
Thomas Coleman Andrews (VA)

CANDIDATE FOR VICE PRESIDENT:
Thomas Harold Werdel (CA)

CONVENTION:

August 27–28, 1956, Fort Worth (TX)

Seventy-five delegates gathered from seventeen states.

PLATFORM HIGHLIGHTS:

SUPPORTED:

- states' rights
- repeal of the income tax
- reductions in government spending, the national debt, and foreign aid giveaways
- the Bricker Amendment
- the elimination of government from competition with private enterprise
- restoration of the system of checks and balances to restrain the Supreme Court
- suspension of all relations with Communist nations
- enforcement of selective and protective immigration
- a return of the power to issue money to Congress

ALSO:

These planks were supplemented with resolutions urging that Social Security be made a voluntary program, that the entire Supreme Court be impeached and removed from office, and that the federal government not be involved in education. Other resolutions supported the doctrine of interposition, the teaching of Americanism and free enterprise, a repeal of the Status of Forces Treaty, withdrawal from the United Nations, an end to farm subsidies, and "right to work" laws. The platform opposed "socialized medicine," defined appropriate methods for constructing constitutional intent, and demanded the return of U.S. servicemen and other U.S. citizens held as prisoners in the People's Republic of China.

DEMOCRATIC PARTY

CANDIDATE FOR PRESIDENT:

Adlai Ewing Stevenson

CANDIDATE FOR VICE PRESIDENT:

Carey Estes Kefauver

CANDIDATES FOR PRESIDENTIAL NOMINATION:

John Stewart Battle (VA)
Albert Benjamin Chandler (KY)
James Curran Davis (GA)
Dwight David Eisenhower (PA)
William Averell Harriman (NY)
Lyndon Baines Johnson (TX)
Carey Estes Kefauver (TN)
John Fitzgerald Kennedy (MA)
Frank John Lausche (OH)
John William McCormack (MA)
Adlai Ewing Stevenson (IL)
William Stuart Symington (MO)
George Bell Timmerman, Jr. (SC)

CANDIDATES FOR VICE-PRESIDENTIAL NOMINATION:

Clinton Presba Anderson (NM)

Edmund Gerald Brown, Sr. (CA)
Frank Goad Clement (TN)
Thomas LeRoy Collins (FL)
Albert Arnold Gore, Sr. (TN)
Luther Hartwell Hodges (NC)
Hubert Horatio Humphrey (MN)
Lyndon Baines Johnson (TX)
Carey Estes Kefauver (TN)
John Fitzgerald Kennedy (MA)
Pitt Tyson Maner (AL)
William Stuart Symington (MO)
Robert Ferdinand Wagner (NY)

PRIMARIES:

MARCH 13, 1956 (NH):

Kefauver 21,701
others 3,945

MARCH 20, 1956 (MN):

Kefauver 245,885
Stevenson 186,723
others 48

APRIL 3, 1956 (WI):

Kefauver 330,665

APRIL 10, 1956 (IL):

Stevenson 717,742
Kefauver 34,092
others 1,640

APRIL 17, 1956 (NJ):

Kefauver 117,056
others 5,230

APRIL 24, 1956 (AK TERRITORY):

Stevenson 7,123
Kefauver 4,536

APRIL 24, 1956 (MA):

McCormack 26,128
Stevenson 19,024
Kefauver 4,547
Eisenhower 1,850
Kennedy 949
Harriman 394
Lausche 253
others 1,379

APRIL 24, 1956 (PA):

Stevenson 642,172
Kefauver 36,552
others 7,482

MAY 1, 1956 (DC):

Stevenson 17,306
Kefauver 8,837

MAY 7, 1956 (MD):

Kefauver 112,768
unpledged delegates 58,366

MAY 8, 1956 (IN):

Kefauver 242,842

MAY 8, 1956 (OH):
Lausche 276,670

MAY 8, 1956 (WV):
unpledged delegates 112,832

MAY 15, 1956 (NE):
Kefauver 55,265
others 3,556

MAY 18, 1956 (OR):
Stevenson 98,131
Kefauver 62,987
Harriman 1,887

MAY 29, 1956 (FL):
Stevenson 230,285
Kefauver 216,549

JUNE 5, 1956 (CA):
Stevenson 1,139,964
Kefauver 680,722

JUNE 5, 1956 (MT):
Kefauver 77,228

JUNE 5, 1956 (SD):
Kefauver 30,940

32ND CONVENTION:
August 13–17, 1956, International Amphitheatre, Chicago (IL)
Frank Goad Clement (TN), temporary chairman
Samuel Taliaferro Rayburn (TX), permanent chairman

The Democratic platform ridiculed the Eisenhower administration as a government of "political amateurs." It asserted that the nation lacked leadership in foreign affairs and pledged support for the United Nations, urged efforts to obtain the release of U.S. servicemen and citizens detained by the People's Republic of China, advocated effective disarmament and adequate defense forces, and endorsed national defense student loans.

PLATFORM HIGHLIGHTS:
SUPPORTED:
- collective security and a strong civil defense
- economic development in third world countries
- freedom for the captive European nations (i.e., those behind the "Iron Curtain")
- self-determination for small nations
- expanded reciprocal trade
- movement toward European unity
- peaceful settlement of the differences between Israel and the Arab states
- open access to the Suez Canal
- support for Free Asia and the Latin American republics
- progressive immigration policies
- a humane refugee policy toward victims of Communist oppression
- achievement of a balanced budget

- equitable tax revisions and monetary reforms
- repeal of the Taft-Hartley Act
- expanded world trade
- full parity for agriculture
- the elimination of poverty in the United States
- a competitive free enterprise system with special incentives for small businesses
- improvements in law enforcement, the merchant marine, transportation, highways, and rivers and harbors
- an increase in the minimum wage to $1.25 per hour, full enforcement of the Fair Labor Standards Act, honest administration of the Walsh-Healey Contracts Act, equal pay for equal work, protection for migratory workers, employment for persons with disabilities, and programs to provide jobs in depressed areas (a "Magna Carta for Labor")
- conservation, family farming, strategic stockpiles of agricultural commodities, creation of an International Food Reserve, and 100-percent parity
- price supports for feed grains and other nonbasic storables
- a food stamp program
- expanded school lunch and special milk programs
- improved distribution of food to public institutions and charitable agencies
- lower rates for farm credit
- rural electric and telephone service
- cooperatives
- increased research and price reporting on timber products
- improved Social Security, unemployment insurance, and public assistance programs
- hospital construction and medical training
- expanded medical research
- federal aid for education, school construction, teacher training, cultural exchange, and vocational education
- expanded program of child welfare grants and support for day care centers
- the rehabilitation and employment of physically handicapped individuals
- an increase in the personal tax exemption
- better debt management
- protection for investors
- improvements in the merit system and civil service
- a fair and nonpolitical loyalty program
- modernization and restoration of efficiency in the postal service
- the highest standards of honesty in government and denounced conflicts of interest
- freedom of information and full disclosure of campaign expenditures and contributions
- an equal rights amendment to the Constitution
- better administration of programs and enhanced benefits for veterans
- statehood for Alaska and Hawaii and commonwealth status for Puerto Rico
- home rule and national representation for the District of Columbia

- self-government for Guam, the Virgin Islands, and other territories
- full backing for treaty rights and the rights of citizenship for American Indians
- reform of congressional procedures
- development, management, protection, and conservation of land, water, energy, soil, recreation, national parks, wildlife, domestic fisheries, forest and grazing lands, and other natural resources
- preferences for public power projects
- restoration of integrity to the atomic energy program and acceleration of nuclear development while maintaining a nuclear stockpile sufficient for national defense purposes
- continued efforts to eliminate discrimination in voting, employment, personal security, and education

DEMOCRATIC PARTY
VOTE FOR PRESIDENTIAL NOMINATION:

Candidate	Ballot: 1
Stevenson	905½
Harriman	210
Johnson	80
Symington	45½
Chandler	36½
Davis	33
Battle	32½
Timmerman	23½
Lausche	5½

VOTE FOR VICE-PRESIDENTIAL NOMINATION:

Candidate	Ballot: 1	2a	2b
Kefauver	466½	551½	755½
Kennedy	294½	618	589
Gore	178	110½	13½
Wagner	162½	9½	6
Humphrey	134	74½	2
Hodges	40	½	0
Maner	33	0	0
Collins	28½	0	0
Anderson	16	0	0
Clement	13½	½	½
Brown	1	½	0
Symington	1	0	0
Johnson	½	0	0
not cast	0	0	5½

GREENBACK PARTY
CANDIDATE FOR PRESIDENT:
Frederick C. Proehl (WA)

CANDIDATE FOR VICE PRESIDENT:
Edward Kirby Meador (MA)

Candidates were chosen by mail referendum.

PLATFORM HIGHLIGHTS:
The party's platform promised to reverse the "present order of things and put money into the hands of the industrious people first." It demanded the conscription of property without compensation for the defense of the nation. It also required the replacement of charity through government programs for the disabled and needy, the elimination of child labor, and payment of old age pensions. The party also sought a "just and fair" wage law and abolition of special privilege and monopolies.

INDUSTRIAL GOVERNMENT PARTY
The Industrial Government Party was the Minnesota and New York state affiliate of the Socialist Labor Party.

LIBERAL PARTY
CANDIDATE FOR PRESIDENT:
Adlai Ewing Stevenson (IL)
CANDIDATE FOR VICE PRESIDENT:
Carey Estes Kefauver (TN)

CONVENTION:
September 11, 1956, Manhattan Center, New York (NY)

The Liberal Party was a New York State third party. It normally endorsed the national Democratic ticket.

MILITANT WORKERS PARTY
The Militant Workers Party was a state affiliate of the Socialist Workers Party.

PIONEER PARTY
CANDIDATE FOR PRESIDENT:
William Langer (ND)
CANDIDATE FOR VICE PRESIDENT:
Burr McCloskey (IL)

CONVENTION:
November 26–27, 1955, Wisconsin Hotel, Milwaukee (WI)

The Pioneer Party was an offshoot of the American Rally, a nonpartisan educational association. Thirty delegates attended the convention.

PLATFORM HIGHLIGHTS:
SUPPORTED:
- a return to constitutional government
- a "golden rule" foreign policy
- demilitarization

- free health services
- economic reforms
- "temperance and control of alcoholic beverages at the local level"

ALSO:
- repudiated war and conscription, sought an end to the Cold War, demanded financial and military withdrawal from abroad, and advocated noninterference in the affairs of other nations
- reaffirmed a belief in individual worth and freedom

PIONEER PARTY
VOTE FOR PRESIDENTIAL NOMINATION: LANGER WAS THE DELEGATES' UNANIMOUS CHOICE TO HEAD THE TICKET. BURR MCCLOSKEY (IL) WAS SELECTED AS THE VICE-PRESIDENTIAL NOMINEE.

PROHIBITION PARTY

CANDIDATE FOR PRESIDENT:
Enoch Arden Holtwick (IL)

CANDIDATE FOR VICE PRESIDENT:
Edwin M. Cooper (CA) (Herbert Charles Holdridge [CA] resigned)

22ND CONVENTION:
September 4–6, 1955, Camp Mack, Milford (IN)

The Prohibition Party's platform expressed belief in the Constitution and opposition to totalitarianism.

PLATFORM HIGHLIGHTS:
SUPPORTED:
- a peace initiative, calling for immediate outlawing of all weapons of annihilation and adoption of a progressive, multilateral arms limitation
- foreign relief and economic aid
- new systems to distribute the fruits of an economy of abundance
- governmental reorganization
- tax reduction and economic freedom
- cooperatives and compulsory arbitration of labor disputes
- congressional control over the issuance of money
- religious liberty and the separation of church and state
- Social Security, old age pensions, and unemployment compensation
- enforcement of laws against gambling, narcotics, and commercialized vice
- a return to honesty in government
- enactment of uniform marriage and divorce laws
- ballot law reform
- direct election of the president and vice president
- home rule and congressional representation for the District of Columbia
- immediate statehood for Alaska and Hawaii

- self-government for Guam, Puerto Rico, Samoa, and the Virgin Islands
- recognition of the full citizenship rights of American Indians

OPPOSED:
- universal military training
- the creation of artificial scarcity of agricultural goods through crop limits
- racial discrimination

ALSO:
- regarding the liquor question, wanted to remove the causes of drinking by raising the economic standards of the country, providing psychiatric aid to treat alcoholics, developing recreational programs as an alternative to the tavern, publicizing scientific facts about alcoholic beverages, and enacting laws that would prohibit the manufacture, distribution, and sale of alcoholic beverages.

PROHIBITION PARTY
VOTE FOR THE PRESIDENTIAL NOMINATION: THERE IS NO INFORMATION AVAILABLE ON THE BALLOTING FOR THE PRESIDENTIAL NOMINATION.

VOTE FOR VICE-PRESIDENTIAL NOMINATION: HOLDRIDGE WAS NOMINATED BY THE CONVENTION FOR VICE PRESIDENT, BUT RESIGNED HIS NOMINATION ON FEBRUARY 15, 1956. THE NATIONAL COMMITTEE APPOINTED COOPER TO FILL THE VACANCY ON THE TICKET.

REPUBLICAN PARTY

CANDIDATE FOR PRESIDENT:
Dwight David Eisenhower

CANDIDATE FOR VICE PRESIDENT:
Richard Milhous Nixon (CA)

CANDIDATES FOR PRESIDENTIAL NOMINATION:
Steve C. Arnold (MT)
John William Bricker (OH)
John Bowman Chapple (WI)
Lawrence Joseph Sarsfield "Lar" Daly (IL)
Dwight David Eisenhower (NY)
Christian Archibald Herter (MA)
William Fife Knowland (CA)
John William McCormack (MA)
Richard Milhous Nixon (CA)
Adlai Ewing Stevenson (IL)

PRIMARIES:
MARCH 13, 1956 (NH):
Eisenhower 56,464
others 600

MARCH 20, 1956 (MN):
Eisenhower 198,111

Knowland 3,209
others 51

April 3, 1956 (WI):
Eisenhower 437,089
Chapple 18,743

April 10, 1956 (IL):
Eisenhower 781,710
Knowland 33,534
Daly 8,364
others 91

April 17, 1956 (NJ):
Eisenhower 357,066
others 23

April 24, 1956 (AK TERRITORY):
Eisenhower 8,291
Knowland 488

April 24, 1956 (MA):
Eisenhower 51,951
Stevenson 604
Herter 550
Nixon 316
McCormack 268
Knowland 250
others 700

April 24, 1956 (PA):
Eisenhower 951,932
Knowland 43,508
others 976

May 1, 1956 (DC):
Eisenhower 18,101

May 7, 1956 (MD):
Eisenhower 66,904
unpledged delegates 3,131

May 8, 1956 (IN):
Eisenhower 351,903
Daly 13,320

May 8, 1956 (OH):
Bricker 478,453

May 8, 1956 (WV):
unpledged delegates 111,883

May 15, 1956 (NE):
Eisenhower 102,576
others 230

May 18, 1956 (OR):
Eisenhower 231,418

May 29, 1956 (FL):
Eisenhower 39,690
Knowland 3,457

June 5, 1956 (CA):
Eisenhower 1,354,764

June 5, 1956 (MT):
Arnold 32,732
Daly 5,447

June 5, 1956 (SD):
unpledged delegates 59,374

26TH CONVENTION:
August 20–23, 1956, Cow Palace, San Francisco (CA)
William Fife Knowland (CA), temporary chairman
Joseph William Martin, Jr. (MA), permanent chairman
Arthur B. Langlie (WA), keynoter

The Republican platform praised President Eisenhower and claimed that peace and prosperity were the products of Republican leadership.

PLATFORM HIGHLIGHTS:
SUPPORTED:
- the "Atoms for Peace" and "open skies" initiatives
- the United Nations
- a strong national defense
- a balanced budget
- gradual reduction in the national debt
- tax reductions
- growth in the private-sector transportation, aviation, and merchant marine industries
- expanded small business participation in federal procurement programs
- low-cost small business loans
- technical research on small business problems
- enforcement of the antitrust laws
- elimination of government red tape
- improved job safety programs
- expanded employment services
- equal pay for equal work
- revision of the Taft-Hartley Act
- crop research, education, and price support differentials
- conservation
- voluntary crop insurance
- expanded school lunch and milk programs
- family farms and cooperatives
- extended rural electrification and communications systems
- improved rural mail delivery
- "agricultural producers in their efforts to seek solutions to their own production and price problems"
- immediate statehood for Alaska and Hawaii
- "sympathetic and constructive execution of the federal trusteeship" for American Indians
- self-government, national suffrage, and congressional representation for the District of Columbia
- Puerto Rico's right of self-determination
- submission of an equal rights amendment to the states for ratification
- civil rights and the Supreme Court decision outlawing segregation in public schools
- extension of the Refugee Relief Act of 1953
- the use of collective security agreements to preserve peace

- an independent Jewish state in the Middle East but within the context of "impartial friendship for the peoples of the Arab states and Israel"
- the reunification of Germany
- gradual and selective reduction of trade barriers on a reciprocal basis
- "people-to-people" exchanges (e.g., sending exchange students, trade delegations, and cultural programs overseas, thus bypassing governmental diplomatic problems) and a bipartisan foreign policy
- increased emphasis on military research and science education for young people
- civil defense programs and federal agencies devoted to keeping "our Government, and our people, safely guarded against all enemies from within"
- adequate benefits for veterans
- conservation management of recreation lands and parks, forest resources, minerals, water resources, and fisheries
- continuous, vigorous development of atomic energy through a partnership between government and private enterprise

OPPOSED:
- the seating of Communist China in the United Nations

ALSO:
- recited its accomplishments in the areas of health, education, and welfare, but promised only to extend Social Security and work with the states to reduce highway fatalities
- lauded honesty and efficiency in government and hailed the merit system for the civil service
- pledged continued efforts to make the postal service self-sustaining

---

REPUBLICAN PARTY
VOTE FOR PRESIDENTIAL NOMINATION: EISENHOWER WAS NOMINATED FOR PRESIDENT BY ACCLAMATION ON THE FIRST BALLOT.

VOTE FOR VICE-PRESIDENTIAL NOMINATION: ALTHOUGH GOVERNOR HAROLD STASSEN OF MINNESOTA HAD PUSHED HERTER'S CANDIDACY FOR VICE PRESIDENT, BY THE TIME THE ROLL WAS CALLED ONLY NIXON WAS FORMALLY PLACED IN NOMINATION. ONE NEBRASKA DELEGATE, TERRY CARPENTER, ATTEMPTED TO OFFER THE NAME OF "JOE SMITH" FOR NOMINATION, BUT HE WAS RULED OUT OF ORDER. NIXON'S NOMINATION WAS THEN MADE UNANIMOUS.

SOCIALIST LABOR PARTY
CANDIDATE FOR PRESIDENT:
Eric Hass (NY)

CANDIDATE FOR VICE PRESIDENT:
Georgia Cozzini (WI)

24TH CONVENTION:
May 5–7, 1956, Henry Hudson Hotel, New York (NY)
Nathan Karp (NJ), temporary and permanent chairman

Thirty-six delegates from sixteen states and the District of Columbia and two ethnic federations attended this convention. The platform of the Socialist Labor Party presented a Marxist analysis of the state of the nation and the world. Two major props were seen as supporting capitalism in its final days: the bubble of consumer credit and the government's spending on the arms race (i.e., artificial levels of spending, which were unsustainable, were keeping the factories open and employment up). The party raised the specter of nuclear warfare as a consequence of the rival imperialism of the United States and the Soviet Union. Socialism was seen as the only alternative to social ruin and atomic war.

PLATFORM HIGHLIGHTS:
SUPPORTED:
- industrial democracy and social ownership of factories, mills, mines, railroads, and land
- elimination of bureaucracies and the exploitation of man by man
- socialism as the answer to crime, juvenile delinquency, mental illness, alcoholism, dope addiction, and other manifestations of capitalist insanity

---

SOCIALIST LABOR PARTY
VOTE FOR PRESIDENTIAL AND VICE-PRESIDENTIAL NOMINATIONS: HASS AND COZZINI WERE UNANIMOUSLY NOMINATED FOR PRESIDENT AND VICE PRESIDENT, RESPECTIVELY. NO OTHER NOMINEES WERE PRESENTED TO THE CONVENTION.

SOCIALIST PARTY
CANDIDATE FOR PRESIDENT:
Darlington Hoopes (PA)

CANDIDATE FOR VICE PRESIDENT:
Samuel Herman Friedman (NY)

CONVENTION:
June 8–10, 1956, Chicago (IL)

The Socialist Party's platform pledged the building of a new, more democratic society in which human rights came before property rights.

PLATFORM HIGHLIGHTS:
SUPPORTED:
- social ownership and democratic control over the means of production, but carefully defined "social ownership" as cooperatives not government ownership
- social ownership of banks and insurance companies, public utilities, and basic industries

- a strong United Nations, universal disarmament, international supervision and control of nuclear weapons, and conservation of natural resources
- social insurance programs covering old age pensions, unemployment compensation, death benefits, and medical care
- the guaranteed right to a job
- decentralization of socialist enterprises so that they would be controlled by workers and consumers, be organized by the people themselves, and be "at least one step removed from government control"
- the Supreme Court decision abolishing segregation
- improvements in the citizens' standard of living through an economic recovery program for the United States
- taxation based on the ability to pay
- the family farm and alleviation of the plight of migrant workers
- removal of ballot restrictions
- repeal of the Taft-Hartley Act and "right to work" laws
- the protection against prosecution for personal political beliefs, repeal of the Smith Act, and restriction of loyalty tests to jobs clearly involving national security

OPPOSED:
- colonialism, racism, and imperialism
- crop limits

SOCIALIST WORKERS PARTY

CANDIDATE FOR PRESIDENT:
Farrell Dobbs (NY)

CANDIDATE FOR VICE PRESIDENT:
Myra Tanner Weiss (NY)

CONVENTION:
August 19, 1956, Adelphi Hall, New York (NY)

In 1956, the platform of the Socialist Workers Party noted a universal demand for industrialization throughout the world. This revolution of rising expectations was coupled with an intensified struggle to throw off colonial domination by imperialist powers. Nikita Khrushchev's denunciation of Joseph Stalin was heralded as a positive change for the working class, although the party warned of capitalist alliances that would counteract the revolutionary masses abroad.

PLATFORM HIGHLIGHTS:
SUPPORTED:
- curbs on inflationary pressures caused by war spending and consumer credit
- the struggle of African Americans for equality
- the formation of unions for migratory workers
- political action through a united Labor Party
- nationwide referenda on questions of war and peace
- withdrawal of all U.S. troops from foreign soil and a halt to all nuclear weapon tests
- recognition of Communist China (PRC) and a "hands-off" policy toward Egypt

- a thirty-hour work week without reductions in pay
- jobless benefits at full union rates
- government operation of idle factories but under worker control
- a ban on production speedups
- equal pay for equal work
- maternity, day care, and summer camp benefits
- adequate old age pensions
- free medical care and hospitalization
- a government-guaranteed college education for all youth
- mandatory cost-of-living adjustments for wages, pensions, and other benefits
- liberalization of election laws
- repeal of the Taft-Hartley and Humphrey-Butler acts, right to work laws, and antilabor legislation
- abolition of the list of subversives and all political prosecutions
- amnesty for the victims of the Smith Act
- full economic, political, and social equality for African Americans and other minorities
- antilynching and anti-poll tax legislation
- price supports for small farms, an all-risk crop insurance program, removal of crop limits, and government food programs for families living on substandard diets
- low-cost agricultural credits and a moratorium on repayment of distress loans
- abolition of the draft, with the military placed under democratic control and servicemen electing their officers and engaging in collective bargaining
- nationalization of all banks, basic industries, food trusts, natural resources, and nuclear power so that these activities could be operated through democratically elected committees of workers and technicians and through the institution of a system of planned economy

OPPOSED:
- both U.S. imperialism and Stalinism
- loyalty purges and witch-hunts
- secret diplomacy and all military alliances and trade restrictions against anti-imperialist countries
- anti-Semitism and police brutality
- commodity speculation and sharecropping

ALSO:
- declaring a national housing emergency, promised to generate 20 million new housing units and to impose rigid rent controls
- would impose no taxes on incomes under $7,500 per year, but would tax incomes over $25,000 per year at 100 percent

SOUTH CAROLINIANS FOR INDEPENDENT ELECTORS

CANDIDATE FOR PRESIDENT:
Harry Flood Byrd (VA)

STATES' RIGHTS PARTY

CANDIDATE FOR PRESIDENT:
Thomas Coleman Andrews (VA)

CANDIDATE FOR VICE PRESIDENT:
Thomas Harold Werdel (CA)

CONVENTION:
October 15, 1956, Mosque Auditorium, Richmond (VA)

The States' Rights Party was a conservative party whose platform endorsed states' rights and a strict interpretation of the Constitution.

STATES' RIGHTS PARTY OF KENTUCKY

CANDIDATE FOR PRESIDENT:
Harry Flood Byrd (VA)

CANDIDATE FOR VICE PRESIDENT:
William Ezra Jenner (IN)

TEXAS CONSTITUTION PARTY

CANDIDATE FOR PRESIDENT:
William Ezra Jenner (IN)

CANDIDATE FOR VICE PRESIDENT:
Joseph Bracken Lee (UT)

The Texas Constitution Party endorsed states' rights and a strict interpretation of the Constitution.

GENERAL ELECTION SUMMARY FOR 1956			
Candidate	*Electoral Votes*	*States*	*Popular Votes*
Eisenhower (R)	457	41	35,581,003
Stevenson (D)	73	7[1]	25,738,765
Stevenson (LIB NY)	0	0	292,557
Andrews (STA RIT)	0	0	109,961[2]
SC Independent Electors	0	0	42,961
Holtwick (PROH)	0	0	41,937
Hass (SL)	0	0	41,159[3]
Jenner (TX CONS)	0	0	30,999
Dobbs (SOC WOR)	0	0	5,549
Conservative Party of NJ	0	0	5,317
Black & Tan GOP	0	0	4,313
Byrd (STA RT KY)	0	0	2,657
Industrial Government	0	0	2,080
Militant Workers	0	0	2,035
Karjewksi (AM THIR)	0	0	1,829
Hoopes (SOC)	0	0	928
American Party	0	0	483
New Party	0	0	364
Smith (CHR NAT)	0	0	11
Langer (PION)	0	0	0
Proehl (GRE)	0	0	0
Shelton (AM VEG)	0	0	0
unpledged	0	0	153,352
unknown	0	0	5,488

[1] Walter Burgwyn Jones (AL) received one electoral vote from an Alabama elector.
[2] An additional 1,027 write-in votes for Andrews were recorded in New York, along with 492 write-in votes for Werdel.
[3] An additional 150 write-in votes for Hass were recorded in New York.

ELECTION OF NOVEMBER 8, 1960

President
JOHN FITZGERALD KENNEDY
Vice President
LYNDON BAINES JOHNSON

HIGHLIGHTS

In October 1957, the Soviet Union launched Sputnik, the first artificial satellite to orbit the earth. The event sent shock waves through a complacent U.S. society and set the stage for the space race issue in the 1960 presidential campaign. The Democrats charged that Dwight Eisenhower was "asleep at the switch," allowing the Soviet Union to establish superiority in space and to pose a threat in the defense arena. Escalating racial tensions, the U.S. military action in Lebanon, widespread anti-U.S. demonstrations abroad, and the collapse of summitry resulting from the U-2 incident in May 1960 all raised questions about Republican leadership. The Democrats fielded four strong candidates—Senators Hubert H. Humphrey, Lyndon B. Johnson, John F. Kennedy, and Stuart Symington—for the nomination, and a host of favorite sons. A coy Adlai Stevenson waited in the background. Kennedy had the best political machine but was hampered by the prevalent opinion that a Roman Catholic could not be elected. When he demonstrated strength in the Protestant stronghold of West Virginia, his bandwagon became unstoppable. Kennedy achieved a first ballot victory at the convention and named Johnson as his running mate.

On the Republican side, Eisenhower was still popular, and his vice president, Richard Nixon, was the odds-on favorite for the Republican nomination to succeed him. Nixon was challenged by Governor Nelson Rockefeller of New York, who represented the liberal wing of the party. After Nixon made certain platform assurances to the governor, the Rockefeller boom faded, and Nixon was nominated without significant opposition. The Republicans chose Henry Cabot Lodge, the U.S. ambassador to the United Nations, to fill the second spot. A series of four debates—the first ever to be televised—highlighted the fall campaign. Nixon fared poorly in the events, looking pale, nervous, and unshaven under the camera lights. His debate style was traditional and logical while Kennedy, who quickly mastered the emergent medium of television, spoke directly to the viewers and established his presidential stature in the process. Kennedy urged an activist government to help get the United States "moving again" and warned against the growing inroads of communism. He also faced the question of his religion squarely and pledged his devotion to the Constitution. In contrast, Nixon simply articulated a traditional Republican view of limited government. In the waning days of the campaign, Nixon also featured Ike's endorsement of his candidacy. The race went down to the wire. Each candidate received less than half of the vote (with the balance being divided among several minor parties), and less than one-tenth of 1 percent separated the victorious Kennedy from his crestfallen rival. Nixon even carried four more states than Kennedy.

AMERICA FIRST PARTY

CANDIDATE FOR PRESIDENT:
Lawrence Joseph Sarsfeld "Lar" Daly (IL)

The platform of the America First Party was conceived and written in its entirety by Daly in Chicago on July 22, 1959.

PLATFORM HIGHLIGHTS:
The America First Party had a three-point program of assertions: the United States could defend itself and the Western Hemisphere without help from anyone else;

the United States must be prepared to "shoot first" if the need arose, including a willingness to use atomic weapons for the immediate destruction of the People's Republic of China; and that any military assistance from other nations must be under the control of the United States.

AMERICAN BEAT CONSENSUS PARTY

CANDIDATE FOR PRESIDENT:
William Lloyd "Bill" Smith (IL)

CONVENTION:
   July 17–24, 1960, College of Complexes, New York
   (NY)

AMERICAN THIRD PARTY

CANDIDATE FOR PRESIDENT:
   Henry B. Krajewski (NJ)

CANDIDATE FOR VICE PRESIDENT:
   Anna Marie Yezo (NJ)

The platform of the American Third Party promised "no piggie deals in Washington." It advocated a square-deal program for all, with the threshold on taxable income beginning at one thousand dollars, instead of six hundred dollars, per person.

PLATFORM HIGHLIGHTS:

SUPPORTED:
- an "open door" policy for countries that wanted to become part of the United States
- government-sponsored homeowners' insurance for veterans
- legalized gambling

OPPOSED:
- the floating of outrageous bonds for government improvement
- foreign aid for freeloaders
- monopolies

ALSO:
- threatened to jail all corrupt politicians
- urged a one-year mandatory agricultural training program for boys, who would be permitted to "rock and roll with the chickens, pigs, and cows at 5 a.m."
- advocated a two-month compulsory outdoor life-training program for girls as an alternative to "hot rods, drag racing, or juvenile destruction"
- wanted the nation to "stop pussy footing with the Communists and finish the war of nerves" and deploy atomic missiles to threaten the Soviet Union
- concluded by observing, "It is a survival of the fittest and now is the hour"

AMERICAN VEGETARIAN PARTY

CANDIDATE FOR PRESIDENT:
   Symon Gould (NY)

CANDIDATE FOR VICE PRESIDENT:
   Christopher Gian-Cursio (FL)

PLATFORM HIGHLIGHTS:

SUPPORTED:
- vegetarianism as a path to world harmony and cultured living and as a way of helping people attain their highest level of understanding, beauty, and living
- universal brotherhood and peace
- natural healing methods

- organic agriculture
- preservation of natural resources
- child welfare programs
- world resource planning to eliminate want and deprivation
- the peaceful protests of the civil rights movement
- the appointment of a cabinet-level secretary of peace

OPPOSED:
- the destruction of any living thing
- the use of animals in scientific experimentation and urged a social view that recognized the unity of all life

CONSERVATIVE PARTY OF NEW JERSEY

CANDIDATE FOR PRESIDENT:
   Joseph Bracken Lee (UT) (Barry Morris Goldwater [AZ] declined)

CANDIDATE FOR VICE PRESIDENT:
   Kent H. Courtney (LA)

CONSERVATIVE PARTY OF VIRGINIA

CANDIDATE FOR PRESIDENT:
   Claiborne Benton Coiner (VA) (Harry Flood Byrd [VA] declined)

CANDIDATE FOR VICE PRESIDENT:
   Edward Joseph Silverman (VA) (Barry Morris Goldwater [AZ] declined)

The party supported the candidacies of Byrd for president and Goldwater for vice president. The formal candidates were "stand-ins" for Byrd and Goldwater, who declined the nominations.

CONSTITUTION PARTY OF TEXAS[1]

CANDIDATE FOR PRESIDENT:
   Charles Loten Sullivan (MS)

CANDIDATE FOR VICE PRESIDENT:
   Merritt Barton Curtis (DC)

PLATFORM HIGHLIGHTS:

SUPPORTED:
- restoration of states' rights under the Ninth and Tenth Amendments to the Constitution
- a balanced federal budget and retirement of the national debt
- repeal of the Sixteenth Amendment and all federal income tax laws
- the superiority of the Constitution above international treaties
- removal of government from competition with free enterprise
- restraint of the Supreme Court through restored checks and balances

[1]Party listed itself as Texas Constitution Party in 1956.

- only selective and protective immigration
- exclusive congressional issuance of money
- individual ownership of precious metals
- free market agriculture without government regulations
- withdrawal from the United Nations
- withdrawal of foreign aid
- suspension of diplomatic relations with Communist nations

CONSTITUTION PARTY

CANDIDATE FOR PRESIDENT:
Merritt Barton Curtis (DC)

CANDIDATE FOR VICE PRESIDENT:
Bryan M. Miller (VA)

CONVENTION:
April 20–24, 1960, Indianapolis (IN)

Proclaiming that "this is a Christian nation," the national platform of the Constitution parties of the United States demanded restoration of states' rights under the Ninth and Tenth Amendments to the Constitution.

PLATFORM HIGHLIGHTS:
SUPPORTED:
- a balanced federal budget and retirement of the national debt
- repeal of the Sixteenth Amendment and all federal income tax laws
- the superiority of the Constitution above international treaties
- the removal of government from competition with free enterprise
- restraint of the Supreme Court through restored checks and balances
- guaranteed individual freedom of choice in associating with others
- deregulation of agriculture and equal application of laws against monopolies to business, labor, agriculture, or cooperatives
- restriction of immigration to the quotas imposed by the McCarran-Walter Act
- exclusive congressional issuance of money
- individual ownership of precious metals
- abolition of the Federal Reserve System
- legislation to outlaw the Communist Party
- mandatory instruction in free enterprise economics in public schools
- withdrawal from the United Nations
- abolition of foreign aid
- suspension of diplomatic relations with Cuba, the Soviet Union, and satellite nations
- a protective tariff
- prevention of U.S. participation in the General Agreements on Tariff and Trade

DEMOCRATIC PARTY

CANDIDATE FOR PRESIDENT:
John Fitzgerald Kennedy

CANDIDATE FOR VICE PRESIDENT:
Lyndon Baines Johnson (TX)

CANDIDATES FOR PRESIDENTIAL NOMINATION:
Ross Robert Barnett (MS)
Edmund Gerald Brown, Sr. (CA)
Lawrence Joseph Sarsfield "Lar" Daly (IL)
Michael Vincent DiSalle (OH)
George Docking (KS) (declined)
Andrew J. Easter (MD)
Orval Eugene Faubas (AR)
Paul Cary Fisher (CA)
Hubert Horatio Humphrey (MN)
Lyndon Baines Johnson (TX)
John Fitzgerald Kennedy (MA)
John Hugh Latham (IN)
Herschel Cellel Loveless (IA)
George Henry McLain (CA)
Robert Baumle Meyner (NJ)
Wayne Lyman Morse (OR)
Richard Milhous Nixon (NY)
Nelson Aldrich Rockefeller (NY)
Albert Dean Rosellini (WA)
George Armistead Smathers (FL)
Adlai Ewing Stevenson (IL)
Stuart Symington (MO)

PRIMARIES:
MARCH 8, 1960 (NH):

Kennedy	43,372
Fisher	6,853
others	674

APRIL 5, 1960 (WI):

Kennedy	476,024
Humphrey	366,753

APRIL 12, 1960 (IL):

Kennedy	34,332
Stevenson	8,029
Symington	5,744
Humphrey	4,283
Johnson	442
others	337

APRIL 19, 1960 (NJ):

unpledged delegates	217,608

APRIL 26, 1960 (MA):

Kennedy	91,607
Stevenson	4,684
Humphrey	794
Nixon	646
Symington	443
Johnson	268
others	721

APRIL 26, 1960 (PA):

Kennedy 183,073
Stevenson 29,660
Nixon 15,136
Humphrey 13,860
Symington 6,791
Johnson 2,918
Rockefeller 1,078
others 4,297

MAY 3, 1960 (DC):

Humphrey 8,239
Morse 6,127

MAY 3, 1960 (IN):

Kennedy 353,832
Latham 42,084
Daly 40,853

MAY 3, 1960 (OH):

DiSalle 315,312

MAY 10, 1960 (NE):

Kennedy 80,408
Symington 4,083
Humphrey 3,202
Stevenson 1,368
Johnson 962
others 669

MAY 10, 1960 (WV):

Kennedy 236,510
Humphrey 152,187

MAY 17, 1960 (MD):

Kennedy 201,769
Morse 49,420
Daly 7,536
Easter 3,881
uninstructed delegates 24,350

MAY 20, 1960 (OR):

Kennedy 146,332
Morse 91,715
Humphrey 16,319
Symington 12,496
Johnson 11,101
Stevenson 7,924
others 1,210

MAY 24, 1960 (FL):

Smathers 322,235

JUNE 7, 1960 (CA):

Brown 1,354,031

JUNE 7, 1960 (SD):

Humphrey 24,773

33RD CONVENTION:

July 11–15, 1960, Los Angeles Memorial Sports
   Arena and Coliseum, Los Angeles (CA)
Frank Forrester Church (ID), temporary chairman
Thomas LeRoy Collins (FL), chairman

The Democratic platform bemoaned the loss of U.S. leadership in the race for space and alleged the existence of a missile gap with the Soviet Union.

PLATFORM HIGHLIGHTS:

SUPPORTED:

- increases in U.S. deterrent military power and balanced conventional forces to permit measured responses to any threat
- collective security arrangements, civil defense, and arms control efforts
- selection of more sensitive diplomatic representatives, balanced information programs, and expansion of cultural exchange programs in an effort to prevent the "ugly American" image abroad
- a restructuring of the National Security Council
- growth in foreign trade, expanded trade opportunities with the Common Market and the "Outer Seven" (i.e., European nations not in the Common Market), and a favorable balance of trade
- an end to discrimination in immigration policy
- a shift in foreign assistance from military to economic aid
- recognition and support for emerging nations
- unrestricted use of the Suez Canal
- creation of world food banks to combat famine
- peaceful negotiations between Israel and the Arab peoples in the Middle East
- advances in European unity
- peaceful competition and negotiations with the Communist world and continued resistance to Communist encroachments, whether in Berlin, Cuba, or Formosa (Taiwan)
- the aspirations of the "captive" nations behind the Iron Curtain
- the United Nations and sought repeal of the "self-judging reservation" by which the United States participated in the World Court
- control of inflation
- full employment, aid to depressed areas, an end to discrimination in employment, protection of the right of collective bargaining and the repeal of Taft-Hartley and "right to work" laws, and advance planning for automation to lessen the impact on displaced workers
- an increase in the minimum wage to $1.25 per hour
- extended social benefits to uncovered workers on farms and in industry
- full parity for farmers
- food stamps and school lunch and milk programs
- family farms, liberalized farm credit, strengthened cooperatives, expanded rural electrification, and improved standards of living in rural communities
- aid for small businesses in obtaining credit and equity capital, accelerated loans from the Small Business Administration, and increased enforcement of antimonopoly and antitrust laws

- construction of more than 2 million new homes per year and a willingness to use government loans to facilitate achievement of that goal
- expansion of Social Security to provide medical care benefits for the aged, more research on major fatal and crippling diseases, and more medical schools, hospitals, and research laboratories
- elimination of age discrimination in employment, raises in retirement benefits under Social Security, expansion of senior housing, and improved conditions in nursing homes and other institutions for the aged
- liberalized disability insurance and improved rehabilitation programs for the physically handicapped
- unemployment benefits subject to uniform minimum standards
- guarantees to women of equal pay for equal work
- expansion of child welfare programs
- expanded federal government participation in public assistance programs
- creation of a new Federal Bureau of Intergroup Relations to resolve problems of discrimination
- federal aid to education for construction of facilities, promotion of vocational education, and payment of teachers' salaries
- creation of a Youth Conservation Corps for underprivileged young people as a way of providing a "rewarding experience in a healthful environment"
- conservation of natural resources under a multiple-use concept, construction of new sewage treatment plants, control of air and water pollution, protection of fish and wildlife, and improvements in the National Park System
- study of alternative energy sources such as the sun and wind, establishment of a national fuels policy, and continued development of sources of power (including water, tidal, and nuclear power)
- intensive forest management on a multiple-use, sustained-yield basis including reforestation of burned-over areas and construction of public access roads
- research for the domestic mining industry and public planning and budgeting to put resources "on a businesslike basis"
- a ten-year action plan to eliminate slums and blight, to encourage metropolitan planning, to assist bus and rail mass transit, to combat air and water pollution, and to expand the nation's park system to meet the recreation needs of a growing population
- improvements in air transportation and development of inland waterways, harbors, roads, and rail systems
- increased studies in basic and applied science in an effort to win the space race
- international regulation of space and a balanced and flexible nuclear defense capability
- oceanographic research

- adoption of a federal code of ethics, modernization of the civil service, reform of federal regulatory agencies, improvements in the postal system, and prosecution of "underworld" crime figures
- rejection of government secrecy
- limits on campaign contributions and expenditures, full disclosure, and provision of a tax credit for campaign contributions
- congressional representation, home rule, and the right to vote in presidential elections for the District of Columbia and the Virgin Islands
- reform of congressional procedures to prevent the frustration of majority rule
- a strengthened Food and Drug Administration and a consumer counsel to speak on behalf of consumers in administrative hearings
- expanded vocational rehabilitation programs, quality medical care, full pension benefits, home loan guarantees, and educational benefits for veterans.
- a balanced budget
- closure of tax loopholes
- the full use of federal powers under the Civil Rights acts of 1957 and 1960 to secure the right to vote for all U.S. citizens
- an end to literacy tests and poll taxes and full enforcement of the Supreme Court's school desegregation decision

OPPOSED:
- recognition of Communist China (PRC)
- the high-interest, tight-money policy of the Eisenhower administration
- discrimination in housing and employment

DEMOCRATIC PARTY
VOTE FOR PRESIDENTIAL NOMINATION:

Candidate	Ballot: 1
Kennedy	806
Johnson	409
Symington	86
Stevenson	79½
Meyner	43
Humphrey	41½
Smathers	30
Barnett	23
Loveless	1½
Brown	½
Faubus	½
Rosellini	½

VOTE FOR VICE-PRESIDENTIAL NOMINATION: JOHNSON WAS NOMINATED FOR VICE PRESIDENT ON THE FIRST BALLOT. THE VOTE WAS MADE UNANIMOUS.

GREENBACK PARTY

CANDIDATE FOR PRESIDENT:
Whitney Hart Slocomb (CA)

CANDIDATE FOR VICE PRESIDENT:
Edward Kirby Meador (MA)

Candidates were chosen by mail referendum.

PLATFORM HIGHLIGHTS:
The platform promised to reverse the "present order of things and put money into the hands of the industrious people first." It demanded the conscription of property without compensation for the defense of the nation. It also required the replacement of charity through government programs for the disabled and needy, the elimination of child labor, and payment of old age pensions. The party also sought a "just and fair" wage law and abolition of special privilege and monopolies.

INDEPENDENT

CANDIDATES FOR PRESIDENT:
Thomas Coleman Andrews (VA)
Stuart Symington (MO)
Agnes Waters (DC)[1]

INDEPENDENT AFRO-AMERICAN UNITY PARTY

CANDIDATE FOR PRESIDENT:
Clennon W. King (GA)

CANDIDATE FOR VICE PRESIDENT:
Reginald Carter (IL)

The party platform declared that "race is America's number one problem."

NATIONAL STATES' RIGHTS PARTY

CANDIDATE FOR PRESIDENT:
Orval Eugene Faubus (AR)

CANDIDATE FOR VICE PRESIDENT:
John Geraerdt Crommelin (AL)

CONVENTION:
March 19–20, 1960, Dayton (OH)

The National States' Rights Party was formed at a convention in Knoxville, Tennessee, on August 30, 1958. At that time, the States' Rights Party and the United White Party agreed to merge to create the new entity.

Delegates from twenty-eight states attended the convention. Supported by various branches of the Ku Klux Klan, the party was strongly nationalistic and anti-Semitic.

PLATFORM HIGHLIGHTS:
SUPPORTED:
- white supremacy and creation of a "White Folk Community"
- states' rights
- free enterprise
- full employment and high wages
- large old age pensions
- racial separation
- segregation in schools and the military
- a whites-only policy for participation in government or service in the courts
- preservation of the "national life" of American Indians with unlimited development of reservation facilities
- labor unions run by honest white men
- a fair price for farm products
- limitations on foreign trade to protect white U.S. producers
- abolition of confiscatory taxation
- elimination of slums, floods, and dust bowls through combined civic efforts in individual states
- racial instruction for white youth
- restructuring of the educational system to afford all white citizens full opportunity to achieve their vocational ambitions
- censorship to prevent unwanted ideologies and influences in the media
- exclusive congressional authority in the issuance of money
- abolition of federal control over the National Guard and state law enforcement agencies, federal judicial decrees that violated state sovereignty, federal "thought control," and secret police tactics
- the states' right to investigate and prosecute subversives
- limitations on immigration solely to white Christian immigrants
- efforts to locate a country in Africa for the repatriation of African Americans
- strengthened cultural and moral ties with other white nations and an end to "alien minority wars" that force white Christian boys to die on foreign soil
- expulsion of all Communists from the United States

OPPOSED:
- foreign "giveaways" (i.e., foreign aid) and international entanglements
- the United Nations

[1]The platform of Agnes Waters opposed all "so-called" civil rights bills and pledged the candidate to restore constitutional government. Waters wanted to repeal U.S. defense commitments to Berlin and Formosa (Taiwan). She denounced "race mixing" and argued against war. Her platform statements were vitriolic, racist, and anti-Semitic.

NATIONAL STATES' RIGHTS PARTY
VOTE FOR THE PRESIDENTIAL NOMINATION:
FAUBUS WAS NOMINATED AGAINST HIS WISHES.

- world government
- race mixing and intermarriage
- communism

OUTER SPACE (FLYING SAUCER) PARTY

CANDIDATE FOR PRESIDENT:
Gabriel Green (CA)

CANDIDATE FOR VICE PRESIDENT:
Addison Brown (OR)

CONVENTION:
August 13–14, 1960, Shrine Auditorium, Los Angeles (CA)
Daniel William Fry (OR), chairman
Gabriel Green (CA), keynoter

The Outer Space, or Flying Saucer, Party was an outgrowth of the Amalgamated Flying Saucer Clubs of America (AFSCA).

PLATFORM HIGHLIGHTS:
The "Space Age" platform was officially adopted on July 4, 1960, in anticipation of the August convention of AFSCA. It recommended "prior choice economics," which would make possible automatic retirement without a reduction in living standards, fair wages, free permanent insurance on everything, guaranteed profits, abundance, elimination of poverty and starvation, free medical and dental care, free college education, emancipation for economic slavery, and retention of free enterprise. The party affirmed the existence of flying saucers and decried the government's withholding of information about them. It advocated building a "true free-energy-powered, man-carrying spaceship" to send to the moon and Mars, broadcasting a message of friendship to space people and offering to exchange diplomats with them, and opening top-secret government files relating to flying saucers.

According to the platform, "As our friends from Space have told us, there are no clean bombs and all radiation from them is harmful to the health and well-being of an earthly life." Despite the detail of the platform, it offered no explanation of what "prior choice economics" meant. The document also advertised tape-recorded messages from space people under such titles as "To Men of Earth" by Voltra, "Monka and Merku Speak" by Monka and Merku, and "Solar Government" by Sutko.

SUPPORTED:
- greater use of television in classrooms
- adoption of the metric system
- repeal of the Taft-Hartley Act and the Landrum-Griffin Bill
- defense of human rights for all citizens
- discontinuation of bomb tests
- inauguration of public works projects
- admission of Puerto Rico as the fifty-first state

- adoption of uniform laws to prevent discrimination
- maintenance of a strong defense
- science
- recognition of the People's Republic of China under a "two-China" policy
- expansion of foreign aid to include free distribution of food surpluses to starving people
- disarmament, but only after the causes of war have been eliminated through the application of prior choice economics
- distribution of information on family planning
- preservation of historical shrines
- application of prior choice economics to fund television programs in lieu of commercial advertising
- the creation of a department of peace

OPPOSED:
- the Connally amendment
- the unnecessary torture of animals and vivisection

PEACE PARTY

CANDIDATE FOR PRESIDENT:
Mihran Nicholas Ask (CA)

PLATFORM HIGHLIGHTS:
The Peace Party's platform consisted of ten planks:
1. To prevent World War 3 without war and weapons
2. To assure peace and plenty to all nations regardless of race, religion, and political connections forced upon them
3. A job for every unemployed
4. Elimination of Beaurocracies [sic]
5. Reduction by 50 percent of all taxes
6. The right to work
7. The right to vote for those who believe and uphold the Constitution of the U.S.A. and have at least a high school education
8. No suppression of press, radio and pulpit
9. The Bible as an obligatory study project in all schools and on all levels
10. Restoration of the Biblical right of men as the head of the home

PROHIBITION PARTY

CANDIDATE FOR PRESIDENT:
Rutherford Losey Decker (MO)

CANDIDATE FOR VICE PRESIDENT:
Earle Harold Munn, Sr. (MI)

23RD CONVENTION:
September 1–3, 1959, Westminster Hotel, Winona Lake (IN)

Nearly three hundred delegates and observers from seventeen states and the District of Columbia attended the convention. Ninety-five delegates cast ballots.

The ticket was announced at the first convention, and a second "nominating convention," to nominate candidates, was held at the Central Free Methodist Church in Lansing (MI), on August 27, 1960.

PLATFORM HIGHLIGHTS:

SUPPORTED:

- constitutional government
- the efforts of agencies that exposed subversive activities and groups
- economy in government, a balanced budget, reduction of the national debt, lowered taxes, and elimination of unnecessary public departments, bureaus, and vested interests
- a possible return to the gold standard
- a sound currency under the control of Congress
- careful study of foreign aid issues, acknowledging "that complex and baffling problems are involved in this area of international relations"
- free enterprise over government restraints and government withdrawal from all activities that compete with private industry
- compulsory arbitration, "right to work" laws, and prohibitions on secondary boycotts and industry-wide bargaining
- states' rights
- enforcement of laws against gambling, narcotics, and commercialized vice
- world peace as a priority
- suspension of testing of nuclear weapons
- religious liberty and separation of church and state
- enactment of uniform marriage and divorce laws
- "an actuarially sound social security program"
- ballot reform to assist minor parties
- a free market agricultural program
- an honest and efficient administration

OPPOSED:

- communism and totalitarianism
- universal military training
- federal aid to education
- mass medication programs and involuntary mental health treatment

ALSO:

- insisted that all laws legalizing the liquor traffic be repealed and that there be rigorous enforcement of new laws prohibiting the manufacture, distribution, and sale of alcoholic beverages

---

PROHIBITION PARTY

VOTE FOR PRESIDENTIAL NOMINATION:
DECKER WAS UNANIMOUSLY NOMINATED
FOR PRESIDENT.

VOTE FOR VICE-PRESIDENTIAL NOMINATION:
MUNN WAS UNANIMOUSLY NOMINATED FOR
VICE PRESIDENT.

REPUBLICAN PARTY

CANDIDATE FOR PRESIDENT:
Richard Milhous Nixon

CANDIDATE FOR VICE PRESIDENT:
Henry Cabot Lodge (MA)

CANDIDATES FOR PRESIDENTIAL NOMINATION:
Pastor Mihran Nicholas Ask (CA)
Frank Roscoe Beckwith (IN)
Dwight David Eisenhower (PA)
Paul Cary Fisher (CA)
Barry Morris Goldwater (AZ)
John Fitzgerald Kennedy (MA)
Clennon W. King (GA)
Henry Cabot Lodge (MA)
Richard Milhous Nixon (NY)
Nelson Aldrich Rockefeller (NY)
Adlai Ewing Stevenson (IL)

PRIMARIES:

MARCH 8, 1960 (NH):

Nixon	65,204
Rockefeller	2,745
Fisher	2,388
Kennedy	2,196
others	498

APRIL 5, 1960 (WI):

Nixon	339,383

APRIL 12, 1960 (IL):

Nixon	782,849
others	442

APRIL 19, 1960 (NJ):

unpledged Delegates	304,766

APRIL 26, 1960 (MA):

Nixon	53,164
Rockefeller	4,068
Kennedy	2,989
Lodge	373
Stevenson	266
Goldwater	221
Eisenhower	172
others	592

APRIL 26, 1960 (PA):

Nixon	968,538
Rockefeller	12,491
Kennedy	3,886
Stevenson	428
Goldwater	286
others	1,202

MAY 3, 1960 (DC):

unpledged Delegates	9,468

MAY 3, 1960 (IN):

Nixon	408,408
Beckwith	19,677

MAY 3, 1960 (OH):
Nixon 504,072

MAY 10, 1960 (NE):
Nixon 74,356
Rockefeller 2,028
Goldwater 1,068
others 1,805

MAY 10, 1960 (WV):
unpledged delegates 123,756

MAY 20, 1960 (OR):
Nixon 211,276
Rockefeller 9,307
Kennedy 2,864
Goldwater 1,571
others 2,015

MAY 24, 1960 (FL):
Nixon 51,036

JUNE 7, 1960 (CA):
Nixon 1,517,652

JUNE 7, 1960 (SD):
unpledged delegates 48,461

27TH CONVENTION:
July 25–28, 1960, International Amphitheatre,
    Chicago (IL)
Cecil H. Underwood (WV), temporary chairman
Charles Abraham Halleck (IN), chairman
Walter Henry Judd (MN), keynoter

The Republican platform described the dramatic changes occurring in the world—new nations, new machines, new weapons, and new ideas. The threat of communism was raised, and it stressed the quality of U.S. leadership, as exemplified by the "Eisenhower-Nixon administration," as a critical factor in the "fate of the world."

PLATFORM HIGHLIGHTS:
SUPPORTED:
- a resolute foreign policy, standing fast for Berlin, the Formosa Straits, and Lebanon
- the Monroe Doctrine, the independence of all the states of the Middle East (including Israel and the Arab states), and an end to trade restrictions and blockades
- regional defense pacts such as the Central Treaty Organization (CENTO), the North Atlantic Treaty Organization (NATO), the Organization of American States (OAS),and the Southeast Asia Treaty Organization (SEATO)
- work within the UN framework for the peaceful settlement of international disputes and the peaceful use of space
- disarmament efforts and a willingness to reevaluate the resumption of underground nuclear tests if the Geneva Conference failed
- foreign aid
- assistance to "captive nations" in their efforts to break away from communism and pointed to the "trained, ex-

perienced, mature, and courageous leadership" of the Republican Party
- reliance on military might to ensure a second-strike capability and mobile and versatile forces
- the Polaris submarine and ballistic missiles, a stronger civil defense program, constant intelligence operations, and development of antimissile missiles
- free enterprise through broad-based tax reform
- elimination of feather-bedding
- maintenance of a stable dollar
- enforcement of antitrust laws
- consumer protection and a strengthened Food and Drug Administration
- a halt to government competition with private businesses
- continuation of the national highway program and the Trade Agreements Act
- further improvements in hours, wages, and working conditions for all workers, including equal pay for equal work for women
- utilization of farm surpluses through a food-for-peace program and creation of a strategic food reserve, school lunch programs, and nutritional supplements for low-income and needy citizens
- agricultural research and price supports
- water and soil conservation
- easier farm credit
- family farms and cooperatives
- increased emphasis on rural electrification and communications
- expansion of the Rural Development Program and the Great Plains Program and a greater direct voice for farmers in agricultural policy development
- wise conservation measures for water resources, promotion of fisheries, the marketing of federal power, reclamation, and the use of federal lands
- improvement of national parks and recreation facilities along with a "keep our great out-of-doors beautiful, green, and clean" campaign
- assistance to mining and other commercial interests seeking development of the nation's natural resources
- government austerity and a conservative approach to public expenditures
- a strengthened Federal Reserve System and a line item veto in authorization and appropriation bills
- additional reorganization of the executive branch and further strengthening of the merit system
- efforts to make the U.S. Post Office self-sustaining
- modification of the electoral college to make it more reflective of the popular vote
- self-government and the right to vote in national elections for the District of Columbia, statehood for Puerto Rico, eventual statehood for the Virgin Islands, and self-government for Guam
- an equal rights amendment to the Constitution that would ensure women equal rights under the law
- the National Defense Education Act and federal selective grants-in-aid to strengthen vocational education,

promote special education for handicapped and gifted-children, foster library development, and stimulate basic educational research

- more vigorous federal support for higher education and research in science and technology
- expanded Social Security and programs for handicapped individuals, improved standards for nursing homes, and enhanced care and treatment of the chronically and mentally ill
- health care relief for the aged to be channeled through private insurance carriers without intruding upon the personal relationship of patient and physician
- a state-oriented health care model
- a new federal-state program for personal care for handicapped persons
- federal aid to combat juvenile delinquency
- urban planning for "wise" land use
- continued support for medical research on both the national and international levels
- research to combat water and air pollution
- additional resources for radiological medicine research and new programs to assist medical education to stem personnel shortages in health and medical fields
- school desegregation
- a ban on discrimination in federally assisted housing and public facilities and services
- the right to boycott businesses to overcome racial discrimination
- liberalization of the immigration laws

OPPOSED:

- recognition of Red China (PRC) and its admission to the United Nations
- mandatory retirement and prompt consideration of the recommendations of the forthcoming White House Conference on Aging, set for January 1961.

ALSO:

- on the domestic front, stressed past successes and the current prosperity, while maintaining the need for "vigorous economic growth"
- acknowledged the housing problem was nearly intractable; nonetheless, promised efforts to clear slums, promote rebuilding, and stimulate the development of nursing homes and specialized types of housing for the elderly
- applauded the Taft-Hartley Act and pointed to an increase in the minimum wage and workmen's compensation benefits, better benefits for railroad workers, and extended unemployment coverage as examples of the party's commitment to labor
- pointed with pride to the Civil Rights acts of 1957 and 1960, the increase in the number of African Americans employed in the federal government and in the number of African-American voters in general, and the strides made in ensuring African Americans equal opportunities in various aspects of society

ROCKING CHAIR PARTY

CANDIDATE FOR PRESIDENT:
Connie N. Watts (GA)

CANDIDATE FOR VICE PRESIDENT:
Ralph Raper (GA)

PLATFORM HIGHLIGHTS:
The platform of the Rocking Chair Party urged abolition of the National Democratic Convention, because it had become a "parlor game." Watts stated that he did not "plan to attend the National Democratic Convention, personally or by proxy—just sit on the front porch and listen to the songs of the birds and enjoy the cool breeze." He was apparently prompted to declare his candidacy because people allegedly kept putting campaign stickers on the tomatoes in his garden.

SOCIALIST LABOR PARTY

CANDIDATE FOR PRESIDENT:
Eric Hass (NY)

CANDIDATE FOR VICE PRESIDENT:
Georgia Cozzini (WI)

25TH CONVENTION:
May 7–9, 1960, Henry Hudson Hotel, New York (NY)
Nathan Karp (NJ), temporary and permanent chairman

The platform of the Socialist Labor Party posed one overriding issue: socialism and survival versus capitalism and catastrophe. This conclusion was drawn from a Marxist analysis of the arms race and the international struggle between the United States and the Soviet Union.

PLATFORM HIGHLIGHTS:
SUPPORTED:

- creation of an industrial democracy in which the factories, mills, mines, railroads, and land were under collective ownership
- administration of all industries by the workers themselves
- abolition of the existing capitalist unions with a new, all-embracing Socialist Industrial Union to be created in their stead

ALSO:

- believed that a united working class could seize the government through the ballot box and accomplish the

---

REPUBLICAN PARTY

VOTE FOR PRESIDENTIAL NOMINATION: NIXON WAS NOMINATED BY ACCLAMATION AFTER GOLDWATER WITHDREW HIS NAME FROM CONSIDERATION.

VOTE FOR VICE-PRESIDENTIAL NOMINATION: LODGE WAS UNANIMOUSLY NOMINATED FOR VICE PRESIDENT ON THE FIRST BALLOT.

Socialist revolution in a peaceful and civilized way, resulting in a Socialist commonwealth of peace, plenty, and international brotherhood

---

SOCIALIST LABOR PARTY
VOTE FOR PRESIDENTIAL AND VICE-PRESIDENTIAL NOMINATIONS: HASS AND COZZINI WERE UNANIMOUSLY NOMINATED BY RISING VOTE FOR PRESIDENT AND VICE PRESIDENT, RESPECTIVELY. NO OTHER NAMES WERE PLACED IN NOMINATION BEFORE THE CONVENTION.

SOCIALIST PARTY

CONVENTION:
May 28–30, 1960, Washington (DC)

No candidates were named, although a lengthy platform was adopted.

SOCIALIST WORKERS PARTY

CANDIDATE FOR PRESIDENT:
Farrell Dobbs (NY)

CANDIDATE FOR VICE PRESIDENT:
Myra Tanner Weiss (NY)

The party's platform presented three questions for humanity: (1) How can the world be freed from the threat of nuclear destruction? (2) How can hunger and poverty be wiped out? (3) How can equality and democracy be won and maintained? The party answered these questions by asserting that socialism could bring peace, prosperity, and equality to all. After indicting U.S. foreign policy, the platform also criticized the Soviet Union and its allies as "bureaucratic police regimes." It argued that the nation's first concern must be "the shape of things at home."

PLATFORM HIGHLIGHTS:
SUPPORTED:
- a planned economy to produce abundance for everyone
- withdrawal of all U.S. troops abroad
- a halt to tests of nuclear weapons and the dismantling of nuclear stockpiles
- all colonial struggles against imperialism, particularly noting the need to recognize the People's Republic of China and to befriend the Cuban revolution
- efforts to turn the arms budget into a peace budget, end the draft, democratize the military by allowing the election of officers, and extend to soldiers the right to collective bargaining
- a thirty-hour work week at forty hours' pay, extended unemployment insurance, government seizure and operation under worker control of idle factories, and equal pay for equal work

- federally financed nurseries and summer camps
- government-guaranteed college education
- full disability benefits, medical care and hospitalization for the elderly, passage of the Forand bill, and adequate pensions for all
- repeal of the Kennedy-Landrum-Griffin, Taft-Hartley, and Humphrey-Butler acts and right to work laws
- liberalized election laws and a lowered voting age to eighteen years
- full economic, social, and political equality for African Americans and other minority groups
- an end to police brutality, abolition of the death penalty, and reform of the prison system
- government underwriting of the full cost of production of farm commodities without crop limits
- government-provided nutritional subsidies for families in the United States living on a substandard diet
- abolition of sharecropping and landlordism
- a moratorium on repayment of distress loans to farmers
- an emergency federal housing and public works program supplemented by rent controls on private housing
- full-scale flood-control, water supply, irrigation, electricity generation, and natural resource conservation programs
- abolition of all payroll and sales taxes and the repeal of all taxes on annual incomes under $7,500, taxes at 100 percent on annual incomes in excess of $25,000, and placing the tax returns of the rich open to public scrutiny
- nationalization of the banks, basic industries, food trusts, medical monopolies, and all natural resources (including nuclear power) under democratic worker management

OPPOSED:
- Jim Crow laws and bigotry
- war as an instrument of foreign policy
- restrictions on organized labor
- loyalty oaths and purges, the Smith Act, the McCarran Internal Security and Immigration laws, political deportations, use of subversive lists, the House Un-American Activities Committee and the Senate Internal Security Subcommittee, and other devices to deny citizens their rights under the Constitution

TAX CUT (AMERICA FIRST; AMERICAN) PARTY

CANDIDATE FOR PRESIDENT:
Lawrence Joseph Sarsfeld "Lar" Daly (IL)

CANDIDATE FOR VICE PRESIDENT:
Merritt Barton Curtis (DC)

PLATFORM HIGHLIGHTS:
The Tax Cut Party had a three-point program of assertions: the United States could defend itself and the Western Hemisphere without help from anyone else; the United States must be prepared to "shoot first" if the need

arose, including a willingness to use atomic weapons for the immediate destruction of the People's Republic of China; and that any military assistance from other nations must be under the control of the United States (i.e., no U.S. forces would be under the command of the UN).

THEOCRATIC PARTY

CANDIDATE FOR PRESIDENT:
Homer Aubrey Tomlinson (NY)

CANDIDATE FOR VICE PRESIDENT:
Raymond L. Teague (AK)

CONVENTION:
March 21, 1960, Church of God, Fulton (MO)

The Theocratic Party was organized on March 21, 1960, at the Church of God in Fulton, Missouri. It was the successor party to the Church of God Party, which was active in 1952.

PLATFORM HIGHLIGHTS:
The Theocratic Party's platform consisted of twelve planks:
* 1. For union of Church and State in Jesus, Prince of Peace
  2. To keep U.S. Constitution, freedom of worship, liberty
  3. For 10-percent tithes for church and nation, instead of taxes
  4. To maintain 1960 scale of wages, profits, progress
  5. For unlimited production, 10-percent profits for farmers
  6. To end wars, crime, delinquency
  7. To unite families, end divorces
  8. To end use of tobacco, intoxicants, narcotics, gambling
  9. To assure equality for all races, nations
  10. To abandon Roman law, English common law, establish new codes, civil and criminal
  11. Establish King James Bible as Foundation of Righteousness
  12. Follow new revelations in government and peace

WRITE-IN

CANDIDATES FOR PRESIDENT:
Thomas Jefferson Anderson (TN)
Hoyt Arlington
Ellis Gibbs Arnall (GA)
Wee Willie B., Jr.
John Sammons Bell
Richard Bell
Nick Belluso (GA)
Iris Blitch
E. S. Bower
J. M. Branch
Hugh Brent
Louis L. Brown
S. Y. Brown
Ralph J. Bunche (NY)
Lester Burns
Harry Flood Byrd (VA)
Robert J. Carter
Charles R. Crisp
Earl Davis
James Curran Davis (GA)
Jefferson Davis
Thomas Joseph Dodd (CT)
Carl Duncan
Bruce Edwards
Jule W. Felton
Huckleberry Finn (Satire)
E. L. "Tic" Forrester (GA)
A. L. Hadden, Jr.
Roy V. Harris
J. B. Hatchett
Bob Humphreys
William Ingram
Ralph Ivie
M. C. "Country" Johnson
Bob Jones (GA)
Vince Kane
Bill Kennedy
Martin Luther King, Jr. (GA)
Lamar Knight
George D. Lawrence
Wade Leonard
George Lilly
Forrester Little
Henry Cabot Lodge (MA)
Oscar Long
H. W. Lott
Douglas MacArthur (WI)
James Mackey
Lester Garfield Maddox (GA)
W. O. McCord
Bob McDyer
Roy McLain
J. A. Milteer
Thomas H. Mitchell
Virlyn B. Moore, Jr.
Walter Morrison
George V. Mosley
J. D. Muse
Marshall Nelms
Fred Orr
J. L. Pilcher (GA)
Sallie Lou Rabun
Mary A. Rambo
C. C. Ramsey
Asa Philip Randolph (NY)
Nelson Aldrich Rockefeller (NY)
Richard Brevard Russell (GA)
Tom Sawyer (Satire)

V. M. Scott
Joe Smith
Sam Smith
Adlai Ewing Stevenson (IL)
Charles E. Stewart
Samuel Stratton (NY)
Harold Symons
Eugene Talmadge (GA)
Herman Talmadge (GA)
Norman Mattoon Thomas (NY)
James Strom Thurmond (SC)

Carl Vinson (GA)
Forbes Warren
James H. Whitaker
Gene Yawn
Bernard A. Young
Billy Young

CANDIDATES FOR VICE PRESIDENT:
James Eastland (MS)
Barry Morris Goldwater (AZ)
Herman Talmadge (GA)

GENERAL ELECTION SUMMARY FOR 1960			
Candidate	Electoral Votes	States	Popular Votes
Kennedy (D)	303	22	34,227,096
Nixon (R)	219	26	34,107,647
Faubus (NSR)	0	0	214,205
Harry Flood Byrd	15	3[1]	116,250
Hass (SL)	0	0	47,881[2]
Decker (PROH)	0	0	45,920
Dobbs (SOC WOR)	0	0	39,542
Sullivan (CONS TX)	0	0	18,169
Lee (CONS NJ)	0	0	8,708
Coiner (CONS VA)	0	0	4,204
unknown	0	0	2,177
Daly (TC)	0	0	1,767
King (IAAU)	0	0	1,485
Curtis (CONS)	0	0	1,401[3]
Independent American	0	0	539
H. Talmadge (WR)	0	0	29
Russell (WR)	0	0	13
Goldwater (WR)	0	0	7
Stevenson (WR)	0	0	6
Andrews (I)	0	0	5
Belluso (WR)	0	0	4
Forrester (WR)	0	0	4
Harris (WR)	0	0	4
Wee Willie B., Jr. (WR)	0	0	3
J. C. Davis (WR)	0	0	3
Anderson (WR)	0	0	2
Byrd (WR)[4]	0	0	2
Johnson (WR)	0	0	2
B. Kennedy (WR)	0	0	2
King (WR)	0	0	2
Mackey (WR)	0	0	2
Muse (WR)	0	0	2
Pilcher (WR)	0	0	2
Rockefeller (WR)	0	0	2
Scott (WR)	0	0	2
Thurmond (WR)	0	0	2
Arlington (WR)	0	0	1
Arnall (WR)	0	0	1
			(continued)

GENERAL ELECTION SUMMARY FOR 1960 (cont.)			
Candidate	Electoral Votes	States	Popular Votes
J.S. Bell (WR)	0	0	1
R. Bell (WR)	0	0	1
Blitch (WR)	0	0	1
Bower (WR)	0	0	1
Branch (WR)	0	0	1
Brent (WR)	0	0	1
S. Y. Brown (WR)	0	0	1
L. L. Brown (WR)	0	0	1
Bunche (WR)	0	0	1
Burns (WR)	0	0	1
Carter (WR)	0	0	1
Crisp (WR)	0	0	1
E. Davis (WR)	0	0	1
J. Davis (WR)	0	0	1
Dodd (WR)	0	0	1
Duncan (WR)	0	0	1
Edwards (WR)	0	0	1
Felton (WR)	0	0	1
Huckleberry Finn (WR)	0	0	1
Gould (AM VEG)	0	0	1
Hadden (WR)	0	0	1
Hatchett (WR)	0	0	1
Hoopes (WR)	0	0	1
Humphreys (WR)	0	0	1
Ingram (WR)	0	0	1
Ivie (WR)	0	0	1
Jones (WR)	0	0	1
Kane (WR)	0	0	1
Knight (WR)	0	0	1
Lawrence (WR)	0	0	1
Leonard (WR)	0	0	1
Lilly (WR)	0	0	1
Little (WR)	0	0	1
Lodge (WR)	0	0	1
Long (WR)	0	0	1
Lott (WR)	0	0	1
MacArthur (WR)	0	0	1
Maddox (WR)	0	0	1
McCord (WR)	0	0	1
McDyer (WR)	0	0	1
McLain (WR)	0	0	1
Milteer (WR)	0	0	1
Mitchell (WR)	0	0	1
Moore (WR)	0	0	1
Morrison (WR)	0	0	1
Mosley (WR)	0	0	1
Nelms (WR)	0	0	1
Orr (WR)	0	0	1
Rabun (WR)	0	0	1
Rambo (WR)	0	0	1
Ramsey (WR)	0	0	1
Randolph (WR)	0	0	1

(continued)

GENERAL ELECTION SUMMARY FOR 1960 (cont.)

Candidate	Electoral Votes	States	Popular Votes
Tom Sawyer (WR)	0	0	1
J. Smith (WR)	0	0	1
S. Smith (WR)	0	0	1
Stewart (WR)	0	0	1
Stratton (WR)	0	0	1
Symington (I)	0	0	1
Symons (WR)	0	0	1
E. Talmadge (WR)	0	0	1
Thomas (WR)	0	0	1
Vinson (WR)	0	0	1
Warren (WR)	0	0	1
Whitaker (WR)	0	0	1
Yawn (WR)	0	0	1
B. A. Young (WR)	0	0	1
B. Young (WR)	0	0	1
Ask (PEACE)	0	0	none recorded
Watts (ROCK C)	0	0	none recorded
Krajewski (AM THIRD)	0	0	none recorded
Slocomb (GRE)	0	0	none recorded
W. L. Smith (AM BEAT)	0	0	none recorded
Tomlinson (THEO)	0	0	none recorded
Waters (I)	0	0	none recorded

[1] Byrd received six electoral votes from Alabama, eight from Mississippi, and one from Oklahoma.

[2] In addition, Hass received three write-in votes in New York.

[3] Curtis also received one write-in vote in New York.

[4] Byrd received the write-in votes from state where he was not a candidate.

ELECTION OF NOVEMBER 3, 1964

President
LYNDON BAINES JOHNSON
Vice President
HUBERT HORATIO HUMPHREY

HIGHLIGHTS

The outcome of the 1964 campaign was never in significant doubt. The memory of John F. Kennedy's assassination was still fresh, and most voters seemed to think Lyndon Johnson deserved the opportunity to carry on the tasks he had begun as the slain president's successor. On the Republican side, the liberal wing of the party suffered a crushing defeat with the nomination of conservative Sen. Barry Goldwater. Despite efforts by moderates and liberals to amend the party's platform specifically to denounce the Communist Party, Ku Klux Klan, and John Birch Society, Goldwater had refused to condemn extremism. Johnson capitalized on Goldwater's unwavering conservatism in a series of harsh television ads, which painted the Republican as an enemy of Social Security and a proponent of nuclear warfare, and Johnson crushed him in the general election. Two interesting footnotes to the election were the candidacy of Clifton DeBerry as the standard-bearer of the Socialist Workers Party and Margaret Chase Smith's campaign for the Republican nomination. DeBerry was the first African-American presidential candidate to ever appear on a state ballot. Senator Smith was the first woman to contest a major party's nomination in primary elections.

AMERICA FIRST PARTY

CANDIDATE FOR PRESIDENT:
Lawrence Joseph Sarsfeld "Lar" Daly (IL)

PLATFORM HIGHLIGHTS:
The platform of the America First Party asserted that the United States could defend itself and the Western Hemisphere without help from any other country; that the United States must be prepared to "shoot first" if the need arose, including a willingness to use atomic weapons for the immediate military destruction of the People's Republic of China; that any military assistance from other nations must be under U.S. control; and that a "Lincoln Free State" should be created for African-American separatists.

AMERICAN PARTY

CANDIDATE FOR PRESIDENT:
Louis Ellsworth Jaeckel (SC) (James Strom Thurmond [CA] declined)

CANDIDATE FOR VICE PRESIDENT:
James Boyd Utt (CA) (declined)

The American Party's platform declared, "Let the Redeemed of the Lord say so with their votes, because the government was "upon His shoulders." The party presented a conservative, patriotic, and nationalistic perspective.

AMERICAN NAZI PARTY

CANDIDATE FOR PRESIDENT:
George Lincoln Rockwell (VA)

The platform of the American Nazi Party demanded that all "White Aryans" in North America unite in a "White People's Republic."

PLATFORM HIGHLIGHTS:
SUPPORTED:
- the restriction of citizenship to persons of white, non-Jewish ancestry
- the strengthening of the family farm by eliminating speculation and ensuring a stable market
- government programs to protect white people's rights to housing, medical care, and old age benefits
- incorporation of physical and character training into the school system
- a debt-free economic system, with public control over banking and credit, "based solely on the productive capacity of the white worker"
- the phasing out of polluting forms of energy
- Aryan cultural endeavors
- state subsidies for science and space exploration
- a strong military
- the promotion of traditional Aryan spiritual values by the state, along with positive eugenic measures to improve the white race

ALSO:
- deemed motherhood as the "noblest profession to which any white woman can aspire"
- condemned "modern art" and "modern music" as being "pseudo-artistic"

AMERICAN VEGETARIAN PARTY

CANDIDATE FOR PRESIDENT:
Symon Gould (NY)

CANDIDATE FOR VICE PRESIDENT:
Abram Wolfson (FL)

The platform of the American Vegetarian Party favored pacifism and vegetarianism for a longer, healthier, and happier life. It also stressed conserving natural resources and urged stiff penalties for the manipulation and certain processing of foods.

THE BEST PARTY

CANDIDATE FOR PRESIDENT:
Yetta Bronstein (NY)

The Best Party was a satire effort by Jeanne Abel, who created the fictitious Yetta Bronstein. The party's platform urged better and stronger government, fluoridation, national bingo, sex education, and lowering the voting age to eighteen. Bronstein campaigned on the slogan "Put a Jewish mother in the White House."

CAR AND DRIVER PARTY

CANDIDATE FOR PRESIDENT:
Daniel Sexton Gurney

The Car and Driver Party was the creation of Car and Driver magazine. It intended to focus attention on the problems of the motoring public.

CONSERVATIVE PARTY OF NEW YORK

CANDIDATE FOR PRESIDENT:
Barry Morris Goldwater (AZ)

CANDIDATE FOR VICE PRESIDENT:
William Edward Miller (NY)

The Conservative Party, as its name suggests, was a right-wing organization based in New York State. It was formed in 1962 in opposition to Nelson Rockefeller's ascendancy within the state's Republican Party.

CONSTITUTION PARTY

CANDIDATE FOR PRESIDENT:
Joseph Benton Lightburn (WV)

CANDIDATE FOR VICE PRESIDENT:
Theodore Conrad Billings (CO)

CONVENTION
July 23–25, 1964, Rice Hotel, Houston (TX)

Fifty-four delegates from twelve states attended the convention.

PLATFORM HIGHLIGHTS:
SUPPORTED:
- the restoration of Congress as the sole authority to issue currency
- the abolition of the Federal Reserve System
- the establishment of a state militia in every state
- the repeal of the Mental Health Act
- the safeguarding of the Constitution's supremacy over treaties
- limitations on the Supreme Court's powers through checks and balances
- the removal of the government from competition with private businesses
- the elimination of government agricultural subsidies
- a balanced federal budget and retirement of the national debt
- a repeal of the Sixteenth Amendment (income tax) and implementing laws, federal inheritance taxes, and estate taxes
- limits on immigration to the quotas established by the McCarran-Walter Act and supported the deportation of illegal aliens
- vigorous prosecution of Communist conspirators for treason
- a repeal of the Civil Rights Act
- the teaching of free enterprise and patriotism in the schools, the elimination of federal aid to education, and the freedom of public schools to hold Bible readings and prayers
- the protection of a person's right to associate freely with whomever he or she chooses
- the Ninth and Tenth amendments to the Constitution
- the withdrawal of the United States from the United Nations
- the repeal of the Nuclear Test Ban Treaty, Disarmament Act, reciprocal trade agreements, and the General Agreement on Tariff and Trade (GATT)
- the elimination of foreign aid
- the suspension of diplomatic relations with Communist countries
- the return of U.S. servicemen stationed abroad
- the abolition of the Council on Foreign Relations and the Business Council, based on the party's claims that they were "prime movers" for world dictatorship

ALSO:
- declared that the United States was a "Christian nation"

CONSTITUTION PARTY
OF PENNSYLVANIA

CANDIDATE FOR PRESIDENT:

James Strom Thurmond (SC) (declined)

DEMOCRATIC PARTY

CANDIDATE FOR PRESIDENT:

Lyndon Baines Johnson

CANDIDATE FOR VICE PRESIDENT:

Hubert Horatio Humphrey

CANDIDATES FOR PRESIDENTIAL NOMINATION:

Daniel Baugh Brewster (MD)
Fay T. Carpenter-Swain (KY)
Lawrence Joseph Sarsfield "Lar" Daly (IL)
Andrew J. Easter (MD)
Barry Morris Goldwater (AZ)
Hubert Horatio Humphrey (MN)
Lyndon Baines Johnson (TX)
Edward Moore Kennedy (MA)
Robert Francis Kennedy (NY)
John Hugh Latham (IN)
Henry Cabot Lodge (MA)
Richard Milhous Nixon (CA)
Albert S. Porter (OH)
John W. Reynolds (WI)
Nelson Aldrich Rockefeller (NY)
William Warren Scranton (PA)
Adlai Ewing Stevenson (IL)
George Corley Wallace (AL)
Matthew Empson Welsh (IN)

CANDIDATES FOR VICE-PRESIDENTIAL NOMINATION:

Thomas Joseph Dodd (CT)
Eugene Joseph McCarthy (MN)
Carl Sanders (GA)

PRIMARIES:

MARCH 10, 1964 (NH):

Johnson 29,317
R. F. Kennedy 487
Lodge 280
Nixon 232
Goldwater 193
Rockefeller 109
write-in 159

APRIL 7, 1964 (WI):

Reynolds 522,405
Wallace 266,136

APRIL 14, 1964 (IL):

Johnson 82,027
Wallace 3,761
R. F. Kennedy 2,894
others 841

APRIL 21, 1964 (NJ):

Johnson 4,863

Wallace 491
R. F. Kennedy 431
others 124

APRIL 28, 1964 (MA):

Johnson 61,035
R. F. Kennedy 15,870
Lodge 2,269
E. M. Kennedy 1,259
Wallace 565
Stevenson 452
Humphrey 323
others 1,436

APRIL 28, 1964 (PA):

Johnson 209,606
Wallace 12,104
R. F. Kennedy 12,029
Scranton 8,156
Lodge 4,895
others 6,438

MAY 5, 1964 (DC):

unpledged delegates 41,095

MAY 5, 1964 (IN):

Welsh 376,023
Wallace 172,646
Daly 15,160
Latham 8,067
Carpenter-Swain 7,140

MAY 5, 1964 (OH):

Porter 493,619

MAY 12, 1964 (NE):

Johnson 54,713
R. F. Kennedy 2,099
Wallace 1,067
Lodge 1,051
Nixon 833
Goldwater 603
others 904

MAY 12, 1964 (WV):

unpledged delegates 131,432

MAY 15, 1964 (OR):

Johnson 272,099
Wallace 1,365

MAY 19, 1964 (MD):

Brewster 267,106
Wallace 214,849
Easter 8,275
unpledged delegates 12,377

MAY 26, 1964 (FL):

Johnson 393,339

JUNE 2, 1964 (CA):

unpledged (Edmund Gerald Brown, Sr. [CA]) slate of
    delegates 1,693,813

unpledged (Samuel William Yorty [CA]) slate of delegates, ... 798,431

JUNE 2, 1964 (SD):
unpledged delegates 28,142

34TH CONVENTION:
August 24–27, 1964, Convention Hall, Atlantic City (NJ)
John Orlando Pastore (RI), temporary chairman
John William McCormack (MA), permanent chairman

The 1964 Democratic platform identified peace and the need for a strong national defense as top U.S. priorities.

PLATFORM HIGHLIGHTS:
SUPPORTED:
- the Nuclear Test Ban Treaty
- the United Nations
- the Alliance for Progress and the isolation of "Castroism"
- an expansion of the Peace Corps and Food for Peace programs
- the reassertion of U.S. leadership in the conquest of space
- public scholarships for worthy students and increased aid for education
- health care programs and increased benefit levels for senior citizens under the Social Security Act
- better housing and improved retirement benefits for the elderly
- an expansion of health facilities and research activities
- increased benefits for veterans, including a reopening of the National Service Life Insurance program
- effective enforcement of the Civil Rights Act of 1964
- a revision of the immigration laws to reunite families
- full equality of opportunity for men and women, including older U.S. citizens
- the continuation of the War on Poverty
- "help" for the physically and mentally handicapped to "develop to the full limit of their capabilities"
- assistance for American Indians in achieving self-sufficiency and the privileges of equal citizenship
- the encouragement of science, technology, and the arts
- low interest rates, tax reductions, and strict economy in federal expenditures
- a balanced budget, price stability, and full employment
- an extension of the Fair Labor Standards Act to all workers
- the revision of the unemployment insurance program
- legal protection and economic encouragement for agricultural and migratory workers
- more manpower training and small business stimulation
- the enforcement of antitrust laws
- a repeal of section 14 (b) of the Taft-Hartley Act
- consumer protection initiatives
- strengthened commodity programs and expansion of the Food Stamp program
- the development of rural community programs and agricultural cooperatives to ensure decent housing and economic security
- continued support for rural electrification and communications
- the conservation of natural resources
- flood control
- irrigation and reclamation
- the promotion of water, nuclear, and tidal power generation
- improvements in municipal water supplies and navigation
- an attack on air pollution
- expanded efforts in desalinization
- the encouragement of the mineral and fuel industries
- the preservation of the Tennessee Valley Authority
- fish and wildlife enhancement
- the development of a "balanced" outdoor recreation program
- the preservation of wilderness areas
- intensive forest management
- improvements in transportation
- initiatives against drug abuse
- urban renewal, community development, and mass transit programs
- the creation of a cabinet-level Department of Urban Affairs
- a high standard of government ethics
- a revision of congressional procedures to make them more democratic
- home rule and congressional representation for the District of Columbia
- self-determination for Puerto Rico and self-government for the Virgin Islands

---

DEMOCRATIC PARTY

VOTE FOR PRESIDENTIAL NOMINATION: JOHNSON WAS UNANIMOUSLY NOMINATED FOR PRESIDENT ON THE FIRST BALLOT.

VOTE FOR VICE-PRESIDENTIAL NOMINATION: PRIOR TO THE CONVENTION, SPECULATION REGARDING THE VICE-PRESIDENTIAL NOMINATION HAD CENTERED ON HUMPHREY AND MCCARTHY, BUT MCCARTHY WITHDREW HIS NAME FROM CONSIDERATION WHEN IT APPEARED THAT JOHNSON HAD SELECTED HUMPHREY. JOHNSON, HOWEVER, INVITED BOTH HUMPHREY AND DODD TO THE WHITE HOUSE DURING THE CONVENTION, SPARKING RUMORS THAT BOTH WERE UNDER REVIEW FOR THE SECOND SPOT ON THE TICKET. WHEN THE NOMINATIONS WERE MADE, SANDERS WAS OFFERED FOR CONSIDERATION, BUT HE DECLINED. HUMPHREY WAS THEN UNANIMOUSLY NOMINATED FOR VICE PRESIDENT ON THE FIRST BALLOT.

OPPOSED:
- the admission of the People's Republic of China to the United Nations
- quota systems and "preferential practices" in civil rights

ALSO:
- paid homage to John F. Kennedy
- vowed to end to hatred and violence by condemning extremism and naming the Communist Party, Ku Klux Klan, and John Birch Society as examples of "misguided zeal and twisted logic"
- ending with a lengthy "Accounting of Stewardship, 1961–1964," recited the Democrats' record under the Kennedy-Johnson administration, matching its pledges of 1960 against its accomplishments, and made the following plea: "In the 1,000 days of John F. Kennedy, in the eventful and culminating months of Lyndon B. Johnson, there has been born a new American greatness. . . . Let us continue."

FREEDOM DEMOCRATIC PARTY

CANDIDATE FOR PRESIDENT:
Lyndon Baines Johnson (TX)

CANDIDATE FOR VICE PRESIDENT:
Hubert Horatio Humphrey (MN)

This party was the Democratic Party's organization in Mississippi that was loyal to the national ticket. Accordingly, it endorsed the Democratic candidates.

INDEPENDENT

CANDIDATES FOR PRESIDENT:
Richard Brevard Russell (GA)
George Corley Wallace (AL)

LIBERAL PARTY OF NEW YORK

CANDIDATE FOR PRESIDENT:
Lyndon Baines Johnson (TX)

CANDIDATE FOR VICE PRESIDENT:
Hubert Horatio Humphrey (MN)

Nominations were made September 1, 1964, by the state committee, which met in New York (NY).

METROPOLITAN PARTY

CANDIDATE FOR PRESIDENT:
Wilbur Allen Huckle

CANDIDATE FOR VICE PRESIDENT:
Marvin Eugene Throneberry (TN)

This party was a promotional effort for the New York Mets baseball team. Its platform advocated more leisure time and a shorter work week.

NATIONAL STATES RIGHTS PARTY

CANDIDATE FOR PRESIDENT:
John Kasper

CANDIDATE FOR VICE PRESIDENT:
Jesse Benjamin Stoner

CANDIDATES FOR PRESIDENTIAL NOMINATION:
John Kasper (TN)
Ross Robert Barnett (MI)

CANDIDATES FOR VICE-PRESIDENTIAL NOMINATION:
Violet Lloyd (IL)
Jesse Benjamin Stoner (GA)
Dewey Taft (FL)

CONVENTION:
March 1–2, 1964, Louisville (KY)
Ned Dupes (GA), national chairman
Matt H. Murphy, Jr. (AL), keynoter

The party challenged the United Nations, world government, and race mixing and intermarriage. It also sought to expel all Communists from the country. The party was supported by various branches of the Ku Klux Klan and was strongly anti-Semitic.

PLATFORM HIGHLIGHTS:
SUPPORTED:
- "White supremacy" and creation of a "White Folk Community"
- states' rights
- free enterprise
- full employment
- high wages
- large old age pensions
- racial separation
- the restoration of segregation in schools and the military
- restrictions against non-Caucasians from participating in government or serving in the courts
- the preservation of the "national life" of American Indians with unlimited development of reservation facilities
- labor unions run by "honest White men"
- a fair price for farm products
- limits on foreign trade to protect Caucasian producers
- the abolishment of confiscatory taxation
- the elimination of slums, floods, and dust bowls through combined civic efforts in individual states
- racial instruction for Caucasian youth
- the restructuring of the educational system to afford all Caucasian citizens the full opportunity to achieve their vocational ambitions
- censorship to prevent unwanted ideologies and influences in the media
- the establishment of Congress as the sole authority to issue money
- the end of federal control over the National Guard and state law enforcement agencies

- the abolishment of federal judicial decrees that violate state sovereignty
- the elimination of federal "thought-control"
- an end to secret police tactics
- the right of states to investigate and prosecute subversives
- limits on immigration solely to Caucasian, Christian immigrants
- efforts to locate a country in Africa for the repatriation of African Americans
- the strengthening of cultural and moral ties with other "White nations" and an end to "alien minority wars" that force "White Christian boys to die on foreign soil"

OPPOSED:
- foreign "giveaways" and international entanglements

NATIONAL STATES RIGHTS PARTY
VOTES FOR PRESIDENTIAL AND VICE-PRESIDENTIAL NOMINATION: PRIOR TO THE CONVENTION, THE NATIONAL EXECUTIVE COMMITTEE MET ON FEBRUARY 30 TO SELECT CANDIDATES TO RECOMMEND AT THE CONVENTION. BARNETT AND KASPER WERE DISCUSSED AS POTENTIAL PRESIDENTIAL CANDIDATES WHILE LLOYD, STONER, AND TAFT WERE OFFERED AS POTENTIAL VICE-PRESIDENTIAL CANDIDATES. KASPER AND STONER RECEIVED THE OVERWHELMING VOTES OF THE NATIONAL EXECUTIVE COMMITTEE. WHEN THE CONVENTION CONVENED, THE NATIONAL EXECUTIVE COMMITTEE'S RECOMMENDATIONS WERE PRESENTED, AND BARNETT AND LLOYD WERE NOMINATED FROM THE FLOOR FOR PRESIDENT AND VICE PRESIDENT, RESPECTIVELY. THE NATIONAL EXECUTIVE COMMITTEE'S SLATE RECEIVED MORE THAN 90 PERCENT OF THE VOTES.

NATIONAL TAX SAVERS PARTY

CANDIDATE FOR PRESIDENT:
Daniel X. B. "Dixbie" Schwartz (NY)

PLATFORM HIGHLIGHTS:
The National Tax Savers Party had a three-point platform for helping the "little man."

SUPPORTED:
- a compulsory, perpetual monthly public referendum by electronic computer before any president could sign a bill into law
- new income tax deductions for normal expenses such as food, rent, and taxes
- the appointment of a secretary of taxation from the common people as a member of the president's cabinet

PATRIOTIC PROTESTANTS OF AMERICA

CANDIDATE FOR PRESIDENT:
L. D. Westerbeek (AZ)

Denouncing Communists and atheists, the self-proclaimed prophet and seer, Mrs. L. D. Westerbeek, promoted a religious message through tent meetings.

PEACE PARTY

CANDIDATE FOR PRESIDENT:
Mihran Nicholas Ask (CA)

PLATFORM HIGHLIGHTS:
SUPPORTED:
- the prevention of World War III by eliminating war and weapons
- a pledge of peace and plenty to all nations regardless of race, religion, and political connections forced upon them
- a job for every unemployed person
- the elimination of bureaucracies
- a reduction of all taxes by 50 percent
- the right to work
- the right to vote for those who believe in and uphold the U.S. Constitution and have at least a high school education
- no suppression of the press, radio, or pulpit
- the Bible as an obligatory study project in all schools and on all levels
- a restoration of the biblical right of men as the head of the home

PEACE PARTY

CANDIDATE FOR PRESIDENT:
Herbert Franklin Hoover (IA)

CANDIDATE FOR VICE PRESIDENT:
Rebecca Shelley

CANDIDATES FOR VICE-PRESIDENTIAL NOMINATION:
Hugh Bryant Hester (NC)
Rebecca Shelley (MI)

The Peace Party was formed at the 1964 annual meeting of the Iowa Farmers Association. At that time, Hoover, fourth cousin to former president Herbert Hoover, was urged to run on a write-in ticket with Brigadier General Hester, USA (retired); however, Hester declined. On October 16, 1964, Shelley was substituted for the second spot on the ticket.

PLATFORM HIGHLIGHTS:
The party's platform spoke out against the "bipartisan Cold Warriors, the military-industrial complex," and nuclear brinkmanship. It opposed the war in Vietnam, graft, corruption, and influence peddling in Washington.

POOR MAN'S PARTY

CANDIDATE FOR PRESIDENT:
Henry B. Krajewski (NJ)

CANDIDATE FOR VICE PRESIDENT:
Anna Marie Yezo (NJ)

PLATFORM HIGHLIGHTS:

SUPPORTED:

- "No Piggie Deals in Washington"
- a square deal program for all, with income taxes starting from $1,000, instead of $600, per person
- an end to floating outrageous bonds for government improvement, instead preferring to finance projects on a cash-and-carry basis
- a termination of foreign aid for "freeloaders"
- the incarceration of all corrupt politicians
- an open-door policy for countries that wanted to become part of the United States
- government-sponsored homeowners' insurance for veterans
- a one-year mandatory agricultural training program for boys, who would be permitted to "Rock and Roll with the chickens, pigs, and cows at 5 a.m."
- a two-month compulsory outdoor life-training program for girls as an alternative to "Hot Rods, Drag Racing, or juvenile destruction"
- an elimination of farm subsidies
- the abolition of the Ku Klux Klan, Communist Party, Nazis, and Progressive Party
- the abolishment of the electoral college
- Golden Age opportunities for everyone
- the legalization of gambling
- a pledge to "stop pussyfooting with the Communists and finish the war of nerves"
- the deployment of atomic missiles over the Soviet Union as a threat

OPPOSED:

- monopolies

PROHIBITION PARTY

CANDIDATE FOR PRESIDENT:
Earle Harold Munn, Sr.

CANDIDATE FOR VICE PRESIDENT:
Mark Revell Shaw (MA)

CANDIDATES FOR PRESIDENTIAL NOMINATION:
Milton Conover (NJ)
Rutherford Losey Decker (MO)
Roy S. Hollomon (KS)
Enoch Arden Holtwick (IL)
Earle Harold Munn, Sr. (MI)
Mark Revell Shaw (MA)
Claude Alonzo Watson (CA)

24TH CONVENTION:
August 29–30, 1963, Hotel Mark Twain, St. Louis (MO)
Earle Harold Munn, Sr. (MI), temporary chairman

PLATFORM HIGHLIGHTS:

SUPPORTED:

- loyalty to the Constitution and Bill of Rights
- governmental economy and tax reduction
- an end to inflation
- price stabilization
- a return to a sound currency (such as the gold standard) under congressional control
- a balanced budget
- the reexamination of the concept of foreign aid
- less government regulations
- a halt to public government competition with private businesses
- an end to monopolies and unethical practices as a way of strengthening free enterprise
- a balanced approach to labor and industrial relations that places the common good before the interests of either business or labor
- compulsory arbitration of labor disputes
- right-to-work laws
- prohibitions against secondary boycotts and industry-wide bargaining
- individual and states' rights
- full civil rights for all
- a return of public morality and law enforcement
- world peace based on the teachings of the "Prince of Peace"
- national sovereignty and preparedness
- restraints in nuclear bomb testing
- the protection of religious liberty and the enactment of uniform marriage and divorce laws
- "actuarially sound voluntary social security programs"
- ballot law reform to assist minor parties in gaining ballot access
- the separation of church and state
- tax exemptions for educational and religious institutions
- a return to a free-market program for agriculture
- the formation of a citizens' coalition against liquor traffic
- stronger efforts at alcohol education and the control (and eventual elimination) of alcoholic beverages

OPPOSED:

- communism and totalitarianism
- militarism
- the overcentralization of government
- the destruction of neighborhood schools
- special privileges for minority groups and the use of "pressure tactics" to achieve civil rights
- universal military training
- limitations on the use of the Bible in public settings (e.g., schools)
- federal aid to education
- unjust incarcerations of persons in mental health cases
- programs of mass medication (e.g., fluoridation)
- the spoils system

REPUBLICAN PARTY

CANDIDATE FOR PRESIDENT:
Barry Morris Goldwater

CANDIDATE FOR VICE PRESIDENT:
William Edward Miller (NY)

CANDIDATES FOR PRESIDENTIAL NOMINATION:
Mihran Nicholas Ask (CA)
Frank Roscoe Beckwith (IN)
John William Byrnes (WI)
Robert Ellsworth Ennis (MD)
Joseph George Ettl (IN)
Hiram Leong Fong (HI)
Barry Morris Goldwater (AZ)
Lyndon Baines Johnson (TX)
Walter Henry Judd (MN)
Norman LePage (NH)
George Cabot Lodge (MA)
Henry Cabot Lodge (MA)
Richard Milhous Nixon (CA)
James Allen Rhodes (OH)
Nelson Aldrich Rockefeller (NY)
George Wilcken Romney (MI)
William Warren Scranton (PA)
Margaret Chase Smith (ME)
Harold Edward Stassen (PA)
John Wesley Steffey (MD)
George Corley Wallace (AL)

PRIMARIES:

MARCH 10, 1964 (NH):
H. Lodge 33,007
Goldwater 20,692
Rockefeller 19,504
Nixon 15,587
Smith 2,120
Stassen 1,373
Scranton 105
LePage 82
others 383

APRIL 7, 1964 (WI):
Byrnes 299,612
unpledged delegates 816

APRIL 14, 1964 (IL):
Goldwater 512,840
Smith 209,521
H. Lodge 68,122
Nixon 30,313
Wallace 2,203
Rockefeller 2,048
Scranton 1,842
Romney 465
others 437

APRIL 21, 1964 (NJ):
H. Lodge 7,896
Goldwater 5,309
Nixon 4,179
Scranton 633
Rockefeller 612
others 304

APRIL 28, 1964 (MA):
H. Lodge 70,809
Goldwater 9,338
Nixon 5,460
Rockefeller 2,454
Scranton 1,709
Johnson 600
Smith 426
G. Lodge 365
Romney 262
others 711

APRIL 28, 1964 (PA):
Scranton 235,222
H. Lodge 92,712
Nixon 44,396
Goldwater 38,669
Johnson 22,372
Rockefeller 9,123
Wallace 5,105
others 5,269

MAY 2, 1964 (TX):
Goldwater 104,137
H. Lodge 12,324
Rockefeller 6,207
Nixon 5,390
Stassen 5,273
Smith 4,816
Scranton 803
others 373

MAY 5, 1964 (IN):
Goldwater 267,935
Stassen 107,157
Beckwith 17,884
Ettl 6,704

MAY 5, 1964 (OH):
Rhodes 615,754

MAY 12, 1964 (NE):
Goldwater 68,050
Nixon 43,613
H. Lodge 22,622
Rockefeller 2,333
Scranton 578
Johnson 316
others 1,010

MAY 12, 1964 (WV):
Rockefeller 115,680

MAY 15, 1964 (OR):
Rockefeller 94,190
H. Lodge 79,169
Goldwater 50,105
Nixon 48,274
Smith 8,087
Scranton 4,509
others 1,152

MAY 19, 1964 (MD):
Steffey 22,135
Ennis 18,859
unpledged delegates 57,004

MAY 26, 1964 (FL):
Goldwater 42,525
unpledged delegates 58,179

JUNE 2, 1964 (CA):
Goldwater 1,120,403
Rockefeller 1,052,053

JUNE 2, 1964 (SD):
Goldwater 27,076
unpledged delegates 57,653

28TH CONVENTION:
July 13–16, 1964, Grand National Livestock Pavilion (Cow Palace), San Francisco (CA)
Mark Odom Hatfield (OR), temporary chairman and keynoter
Thruston Ballard Morton (KY), permanent chairman

PLATFORM HIGHLIGHTS:
The Republican Party's platform reflected the conservative tilt of the party's Goldwater faction. It cast the 1964 contest as a competition between the forces of freedom and slavery. The Democrats were condemned as "Federal extremists," who recklessly promoted the centralization of power.

SUPPORTED:
- the right of individuals to "govern themselves" with a minimum of government interference
- "check[s]" and restraints on the powers and appetites of the federal government
- equal opportunity (but not an equal outcome)
- the competitive free enterprise system
- limited government
- the use of tax credits to assist needy senior citizens in meeting medical and hospital costs
- a revision of Social Security's earning limitations
- tax incentives to reduce the burden of financing college education
- exemptions to the minimum-wage laws to encourage the employment of teenagers
- the enactment of legislation to restrict the flow of obscene materials through the mail
- a repeal of the "bread tax"
- the creation of an all-volunteer army
- the enforcement of the Civil Rights Act
- immigration reform to reunite families
- a constitutional amendment authorizing the voluntary and nondiscriminatory observation of religious practice in public places
- a reduction in government spending
- an end to deficit financing
- a reduction in individual and corporate income taxes
- the repayment of the public debt
- a reduction in government red tape

- a strong defense
- the removal of federal excise taxes
- a simplification of federal and state tax and regulatory requirements affecting small businesses
- limits on the authority of federal agencies
- a reduction in paperwork
- a reduction in trade restrictions
- the enforcement of antitrust laws
- the elimination of excessive bureaucracy and the adoption of the Hoover Commission's recommendations
- a development of voluntary commodity programs
- a "balanced use" of natural resources
- a restoration of collective bargaining responsibility to labor and management
- the beneficial use of public lands
- water-resource planning
- the reliance on sustained yield in forestry practices
- the development of domestic fishing and mineral resources
- the development of atomic power and encouragement of the oil and coal industries
- an accelerated space program
- a reevaluation of grants-in-aid programs
- more emphasis on private enterprise to revitalize urban areas and expand housing
- a constitutional amendment to permit state senates to be apportioned on a geographical basis instead of a population basis
- budgetary reform
- the maintenance of a strong dollar at home and abroad
- "victory for freedom" and denounced communism
- consultation with U.S. allies
- the Open Skies policy proposed by President Dwight Eisenhower
- the captive nations of Eastern Europe
- the United Nations, although the party wanted to revise the charter to "more accurately reflect the power realities of the world"
- the North Atlantic Treaty Organization (NATO), Southeast Asia Treaty Organization (SEATO), and Central Treaty Organization (CENTO)
- quick and decisive action to ensure victory in South Vietnam
- the destruction of the Berlin Wall
- the renunciation and economic boycott of Fidel Castro's Cuba by American nations
- the upholding of the Panama Canal Treaty (while supporting exploration of alternative canal routes and greater involvement of Panama in the economic benefits of the canal)
- the United States in "tak[ing] the Cold War offensive"
- an extension of the free enterprise system to emergent nations with U.S. assistance
- military superiority, not equality, as "freedom's shield"
- the development of new weapon systems
- professionalism in the armed forces
- strong civilian control over the military

OPPOSED:
- efforts to weaken neighborhood schools and to promote "reverse discrimination"
- federal controls on agriculture
- lawlessness and violence
- wasteful spending
- aid to Communist nations unless that aid reduces their power and influence
- recognition of the People's Republic of China
- unilateral disarmament

REPUBLICAN PARTY VOTE FOR PRESIDENTIAL NOMINATION:	
Candidate	*Ballot: 1*
Goldwater	883
Scranton	214
Rockefeller	114
Romney	41
Smith	27
Judd	22
Fong	5
H. Lodge	2

Goldwater's nomination was made unanimous.

VOTE FOR VICE-PRESIDENTIAL NOMINATION: MILLER WAS UNANIMOUSLY CHOSEN AS THE VICE-PRESIDENTIAL NOMINEE ON THE FIRST BALLOT.

SOCIALIST LABOR PARTY

CANDIDATE FOR PRESIDENT:
Eric Hass (NY)

CANDIDATE FOR VICE PRESIDENT:
Henning Albert Blomen (MA)

26TH CONVENTION:
May 2–3, 1964, Henry Hudson Hotel, New York (NY)
Nathan Karp (NJ), temporary and permanent chairman

Twenty-nine delegates from fifteen states, the District of Columbia, and two ethnic federations attended this convention.

PLATFORM HIGHLIGHTS:
The platform of the Socialist Labor Party once again declared that humanity stood on the threshold of a new social order. It announced the death rattle of capitalism, spurned Lyndon Johnson's "phony antipoverty wars," rejected "self-styled radicals and liberals," and argued that capitalism's best-kept secret was that poverty could no longer be justified. In a changing work world, the party maintained, capitalism prevented humanity's achievement

of its highest potential. In a Socialist world, workers would derive full benefits from their production and "democracy would be a vibrant, meaningful reality." Under Socialist leadership, administrators and planners would act on behalf of workers, creating a "heaven on earth." The party's platform called on workers to consolidate their economic forces into one integral Socialist Industrial Union under democratic control. That union would back up the peaceful Socialist ballot and usher in the new age of affluence and enduring peace.

SOCIALIST LABOR PARTY
VOTES FOR PRESIDENTIAL AND VICE-PRESIDENTIAL NOMINATION: HASS AND BLOMEN WERE UNANIMOUSLY NOMINATED FOR PRESIDENT AND VICE PRESIDENT, RESPECTIVELY. NO OTHER NAMES WERE PLACED BEFORE THE CONVENTION.

SOCIALIST WORKERS PARTY

CANDIDATE FOR PRESIDENT:
Clifton DeBerry (NY)

CANDIDATE FOR VICE PRESIDENT:
Edward Shaw (NY)

CONVENTION:
December 28, 1963, New York (NY)

PLATFORM HIGHLIGHTS:
The platform of the Socialist Workers Party painted a bleak future under capitalism, citing the poverty and exploitation of workers and minorities as needless social evils.

SUPPORTED:
- a "Freedom Now" Party
- a peaceful foreign policy
- the recognition of the PRC government (China)
- the creation of a Fair Employment Practices Commission
- the teaching African-American history in public schools
- the abolition of lists of subversives and "red-baiting"
- a liberalization of election laws
- organized labor
- increased benefits for workers
- a ban on racial and sexual discrimination
- guaranteed college educations for young people
- adequate pensions and free medical care for seniors
- aid to farmers to raise their standard of living
- an immediate emergency housing and public works program
- steeply progressive taxes with exemptions for low-income families
- the nationalization of all banks, basic industries, food trusts, and natural resources, including nuclear power
- the election of workers and technicians to manage facilities in the interests of producers and consumers

OPPOSED:

- U.S. intervention abroad
- the "token" civil rights legislation of the Johnson administration
- Democratic policies as antilabor
- congressional inquisitions because they infringed on individual rights
- unions as too conservative
- anticrime laws as repressive and dangerous
- capitalist imperialism
- all forms of anti-Semitism

THEOCRATIC PARTY

CANDIDATE FOR PRESIDENT:
Homer Aubrey Tomlinson (NY)

CANDIDATE FOR VICE PRESIDENT:
William Richard Rogers (MO)

CONVENTION:
May 21, 1964, Fulton (MO)

PLATFORM HIGHLIGHTS:
The Theocratic Party's platform pledged that its candidates, "Mighty Men of God," would bring about a "Government under God."

SUPPORTED:

- the union of church and state
- the full restoration of the Constitution
- an end to taxes and the institution of a 10 percent tithe instead
- the establishment of the U.S. wage scale in all countries
- support for free enterprise
- an end to wars, crime, and civil strife
- substituting Roman law for 1964 legal codes
- prayer and Bible reading in schools
- an end to divorce, gambling, and liquor
- new revelations affecting government and peace

UNITED NATIONS PARTY

CANDIDATE FOR PRESIDENT:
Emil Matalik (WI)

A Wisconsin farmer, Matalik offered the United Nations sixty acres of his farmland. When it ignored his offer, he sent deeds for five-acre parcels to the heads of state of 177 nations. He then decided to seek the presidency on a United Nations Party platform, which urged a return to an agrarian society in which everyone was given five acres to farm. He supported a program to turn cities into farmlands and favored strict birth control, bidding all couples with more than two children be drafted into the military. His platform called for abolishing tobacco, liquor, and gambling; disbanding all religions; and relocating the United Nations on the Matalik homestead. Matalik maintained that Catholics controlled the Democratic Party and that the Central Intelligence Agency and Protestants controlled the Republican Party. Believing that speech patterns put the most important things first, the candidate always signed himself "Matalik, Emil."

UNITED PARTY

CANDIDATE FOR PRESIDENT:
Grant Van Tilborg (unknown)

CANDIDATE FOR VICE-PRESIDENT:
Harold L. Putnam (MA)

PLATFORM HIGHLIGHTS:
The United Party's platform demanded the expulsion of all groups that tended to break up the "united" character of the nation. More than one hundred organizations were listed as undesirable, including the Communists, Socialists, Ku Klux Klan, John Birch Society, American Federation of Labor-Committee for Industrial Organization (AFL-CIO), and the National Association for the Advancement of Colored People (NAACP).

UNIVERSAL PARTY

CANDIDATE FOR PRESIDENT:
Kirby James Hensley (CA)

CANDIDATE FOR VICE PRESIDENT:
John Orville Hopkins (IA)

1ST CONVENTION:
August 8, 1964, Hotel Leamington, Oakland (CA)
John W. Hopkins (CA), chairman

The Universal Party was formed on July 4, 1963, at a gathering of persons who had been contacted by UFOs (unidentified flying objects) and "New Age" thinkers in Berkeley (CA).

PLATFORM HIGHLIGHTS:
A preliminary platform was drafted at the party's organizational meeting in 1963. It was subsequently submitted to the first convention, where the original document was expanded.

SUPPORTED:

- a general revision of the election system and elimination of national conventions, the electoral college, and other representative structures
- a direct election of public officials by the people
- the recall of public officials
- a prohibition on lobbying
- the participation of women in elective and appointive offices
- equal pay for equal work for women
- the abolition of usury
- a reassertion of congressional control over money
- an expansion of credit unions for future banking
- the elimination of taxes by Congress's printing enough money to pay its obligations

- the government's withdrawal from activities that compete with the private sector
- a World Congress with equal representation of nations
- a World Supreme Court assisted by national appellate courts
- an end to unemployment
- the guild system and creation of specialized craft unions
- village and farm development on unused public lands as a solution to urban crowding
- small farm owners over large corporate farming interests
- the control of speculation and the subsidizing of "start-up" farmers for up to five years
- the conservation of all natural resources
- the substitution of free or cosmic energy for oil and gas
- free education
- the encouragement of private schools
- equal support for the humanities and for the sciences
- a fostering of spiritual (not religious) training and research
- the standardization of marriage laws and the handling of divorce matters by domestic specialists and counselors
- the stimulation of small businesses and enforcement of fair trade practices
- limits on the dramatization of crimes and vices on television or in movies

- the prevention of juvenile delinquency
- karmic justice
- full recognition of civil rights
- improvements in old age and unemployment benefits and medical assistance programs

OPPOSED:

- zoning laws and highway condemnation as interferences with private property
- labor or management monopolies

ALSO:

- claimed that messages from greater worlds that often contact earth confirm the truth of reincarnation

---

UNIVERSAL PARTY

VOTE FOR PRESIDENTIAL NOMINATION: J. W. HOPKINS WAS PLACED IN NOMINATION FOR PRESIDENT, BUT HE DECLINED. HENSLEY WAS THEN NOMINATED BY ACCLAMATION.

VOTE FOR VICE-PRESIDENTIAL NOMINATION: J. O. HOPKINS (FATHER OF J. W. HOPKINS) WAS UNANIMOUSLY NOMINATED FOR VICE PRESIDENT.

GENERAL ELECTION SUMMARY FOR 1964:

Candidate	Electoral Votes	States	Popular Votes
Johnson (D)	486	44 (+DC)	43,167,895[1]
Goldwater (R)	52	6	27,175,770
unpledged Democrat	0	0	210,732
blank and void[2]	0	0	199,675
Hass (SOC LAB)	0	0	42,642
Munn (PROH)	0	0	23,267
DeBerry (SOC WOR)	0	0	22,249
Kasper (NSR)	0	0	6,957
Lightburn (CONST)	0	0	5,060
Wallace (I)	0	0	60
Russell (I)	0	0	50
Hensley (UNIV)	0	0	19
unknown	0	0	30,388

[1]Includes the votes of the Freedom Democratic Party and Liberal Party
[2]blank and void = ballots improperly marked or ballots cast but not marked at all

ELECTION OF NOVEMBER 5, 1968

President
RICHARD MILHOUS NIXON
Vice President
SPIRO THEODORE AGNEW

HIGHLIGHTS

The 1968 election was like no other in U.S. history in the intensity of the unfolding drama and the bitter legacy left in its wake. Throughout the 1960s, the Vietnam War continued to escalate, dividing the United States into emotional factions that either supported or opposed U.S. involvement in Southeast Asia. By 1968, the war and its concomitant social unrest had become the dominant political issues facing the electorate. When Sen. Eugene Joseph McCarthy challenged the incumbent president of his own party, Lyndon Baines Johnson, in opposition to the war, young people rallied to McCarthy's banner. His strong second-place showing in New Hampshire contributed to President Johnson's surprise announcement that he would not seek reelection. With Johnson's withdrawal, Vice President Hubert Horatio Humphrey entered the race and assumed the role of defender of administration policy. Meanwhile, McCarthy's leadership of the antiwar faction of the Democratic Party was contested by Robert Francis Kennedy's entrance into the competition for the presidential nomination. On the Republican side, Sen. Barry Goldwater's conservatism was discredited, and the more moderate Richard Milhous Nixon became the favorite for nomination. In April, Martin Luther King, Jr., was assassinated, and urban riots spread across the country. On June 6, 1968, on the verge of the Democratic Convention, Kennedy was assassinated moments after declaring his victory in the California primary. The Democratic Convention in Chicago was marked by violence and discord, but Humphrey emerged with the nomination and the tattered reigns of his party. The fall campaign was made more complex by the third-party candidacy of Gov. George Corley Wallace of Alabama, who appealed to the extreme conservative elements in the nation. When the final vote was counted, Nixon had achieved a narrow victory (43.41 percent) over Humphrey (42.72 percent), and Wallace had scored the highest third-party vote (13.52 percent) since Sen. Robert LaFollette's campaign in 1924. As a footnote, the 1968 election saw the return of the Communist Party to electoral politics. Its candidate for president, Charlene Mitchell, was the first African-American woman ever to appear on a ballot for national office.

AMERICAN INDEPENDENT (AMERICAN; COURAGE; CONSERVATIVE; GEORGE WALLACE; INDEPENDENT) PARTY

CANDIDATE FOR PRESIDENT:
George Corley Wallace (AL)

CANDIDATE FOR VICE PRESIDENT:
Curtis Emerson LeMay

CANDIDATES FOR VICE-PRESIDENTIAL NOMINATION:
Albert Benjamin Chandler (KY)
Richard Joseph Daley (IL)
Samuel Marvin Griffin (GA)
John Edgar Hoover (DC)
Curtis Emerson LeMay (OH)

PRIMARY:
MAY 14, 1968 (NE):
Wallace 493
others 11

CONVENTION:
Miami (FL), following the Democratic and Republican conventions

William K. Shearer of California formed this party in 1967.

PLATFORM HIGHLIGHTS:
The platform of the American Independent Party appealed to the "average American." It denounced the decay and turmoil in the nation's cities and the weakness and drift that characterized U.S. foreign policy.

SUPPORTED:

- the restoration of states' rights
- an amendment to the Constitution subjecting federal judges to the electorate and compelling Supreme Court justices to be reconfirmed at periodic intervals
- local law enforcement agencies
- the restoration of order in urban areas and the prosecution of persons engaged in anarchy and social disorder
- the use of block grants to state and local governments
- an expansion of rehabilitation programs
- efforts to combat drug addiction and deter juvenile delinquency
- public programs to care for children who have no other responsible parties to care for them
- increases in Social Security benefits and improvements in Medicare, including coverage for long-term care
- the right to private property and home ownership
- a policy of industrial diversification and decentralization and free enterprise
- job training and a partnership with the private sector to create jobs
- a reduction in the size of the bureaucracy
- assistance to small businesses
- lower taxes for everyone
- increased government efficiency
- the termination of tax exemptions for giant nonprofit foundations and institutions
- import restrictions to protect U.S. industry
- lowered trade barriers in other countries and the restoration of a favorable balance of payments
- agricultural price supports at 90 percent of parity (increasing to 100 percent by congressional action)
- the preservation of the family farm
- the creation of a national feed grain authority
- restrictions on the sale price of surplus food reserves
- self-determination on the need for crop controls
- tariffs on foreign farm and meat products
- the development of foreign agricultural markets
- expanded programs of disease and insect control
- the Rural Electrification Administration, Farm Home Administration, and agricultural colleges and extension services
- soil conservation
- improvements in farm production reporting
- the elimination of red tape within the Department of Agriculture
- improved working and living conditions for labor
- democratic unions free from governmental intrusions
- the right of collective bargaining
- good-faith bargaining without coercive action by the government
- a return of education to local control with fewer strings on federal aid to schools
- school prayer
- scientific research, with an emphasis on the space program

- the development of mass transit systems, including high-speed passenger trains between urban areas
- improvements in air traffic control
- the modernization of the merchant marine and ship-building industries
- the development of the Interstate Highway System and further progress in highway safety
- efforts to combat air and water pollution
- the development of biological and other less toxic pest controls
- the protection of wetlands, estuaries, and endangered wildlife
- streamlined federal assistance to state fish and game programs
- improvements for outdoor recreational areas and parks
- the management of timber resources to avoid depletion and to ensure reforestation
- an end to discrimination in public programs and full participation in the benefits of citizenship for American Indians and Eskimos
- the North Atlantic Treaty Organization (NATO), Organization of American States (OAS), and Monroe Doctrine
- aid for Latin America
- stiffened resistance to Fidel Castro's Cuba
- a lifting of sanctions against Rhodesia and South Africa
- the installation of an antiballistic missile defense system
- a strong national defense, including improved intelligence capabilities
- the retention of the selective service
- a buildup of the reserve system
- veterans and their families
- enhanced benefits for military personnel

OPPOSED:

- federal gun controls
- massive federal aid to cities
- the government's intrusion in business affairs
- the use of schools for social experimentation

ALSO:

- promised not to "abandon the United Nations Organization unless it first abandons us"
- declared national self-interest was the only justification for foreign aid
- planned to reduce military expenditures abroad by making allies assume more of the burden
- promised an even-handed approach to the Middle East, with an emphasis on getting all parties to negotiate their differences
- with regard to Vietnam, declared that "the prime consideration at this time is the honorable conclusion of hostilities"; favored a negotiated end to the fighting, but acknowledged that a military solution—based on

the use of conventional weapons—might be necessary; and demanded the definition of national objectives in Vietnam, promising that civilian control of the military would not impede the attainment of tactical objectives as determined by military commanders

---

AMERICAN INDEPENDENT (AMERICAN; COURAGE; CONSERVATIVE; GEORGE WALLACE; INDEPENDENT) PARTY VICE-PRESIDENTIAL NOMINATION: GRIFFIN WAS CHOSEN ON FEBRUARY 14, 1968, AS THE TICKET'S VICE-PRESIDENTIAL CANDIDATE TO PERMIT THE FILING OF BALLOT PETITIONS. WHEN WALLACE NAMED LEMAY AS HIS RUNNING MATE, GRIFFIN WITHDREW.

BERKELEY SELF-DEFENSE GROUP

CANDIDATE FOR PRESIDENT:
Kent M. Soeters (CA)

CANDIDATE FOR VICE PRESIDENT:
James P. Powers (CA)

The Berkeley Self-Defense Group called itself "an anti-Establishment organization opposed to the Selective Service and the income tax." Its presidential candidate kicked off his campaign with a "Potato Execution and Machine Smashing" on the campus of the University of California at Berkeley. Purportedly, Soeters wanted to demonstrate that people will attend political rallies regardless of their content or lack of content.

THE BEST PARTY

CANDIDATE FOR PRESIDENT:
Yetta Bronstein (NY)

The Best Party was the creation of Alan Abel and his wife, Jeanne Abel, who posed as Mrs. Yetta Bronstein. This successful satire effort was not discovered as a ruse until well after the 1968 election. The party's platform called for the election of a "Jewish mother" to the White House, the use of a suggestion box on the White House fence, the teaching of boring sex education, the withdrawal of the United States from Vietnam, and the printing of Brigitte Bardot's likeness on a postage stamp. It urged lowering the voting age to eighteen, improving and strengthening government, maintaining fluoridation programs, and playing national bingo.

While no vice-presidential candidate was nominated, Bronstein briefly considered the comedian Godfrey Cambridge and Dennis Eskow, a reporter for the New York Daily News, as her running mate.

COMMUNIST (FREE BALLOT) PARTY, USA

CANDIDATE FOR PRESIDENT:
Charlene Mitchell

CANDIDATE FOR VICE PRESIDENT:
Michael Zagarell (NY)

CANDIDATES FOR PRESIDENTIAL NOMINATION:
Charlene Mitchell (CA) (Gus Hall [NY] declined)

19TH CONVENTION:
July 3–7, 1968, Diplomat Hotel, New York (NY)
Gus Hall (NY), chairman

The convention was attended by 179 delegates and alternates from twenty-nine Communist Party districts. The 1968 election was the first presidential election the Communists had entered since 1940.

PLATFORM HIGHLIGHTS:
The platform condemned U.S. involvement in Vietnam, denounced the greed of giant corporations, rejected racism and poverty, and called for an end to the arms race. It declared the need for revolutionary changes in the country's social system to destroy capitalism and inaugurate socialism. The Communists wanted to end the bombing of Vietnam and to withdraw U.S. troops.

SUPPORTED:

- the recognition of the National Liberation Front
- servicemen's unions and democratization of the armed forces
- the abolition of the draft
- amnesty for draft resisters
- revisions in the Code of Military Justice
- a diversion of military funds to food programs
- reduction in troop strength and the withdrawal of U.S. troops abroad
- restrictions on the president's war-making powers, with any decision to send troops abroad for war purposes subject to a national referendum
- an end to the Cold War and the arms race
- a ban against nuclear, chemical, and bacteriological weapons
- the destruction of the military-industrial complex through nationalization of the armament, nuclear power, and space industries
- an end to all military alliances, including the abolition of NATO and the Southeast Asia Treaty Organization (SEATO)
- a halt to intervention in Latin America
- a lifting of the blockade against Cuba and the establishment of diplomatic relations with Fidel Castro
- the recognition of the People's Republic of China
- independence for Puerto Rico
- full equality for minorities, including the right to self-determination and self-defense

- African Americans having control of African-American communities
- full implementation of American Indian and Mexican treaty rights
- increased participation of minorities in the political life of the nation
- community control of police departments
- the release of political prisoners such as Rap Brown, Huey Newton, and Herman Ferguson
- taxes for the rich and tax relief for the poor
- curbs on government subsidies and tax breaks for businesses and wealthy individuals in industry and agriculture
- an end to exorbitant profits for monopolies
- requirements that nonprofit foundations, institutions, and churches pay taxes
- the imposition of price controls
- the nationalization of the pharmaceutical industry and public utilities
- subsidies for family farmers instead of corporate agriculture
- an end to crop production controls
- the reorganization of the Federal Communications Commission, with guaranteed equal and free time to all democratic organizations, and the elimination of the big business monopoly over the mass media
- the abolishment of the Federal Bureau of Investigation (FBI), the Central Intelligence Agency (CIA), the House Un-American Activities Committee (HUAAC), and the Senate Internal Security Subcommittee
- a repeal of the McCarran-Walter Act
- the removal of legal impediments against Communist political activities
- the abolishment of the congressional seniority system
- free and available public education from grade school to the university level
- adult education, with students provided a living stipend
- the lowering of the voting age to eighteen
- a massive public building program to provide jobs, increase housing, and end slums
- the development of free, public rapid-transit systems
- the creation of a national health care system
- a thirty-hour work week
- the right of workers to veto any labor-saving machinery in plants
- the repeal of antilabor laws
- labor's rights to organize and to strike
- the democratization of unions, including an end to discriminatory union practices
- an increase in the minimum wage
- special protection for young workers and a system of upgrading job skills
- equal pay for equal work guaranteed to women
- free lunches and day care for children
- reforms in the welfare system to provide jobs and a decent income for all
- the right to reproductive freedom, including the right to free abortions on demand, for women
- ninety days' maternity leave with pay for new mothers

OPPOSED:
- anti-Semitism and racism
- police brutality
- military and corporate influences in colleges and universities

Prior to the convention, Hall was widely considered to be the favorite for the nomination, but he declined.

CONSTITUTION PARTY

CANDIDATE FOR PRESIDENT:
Richard Kimball Troxell (TX)

CANDIDATE FOR VICE PRESIDENT:
Merle Melvin Thayer (IA)

CANDIDATES FOR PRESIDENTIAL NOMINATION:
Richard Kimball Troxell (TX) (George Corley Wallace [AL] declined)

CONVENTION:
July 18–21, 1968, Denver (CO)

PLATFORM HIGHLIGHTS:
The Constitution Party's platform declared that the United States was a "Christian nation."

SUPPORTED:
- the restoration of Congress as the sole power to issue money
- the abolishment of the Federal Reserve System
- the establishment of a state militia in every state
- the supremacy of the Constitution over treaties
- limits on the powers of the Supreme Court through checks and balances
- the removal of the government from competition with private businesses
- a balanced federal budget and retirement of the national debt
- a repeal of the Sixteenth Amendment (income tax and implementing laws, federal inheritance taxes, and estate taxes
- limits on immigration to the quotas established by the McCarran-Walter Act and deportations of illegal aliens
- the vigorous prosecution of Communist conspirators for treason
- a repeal of the Civil Rights Act
- the elimination of government agricultural subsidies
- a repeal of the Alaska Mental Health Act
- the teaching of free enterprise and patriotism in the schools
- the elimination of federal aid to education
- Bible readings and prayers in public schools
- the protection of a person's right to associate freely with whomever he or she chooses

- restoration of states' rights under the Ninth and Tenth amendments to the Constitution
- the repeal of the United Nations Charter, the Nuclear Test Ban Treaty, the Disarmament Act, the Consular Treaty, the Participation Act of 1945, reciprocal trade agreements, and the General Agreement on Tariff and Trade (GATT)
- the elimination of foreign aid
- a suspension of diplomatic relations with Communist countries
- the return of U.S. servicemen stationed abroad
- the outlawing of the Council on Foreign Relations and the Business Council, claiming they were "prime movers" for world dictatorship

The party initially supported George Wallace for president, but he did not accept the party's nomination.

COSMIC LOVE PARTY
CANDIDATE FOR PRESIDENT:
Louis Abolafia (NY)

CONVENTION:
May 2–5, 1967, Village Theatre, New York (NY)

About sixty-five persons attended the "happening" and "Freakathon" for hippies and saints.

PLATFORM HIGHLIGHTS:
The platform of the Cosmic Love Party called for the promotion of love of all kinds—art, beauty, and culture—and an uplifting of all moral values in the country and the world. It also urged the creation of culture centers around the country. The party's candidate for president posed in the nude (with a strategically placed derby) for campaign publicity, asking, "What have I got to hide?"

DEMOCRATIC PARTY
CANDIDATE FOR PRESIDENT:
Hubert Horatio Humphrey

CANDIDATE FOR VICE PRESIDENT:
Edmund Sixtus Muskie

CANDIDATES FOR PRESIDENTIAL NOMINATION:
Roger Douglas Branigan (IN)
Paul E. Bryant (AL)
John Geraerdt Crommelin (AL)
Paul Cary Fisher (CA)
Jacob John Gordon (MA)
James Harrison Gray (GA)
Lyndon Baines Johnson (TX)
Hubert Horatio Humphrey (MN)
Edward Moore Kennedy (MA)
Robert Francis Kennedy (NY)
Richard E. Lee (MD)
Eugene Joseph McCarthy (MN)
George Stanley McGovern (SD)

Daniel Killian Moore (NC)
Richard Milhous Nixon (CA)
Grady O'Cummings III (NY)
Channing Emery Phillips, (DC)
Ronald Wilson Reagan (CA)
Nelson Aldrich Rockefeller (NY)
George Armistead Smathers (FL)
George Corley Wallace (AL)
Stephen Marvin Young (OH)

CANDIDATES FOR VICE-PRESIDENTIAL NOMINATION:
Julian Bond (GA)
Richard Joseph Daley (IL)
James Burrows Edwards (SC)
Paul Cary Fisher (CA)
James William Fulbright (AR)
David Charles Hoeh (NH)
Hubert Horatio Humphrey (MN)
Lyndon Baines Johnson (TX)
Edward Moore Kennedy (MA)
Robert Francis Kennedy (NY)
Claude Roy Kirk, Jr. (FL)
Allard Kenneth Lowenstein (NY)
Eugene Joseph McCarthy (MN)
George Stanley McGovern (SD)
Robert Evander McNair (SC)
Edmund Sixtus Muskie (ME)
Richard Milhous Nixon (CA)
Peter Paul O'Dwyer (NY)
Henry Schoellkopf Reuss (WI)
Abraham Alexander Ribicoff (CT)
Ryan (PA)
James Terry Sanford (NC)
Robert Sargent Shriver (IL)
James Hugh Joseph Tate (PA)
John Anthony Volpe (MA)
George Corley Wallace (AL)

PRIMARIES:
MARCH 12, 1968 (NH):
Johnson 27,243
McCarthy 23,280
Nixon 2,529
R. F. Kennedy 600
Fisher 504
Rockefeller 243
Wallace 197
Crommelin 186
Lee 170
Gordon 77
scattering 152

Vice-presidential primary:
Humphrey 7,610
R. F. Kennedy 2,833
McCarthy 1,105
Fisher 858

Johnson 381
Kirk 339
Volpe 205
Nixon 158
Wallace 44
scattering 1,260

APRIL 2, 1968 (WI):
McCarthy 412,160
Johnson 253,696
R. F. Kennedy 46,507
Wallace 4,031
Humphrey 3,605
unpledged delegates 11,861
others 1,142

APRIL 23, 1968 (PA):
McCarthy 428,259
R. F. Kennedy 65,430
Humphrey 51,998
Wallace 24,147
Johnson 21,265
Nixon 3,434
others 2,556

APRIL 30, 1968 (MA):
McCarthy 122,697
R. F. Kennedy 68,604
Humphrey 44,156
Johnson 6,890
Rockefeller 2,275
Wallace 1,688
others 2,593

MAY 7, 1968 (DC):
R. F. Kennedy 57,555
Humphrey 32,309
independent slate for Humphrey 2,250

MAY 7, 1968 (IN):
R. F. Kennedy 328,118
Branigan 238,700
McCarthy 209,695

MAY 7, 1968 (OH)
Young 549,140

MAY 14, 1968 (NE):
R. F. Kennedy 84,102
McCarthy 50,655
Humphrey 12,087
Johnson 9,187
Nixon 2,731
Reagan 1,905
Wallace 1,298
others 646

MAY 14, 1968 (WV):
unpledged delegates 149,282

MAY 28, 1968 (FL):
Smathers 236,242

McCarthy 147,216
unpledged delegates 128,899

MAY 28, 1968 (OR):
McCarthy 163,990
R. F. Kennedy 141,631
Johnson 45,174
Humphrey 12,421
Reagan 3,082
Nixon 2,974
Rockefeller 2,841
Wallace 957

JUNE 4, 1968 (CA):
R. F. Kennedy 1,472,166
McCarthy 1,329,301
unpledged delegates 380,286

JUNE 4, 1968 (NJ):
McCarthy 9,906
R. F. Kennedy 8,603
Humphrey 5,578
Wallace 1,399
Nixon 1,364
others 596

JUNE 4, 1968 (SD):
R. F. Kennedy 31,826
Johnson 19,316
McCarthy 13,145

JUNE 11, 1968 (IL):
McCarthy 4,646
E. M. Kennedy 4,052
Humphrey 2,059
others 1,281

35TH CONVENTION:
August 26–29, 1968, International Amphitheater, Chicago (IL)
Daniel Ken Inouye (HI), temporary chairman and keynoter
Carl Bert Albert (OK), chairman

PLATFORM HIGHLIGHTS:
The Democratic platform reflected the divisions within the party and the nation, calling for a return to the rule of law, patriotism, and "orderly progress." It recited the achievements of the Johnson administration. The platform went on to urge continued U.S. leadership in international affairs, but it warned against making the nation the policeman of the world.

SUPPORTED:
• a strong and balanced national defense, anchored in vigorous research and development
• NATO and arms control
• Israel and peace negotiations in the Middle East
• "an honorable and lasting settlement" with Vietnam
• the Paris Peace talks

- a broad-based peace initiative advocating U.S. and UN technical assistance and development programs for undeveloped nations
- the Peace Corps, the United Nations, the Alliance for Progress, and the Charter of Punta del Este (a foreign policy pact promoting Latin American development)
- mutually beneficial trade agreements and investment programs
- progress toward freer international trade based on the Trade Expansion Act and the Kennedy Round
- improvements in the international monetary system
- the use of tax policies to help regulate economic growth
- tax relief for persons with lower incomes
- a balanced budget
- price stability and full parity for farm products
- the preservation of the family farm
- an expansion of the Food for Peace program
- the creation of a Strategic Food and Feed Reserve Plan
- collective bargaining rights for farmers in the market place
- easier farm credit policies
- cooperatives, crop insurance, and rural electrification and communications programs
- small businesses
- organized labor by promising to repeal compulsory open shop laws, to permit situs picketing, and to modernize the National Labor Relations Act
- the strengthening of consumer education, the expansion of consumer representation in the councils of government, and the enforcement of consumer protection laws
- automatic cost-of-living adjustments in Social Security benefits, coverage for prescription drugs under Medicare, and an enriched life in the community for the elderly
- improved medical care and increased benefits for veterans
- the need to increase housing stock, especially for low-income families, rural citizens, migrant workers, Native Americans on reservations, the elderly, and the physically handicappe
- efforts to strengthen the merchant marine, modernize the Panama Canal, increase transportation research, develop ports and inland waterways, improve air traffic congestion, and expand mass transit
- efforts to address communication, science, and technological needs
- continued leadership in space and energy development
- antipoverty programs, such as Head Start and Community Action
- the strict enforcement of all civil rights laws
- the need to create a "Federal-Indian partnership" to improve living conditions for Native Americans
- promises to find new ways, such as the successful Model Cities program, to lure private investment capital into inner city areas
- the creation of new jobs in rural areas

- expanded efforts to make rural citizens receive decent housing, education, health care, and public services
- job training and the continuation of programs such as the Neighborhood Youth Corps and the Job Opportunities in the Business Sectors (JOBS) program
- the idea that the government should be the "employer of last resort" for those who could not obtain other employment
- efforts to raise the minimum wage, strengthen occupational safety and health regulations, protect workers against "green card" competition, and modernize the unemployment compensation program
- federal assumption of responsibility for welfare, expansion of food programs for the hungry, and other improvements in assistance programs for the needy
- the creation of maternal and child health centers and voluntary family planning information centers around the country
- uniform standards for Medicaid to cover prenatal and child care and a new program like Medicare to finance prenatal care for mothers and postnatal care for children
- more medical research
- the construction of new medical schools
- the development of coordinated approaches between the public and private sectors to contain health care costs
- preschool education, improved teacher recruitment and training, expanded educational research, full funding for Title I schools, enlargement of the federal scholarship program, enhanced support for the arts and humanities, and more federal aid to education
- the right of eighteen year olds to vote
- increased representation of young people in civic affairs
- the restructuring of local draft boards to make them more representative of their communities
- efforts to combat air, water, and visual pollution
- controls over the dumping of industrial wastes
- the enhancement of outdoor recreation opportunities
- reclamation of land
- sustained yield management of forests
- multiple-use development of public lands
- the expansion of national systems of scenic and wild rivers, wilderness preservation areas, redwood forest preserves, and protected marshland and estuaries
- oceanologic research and development
- cooperation among federal, state, and local governments to make government more efficient and responsive
- improvements in the working conditions of federal employees
- the elimination of barriers to voting
- reforms in the electoral college
- calls to permit limited campaign contributions to be treated as tax credits
- full citizenship for residents of the District of Columbia, with voting representation in Congress

- the continuation of the commonwealth status of Puerto Rico and nonvoting representation of Guam and the Virgin Islands in Congress
- local police officers
- a sustained campaign against lawlessness and crime with streamlined procedures to end court congestion, increased efforts to rehabilitate offenders, modernized equipment and techniques of police control, expanded police-community relationships

- the passage of gun control legislation
- the focus on riots, organized crime, and trafficking in narcotics as areas needing special attention

OPPOSED:
- unilateral withdrawal from Vietnam and denied a demand for the unconditional surrender of the Communist force there
- the repression of Jews in the Soviet Union

DEMOCRATIC PARTY
VOTE FOR PRESIDENTIAL NOMINATION:
R. F. KENNEDY MOUNTED A VIGOROUS CAMPAIGN FOR THE PRESIDENTIAL NOMINATION, BUT HE WAS ASSASSINATED BEFORE THE CONVENTION. HUMPHREY WAS NOMINATED FOR PRESIDENT ON THE FIRST BALLOT.

Candidate	Ballot: 1
Humphrey	1,761¼
McCarthy	601
McGovern	146½
Phillips	67½
Moore	17½
Kennedy, E. M.	12¾
Bryant	1½
Wallace	1
Gray	½
not voting	15

VOTE FOR VICE-PRESIDENTIAL NOMINATION:
MUSKIE WAS NOMINATED FOR VICE PRESIDENT ON THE FIRST BALLOT. ALTHOUGH ALL STATES WERE CALLED IN THE ROLL, THE VOTE WAS NEVER COMPLETED. UNDER SUSPENSION OF THE RULES, MUSKIE WAS NOMINATED BY ACCLAMATION.

Candidate	Ballot: 1
Muskie	1,942½
Bond	48½
Hoeh	4
Kennedy, E. M.	3½
McCarthy	3
Ribicoff	2
McGovern	2
Edwards	2
Daley	1½
McNair	1½
Tate	1½
Sanford	1
Shriver	1
Lowenstein	1
Reuss	1
O'Dwyer	1
Ryan	¾
not voting	604¼

FREEDOM AND PEACE (NEW; PEACE AND FREEDOM ALTERNATIVE) PARTY

CANDIDATE FOR PRESIDENT:
Richard Claxton "Dick" Gregory (Coretta Scott King declined)

CANDIDATES FOR VICE PRESIDENT:
David Frost (NJ)
Mark Lane (NY)
Benjamin McLane Spock (VI)

CANDIDATES FOR PRESIDENTIAL NOMINATION:
Richard Claxton "Dick" Gregory (IL)
Coretta Scott King (GA)
John Vliet Lindsay (NY)
Eugene Joseph McCarthy (MN)
George Stanley McGovern (SD)

CONVENTION:
August 31, 1968, Chicago (IL)

This New York-based group included Communists and members of the National Conference for New Politics.

PLATFORM HIGHLIGHTS:
SUPPORTED:
- the immediate withdrawal of all U.S. troops from Vietnam
- African-American control of African-American communities, schools, police, and health services
- the abolition of the draft and amnesty for draft resistors
- the repeal of repressive laws (e.g., stop and frisk, shoot to kill, and McCarran-Walter Act)
- lower taxes for workers and higher taxes for the rich and corporations
- strict enforcement of civil rights, open housing, and equal employment laws
- free health care for all
- a repeal of antilabor laws, especially the Taft-Hartley, Taylor, and Landrum-Griffith acts
- independence for Puerto Rico
- an expropriation of inadequately maintained slum dwellings

Dick Gregory also offered planks from his personal platform.

SUPPORTED:
- an end to "moral pollution"

- the prosecution of the criminal syndicate
- the creation of better police-community relations
- improvements in the salaries of police officers
- an end to hostilities in Vietnam
- reforms in the welfare system to ensure realistic allowances and open opportunities for employment
- reductions in unemployment by building "industrial complexes" as the focus for new communities
- an end to starvation in the United States
- the lowering of the voting age to eighteen
- the integration of American Indians from the reservation into the mainstream of U.S. life
- the basing of foreign aid on humanitarian principles
- the creation of a Youth Commission to promote constructive activities for young people
- the initiation of preschool education, college student stipends, and culturally relevant courses
- the enforcement of civil rights
- the mandatory registration of firearms and prohibitions against handguns
- efforts to declare families of soldiers killed in the Vietnam War as wards of the state, entitled to all of the basic requirements of a decent life

---

FREEDOM AND PEACE (NEW; PEACE AND FREEDOM ALTERNATIVE) PARTY
VOTE FOR PRESIDENTIAL NOMINATION: THE FREEDOM AND PEACE PARTY INITIALLY SUPPORTED MCCARTHY'S NOMINATION FOR PRESIDENT. WHEN CORETTA SCOTT KING WAS NOMINATED, SHE ALSO DECLINED. LINDSAY AND MCGOVERN WERE ALSO CONSIDERED FOR THE NOMINATION.

VOTE FOR VICE-PRESIDENTIAL NOMINATION: SPOCK WAS NOMINATED FOR VICE PRESIDENT, BUT HE DECLINED.

INDEPENDENT

CANDIDATES FOR PRESIDENT:
Johnnie Mae Hackworthe (TX)[1]
Americus Liberator (NE)[2]
Eugene Joseph McCarthy (MN)[3]
Guy H. Rouse (FL)[4]

[1]Hackworthe, a perennial candidate for public office in Texas, claimed God inspired her to seek the presidency. She simultaneously sought the governorship of Texas.
[2]Liberator refused to discuss any issues during the campaign, fearing other candidates would steal his ideas.
[3]McCarthy did not seek the presidency on a third-party ticket in 1968, but many of his followers advanced his candidacy and cast ballots for him anyway. His name appeared on several ballots under various party designations.
[4]Rouse campaigned on a platform calling for an end to race riots, keeping prayer in schools, and "getting the Sting out of the United States Government." When asked what was meant by the phrase "getting the Sting out" of government, he replied, "That's the whole secret. Ah'd rather not express mahself right now. . . ."

LIBERAL PARTY

CANDIDATE FOR PRESIDENT:
Hubert Horatio Humphrey (MN)
CANDIDATE FOR VICE PRESIDENT:
Edmund Sixtus Muskie (MN)

The Liberal Party was a New York State third party that usually endorsed the national Democratic Party ticket.

CONVENTION:
September 24, 1968, Hotel Roosevelt, New York (NY)

Although Edward Moore Kennedy of Massachusetts had some support for the presidential nomination, the Liberal Party endorsed the candidates of the Democratic Party.

NATIONAL TAX SAVERS PARTY

CANDIDATE FOR PRESIDENT:
Daniel X. B. "Dixbie" Schwartz (NY)

The National Tax Savers Party had a three-point platform for helping the "little man."

SUPPORTED:
- a compulsory, perpetual monthly public referendum by computer before any president could sign a bill into law
- new income tax deductions for normal expenses such as food, rent, and taxes
- the appointment of a secretary of taxation from the common people as a member of the president's cabinet

NEW PARTY

CANDIDATE FOR PRESIDENT:
Eugene Joseph McCarthy (MN) (withdrew)
CANDIDATE FOR VICE PRESIDENT:
John Vliet Lindsay (NY) (withdrew)

The New Party was created by McCarthy's supporters who were formerly in the Democratic Party. It eventually affiliated with the Peace and Freedom Party.

NEW PARTY OF ARIZONA

CANDIDATE FOR PRESIDENT:
Eugene Joseph McCarthy (MN)
CANDIDATE FOR VICE PRESIDENT:
John Vliet Lindsay (NY)

The New Party of Arizona was created by McCarthy's supporters in Arizona. It eventually affiliated with the Peace and Freedom Party.

NEW PARTY OF COLORADO

CANDIDATE FOR PRESIDENT:
Richard Claxton "Dick" Gregory (IL)

CANDIDATE FOR VICE PRESIDENT:
Mark Lane (NY)

The New Party of Ohio was affiliated with the Peace and Freedom Party.

NEW PARTY OF OHIO

CANDIDATE FOR PRESIDENT:
Eugene Joseph McCarthy (MN)

CANDIDATE FOR VICE PRESIDENT:
Coretta Scott King (GA) (withdrew)

The New Party of Ohio was created by McCarthy's supporters in Ohio. It eventually affiliated with the Peace and Freedom Party.

NEW PARTY OF OREGON

CANDIDATE FOR PRESIDENT:
Charles McKinley (OR) (McKinley's name went forward on election ballot when Eugene Joseph McCarthy [MN] declined)

CANDIDATE FOR VICE-PRESIDENT:
Robin Arthur Drews (OR)

The New Party of Oregon was created by McCarthy's supporters in Oregon. It eventually affiliated with the Peace and Freedom Party.

CONVENTION:
August 26, 1968, Portland (OR)

NEW POLITICS PARTY

CANDIDATE FOR PRESIDENT:
Leroy Eldridge Cleaver (CA)

CANDIDATE FOR VICE PRESIDENT:
Larry Hochman (MI)

The New Politics Party was based in Michigan and was affiliated with the Peace and Freedom Party.

PLATFORM HIGHLIGHTS:
The party's platform sought a society in which decisions were made from below. It opposed racism, repression, war, and exploitation of the people.

SUPPORTED:
• an end to the Vietnam War
• oppressed people around the world
• the creation of institutions to provide economic equality, personal freedom, and popular control
• the program of the Black Panther Party

NEW REFORM PARTY

CANDIDATE FOR PRESIDENT:
Eugene Joseph McCarthy (MN) (withdrew)

CANDIDATE FOR VICE PRESIDENT:
Peter Paul O'Dwyer (NY) (withdrew)

The New Reform Party was created by McCarthy's supporters in several states. It eventually affiliated with the Peace and Freedom Party.

THE 1976 COMMITTEE

CANDIDATE FOR PRESIDENT:
Ezra Taft Benson (UT)

CANDIDATE FOR VICE PRESIDENT:
James Strom Thurmond (SC)

This group, which sought to influence both the Democratic and the Republican parties, was organized on April 30, 1966, in Chicago (IL). It was composed of members of the John Birch Society and other conservative organizations.

PATRIOTIC PARTY

CANDIDATE FOR PRESIDENT:
George Corley Wallace (AL)

CANDIDATE FOR VICE PRESIDENT:
William Penn Patrick (CA) (withdrew)

1ST CONVENTION:
July 2–4, 1967, Town House Motor Inn, Kansas City (KS)
Robert Bolivar DePugh (MO), temporary chairman

The Patriotic Party was founded on July 3 and July 4, 1966, in Kansas City (MO). Nearly five hundred delegates from forty-seven states attended the founding convention. The party grew out of the right-wing Minutemen organization.

One hundred fifty delegates attended the nominating convention.

PLATFORM HIGHLIGHTS:
The Patriotic Party's platform consisted of fifty-one planks espousing radical right-wing views. They included withdrawing from the United Nations and substituting a sales tax for taxes on personal and corporate incomes. It called for "severely limited government and a maximum of individual freedom." The document was drawn from Robert DePugh's book, *Blueprint for Victory,* which outlined a paramilitary approach to anticommunism.

PATRIOTIC PARTY
VOTE FOR PRESIDENTIAL NOMINATION: WALLACE WAS NOMINATED FOR PRESIDENT BY ACCLAMATION.

PEACE AND FREEDOM ALTERNATIVE

CANDIDATE FOR PRESIDENT:
Richard Claxton "Dick" Gregory (IL)

CANDIDATE FOR VICE PRESIDENT:
David Frost (NJ)

The Peace and Freedom Alternative was a New Jersey-based party.

PLATFORM HIGHLIGHTS:
The party's platform called for the immediate cessation of all efforts to impose the will of the United States on Vietnam.

SUPPORTED:
- an end to government violence in international and domestic affairs
- the adoption of a constitutional prohibition against military and civilian conscription
- the release of all draft resistors and amnesty for those who fled the country to avoid the draft
- the reallocation of military appropriations to improve the lives of African Americans and other deprived groups
- full cooperation with the United Nations in promoting progress abroad

PEACE AND FREEDOM PARTY

CANDIDATE FOR PRESIDENT:
Leroy Eldridge Cleaver (CA)
Richard Claxton "Dick" Gregory

CANDIDATES FOR VICE PRESIDENT:
Rudolfo "Corky" Gonzales (CO)
Larry Hochman (MI)
Judith Mage (NY)
David M. Rehfield (AZ)
Peggy Terry (IL)
Calvin Winslow (WA)

The Peace and Freedom Party was founded on March 18, 1968, in California. It was the outgrowth of a New Politics conference on September 17, 1967, in San Luis Obispo (CA).

1ST CONVENTION:
August 17–18, 1968, University of Michigan Campus, Ann Arbor (MI)

Attending this convention were 218 delegates from twenty states. The party adopted a "statement of principles" that supported the right of self-determination for all peoples of the world and denounced U.S. imperialism.

PLATFORM HIGHLIGHTS:
SUPPORTED:
- the liberation struggle of the Vietnamese people
- the immediate withdrawal of U.S. troops from Vietnam
- the domestic liberation struggles of the African-American, Spanish-speaking, American Indian, and poor Caucasian peoples
- community control and the right of armed self-defense

- workers who wanted to gain control over their unions, to end racism, and to organize the unorganized (e.g., migrant farm workers)
- the right of public employees to strike
- the rights of women to self-determination and liberation
- the rights of servicemen to organize themselves and engage in free speech
- draft resistance
- student control over educational institutions
- "the prosecution of our struggle not only through electoral means, but also through mass direct action"

OPPOSED:
- the Selective Service system

The platform of the California Peace and Freedom Party, adopted on March 18, 1968, is one of several separate platforms promoted by the Peace and Freedom Party.

SUPPORTED:
- the need for the people themselves to make the decisions that affect their lives, especially economic decisions (and pointed out how capitalism, racism, militarism, and imperialism deny people opportunities to make such decisions for themselves)
- demands for Huey Newton's freedom
- the program of the Black Panther Party
- participation in "Stop the Draft Week" and abolition of the Selective Service system
- the right of eighteen year olds to vote
- expanded rights for servicemen and -women
- denouncements of the repression of the student movement in Poland
- the immediate withdrawal of U.S. troops from Vietnam

OPPOSED:
- U.S. interference in the liberation struggles of other nations and gave a lengthy analysis of business and military domination of U.S. foreign policy
- imperialism by any other nation

The platform of the New York Peace and Freedom Party is further illustrative of the general approach of the party.

SUPPORTED:
- the immediate and unconditional withdrawal of U.S. troops from Thailand, Vietnam, and other foreign nations
- an end to foreign economic and military aid
- an end to NATO and SEATO
- an end to compulsory military service
- amnesty for draft resistors
- national liberation movements
- the withdrawal of police from ghettos and self-determination for minority peoples through community control of basic institutions
- the fulfillment of treaty obligations to Spanish-Americans, Mexican-Americans, and American Indians
- freedom for political prisoners

- an end to police attacks on demonstrators, wiretapping, and other methods of suppressing political opposition
- the redirection of the economy toward the elimination of poverty and slums
- the Black Panther's ten-point program
- increased taxation of the rich and relief for the working class
- an unrestricted right to organize, strike, boycott, and bargain
- the democratization of unions
- community-parent-student-teacher control of schools and universities
- an end to corporate and military interference in university affairs
- increased access to higher education for minorities and working-class youth
- relevance in instruction (i.e., that the basics were not relevant; that instead such subjects as black studies, community organizing, and socialist economics should be taught)
- student and worker protests in Europe and New York
- an end to harassment of youth
- the legalization of marijuana
- the right of eighteen year olds to vote
- the destruction of cultural monopolies
- the subsidization of students and artists
- an end to water and air pollution
- the preservation of natural resources
- the transformation of cities into livable human environments
- free public health care, day care, transportation, and communications
- women's rights, including the elimination of employment discrimination, the legalization of abortions, and the provision of free medical facilities for birth control

---

PEACE AND FREEDOM PARTY
VOTE FOR PRESIDENTIAL NOMINATION: CLEAVER, WHO DECLARED HIS CANDIDACY ON MAY 14, 1968, WAS NOMINATED ON THE FIRST BALLOT.

Candidate	Ballot: 1
Cleaver	161½
Gregory	54

PEOPLE'S CONSTITUTIONAL PARTY

CANDIDATE FOR PRESIDENT:
Ventura Chavez (NM)

CANDIDATE FOR VICE PRESIDENT:
Adelicio Moya (NM)

CONVENTION:
August 3, 1968, Albuquerque (NM)
Marical Jimenez, chairman

The People's Constitutional Party was founded by followers of Reies Lopez Tijerina and the Alianza Federal de Mercedes. The Alianza sought to compel the U.S. government to honor Spanish land grants in the western United States and turn over millions of acres to Hispanic people. The articles of incorporation of the People's Constitutional Party identified the party's purpose as guaranteeing "to the poor people of New Mexico all those rights and benefits which have been denied them for centuries."

PLATFORM HIGHLIGHTS:
SUPPORTED:

- an end to discrimination against Indo-Hispanic, American-Indian, and African-American peoples
- a reform of the educational system to make it multilingual and culturally relevant
- the development of agriculture and industry to provide jobs for all
- the Alianza's demand for restoration of Spanish land grants to the original owners' descendants

PROHIBITION PARTY

CANDIDATE FOR PRESIDENT:
Earle Harold Munn, Sr.

CANDIDATE FOR VICE PRESIDENT:
Rolland Ernest Fisher

CANDIDATES FOR PRESIDENTIAL NOMINATION:
Benjamin Calvin Bubar (ME)
Rolland Ernest Fisher (KS)
Earle Harold Munn, Sr. (MI)
Mark Revell Shaw (MA)

CANDIDATES FOR VICE-PRESIDENTIAL NOMINATION:
Benjamin Calvin Bubar (ME)
Rolland Ernest Fisher (KS)
Mark Revell Shaw (MA)

25TH CONVENTION:
June 28–29, 1967, Young Women's Christian Association, Detroit (MI)
Earle Harold Munn, Sr. (MI), temporary chairman, morning, June 28, 1967
Roger E. Bohall (NY), chairman, afternoon, June 28, 1967
Delmar D. Gibbons (MI), chairman, evening, June 28, 1967
Rolland Ernest Fisher (KS), chairman, June 29, 1967

Approximately 130 delegates and visitors attended the convention.

PLATFORM HIGHLIGHTS:
SUPPORTED:

- constitutional government and the system of checks and balances
- governmental economy, with a reduction in the national debt and in taxes

- a call to Congress to block inflation, ensure a sound currency, stabilize prices, and retire the national debt
- the careful consideration of a return to the gold standard
- a program of general revenue sharing, a balanced budget, and review of tax policies
- limits on foreign aid to repayable loans
- the free enterprise system
- compulsory arbitration in labor disputes, right-to-work laws, and equal enforcement of antitrust laws
- civil service reform as the antidote to the traditional "spoils system" pursued by the major parties
- states' rights and promises to address the two causes of the erosion of states' rights—the growth of the military-industrial complex and the demand of groups for federal protection of individual rights
- human rights for all (This was a hedge against criticism for opposing affirmative action and "groups" seeking federal protection.)
- strengthened enforcement of laws against gambling, narcotics, and commercialized vice
- efforts to work for peace based on the teachings of the Prince of Peace
- national preparedness and an all-volunteer military
- a suspension of testing nuclear weapons
- uniform marriage and divorce laws
- revisions to Social Security to make it actuarially sound and less politically sensitive
- ballot law reform
- religious liberty
- the continued separation of church and state (while recognizing the Bible as a "non-sectarian book")
- restrictions on involuntary mental health treatments and mass medication programs
- state efforts to ensure pure water and unpolluted air
- increased efforts to control the use of tobacco and narcotic or psychedelic drugs

Opposed:
- communism and totalitarianism
- monopolies and unethical practices by unscrupulous groups
- excessive government regulation
- the government's involvement in competitive business activity, urging it to sell such business enterprises to private industry
- arbitrary pressure tactics and efforts to destroy neighborhood schools
- compulsory military training
- direct federal aid to education
- agricultural supports and subsidies

Also:
- deplored the repeal of the Eighteenth Amendment and attributed the moral decline in the United States to liquor traffic
- ultimately designed its program to eliminate the alcoholic beverage industry altogether

PROHIBITION PARTY

VOTE FOR PRESIDENTIAL NOMINATION: UNDER THE RULES OF THE CONVENTION, EACH STATE COULD ONLY CAST ONE VOTE FOR EACH ELECTORAL VOTE THAT THE STATE COULD CAST IN THE ELECTORAL COLLEGE

Candidate	Ballot: 1	2
Munn	23	33
Bubar	9	0
Fisher	8	0
Shaw	6	13

VOTE FOR VICE-PRESIDENTIAL NOMINATION: FISHER WAS NOMINATED FOR VICE PRESIDENT ON THE FIRST BALLOT, DEFEATING BUBAR AND SHAW.

REPUBLICAN PARTY

CANDIDATE FOR PRESIDENT:
Richard Milhous Nixon

CANDIDATE FOR VICE PRESIDENT:
Spiro Theodore Agnew

CANDIDATES FOR PRESIDENT:
Frank Carlson (KS)
Clifford Philip Case (NJ)
Elmer William Coy (OH)
Donald Halleck Dumont (IL)
William Wadsworth Evans, Jr. (NJ)
Paul Cary Fisher (CA)
Hiram Leong Fong (HI)
James Maurice Gavin (MA)
Herbert Franklin Hoover (IA)
Hubert Horatio Humphrey (MN)
Lyndon Baines Johnson (TX)
Robert Francis Kennedy (NY)
Curtis Emerson LeMay (OH)
Americus Liberator (NE)
John Vliet Lindsay (NY)
Eugene Joseph McCarthy (MN)
Richard Milhous Nixon (NY)
Ronald Wilson Reagan (CA)
James Allen Rhodes (OH)
Nelson Aldrich Rockefeller (NY)
Winthrop Rockefeller (AR)
George Wilcken Romney (MI)
Raymond Philip Shafer (PA)
Harold Edward Stassen (MN)
Willis Emerson Stone (CA)
John Anthony volpe (MA)
George Corlay Wallace (AL)
David Watumull (HI)

CANDIDATES FOR VICE PRESIDENT:
Spiro Theodore Agnew (MD)
Edward William Brooke (MA)

Austin Marion Burton (KY)
Paul Cary Fisher (CA)
Claude Roy Kirk, Jr. (FL)
John Vliet Lindsay (NY)
Ronald Wilson Reagan (CA)
James Allen Rhodes (OH)
George Wilcken Romney (MI)
Laurence Cortelyou Smith (MO)
John Anthony Volpe (MA)

PRIMARIES:

MARCH 12, 1968 (NH):

Nixon	80,666
Rockefeller, N. A.	11,241
McCarthy	5,511
Johnson	1,778
Romney	1,743
Stone	527
Stassen	429
Fisher	374
Reagan	362
Hoover	247
Watumull	161
Evans	151
Coy	73
Dumont	39
scattering	636

Vice-presidential primary:

Burton	10,987
Smith	9,291
Volpe	5,611
Kirk	4,842
Reagan	4,108
Romney	1,035
Fisher	998
scattering	5,261

APRIL 2, 1968 (WI):

Nixon	390,368
Reagan	50,727
Stassen	28,531
Rockefeller	7,995
Romney	2,087
unpledged delegates	6,763
others	3,382

APRIL 23, 1968 (PA):

Nixon	171,815
Rockefeller, N. A.	52,915
McCarthy	18,800
Wallace	13,290
Kennedy, R. F.	10,431
Reagan	7,934
Humphrey	4,651
Johnson	3,027
Shafer	1,223
others	3,487

APRIL 30, 1968 (MA):

Rockefellerr, N. A.	31,964
Volpe	31,465
Nixon	27,447
McCarthy	9,758
Reagan	1,770
Kennedy, R. F.	1,184
others	2,933

MAY 7, 1968 (DC):

Nixon/Rockefeller, N. A. joint ticket	12,102
unpledged delegates	1,328

MAY 7, 1968 (IN):

Nixon	508,362

MAY 7, 1968 (OH):

Rhodes	614,492

MAY 14, 1968 (NE):

Nixon	140,336
Reagan	42,703
Rockefeller, N. A.	10,225
Stassen	2,638
McCarthy	1,544
Liberator	1,302
others	1,728

MAY 14, 1968 (WV):

unpledged delegates	81,039

MAY 28, 1968 (FL):

unpledged delegates	51,509

MAY 28, 1968 (OR):

Nixon	203,037
Reagan	63,707
Rockefeller, N. A.	36,305
McCarthy	7,387
Kennedy, R. F.	1,723

JUNE 4, 1968 (CA):

Reagan	1,525,091

JUNE 4, 1968 (NJ):

Nixon	71,809
Rockefeller, N. A.	11,530
Reagan	2,737
McCarthy	1,358
others	1,158

JUNE 4, 1968 (SD):

Nixon	68,113

JUNE 11, 1968 (IL):

Nixon	17,490
Rockefeller, N. A.	2,165
Reagan	1,601
others	1,147

29TH CONVENTION:

August 5–8, 1968, Convention Hall, Miami Beach (FL)

Edward William Brooke (MA), temporary chairman

Gerald Rudolph Ford (MI), chairman
Daniel Jackson Evans (WA), keynoter

PLATFORM HIGHLIGHTS:

The Republican platform in 1968 pointed to a nation in turmoil and laid the blame squarely at the feet of the Democratic Party. The Republican Party's "overriding domestic goal" was "a peaceful, reunified America, with opportunity and orderly progress for all." New cities were envisioned, free from blight and slums, crimes, and pollution.

SUPPORTED:

- the streamlining of federal aid to assist in the rebuilding of cities
- the protection of civil rights
- the engagement of private enterprise to improve urban life
- the promotion of housing and home ownership through reduced interest rates, the use of "sweat equity," the modernization of building codes, and other means
- improvements in urban mass transit
- a restoration of law and order, tough actions against lawlessness and crime, and the targeting of drug traffickers, members of organized crime, racketeers, and juvenile delinquents in Republican anticrime efforts
- the creation of a federal corrections service
- the modernization of the judicial system
- the enactment of legislation to control the indiscriminate availability of firearms (while safeguarding the right to own and use guns)
- state action to reduce the voting age to eighteen
- a reform of the Selective Service system
- the eventual transition to an all-volunteer military
- the creation of a national commission to study the quality and relevance of U.S. education
- increased emphasis on preschool education
- improvements in teacher training (and support for voluntary bilingual education)
- an extension of federal assistance for nonpublic school children
- increased attention to vocational education
- the creation of an industry youth program combined with a sub-minimum wage for entry-level workers
- grants, work opportunities, and loan programs for college students
- federal aid to expand university and college facilities
- the use of tax credits and deductions to relieve the financial strain on families paying for higher education for their children
- federal revenue sharing
- an enactment of the Human Investment Act, which offered tax credits to employers providing job training for disadvantaged individuals
- the creation of a job opportunity data bank
- the use of local business advisory boards to design training programs
- a simplification of all national job programs
- welfare reform to reduce "debilitating dependence" and to motivate individuals to seek work
- community development corporations and inner-city insurance programs
- lower-income representation in welfare program decisions
- a unified federal food-distribution program
- consumer protection measures
- the expansion of private health insurance plans
- increased numbers of health care professionals and the construction of new facilities
- the promotion of preventive and community-based care (including private insurance coverage and appropriate care for persons with mental illnesses)
- the elimination of architectural barriers for persons with physical handicaps
- increases in research on medical treatments
- automatic Social Security and Railroad Retirement Act cost-of-living adjustments, an increased earnings exemption, higher benefits for widows, reduction in the age of universal coverage, and other reforms for the elderly
- assurances to returning Vietnam War veterans of jobs and other assistance, with a special rehabilitation allowance for paraplegics
- increased benefits and adequate medical and hospital care for all veterans
- offers of equal opportunity to American Indians and Eskimos
- the use of block grants and revenue sharing to strengthen state and local governments
- a reform of the electoral college system
- self-government and congressional representation for the District of Columbia
- statehood for Puerto Rico
- an election reform act to control political spending and fund-raising
- protections for federal workers against government intrusion into their privacy
- congressional and Postal Service reforms
- a restoration of fiscal integrity, sound monetary policies, and sustained economic vitality without wage and price controls
- reductions in the national debt
- simplifications in and reforms of the tax structure
- aid to small businesses
- the updating of antitrust policies and the elimination of improper federal competition with private enterprise
- a convening of a special governmental efficiency commission
- an equitable minimum wage along with a reexamination of the forty-hour work week
- strict enforcement of the Taft-Hartley and Landrum-Griffin acts
- a development of permanent, long-range solutions to national labor emergencies

- the promotion of air transportation and safety, along with continued improvements in other modes of transportation
- offers to farmers of "fair prices," "sympathetic consideration," "sound economic policies," and protection against unfair foreign competition
- calls for reorganization of the Commodity Credit Corporation
- improvements in the distribution of food and milk to schools and low-income citizens
- a strengthened Food for Peace program
- assistance to rural electric, telephone, and other cooperatives
- increased agricultural research
- improved credit programs for farmers
- a more direct farmer voice in agricultural policy
- the "revitalization of rural America"
- the "sound conservation and development of natural resources" by endorsing the depletion allowance and other methods of encouraging the discovery and development of minerals and fuel deposits
- the implementation of a "multiple-use" land use policy
- an expansion of recreational, green space, park, and wilderness areas
- improved forestry practices and protection of watersheds, increased flood-control and reclamation efforts, and more emphasis on weather modification and desalinization research
- an adoption of a national fisheries policy and further exploration of the sea and polar regions
- calls for more skilled scientists and engineers, a stronger research effort, and more emphasis on the space program
- the United Nations and the International Court of Justice
- international efforts to address the population explosion
- demands that foreign aid be linked to foreign policy
- pledges to tighten passport administration and to administer strictly the Export Control Act
- the restoration of the balance of payments
- freer trade with other nations, subject to "hard-headed bargaining"
- the Monroe Doctrine
- expressions of hostility toward Fidel Castro's Cuba
- Israel and the need for a stable peace in the Middle East
- an end to the arms race
- the restoration of U.S. relations with Western Europe and NATO
- the captive nations in Eastern Europe in their struggle for freedom

OPPOSED:

- government-coerced strike settlements
- the oppression of Jews and other minorities in the Soviet Union
- the People's Republic of China's bid for U.S. diplomatic recognition and for admission to the United Nations

ALSO:

- castigated their opponents
- promoted the policy of "progressive de-Americanization" of the Vietnam War while promising full military support for U.S. servicemen and -women and insisting on South Vietnam's greater assumption of responsibility and on progress toward a fair and equitable settlement
- promised to pursue peace negotiations, asserting that U.S. soldiers deserve "our total support, our encouragement, and our prayers"
- to counter the Democratic administration's seriously weakened national defense, pledged that the United States would once again enjoy preeminent military strength under the Republicans
- advocated extension of the Polaris-Poseidon concept, strengthening of intelligence gathering, more effective use of defense dollars, reinvigoration of the National Security Council, improvements in the merchant marine, deployment of advanced weapons concepts, a commitment to military research, and a thorough review of America's preparedness

REPUBLICAN PARTY
VOTE FOR PRESIDENTIAL NOMINATION:

Candidate	Ballot: 1	2
Nixon	692	1238
Rockefeller, N. A.	277	93
Reagan	182	2
Rhodes	55	0
Romney	50	0
Case	22	0
Carlson	20	0
Rockefeller, W.	18	0
Fong	14	0
Stassen	2	0
Lindsay	1	0

VOTE FOR VICE-PRESIDENTIAL NOMINATION:

Candidate	Ballot: 1
Agnew	1119
Romney	186
Lindsay	10
Brooke	1
Rhodes	1
not voting	16

SOCIALIST LABOR (INDUSTRIAL GOVERNMENT) PARTY

CANDIDATE FOR PRESIDENT:

Henning Albert Blomen (MA)

CANDIDATE FOR VICE PRESIDENT:
George Sam Taylor (PA)

27TH CONVENTION:
May 4–7, 1968, Towers Hotel, Brooklyn (NY)
Nathan Karp (NJ), temporary and permanent chairman

Thirty-four delegates from fifteen states, the District of Columbia, and two ethnic federations (These were "old country" labor/social organizations of German-Americans, Swedish immigrants, Hungarian socialists, and so forth in the United States) attended this convention.

PLATFORM HIGHLIGHTS:
The platform of the Socialist Labor Party declared that the pervasive social unrest in the United States was the legacy of capitalism and the "revolution of rising expectations." It announced that "the alternative to the rapidly disintegrating capitalist world is a world organized on a sane foundation of social ownership. . . ." Under the party's agenda, society would be reconstructed along socialist principles, with production determined by human needs and desires and political representation based on industrial constituencies. Thus, Socialist planners and administrators would be democratically elected. Workers would be organized into one integral Socialist Industrial Union to back up the Socialist ballot with a power capable of overthrowing capitalism. When socialism is achieved, the party asserted, peace, liberty, abundance, cooperation, and brotherhood would prevail.

SOCIALIST LABOR (INDUSTRIAL GOVERNMENT) PARTY
VOTES FOR PRESIDENTIAL AND VICE-PRESIDENTIAL NOMINATION: BLOMEN AND TAYLOR WERE UNANIMOUSLY NOMINATED FOR PRESIDENT AND VICE PRESIDENT, RESPECTIVELY. NO OTHER NAMES WERE PRESENTED TO THE CONVENTION.

SOCIALIST WORKERS PARTY

CANDIDATE FOR PRESIDENT:
Fred Halstead (NY)

CANDIDATE FOR VICE PRESIDENT:
Paul Benjamin Boutelle (NJ)

CONVENTIONS:
On August 30, 1967, at the Socialist Workers Party Headquarters in New York the 1968 ticket was officially announced. The nominations were agreed to at a meeting of its national committee in June 1967 and confirmed by a poll of committee members who had not participated in the original meeting. A ratification convention was held on October 27, 1967.

PLATFORM HIGHLIGHTS:
The platform of the Socialist Workers Party denounced the bipartisan policies of the Democrats and Republicans as reflecting the capitalist system's need to exploit workers, foster racism, and pursue imperialist objectives.

SUPPORTED:
- calls for an end to the Vietnam War through a popular referendum and an immediate withdrawal of U.S. troops
- the abolition of the draft
- the protection of GIs' right to protest the war
- the right of self-determination of all oppressed national minorities
- hands off policy toward Cuba and the People's Republic of China and the encouragement of national liberation movements abroad
- the right of African Americans to keep arms and organize themselves for self-defense
- recognition of the "Black power" movement and community control over basic institutions affecting African-Americans' lives
- preferential hiring and guaranteed jobs for African Americans
- a development of nonprofit cooperative shops and housing projects for African Americans
- citizen review boards to control "the cops" until the police could be removed from African-American communities and replaced by elected community representatives
- an independent African-American political party and an independent labor party
- a repeal of all antilabor laws and the defense of the unconditional right to strike
- union escalator clauses
- elections of community price committees to police prices charged by businesses
- a reduced work week without cuts in pay and unemployment compensation at union wages
- a crash program of public housing and public works paid out of saved military funds
- the right to vote for eighteen year olds
- free public education through the university level, with stipends paid to students
- the involvement of students in all university decisions

OPPOSED:
- wage freezes
- union discrimination against African-American workers

ALSO:
- accepted young people's rejection of the "sterile cultural values" of society
- sought nationalization of major corporations and banks under control of elected worker committees
- welcomed the advent of a planned, democratic Socialist United States

STRAIGHT TALKING AMERICAN GOVERNMENT PARTY

CANDIDATE FOR PRESIDENT:
Patrick Layton Paulsen (CA)

The Straight Talking American Government (STAG) Party was the creation of television comedian Patrick Layton Paulsen. Paulsen was a regular on the Smothers Brothers' television comedy program. The STAG Party's platform argued that "issues have no place in a presidential campaign."

THEOCRATIC PARTY

CANDIDATE FOR PRESIDENT:
William Richard Rogers (MO)

PLATFORM HIGHLIGHTS:

The Theocratic Party's platform reiterated the Ten Commandments, adding two additional "laws for individuals:" (1) "this is my beloved son: hear ye Him" and (2) love one another. Paralleling these twelve "laws" were twelve laws for world government, twelve rules for individual nations, and twelve policies for a new civil and criminal code. For world government, the platform advised:

- (1) one gathering of nations, one world ruler
  (2) each nation should choose its own ruler, subject to approval by the world ruler
  (3) nations that do not unite would suffer drought and plague
  (4) so, too, would nations that resorted to war
  (5) all nations were to gather yearly in Jerusalem in October
  (6) the world ruler would prepare the program
  (7) men would be heard in October gatherings, but women would remain silent
  (8) these gatherings would not enact laws but would make recommendations
  (9) the Twelve Commandments for Individuals would be binding on nations
  (10) adherence to the forty-eight laws would be by teaching, not by force
  (11) all nations would pay a 10 percent tithe on national income each October
  (12) decisions made in October gatherings would be subject to change the following October. Individual nations were to unite church and state under Jesus, Prince of Peace, but maintain freedom of worship and liberty. The ten percent tithes would be paid to the church and nation instead of taxes.

SUPPORTED:

- promises to maintain the 1965 scale of wages, profits, and progress, while promoting unlimited production and free enterprise
- an end to wars, crimes, and delinquency
- the union of families and an end to divorces
- the elimination of the use of tobacco, intoxicants, narcotics, and gambling
- the promotion of equality for all races and nations
- Bible reading and prayer in schools
- new revelations in government and peace
- the abandonment of Roman and English common law for newly established civil and criminal codes that ad-

vocated forgiving repentant criminals up to 490 times, per the new "law of grace," and punishing the unrepentant according to present codes of law
- the discontinuation of the jury system and holding trials before "godly" judges
- an execution of judgment by word of the judge, not by force
- the conversion of prisons into "refuge" cities for society's safety and time to repent for criminals
- the use of fourfold restitution to demonstrate repentance for convicted criminals
- complete forfeiture for the covetous
- requirements that the losing civil litigants should award their adversaries doubly
- freedom for repentant prisoners
- calls for all present litigants to withdraw their actions and reconsider

UNIVERSAL PARTY

CANDIDATE FOR PRESIDENT:
Kirby James Hensley (CA)

CANDIDATE FOR VICE PRESIDENT:
Roscoe Bernard MacKenna

CONVENTION:
March 2, 1968, Denver (CO)
John W. Hopkins (CA), chairman

PLATFORM HIGHLIGHTS:

The Universal Party's platform called for a general revision of the election system, with the elimination of national conventions, the electoral college, and other representative structures. Instead, public officials—including Supreme Court justices—would be directly elected by the people and subject to recall. Lobbying would be prohibited. The party encouraged women to participate in elective and appointive offices and demanded equal pay for equal work. Usury would be abolished, Congress would reassert its control over money, and credit unions would be expanded for future banking. Instead of taxes, the platform urged Congress to print enough money to pay its obligations and advocated the government's withdrawal from activities that compete with the private sector.

SUPPORTED:

- a World Congress with equal representation of nations and a World Supreme Court assisted by national appellate courts
- calls for giving Congress the ability to declare war but making it subject to the president's approval
- an end to unemployment and the promotion of the Guild System and creation of specialized craft unions
- village and farm development on unused public lands as a solution to urban crowding
- small farm owners over large corporate farming interests
- the control of speculation and subsidization of "start-up" farmers for up to five years

- the conservation of all natural resources and the substitution of free or cosmic energy for oil and gas
- the protection of all life against contamination of air, water, and foodstuffs
- free education and private schools, with the humanities receiving equal support with the sciences and spiritual (not religious) training and research being fostered
- standardized marriage laws and domestic relations courts for divorce matters
- the stimulation of small businesses and enforcement of fair trade practices
- uniform traffic laws
- the abolition of capital punishment
- the elimination of conflicts of interest among public officials
- federal financing of elections
- the extension of bulk postal rates to political parties
- a change in the one-man-one-vote reapportionment ruling
- due process rights for mental patients charged with crimes
- the participation of public employees in politics
- the release of secret job or medical examination information by employers to applicants
- karmic justice as well as full recognition of civil rights

- the claim that messages from greater worlds that often contact earth confirm the truth of reincarnation
- the extension of civil treatment and protection, rather than being confined to jail, to visitors from outer space
- improvements in old age and unemployment benefits and medical assistance programs

OPPOSED:
- zoning laws and highway condemnation as interferences with private property
- labor or management monopolies

ALSO:
- intended to limit dramatization of crimes and vices on television or in movies and to take steps to prevent juvenile delinquency

YOUTH INTERNATIONAL PARTY

CANDIDATE FOR PRESIDENT:
Pigasus J. Pig (IL)

The Youth International Party was a radical organization of young people with left-wing views. The party was noted for outrageous protest activities and its anarchistic tendencies. The slogan of the "Yippie" candidate was "Join the Groundswill."

GENERAL ELECTION SUMMARY FOR 1968:			
Candidate	Electoral Votes	States	Popular Votes
Nixon (R)	301	32	31,710,470
Humphrey (D)	191	13 (+DC)	31,209,677[1]
Wallace (AI)	46	5	9,893,952
Cleaver (PF)	0	0	74,014
Blomen (SOC LAB)	0	0	52,247
Gregory (FP [NEW; PFA])	0	0	47,097[2]
Halstead (SOC WOR)	0	0	38,011
McCarthy (I)	0	0	27,002[3]
Munn (PROH)	0	0	14,787
AIDA	0	0	10,960
Cleaver (NEW POL)	0	0	4,585
PET	0	0	3,377
Chavez (PEO CON)	0	0	1,519
Mitchell (COM)	0	0	438
Hensley (UNIV)	0	0	142
Rockefeller (I)	0	0	69
Troxell (CONST)	0	0	34
Soeter (BSDG)	0	0	17
unknown	0	0	6,627[4]

[1]Includes 311,622 votes from the Liberal Party
[2]Includes 1,393 votes from the New Party of Colorado and from the Peace and Freedom Alternative
[3]Includes 1,000 votes from the New Party, 2,751 votes from the New Party of Arizona, and 470 votes from the New Reform Party
[4]Includes 2,645 votes for write-in candidates

ELECTION OF NOVEMBER 7, 1972

President
RICHARD MILHOUS NIXON
Vice President
SPIRO THEODORE AGNEW

HIGHLIGHTS

The 1972 electorate was noticeably apathetic, perhaps exhausted from the tumult of 1968. The incumbent president, Richard Milhous Nixon, had carefully positioned himself in the mainstream of public opinion, while maintaining his basically conservative credentials. He continued that practice as the election approached. His February trip to China strengthened Nixon's image among moderates as a "peace-maker," even as the end of the Vietnam war eluded his grasp. On the other hand, his hold on the conservative element in the country was weakened by this same gambit, creating a potential future opening for Democratic Governor George Wallace of Alabama. But Wallace, who was courting right-wing Democrats for his party's nomination, never made it to the general election campaign. His bid for the Democratic nomination was cut short when he was gunned down and seriously wounded while campaigning in a Laurel, Maryland, shopping center, May 15th.

Throughout the primaries, the president spent most of the campaign aloof in the White House. He continued to play the statesman after the Democratic nominee was selected. Despite a seemingly clear-cut choice between the president and the Democratic candidate, Sen. George Stanley McGovern of South Dakota, Nixon's liberal challenger searched in vain for an issue that could turn the tide in his favor. McGovern suffered a serious humiliation in the selection of his vice-presidential running mate when he was forced to dump his initial choice, Sen. Thomas Eagleton of Missouri, in favor of Sargent Shriver after Eagleton admitted to receiving mental health treatment for depression. McGovern needed a jumpstart for his campaign, but it never happened.

McGovern remained hopeful, however, for the Democratic Party had radically reformed to be more inclusive. The 1972 election was the first in which eighteen to twenty year olds could vote (the 26th Amendment of the Constitution having been ratified July 1, 1971), and sentiment against the war in southeast Asia seemed to keep rising. But the nation apparently was not in as liberal a mood as McGovern, and the Nixon administration's promise that "peace was at hand" effectively removed the war issue, which had rallied so many young people. The polls consistently and correctly predicted a massive defeat for McGovern, who inherited a fragmented party after Hubert Humphrey's 1968 race. Nixon's margin of 17.9 million votes was the largest in U.S. history. Yet Nixon's victory proved Pyrrhic, as later charges against his campaign committee for breaking into the Democratic National Committee headquarters led to the unraveling Watergate scandal and to his resignation on August 9, 1974.

In a historic footnote, the 1972 election saw the first electoral vote ever cast for a woman when a Republican elector from Virginia broke ranks and voted for the Libertarian Party's candidates, John Hospers of California and Theodora Nathan of Oregon. Incidentally that same elector, Roger MacBride, went on to become the Libertarian Party's candidate for president in 1976.

AMERICA FIRST PARTY

CANDIDATE FOR PRESIDENT:
John Val Jean Mahalchik (NJ)

CANDIDATE FOR VICE PRESIDENT:
Irving Homer (PA)

Claiming to be broke, Mahalchik ran a "penniless" campaign in New Jersey, attacking professional politicians, millionaires, and lawyers. Mahalchik lived in a teepee on the grounds of his junkyard (which he insisted was a "surplus dealership"). He advocated an anarchistic approach to "getting the government back."

AMERICAN (AMERICAN INDEPENDENT; COURAGE) PARTY

CANDIDATE FOR PRESIDENT:

John George Schmitz

CANDIDATE FOR VICE PRESIDENT:

Thomas Jefferson Anderson

CANDIDATES FOR PRESIDENTIAL NOMINATION:

Thomas Jefferson Anderson (TN)
Charles C. Compton (CA)
Evilyn Evelyn (CA)
Lester Maddox Garfield (GA)
L. Allen Greer (FL)
Richard Broughton Kay (OH)
Tim Salay (OH)
John George Schmitz (CA)
George Corley Wallace (AL)

CANDIDATES FOR VICE-PRESIDENTIAL NOMINATION:

Thomas Jefferson Anderson (TN)
Homer Fikes (TX)
Richard Broughton Kay (OH)
Robert Bruce Mess (TN)
Claiborne W. "Clay" Smothers (TX)

PRIMARY:

JUNE 6, 1972 (CA):

Evelyn
Compton
Salay

1ST CONVENTION:

August 3–5, 1972, Freedom Hall, Louisville (KY)
Keith Greene (CA), chairman
Thomas Jefferson Anderson (TN), keynoter

Two thousand delegates from forty states, with a total of 460 votes, participated in the convention.

PLATFORM HIGHLIGHTS:

SUPPORTED:

- local government and individual rights
- the elimination of government competition with private enterprise
- the elimination of judicial usurpation of authority and periodic reconfirmation of judges
- local law enforcement
- maximum penalties for skyjacking
- the right of states to impose the death penalty
- stiff mandatory penalties for drug trafficking and a break in relations with the People's Republic of China, which was viewed as a major source of illicit drugs
- criminal penalties for obscenity and the public display of homosexuality
- stiff mandatory sentences for the commission of a crime involving a firearm
- the protection of Social Security trust funds, but sought to make the program voluntary
- state educational and employment programs for persons with disabilities
- freedom of choice in health care
- the return to the gold standard, abolition of the Federal Reserve System, and a balanced budget
- the closure of tax loopholes for the rich and tax relief for the lower and middle classes
- modest consumer protection programs
- collective bargaining and portable retirement benefits
- the end of public housing projects unless locally approved by the voters
- private education
- local control of schools and the right of voluntary, nondenominational school prayer
- the conservation and protection of the environment
- disclosure of campaign contributions
- the elimination of discriminatory laws against new political parties
- "sunshine" laws
- the abolition of regional governments
- the gradual phaseout of government agricultural subsidies, controls, and restrictions
- the withdrawal of the United States from the United Nations
- the adoption of a constitutional amendment to limit the treaty-making authority of the federal government
- U.S. prisoners of war (POWs) in Vietnam
- Cuban exiles
- a break in trade relations with Communist nations
- continued friendship with Nationalist China
- U.S. neutrality in the Middle East
- friendly relations with Rhodesia and South Africa
- the collection of foreign debts
- calls for the withdrawal of the United States from the General Agreement on Tariffs and Trade (GATT) but espoused a pro-tariff position

---

AMERICAN (AMERICAN INDEPENDENT; COURAGE) PARTY
VOTE FOR PRESIDENTIAL NOMINATION:

Candidate	Ballot: 1
Schmitz	329¼
Maddox	55¹³/₂₀
Greer	25½
Anderson	23⅓
Kay	16
Wallace	8

After Wallace declined to run in a dramatic telephone broadcast to the convention, Schmitz was nominated for president on the first ballot.

VOTE FOR VICE-PRESIDENTIAL NOMINATION:
ANDERSON WAS NOMINATED FOR VICE PRESIDENT BY ACCLAMATION, AFTER THE OTHER FOUR CANDIDATES WITHDREW THEIR NAMES.

- an all-volunteer military
- appropriate veterans' benefits
- the elimination of war profiteering
- the redirection of military expenditures to domestic use
- the rejection of the Equal Rights Amendment (ERA)

OPPOSED:

- the legalization of marijuana
- abortion and euthanasia
- all forms of gun control
- federal welfare programs
- federal health insurance
- wage and price controls
- government-maintained monopolies
- unjust foreign imports from slave nations
- forced school busing
- sex education and sensitivity training curricula
- the "criminal Communist conspiracy"
- aid to North Vietnam and amnesty for draft dodgers
- all foreign aid
- statehood for the remaining territories, preferring that they become commonwealths

ALSO:

- advocated that only "modest quotas" of immigrants from Europe and the Western Hemisphere be admitted to the country and that they be subjected to loyalty tests
- criticized the State Department and called for the elimination of the Peace Corps and the U.S. Information Agency
- identified the Council of Foreign Relations as a "conspiratorial apparatus" seeking one world government
- proposed repealing the Arms Control and Disarmament Act and not adopting further disarmament treaties without sufficient evidence of good faith by all parties
- declared in favor of a redefinition of America's fishing rights in commercial waters

BUREAUCRATIC PARTY

CANDIDATE FOR PRESIDENT:
James Harlan Boren (VA)

Billed as a "dark, dark horse," Boren launched his Bureaucratic Party's campaign for president with the motto "When in doubt, mumble." Instead of busing students to school, Boren advocated busing schools to the students. He refused to talk about his plan for world peace "until he had a chance to discuss it with Dr. [Henry] Kissinger" (which he never did).

PLATFORM HIGHLIGHTS:
Claiming that bureaucracy is the highest and most beautiful form of self expression, Boren articulated the virtues of red tape and advocated "dynamic inaction" as a way of life.

SUPPORTED:

- ways to put people to work by studying the problem of unemployment and switching the objectives of the De-

fense Department and the Postal Service, so that the Defense Department would deliver the mail and the Post Office would deliver munitions

- government leaks that promoted memos and "orbital dialogue," but not paper shredding
- an international Bureaucrats' Olympics, featuring an executive shot put competition over lunchtime
- one resolution to the population problem—lengthening the gestation period
- a regulation of the economy "in order to meet the proliferation of standards of wage-price harmonics and monetary proficiency within the spectral contingencies of the corporate linkage with the anticipatory disparity of domestic portfolios"

COMMUNIST PARTY

CANDIDATE FOR PRESIDENT:
Gus Hall (NY)

CANDIDATE FOR VICE PRESIDENT:
Jarvis Tyner (NY)

20TH CONVENTION:
February 18, 1972, Towers Hotel, New York (NY)
Henry Winston, national chairman

There were 275 delegates from thirty-four states at this Convention.

PLATFORM HIGHLIGHTS:

SUPPORTED:

- the Hall-Tyner ticket as a "meaningful and forceful" protest vote
- an end to the war in Indochina through unconditional withdrawal, payment of reparations, and the establishment of peaceful relations with North Vietnam
- the closure of all foreign military bases and the halt to intervention abroad against people's liberation movements (in places like Angola, Chile, Greece, Rhodesia, and South Africa)
- urged full diplomatic relations with Communist countries
- independence for Puerto Rico
- a hands-off policy in Ireland
- the Palestinians against Israel
- interest-free loans to underdeveloped nations
- an end to poverty and a repeal of the wage freeze and the Pay Board
- an end to restrictions on the right to strike
- the repeal of the Taft-Hartley and Landrum-Griffin acts
- the prohibition against discrimination in employment and union membership
- an increase in welfare benefits and Social Security (with full retirement at fifty-five)
- the creation of a comprehensive unemployment program at full take-home pay wages
- an increase in the minimum wage to $5.00 per hour and a reduction in the work week to thirty hours at forty hours' pay

- massive public housing and urban transit programs
- national health care
- the prosecution of drug profiteers and pushers
- a guaranteed minimum income for small farm operations
- the organization of agricultural workers into unions
- stronger occupational health and safety laws
- resistance to the introduction of "speed-up" machinery
- nationalization of the major industries of the country
- local self-government in ghettos and barrios and recommended adoption of proportional representation to encourage minority political participation
- the honoring of federal treaty obligations to American Indian and Chicano people regarding land and natural mineral rights
- curbs on police brutality, with the right of self-defense protected
- freedom for Angela Davis and other political prisoners
- an end to racism in the armed forces
- a democratization of the military and the freedom of servicemen to unionize
- a sharply graduated tax on corporate profits and the closing of tax loopholes for businesses
- the abolishment of taxes on family incomes below $15,000, along with property taxes on homes assessed at less than $25,000
- a reform of the federal bureaucracy by curtailing the powers of the president and abolishing the Federal Bureau of Investigation (FBI) and the various agencies that had jurisdiction over internal security
- the removal of restrictions on the Communist Party and other minority parties
- an end to the congressional seniority system
- an end to bias in the legal system
- a prohibition against the National Guard or military in suppressing labor and people's struggles
- an end to the military draft
- the creation of a jobs program for all veterans and soldiers
- the elimination of America's military presence abroad
- a reduction in domestic armed forces
- the enactment of a National Youth Act to provide jobs and training for young people, with special emphasis on minority youth
- free education from grade school through graduate school, with government subsidies to help students with their living expenses
- integration "by any means necessary," and the eradication of military and corporate influences in education
- a national students' bill of rights, to be enacted by a nationwide student referendum
- student participation in all levels of government (particularly within the special youth projects) and student exchange programs
- a labor bill of rights to guarantee equal pay for equal work for working women
- an end to menial work
- a jobs training program

- strict enforcement of occupational health and safety laws
- six months' maternity and abortion leave
- the passage of a Child Development Act
- the creation of a nationwide, twenty-four-hour child care facilities program
- the abolition of the existing welfare system and adoption of a guaranteed family income of $6,500 per year
- enhanced participation in the political life of the nation for the disenfranchised
- the Vietnamese "war of liberation"

OPPOSED:
- capitalism as the handmaiden of imperialism
- the arms race
- the wage freeze
- the oppression of minorities
- both major parties, condemned as representatives of big business
- racism, anti-Semitism, and bigotry and urged that they be made federal crimes

CONSERVATIVE PARTY OF NEW YORK

CANDIDATE FOR PRESIDENT:
Richard Milhous Nixon

CANDIDATE FOR VICE PRESIDENT:
Spiro Theodore Agnew (MD)

CANDIDATES FOR PRESIDENTIAL NOMINATION:
Richard Milhous Nixon (CA)
John G. Schmitz (CA)

The Conservative Party was a New York State third party that normally endorsed the Republican presidential ticket.

CONSTITUTION PARTY

CANDIDATE FOR PRESIDENT:
John George Schmitz (CA)

CANDIDATE FOR VICE PRESIDENT:
Thomas Jefferson Anderson (TN)

CONVENTION:
July 21–22, 1972, Embassy Motor Inn, Chicago (IL)
Joan Van Poperin, national chairman

The Constitution Party supported the candidates of the American Party.

PLATFORM HIGHLIGHTS:
The Constitution Party's platform was adopted on June 15, 1971, in Springfield (IL).

SUPPORTED:
- freedom of religion
- the right of Congress to control the issuance of money
- a militia in every state
- a limit on immigration to the quotas established by the McCarran-Walter Act

- national sovereignty over international treaties
- restrictions on the Supreme Court
- the elimination of government competition with private businesses
- the deregulation of agriculture
- states' rights
- a repeal of the income, inheritance, and estate taxes
- reductions in government spending, the national debt, and foreign aid giveaways
- the prosecution of domestic Communists
- prayer and Bible reading in schools
- the teaching of free enterprise
- the repeal of the Civil Rights Act and other infringements on the right of free association
- the repeal of the Alaska Mental Health Act
- the repeal of the United Nations Charter, the Participation Act of 1945, the Consular Treaty, the Nuclear Test Ban Treaty, Disarmament Act, and reciprocal trade agreements
- a suspension of diplomatic relations with Communist nations

OPPOSED:
- Zionism
- forced busing
- federal aid to education
- the Council on Foreign Relations and the Business Council

CONSTITUTIONAL PARTY
CANDIDATE FOR PRESIDENT:
Talmadge Martin Warren (VA)

A school teacher, Warren sought the presidency as a learning experience for his eighth-grade students.

PLATFORM HIGHLIGHTS:
SUPPORTED:
- equal media space for all candidates in a primary
- a "none of the above" ballot line
- the direct election of Supreme Court justices
- a 20 percent cut in the federal payroll
- restrictions on U.S. investment in Mexico and foreign investments in U.S. businesses
- periodic open bidding for privatized government monopolies like Amtrak and the Postal Service
- foreign aid shifted from the government to voluntary channels
- a national informational network
- the tracking and prosecution of industrial spying
- a nuclear-free world
- the deployment of the military to aid the war on drugs
- full government-provided health care for all citizens, who, with their families, would closely check all charges
- the monitoring of the possession of semiautomatic and assault weapons

- criminals being held responsible for compensating their victims
- a child allowance to married couples with preschool children when the mother does not work outside the home for more than sixteen hours per week

OPPOSED:
- the "borrow and pay" approach to government financing

DEMOCRATIC PARTY
CANDIDATE FOR PRESIDENT:
George Stanley McGovern

CANDIDATE FOR VICE PRESIDENT:
Robert Sargent Shriver (IL) (Thomas Eagleton [MO] resigned)

CANDIDATES FOR PRESIDENTIAL NOMINATION:
William Robert Anderson (TN)
Walter Ralph Buchanan (CA)
Shirley Anita St. Hill Chisholm (NY)
William Ramsey Clark (TX)
Edward Thomas "Ned" Coll (CT)
Charles C. Compton (CA)
Evilyn Evelyn (CA)
Walter Edward Fauntroy (DC)
John Gardner (DC)
John Joyce Gilligan (OH)
Rupert Vance Hartke (IN)
Wayne Levere Hays (OH)
Hubert Horatio Humphrey (MN)
Henry Martin Jackson (WA)
Edward Moore Kennedy (MA)
John Vliet Lindsay (NY)
Lester Garfield Maddox (GA)
Eugene Joseph McCarthy (MN)
George Stanley McGovern (SD)
Wilbur Daigh Mills (AR)
Patsy Takemoto Mink (HI)
Walter Frederick Mondale (MN)
Edmund Sixtus Muskie (ME)
Ralph Nader (CT)
Grady O'Cummings III (NY)
James Terry Sanford (NC)
Robert Sargent Shriver (IL)
John Varick Tunney (CA)
George Corley Wallace (AL)
Samuel William Yorty (CA)

CANDIDATES FOR VICE-PRESIDENTIAL NOMINATION:
Bruno Agnoli (NJ)
Grady Albright (FL)
Wendell Richard Anderson (MN)
Stanley Norman Arnold (NY)
Reubin O'Donovan Askew (FL)
Herman Badillo (NY)
Pat Barrett (IL)
Birch Evan Bayh (IN)

Robert Selmer "Bob" Bergland (MN)
Daniel J. Berrigan (NY)
Philip Francis Berrigan (MD)
Horace Julian Bond (GA)
Edmond J. Bonnette (NJ)
Chester Bliss Bowles(CT)
Edward Thompson Breathitt, Jr. (KY)
Archie Bunker (fictitious)
Philip Burton (CA)
James Earl "Jimmy" Carter (GA)
William Hodding Carter III (MS)
William Venroe Chappell, Jr. (FL)
Cesar Estrada Chavez (CA)
Lawton Mainor Chiles, Jr. (FL)
Shirley Anita St. Hill Chisholm (NY)
Frank Forrester Church, Jr. (ID)
William Ramsey Clark (NY)
Leon Frederick Cook (MN)
Richard Joseph Daley (IL)
John Paul DeCarlo (AL)
Ronald Vernie Dellums (CA)
George A. Dowdy (TN)
Robert Frederick Drinan (MA)
Thomas Francis Eagleton (MO)
Tarlton "Sissy" Farenthold (TX)
Nick Galifianakis (NC)
Glenn A. Goodrich
Maurice Robert "Mike" Gravel (AK)
Martha Wright Griffiths (MI)
Ernest Henry Gruening (AK)
William Lewis Guy (ND)
Charles Granville Hamilton (MS)
Richard Gordon Hatcher (IN)
John Joseph Houlihan (IL)
Harold Everett Hughes (IA)
James Baxter Hunt, Jr. (NC)
Henry Martin Jackson (WA)
Robert Kariss (FL)
Edward Moore "Ted" Kennedy (MA)
Moon Landrieu (LA)
Allard Kenneth Lowenstein (NY)
Eugene Joseph McCarthy (MN)
Eleanor Stegeberg McGovern (SD)
Wilbur Daigh Mills (AR)
Marth Elizabeth Beall Jennings Mitchell (NY)
Roberto A. Mondragon (NM)
Joseph Mamiel Montoya (NM)
Roger Harrison Mudd (VA)
Edmund Sixtus Muskie (ME)
Ralph Nader (CT)
George E. Norcross (NJ)
Endicott Peabody (MA)
Claiborne de Borda Pell (RI)
Claude Denson Pepper (FL)
Abraham Alexander Ribicoff (CT)
Peter Wallace Rodino, Jr. (NJ)

Jerry Clyde Rubin (CA)
James Terry Sanford (NC)
Fred Seaman (TX)
Joe Smith (fictitious)
Claiborne W. "Clay" Smothers (TX)
Benjamin McLane Spock (VI)
Adlai Ewing Stevenson III (IL)
Ann Tavolacci (MI)
Hoyt Patrick Taylor, Jr. (NC)
George Corley Wallace (AL)
Leonard Freel Woodcock (MI)

PRIMARIES:
MARCH 7, 1972 (NH):
Muskie 41,235
McGovern 33,007
Yorty 5,401
Mills 3,563
Hartke..................................... 2,417
Kennedy.................................... 954
Humphrey................................... 348
Jackson..................................... 197
Wallace 175
Coll 280
others 1,277

MARCH 14, 1972 (FL):
Wallace................................. 526,651
Humphrey.............................. 234,658
Jackson 170,156
Muskie 112,523
Lindsay 82,386
McGovern 78,232
Chisholm 43,989
McCarthy 5,847
Mills 4,539
Hartke.................................... 3,009
Yorty 2,564

MARCH 21, 1972 (IL):
Muskie 766,914
McCarthy 444,260
Wallace................................... 7,017
McGovern 3,687
Humphrey................................. 1,476
Chisholm 777
Jackson.................................... 442
Kennedy................................... 242
Lindsay 118
others 211

APRIL 4, 1972 (WI):
McGovern 333,528
Wallace................................. 248,676
Humphrey.............................. 233,748
Muskie 115,811
Jackson 88,068
Lindsay 75,579
McCarthy 15,543

Chisholm 9,198
Yorty 2,349
Mink 1,213
Mills 913
Hartke 766
Kennedy 183
none of the above 2,450
others 559

APRIL 25, 1972 (MA):
McGovern 325,673
Muskie 131,709
Humphrey 48,929
Wallace 45,807
Chisholm 22,398
Mills 19,441
McCarthy 8,736
Jackson 8,499
Kennedy 2,348
Lindsay 2,107
Hartke 874
Yorty 646
Coll 589
others 760

APRIL 25, 1972 (PA):
Humphrey 481,900
Wallace 292,437
McGovern 280,861
Muskie 279,983
Jackson 38,767
Chisholm 306
others 585

MAY 2, 1972 (DC):
Fauntroy 21,217
unpledged 8,343

MAY 2, 1972 (IN):
Humphrey 354,244
Wallace 309,495
Muskie 87,719

MAY 2, 1972 (OH):
Humphrey 499,680
McGovern 480,320
Muskie 107,806
Jackson 98,498
McCarthy 26,026

MAY 4, 1972 (TN):
Wallace 335,858
Humphrey 78,350
McGovern 35,551
Chisholm 18,809
Muskie 9,634
Jackson 5,896
Mills 2,543
McCarthy 2,267
Hartke 1,621

Lindsay 1,476
Yorty 692
others 24

MAY 6, 1972 (NC):
Wallace 413,518
Sanford 306,014
Chisholm 61,723
Muskie 30,739
Jackson 9,416

MAY 9, 1972 (NE):
McGovern 79,309
Humphrey 65,968
Wallace 23,912
Muskie 6,886
Jackson 5,276
Yorty 3,459
McCarthy 3,194
Chisholm 1,763
Lindsay 1,244
Mills 377
Kennedy 293
Hartke 249
others 207

MAY 9, 1972 (WV):
Humphrey 246,596
Wallace 121,888

MAY 16, 1972 (MD):
Wallace 219,687
Humphrey 151,981
McGovern 126,978
Jackson 17,728
Yorty 13,584
Muskie 13,363
Chisholm 12,602
Mills 4,776
McCarthy 4,691
Lindsay 2,168
Mink 573

MAY 16, 1972 (MI):
Wallace 809,239
McGovern 425,694
Humphrey 249,798
Chisholm 44,090
Muskie 38,701
Jackson 6,938
Hartke 2,862
unpledged 10,700
others 51

MAY 23, 1972 (OR):
McGovern 205,328
Wallace 81,868
Humphrey 51,163
Jackson 22,042
Kennedy 12,673

Muskie 10,244
McCarthy 8,943
Mink 6,500
Lindsay 5,082
Chisholm 2,975
Mills 1,208
others 618

MAY 23, 1972 (RI):
McGovern 15,603
Muskie. 7,838
Humphrey 7,701
Wallace. 5,802
McCarthy. 245
Jackson. 138
Mills. 41
Yorty. 6
unpledged. 490

JUNE 6, 1972 (CA):
McGovern. 1,550,652
Humphrey 1,375,064
Wallace. 268,551
Chisholm 157,435
Muskie 72,701
Yorty 50,745
McCarthy 34,203
Jackson 28,901
Lindsay 26,246
Buchanan
Evelyn
Compton
others 20

JUNE 6, 1972 (NJ):
Chisholm 51,433
Sanford 25,401

JUNE 6, 1972 (NM):
McGovern 51,011
Wallace. 44,843
Humphrey. 39,768
Muskie. 6,411
Jackson 4,236
Chisholm 3,205
none of the above. 3,819

JUNE 6, 1972 (SD):
McGovern 28,017

36TH CONVENTION:
July 10–13, 1972, Convention Hall, Miami Beach
   (FL)
Lawrence F. O'Brien (MA), permanent chairman
(temporary chairman position abolished)

PLATFORM HIGHLIGHTS:
The Democratic platform of 1972 was a huge document addressing a lengthy list of policy issues facing the country, only a portion of which can be enumerated below. Citizens were asked to decide "whether they want their country back again." After condemning the Nixon administration, the Democrats declared that "full employment—a guaranteed job for all—is the primary economic objective" of their party.

SUPPORTED:
• tax reform
• the enforcement of equal opportunity laws
• improvements in education, job training, and employment placement
• economic development
• the adoption of an industrial relocation policy
• a use of the government as the "employer of last resort" to ensure a job to everyone who wants one
• stepped-up antitrust enforcement
• adjustments in rate-making and regulatory activities
• heightened efforts to curb monopolies
• the regulation of multinational and international corporations
• raised Social Security ceilings on earned income
• increased federal support for education to relieve the property tax burden
• a repeal of section 14 (b) of the National Labor Relations Act, which allows states to legislate the open shop
• the minimum wage increases to $2.50 per hour, maternity benefits for all working women, and strengthened occupational health and safety laws
• the lettuce boycott
• the rights of children, the mentally retarded and mentally ill, and prisoners
• the right of privacy and the right to be different
• children as the first priority as the nation moved toward National Health Insurance
• the rights of women, emphasized through a call to ratify the ERA and to enact legislation guaranteeing equal pay for equal work
• family planning
• an end to government secrecy in most areas
• efforts to eliminate the seniority system in Congress and to reform administrative agencies
• full disclosure in campaign finance and potential conflicts of interest
• increased regulation of lobbyists
• universal voter registration by post card
• a revision of the Hatch Act
• home rule for the District of Columbia
• the abolition of the electoral college
• other systemic changes to expand participation in the political process
• greater federal grants-in-aid for the territories and the continuation of the commonwealth status of Puerto Rico
• a partnership among federal, state, and local governments, using general revenue sharing as a way to rebuild the nation's infrastructure
• an urban growth policy, increased attention to housing and community development, and more support for the New Town program

- urban mass transit with a pledge to convert the Highway Trust fund into a Transportation Trust Fund
- environmental protection without sacrificing jobs, further development of science and technology, creation of a national energy policy emphasizing alternative energy sources, and conservation of ocean and public land resources
- early childhood education
- school finance reform
- bilingual education
- career education
- increased federal aid to schools, especially for programs for handicapped and disadvantaged children
- an expanded higher-education loan fund for students
- enhanced arts and humanities
- crime prevention plans that stressed law enforcement planning, expanded training for police, a streamlined legal system, and increased treatment opportunities for substance abusers but opposed repressive measures
- handgun control
- massive efforts to stop drug suppliers and distributors and to root out organized and professional criminal syndicates
- an emphasis on rehabilitation, not retribution, in corrections
- a revitalization of the rural United States and a of the strengthening of the family farm
- equitable price controls based on 110 percent of parity, and production adjustments that would ensure adequate food and fiber for domestic use
- policies that would ensure farm people a voice in the programs affecting their lives

- an end to the Vietnam War before October 1, 1972
- the enactment of a full GI bill of rights for Vietnam War veterans
- a military posture of strength, while reducing bases overseas and wasteful expenditures
- an end to the draft
- the ratification of the Strategic Arms Limitations Talks (SALT) agreement
- the ratification of the Protocol on Chemical Warfare
- a reduction in North Atlantic Treaty Organization (NATO) forces while reiterating a continued commitment to collective defense
- an endorsement of Israel, as well as Bangladesh, India, and Japan
- diplomatic relations with the People's Republic of China and the reexamination of U.S. relations with Cuba
- a strengthened United Nations, a good-neighbor policy in Latin America, renegotiated foreign trade barriers, a reform of the international monetary system, and U.S. aid to developing nations through international organizations (with a reduced emphasis on military aid)
- collective bargaining rights for government employees, and portable pension rights

OPPOSED:
- wage and price controls
- the oil import quota
- tax loopholes for the rich and powerful corporate interests
- the ban on common-site picketing
- the set-aside program and programs that worked against the family farmer and small-town rural United States
- subsidies for large farming operations

DEMOCRATIC PARTY
VOTE FOR PRESIDENTIAL NOMINATION:

Candidate	Ballot: 1	2
McGovern	1728½₀	1,864¹⁹⁄₂₀
Jackson	525	485¹³⁄₂₀
Wallace	381⁷⁄₁₀	377½
Chisholm	151¹⁹⁄₂₀	101²⁄₂₀
Sanford	77½	69½
Humphrey	66⁷⁄₁₀	35
Mills	33⁸⁄₁₀	32²⁄₁₀
Muskie	24¹⁄₁₀	20²⁄₁₀
Kennedy	12⁷⁄₁₀	10¹³⁄₂₀
Hays	5	5
McCarthy	2	2
Mondale	1	1
Clark	1	0
abstentions	5	9⁷⁄₁₀

Hartke, Gardner, Shriver, Nader, Tunney, Anderson, Gilligan, Yorty, Mink, and Maddox were also contenders prior to the convention. McGovern was nominated for president on the first ballot.

(continued)

DEMOCRATIC PARTY (cont.)
VOTE FOR VICE-PRESIDENTIAL NOMINATION:

Candidate	Ballot: 1	Candidate	Ballot: 1
Eagleton	1,741^{81}/₁₀₀	Taylor	2
Farenthold	404^3/₁₀₀	Woodcock	2
Gravel	225^{38}/₁₀₀	Gruening	1^5/₂₂
Peabody	107^{26}/₁₀₀	Agnoli	1
Smothers	74	Albright	1
Bayh	62	Barrett	1
Rodino	56½	D. Berrigan	1
Carter	30	P. Berrigan	1
Chisholm	20	Bond	1
Landrieu	18½	Bonnette	1
Breathitt	18	Bowles	1
Kennedy	15	Bunker	1
Kariss	14½	Burton	1
Hatcher	11	Chappell	1
Hughes	10	Chiles	1
Montoya	9	Church	1
Stevenson	8	Cook	1
Guy	7¹/₁₀	Dowdy	1
Bergland	5	Drinan	1
Carter	5	Galifianakis	1
Chavez	5	Goodrich	1
Mills	6	Griffiths	2
Anderson	4	Hamilton	1
Arnold	4	Hunt	1
Dellums	4	Jackson	1
Houlihan	4	Lowenstein	1
Mondragon	4	McGovern	1
Askew	3	Nader	1
McCarthy	3	Norcross	1
Sanford	3	Rubin	1
Pell	2¹⁵/₂₂	Seaman	1
Badillo	2½	Smith	1
Clark	2	Spock	1
Daley	2	Tavolacci	1
DeCarlo	2	Wallace	1
Mudd	2	Mitchell	⅚
Muskie	2	not voting	74⁷/₁₀
Pepper	2	unknown	1
Ribicoff	2		

Eagleton was nominated for vice president on the first ballot, but he resigned nineteen days later. On August 8, 1972, the Democratic National Committee named Shriver to replace Eagleton as the Democratic vice-presidential candidate.

- the Greek military government, Soviet policy toward Jewish emigration, and the racist regimes of South Africa and Southern Rhodesia

ALSO:

- addressed the rights of various special populations, including youth, poor people, American Indians, persons with disabilities, the elderly, veterans and servicemen and -women, the mentally retarded, and consumers

GERONIMO PARTY
CANDIDATE FOR PRESIDENT:
Phillip Cassadore (AZ)

The Geronimo Party's platform promised to "paint the White House red, make it circular instead of square, and move it to the reservation." It urged the adoption of the Apache way of life and a more spiritual and mystical way of looking at the world, without reliance on modern technology. The party urged that all men be treated alike under the same set of laws and that they be given an even chance to live and grow.

INDEPENDENT
CANDIDATES FOR PRESIDENT:
Mihran Nicholas Ask (CA)[1]
John Beno (CO)
Harry Cohen (NJ)
James R. Goodluck (OH)
Clennon W. King (GA)[2]
John J. Kusic (OH)
Rev. J. Christopher Johnston (OH)
Shawn P. O'Malley (OH)
John L. Ruffing, Jr. (OH)
Dean Templeton (WA)

INDEPENDENT PARTY
CANDIDATE FOR PRESIDENT:
Edward Arthur Wallace (OH)
CANDIDATE FOR VICE PRESIDENT:
Robert Bruce Mess (AL)

LIBERAL PARTY OF NEW YORK
CANDIDATE FOR PRESIDENT:
George Stanley McGovern (SD)
CANDIDATE FOR VICE PRESIDENT:
Robert Sargent Shriver (MD)

The Liberal Party was a New York State third party that normally endorsed the Democratic presidential ticket.

LIBERTARIAN PARTY
CANDIDATE FOR PRESIDENT:
John Hospers
CANDIDATE FOR VICE PRESIDENT:
Theodora "Tonie" Nathan
CANDIDATES FOR PRESIDENTIAL NOMINATION:
James G. Bryan (OR)
John Hospers (CA)

[1]Pastor Ask's platform consisted of the same ten planks he had promoted since 1960: "1. To prevent World War 3 without war and weapons. 2. To assure peace and plenty to all nations regardless of race, religion, and political connections forced upon them. 3. A job for every unemployed. 4. Elimination of Beaurocracies (sic). 5. Reduction by 50 percent of all taxes. 6. The right to work. 7. The right to vote [for those] who believe and uphold the Constitution of the U.S.A. and has at least a High School education. 8. No suppression of press, radio and pulpit. 9. The Bible as an obligatory study project in all schools and on all levels. 10. Restoration of the Biblical right of men as the head of the home."
[2]King's platform suggested that the solution to the race problem was to declare everyone white. He argued that the next president would be a reincarnation of Jesus and urged voters to "vote for Jesus" to usher in the new utopia of human peace and unity.

CANDIDATES FOR VICE-PRESIDENTIAL NOMINATION:
Diana Amsden (NM)
Theodora "Tonie" Nathan (OR)
1ST CONVENTION:
June 16–18, 1972, Hotel Radisson, Denver (CO)
David F. Nolan (CO), temporary chairman

It was attended by eighty-nine delegates from twenty-three states.

PLATFORM HIGHLIGHTS:
The platform began with a statement of principles that challenged the "omnipotent state" and defended the rights of the individual.

SUPPORTED:
• a repeal of all victimless crimes statutes (e.g., governing sexual relations, drug use, gambling, and attempted suicide)
• stronger due process for persons accused of crimes
• restitution laws
• the repeal of pornography laws
• calls for making the National Census voluntary
• the right to keep and bear arms
• a volunteer army, while advocating unconditional amnesty for military deserters and draft evaders
• voluntary contracts between employers and employees, along with an unfettered right to engage in collective bargaining
• private ownership of gold and a repeal of all legal tender laws
• a reduction in taxes and government spending
• the elimination of the Federal Reserve System
• total free trade
• a repeal of wage and price controls
• the elimination of governmental subsidies
• an adoption of the Liberty Amendment, which prohibited the Federal government from competing with private enterprises
• an "eventual repeal of all taxation"
• laws against fraud and misrepresentation, but consumer protection legislation was viewed as an infringement on voluntary trade
• a withdrawal from all international alliances not essential to protect the freedom of U.S. citizens
• abortion rights but denounced all forms of coercive population control
• the right of political units to secede from the entities with which they disagree
• United States withdrawal from the United Nations
• an end to foreign trade

OPPOSED:
• censorship in all its forms
• the Federal Communications Commission, National Labor Relations Board, Interstate Commerce Commission, the Department of Agriculture, Tariff Commission, and Customs Court

- the draft
- restrictions on property rights
- all government regulation of the economy
- government intervention, which was to blame for pollution, overpopulation, educational problems, poverty, and unemployment
- compulsory education and busing, along with federal aid to schools
- minimum wage laws, "protective" legislation for women and children, regulation of day care centers, welfare and relief projects, and programs to "aid the poor" as being outside the proper role of government
- efforts to regulate currency exchange rates
- the claims of international entities to ownership of unclaimed ocean floor and planetary bodies

ALSO:
- did not recognize the legitimacy of totalitarian governments
- argued that, as allies assumed a larger share of the burden of their own defense, the United States should be able to reduce expenditures for its conventional war capability

---

LIBERTARIAN PARTY
VOTE FOR PRESIDENTIAL NOMINATION: HOSPERS WAS NOMINATED FOR PRESIDENT ON THE FIRST BALLOT, WINNING BY A 3 TO 1 MARGIN OVER BRYAN. SEVERAL OTHER INDIVIDUALS WERE OFFERED FOR CONSIDERATION, BUT THEY DECLINED.

VOTE FOR VICE-PRESIDENTIAL NOMINATION: NATHAN WAS NOMINATED FOR VICE PRESIDENT ON THE FIRST BALLOT.

LIBERTY UNION PARTY

CANDIDATE FOR PRESIDENT:
Benjamin McLane Spock (AR)

CANDIDATE FOR VICE PRESIDENT:
Julius Hobson (DC)

The Liberty Union Party was based in Vermont and supported the People's Party candidates.

LOYAL U.S.A. PARTY

CANDIDATE FOR PRESIDENT:
Billy Joe Clegg (OK)

CANDIDATE FOR VICE PRESIDENT:
William Franklin Graham (declined)

CANDIDATES FOR VICE-PRESIDENTIAL NOMINATION:
Barry Morris Goldwater (AZ)
William Franklin "Billy" Graham (MN)
Richard Claxton "Dick" Gregory (IL)

Henry Martin "Scoop" Jackson (WA)
Jesse Louis Jackson (IL)
George Corley Wallace (AL)

CONVENTION:
February 1972

The Loyal U.S.A. Party was formed on November 10, 1970.

PLATFORM HIGHLIGHTS:
The platform of the Loyal U.S.A. Party demanded a "President who will either go to the bathroom or get off the pot." As a Christian organization, the party was staunchly anti-Communist. Its founder, Reverend Clegg, admitted to committing "about every sin in the book" before he found the spirit of God and answered the call to run for president. The party's plan for Vietnam consisted of flying two large empty aircraft to Vietnam, loading the planes with half combat and half support troops of young South Vietnamese, and flying them to the United States for training and exposure to U.S. ways of life. Upon their return to Vietnam, these troops would be released, and the planes would be filled with U.S. troops for the return flight. This replacement strategy would be continued until all U.S. troops were removed. The platform rejected forced busing, trade with the People's Republic of China, the wage-price freeze, and lifetime appointments for Supreme Court justices. It endorsed a four-day work week, revenue sharing, a massive public works project built around the Anti-Pollution Association, and compulsory, one-year active military service for all (to be deemed equivalent to one year of college education).

LOYAL U.S.A. PARTY
VOTE FOR VICE-PRESIDENTIAL NOMINATION: DELEGATES TO THE CONVENTION SELECTED WILLIAM GRAHAM FOR VICE PRESIDENT, WITH 55 PERCENT OF THE VOTE. RICHARD CLAXTON "DICK" GREGORY OF ILLINOIS RECEIVED 25 PERCENT OF THE VOTE; BARRY MORRIS GOLDWATER OF ARIZONA GOT 5 PERCENT; JESSE LOUIS JACKSON OF ILLINOIS OBTAINED 5 PERCENT; HENRY MARTIN "SCOOP" JACKSON OF WASHINGTON, 5 PERCENT; AND GEORGE CORLEY WALLACE OF ALABAMA GOT 5 PERCENT.

NATIONAL SURREALIST PARTY

CANDIDATE FOR PRESIDENT:
George G. Papoon (KS)

CANDIDATE FOR VICE PRESIDENT:
George Leroy Tirebiter (CA)

The National Surrealist Party was founded by the Firesign Theatre in 1968 in Hollywood (CA). Its platform advocated "one organism, one vote" and "one man, one channel." Membership in the party was open to animals of all kinds, including aliens from outer space. The party was concerned with the question, "What is reality?" and hoped to raise awareness of multiple realities. The platform called for "miniaturizing the bureaucracy, diversifying the income tax, freeing the banks, bringing the natural resources of the country under the control of the people, and encouraging local governments to return power to their constituents."

PEACE AND FREEDOM PARTY

CANDIDATE FOR PRESIDENT:
Benjamin McLane Spock (AR)

CANDIDATE FOR VICE PRESIDENT:
Julius Hobson (DC)

The Peace and Freedom Party supported the People's Party ticket.

PRIMARY:
(While not listed, the following candidates were registered with the California secretary of state to require that their vote be tallied. None received recorded votes, although the Peace and Freedom Party did hold a primary in California.)

JUNE 6, 1972 (CA):
Evelyn
Compton
Slocum

PEOPLE'S PARTY

CANDIDATE FOR PRESIDENT:
Benjamin McLane Spock

CANDIDATE FOR VICE PRESIDENT:
Julius Hobson (DC)

CANDIDATES FOR PRESIDENTIAL NOMINATION:
Jack Hampton (CA)
Nicholas Johnson (DC)
Eugene Joseph McCarthy (MN)
Ralph Nader (CT)
Benjamin McLane Spock (AR)

The People's Party was formed through a coalition of the Peace and Freedom Party, the New Party, and the D.C. Statehood Party.

CONVENTION:
July 27–30, 1972, St. Louis (MO)

Spock was nominated for president on November 27, 1971, at a peace convention in Dallas (TX). Two hundred delegates from twenty-seven states attended this first convention. Spock accepted the presidential nomination on the understanding that he would withdraw if the party could persuade McCarthy, Ralph Nader of Connecticut, or Johnson to head the ticket. On July 27–30, 1972, the People's Party ratified the earlier choices.

PLATFORM HIGHLIGHTS:
The platform of the People's Party was a lengthy document espousing a radical perspective.

SUPPORTED:
- a repeal of age-based laws limiting eligibility for political activity
- the recognition of full rights and responsibilities for young people, including the right to be independent of one's parents
- the right of young people to have equal say in their education
- an extension of the right to equal treatment under law to young people
- the granting of the right to determine one's own lifestyle to those who choose to be different
- seniors were to be accorded (1) the right to work productively, with no mandatory retirement age; (2) the right to guaranteed annual income; (3) the right to make decisions about one's life; (4) the right to control institutions controlling their lives; and (5) the right to decent housing (without the burden of a property tax) and good transportation
- the creation of a Department of Culture and the Arts, which would fund and encourage the development of the arts
- the maximization of human potential "to the fullest"
- conservation and environmental protection
- a revision of the nation's energy policy to halt nuclear energy development, decrease energy consumption, and encourage alternative energy sources
- the construction of rapid mass transit systems
- voluntary population control through sex education, legalization of abortions, and free distribution of contraceptives
- greater reliance on biodegradable and recyclable products
- strict enforcement of the Clean Water Act
- adequate health and safety testing of new products and drugs
- a reorganization of the government to make federal environmental and energy agencies more responsive to the public
- a change in the economic system to allow people to control the institutions that affect their lives
- the reconstitution of corporations as public trusts, subsidies to support the production of critical goods and services for communities, the establishment of minimum and maximum annual incomes, an increase in the supply of the necessities of life, and other features of a "populist economic system" controlled by a people's national planning and review board
- plugging tax loopholes, a progressive income tax, the enactment of an excess profits tax, and an end to the wage freeze
- the creation of a guaranteed jobs program
- an end to tax incentives for U.S. investments abroad

- the National Welfare Rights Organization program
- the thirty-hour week at forty-hours' pay
- portable pension rights
- free mass transportation, child care, and medical care
- the abolition of compulsory education but endorsed the concept of community control over schools, recommended experimental education, accepted busing as a temporary means to achieve racial balance, and promoted a bill of rights for students
- education financed through a national progressive income tax, rather than by relying on local property taxes
- price supports on storable grains, prohibitions against selling storable grains at less than parity, retention of Commodity Credit Corporation bins, inclusion of farmers under the minimum wage law, and enforcement of the right of agricultural workers to organize under the Wagner Act
- small family farmers over large corporate agricultural interests
- freedom for Guam, Puerto Rico, and all other territories
- community boards to govern the police, welfare agencies, and educational services
- the development of new methods of measuring popular opinion and encouraging participatory democracy
- the adoption of a fair campaign practices code
- statehood for the District of Columbia
- an end to the draft
- the creation of a cabinet-level Department of Peace and Priorities
- massive voter registration drives among young people and minorities
- the recognition of the sovereignty of the American Indian nations
- free medical care for everyone
- participatory democracy in unions and apprenticeship programs, job retraining programs, protection of the rights to strike, and nondiscrimination in employment and promotions
- a ban on forced labor
- an expansion of access to legal services
- efforts to ensure constitutional rights for minors
- calls to provide for community-control over law enforcement and greater controls over corporate crime
- an adoption of an elective judiciary, supplemented with community courts
- a prisoners' union and a bill of rights for prisoners
- the decriminalization of psychoactive drugs
- the payment of reparations to foreign and domestic peoples who have been victims of oppression
- an abolition of the Universal Code of Military Justice
- a repeal of victimless crime laws, along with laws permitting preventive detention, domestic spying, and no-knock arrests
- the abolition of the present penal system, replacing it with a system of community-controlled reeducation centers

- national autonomy for African-Americans, Chicanos, and Native Americans
- ratification of the ERA
- the right to an abortion
- paid maternity leave benefits on a voluntary basis for the mother, government programs to provide child care services, and the elimination of gender-based stereotypes
- the immediate, unilateral withdrawal of U.S. troops from Southeast Asia and an end to all military aid
- the abolishment of the Central Intelligence Agency (CIA) and Agency for International Development
- the abolition of all U.S. armed forces except the Coast Guard and local militia
- a halt to the space program, with future space research to be conducted on an international cooperative basis
- the abolition of the electoral college and gerrymandering
- "all consciousness-raising alternatives" to the status quo

Opposed:
- sexism
- racism and oppression of minorities, workers, gay people, seniors, farmers, and young people
- big finance, big corporations, and the big military establishment, which were blamed for the nation's ills and were accused of controlling the two major parties
- medical research on Third World peoples without their consent as well as forced sterilization and lobotomies
- laws regulating sexual behavior (including homosexuality), marriage, and divorce

PROHIBITION PARTY

CANDIDATE FOR PRESIDENT:
Earle Harold Munn, Sr.

CANDIDATE FOR VICE PRESIDENT:
Marshall Eugene Uncapher

CANDIDATES FOR PRESIDENTIAL NOMINATION:
Joseph Lee Autenrieth (MO)
Charles Wesley Ewing (MI)
Earle Harold Munn, Sr. (MI)
Mark Revell Sadler (MA)
Marshall Eugene Uncapher (KS)

CANDIDATES FOR VICE-PRESIDENTIAL NOMINATION:
Marshall Eugene Uncapher (KS)
Roger Irving Williams (RI)

26TH CONVENTION:
June 24–25, 1971, Wichita (KS)

PLATFORM HIGHLIGHTS:
Supported:
- a constitutional government
- governmental economy (i.e., reduced expenditures)
- a reduction of the national debt
- a reduction in taxes
- a balanced budget
- a favorable balance of payments
- a financial program to curb inflation

- a thorough review of tax policies
- a program of general revenue sharing
- a stabilization of wages and prices
- increased environmental awareness
- an emphasis on tertiary treatment of sewage
- the development of atomic fusion
- a substitution of nonpolluting sources of power in automobiles
- the promotion of peace and reduced international tension but believed foreign aid should be limited to repayable loans (except in the case of disaster relief)
- the free enterprise system
- compulsory arbitration in labor disputes, promising to enforce stringently laws prohibiting strikes by public employees
- states' rights and right-to-work laws
- neighborhood schools
- strengthened enforcement of laws against gambling, narcotics, and commercialized vice
- an all-volunteer military
- the establishment of year-round Daylight Savings Time
- the protection of the civil service
- the overhaul of the welfare system
- an enactment of uniform marriage and divorce laws
- ballot law reform
- continued separation of church and state (while recognizing the Bible as a "non-sectarian book")
- restrictions on involuntary mental health treatments
- an increased effort to control the use of tobacco and narcotic or psychedelic drugs

OPPOSED:
- communism and totalitarianism
- monopolies
- excessive government regulations
- the government being engaged in competitive business activity

- the news media's sensationalized reports of permissiveness
- a guaranteed annual income
- tax discrimination against evangelical Christian institutions
- the use of Social Security for political purposes
- direct federal aid to education

ALSO:
- deplored the repeal of the Eighteenth Amendment and attributed the moral decline in the United States to liquor traffic
- wanted to eliminate the alcoholic beverage industry altogether

REPUBLICAN PARTY

CANDIDATE FOR PRESIDENT:
Richard Milhous Nixon

CANDIDATE FOR VICE PRESIDENT:
Spiro Theodore Agnew

CANDIDATES FOR PRESIDENTIAL NOMINATION:
John Milan Ashbrook (OH)
Charles C. Compton (CA)
Evilyn Evelyn (CA)
Paul Norton McCloskey, Jr. (CA)
Richard Milhous Nixon (CA)
Patrick Layton Paulsen (CA)
Will Slocum (CA)
George Corley Wallace (AL)

CANDIDATES FOR VICE-PRESIDENTIAL NOMINATION:
Spiro Theodore Agnew (MD)
Edward William Brooke (MA)
David Brinkley (NY)
Chief Burning Wood (aka Austin Marion Burton) (KY)

PRIMARIES:
MARCH 7, 1972 (NH):

Nixon	79,239
McCloskey	23,190
Ashbrook	11,362
Paulsen	1,211
others	2206

Vice-presidential primary:

Agnew	
Brooke	
Burning Wood	

MARCH 14, 1974 (FL):

Nixon	360,278
Ashbrook	36,617
McCloskey	17,312

MARCH 21, 1972 (IL):

Nixon	32,550
Ashbrook	170

PROHIBITION PARTY
VOTE FOR PRESIDENTIAL NOMINATION:

Candidate	Ballot: 1	2	3
Munn, Sr.	19	26	31
Ewing	12	22	19
Uncapher	6	1	0
Autenrieth	6	1	0
Shaw	5	0	0

VOTE FOR VICE-PRESIDENTIAL NOMINATION:

Candidate	Ballot: 1
Uncapher	30
Williams	22

McCloskey 47
others 802

APRIL 4, 1972 (WI):
Nixon 277,601
McCloskey 3,651
Ashbrook 2,604
none of the above 2,315
others 273

APRIL 25, 1972 (MA):
Nixon 99,150
McCloskey 16,435
Ashbrook 4,864
others 1,690

APRIL 25, 1972 (PA)
Nixon 153,886
Wallace 20,472
others 10,443

MAY 2, 1972 (IN):
Nixon 417,069

MAY 2, 1972 (OH):
Nixon 692,828

MAY 4, 1972 (TN):
Nixon 109,696
Ashbrook 2,419
McCloskey 2,370
others 4

MAY 6, 1972 (NC):
Nixon 159,167
McCloskey 8,732

MAY 9, 1972 (NE):
Nixon 179,464
McCloskey 9,011
Ashbrook 4,996
others 801

MAY 9, 1972 (WV):
unpledged 95,813

MAY 16, 1972 (MD):
Nixon 99,308
McCloskey 9,223
Ashbrook 6,718

MAY 16, 1972 (MI):
Nixon 321,652
McCloskey 9,691
unpledged 5,370
others 30

MAY 23, 1972 (OR):
Nixon 231,151
McCloskey 29,365
Ashbrook 16,696
others 4,798

MAY 23, 1972 (RI):
Nixon 4,953

McCloskey 337
Ashbrook 175
unpledged 146

JUNE 6, 1972 (CA):
Nixon 2,058,825
Ashbrook 224,922
others 175
Slocum . . . .
Evelyn . . . .
Compton . . . .

JUNE 6, 1972 (NJ):
unpledged 215,719

JUNE 6, 1972 (NM):
Nixon 49,067
McCloskey 3,367
none of the above 3,035

JUNE 6, 1972 (SD):
Nixon 52,820

30TH CONVENTION:
August 21–23, 1972, Convention Hall, Miami
   Beach (FL)
Ronald Reagan (CA), temporary chairman
Gerald Rudolph Ford, Jr. (MI), permanent chairman
Anne Legendre Armstrong (TX), co-keynoter
Richard Green Lugar (IN), co-keynoter

PLATFORM HIGHLIGHTS:
The lengthy 1972 Republican platform reminded voters about how bad things were in 1968 and claimed that the Nixon administration had turned the nation back on course with a new, buoyant, and confident spirit. It outlined a program for the future that included the "Nixon Doctrine," which proclaimed "that America will remain fully involved in world affairs, and do this in ways that will elicit greater effort by other nations and the sustaining support of our people."

SUPPORTED:
- military and economic aid for U.S. allies
- an international partnership
- a willingness to negotiate
- arms reductions
- expanded contacts with formerly isolated Communist nations
- an honorable end to the conflict in Vietnam with a full accounting of POWs and personnel missing in action (MIA)
- a continued movement toward "Vietnamization" of the war (i.e., withdrawal of U.S. troops and their replacement by South Vietnamese soldiers)
- the cease-fire in the Middle East
- a reform of immigration policy and enforcement of restrictions on illegal aliens' entry into the United States
- assistance for international multilateral agencies, including the United Nations (albeit mandating some changes in the United Nations)

- freedom for Soviet Jews to emigrate to Israel or elsewhere
- Israel and a promise to maintain a military balance in the Middle East by providing Israel the weapons necessary to defend itself
- pledges to maintain the U.S. naval presence in the Mediterranean Sea and technical forces in Europe
- NATO
- friendship with Japan
- improved relations with the Soviet Union and the People's Republic of China
- the common long-range interests between the United States and Latin America, although Cuba was still considered ineligible for reentry to the community of American states
- calls for encouraging nonviolent, evolutionary change in southern Africa and throughout the continent, while declaring minority rule and apartheid to be "seemingly intractable problems"
- a strong national defense, with a modern, well-equipped force (including the F-155, the Trident submarine, and the B-1 bomber)
- shared responsibility for mutual defense with other nations
- an all-volunteer armed force
- pay raises for service personnel
- increases in military housing
- better defense management and elimination of waste
- an abolition of unnecessary or obsolete federal programs
- the approval of the SALT agreements
- continued efforts to control inflation
- the eventual removal of wage and price controls
- tax revisions to encourage work, innovation, and investment
- improvements in federal manpower programs
- greater competition and support for free enterprise
- international monetary reform
- a restoration of the right of U.S. citizens to own gold
- a reform of the congressional budgeting process
- comprehensive tax reform
- the elimination of government waste
- general revenue sharing
- a more open world market, with federal aid to assist readjustment by workers, businessmen, and communities adversely affected by changing patterns of trade
- increased efforts to promote export opportunities
- increased financing for small businesses through the Small Business Administration (SBA)
- more incentives for the private sector to join SBA direct action programs
- the strengthening of the SBA's Community Development program
- a rejuvenation of the Small Business Investment Company program and other actions to bolster small firms
- promises to help graduate more primary care physicians and allied health personnel

- health maintenance organizations and other delivery system innovations
- a comprehensive health insurance program to be financed by employers, employees, and the federal government, while maintaining opposition to nationalized compulsory health insurance
- prevention and physical fitness
- expanded medical research in such areas as cancer, mental retardation, and sickle cell anemia
- encouragements for private insurance to cover mental illness
- the further development of comprehensive community mental health centers
- an improvement in consumer protection in the health care marketplace
- vocational and continuing education programs
- career education, student loan programs, and special programs for children with dyslexia and hyperkinesis
- public financial assistance for children in parochial and private schools
- special general revenue sharing for education
- reforms in the welfare system, including more job training, uniform federal welfare standards, family planning; an end to abuse of the system; and expanded employment opportunities
- promises to keep the organized syndicates and lawless elements in society "on the run"
- rehabilitation
- local police forces
- a reform of the federal criminal code
- relief for crowded federal court dockets
- an intensified effort to prevent criminal access to all weapons, including handguns, without restricting legitimate gun ownership
- arguments that the nation was winning the war on drugs but needed to obtain international agreements relating to the production and movement of dangerous drugs
- research on drug usage
- expanded drug abuse education, rehabilitation, training, and treatment programs
- further expansion of the agricultural export market
- a reduction in farm loan interest rates and easier credit
- family farming
- favorable tax treatment of farm estates
- the development of new farm products through research
- the conservation of land and water resources
- technical assistance and environmental enhancement for rural communities
- general revenue sharing and special general revenue sharing for urban development as ways of assisting community development, along with programs to address the problem of abandoned buildings and further implementation of the "new towns" concept
- new private-sector housing initiatives, expanded subsidy programs and more liberal mortgage credit activi-

ties of federal housing agencies, and technological and management innovations to lower housing costs

- a revitalization of surface freight transportation, modernization of railway equipment and operations, and development of new methods of transporting people in urban areas
- the enactment of President Nixon's legislative agenda on the environment
- the conservation of natural resources and energy
- flood control, navigation improvement, and land reclamation
- the acceleration of research on thermonuclear, geothermal, and other alternative energy sources, including a liquid-metal fast breeder reactor
- a new cabinet-level Department of Natural Resources
- the development of coastal zone management systems, environmental protection for the oceans and marine species, management of the mineral and fish resources of the sea, and support for the United Nations Conference on the Law of the Sea
- boosted scientific research for programs relating to clean energy, pollution-free transportation, addiction control and rehabilitation, and other areas of vital public concern
- priority attention for the space program, communications, exploration of the seabeds, and efforts to mobilize unemployed scientists and engineers
- voluntary school prayer
- "balanced" self-government and representation in Congress for the District of Columbia
- self-determination for Puerto Rico
- expanded rights for American Samoa, Guam, Micronesia, and the Virgin Islands
- volunteerism in the community
- the arts and humanities
- improvements in the lives of children and youth
- the ratification of the ERA, an expansion of child care services, and the need for more employment opportunities for women
- increased widow, widower, and delayed retirement benefits
- improvements in Medicare
- tax breaks for seniors
- senior volunteer programs and other opportunities to achieve "self-reliance, fulfillment, and dignity"
- collective bargaining
- the stronger enforcement of mine health and safety laws
- improvements in pension systems
- the modernization of the civil service
- a reduction in seasonal fluctuations in the construction industry
- improved labor-management relations
- an end to discrimination by enforcing the Voting Rights Act, extending bilingual education, and providing more job opportunities for minorities
- a new relationship with American Indians, Alaskan Natives, and Hawaiians, stating special concern for off-reservation American Indians and insisting on favorable treatment for American Indian, Alaskan Native, and Hawaiian land claims
- a consumers' bill of rights and creation of an independent Consumer Protection Agency
- an independent system of Veterans Administration health care facilities
- special consideration for the needs of Vietnam War veterans
- a better coordinated national policy on cemeteries and burial benefits for veterans

OPPOSED:

- "Big Brother" (i.e., government paternalism and control)
- defense cuts, particularly those affecting the Minuteman III, Poseidon program, and the U.S. fleet of aircraft carriers
- the relocation of plants to foreign countries to take advantage of lower wage rates
- forced busing and the enactment of the Equal Educational Opportunities Act
- quotas in educational institutions, whether applied to students or faculty
- a guaranteed annual income
- the legalization of marijuana

REPUBLICAN PARTY	
VOTE FOR PRESIDENTIAL NOMINATION:	
Candidate	Ballot: 1
Nixon	1,347
McCloskey	1
VOTE FOR VICE-PRESIDENTIAL NOMINATION:	
Candidate	Ballot: 1
Agnew	1,345
Brinkley	1
abstention	2

SOCIALIST LABOR PARTY

CANDIDATE FOR PRESIDENT:
Louis Fisher (IL)

CANDIDATE FOR VICE PRESIDENT:
Genevieve Gunderson (MN)

28TH CONVENTION:
April 8–11, 1972, Detroit Hilton, Detroit (MI)
Joseph Pirincin (OH), temporary chairman
Joseph Pirincin (OH), chairman, April 8–9, 1972
George Sam Taylor (PA), chairman, April 10, 1972
Thirty-three delegates from fifteen states and the District of Columbia attended this convention.

PLATFORM HIGHLIGHTS:
The platform declared that "social systems are mortal" and announced that capitalism was on the verge of death. In Marxist terms, it explained why capitalism "overproduces" and why the Vietnam War accelerated the tendency toward inflation. Workers were called upon to perform an "historic task," that is, to seize the revolutionary moment, to bring about Socialist Industrial Unions, and to achieve industrial self-government.

SOCIALIST LABOR PARTY
VOTES FOR PRESIDENTIAL AND VICE-PRESIDENTIAL NOMINATION: FOURTEEN PERSONS WERE INTERVIEWED BY THE NOMINATION COMMITTEE. FISHER AND GUNDERSON WERE UNANIMOUSLY NOMINATED FOR PRESIDENT AND VICE PRESIDENT, RESPECTIVELY, WITH NO OTHER NAMES BEING PLACED BEFORE THE CONVENTION.

SOCIALIST WORKERS PARTY

CANDIDATE FOR PRESIDENT:
Linda Jenness (GA)
Evelyn Reed (NY) (on the ballots in IN, NY, WI)

CANDIDATE FOR VICE PRESIDENT:
Clifton DeBerry (NY) (on the ballots in IN, NY, WI)
Andrew Pulley (IL)

CONVENTION:
Detroit (MI)

PLATFORM HIGHLIGHTS:
The platform of the Socialist Workers Party denounced both the Republican and Democratic parties, accusing them of being responsible for the war in Indochina, inflation, police brutality, and the erosion of civil liberties. The capitalist system was blamed for racism and exploitation of the poor. Support for reformist elements in the two capitalist parties was viewed as wasted effort, since only fundamental Socialist changes could alter present circumstances.

SUPPORTED:
- an immediate withdrawal of U.S. troops from Southeast Asia
- the dismantling of military bases around the world
- the abolition of the draft
- unconditional amnesty for draft evaders and deserters
- a national referendum on the Vietnam War
- the "liberation" struggles in Africa, Arab lands, Asia, and Latin America
- unity among workers in opposition to wage controls and war spending
- cost-of-living escalator clauses in all contracts
- a shorter work week
- public works projects
- guaranteed unemployment compensation

- the elimination of restrictions on the right to strike
- rank-and-file control over unions
- a repeal of the Taft-Hartley Act
- the abolition of all taxes on incomes below $10,000 and confiscation of all war profits
- taxes at 100 percent on incomes above $25,000
- a rollback on rents
- free medical and dental care for everyone
- the promotion of mass transit and free rides to the needy
- African-American control over African-American communities, including schools, police, housing, medical care, and other institutions
- the right of self-defense for African Americans
- a mass Black Political Party
- Chicano and Mexican worker parties like La Raza Unida
- equal rights for women, including reproductive freedom, promotion of birth control, equal pay legislation, ratification of the ERA, and expansion of free government child care facilities
- a 100 percent tax on profits from pollution
- the mandatory installation of pollution-control equipment
- a halt to the destruction of the environment
- free education through the university level, with appropriate government stipends to assist students, and guaranteed jobs upon graduation
- student and faculty control over education and full constitutional rights for all students
- basic civil and human rights for prison inmates, including the right to receive union wages, and condemned censorship in prisons
- the liberalization of the election laws to ease the burden on smaller parties
- the enactment of laws to protect the full civil and human rights of gay people and political activists
- a nationalization of major corporations and banks under worker control
- the need to organize an independent labor party, which, of course, would be the Socialist Workers Party, for African Americans, Chicanos, and women

---

SOCIALIST WORKERS PARTY
VOTES FOR PRESIDENTIAL AND VICE-PRESIDENTIAL NOMINATION: BOTH CANDIDATES—JENNESS AND PULLEY—WERE INELIGIBLE BECAUSE THEY WERE BELOW THE CONSTITUTIONAL AGE REQUIREMENT. REED AND DEBERRY WERE SUBSTITUTED AS THE PRESIDENTIAL AND VICE-PRESIDENTIAL CANDIDATES ON THE BALLOTS OF INDIANA, NEW YORK, AND WISCONSIN.

UNIVERSAL PARTY

CANDIDATE FOR PRESIDENT:
Gabriel Green

CANDIDATE FOR VICE PRESIDENT:
Daniel William Fry (OR)

CANDIDATES FOR PRESIDENTIAL NOMINATION:
Mark Brownell (CA)
Gabriel Green (CA)
Samuel G. Partridge (CA)
Arthur Rosenblum (PA)

CONVENTION:
April 8–10, 1972, Holiday Inn, Flagstaff (AZ)
John W. Hopkins (CA), chairman

PLATFORM HIGHLIGHTS:
The Universal Party's platform called for the general revision of the election system, with the elimination of national conventions, the electoral college, and other representative structures. Instead, public officials—including Supreme Court justices—would be directly elected by the people and subject to recall.

SUPPORTED:
- encouragements for women to participate in elective and appointive offices and equal pay for equal work
- the reassertion of congressional control over money
- the expansion of credit unions for future banking
- the printing of enough money to pay congressional obligations, instead of levying taxes
- the government's withdrawal from activities that compete with the private sector
- a World Congress with equal representation of nations
- a World Supreme Court assisted by national appellate courts
- a provision that only Congress could declare war, subject to approval by the president
- an end to unemployment
- a promotion of the Guild System and the creation of specialized craft unions, while opposing labor or management monopolies
- village and farm development on unused public lands as a solution to urban crowding
- small farm owners over large corporate farming interests
- subsidies for "start-up" farmers for up to five years
- the conservation of all natural resources and the use of free, or cosmic, energy substituted for oil and gas
- the protection of all life against contamination of air, water, and foodstuffs
- free education
- private schools
- the humanities and the sciences equally
- spiritual (not religious) training and research
- standardized marriage laws and the handling of divorce matters in domestic relations courts
- the stimulation of small businesses and the enforcement of fair trade practices
- controls on speculation
- an intention to limit the dramatization of crimes and vices on television or movie screens and to take steps to prevent juvenile delinquency
- uniform traffic laws
- the abolition of capital punishment
- the elimination of conflicts of interest among public officials
- federal financing of elections
- the extension of bulk postal rates to political parties
- a change in the one-man one-vote reapportionment ruling
- due process rights for mental patients charged with crimes
- the freedom of public employees to participate in politics
- Karmic justice
- full recognition of civil rights
- the equality of all persons regardless of race, color, gender, creed, or national origin
- improved old age and unemployment benefits and medical assistance programs
- the claims that messages from greater worlds that often contact earth confirm the truth of reincarnation
- the provision of civil treatment and protection to visitors from outer space, rather than confinement to jail

OPPOSED:
- usury
- zoning laws and highway condemnation as interferences with private property
- lobbying
- secret job or medical examination information by employers being withheld from applicants

---

UNIVERSAL PARTY
VOTE FOR PRESIDENTIAL NOMINATION:

Candidate	Ballot: 1
Green	20
Brownell	5
Partridge	2
Rosenblum	2

VOTE FOR VICE-PRESIDENTIAL NOMINATION:
FRY WAS NOMINATED.

GENERAL ELECTION SUMMARY FOR 1972:

Candidate	Electoral Votes	States	Popular Votes
Nixon (R)	520	49	47,108,459[1]
McGovern (D)	17	1 (+DC)	29,084,726[2]
Hospers (LIBRTN)	1	0	2,691
Spock (LIBUN)	0	0	78,751
(PFP)	0	0	55,167
Schmitz (A)	0	0	1,063,792[3]
Jenness (SOC WOR)	0	0	96,176
Fisher (SOC LAB)	0	0	53,617
ND	0	0	37,815
Hall (COM)	0	0	25,222
Munn (PROH)	0	0	13,444
IGP	0	0	2,855
UNI CIT	0	0	2,265
Mahalchik (AM FIR)	0	0	1,743
IP (WI)	0	0	506
Wallace (IP)	0	0	460
Green (UNIV)	0	0	199
Beno (I)	0	0	6
Boren (BUREAU)	0	0	2
unknown	0	0	12,915

[1]Includes 183,128 votes from the Conservative Party of New York
[2]Includes 368,136 votes from the Liberal Party of New York
[3]Includes 70,593 votes from the Constitution Party

ELECTION OF NOVEMBER 2, 1976

President
EARL "JIMMY" CARTER, JR.

Vice President
WALTER FREDERICK MONDALE

HIGHLIGHTS

The campaign of 1976 began with President Gerald Rudolph Ford, Jr., on shaky ground. Still suffering the ill effects of his pardon of President Richard Nixon, Ford appeared weak. This public perception encouraged Gov. Ronald Wilson Reagan of California to challenge him for the Republican nomination. Reagan was the darling of the right wing of the party, but his supporters were unable to overcome the advantage of Ford's incumbency. At the Republican Convention, Reagan gambled on a novel idea: he named his vice-presidential running mate, Sen. Richard Schultz Schweiker of Pennsylvania, before the balloting began for the presidential nomination. It did not work, and Ford received the nomination. On the Democratic side, a little-known former governor of Georgia, James Earl "Jimmy" Carter, Jr., slowly moved from obscurity to take the Democratic nomination. He defeated one congressman, four senators, three governors, and a former vice-presidential candidate. Promising "a government as good as the American people," Carter went on to beat Ford, who had made several missteps in the debates and along the campaign trail, and Ford's fragmented Grand Old Party in the general election. One interesting feature of the campaign was the candidacy of another former governor of Georgia, Lester Garfield Maddox, who ran on the American Independent ticket and had once served as Carter's lieutenant governor. Also, a New York housewife, Ellen Cullen McCormack, made history when she sought the Democratic nomination on an antiabortion platform and garnered enough support to qualify for federal matching funds.

ACE-ELI PARTY

CANDIDATE FOR PRESIDENT:
Robin Rex Burns (CA)

AMERICAN FREEDOM PARTY

CANDIDATE FOR PRESIDENT:
Larry Brant Sargeant (NV)

AMERICAN INDEPENDENT PARTY

CANDIDATE FOR PRESIDENT:
Lester Garfield Maddox

CANDIDATE FOR VICE PRESIDENT:
William Daniel Dyke

CANDIDATES FOR PRESIDENTIAL NOMINATION:
Thomas M. Goodloe, Jr. (CA)
Jesse Alexander Helms, Jr. (NC)
Christian F. Larson (NJ)
Lester Garfield Maddox (GA)
Ellen Cullen McCormack (NY)
Robert Morris (TX)
Alberta Procell (CA)
John Richard Rarick (LA)

Ronald Wilson Reagan (CA)
George J. Shea (CA)
Steven Douglas Symms (ID)
Meldrim Thomson, Jr. (NH)
Richard Art Viguerie (VA)
George Corley Wallace (AL)
Andrew J. Watson (PA)

CANDIDATES FOR VICE-PRESIDENTIAL NOMINATION:
William Daniel Dyke (WI)
Daniel Hansen (NV)
Edmund Otto Matzal (NJ)
Eileen Knowland Shearer (CA)
Tom Sloan (NJ)
Richard Art Viguerie (VA)

PRIMARIES:
JUNE 8, 1976 (CA):

Shea	3,447
Rarick	2,922
Watson	2,447
Procell	1,719
Goodloe	1,523
others	7

2ND CONVENTION:
> August 26–28, 1976, Conrad Hilton Hotel, Chicago
> (IL)
> William K. Shearer (CA), cochairman
> Arthur Cain (OH), cochairman

The American Independent Party split from George Wallace's American Party after the 1972 elections. Approximately seven hundred delegates attended the convention.

PLATFORM HIGHLIGHTS:
The lengthy platform of the American Independent Party expressed faith in God, loyalty to the nation, a belief in personal liberty and individual rights, and support for free enterprise.

SUPPORTED:
- the unrestricted right to bear arms but endorsed stiff mandatory prison sentences for the commission of crimes involving firearms
- local law enforcement agencies but wanted to abolish the Law Enforcement Assistance Administration
- the right of states to impose capital punishment
- mandatory penalties for drug offenses
- the breaking of diplomatic relations with the People's Republic of China because of its role in drug trafficking
- the "right to life" cause
- the development of private schools and the withdrawal of federal aid to education
- voluntary, nondenominational school prayer
- campaign finance disclosure
- curbs on the use of executive orders
- states' rights
- the transferring of all federal lands to the states
- nuclear power
- the construction of dams for flood control, navigation, recreation, and pollution-free power
- the gradual elimination of agricultural price supports and subsidies, but favored a protective tariff
- the restraint of regulatory agencies
- a strong merchant marine
- an end to U.S. participation in the General Agreement on Tariffs and Trade (GATT)
- a 200-mile limit on U.S. territorial fishing rights
- equal opportunity for all
- the right to collective bargaining
- limitations on immigration
- the need for "reasonable" programs of consumer protection
- a balanced budget and tax reductions, with the elimination of the graduated income tax and estate and gift taxes
- the repeal of the federal telephone tax
- an adoption of the Liberty Amendment
- the right of individuals to possess, use, and trade precious metals
- welfare reform to reduce fraud and subsidies to able-bodied persons who refuse to work

- the right to choose one's own healing practitioner or type of treatment
- the establishment of Social Security as a voluntary program, with no earnings test and protections for the integrity of the trust fund
- the withdrawal of the United States from the United Nations and ratification of the Bricker Amendment
- the retention of the Panama Canal
- friendly relations with the Republic of China on Taiwan
- the disengagement of the United States from the politics of the Middle East
- an end to hostile acts against Rhodesia and South Africa
- an end to foreign aid programs
- the abrogation of the Strategic Arm Limitations Talks Treaty
- improvements in the Reserves and National Guard
- veterans and the nation's special responsibility to servicemen missing in action (MIA) and in prisoner-of-war (POW) camps
- the recomputation of military retirement pay to correct inequities created by the Democratic Congress
- the direct election of federal judges at the district level and requirements that all other federal judges and justices be periodically reconfirmed
- the right to choose one's own counsel, rather than being restricted to choosing among members of the American Bar Association
- the restoration of the rights of juries

OPPOSED:
- regional governments and zoning laws
- the legalization of marijuana
- all forms of abortion
- federal child care programs
- the Equal Rights Amendment (ERA)
- homosexuality and obscenity
- sex education, sensitivity training, child advocacy, and other programs of agencies such as the National Institute of Mental Health
- forced busing
- election laws that discriminated against new parties and promoted an amendment of the Voting Rights Act to ensure the equality of all states in its application
- secrecy in government, demanding investigations into Watergate, John F. Kennedy's assassination, and the possible infiltration of the KGB (Soviet intelligence agency) into the Central Intelligence Agency (CIA) and Federal Bureau of Investigation (FBI)
- communism, seeking a congressional investigation into the Council on Foreign Relations and the Foreign Policy Association
- federal administration of water rights
- federal revenue sharing as a fraud on the public
- quota systems and reverse discrimination
- any government red tape that impedes small businesses, such as the Humphrey-Hawkins bill

- monopolies
- public housing and government-controlled medicine
- compulsory mass medication (i.e., fluoridation) but recognized the needs of handicapped persons to state educational and employment programs
- détente with communist nations
- a blanket amnesty for draft dodgers
- aid to Vietnam

Also:
- demanded that the United States should "never again" be engaged in battle without a declaration of war
- voiced suspicion about the loyalty of State Department personnel

---

AMERICAN INDEPENDENT PARTY
VOTE FOR PRESIDENTIAL NOMINATION:
BOTH WALLACE AND REAGAN WERE SENTIMENTAL FAVORITES FOR THE PRESIDENTIAL NOMINATION, BUT NEITHER EXPRESSED INTEREST. WILLIAM RUSHER (A CONSERVATIVE PUBLISHER) AND VIGUERIE THEN FAILED TO ENLIST SENATOR HELMS, GOVERNOR THOMSON, OR REP. PHILIP MILLER CRANE OF ILLINOIS FOR THE TOP POSITION. MADDOX WAS THUS NOMINATED ON THE FIRST BALLOT, DEFEATING MORRIS AND RARICK.

VOTE FOR VICE-PRESIDENTIAL NOMINATION:
DYKE WAS NAMED AS THE VICE-PRESIDENTIAL NOMINEE OVER VIGUERIE, WHO HAD CAMPAIGNED WITH MORRIS ON A JOINT TICKET.

AMERICAN INDEPENDENT PARTY OF NEW MEXICO

CANDIDATE FOR PRESIDENT:
Ronald Wilson Reagan (CA) (declined)

CANDIDATE FOR VICE PRESIDENT:
Edmund Gerald "Jerry" Brown, Jr. (CA)

AMERICAN MANDATE PARTY

CANDIDATE FOR PRESIDENT:
John Cole (WA)

PLATFORM HIGHLIGHTS:
The platform of the American Mandate Party demanded full national employment in eighteen months, an end to inflation in a year, and a 50 percent reduction in state, federal, and property taxes. It also called for 5l-cent first-class postage stamps.

AMERICAN MUGWUMP PARTY OF 1884

CANDIDATE FOR PRESIDENT:
William H. "Lucky Buck" Rogers (CA)

PLATFORM HIGHLIGHTS:
The American Mugwump Party had four planks in its platform: (1) complete price control, (2) no unemployment, (3) a youth opportunity program, and (4) no petroleum imports. It claimed that reduced spending and reduced employment "go hand in hand."

AMERICAN PARTY

CANDIDATE FOR PRESIDENT:
Otho Richard Barton (CA)

PLATFORM HIGHLIGHTS:
Barton called himself "the Lamb, the Lion of God, Alfla (sic) Omega, Jesus Christ Super Star, Oneness of the True Church of God." He claimed to stand "for God and Country—the United States of America—the Red, White and Blue, Stars and Stripes forever."

AMERICAN PARTY

CANDIDATE FOR PRESIDENT:
Thomas Jefferson Anderson

CANDIDATE FOR VICE PRESIDENT:
Rufus E. Shackleford

CANDIDATES FOR PRESIDENTIAL NOMINATION:
Thomas Jefferson Anderson (TN)
Ezra Taft Benson (UT)
William Harrison Bowler (AZ)
Carmen Christopher Chimento (NH)
John Bertrand Conlan, Jr. (AZ)
Marvin Lamar Cooley
Paul Edward Cunningham (PA)
Curtis Bean Dall (VA)
Richard Marvin De Vos (MI)
John Louellen Grady (FL)
Percy Laurie Greaves, Jr. (NY)
Jesse Alexander Helms, Jr. (NC)
Richard Broughton Kay (OH)
Lawrence Patton McDonald (GA)
Cecil Fay Moore (GA)
Grady Ray Motsinger, Jr. (NC)
John Richard Rarick (LA)
Ronald Wilson Reagan (CA)
Paul Emanuel Sanger (PA)
Phyllis Stewart Schlafly (IL)
David Lee Stallard (KS)
Meldrim Thomson, Jr. (NH)
Lawrence Rey Topham (UT)
George Corley Wallace (AL)

CANDIDATES FOR VICE-PRESIDENTIAL NOMINATION:
Bruce Rudolph Bangerter (UT)
William Harrison Bowler (AZ)
Marvin Lamar Cooley (AZ)
William Edward Parker (KY)
Rufus E. Shackelford (FL)

PRIMARIES:

MARCH 2, 1976 (MA):
(no names on ballot)
Wallace 86
no preference 98
others 509

APRIL 6, 1976 (WI):
(no names on ballot)
scattered write-in votes 1,033

MAY 25, 1976 (ID):
Rarick 409
Anderson 261
uncommitted delegates 92

2D CONVENTION:
June 16–20, 1976, Salt Palace, Salt Lake City (UT)
Thomas Jefferson Anderson (TN), chairman
Scott Stanley, Jr., keynoter

Although the American Party had allotted 535 delegates, only 291 members from 33 states actually participated in the convention.

PLATFORM HIGHLIGHTS:

SUPPORTED:

- the phased termination of agricultural subsidies, production and price controls, and government-owned reserves
- a protective tariff for agricultural products
- the government's divestment of Amtrak and the Postal Service
- the abolition of the Interstate Commerce Commission and the Occupational Safety and Health Administration (OSHA)
- a hands-off attitude toward business
- the restoration of the death penalty
- the elimination of plea bargaining
- a reform of the "over-permissive" parole system but demanded stiff mandatory state penalties for crimes committed with a gun
- the breaking of diplomatic relations with the People's Republic of China because of its role in illicit drug trafficking
- voluntary, nondenominational school prayer and local control of school systems
- the removal of price controls and taxes on the production and distribution of energy
- restraint by federal bureaucracies involved in consumer protection
- the abolition of the Environmental Protection Agency
- the defeat of the ERA
- the control of illegal aliens
- the constriction of the jurisdiction of federal courts and the president's authority to issue executive orders
- a phasing out of federal health care programs and the abolishment of the Professional Services Review organizations

- the gradual elimination of Social Security
- the control of welfare programs turned over to charities and state and local governments
- freedom of choice in pursuing alternative medical treatments
- the abolishment of the Federal Reserve System
- the restoration of the gold standard
- a balanced budget
- restrictions on the political activities of labor unions and on the right of government employees to engage in collective bargaining
- "right to work" laws
- an end to all zoning and land use laws and compulsory federal flood-control insurance
- the restoration of the House and Senate Internal Security committees and the Subversive Activities Control Board
- the right of states to legislate on public morality
- the abolishment of regional governments and revenue sharing
- tax reforms to level the progressivity of the income tax
- investigations of tax-exempt foundations
- the breaking of diplomatic and trade relations with all Communist countries
- the discontinuation of all foreign aid programs
- nonmilitary assistance to anti-Fidel Castro Cubans
- a ban on imports from countries employing slave labor
- the withdrawal of the United States from the Middle East and the adoption of a policy of noninvolvement
- protections for the nation's offshore resources and fishing rights to a distance of 200 miles
- U.S. sovereignty over the Panama Canal
- the ratification of the Bricker Amendment, along with the withdrawal of the United States from the United Nations
- a requirement that no foreign military action could be pursued for more than seventy-two hours without a declaration of war by Congress

OPPOSED:

- conversion to the metric system
- all gun control efforts
- federal initiatives in child care
- a repeal of compulsory education laws
- busing to achieve racial balance and all federal aid to schools
- fluoridation of water
- "socialized medicine"
- open housing laws
- the quota system
- all abortions, except when necessary to save the mother's life
- urban renewal programs
- minimum wage laws
- federal financing of elections
- secret diplomacy and the "scandal-ridden" State Department

AMERICAN PARTY
VOTE FOR PRESIDENTIAL NOMINATION:

Candidate	Ballot: 1
Anderson	160
Bowler	42⅔
Greaves	29⅔
Moore	11⅔
Cooley	10
Topham	5
Stallard	0

VOTE FOR VICE-PRESIDENTIAL NOMINATION:

Candidate	Ballot: 1
Shackelford	165½
Bowler	74⅔
Cooley	11
Parker	9
Bangerter	0

AMERICAN PARTY OF NEW JERSEY
CANDIDATE FOR PRESIDENT:
Christian F. Larson (NJ) (Lester Maddox [GA] declined)

CANDIDATE FOR VICE PRESIDENT:
Edmund Otto Matzal (NJ)

AMERICAN PEOPLE'S FREEDOM PARTY
CANDIDATE FOR PRESIDENT:
Charles Norton Averill (MD)

The American People's Freedom Party asserted a belief in the right of all citizens to govern themselves at whatever level they choose. Averill promised to "take the job" at $12,000 a year for the four-year term.

PLATFORM HIGHLIGHTS:
SUPPORTED:

- an immediate halt in the use of nuclear and atomic energy for destructive purposes and a moratorium on their peaceful use until a study was completed on the disposal of waste materials
- the direct election of the president, vice president, cabinet heads, and directors of the FBI and CIA
- limits on congressional salaries to $25,000 per year
- tax reforms to close loopholes and increase personal exemptions for low-income individuals
- the breakup of giant corporations and the immediate imposition of price controls
- a comprehensive study of the most beneficial pupil-to-teacher cost ratio and its implementation nationwide
- free college education for those unable to afford it
- full pardons for all Vietnam War resistors
- prohibitions against military service before the age of twenty-one
- freedom of choice in abortions
- restrictions on all handguns
- special status for American Indians (including the right to the sacramental use of drugs)
- the legalization of marijuana
- an end to foreign military aid
- the reestablishment of Panamanian sovereignty over the Panama Canal

AMERICAN PEOPLE'S PARTY
CANDIDATE FOR PRESIDENT:
Cecilia M. Pizzo (LA)

PLATFORM HIGHLIGHTS:
The American People's Party sought to nullify the Louisiana Purchase and the Charter of the United Nations. The platform promised to reorganize the federal government, to abolish the Federal Reserve System, and to investigate President Gerald Ford to determine his possible involvement in the Bilderbergers international financial conspiracy. Thirty-three planks enumerated assorted demands for investigations, including investigations of "the strange death of ex-FBI agent Guy Banister," the Roman Catholic Church, "internationalism," the construction of the Super Dome in New Orleans, the gold at Fort Knox, and Avondale Shipyard's contracts.

AMERICAN PEOPLE'S PARTY
CANDIDATE FOR PRESIDENT:
Thomas William Bailey (PA)

The American People's Party wanted to "give America back to the people." It promised to "save America from the present corrupt and scandal-ridden" Republican and Democratic parties. According to its candidate, it was "time for the nation to return to God."

ARCHONIST PARTY
CANDIDATE FOR PRESIDENT:
William Lyle Knaus (MN)

Archonism was defined as a "positive interpretation of the Divine Will in relation to political matters." The Archonist Party was anti-Zionist and anti-Israel, advocating an Archonist Constitution for America.

PLATFORM HIGHLIGHTS:
SUPPORTED:

- the disengagement from foreign entanglements
- the repudiation of all special interest groups
- an end to reverse discrimination
- the development of alternative energy sources

- rational and equitable controls on prices, wages, and profits
- tax reforms
- the encouragement of maximum public participation by competent leaders and qualified citizens and recommended limitations on the civic influence of unqualified and unprepared individuals

THE BLACK ASSEMBLY

CANDIDATE FOR PRESIDENT:
Frederick Douglass Kirkpatrick (NY)

CANDIDATES FOR PRESIDENTIAL NOMINATION:
Horace Julian Bond (GA)
John James Conyers, Jr. (MI)
Ronald Vernie Dellums (CA)
Richard Claxton "Dick" Gregory (IL)
Richard Gordon Hatcher (IN)
Frederick Douglass Kirkpatrick (NY)
William Owens (MA)
Barbara Ann Sizemore (PA)

PLATFORM HIGHLIGHTS:
Folk singer Kirkpatrick's platform sought full employment, health care, and insurance for all; forty acres and a tractor for African Americans; the abolition of tax loopholes; and the preservation of nature. Calling himself "a man of the common people," Kirkpatrick wanted to "take crime out of the suites" (i.e., white collar crime) and create a nonviolent economy. Kirkpatrick proclaimed his central theme—"We need each other"—through his "Declaration of Interdependence."

SUPPORTED:
- a 30 percent cut in the military budget
- the abandonment of the B-1 bomber
- the withdrawal of U.S. troops from the Philippines, Republic of Korea, and other foreign lands
- a revision of the educational curricula to teach people how to use their hands and their minds
- the return of U.S. industry from abroad
- a socialized food program that would limit food costs to 10 percent of income
- the preservation of the family farm
- the creation of socialized housing
- an end to the oil monopoly and the elimination of the oil depletion allowance
- the enforcement of the antitrust laws and an imposition of heavy fines for price fixing
- "world citizenship"
- a rotating grassroots world council on basic human needs
- an international exchange program
- reasonable defense measures
- foreign aid based on humanitarian concerns
- a return to an agriculturally dominated society and an educational system that emphasizes "sane and healthy living" and nonviolent work-education

- the defense and promotion of basic human rights
- the condemnation of the role of big business in racial discrimination and bigotry
- an attack on white-collar crime and the criminal abuses of authority in the FBI and CIA
- a decentralization of power in the cities and a respect for "seasoned citizens"

CHRISTIAN BULL MOOSE-FLYING TIGER PARTY

CANDIDATE FOR PRESIDENT:
Morton Frederick Meads (Philippine Islands)

CANDIDATE FOR VICE PRESIDENT:
William Lawrence Fields (Philippine Islands)

CONVENTION:
August 24, 1976, Manila, Philippine Islands

The Christian Bull Moose-Flying Tiger Party was also known as the "New Frontier Party."

CITIZENS' WRITE-IN VOTES FOR BETTER GOVERNMENT

CANDIDATE FOR PRESIDENT:
Tilden William Johnson (CA)

COMMANDMENTS PARTY

CANDIDATE FOR PRESIDENT:
Ivar Blomberg (MI)

The Commandments Party sought an end to such "national" vices as immorality, lack of vision, and labor union dictatorship in the United States. Proclaiming himself a "prophet," Blomberg urged free trade, capitalism, the restoration of the death penalty, and the removal of all soldiers and weapons of war from foreign lands. He asked his fellow citizens to "think about it—long and fervently."

COMMON AMERICAN PARTY

CANDIDATE FOR PRESIDENT:
Danny Page Sell (OH)

Sell formed the Common American Party because he believed it was time to return the nation to the common people. He promised to provide the country a new system, "one that offers more and for less." Also, he planned to "declare . . . unconstitutional" the section of the Constitution relating to the qualifications for president.

COMMONWEALTH PARTY OF THE UNITED STATES

CANDIDATE FOR PRESIDENT:
Anton Pirman (IL)

CANDIDATE FOR VICE PRESIDENT:
Morris Relante (TX)

The Commonwealth Party sought to create deep sea ports in Arizona and Nevada via the Gulf of California.

COMMUNIST PARTY, USA
CANDIDATE FOR PRESIDENT:
Gus Hall (NY)

CANDIDATE FOR VICE PRESIDENT:
Jarvis Tyner (NY)

21ST NATIONAL CONVENTION:
June 26–29, 1975, Ambassador West Hotel, Chicago (IL)

Approximately 150 delegates from thirty-eight states attended the convention.

PLATFORM HIGHLIGHTS:
The Communist Party's slate was announced at a press conference in New York City on February 18, 1976.

SUPPORTED:
- as its top priority, the enactment of a comprehensive national health act
- a cut in the military budget of 80 percent and using the savings to rebuild cities, to provide low-rent housing and low-interest loans for home owners, to develop mass transit, and to generate new schools and hospitals
- a thirty-hour work week without reductions in pay
- a shift in the tax burden from working people to the rich and a move to close tax loopholes
- an end to sales taxes
- an exemption from all taxes of any family incomes under $25,000
- an end to the Cold War and a normalization of relations with Cuba and the Socialist world
- reparation payments to Vietnam
- the prevention of a nuclear holocaust
- a halt to the CIA's and the Pentagon's intervention in other lands
- independence for Puerto Rico
- the abolishment of racism and racist or anti-Semitic organizations
- an expansion and enforcement of civil rights laws
- a guarantee of a secure future for youth by providing jobs and educational opportunities
- the passage of a National Youth Act and extension of unemployment benefits to young people
- an end to discrimination against women through affirmative action, criminal penalties, and guarantees of equal pay for equal work
- cost-of-living escalator clauses for Social Security benefits
- an elimination of the Medicare deductible
- free fares on local and interurban bus, rail, or air travel for the elderly
- an increase in the elderly's level of permissible earnings without risking the loss of Social Security
- the abolishment of the FBI, the CIA, and other anti-democratic agencies
- the repeal of repressive laws such as those restricting ballot access of minority parties, or S.1 (Senate bill 1), a proposal to revise the judicial code

CONSERVATIVE PARTY OF NEW YORK
CANDIDATE FOR PRESIDENT:
Gerald Rudolph Ford, Jr. (MI)

CANDIDATE FOR VICE PRESIDENT:
Robert Joseph Dole (KS)

The Conservative Party was a New York State third party. It normally endorsed the national ticket of the Republican Party.

CONSTITUTIONAL PARTY
CANDIDATE FOR PRESIDENT:
Talmadge Martin Warren (VA)

A schoolteacher, Warren sought the post as a learning experience for his eighth-grade students.

PLATFORM HIGHLIGHTS:
SUPPORTED:
- efforts to give all candidates in a primary equal media space
- a "none of the above" ballot line
- the direct election of Supreme Court justices
- a 20 percent cut in the federal payroll
- restrictions on U.S. investment in Mexico and foreign investments in U.S. businesses
- periodic open bidding for privatized government monopolies such as Amtrak and the Postal Service
- a shifting of foreign aid from the government to voluntary channels
- a national informational network in the United States
- the tracking and prosecution of industrial spies
- a nuclear-free world
- the deployment of the military in the war on drugs
- full government-provided health care for all citizens, who would closely check all health care charges
- the monitoring of the possession of semiautomatic and assault weapons
- criminals being held responsible for compensating their victims
- a child allowance for married couples with preschool children when the mother does not work outside the home for more than sixteen hours per week

OPPOSED:
- the "borrow and pay" approach to government financing

CONSTITUTIONAL PARTY OF PENNSYLVANIA

CANDIDATE FOR PRESIDENT:
Paul Edward Cunningham (PA)

PRIMARY:

APRIL 27, 1976 (PA):
Cunningham. 1,333
others 87

PLATFORM HIGHLIGHTS:

SUPPORTED:
- stronger law enforcement
- reduced government spending
- an end to inflation and deficit financing
- regular repayments on the national debt
- support payments for the aged and physically handicapped
- a constitutional amendment to limit income taxes and prohibit progressive taxation
- the removal of the Social Security programs' limits on earnings
- a repeal of federal poverty programs
- legislation to control political expenditures by organizations
- the free enterprise system
- parental freedom of choice in public schools
- improved neighborhood schools under local control
- voluntary community action to clean up the environment
- the prosecution of violators of health laws
- the jurisdiction of federal courts over labor disputes
- an end to crop subsidies and agricultural price controls
- strict limits on the use of eminent domain laws
- the privatization of all federally owned businesses that compete with private enterprise
- voluntary prayer and Bible readings in the public schools, defended by a constitutional amendment if necessary
- strong mandatory sentences for crimes committed with a gun
- the deportation of subversive aliens
- legislation to outlaw the Communist Party
- a policy of "total victory over Communism," asserting the Monroe Doctrine against Communist aggression in the Western Hemisphere
- discontinued aid and trade with Communist nations
- a foreign policy designed to preserve the "American way of life" and "sovereignty"
- a policy of burden sharing with U.S. allies, which were expected to pay for a greater share of mutual defense arrangements

OPPOSED:
- a guaranteed annual income for all
- socialism
- excessive U.S. financial support for the United Nations
- unionization and strikes by public employees
- forced busing for education
- a "giveaway" appeasement policy in foreign affairs
- gun control

CONSTRUCTIONALIST PARTY

CANDIDATE FOR PRESIDENT:
Clifford Hersted (IL)

CORRECTION, PUNISHMENT, AND REMEDY PARTY

CANDIDATE FOR PRESIDENT:
James Zalmer Hardy (KY)

PLATFORM HIGHLIGHTS:

SUPPORTED:
- a minimum-assistance welfare system, based on the recipient's age, and designed to help the destitute, disabled, and unemployed
- a retirement system that provided enough money for a decent standard of living
- computerized at-home voting
- federal and state television networks
- the promotion of health foods
- a new, unified court system to handle all cases, whether civil, criminal, or tax-related
- a "total taxpayer's clinic for all minor illnesses"
- federal domestic aid and assistance
- direct payment to taxpayers for lengthy and terminal medical cases
- a full educational curricula
- student stipends
- classes in constitutional law available to the general public
- more democratic procedures of governance
- the re-creation of the nation, dividing it into states no larger than 25 square miles in size that would ensure open residency to "unanimous thinkers"

OPPOSED:
- slavery
- criminal rule
- the "church"
- political parties

ALSO:
- condemned the existing political leadership of the country as "sick and bigoted"

CRISPUS ATTUCKS PARTY

CANDIDATE FOR PRESIDENT:
Theadore Marcus Pryor (CT)

CRUSADE FOR LOGIC

CANDIDATE FOR PRESIDENT:
John Cherry "Jack" Briggs (NM)

DEMOCRATIC PARTY

CANDIDATE FOR PRESIDENT:

James Earl "Jimmy" Carter, Jr.

CANDIDATE FOR VICE PRESIDENT:

Walter Frederick Mondale

CANDIDATES FOR PRESIDENTIAL NOMINATION:

Conrad Abbott (MA)
Frank Ahern (LA)
Stanley Norman Arnold (NY)
Reubin O'Donovan Askew (FL)
Phillip Vernon Baker (KY)
Birch Evan Bayh (IN)
Lloyd Millard Bentsen, Jr. (TX)
Arthur Owen Blessitt (FL)
Frank Joseph Bona (NY)
Horace Julian Bond (GA)
Robert L. Brewster (FL)
George Gittion Britt, Jr. (PA)
Mary Jane Britt (PA)
David V. Brooks (NC)
Edmund Gerald "Jerry" Brown, Jr. (CA)
Walter Ralph "Buck" Buchanan (CA)
James Allen Burner (WV)
Accountability Einstein Belcher Burns (OK)
Robert Carlyle Byrd (WV)
Hugh Leo Carey (NY)
Charles Joseph Carney (OH)
James Earl "Jimmy" Carter, Jr. (GA)
Albert Castro, Jr. (WI)
Caesar Estrada Chavez (CA)
Frank Forrester Church (ID)
Guy Walters Clay (KY)
Billy Joe Clegg (OK)
Charles D. Cockburn (PA)
Charles C. Compton (CA)
August "Gemini" Cook (OR)
Gilbert Cope (PA)
Norman Cousins (NY)
Vernon Mathew Dabbs (aka Josphy Edgar Hoover, Jr.) (NC)
Lawrence Joseph Sarsfield "Lar" Daly (IL)
Ronald Vernie Dellums (CA)
Gertrude Walton Donahey (OH)
Jack Dorsey (GA)
Charles Frederick Francis Eaton, Sr. (OH)
Abram Eisenman (GA)
David Cornelius Eley (MI)
Martha M. Evert (PA)
Lee Charles Falke (OH)
Walter Fauntroy (DC)
Richard E. "Bud" Flynn (CA)
Carl Floyd Freeman (GA)
Kenneth Fregoe (NY)
Louis Joseph Friedman (CA)
John Herschel Glenn, Jr. (OH)

John Samuel Gonas (IN)
Jesse Gray (NY)
David Hanley (MO)
Fred Roy Harris (OK)
Wayne Levere Hays (OH)
Hubert Horatio Humphrey (MN)
Donald L. Jackson (NY)
Henry Martin Jackson (WA)
Leon Jaworski (TX)
John H. Jenkins (TX)
Barbara Charlene Jordan (TX)
Robert Lee Kelleher (MT)
Edward Moore Kennedy (MA)
Caroline P. Killeen (NM)
Reed Larson (VA)
Rick Loewenherz (OK)
Frank M. Lomento (PA)
Brian F. Lucey (NY)
Floyd L. Lunger (NJ)
Catherine III Trinity Victoria Alix Meda Magnifico (CA)
Lucy Mayberry (DC)
John Henry McCabe (MI)
Ellen Cullen McCormack (NY)
George Stanley McGovern (SD)
Lillian A. McNally (DC)
Gary Franklin Merrill (ME)
Walter Frederick Mondale (MN)
Richard Arlis Moore (FL)
Thomas Ellsworth Morgan (PA)
Ronald Milton Mottl (OH)
Daniel Patrick Moynihan (NY)
Edmund Sixtus Muskie (ME)
Loretta M. O'Connor (NY)
Grady O'Cummings III (NY)
Walter Joseph O'Malley, Jr. (CA)
Ancel Elvin "Pat" Patton (CA)
Ralph "Shorty" Price (AL)
Jennings Fitz Randolph (WV)
James Harold Roark (FL)
Joseph Claude "Jay" Roberts (CA)
Fifi Rockefeller (KY)
George Buchanan Roden (TX)
Peter Wallace Rodino, Jr. (NJ)
Raymond Allen Peter Rollinson (NJ)
Robert John Roosevelt (MD)
Chester M. Rudnicki (MA)
Joseph A. Ryan (HI)
Vincent J. Sabitini (TX)
James Terry Sanford (NC)
Bernard B. Schechter (CA)
John Frederick Seiberling (OH)
Mitchell Francis Shaker (OH)
Milton Jerrold Shapp (PA)
Robert Sargent Shriver (MD)
John Joseph Sirica (DC)

Adlai Ewing Stevenson III (IL)
Louis Stokes (OH)
Fred William Stover (IA)
John J. Sussina (CT)
William Sweeney (MA)
Torfin Austin Teigen (ND)
Reginald Sullivan Voyle Towers (CA)
Morris King Udall (AZ)
Charles Albert Vanik (OH)
Charles Gordon Vick (TN)
Calvin J. Voelker (MN)
Donald James Von Rase (WI)
Daniel Walker (IL)
George Corley Wallace (AL)
Robert Lee Washington, Jr. (WI)
Walter Washington (DC)
Lawrence Welk (CA)
Lyle Leonard Willis (KY)
Kenneth Raymond Woodruff (MO)

CANDIDATES FOR VICE-PRESIDENTIAL NOMINATION:

Carl Bert Albert (OK)
Wendell Richard Anderson (MN)
Jerry Apodaca (NM)
Gary Edward Benoit (MA)
Thomas Bradley (CA)
Fay T. Carpenter-Swain (aka H. R. H. Fifi Rockefeller) (KY)
Frank Forrester Church (ID)
Ronald Vernie Dellums (CA)
Fritz Efaw (Great Britain) (a U.S. citizen; leader of Democrats abroad)
Peter F. Flaherty (PA)
John Herschel Glenn, Jr. (OH)
Ella Tambussi Grasso (CT)
Fred Roy Harris (OK)
Philip Aloysius Hart (MI)
Ernest Frederick "Fritz" Hollings (SC)
Barbara Charlene Jordan (TX)
Edward Moore Kennedy (MA)
Allard Kenneth Lowenstein (NY)
Edmund Sixtus Muskie (ME)
Auburn Lee Packwood (MO)
Peter Wallace Rodino, Jr. (NJ)
Raymond Allen Peter Rollinson (NJ)
Josephine E. R. A. Smith (fictitious)
Hunter Stockton Thompson (CO)
Morris King Udall (AZ)
George Corley Wallace (AL)

PRIMARIES:
FEBRUARY 24, 1976 (NH):
Carter 23,373
Udall 18,710
Bayh 12,510
Harris 8,863
Shriver 6,743

Humphrey 4,596
Jackson 1,857
Wallace 1,061
McCormack 1,007
Blessitt 828
Arnold 371
Clegg 174
Schechter 173
Bona 135
Kelleher 87
Sanford 53
Loewenherz 49
MacBride (VA) . . . .
others 1,791

Vice-presidential primary:
Packwood . . . .
Rollinson . . . .

MARCH 2, 1976 (MA):
Jackson 164,393
Udall 130,440
Wallace 123,112
Carter 101,948
Harris 55,701
Shriver 53,252
Bayh 34,963
McCormack 25,772
Shapp 21,693
Humphrey 7,851
Kennedy 1,623
Kelleher 1,603
Bentsen 364
Sanford 351
no preference 9,804
others 2,951

MARCH 2, 1976 (VT):
Carter 16,335
Shriver 10,699
Harris 4,893
McCormack 3,324
others 3,463

MARCH 9, 1976 (FL):
Carter 448,844
Wallace 396,820
Jackson 310,944
Shapp 32,198
Udall 27,235
Bayh 8,750
Blessitt 7,889
McCormack 7,595
Shriver 7,084
Harris 5,397
Byrd 5,042
Church 4,906
no preference 37,626

MARCH 16, 1976 (IL):

Carter	630,915
Wallace	361,798
Shriver	214,024
Harris	98,862
others	6,315

MARCH 23, 1976 (NC):

Carter	324,437
Wallace	210,166
Jackson	25,749
Udall	14,032
Harris	5,923
Bentsen	1,675
no preference	22,850

APRIL 6, 1976 (WI):

Carter	271,220
Udall	263,771
Wallace	92,460
Jackson	47,605
McCormack	26,982
Harris	8,185
Shriver	5,097
Bentsen	1,730
Bayh	1,255
Shapp	596
others	14,473
none of the above	7,154

APRIL 27, 1976 (PA):

Carter	511,905
Jackson	340,340
Udall	259,166
Wallace	155,902
McCormack	38,800
Shapp	32,947
Bayh	15,320
Harris	13,067
Humphrey	12,563
others	5,032

MAY 4, 1976 (DC):

Carter	10,521
Fauntroy	10,149
Udall	6,999
Washington, W.	5,161
Harris	461

MAY 4, 1976 (GA):

Carter	419,272
Wallace	57,594
Udall	9,755
Byrd	3,628
Jackson	3,358
Church	2,477
Ahern	1,487
Shriver	1,378
Bayh	824

Harris	699
McCormack	635
Eisenman	351
Bentsen	277
Bona (NY)	263
Shapp	181
Roden	153
Kelleher	139

MAY 4, 1976 (IN):

Carter	417,480
Wallace	93,121
Jackson	72,080
McCormack	31,708

MAY 11, 1976 (NE):

Church	67,297
Carter	65,833
Humphrey	12,685
Kennedy	7,199
McCormack	6,033
Wallace	5,567
Udall	4,688
Jackson	2,642
Harris	811
Bayh	407
Shriver	384
others	1,467

MAY 11, 1976 (WV):

Byrd	331,639
Wallace	40,938

MAY 18, 1976 (MD):

Brown	286,672
Carter	219,404
Udall	32,790
Wallace	24,176
Jackson	13,956
McCormack	7,907
Harris	6,841

MAY 18, 1976 (MI):

Carter	307,559
Udall	305,134
Wallace	49,204
Jackson	10,332
McCormack	7,623
Shriver	5,738
Harris	4,081
uncommitted delegates	15,853
others	3,142

MAY 25, 1976 (AR):

Carter	314,306
Wallace	83,005
Udall	37,783
Jackson	9,554
uncommitted delegates	57,152

MAY 25, 1976 (ID):
Church 58,570
Carter 8,818
Humphrey 1,700
Brown 1,453
Wallace 1,115
Udall 981
Jackson 485
Harris 319
uncommitted delegates 964

MAY 25, 1976 (KY):
Carter 181,690
Wallace 51,540
Udall 33,262
McCormack 17,061
Jackson 8,186
Rockefeller 2,305
uncommitted delegates 11,962

MAY 25, 1976 (NV):
Brown 39,671
Carter 17,567
Church 6,778
Wallace 2,490
Udall 2,237
Jackson 1,896
none of the above 4,603

MAY 25, 1976 (OR):
Church 145,394
Carter 115,310
Brown 106,812
Humphrey 22,488
Udall 11,747
Kennedy 10,983
Wallace 5,797
Jackson 5,298
McCormack 3,753
Harris 1,344
Bayh 743
others 2,963

MAY 25, 1976 (TN):
Carter 259,243
Wallace 36,495
Udall 12,420
Church 8,026
Jackson 5,672
McCormack 1,782
Harris 1,628
Brown 1,556
Shapp 507
Humphrey 109
uncommitted delegates 6,148
others 492

JUNE 1, 1976 (MT):
Church 63,448

Carter 26,329
Udall 6,708
Wallace 3,680
Jackson 2,856
no preference 3,820

JUNE 1, 1976 (RI):
Carter 18,237
Church 16,423
Udall 2,543
McCormack 2,468
Jackson 756
Wallace 507
Bayh 247
Shapp 132
uncommitted delegates 19,035

JUNE 1, 1976 (SD):
Carter 24,186
Udall 19,510
McCormack 4,561
Wallace 1,412
Harris 573
Jackson 558
no preference 7,871

JUNE 8, 1976 (CA):
Brown 2,013,210
Carter 697,092
Church 250,581
Udall 171,501
Wallace 102,292
Jackson 38,634
McCormack 29,242
Harris 16,920
Bayh 11,419
uncommitted delegates 78,595
others 215

JUNE 8, 1976 (NJ):
Carter 210,655
Church 49,034
Jackson 31,820
Wallace 31,183
McCormack 21,774
Lunger 3,935
Gray 3,574
Lomento 3,555
Rollinson 3,021
Gonas 2,288

JUNE 8, 1976 (OH):
Carter 593,130
Udall 240,342
Church 157,884
Wallace 63,953
Donahey 43,661
Jackson 35,404

37TH CONVENTION:

> July 12–15, 1976, Madison Square Garden, New York (NY)
> Lindy Boggs (LA), chairman
> Barbara Charlene Jordan (TX), keynote speaker
> John Herschel Glenn, Jr., (OH), keynote speaker

Attending this convention from every state and territory were 3,048 delegates.

PLATFORM HIGHLIGHTS:

Stating "the platform is the party's contract with the people," the lengthy 1976 Democratic Convention pledged to work for full employment, price stability, and balanced growth. The platform called on the Federal Reserve to become "a full partner" in national economic decisions and be more responsive to Congress and the president.

SUPPORTED:

- careful economic planning with annual employment, production, and price stability targets
- federal antirecession grant programs to state and local governments, public works projects, and direct stimulus to the private sector as countercyclical recession measures
- the creation of a domestic development bank and the use of federally insured taxable state and local bonds, or similar mechanisms, to encourage private-sector investment in chronically depressed areas
- the consolidation of youth employment programs
- improved training and apprenticeship, internship, and job counseling programs
- youth participation in public employment projects
- vigorous enforcement of equal opportunity laws
- the establishment of a comprehensive anti-inflation policy
- the reexamination and reform of the government regulatory structure
- the promotion of freer international trade
- lower interest rates
- the use of tax policy to maintain the real income of workers
- competition in the private sector
- a strong domestic council on price and wage stabilization that would be more selective than the comprehensive system of mandatory controls imposed by the Republican administration
- a move against anticompetitive concentrations of economic power under the antitrust laws and through encouragement of small businesses and the family farm
- aid for minority-owned small businesses and similar programs for women
- the elimination of government red tape
- the use of federal contract and procurement opportunities to expand the involvement of small firms in government business
- tax reforms to ensure equity in the tax burden, to close loopholes, to end special privileges for multinational corporations, to overhaul estate and gift tax provisions, to discourage corporate mergers and takeovers, to end discrimination against individuals on the basis of gender or marital status, and to curb expense-account deductions
- a denouncement of abuses by the Internal Revenue Service
- revisions in the Social Security tax and its programs to ensure greater equity for women and the poor
- comparable pay for comparable worth
- full enforcement of the Equal Credit Opportunity Act
- the right of agricultural workers and public employees to organize and collectively bargain
- a more efficient administration and fair enforcement of the National Labor Relations Act and the Fair Standards Act
- job-site picketing by construction workers
- the repeal of section 14 (b) of the Taft-Hartley Act
- the strengthening of OSHA laws
- a new mine safety law
- adequate compensation for the victims of black lung disease and their dependents
- the adoption of zero-based budgeting, mandatory reorganization timetables, and sunset laws to reform government
- an expanded role for the General Accounting Office and congressional agency oversight
- a restraint on the part of the president in exercising executive privilege
- government processes and members' participation open to citizen scrutiny
- an overhaul of the Hatch Act and the civil service laws to protect the Civil Service from political abuse while guaranteeing civil rights for public servants
- a revision of ethics laws to require divestiture when a potential conflict of interest might arise
- full public disclosure of financial status of major public officials
- restrictions on "revolving door" careerism
- the selection of diplomats, federal judges, and other major officials on the basis of merit instead of politics
- the regulation of lobbyists
- public financing of presidential and congressional elections
- the creation of an office of citizen advocacy in the executive branch
- government responsiveness under the Freedom of Information Act
- reductions in excessive paperwork and red tape
- a process of business accountability through strengthening "consumer sovereignty"
- the enforcement of antitrust, health, and safety laws
- a greater use of paraprofessionals to reduce costs
- federal standards for state no-fault insurance programs
- full funding for neighborhood legal services for the poor
- the development of product performance standards
- improved labeling and advertising requirements

- stronger consumer grievance and small claims court procedures
- improvements in the U.S. Postal Service
- wholesomeness of consumer products
- a comprehensive national health insurance system with universal and mandatory coverage that would "not discriminate against the mentally ill"
- a health care program that would emphasize prevention, protections for the personal relationships between physicians and their patients, an increase in aid to government laboratories and private institutions searching for the cures to dread diseases, and more community-based care and primary health care providers within the system
- community mental health centers and ways to increase their access by underserved populations
- "fundamental welfare reform"—a simplified system of income maintenance based on available work for those able to perform it
- a phased reduction of local and state contributions to welfare
- "compensatory opportunities" for historically denied populations (e.g., affirmative action programs)
- the ratification of the ERA and full implementation of Title IX program's requirements
- a liberalization of voting rights laws, including mail registration
- home rule and congressional representation for the District of Columbia
- self-determination for Puerto Rico
- the observance of Dr. Martin Luther King's birthday as a federal holiday
- pardons for war resistors (on a case-by-case basis for deserters)
- protections for citizens' right to privacy
- the Supreme Court decision in Roe v. Wade
- respect for and implementation of American Indian treaty rights and reexamination of the role of the Bureau of Indian Affairs
- the easier attainment of citizenship by resident aliens
- compensatory education programs such as Title 1 and Head Start
- promises of federal aid for programs for the handicapped and bilingual, vocational, adult, and early childhood education
- the creation of developmental and educational child care programs
- demands for compliance with civil rights requirements in hiring and promotion within school systems
- state-based school district equalization
- libraries, teacher traineeships and internships, and basic and applied research (in the liberal arts, humanities, and professions)
- school desegregation, while proclaiming busing was "a judicial tool of last resort"
- federal aid for pupils in nonsegregated private and parochial schools
- a commitment to Basic Educational Opportunity grants and other aid and loan programs to help young people attend the college or university of their choice
- raises in social service grant programs to compensate for inflation
- the recognition of the needs of disabled citizens (including affirmative action in employment)
- health security for older citizens
- protections of the elderly's Social Security benefits
- the enforcement of nursing home standards
- employment, nutrition, and transportation programs
- efforts to address concerns regarding employment, job training, health care, and pension benefits for veterans
- adequate funding for the National Endowment for the Arts and Humanities, along with a revision of tax laws that penalize creative work
- funding for public broadcasting as well as antirecessionary job programs for artists, authors, and performers
- the development of the nations' first urban policy of emergency antirecession aid to states and cities
- general revenue sharing between the Federal government and the states
- a revitalized housing program with direct federal subsidies and low-interest loans to encourage construction of low- and moderate-income housing and housing for the elderly and to rehabilitate existing housing stock
- the preservation of historic landmarks
- a reinvigoration of the Federal Housing Administration
- the enforcement of the Fair Housing Act
- demands for a swift, certain, and just criminal justice system
- the prosecution of white-collar crime and consumer fraud
- programs to combat abuse of children and the elderly
- a major reform of the justice system, while reaffirming the importance of civil liberties in any criminal code revision
- criticism of the Law Enforcement Assistance Agency
- the value of law enforcement's community relations activities
- a strong effort to end "the vicious cycle of drug addictions and crime"
- stronger gun control laws along with mandatory sentences for people who commit crimes involving guns
- local police forces (e.g., in recruitment, training, equipment, working conditions, and benefits), a reform of bail and pretrial detention procedures, an increased number of judges and prosecutors, and better courtroom management and record keeping
- efforts to give victimless crimes lower priority than crimes against the person and revisions of rape laws to eliminate discriminatory features directed against the victims
- infrastructure improvements to roads, bridges, and highways; mass transit; and a revitalization of the railroads, trucking, bus, inland waterway, and air transportation systems
- the expanded use of renewable energy resources

- the promotion of energy conservation through the establishment of national building performance standards, reforms of utility rate structures, automobile efficiency standards and appliance labeling requirements, and home owners' incentives to make conservation investments
- increased coal production but subject to environmental and occupational safety controls
- revisions in the leasing of federal reserves on public lands and the outer continental shelf to increase the benefit to the federal treasury and to ensure greater protection for the environment
- more research directed toward resolving the problems of nuclear waste, reactor safety, and nuclear safeguards but a de-emphasis on nuclear power
- calls for a long-range assessment of mineral reserves
- full implementation of the Rural Development Act of 1972
- family farms and the condemnation of nonfarm conglomerates but applauded farm cooperatives and bargaining associations
- improvements in the living conditions of rural citizens
- a simplification of the federal grant process
- expansions of the international market for agricultural products
- import restrictions on agricultural goods
- parity for farm commodities
- "full production" of crops with excess crops stored for famine
- the Capper-Volstead Act
- easier access to farm credit, energy resources, transportation, and utilities
- soil conservation and the elimination of tax shelter farming
- a tax overhaul to protect family farms
- the development of domestic fisheries through ecologically sound conservation practices
- stronger enforcement of environmental protections against air and water pollution and harmful chemicals
- the management of public lands—whether forests, wilderness areas, deserts, coastal beaches, barrier dunes, or other "precious resources"—to protect them for future generations
- recycling and environmental research and development
- promises to involve Congress in foreign policy decisions and to pursue the expansion of human rights as a basic objective of diplomacy
- reciprocal and orderly reductions in trade barriers
- the coordination of U.S. monetary policies with European and Japanese allies
- a stronger merchant marine
- the establishment of international mechanisms for the control of multinational corporations
- limits on international development of atomic energy and the proliferation of nuclear weapons

- the International Fund for Agricultural Development and revisions of the Food for Peace program
- efforts to tie foreign aid to human rights
- the promotion of effective family planning and population control
- the work on international environmental concerns within the structure of the United Nations
- the protection of the criminal justice rights of U.S. citizens abroad
- diplomatic efforts to curb international drug traffic
- reductions in defense spending while ensuring a strong military deterrent capability with upgrades in U.S. conventional forces, especially the navy
- strong congressional oversight of covert intelligence activities
- stable relations between the United States and the Soviet Union, avoiding excesses, hope, or fear
- negotiations with nuclear nations for nuclear disarmament and arms control and to expand trade opportunities, all within a human rights context
- the United Nations but called for certain reforms
- the North Atlantic Treaty Organization (NATO), the European Community, and peaceful settlements of the conflicts in Cyprus and Northern Ireland

DEMOCRATIC PARTY
Vote for Presidential Nomination:

Candidate	Ballot: 1	1a
Carter	2,238½	2,468½
Udall	329½	329½
Brown	300½	70½
Wallace	57	57
McCormack	22	0
Church	19	0
Humphrey	10	0
Jackson	10	0
Harris	9	0
Shapp	2	0
Byrd	1	0
Chavez	1	0
Jaworski	1	0
Jordan	1	0
Kennedy	1	0
Randolph	1	0
Stover	1	0
"Nobody"	½	
not voting	3	

Carter was subsequently nominated by acclamation, the rules having been suspended after the switches.

Vote for Vice-Presidential Nomination:
MONDALE WAS NOMINATED FOR VICE PRESIDENT ON THE FIRST BALLOT.

- Israel's independence and a peaceful resolution of the tensions in the Middle East
- the recognition of Jerusalem as Israel's capital (and calls to move the U.S. Embassy there)
- open access to the Suez
- continued friendship and cooperation with Japan and the Republic of Korea, gradual withdrawal of U.S. troops from the Korean peninsula, and further improvements in U.S. relations with the People's Republic of China
- a new Panama Canal Treaty, the Good Neighbor Policy, and Alliance for Progress and opposed normal relations with Cuba until it met a number of conditions
- the Sanhel Development Plan in Africa, demands for majority rule in Southern Africa and denial of recognition for "pseudo-independent" homelands, UN sanctions against Rhodesia, and ways to normalize relations with Angola

OPPOSED:
- redlining
- government bugging, wiretaps, and mail opening
- the "horizontal" concentration of economic power of energy companies simultaneously engaged in oil and coal production

EAGLE PARTY

CANDIDATE FOR PRESIDENT:
Lucy Mayberry (DC)

CANDIDATE FOR VICE PRESIDENT:
Edmund Gerald "Jerry" Brown, Jr. (CA)

FEDERALIST DEMOCRATIC-REPUBLICAN PARTY

CANDIDATE FOR PRESIDENT:
David G. Hamby (IL)

FEDERALIST PRESERVER PARTY

CANDIDATE FOR PRESIDENT:
Wallace Snow, Jr. (NJ)

PLATFORM HIGHLIGHTS:
Calling on Christian churchgoers to support his candidacy, Snow proclaimed his election strategy as a "knowathon" in which people who knew him would contact others in an expanding pyramid of supporters. Snow was also convinced his mail was being confiscated by the Post Office for political reasons.

SUPPORTED:
- the two-party system of government
- efforts to eliminate the deficit and to promote economic recovery
- quality education in safe schools
- efforts to make the urban United States safer

- assistance to the transportation industry
- aid for the American Medical Association in establishing a first-rate medical system
- improvements in the living standard of senior citizens
- "a military of maximum deterrence"
- policemen, firemen, unions, corporations, and industries
- incentives for broad-based international economic, military, and political participation in the common objectives of the United States and its allies

ALSO:
- declared its president would "lead, manipulate, stipulate, procrastinate, manage, correlate, expedite, methodize, trust in God, trust in America, beg, and order"

FREEDOM PARTY

CANDIDATE FOR PRESIDENT:
Ron Veatch (TX)

The Freedom Party announced its formation in a classified advertisement in the New Times magazine. Nothing was heard from the party after its formation.

HEVAN ON EARTH PARTY

CANDIDATE FOR PRESIDENT:
James Leroy Modrell Evans (TX)

The Hevan (sic) on Earth Party condemned the social problems caused by money, asserted the primacy of the Bible, and promised favors to no one. Evans, a deep sea fisherman, was its only member. He railed against usury, opposed gun control, and wanted to abolish the financial system of the country. He believed that the original humans were organized into seven races—white, yellow, black, purple, pink, gray, and red. His lengthy statements suggested that he bore the marks of the crucifixion and that humanity's ancestors came from flying saucers. He suggested rewriting the U.S. Constitution, making children his top priority, creating a "peace rangers" program, and establishing a "Freedom of Love Society" to provide everyone with a mate.

HOLY SPIRIT PARTY

CANDIDATE FOR PRESIDENT:
Paul Willard Engvalson (CA)

According to Engvalson, the Holy Spirit Party was created because God told him to run. Engvalson also asserted that his wife had given birth to John the Harbinger by immaculate conception in 1973. He claimed that a comet from God brought about the Watergate revelations and "broke the negative force field that had been set up" by the Antichrist. In a letter to President Ford, Engvalson admitted his penchant for "swearing" and using four-letter words but suggested he was ready and willing to help the president resolve the nation's problems.

INDEPENDENT
CANDIDATES FOR PRESIDENT:
Joseph R. Abizaid (MA)
Joseph Cockrell Adams, Jr. (TN)
Steven George "Stuart" Aldea (NY)
Victoria Anton (NY)
E. M. Ard (AL)
Jefferson Taswell Baker, Jr. (TX)
Claude Thomas Ballard (TX)
Jack Benny (MS)
Shirley Marie Oakes Bothwell (MD)
Accountability Einstein Belcher Burns (OK)[1]
Jack S. Caldwell (MA)
Vincent J. Carey (NY)
Norman Franklin Cates (FL)
Richard Chandler Collins (CA)
Charles F. Coombs (NY)
Donald Cregan (FL)
Jimmy H. Cude (TX)
Baba Ram Dass (aka Richard Alpert) (CA)
Katherine A. Deanglis (OH) (vice president)
Charles Wesley De Shon (MO)
Richard A. Dickerman (MO)[2]
Milton J. Dukes (SC)
James Henry Eason (CA)
James Holloway Edwards (NY)
Richard Hastings Englefield (OH)
Michael J. Estocin (PA)[3]
Edward Frank Frey (CA)
Jonathan Malcolm Friedman (NJ)
Donald L. Frietas (CA)
Fielding L. Fry II (MD)
Patrick William Gabor (VA)
Edward Earl Gentry (LA)
Malcombe George (CA)
Paul Martin Geyer (NJ)
Herbert R. Ginsberg (MS)
James Irvin Glover (NJ)
Shenandoah Goldenghost (AZ)

Ernest Green (OR)
Jodie Grossman (NY)
Johnnie Mae Hackworthe (TX)[4]
Frank Little John Haile (TN)
Charles A. Hanisco (PA)
Anthony Stephen Harrington (DC)
Aaron Lee Haskew (NM)
Jessie Hatcher (IN)
Paul Anthony Hein, Jr., (MO)[5]
James Lynn Heisterkemp (CA)
Elizabeth B. Henderson (PA)
Robert Vernon Herndon (KY)
Lester Higby, Sr. (CA)
Marie Louise "Peggy" Hoenig (NY)
Guy V. Houston (FL)
Artis Gaines Isaac (OK)
Stanley Jucus (FL)
John M. Kennedy (FL)
Robert J. Kilpatrick (OH)
Clayton Dale Klahre (PA)
Paul T. Lanyhow (unknown)
Otha Leverette (FL)
Americus Liberator (NE)
Monte Harris Liebman (WI)
Catherine III Trinity Victoria Alix Meda Magnifico (CA)
John Herbert Marken (CA)
Sidney A. Marshall (ND)
Jim McCarley (CA)
William J. McCormick (PA)
Eugene James McMahon (NY)
Josephine Ann Rudd Miller (IN)
James Arnold Mobley (TN)
Nora Morome (CA)[6]
Ralph Nader (CT)
Alice K. Nephew (NY)
Terrance O'Connor (MA)
Ethel I. Oliver (MI)
Lucy Parker (IN)
Ancel Elvin "Pat" Patton (CA)

[1]A promoter of the "MARS-EARS Project," Burns claimed the "particulars" of his campaign were a "state secret, being compiled by either the CIA or FBI." His "project" was a nonprofit enterprise for "bringing accountability to the environment." He advocated automation, humanization, and universal and continuous accountability through auditing and evaluation.
[2]Dickerman's candidate for vice president was Lawrence Maxeiner of Missouri.
[3]A serviceman missing in action in Vietnam, Estocin's family sponsored his candidacy to dramatize the plight of the families of POWs and MIAs.
[4]Running because "the Lord told me to," Hackworthe was most noted for her predictions of the destruction of Presidents Dwight Eisenhower and Lyndon Johnson. Both prophecies resulted in her arrests for threatening public officials.
[5]Hein, a doctor, sought a guaranteed right to life for all citizens from the moment of conception. He also urged the repeal of the Sixteenth Amendment, which authorized income taxes, and a drastic reduction in the size of the federal government.
[6]Morome's campaign platform promised to end all antipoverty programs, welfare assistance, social security payments, and unemployment insurance benefits. Instead, the "Morome Plan" offered an $8,000 annual government grant to married women with a family income of $6,000 or less, on the condition that they would make a commitment to remain full-time housewives; single men and women without income would receive food stamps and rent-free housing; unemployed youth would be guaranteed government jobs; and national health insurance would be provided to everyone. Morome favored limiting abortions to the first trimester, opposed school busing, and demanded serious disciplinary action against drug use in schools.

U. Utah Phillips (UT)[1]
Princess Fifi Taft-Clay Pickwildliferunningwaters
    (KY)[2]
Crown Robbins (aka R. C. Hill) (IL)
Orlan Ardell Saucke (TN)
Christopher Schillaci (NY)
O. B. A. Schmidt (TX)
Rochelle M. Scott (PA)
K. Core Seaman (CO)
Donald Joseph Shannon (MI)
Arthur C. Shultz (IN)
H. J. "Jim" Sieger (MO)
Sam "Mr. Clean" Silverstein (NY)[3]
Jerold S. Slate (NY)
Martin Spahr, Sr. (CT)
Carl F. Stelman (NY)
Joan Stoliker (CA)
Florence Joy Talbow (AZ)
Roger H. Taylor (IL)
Ralph Dean Templeton (WA)
Michael Derek Tregenza (England)
Joseph Howard Tucker (GA)
William F. Tucker (RI)
Arthur Tully (CA)
Joseph John Tydlaska (NM)
Ira R. Waggoner (IL)
Sam Wallace (AL)
George Washington (IL)
Byron Chester Wentworth (MA)
Gordon Held Wharton (TX)
Michael Woytowich (PA)
Joseph Peter Zarnowski (NJ)

INDEPENDENT CHRISTIAN PARTY

CANDIDATE FOR PRESIDENT:
Calvin Carl Ehinger (CA)

City Councilman Ehinger hoped to reach all Christians with his political message by traveling across the nation and working at odd jobs. His campaign was marked by his good-natured sense of humor.

[1]Phillips ran as the "sloth and indolence" candidate, urging voters to vote for themselves. If elected, he promised to take possession of the White House and do nothing. His running mate, Mallard Fillmore, was a fictitious character.
[2] Pickwildliferunningwaters had Guy Walters (Rockefeller) Taft of Kentucky as her running mate.
[3] Silverstein was promoted as a candidate by Alan Abel, who, together with his wife, also created the legendary Yetta Bronstein (q.v.). Silverstein "promised nothing," arguing that he could deliver on his promise. His platform demanded that congressmen be taken off salary and placed on commission. He supported gun ownership but urged that the velocity of bullets be decreased 98 percent. He wanted to put nudes on postage stamps, compel physicians to publish their medical school grades, and require insurance companies to sell no-fault suicide insurance. Silverstein would have abolished the income tax and levied a gross weight tax instead, charging one dollar per pound of body weight.

INDEPENDENT (COMMITTEE FOR A CONSTITUTIONAL PRESIDENCY)

CANDIDATE FOR PRESIDENT:
Eugene Joseph McCarthy (MN)

CANDIDATES FOR VICE PRESIDENT:
Dennis McCarty Anderson (OH)
Marlene K. Barrett (MO)
Rollie James Bartlett (KY)
John Francis Callahan (OR)
Sheila Coyne Carnac O'Day (CA)
John Ernest Clay (IL)
Anthony Owen Colby (IA)
Magdalene Ruth Downey (WI)
William Clay Ford (MI) (withdrew)
Karl Gruhn (MN)
M. C. Hansborough (DC)
Patricia O'Brien Holland (NH)
Alma J. Johnson (GA)
Sharon Lee Stone Kilpatrick (VA)
Hugh Wilson Long III (LA)
Donald Layton Lucas (ME)
Carl Maxey (WA)
William Morris (CT)
Phyllis J. Paine (NE)
Sally J. Sommers (MT)
Terrence J. Spencer (NY)
Duane Francis Stein (IA)
John Hartzell Stouffer (MA)
Mary Ann Surges (CO)
Donald H. Taylor (MI)
Robert Augustine Toal (TN)
Patricia Perkins Weymouth (MI)
Sally Louise Wheaton (PA)
Nancy Tate Wood (NY)

CANDIDATES FOR VICE-PRESIDENTIAL NOMINATION:
Dennis McCarty Anderson (OH)
Marlene K. Barrett (MO)
Rollie James Bartlett (KY)
John Francis Callahan (OR)
Sheila Coyne Carnac O'Day (CA)
John Ernest Clay (IL)
Anthony Owen Colby (IA)
Magdalene Ruth Downey (WI)
William Clay Ford (MI) (withdrew)
Karl Gruhn (MN)
M. C. Hansborough (DC)
Patricia O'Brien Holland (NH)
Alma J. Johnson (GA)
Sharon Lee Stone Kilpatrick (VA)
Hugh Wilson Long III (LA)
Donald Layton Lucas (ME)
Charles McCurdy Mathias (MD)
Carl Maxey (WA)
Thomas McCall (OR)

William Morris (CT)
Phyllis J. Paine (NE)
Sally J. Sommers (MT)
Terrence J. Spencer (NY)
Duane Francis Stein (IA)
John Hartzell Stouffer (MA)
Mary Ann Surges (CO)
Donald H. Taylor (MI)
Robert Augustine Toal (TN)
Patricia Perkins Weymouth (MI)
. Sally Louise Wheaton (PA)
Nancy Tate Wood (NY)

INDEPENDENT DEMOCRAT

CANDIDATE FOR PRESIDENT:
John Frank Demko (CT)

INDEPENDENT DEMOCRAT

CANDIDATE FOR PRESIDENT:
Robert Lee Washington, Jr. (WI)

Washington promised, if elected, to "uphold the U.S. Constitution." He was otherwise silent during the campaign.

INDEPENDENT "MAMMON" PARTY

CANDIDATE FOR PRESIDENT:
Reginald Sullivan Voyle Towers (CA)

The Independent "Mammon" Party advocated a guaranteed federal job for everyone under a plan called "Work Well." It proclaimed the right of self-defense but suggested that negotiation was the truer form of "self-knowledge." It cautioned the world to beware the terrorist or individual who might "foist a decision on us all leading to a point of nuclear no-return."

INDEPENDENT OF VERMONT

CANDIDATE FOR PRESIDENT:
James Earl "Jimmy" Carter, Jr. (GA)

CANDIDATE FOR VICE PRESIDENT:
Walter Frederick Mondale (MN)

INDEPENDENT REPUBLICRAT

CANDIDATE FOR PRESIDENT:
Keith Knowles Stone (FL)

Stone promoted an end to inflation by gradually decreasing all federal wages and the wages of all firms doing business with the government to those in 1950. His platform indicated he supported an end capital punishment, to the "dope traffic" and water pollution, and slowing down foreign imports. He opposed government worker unions, crime, dishonesty in government, and compulsory insurance.

INNOVATIVE TICKET

CANDIDATE FOR PRESIDENT:
Thomas Chester Bryant (TN)

PLATFORM HIGHLIGHTS:
SUPPORTED:

- the restoration of prayer and Bible reading in public schools
- the elimination of bureaucratic agencies
- an end to deficit spending and inflation
- incentives for the private sector to increase productivity
- modernization of the military
- the creation of two new states—one in the Deep South and another in the Far West—to be built by the unemployed of the country
- a five-year moratorium on interest being charged on the national debt
- nuclear fusion

KOSMOCRACY TICKET

CANDIDATE FOR PRESIDENT:
Rosa Der Sarkisian (CA)

Claiming to be "Messiah God Rosa the Rose," Der Sarkisian declared, "Time has run out. The funeral of democracy is set. . . . [Now] you are automatically reaffirming my dictatorship of Kosmokracy" (sic). She advised people to "stop asking all your wasteful, idiotic questions!" She defined Kosmocracy as the "counter to centrifugal force." According to Der Sarkisian, "Formerly the entire universe was gyrating to perpetually avoid all centrality and merger in order to eternally perpetuate the absolute camouflage of duality. Now I have personally reset the entire course of things. All directions, polarities, extremities, avoidances, etc., now automatically turn inward rather than outward."

KU KLUX KLAN PARTY

CANDIDATE FOR PRESIDENT:
Dale Richard Reusch (OH)

CANDIDATE FOR VICE PRESIDENT:
Scott Monroe Nelson (TX)

The Ku Klux Klan Party, an outgrowth of the National Knights of the Ku Klux Klan, was also known as the "Americans for America" Party. Its ticket was announced at the annual meeting of the National Knights of the Ku Klux Klan on September 2, 1974, in Atlanta and ratified by the Imperial Board of the National Knights on December 14, 1974, in Stone Mountain (GA).

PLATFORM HIGHLIGHTS:
SUPPORTED:

- a call to move the national capital to Nebraska
- an end to foreign aid
- the tightening of immigration laws

- welfare reform to prevent fraud and abuse by recipients
- the death penalty
- prayer in schools
- a strong national defense
- segregation, with repatriation of "Black people" to Africa
- "White supremacy," with racial identity education taught in the public schools
- agricultural subsidies
- states' rights

OPPOSED:

- intermarriage across racial lines
- communism
- the Federal Reserve System
- compulsory school busing
- the United Nations
- regional government
- gun control
- high taxes

LEAGUE OF WOMEN VOTERS

CANDIDATE FOR PRESIDENT:
Lucy Peters Wilson Benson (MA)

LIBERAL PARTY OF NEW YORK

CANDIDATE FOR PRESIDENT:
James Earl "Jimmy" Carter, Jr. (GA)

CANDIDATE FOR VICE PRESIDENT:
Walter Frederick Mondale (MN)

The Liberal Party was a New York State third party. It normally endorsed the national candidates of the Democratic Party.

LIBERTARIAN PARTY

CANDIDATE FOR PRESIDENT:
Roger Lea MacBride

CANDIDATE FOR VICE PRESIDENT:
David Peter Bergland

CANDIDATES FOR PRESIDENTIAL NOMINATION:
David Peter Bergland (CA)
Kathleen G. "Kay" Harroff (OH)
Robert S. Loomis (CT)
Roger Lea MacBride (VA)
Guy W. Riggs (NY)
Murray Newton Rothbard (NY)

CANDIDATES FOR VICE-PRESIDENTIAL NOMINATION:
David Peter Bergland (CA)
Walter Edward Block (NY)
Manuel Stuart "Manny" Klausner (CA)
Theodore Nathalia "Tomie" Nathan (OR)
Jim Trotter (CA)
John Richard Vernon (OK)

2D CONVENTION:
August 28-September 1, 1975, Statler Hilton Hotel, New York (NY)

Delegates from thirty-five states and the District of Columbia attended this convention.

PLATFORM HIGHLIGHTS:
The platform grounded itself in the "fundamental principle" that no one should initiate force against anyone else (whether individual, group, or government). Impartial and consistent law enforcement was seen as the way to suppress crime.

SUPPORTED:

- the repeal of all "victimless crime" laws, such as those relating to drug use, consensual sexual relations (including prostitution and homosexuality), gambling, and suicide
- due process for those accused of crimes
- restitution laws for those wrongfully injured by criminal proceedings and for the victims of crimes
- an end to certain involuntary mental health treatments (e.g., aversion therapy, psychosurgery, and drug therapy), as well as funding for community mental health centers
- freedom of religion
- a voluntary census
- the rights of gays and lesbians to serve in the military and amnesty for draft evaders and deserters
- the right to hold private property
- the right of collective bargaining and secondary boycotts
- free trade, unfettered by government regulation or subsidies
- private ownership of gold
- a repeal of all legal tender laws, a drastic reduction in taxes and government spending, an end to deficit budgets, and a halt to inflationary monetary policies
- the abolition of the Federal Reserve System
- the repeal of wage and price controls
- the abolishment of the Tariff Commission and Customs Court, the government-owned Postal Service, the Food and Drug Administration, OSHA, the Federal Power Commission, the Environmental Protection Agency, and the Federal Energy Administration
- the right of citizens to challenge the ways in which taxes were spent, the repeal of the Sixteenth Amendment, amnesty for all tax protesters, and the eventual elimination of all taxes
- the decontrol of energy resources and privatization of the atomic energy industry
- private business taking over the public domain, but the rights of private property holders to advance technology and expand production were to be defended
- the reform of the nuisance and negligence laws to cover air, water, and noise pollution
- regulations against consumer fraud and misrepresentation but not paternalistic regulations that restricted free choice

- a tax-credit system to encourage private schools and a steady reduction in tax support for public schools
- welfare reform by eliminating the minimum wage law, protective legislation for women and children, regulation of day care centers, the National Labor Relations Act, and all public "aid to the poor" and relief programs
- the deregulation of the medical insurance industry and malpractice reform
- a repeal of compulsory medical treatment laws
- voluntary restrictive covenants on land use
- the reconfiguration of Social Security as a voluntary system
- the abolition of the Civil Service system
- the abrogation of campaign finance laws
- a liberalization of ballot access laws
- injunctions against "entangling alliances"
- negotiations for international disarmament
- immediate independence for American Samoa, Guam, Micronesia, Puerto Rico, and the Virgin Islands
- the withdrawal of the United States from the United Nations
- a neutral stance toward the Middle East

OPPOSED:

- "no fault" insurance laws
- involuntary commitment for mental health treatment as well as expenditures on behalf of psychiatric and psychological research and treatment
- regulations for broadcasting as an infringement on freedoms of speech and the press (including requirements for "fairness" and "equal time")
- the Federal Communications Act and tax funding for public television and radio
- unwarranted government secrecy
- all invasions of privacy by government, which included abolition of internal security agencies, congressional subpoena powers, the FBI, and the CIA
- gun control in all forms, along with compulsory military service and the Uniform Code of Military Justice
- the National Labor Relations Act, and discrimination against individuals on the basis of gender, race, color, creed, age, national origin, or sexual preference
- government efforts to regulate private discrimination in employment, housing, and so-called public accommodations
- laws governing fluoridation, controlled substances, the 55-mile-per-hour speed limit, safety belts, air bags, and crash helmets
- compulsory education, public financing of schools, and compulsory busing
- public health care programs and national health insurance, Medicare and Medicaid, Professional Standards Review organizations, and health planning activities

- government zoning laws, urban renewal, building codes, eminent domain, and other land use restrictions as violations of property rights
- foreign aid programs
- the Export-Import Bank, World Bank, and International Monetary Fund
- the claims of the United Nations to ocean property
- all international monetary schemes, demanding that the United States withdraw from them
- the president's war powers
- U.S. military forces being stationed abroad
- multilateral and bilateral commitments such as NATO and the Monroe Doctrine
- the Logan Act

ALSO:

- cautioned that "our silence about any other particular government law, regulation, ordinance, directive, edict, control, regulatory agency, activity, or machination should not be construed to imply approval"

LIBERTARIAN PARTY
VOTE FOR PRESIDENTIAL NOMINATION:

Candidate	Ballot: 1
MacBride	142
Bergland	unreported
Harroff	62
Loomis	unreported
Riggs	32
Rothbard	unreported
abstentions	6

VOTE FOR VICE-PRESIDENTIAL NOMINATION:

Candidate	Ballot: 1	2	3
Bergland			
Block			
Klausner			
Nathan			
Trotter			
Vernon			

Votes unrecorded, Bergland was nominated on 3d ballot.

MILLENIUM (SIC) PARTY

CANDIDATE FOR PRESIDENT:
Elton Robert Maas (OR)

CANDIDATE FOR VICE PRESIDENT:
Frank Forrester Church (ID)

The Millenium Party sought to bring about an ideal age based on Edward Bellamy's book, Looking Backward: 2000

1887. Candidate Mass asserted that he would apply "true science" to create a "perfect social order." He urged a reduction in government waste, less advertising, and less insurance. A mystic, Maas supported unconventional cancer cures, technocracy, biblical prophecy, Scientology, and monetary reform.

NATIONAL AMERICAN BICENTENNIAL PARTY

CANDIDATE FOR PRESIDENT:
David Cornelius Eley (MI)

PLATFORM HIGHLIGHTS:

While opposed to segregation, Eley, who was the founder of the National American Bicentennial Party, did not favor forced school busing. Instead, he advocated student choice, with an annual poll among young people determining who would attend segregated schools and who would attend integrated schools. His slogan was "Let's be real."

SUPPORTED:

- a limited, part-time public/private employment program to give jobs to all who need them
- greater judicial latitude in dealing with criminals while opposing more prison construction
- welfare as a way of preventing class warfare, declaring that "punishing the poor for being poor must stop"
- suggestions that Social Security and retirement benefits be phased-in on a coordinated basis with the phaseout of gainful employment
- the free use of agricultural lands idled by crop controls in order to raise food for nutritionally deprived populations

ALSO:

- claimed that "war as a social institution has exhausted its constructive energy" and proposed a twenty-five-year moratorium on war and on the development of new weapon systems
- questioned U.S. foreign policy toward Africa, Cuba, and the Soviet Union

NATIONAL CHRISTIAN PARTY (NPA)

CANDIDATE FOR PRESIDENT:
Ceil Evan Brown (FL)

CANDIDATE FOR VICE PRESIDENT:
Michael Voss (FL)

Brown, an African-American woman, created the National Christian Party on July 26, 1963.

PLATFORM HIGHLIGHTS:
SUPPORTED:

- the legalization of unconventional cancer cures (especially the coffee enema)
- a presidency made up of eight to ten men promoted through the ranks of Congress, instead of the quadrennial "winner-take-all" system
- disarmament

- a cap on interest rates
- a balanced budget
- better working conditions
- "Moral Rearmament"
- a return to the principles of the Bible
- a Peace Corps "in reverse," with teachers from abroad imported to U.S. schools
- a greater emphasis on music, agriculture, small stock farming, carpentry, and other manual skills in school
- the elimination of poverty
- massive reforms in the judiciary, medicine, taxes, housing, land management, and employment

OPPOSED:

- forced integration

NATIONAL INDEPENDENCE PARTY

CANDIDATE FOR PRESIDENT:
Accountability Einstein Belcher Burns (OK)

NATIONAL SURREALIST PARTY

CANDIDATE FOR PRESIDENT:
George G. Papoon (KS)

CANDIDATE FOR VICE PRESIDENT:
George Leroy Tirebiter (CA)

CONVENTION:
July 31-August 1, 1976, La Casa de la Raza, Santa Barbara (CA)

The National Surrealist Party was founded by the Firesign Theatre in 1968 in Hollywood (CA).

PLATFORM HIGHLIGHTS:

Campaigning in the nude, Papoon advocated "one organism, one vote" and "one man, one channel." Membership in the party was open to animals of all kinds, including aliens from outer space. The party was concerned with the question, "What is reality?" and hoped to raise awareness of multiple realities.

SUPPORTED:

- the "miniaturization" of the bureaucracy
- a diversification of the income tax
- deregulation of the banks
- the people's control over the country's natural resources
- local governments returning power to their constituents
- the removal of the "Kissenrockafordafeller rascals" from office to suspend them for eternity over Secaucus (NJ)
- the conversion of "fossil fools" to the cause of renewable resources
- the creation of a cabinet-level Department of Chance to run a national lottery
- a mentholated paper currency

NEW AMERICAN MAJORITY PARTY

CANDIDATE FOR PRESIDENT:
Shannon John Hannah (PA)

NEW WORKERS PARTY

CANDIDATE FOR PRESIDENT:
Leonard Morgensen Andersen (NY)

PLATFORM HIGHLIGHTS:

SUPPORTED:
- a "Workers' Bill of Rights" that included the right and means to participate in politics
- the right to reeducate "parasites" vigorously
- the right to use public media
- the right to employment
- the right to equality and brotherhood
- the right to have children and have them protected
- a federal program to offer young people a choice between productive work and one year of involuntary "labor education"
- legalized gambling
- limits on campaign contributions to the party to $500 per person
- the creation of a "semi-underground election organization" consisting of cells of ten to one hundred people
- limitations in the seniority system in politics and protections for the prior job rights of persons elected to public office as a means to encourage turnover in office
- the notion that politicians should be wage and salary earners while opposing the idea that others should be expected "to fight your battle"

OPPOSED:
- capitalism

ALSO:
- cryptically asked to "let it be known criminals have one nationalism bastard, i.e., ones with no pride and one religion stealing which is in opposition to all others"
- warned that "if there isn't a meaningful political movement in the next four years, there will be a totalitarian regime of one kind or another"

NON-COMMITTEE (INDEPENDENT)

CANDIDATE FOR PRESIDENT:
Paul E. Trent (OK)

The campaign of Paul E. Trent focused on sex, because the candidate claimed he wanted "to turn women on to politics." He argued that people should learn to use tax loopholes and not try to eliminate them.

NON-PARTISAN

CANDIDATE FOR PRESIDENT:
Evylin Martha (Hemple) #501–14–7038 (CA)

NUDE RUN PARTY

CANDIDATE FOR PRESIDENT:
Edward Hicok "Eddie" Collins (IL)

CONVENTION:
July 4, 1976, Sycamore (IL)

PLATFORM HIGHLIGHTS:
The platform of the Nude Run Party expressly wished to usher in a "truly free society" through the promotion of nudity. The party claimed that nudity was an ecologically sound movement.

THE ONE PARTY

CANDIDATE FOR PRESIDENT:
Stella Stevens (CA)

CANDIDATE FOR VICE PRESIDENT:
Joe E. Brown (FL)

The One Party invoked the symbol of "One" to suggest unity, as in "one God, one Now, one Existence." A former actress, Stevens asserted that "all sex is natural" and called marijuana "a gift from God." As a party of idealists, the One Party proclaimed that "God is inside of every human being."

OREGON GOOD TIMES PARTY

CANDIDATE FOR PRESIDENT:
August "Gemini" Cook (OR)

A self-described yogi and universal people preceptor, Cook sought "freedom of speech, press, people to peaceable assembly, religion (Eastern, Western, other)." His party advocated an end to log shipments to Japan, the promotion of tree planting, the creation of a 200-mile fishing zone off the Pacific coast, and environmentalism, including low-cost solutions to energy problems (for example, solar, wind, and geothermal power).

ORGANIC GROWTH PARTY

CANDIDATE FOR PRESIDENT:
Joseph Ignas Miller (FL)

PAINT PONY PARTY

CANDIDATE FOR PRESIDENT:
Tony Champ McCoy (OR)

PEACE PARTY

CANDIDATE FOR PRESIDENT:
Joseph Thomas Robino, Jr. (LA)

Promising that "the size of a person's pocketbook" and "the color of one's skin, one's sex or religious beliefs matters (sic) not to the Peace Party," the platform called for "peace, peace, peace." It sought "peace, brotherhood—right on!" Its final observations noted that "the human tongue is the deadliest of all blunt instruments. The lump in the throat hardest to bear is swallowing your own words. You'll never reap the sheaves of joy from the effects of vice or crime."

PEARL PARTY

CANDIDATE FOR PRESIDENT:
John Joseph Daniel Soldo (NY) (withdrew)

The Pearl Party grew out of Pearl Press, a publishing house specializing in literary works. Its candidate for president, Soldo, was a noted poet of works on gay love, T. S. Eliot, and other subjects. The platform spoke about uniting the right hand with the left hand and made obscure references to classical works, but it did not articulate a political agenda. Soldo challenged his competitors to a debate, but illness forced him to drop out of the race before the election.

PEOPLE'S (PEACE AND FREEDOM; LIBERTY UNION) PARTY

CANDIDATE FOR PRESIDENT:
Margaret Wright

CANDIDATE FOR VICE PRESIDENT:
Benjamin McLane Spock (Maggie Kuhn [PA], declined)

CANDIDATES FOR PRESIDENTIAL NOMINATION:
Margaret Wright (CA)
Frank Paul Zeidler (WI)

CANDIDATES FOR VICE-PRESIDENTIAL NOMINATION:
Zolton A. Ferency (MI)
Benjamin McLane Spock (AR)

PRIMARIES:

MARCH 2, 1976 (LIBERTY UNION PARTY) (VT):
Wright	965
others	150

JUNE 8, 1976 (PEACE AND FREEDOM PARTY) (CA):
Wright	4,351
Zeidler	1,372
others	12

CONVENTION:
August 31, 1975, St. Louis (MO)

PEOPLE'S (PEACE AND FREEDOM; LIBERTY UNION) PARTY
VOTES FOR PRESIDENTIAL AND VICE-PRESIDENTIAL NOMINATION: KUHN WAS NOMINATED FOR VICE PRESIDENT, BUT SHE DECLINED. DOCTOR SPOCK WAS SELECTED TO FILL THE VACANCY.

PEOPLE'S PEACE AND PROSPERITY PARTY

CANDIDATE FOR PRESIDENT:
Kirby James Hensley (CA)

The People's Peace and Prosperity Party was founded on March 3, 1970, in Modesto (CA). It sought to organize in-dependent thinking people into a third political force and to return government control to the people. According to the party's principles, peace could only be achieved through a government that served the people, regardless of age, color, or creed

PROHIBITION PARTY

CANDIDATE FOR PRESIDENT:
Benjamin Calvin Bubar (ME)

CANDIDATE FOR VICE PRESIDENT:
Earl Farwell Dodge (CO)

27TH CONVENTION:
June 26–27, 1975, Beth Eden Baptist Church, Denver (CO)

Attending this convention were 107 delegates from nineteen states.

PLATFORM HIGHLIGHTS:

SUPPORTED:

- the party's commitment to the Constitution
- limits on the power of the federal judiciary
- promises to combat inflation by cutting government expenditures, reducing taxes for the middle class, constitutionally limiting the spending and taxing powers of Congress, balancing the budget, withdrawing government from competition with private enterprise, and reducing the national debt
- limits on foreign aid
- the enforcement of antitrust laws and laws forbidding strikes by federal government employees
- right-to-work laws
- states' rights but condemned regional governments
- a constitutional amendment to protect the life of the unborn except in cases when the mother's life is endangered
- strict enforcement of laws against gambling, narcotics, and commercialized vice
- military preparedness and the concept of the volunteer military
- welfare reform to remove "undeserving persons," to promote self-sufficiency, and to stop the distribution of birth-control devices to minors without parental consent
- uniform marriage and divorce laws
- the separation of church and state, while approving Bible reading in public schools or other institutions
- ballot law reforms to extend access to third parties
- a revision in the Social Security laws to make the program voluntary, to establish it on a sound actuarial basis, to eliminate work restrictions on beneficiaries, and to provide for automatic cost-of-living adjustments
- efforts to curb tobacco use and a ban on harmful drugs
- government antipollution programs

OPPOSED:

- communism
- burdensome restraints on free enterprise

- excessive government regulation, control of monopolies, and restrictions on unethical practices of unscrupulous groups
- anarchistic and arbitrary pressure tactics, forced busing, and quota systems
- euthanasia
- a guaranteed annual income
- efforts to restrict religious broadcasting and the establishment of new churches
- federal aid to education
- government controls and subsidies for agriculture
- socialized medicine, involuntary commitment to mental hospitals, and mass medication programs

Also:
- blamed alcoholic beverages for a host of modern social problems and called for a program of publicity, education, legislation, and administration to eliminate the liquor traffic
- promised to repeal all laws that permitted that traffic and to enforce rigorously laws against the manufacture, distribution, and sale of alcoholic beverages

---

PROHIBITION PARTY
VOTE FOR PRESIDENTIAL NOMINATION:
BUBAR WAS NOMINATED BY ACCLAMATION ON THE FIRST BALLOT.

VOTE FOR VICE-PRESIDENTIAL NOMINATION:
DODGE WAS NOMINATED BY ACCLAMATION ON THE FIRST BALLOT.

PROTECTIONIST DEMOCRAT-CONSERVATIVE REPUBLICAN PARTY

CANDIDATE FOR PRESIDENT:
Jose Antonio Torres II (TX)

PURITAN EPIC, PROHIBITION, AND MAGNETOHYDRODYNAMICS PARTY

CANDIDATE FOR PRESIDENT:
Merrill Keith Riddick (MT)

An aviation pioneer, Riddick ran for president to promote the process of magnetohydrodynamics (MHD), an energy-generation process in which coal is converted to electricity in a superheated chamber using magnets. The party also advocated an end to the misuse of campaign funds, criminal activity in government, and violence as a national policy.

REPUBLICAN PARTY

CANDIDATE FOR PRESIDENT:
Gerald Rudolph Ford, Jr.

CANDIDATE FOR VICE PRESIDENT:
Robert Joseph Dole

CANDIDATES FOR PRESIDENTIAL NOMINATION:
Spiro Theodore Agnew (MD)
Pearl Mae Bailey (CA)
Howard Henry Baker, Jr. (TN)
Winton Everett Barker (MN)
John Brennan (PA)
James Lane Buckley (NY)
Austin Marion Burton (KY)
Carmen Christopher Chimento (NH)
Henry Cleaver (NY)
John Bowden Connally (TX)
Clarence L. Courton (FL)
Joseph Lar Sarsfeld "America First "Daly (IL)
Robert Dane (MO)
Donald Halleck Dumont (IL)
Nell K. Fiola (MN)
Gerald Rudolph Ford, Jr. (MI)
Phillip Arthur Fredette (MA)
John Jacob Gordon (MA)
Thurman Jerome Hamlin (KY)
Jesse Alexander Helms, Jr. (NC)
William Andrew Jolley (OR)
Tommy William Klein (KY)
Kenyon Raymond Knourek (CA)
Robert J. Luellen (IN)
Catherine III Trinity Victoria Alix Meda Magnifico (CA)
Charles McCurdy Mathias (MD)
Walter James McCloud (MO)
Ken Murray (MI)
Mildred Catherine Odorize (IL)
Richard Buell Ogilvie (IL)
Hubert David Patty (TN)
Charles Harting Percy (IL)
Robert L. Persons (OH)
Donald James Butler Poremski (NJ)
Robert D. Ray (IA)
Ronald Wilson Reagan (CA)
Elliot Lee Richardson (MA)
Nelson Aldrich Rockefeller (NY)
Lee Arnold Spiegelman (FL)
Harold Edward Stassen (MN)
Elmer Eugene Thon (AZ)
Lowell Palmer Weicker, Jr. (CT)
Ernest "Utopia '76" Whitford (CA)
Mary E. Humphrey Williams (MI)
R. W. Yeager (KS)

CANDIDATES FOR VICE-PRESIDENTIAL NOMINATION:
James Browning Allen (AL)
John Bayard Anderson (IL)
Anne Legendre Armstrong (TX)
Howard Henry Baker, Jr. (TN)
Raymond Anderson Barnhart (TX)

Robert Edmund Bauman (MD)
Christopher Samuel Bond (MO)
William Emerson Brock III (TN)
Edward William Brooke (MA)
William Frank Buckley, Jr. (NY)
Chief Burning Wood (KY)
Austin Marion Burton (KY)
George Herbert Walker Bush (TX)
John Bowden Connally (TX)
Philip Miller Crane (IL)
Katherine A. Deanglis (OH)
Robert Joseph Dole (KS)
Peter Vichi Domenici (NM)
James Burrows Edwards (SC)
Daniel Jackson Evans (WA)
Louis Frey, Jr. (FL)
Frank S. Glenn (TX)
John Louellen Grady (FL)
Gregory Hansman (MO)
Jesse Alexander Helms, Jr. (NC) (withdrew)
Carla Anderson Hills (CA)
Wallace John Stockman Johnson (CA)
David Arthur Keene (VA)
Paul Dominique Laxalt (NV)
James Albertus McClure (ID)
Louis Dona Gingrass O'Hara (RI)
Nancy Dale Palm (TX)
Ronald Wilson Reagan (CA)
Elliot Lee Richardson (MA)
Nelson Aldrich Rockefeller (NY)
William Doyle Ruckelshaus (WA)
Donald Henry Rumsfeld (IL)
Richard Schultz Schweiker (PA)
William Warren Scranton (PA)
John Patrick Sears (VA)
William Edward Simon (NY)
Roger Thomas Staubach (TX)
Alan Watson Steelman (TX)
Steven Douglas Symms (ID)
David Conner Treen (LA)
Lowell Palmer Weicker, Jr. (CT)
John Alva "Jack" Wellborn (MI)

PRIMARIES:
FEBRUARY 24, 1976 (NH):
Ford 55,156
Reagan 53,569
others 2,949

Vice-presidential primary:
Burton (KY) . . . .
Johnson . . . .

MARCH 2, 1976 (MA):
Ford 115,375
Reagan 63,555

no preference 6,000
others 3,519
MARCH 2, 1976 (VT):
Ford 27,014
Reagan 4,892
others 251
MARCH 9, 1976 (FL):
Ford 321,982
Reagan 287,837
MARCH 16, 1976 (IL):
Ford 456,750
Reagan 311,295
Daly 7,582
others 266
MARCH 23, 1976 (NC):
Reagan 101,468
Ford 88,897
no preference 3,362
APRIL 6, 1976 (WI):
Ford 326,869
Reagan 262,126
none of the above 2,234
others 583
APRIL 27, 1976 (PA):
Ford 733,472
Reagan 40,510
others 22,678
MAY 4, 1976 (GA):
Reagan 128,671
Ford 59,801
MAY 4, 1976 (IN):
Reagan 323,779
Ford 307,513
MAY 11, 1976 (NE):
Reagan 113,493
Ford 94,542
others 379
MAY 11, 1976 (WV):
Ford 88,386
Reagan 67,306
MAY 18, 1976 (MD):
Ford 96,291
Reagan 69,680
MAY 18, 1976 (MI):
Ford 690,180
Reagan 364,052
uncommitted delegates 8,473
others 109
MAY 25, 1976 (AR):
Reagan 20,628
Ford 11,430
uncommitted delegates 483

MAY 25, 1976 (ID):
Reagan 66,743
Ford 22,323
uncommitted delegates 727

MAY 25, 1976 (KY):
Ford 67,976
Reagan 62,683
Klein 1,088
uncommitted delegates 1,781

MAY 25, 1976 (NV):
Reagan 31,637
Ford 13,747
none of the above 2,365

MAY 25, 1976 (OR):
Ford 150,181
Reagan 136,691
others 11,663

MAY 25, 1976 (TN):
Ford 120,6685
Reagan 118,997
uncommitted delegates 2,756
others 97

JUNE 1, 1976 (MT):
Reagan 56,683
Ford 31,100
no preference 1,996

JUNE 1, 1976 (RI):
Ford 9,365
Reagan 4,480
uncommitted delegates 507

JUNE 1, 1976 (SD):
Reagan 43,068
Ford 36,976
uncommitted delegates 4,033

JUNE 8, 1976 (CA):
Reagan 1,604,836
Ford 845,655
others 20

JUNE 8, 1976 (NJ):
Ford 242,122

JUNE 8, 1976 (OH):
Ford 516,111
Reagan 419,646

31ST CONVENTION:
August 16–19, 1976, Kemper Arena, Kansas City (MO)
Robert Joseph Dole (KS), temporary chairman
John Jacob Rhodes (AZ), permanent chairman
Howard Henry Baker, Jr. (TN), keynoter

PLATFORM HIGHLIGHTS:
The 1976 Republican platform emphasized "less government, less spending, less inflation." Claiming that "the number one destroyer of jobs is inflation" and "the number one cause of inflation is the government's expansion of the nation's supply of money and credit," the party demanded an end to deficit spending and the adoption of a balanced budget.

SUPPORTED:
- the renewal of the GATT Multifiber Agreement
- a reduction of taxes and the use of tax credits for college tuition, technical training, and child care expenses
- tax simplification, including new systems of accelerated depreciation, removal of the tax on equity financing, abolition of the double tax on dividends, incentives to expand stock ownership, and an increase in the personal exemption to $1,000
- an increase in the estate tax exemption
- the promotion of a liberalized marital deduction and an end to death taxes on capital gains
- major changes in the laws governing confidentiality of tax returns and Social Security records to protect the individual's privacy
- the declassification of many government records being withheld from public scrutiny
- the Agricultural Act of 1973
- the strengthening of the present grain inspection system
- government's role in regulating the import of foreign commodities to ensure equity in quality
- all-risk crop insurance through government reinsurance of private insurance companies
- the valuation of farm property on the basis of current use and extensions of credit payment deadlines
- the expansion of agricultural research
- the investigations of concerns about regulations issued by the Army Corps of Engineers and demanded agricultural exemptions from their application
- farmer cooperatives, including rural electric and telephone cooperatives, and the Capper-Volstead Act
- changes in the Small Business Administration, reductions in paperwork and red tape (particularly from the Internal Revenue Service and the Census Bureau), and more equitable tax treatment
- the enforcement of antitrust laws against all segments of the economy equally
- general revenue sharing
- block grant programs, including health, child nutrition, education, surface transportation, and social services
- a functional realignment of government
- the repeal of statutes granting members of Congress automatic pay increases
- a public disclosure of financial interests of senators and representatives
- improved lobbying disclosures
- voluntary regional presidential primaries
- improvements in the U.S. Postal Service
- the notion that "fighting crime is—and should be—a local responsibility," and proceeded to endorse the Law Enforcement Assistance Administration

- states' options regarding the death penalty
- stronger state sentencing and parole procedures
- prison reform, with priority given to the young first-time offender, and additional research to help prevent juvenile delinquency
- bail reform
- automatic and mandatory minimum sentences for conviction of crimes involving dangerous weapons while continuing to oppose federal registration of firearms
- stronger antiobscenity laws
- ratification of the treaty on synthetic drugs
- increased emphasis on the prevention of licit drugs being diverted into illicit channels
- more intensive efforts to control the illegal importation of dangerous drugs
- a halt to international terrorism through international collective action
- a sub-minimum wage law to foster youth employment
- families as the "foundation of our nation"
- tax credits for private school tuition payments, direct financial support to nonpublic schools "on a constitutionally acceptable basis," and local discretion concerning the use of nonsectarian prayers in public schools, again, by constitutional amendment if required
- revised guidelines for student loan eligibility
- an end to government interference in the management of college and universities
- catastrophic illness protection for those who cannot afford it, utilizing the private insurance system
- a "comprehensive and equitable approach" to mental health, including a focus on the prevention, treatment, and care of mental illness
- a continuing "public dialogue" on abortion but also endorsed the enactment of a constitutional amendment protecting the "right to life for unborn children"
- equal opportunities and civil rights for all citizens
- more emphasis on minority education, more loans to minority businesses, and more minority opportunities for federal employment
- ratification of the ERA
- the elimination of discriminatory laws against women in employment, taxation, disability programs, and Social Security and promised new efforts to ensure job training, counseling, child care, flexible work, small business assistance, housing equity, and estate tax reform for women
- new incentives for Hispanic Americans to become proficient in English
- Native Americans by honoring the nation's trust relationship with them and by promoting "self-determination without termination"
- self-determination, in principle, for American Samoa, the District of Columbia (including home rule and voting representation in the Senate and House of Representatives), Guam, Puerto Rico (including statehood, if approved by a referendum), and the Virgin Islands

- the right to vote in presidential elections for Guam, Puerto Rico, and the Virgin Islands
- the removal of architectural, communications, and transportation barriers for and attitudes toward disabled persons
- collective bargaining
- section 14(b) of the Taft-Hartley Act and uniform administration of the Hatch Act
- increased efforts to restrict illegal aliens and to punish employers who hired them
- more part-time and flexible-hour work
- "a systematic and complete overhaul of the welfare system" by emphasizing adequate living standards for the "truly needy," ending welfare fraud, excluding illegal aliens, instituting work requirements but not guaranteed annual incomes, providing educational and vocational incentives, and ensuring better coordination between federal efforts and those of local and state welfare agencies without "federalizing" the system
- a streamlined food stamp program
- incentives to families to care for their older members
- the abolishment of mandatory retirement
- expanded Foster Grandparent and Senior Companion programs
- a strengthened Social Security system
- improvements in the Veterans Administration (VA) hospital system
- education, jobs, housing, and other loan and death benefits for younger veterans, especially those from the Vietnam conflict
- a coordinated National Urban Policy of neighborhood self-help groups, community rehabilitation efforts, and neighborhood business investments that would emphasize capital formation and technical assistance for small and minority businesses
- home mortgage deductions
- inflation-impact studies for all government regulations
- the elimination of housing discrimination
- incentives to develop low- and moderate-income housing
- urban homesteading
- the deregulation of airlines and motor carriers
- a commitment to complete the Interstate Highway System and maintain or replace the nation's network of bridges
- more research on fuel-efficient automobiles and airplanes, safer railroads, and more convenient and less expensive urban transportation
- an expansion of the energy supply and improvements in energy efficiency, including incentives for the exploration and development of domestic energy sources and more research on alternative energy options (e.g., solar, geothermal, cogeneration, solid waste, wind, water)
- an immediate end to price controls on oil and "newly discovered" natural gas
- reductions in red tape in all aspects of government

- accelerated development of nuclear energy, oil shale reserves, Alaskan petroleum, and the leasing of the Outer Continental Shelf
- more reliance on coal and the return of mined lands to beneficial use
- continued research on the potential of fusion energy
- clean air and water and scientific and technological research on environmental problems
- the protection of the nation's recreational and scenic areas
- land use planning, desalinization, multiple-use management of public lands, sustained-yield forestry management (including clear-cutting and replanting), and recycling and recovery
- a presidential panel to develop national environmental and energy priorities
- a national science policy (based on a public-private partnership)
- an expansion of the national space program
- the preservation of the cultural heritage of the nation's various ethnic groups as a priority, including the National Endowment for the Arts and the National Endowment for the Humanities
- continued federal assistance for public broadcasting, as well as enhancements in copyright law and tax relief for artists
- bipartisanship in foreign policy
- Alexander Solzhenitsyn
- a superior national defense with growth in the current defense budget
- the development of a new intercontinental ballistic missile, the B-1 bomber, and a new missile-launching submarine
- increased military research
- a stronger and more accountable intelligence system
- NATO allies but wanted them seen ready to assume a greater share of the costs of European defense
- the peaceful resolution of the problems in Cyprus, which was important for the solidarity of the NATO alliance
- the Republican administration's "excellent relations" with the European Economic Community
- Japan, as a "valued friend"
- continued military and economic assistance to the Republic of Korea
- U.S. friendships with Australia, Indonesia, Malaysia, New Zealand, the Philippines, and Singapore
- a demand for a full accounting of U.S. servicemen held as POWs and MIAs in Southeast Asia
- steady growth in the relationship with the People's Republic of China, while keeping the party's commitments to the Nationalist Chinese as well
- the historic friendship of the United States with Canada and U.S. obligations to Mexico and its Central and Latin American neighbors
- the position of keeping Cuba "outside the Inter-American family of nations"

- safeguards for U.S. interests in any renegotiation of the Panama Canal Treaty
- the U.S. commitment to Israel as a cornerstone of foreign policy and to the notion of a negotiated peace agreement among all states involved in the Arab-Israeli conflict and in the civil war in Lebanon
- self-determination in Africa, while opposing any Soviet engagement in the continent
- efforts to "reduce tensions and to arrive at mutually beneficial and self-enforcing agreements in all fields of international activity" and hard-headed bargaining in arms reduction talks with the Soviet Union but denounced the structuring of U.S. farm export policy based on agricultural commodity sales concessions to the Soviets
- calls for holding the Soviet Union accountable for implementing the UN Declaration on Human Rights and the Helsinki Agreements
- the right of Jews and other groups to emigrate from the Soviet Union
- self-determination for Eastern Europe
- the Voice of America, Radio Free Europe, and Radio Liberty
- a reform of the United Nations
- new international structures to deal with terrorism, peacekeeping, drug control, ocean development, and nonproliferation of nuclear weapons
- a threat to withdraw from the International Labor Organization
- a more efficient foreign aid program
- ocean development
- completion of the Law of the Sea Treaty
- an extension of U.S. territorial offshore claims from three to twelve miles from shore (along with the concept of a 200-mile offshore economic zone)
- international safeguards for the use of nuclear technology
- a rejection of corporate bribery as a legitimate business strategy abroad
- a stronger international monetary system and a reduction in trade barriers
- a preference for free market competition over cartels, price-fixing arrangements, and commodity agreements in the international arena

OPPOSED:
- the concept of the government as the employer of last resort
- government-controlled grain reserves and the application of "unrealistic" OSHA and environmental protection laws to farm practices
- post card voter registration, proxy voting in congressional committees, and a national presidential primary
- forced busing (through a constitutional amendment if necessary)
- compulsory national health insurance, along with fraud and abuse in the Medicare and Medicaid programs

- research using live fetuses and "right-to-die" legislation
- the quota system for affirmative action
- the rights of public employees to strike (unless states chose to authorize them)

REPUBLICAN PARTY
VOTE FOR PRESIDENTIAL NOMINATION:

Candidate	Ballot: 1
Ford	1,187
Reagan	1,070
Richardson	1
abstention	1

At this convention, Reagan publicly announced Schweiker as his choice for a vice-presidential running mate before the presidential balloting began. Ford's nomination was made unanimous.

VOTE FOR VICE-PRESIDENTIAL NOMINATION:

Candidate	Ballot: 1	2
Dole	1,921	1,981
Helms	103	99
Reagan	27	23
Crane	23	8
Grady	19	0
Frey	9	0
Baker	6	6
Buckley	4	5
Armstrong	6	4
Connally	4	4
Steelman	3	3
Treen	3	3
Bush	2	2
Laxalt	2	2
Wellborn	2	2
Richardson	2	2
Schweiker	2	2
Bauman	2	0
Sears	1	1
Allen	1	1
Brock	2	1
Edwards	1	1
Keene	1	1
McClure	1	1
Domenici	1	1
Barnhart	1	1
Palm	1	1
Simon	2	1
Staubach	1	1
Symms	1	1
Glenn	1	1
Rumsfeld	1	1
abstentions	103	99

Dole was nominated for vice president on the first ballot.

- unionization of the military and legalization of common-situs picketing
- the atrocities in Cambodia
- secret agreements with other governments

RESTORATION PARTY
CANDIDATE FOR PRESIDENT:
Ernest L. Miller (VA)

CANDIDATES FOR VICE PRESIDENT:
Frank Wasil Gaydosh (PA)
(Roy Nathan Eddy [FL] withdrew)

PLATFORM HIGHLIGHTS:
The Restoration Party argued that a Communist conspiracy (acting as a front for the "Illuminati") was running the U.S. government and had taken control of the press, schools, churches, money, and military forces.

SUPPORTED:
- a protective tariff
- a repeal of the Twenty-fifth Amendment (presidential disability and succession)
- school prayer
- the restoration of national sovereignty and constitutional government
- a superior military
- the elimination of the Federal Reserve System
- the withdrawal of the United States from the United Nations
- a repeal of the Sixteenth Amendment
- a repeal of all mental health legislation
- the unrestricted right to keep and bear arms
- a repeal of State Department Top Secret Publication 7277, Disarmament Series 5
- the outlawing of the Communist Party
- capital punishment
- strict laws against abortion and euthanasia
- local police efforts
- strong laws against the sale, distribution, and use of marijuana and other drugs
- the direct election of all District Court judges, with Supreme Court judges to be appointed for four-year terms

OPPOSED:
- cloud seeding
- liberal immigration policies
- foreign aid
- the Panama Canal Treaty
- the adoption of the Genocide and Seabed treaties
- welfare
- the ERA
- regional government
- fluoridation of water
- trade with Communist countries
- restrictions on the use of unconventional cancer treatments and organic food supplements

ALSO:
- promised to have three shifts of twelve men each praying around the clock at the White House
- demanded that "the Devil, sensitivity training, sex education, One-Worldism, Socialism, Marxism, witchcraft, and brainwashing change techniques" be taken out of the schools and that "the Bible, Prayer, Patriotism, honesty, chastity, personal integrity, and the free enterprise economic system" be allowed to flourish
- promised to eradicate the "evil, Satanic, secret order" known as the "Illuminati"
- pledged itself to reduce taxes "by at least 50 percent"

SOCIALIST LABOR PARTY

CANDIDATE FOR PRESIDENT:
Julius Levin (NJ)

CANDIDATE FOR VICE PRESIDENT:
Constance Blomen (MA)

29TH CONVENTION:
February 7–11, 1976, Stouffer's Northland Inn, Southfield (MI)
George Sam Taylor (PA), temporary chairman and chairman, February 7, 1976
Alan Karp (CA), chairman, February 8–11, 1976

Thirty-one delegates from thirteen states attended this convention.

PLATFORM HIGHLIGHTS:
The party's officials readopted the platform of 1972. It declared that "social systems are mortal" and that capitalism was on the verge of death. In Marxist terms, it explained why capitalism "overproduces" and why the Vietnam War accelerated the tendency toward inflation. Workers were called upon to perform a "historic task," that is, to seize the revolutionary moment and bring about Socialist industrial unions and achieve industrial self-government.

SOCIALIST LABOR PARTY
VOTES FOR PRESIDENTIAL AND VICE-PRESIDENTIAL NOMINATION: LEVIN AND BLOMEN WERE UNANIMOUSLY NOMINATED FOR THE OFFICES OF PRESIDENT AND VICE PRESIDENT, RESPECTIVELY. NO OTHER NAMES WERE PRESENTED TO THE CONVENTION.

SOCIALIST PARTY

CANDIDATE FOR PRESIDENT:
Frank Paul Zeidler

CANDIDATE FOR VICE PRESIDENT:
John Quinn Brisben

CANDIDATES FOR PRESIDENTIAL NOMINATION:
Abraham Bassford IV (WI)
William Briggs (CA)
John Quinn Brisben (IL)
William Davis Edwards (CA)
William Osborne Hart (WI)
David Ernest McReynolds (NY)
Eleanor Miller (DC)
Ann Williams Rosenhaft (NY)
Harry Siitonen (CA)
Frank Paul Zeidler (WI)

CANDIDATES FOR VICE-PRESIDENTIAL NOMINATION:
Merle P. Bigenho (FL)
John Quinn Brisben (IL)
Chester Arthur Graham (MI)
Beatrice Vivian Hermann (WI)
Jeremy "Jerry" Rifkin (CA)
Ann Williams Rosenhaft (NY)
Harry Siitonen (CA)

CONVENTION:
August 30–September 1, 1975, Hotel Wisconsin, Milwaukee (WI)
Frank Paul Zeidler (WI), temporary chairperson and chairperson, August 30, 1975
Harry Siitonen (CA), chairperson, August 31, 1975
William Briggs (CA), chairperson, September 1, 1975

This presidential campaign was the first one in which the Socialist Party participated since 1956. Forty-eight delegates from twelve states attended this convention. Early in the campaign, party officials considered a merger between the Socialist Party and the People's Party presidential campaigns, but the plans for a joint ticket were never realized.

PLATFORM HIGHLIGHTS:
The Socialist platform argued that the "American people should have an opportunity to choose democratic socialism."

SUPPORTED:
- cooperative farming and the rights of farm workers to organize
- the abolition of the Board of Trade and the vertically integrated monopolies of agri-corporations in preference to the family farmer
- a restructuring of communications to provide free access to all points of view and public ownership of telephones and public control of radio and television
- the right of teachers and school employees to strike
- expanded educational opportunities (e.g., the educaid program and free and equal access for all individuals)
- integrated education as essential and busing for that purpose
- self-determination, democracy, and economic justice as vital components of any achievable peace, while condemning inequities between have and have-not nations
- an end to the arms race
- the aspirations of women and minorities and the fulfillment of civil and human rights for all, with an end to exploitation

- the abolition of the CIA and legislation to prevent abuses by other agencies, specifically deploring violations of constitutional rights by federal agencies and local police forces
- concern for the problems of urban dwellers
- a subordination of private property rights to the public need, particularly in regard to the environment
- public ownership of energy production and distribution and the development of public transportation
- efforts to diminish the power of great wealth, comparing the Watergate scandal to the corruption "of every corporate boardroom"
- the notion that "only social control of the production and distribution of goods would create the base for building a new society"
- social control over banking and credit institutions, union democracy, a massive public housing program, and reallocation of the defense budget to domestic social purposes
- amnesty for all war resisters
- a comprehensive national health policy
- workers' control of the workplace
- an expansion in democratic decision making, whether in private or governmental enterprises, to include working people

---

SOCIALIST PARTY

VOTE FOR PRESIDENTIAL NOMINATION: ALL OF THE CANDIDATES FOR PRESIDENT DECLINED THE NOMINATION. ZEIDLER WAS ASKED TO RECONSIDER, AND HE AGREED TO BE PLACED IN NOMINATION. ACCORDINGLY, HE WAS NOMINATED BY ACCLAMATION.

VOTE FOR VICE-PRESIDENTIAL NOMINATION: ALL OF THE VICE-PRESIDENTIAL CANDIDATES DECLINED THE NOMINATION. GRAHAM, HERMANN, RIFKIN, ROSENHAFT, AND SIITONEN WERE NOMINATED FOR VICE PRESIDENT, BUT ALL DECLINED. BRISBEN WAS URGED TO RECONSIDER, AND HE AGREED TO ACCEPT THE NOMINATION. ACCORDINGLY, HE ALSO WAS NOMINATED BY ACCLAMATION.

SOCIALIST WORKERS PARTY

CANDIDATE FOR PRESIDENT:
Peter Miguel Camejo (CA)

CANDIDATE FOR VICE PRESIDENT:
Willie Mae Reid (IL)

CONVENTION:
The national committee nominated the candidates of the Socialist Workers Party at a meeting held at the Jefferson Hotel in St. Louis (MO) from December 28, 1974, through January 1, 1975. At this time, the party also adopted a platform. The meeting coincided with the 14th National Convention of the Young Socialist Alliance, which was chaired by Andrew Pulley and attended by more than one thousand participants from thirty-nine states and 115 college campuses.

PLATFORM HIGHLIGHTS:
The party's platform espoused socialism (à la Trotskyism), women's and minorities' rights, resistance to militarism and imperialism, peace, and increased public assistance for the elderly, poor, and persons with disabilities.

SPACE TICKET

CANDIDATE FOR PRESIDENT:
Jane Ashman (CA)

Claiming to be empowered with the telepathic ability to communicate with people from outer space, Ashman sought to have earth "take its place in the fellowship of the planets." She promised to make the secret government files on unidentified flying objects (UFOs) public.

SYMBIOTIC UNION

CANDIDATE FOR PRESIDENT:
Conrad Flournoy Morrow (OH)

Claiming to be the "Northern Corps" of the Symbionese Liberation Army, the Symbiotic Union urged peace, communism, and harmony among people. It denounced the "Monopoly Capitalists" and praised the "Revolutionary Proletariat." The Symbiotic Union's campaign slogan was "None of the Above. No candidate of the bourgeoisie is acceptable in '76." It promised a "union of all living things" and demanded the government's defeat. Its program sought to "make the rich pay."

THEO-DEMS

CANDIDATE FOR PRESIDENT:
Avo Loyce Lowe Brown (TX)

Brown sought the support of Christian voters in her campaign for the presidency. She claimed her candidacy was the result of "Divine Constraint," but she did not assert any special divine promise that she would be elected. Her campaign was limited to answering mail inquiries.

TUITION CUT PARTY

CANDIDATE FOR PRESIDENT:
Ron Luther (OH)

CANDIDATE FOR VICE PRESIDENT:
James R. Goodluck (OH)

UNITED AMERICAN PARTY

CANDIDATE FOR PRESIDENT:
Frank Taylor (AZ)

CANDIDATE FOR VICE PRESIDENT:
Henry Swan (AZ)

UNITED NATIONS PARTY

CANDIDATE FOR PRESIDENT:
Emil Matalik (WI)

Matalik created the United Nations Party (also known as the # 1 Party and the United Nations Organization, or 1-U.N.O., Party) in 1964 to promote world peace and the abolition of hunger. The party's platform viewed overpopulation as the world's biggest problem and proposed limiting each family to one child (later increased to two children), one animal, and one tree. The party also sought to create a World presidency, a Universal Congress, and a Global Supreme Court. To resolve the urban problems of the world, the platform suggested tearing down the cities and using the land for farming. To that end, each person would be given five usable acres of land for farming. Public use of tobacco, liquor, and gambling would be prohibited. Free world communications would be ensured. The platform also promoted worldwide free love—"especially for single and virginized people"—and coed nudist camps for prison inmates. It advocated the abolition of the monetary system and replacing it with "volunteerism."

Matalik's announced choice for World vice president was Ching Chang, the wife of Mao Tse-tung. For vice president of the United States, he promoted Corrine A. Huff and Angela Davis.

CANDIDATE FOR WORLD VICE PRESIDENT:
Ching Chang (People's Republic of China; the wife of Mao Tse-tung)

CANDIDATES FOR U.S. VICE PRESIDENT:
Corrine A. Huff (NY)
Angela Davis (CA)

Matalik created the United Nations Party (also known as the # 1 Party and the United Nations Organization, or 1-U.N.O., Party) in 1964 to promote world peace and the abolition of hunger.

PLATFORM HIGHLIGHTS:

SUPPORTED:

- limits on each family to one child (later increased to two children), one animal, and one tree to counter the world's biggest problem—overpopulation
- the creation of a World presidency, a Universal Congress, and a Global Supreme Court
- the conversion of cities to farm land, thus resolving the urban problems of the world
- the issuance of five usable acres of land to each person for farming
- prohibitions on the public use of tobacco, liquor, and gambling
- free world communications

- the promotion of worldwide free love—"especially for single and virginized people"—and coed nudist camps for prison inmates
- the abolition of the monetary system, replacing it with "volunteerism"

UNITED NATIONS PARTY
VOTES FOR WORLD VICE-PRESIDENTIAL AND U.S. VICE-PRESIDENTIAL NOMINATION: MATALIK ANNOUNCED HIS CHOICE FOR THE WORLD VICE PRESIDENT. HE ALSO PERSONALLY PROMOTED THE TWO CANDIDATES FOR THE U.S. VICE-PRESIDENTIAL NOMINATIONS.

UNITED PARTY

CANDIDATE FOR PRESIDENT:
J. W. Burdell (TX)

CANDIDATE FOR VICE PRESIDENT:
Dorrice Wright (TX)

The United Party sought to elect a "working man" for president. To promote his candidacy and raise money, Burdell placed a classified advertisement in the Sherman (TX) *Democrat* offering to sell "three horses, six pigs, one seeder, and fertilizer spreader."

U.S. FELLOWSHIP PARTY

CANDIDATE FOR PRESIDENT:
Lloyd Osborne "Alamo" Scott (TX)

U.S. LABOR PARTY

CANDIDATE FOR PRESIDENT:
Lyndon Hermyle LaRouche, Jr. (VA)

CANDIDATE FOR VICE PRESIDENT:
Ronald Wayne Evans (MI)

This election was the first and only one contested by the U.S. Labor Party. After 1976, its followers gravitated to the Democratic Party, where they assumed the role of an unwelcome "fringe" element dominated by LaRouche.

PLATFORM HIGHLIGHTS:

SUPPORTED:

- the impeachment and removal from office of Nelson Aldrich Rockefeller
- international agreements among the United States, the Comecon sector (the Soviet bloc's Council for Mutual Economic Assistance), and Third World forces regarding food production, "brute force"-controlled thermonuclear reactor technology, and the development of "industrially advanced foci"
- the development of groupings of states at the international level as a means of promoting regional coopera-

tion (e.g., the United States, Canada, and Mexico as one group)

- an "orderly debt moratorium" as the solution for the economic depression
- the nationalization of banks (along with pension funds and insurance companies) threatened with collapse and the issuance of government credits and grants to restore full production levels
- nuclear fusion and the development of controlled thermonuclear reactors
- research and development of plasma physics
- the consolidation of unemployment, pension, disability, and government medical payments under Social Security
- socialism (the party claimed to be "committed to the establishment of a workers and farmers government") but relied on the judgment of the population regarding the timing of a transition from capitalism to socialism
- the deployment of excess military forces as emergency logistical and engineering resources in various communities
- the "disbandment" of the CIA, the Law Enforcement Assistance Administration, and the FBI and the development of a new national law enforcement agency under a reorganized Department of Justice
- the replacement of the International Monetary Fund and the World Bank with a new International Development Bank

ALSO:

- saw its foreign economic policies as producing a "giant leap in the social productivity of even the most poorly developed large sectors of the earth" over a period of ten to fifteen years
- drafted proposals for legislation governing agricultural policy, housing, the "Mexican Triage," banking, transportation, natural gas production, and reconstruction of Indochina and the Middle East

U.S. PEOPLE'S PARTY
CANDIDATE FOR PRESIDENT:
Ralph Randolph Reed (VA)

Reed created the U.S. People's Party to promote his effort to abolish all taxes and money. His campaign was based on his reading of the Bible. He proposed making everything free to workers who held an identification card. By making everyone equal, Reed hoped to eradicate poverty and crime. He also sought the elimination of all war-making materials, but if other nations did not follow suit, he urged making the United States "the strongest in the world."

WORLD CITIZEN PARTY
CANDIDATE FOR PRESIDENT:
Sol Gareth "Garry" Davis (DC)

Davis was a self-designated "world citizen," having renounced his U.S. citizenship in 1948 to protest militarism.

The son of band leader Meyer Davis, he urged his followers to "think globally, act locally."

PLATFORM HIGHLIGHTS
SUPPORTED:

- "the Universal Declaration of Human Rights plus ecological rights as outlined in the Stockholm Declaration as well as the rights of ethnic minority groups"
- world citizenship
- the creation of world law and appropriate government organs (e.g., World Legislature, World Courts, World Executive, and World Guard Force) essential to guarantee fundamental human rights and freedoms
- the realignment of local and national law to conform to world law
- the recognition and representation of viable ethnic groups
- representation for stateless persons and refugees
- representation of ecosystems against exploitation
- the mundialization (internationalization—connecting into "one world") of villages, towns, cities, and universities
- the endorsement of existing national and international organizations and associations promoting world peace, human rights, and world government

WORLD GOVERNMENT PARTY
CANDIDATE FOR PRESIDENT:
John Paul Fritz (HI)

PLATFORM HIGHLIGHTS:
SUPPORTED:

- the relocation of the United Nations to Honolulu (HI)
- more jobs
- better transportation
- the construction of "flying saucer-type" airships at Pearl Harbor
- world democracy
- the abolition of the "British caste system"
- a world military establishment
- the irrigation of deserts
- a moderation of the world's climate
- the development and population of other planets

YOUR BULL PARTY
CANDIDATE FOR PRESIDENT:
John L. Predgen (CA)

Predgen created the Your Bull Party to promote an honest presidency. He placed classified ads in newspapers to advertise his candidacy, promising "democracy and leadership." Predgen opposed monopolies and Jimmy Carter. He promoted enactment of a national "bottle bill" (i.e., legislation requiring a refundable deposit on soft drink bottles) and a "minus five miles per hour" speed limit for trucks and buses.

GENERAL ELECTION SUMMARY FOR 1976:			
Candidate	Electoral Votes	States	Popular Votes
Carter (D)	297	23 (+ DC)	40,977,147[1]
Ford (R)[2]	240	27	39,422,671[3]
Reagan	1 (WA)	0	0
McCarthy (I [CCP])	0	0	756,691
MacBride (LIBRTN)	0	0	173,011
Maddox (AI)	0	0	170,531
Anderson (A)	0	0	160,773
Camejo (SOC WOR)	0	0	91,314
Hall (COM)	0	0	58,992
Wright (PEO [PF; LU])	0	0	49,024
LaRouche (US LAB)	0	0	40,043
Bubar (PROH)	0	0	15,934
Levin (SOC LAB)	0	0	9,616
Ziedler (SOC)	0	0	6,038
Miller (REST)	0	0	361
Taylor (UNI AM)	0	0	36

[1]Includes 991 votes from the Independent of Vermont party and 145,393 votes from the Liberal Party of New York

[2]One elector from Washington cast his vote for president for Reagan and Dole for vice president

[3]Includes 274,878 votes from the Conservative Party of New York

ELECTION OF NOVEMBER 4, 1980

President
RONALD WILSON REAGAN

Vice President
GEORGE HERBERT WALKER BUSH

HIGHLIGHTS

Arguing that the country suffered from a "national malaise" that included memories of an energy crisis marked by long lines at the gas pumps, runaway inflation, and the adverse publicity associated with the prolonged captivity of the U.S. Embassy personnel held hostage by Iran, President Jimmy Carter entered the 1980 presidential campaign with uncertain prospects. Republicans were jumping for the opportunity to challenge him—Rep. John Bayard Anderson; Sen. Howard Henry Baker, Jr.; George Bush; former governor John Bowden Connally; Rep. Phil Crane; Sen. Robert Joseph Dole; and Gov. Ronald Reagan. Carter was resilient, however, and most predictions suggested a close contest in November. On the Democratic side, Carter was challenged by Sen. Edward Kennedy, but his lackluster campaign ensured the president's renomination in August. The Republican contest had narrowed by convention time, with Anderson being the only contender standing in Reagan's way. Reagan rolled over Anderson, but the cerebral congressman refused to give up. Instead, he mounted an independent campaign as a third option in November. The popular Reagan espoused a conservative position in stark contrast to Carter's more moderate positions. When the final votes were counted, Reagan trounced the incumbent president, winning forty-three states to Carter's six (plus the District of Columbia).

ALASKAN HOMESTEADER TICKET

CANDIDATE FOR PRESIDENT:
John Cherry "Jack" Briggs (NM)

AMERICAN INDEPENDENT (AMERICAN) PARTY

CANDIDATE FOR PRESIDENT:
John Richard Rarick

CANDIDATE FOR VICE PRESIDENT:
Eileen Shearer

CANDIDATES FOR PRESIDENTIAL NOMINATION:
Percy Laurie Greaves, Jr.(NY)
John Richard Rarick (LA)
James D. Schumacher (AZ)

CANDIDATES FOR VICE-PRESIDENTIAL NOMINATION:
Arthur Lee (WA)
Thomas McCrary (GA)
Eileen Shearer (CA)

PRIMARY:
JUNE 3, 1980 (CA):
Downey 10,838
Rarick 10,358
others 9

CONVENTION:
August 29–30, 1980, Sacramento (CA)

PLATFORM HIGHLIGHTS:
The lengthy platform of the American Independent Party expressed faith in God, loyalty to the nation, a belief in personal liberty and individual rights, and support for free enterprise.

SUPPORTED:
• an end to secrecy in government
• a restraint of regulatory agencies
• the construction of dams but not the extension of federal authority over rivers
• the development of safe nuclear energy
• the need to conserve energy and create alternative sources through the private sector
• a return to the gold standard
• the right of private citizens to own and exchange precious metals
• a balanced federal budget
• an elimination of wage and price controls
• immediate tax reductions, closure of loopholes, a repeal of the Sixteenth Amendment and adoption of the Liberty Amendment, and the repeal of the federal telephone tax

- restrictions on multinational oil companies
- a repeal of the 160-acre limitation on land that a farmer could irrigate from federal projects
- a gradual elimination of agricultural price supports and subsidies
- collective bargaining and portable retirement benefits
- the rejection of the Equal Rights Amendment (ERA)
- an abolition of federally assisted housing projects
- reforms to make welfare less attractive and more locally controlled
- efforts to make Social Security a voluntary program
- education as a purely local matter, abolishing the Department of Education
- school prayer
- private schools
- the reestablishment of the internal security activities of Congress and the executive branch
- the police and local control of law enforcement
- tough criminal sentencing practices
- the imposition of maximum penalties for skyjacking and political assassinations
- reforms to empower juries
- controls over drug trafficking by instituting mandatory sentencing for dealers, making all narcotics illegal except for prescribed medical purposes, and taking all legislation and administrative action necessary to stop the flow of hard drugs from foreign countries
- strong penalties for obscenity and opposed legalization or special preferences for homosexuals
- the reinstatement of all antiabortion laws and opposed euthanasia
- calls for Congress to remove the appellate jurisdiction of the Supreme Court over school prayer, abortion, busing, and racial or sexual quotas
- the disclosure of campaign contributions and expenditures
- fair treatment under the election laws and application of the equal time and fairness doctrine
- a repeal of the Voting Rights Act of 1965
- the withdrawal of the United States from the United Nations
- the Monroe Doctrine
- a distinctly isolationist perspective
- an end to foreign aid
- a new Neutrality Act to prevent U.S. involvement in foreign wars
- a repudiation of the Panama Canal Treaty
- the denial of statehood for U.S. territories
- a strengthening of the War Powers Act
- a disengagement of the United States from the Middle East
- calls for Iran to be treated as an "outlaw nation" subject to severe sanctions
- tariffs through the use of a Tariff Commission
- a strengthened merchant marine

- a termination of U.S. participation in the General Agreement on Tariffs and Trade (GATT)
- the termination of trade with Communist countries
- a 200-mile limit for U.S. fishing rights and other sea resources, with Communist nations being prohibited from fishing in U.S. waters
- severe restrictions on immigration and the rights of immigrants
- a rejection of the SALT II Treaty
- a repeal of the Arms Control and Disarmament Act
- a highly cautious approach to future disarmament discussions

OPPOSED:

- the 55-mile-per-hour speed limit
- mandatory pollution controls on automobiles
- census questions that invaded privacy
- revenue sharing as a fraud on the public
- regional governments and zoning laws
- a repeal of the Environmental Protection Act
- the establishment of a federal land use policy
- U.S. dependence on foreign and domestic oil monopolies
- the Interstate Commerce Commission and Federal Reserve System
- the imposition of a value-added tax and taxes on retirement pensions
- rent controls and high interest rates
- federal welfare and food stamp programs
- sex education and related programs
- forced busing
- the repeal of the Federal Employment Practices Commission, fair housing legislation, quota systems, and affirmative action programs
- government intrusions into the health care arena
- representation of the District of Columbia in Congress "as if it were a state"
- communism
- gun control
- "judicial usurpation of the constitutional process," by requiring a combination of direct election of some judges and periodic reconfirmation of others
- federal matching funds for campaigns
- unconstitutional and unfair wars (such as Vietnam)
- recognition of Cuba

AMERICAN INDEPENDENT (AMERICAN) PARTY

VOTE FOR PRESIDENTIAL NOMINATION:
RARICK WAS EASILY NOMINATED FOR PRESIDENT ON THE FIRST BALLOT, RECEIVING OVER 80 PERCENT OF THE VOTES.

VOTE FOR VICE-PRESIDENTIAL NOMINATION:
SIMILARLY, SHEARER WON MORE THAN TWO-THIRDS OF THE CONVENTION VOTES FOR VICE PRESIDENT.

- the restoration of friendly relations with South Africa
- the State Department for its "security risks"
- compulsory military training and the draft, instead advocating the reorientation of the economy to peacetime purposes
- war profiteering

AMERICAN PARTY

CANDIDATE FOR PRESIDENT:
Percy Laurie Greaves, Jr. (NY)

CANDIDATE FOR VICE PRESIDENT:
Frank L. Varnum (OR)

PRIMARY:

MAY 27, 1980 (ID):

John Richard Rarick (LA) 97
uncommitted delegates 63

3D CONVENTION:
December 8, 1979, Pasadena (CA)

The American Party and the American Independent Party sought a unity ticket, although unsuccessfully. Greaves was replaced on the American Independent ticket by Rarick.

PLATFORM HIGHLIGHTS:

SUPPORTED:

- the phased termination of agricultural subsidies
- production and price controls
- government-owned reserves
- a protective tariff for agricultural products
- government divestment of Amtrak and the Postal Service
- the abolition of the Interstate Commerce Commission and the Occupational Safety and Health Administration (OSHA)
- a hands-off attitude toward business
- restraint by federal bureaucracies involved in consumer protection
- the restoration of the death penalty
- the elimination of plea bargaining
- a greater use of restitution for criminals to pay victims
- a reform of the "over-permissive" parole system
- stiff mandatory state penalties for crimes committed with a gun
- the breaking of relations with the People's Republic of China because it was a major source of illicit drugs
- the creation of a voucher system and a repeal of compulsory education laws
- voluntary, nondenominational school prayer and local control of school systems
- the removal of price controls and taxes on the production and distribution of energy
- the abolition of the Department of Energy and the Environmental Protection Agency
- the control of illegal aliens
- an end to all foreign aid programs

- the severing of diplomatic and trade relations with all Communist countries
- nonmilitary assistance to anti-Fidel Castro Cubans
- the withdrawal of the United States from the Middle East and a policy of noninvolvement
- the protection of the nation's offshore resources and fishing rights to a distance of 200 miles
- the reestablishment of U.S. sovereignty over the Panama Canal
- the ratification of the "Bricker Amendment" and the withdrawal of the United States from the United Nations
- a requirement that no foreign military action could be pursued for more than seventy-two hours without a declaration of war by Congress
- calls for encouraging Congress to constrict the jurisdiction of federal courts and for limiting the president's authority to issue executive orders
- freedom of choice in pursuing alternative medical treatments
- the abolition of the Federal Reserve System
- a restoration of the gold standard
- a requirement for balancing the budget
- restrictions on the political activities of labor unions
- "right to work" laws
- a move to turn over all federal lands to the states
- the elimination of urban renewal programs
- calls for Congress to restore the House and Senate Internal Security committees and to re-create the Subversive Activities Control Board
- states' rights to legislate on public morality
- a phasing out of Social Security
- charities and state and local governments taking over welfare programs
- tax reforms to level the progressivity of the income tax
- an investigation of tax-exempt foundations
- an end to federal financing of elections
- an end to busing to achieve racial balance along with all federal aid to schools
- the defeat of the ERA
- a phasing out of federal health care programs and the abolition of Professional Services Review organizations
- the abolishment of regional governments and revenue sharing

OPPOSED:

- the conversion to the metric system
- federal initiatives in child care
- all gun control efforts
- fluoridation of water
- "socialized medicine"
- the right of government employees to engage in collective bargaining
- an end to all zoning and land use laws and compulsory federal flood-control insurance
- open housing laws

- the quota system as a method of affirmative action
- abortions, except when necessary to save the mother's life

ALSO:
- criticized minimum wage laws
- denounced secret diplomacy, the U.S. failure in Iran, and the "scandal-ridden" State Department
- repudiated the Strategic Arms Limitations Talks (SALT) I and SALT II treaties

AMERICAN PARTY OF KANSAS

CANDIDATE FOR PRESIDENT:
Frank Winfield Shelton (KS) (Ronald Wilson Reagan [CA] declined)

CANDIDATE FOR VICE PRESIDENT:
Marion Ruck Jackson (KS) (Jack French Kemp [NY] declined)[1]

Former governor Meldrim Thomson of New Hampshire formed the Committee of 56 in 1979 to explore the formation of a Constitution Party to promote conservative, patriotic principles of government. When Ronald Reagan emerged as the top contender for the Republican's presidential nomination, funds for the fledgling Constitution Party evaporated and Thomson withdrew his candidacy. Remnants of the party met and decided to work within the American Party's framework. Accordingly, the American Party of Kansas met and nominated Reagan for president and Kemp for vice president. When both declined, Shelton and Jackson were substituted on the ticket.

PLATFORM HIGHLIGHTS:
The American Party of Kansas supported the free enterprise system, opposed rural electric cooperatives, and generally endorsed the platform of the national American Party (see above).

BUREAUCRATIC PARTY

CANDIDATE FOR PRESIDENT:
James Harlan Boren (VA)

Claiming that bureaucracy is the highest and most beautiful form of self expression, Boren articulated the virtues of red tape and advocated "dynamic inaction" as a way of life. His party propounded the principle "When in doubt, mumble."

PLATFORM HIGHLIGHTS:
SUPPORTED:
- ways to put people to work by studying the problem of unemployment
- a switch in the objectives of the Defense Department and the Postal Service, so that the Defense Department would deliver the mail and the Post Office would deliver munitions

[1]Some sources give Marion Jackson's husband, George E. Jackson, as the vice-presidential candidate.

- a resolution of the busing controversy
- government leaks that promoted memos and "orbital dialogue"
- an international Bureaucrats' Olympics, featuring an executive shot put competition over lunchtime

OPPOSED:
- paper shredding

CITIZENS PARTY

CANDIDATE FOR PRESIDENT:
Barry Commoner (MO)

CANDIDATES FOR VICE PRESIDENT:
Wyretha Wiley Hanson
La Donna Crawford Harris (VA)

1ST CONVENTION:
April 11–13, 1980, Cleveland Plaza Hotel, Cleveland (OH)

The Citizens Party was formed on May 15, 1979, as the National Citizens Organizing Committee. In December 1979, it formally registered with the Federal Elections Commission as the Citizens Party.

Approximately 260 delegates from thirty states attended the first nominating convention.

PLATFORM HIGHLIGHTS:
The platform of the Citizens Party charged business with greed and government with incompetence. It sought public control over the energy industry.

SUPPORTED:
- an end to nuclear power development
- solar energy
- the rationing of gasoline to reduce consumption by 20 percent
- the production of ethyl alcohol from crops as an alternative to oil
- cutbacks in military spending
- the imposition of price controls to curb inflation
- public representation on corporate boards
- an end to the arms race
- the elimination of the draft
- the development of a National Health Service
- a full implementation of treaty obligations with Native Americans
- an end to U.S. interference in the affairs of other nations
- the reconstruction of the railroads
- the ratification of the ERA and equal pay for equal work
- affirmative action in education and employment
- local governments and labor unions taking control over government investment and loan guarantees
- family farms and small businesses
- the reindustrialization of basic industries under local community and worker control
- an end to the dumping of toxic wastes
- limits on plant closures

OPPOSED:

- the gentrification of neighborhoods
- condominium conversions
- Iran for taking U.S. hostages
- the Soviet Union for its interference in Afghanistan

CITIZENS PARTY

Vote for Presidential and Vice-Presidential Nomination: Although the presidential and vice-presidential candidates were chosen at the convention, the party's full membership voted on ratifying the slate by mailgram during the week following the convention.

COMMUNIST PARTY

CANDIDATE FOR PRESIDENT:
Gus Hall (NY)

CANDIDATE FOR VICE PRESIDENT:
Angela Yvonne Davis (CA)

PLATFORM HIGHLIGHTS:

SUPPORTED:

- the ratification of the SALT II treaty and an end to the arms race
- normalized relations with the Soviet Union and negotiations for a mutual arms reduction
- proposals to cut the military budget by $100 billion, transferring the savings to domestic programs
- an end to the blockade of Cuba
- independence for Puerto Rico
- a reduction in the work day to six hours without reducing pay
- unions and communities taking control of closed factories
- increases in unemployment benefits to 75 percent of prevailing wages
- the creation of new jobs under an emergency program
- the enactment of a labor bill of rights
- a repeal of the Taft-Hartley and Landrum-Griffin acts
- an end to all restrictions on the rights to organize and strike
- affirmative action programs at all levels of hiring, training, and upgrading employment
- full rights for foreign-born and undocumented workers
- full civil and trade union rights for farm workers
- government guarantees for low-interest loans and free crop insurance for farmers
- 100 percent parity prices for family farm operators
- an end to trade restrictions and embargoes against Socialist and developing countries
- the defeat of section 1722 (a criminal code revision)
- affirmative action programs in housing, education, health care, and political representation, as well as employment
- strong enforcement of civil rights laws and the abolition of the death penalty
- equal access to the ballot and mass media for independent candidates and political parties
- a guaranteed minimum annual income of $15,000 for a family of four
- an end to evictions and forced repossessions
- a prohibition against utility shutoffs
- tax exemptions for family incomes below $25,000
- the ratification of the ERA
- full political representation for women
- comparable pay for comparable work
- the prosecution of employers who discriminate against or harass women on the job
- funding for comprehensive child care, family planning, and abortions
- an end to involuntary sterilization
- the passage of a National Youth Act
- the elimination of the draft
- free education through the college level
- unemployment compensation for first-time job seekers
- expanded cultural and recreational opportunities for young people
- increased Social Security benefits, adjusted for inflation
- free public transportation for seniors
- the elimination of the Medicare deductible and restrictions on senior employment
- special rent, utilities, and mortgage assistance programs for the needy
- the passage of a National Health Care Act to provide free and comprehensive health care for all
- public ownership of the health care industry
- an expansion of public health facilities and stronger enforcement of the Occupational Safety and Health Act
- calls for monopolies to pay for environmental cleanup
- the strengthening and enforcement of antipollution standards
- full compensation at corporate expense for the victims of pollution
- the nationalization of the energy industry, with federal support for the development of alternative energy sources
- the closing of all nuclear plants until their safety was proven

OPPOSED:

- racism
- the Ku Klux Klan
- Nazis
- the Federal Bureau of Investigation (FBI)
- the Central Intelligence Agency (CIA)

CONSTITUTIONAL PARTY

CANDIDATE FOR PRESIDENT:
Talmadge Martin Warren (VA)

A schoolteacher, Warren sought the presidency as a learning experience for his eighth-grade students.

PLATFORM HIGHLIGHTS:

SUPPORTED:

- equal media space for all candidates in a primary
- a "none of the above" ballot line
- the direct election of Supreme Court justices
- a 20 percent cut in the federal payroll
- restrictions on U.S. investment in Mexico and foreign investments in U.S. businesses
- periodic open bidding for such privatized government monopolies as Amtrak and the Postal Service
- a shift in foreign aid from government to voluntary channels
- a national informational network, the tracking and prosecuting of industrial spying, and a nuclear-free world
- the deployment of the military to aid the war on drugs
- the federal government's provision of full health care for all citizens, who, along with their families, would closely monitor all charges
- the monitoring of the possession of semiautomatic and assault weapons
- criminals being held responsible for compensating their victims
- a child allowance for married couples with preschool children when the mother does not work outside the home for more than sixteen hours per week

OPPOSED:

- the "borrow and pay" approach to government financing

CONSTITUTIONAL VALUES PARTY

CANDIDATE FOR PRESIDENT:
    William John Eisenman (NJ)

The Constitutional Values Party sought to have government leaders "obey the simple and absolute words of the Constitution, especially the First and Fourteenth Amendments."

PLATFORM HIGHLIGHTS:

SUPPORTED:

- an end to inflation, which was defined as a national security issue
- judicial reform to reduce the influence of "Big Money"
- alternative cancer therapies
- the streamlining of the Food and Drug Administration
- open and truthful foreign policy
- efforts to ensure the rich bear their "fair share of taxes"
- control over monopolies
- energy alternatives

OPPOSED:

- the notion of "victimless crimes," urging that police efforts be directed toward "real crimes" of violence
- polluters, calling for harsh penalties for companies engaged in environmental pollution
- nuclear power

CORRECTION, PUNISHMENT, AND REMEDY PARTY

CANDIDATE FOR PRESIDENT:
    James Zalmer Hardy (KY)

PLATFORM HIGHLIGHTS:

SUPPORTED:

- a minimum-assistance welfare system based on the age of the recipient
- a welfare system to help the destitute, disabled, and unemployed
- a retirement system that provided enough money for a decent standard of living
- computerized at-home voting
- federal and state television networks
- the promotion of health foods
- a new, unified court system that would handle all cases, whether civil, criminal, or tax related
- a "total taxpayer's clinic for all minor illnesses"
- federal domestic aid and assistance
- direct payment to taxpayers for lengthy and terminal medical cases
- a full educational curriculum
- student stipends
- classes in constitutional law made available to the general public
- more democratic procedures of governance
- the notion of re-creating the nation and dividing it into states no larger than twenty-five square miles in size
- open residency in each state for "unanimous thinkers"

OPPOSED:

- slavery
- criminal rule
- the "church"
- political parties
- the country's existing political leadership, condemned as "sick and bigoted"

DEMOCRATIC PARTY

CANDIDATE FOR PRESIDENT:
    James Earl "Jimmy" Carter, Jr.

CANDIDATE FOR VICE PRESIDENT:
    Walter Frederick Mondale

CANDIDATES FOR PRESIDENTIAL NOMINATION:
    Frank Ahern (LA)
    John Bayard Anderson (IL)
    James William Barton (IL)
    Edward Peter Beard (RI)
    Joseph Thomas Bongiovanni (FL)
    Edmund Gerald "Jerry" Brown, Jr. (CA)
    Orville Harris Brown (KY)
    Dale Leon Bumpers (AR)
    James Harry Burch (VA)
    George Herbert Walker Bush (TX)
    Robert Carlyle Byrd (WV)

Hugh Leo Carey (NY)
James Earl "Jimmy" Carter, Jr. (GA)
Anthony Solomon Chavez (TX)
John Martin Chick (NY)
John Chester Culver (IA)
Ronald Vernie Dellums (CA)
Charles Clifton Finch (MS)
Gerald Rudolph Ford, Jr. (MI)
Carl Floyd Freeman (GA)
Paul King Germani (MA)
James Irvin Glover (NJ)
Lawrence W. Goldberg (PA)
Kent Raymond Hance (TX)
Koryne Emily Horbal (MN)
Richard Broughton Kay (OH)
Edward Moore Kennedy (MA)
Albert Leo LaFontaine (MN)
Lyndon Hermyle LaRouche, Jr. (NY)
Walter Gerhard Lux (FL)
Robert Earl Maddox, Jr. (FL)
Scott Milne Matheson (UT)
Walter Frederick Mondale (MN)
Edmund Sixtus Muskie (ME)
William Leslie Nuckols (AL)
Grady O'Cummings III (NY)
Edward William Proxmire (WI)
Jennings Fitz Randolph (WV)
Ronald Wilson Reagan (CA)
Don Reaux (TX)
Raymond Allen Peter Rollinson (NJ)
Gerald Martin Rothbard (FL)
Daniel Ernest Sanderson (CA)
John Joseph Semensi (MA)
Bobbie Weldon Shofner (NV)
Warren Richard Spannaus (MN)
Thomas Jefferson "Tom" Steed (OK)
Duke Esten Stockton (WA)
Marlin Dale Thacker (AL)
Peter Frederick Tittl (IL)
Alice Tripp (MN)
Charles Gordon Vick (TN)
David Vincent Wade (MA)
Byron Chester Wentworth (MA)

CANDIDATES FOR VICE-PRESIDENTIAL NOMINATION:

Leslie Aspin (WI)
Mario Biaggi (NY)
Melvin Boozer (DC)
Edmund Gerald "Jerry" Brown, Jr. (CA)
Shirley Anita St. Hill Chisholm (NY)
Thomas Andrew Daschle (SD)
Ennis Francis (NY)
Lawrence W. Goldberg (PA)
Michelle Kathleen Gray (CA)
Richard Grayson (NY)
Edward Michael Harrington (NY)

Elihu Mason Harris (CA)
Frank Minis Johnson, Jr. (AL)
Barbara Charlene Jordan (TX)
Paul Koretz (CA)
Maryann Elizabeth Hull Kuharski (WA)
Theodore Ralph Kulongoski (OR)
Patrick Joseph Lucey (WI)
James A. "Jim" McDermott (WA)
George Stanley McGovern (SD)
Barbara Ann Mikulski (MD)
Walter Frederick Mondale (MN)
Roberto A. Mondragon (NM)
George Moody
Rick Mullen
Gaylord Anton Nelson (WI)
George Orwell (satire)
Dennis Peron (CA)
Charley Prine, Sr. (TX)
William Aloysius Redmond (IL)
Edward Gene Rendell (PA)
Eunice Mary Kennedy Shriver (MD)
Gerry Sikorski (MN)
Patricia A. Stone Simon (MA)
Jim Thomas (OK)
Eric Tovar (CA)
Morris King Udall (AZ)
Jim Wheeler
William Wayne Winpisinger (DC)

PRIMARIES:
FEBRUARY 17, 1980 (PR):
Carter 449,681
Kennedy 418,068
Brown 1,660
others 826

FEBRUARY 26, 1980 (NH):
Carter 52,692
Kennedy 41,745
Brown 10,743
LaRouche 2,326
Kay 566
others 3,858

MARCH 4, 1980 (MA):
Kennedy 590,393
Carter 260,401
Brown 31,498
no preference 19,663
others 5,368

MARCH 4, 1980 (VT):
Carter 29,015
Kennedy 10,135
Brown 358
LaRouche 6
others 189

MARCH 11, 1980 (AL):
Carter 193,734
Kennedy 31,382
Brown 9,529
Nuckols 609
Maddox 540
unpledged delegates 1,670

MARCH 11, 1980 (FL):
Carter 666,321
Kennedy 254,727
Brown 53,474
Kay 19,160
no preference 104,321

MARCH 11, 1980 (GA):
Carter 338,772
Kennedy 32,315
Brown 7,255
Finch 1,378
Kay 840
LaRouche 513
unpledged delegates 3,707

MARCH 18, 1980 (IL):
Carter 780,787
Kennedy 359,875
Brown 39,168
LaRouche 19,192
Anderson 1,643
others 402

MARCH 25, 1980 (CT):
Kennedy 98,662
Carter 87,207
LaRouche 5,617
Brown 5,386
unpledged delegates 13,403

MARCH 25, 1980 (NY):
Kennedy 582,757
Carter 406,305

APRIL 1, 1980 (KS):
Carter 109,807
Kennedy 61,318
Brown 9,434
Finch 629
Maddox 632
Ahern 571
Rollinson 364
none of the names shown 11,163

APRIL 1, 1980 (WI):
Carter 353,662
Kennedy 189,520
Brown 74,496
LaRouche 6,896
Finch 1,842
none of the names shown 2,694
others 509

APRIL 5, 1980 (LA):
Carter 199,956
Kennedy 80,797
Brown 16,774
Finch 11,153
Kay 3,362
Maddox 2,830
Reaux 2,255
unpledged delegates 41,614

APRIL 22, 1980 (PA):
Kennedy 736,854
Carter 732,332
Brown 37,669
Anderson 9,182
Bush 2,074
Reagan 1,097
Ford 150
no preference 93,865

MAY 3, 1980 (TX):
Carter 770,390
Kennedy 314,129
Brown 35,585
unpledged delegates 257,250

MAY 6, 1980 (DC):
Kennedy 39,561
Carter 23,697
LaRouche 892

MAY 6, 1980 (IN):
Carter 398,949
Kennedy 190,492

MAY 6, 1980 (NC):
Carter 516,778
Kennedy 130,684
Brown 21,420
no preference 68,380

MAY 6, 1980 (TN):
Carter 221,658
Kennedy 53,258
Brown 5,612
Finch 1,663
LaRouche 925
unpledged delegates 11,515
others 49

MAY 13, 1980 (MD):
Carter 226,528
Kennedy 181,091
Brown 14,313
Finch 4,891
LaRouche 4,388
unpledged delegates 45,879

MAY 13, 1980 (NE):
Carter 72,120
Kennedy 57,826
Brown 5,478

LaRouche 1,169
unpledged delegates 16,041
others 1,247

MAY 20, 1980 (MI):
Brown 23,043
LaRouche 8,948
unpledged delegates 36,385
others 10,048

MAY 20, 1980 (OR):
Carter 208,693
Kennedy 114,651
Brown 34,409
Anderson 5,407
Reagan 2,206
Bush 1,838

MAY 27, 1980 (AR):
Carter 269,375
Kennedy 78,542
Finch 19,469
unpledged delegates 80,904

MAY 27, 1980 (ID):
Carter 31,383
Kennedy 11,087
Brown 2,078
unpledged delegates 5,934

MAY 27, 1980 (KY):
Carter 160,819
Kennedy 55,167
Kay 2,609
Finch 2,517
unpledged delegates 19,219

MAY 27, 1980 (NV):
Carter 25,159
Kennedy 19,296
none of the names shown. 22,493

JUNE 3, 1980 (CA):
Kennedy. 1,507,142
Carter. 1,266,276
Brown 135,962
LaRouche 71,779
unpledged delegates 382,759
others 51

JUNE 3, 1980 (MT):
Carter 66,922
Kennedy 47,671
no preference 15,466

JUNE 3, 1980 (NJ):
Kennedy 315,109
Carter 212,387
LaRouche 13,913
unpledged delegates 19,499

JUNE 3, 1980 (NM):
Kennedy 73,721

Carter 66,621
LaRouche 4,798
Finch. 4,490
unpledged delegates 9,734

JUNE 3, 1980 (OH):
Carter 605,744
Kennedy 523,874
LaRouche 35,268
Kay 21,524

JUNE 3, 1980 (RI):
Kennedy 26,179
Carter 9,907
LaRouche 1,160
Brown. 310
unpledged delegates. 771

JUNE 3, 1980 (SD):
Kennedy 33,418
Carter 31,251
unpledged delegates 4,094

JUNE 3, 1980 (WV):
Carter 197,687
Kennedy 120,247

38TH CONVENTION:
August 11–14, 1980, Madison Square Garden, New
   York (NY)
John White, temporary chairman
Thomas P. "Tip" O'Neill, Jr. (MA), permanent chair
Dianne Feinstein (CA), cochair
Morris King Udall (AZ), keynoter

PLATFORM HIGHLIGHTS:
The 1980 Democratic platform was a lengthy recitation of
the problems confronting the nation—an unusual approach
for the party in power.

SUPPORTED:
• promises to fight the recession and unemployment,
  without sacrificing anti-inflationary initiatives
• a $12 billion antirecession jobs program
• countercyclic assistance for cities
• more youth employment
• expanded training programs for women and displaced
  homemakers
• worker training programs
• increased opportunities for seniors
• railroad rehabilitation
• the restoration of the housing industry
• a strengthening of the National Accord with Labor
• further targeted tax reductions
• restraint in federal spending
• a reduction in the interest rate
• the deregulation of certain industries
• tax simplification and new depreciation rules to stimulate selective capital investment
• patent reform
• investment, innovation, and competitiveness

- increased export trade
- the elimination of unfair trade practices, such as dumping
- technical assistance to firms doing business abroad
- reforms in the Hatch Act to extend civil rights to federal employees
- legislation to permit public employees and agricultural workers to engage in collective bargaining and to allow workers in the building trades to picket
- a repeal of section 14 (b) of the Taft-Hartley Act
- protective measures for workers affected by plant closures
- special assistance to workers in distressed industries
- promises of an adequate minimum benefit for persons who are unemployed or have an employment-related disability or sickness
- small businesses, particularly women's business enterprises and minority businesses, and pledged continued assistance
- the "comparable worth" principle, outlining a series of initiatives to reduce the economic inequities faced by women
- job training and apprenticeship programs for women, youth, minorities, and persons who seem unemployable
- strong consumer protection efforts
- continued funding for Food Stamps and expansion of the Women, Infants, and Children (WIC) program
- legislation to overturn the Illinois Brick case
- the enforcement of antitrust laws and the control of corporate conglomerates
- efforts to provide consumers with the information and education necessary to make informed judgments in the marketplace
- the enactment of a universal and comprehensive national health insurance program, combined with a "Child Health Assurance Program" (under an expanded Medicaid benefit)
- special attention for mental health and long-term care
- the nursing profession and incentives for more women and minorities to pursue nursing and other health-related careers
- the Roe v. Wade decision
- a demand that Medicaid reimbursements be made more equitable
- a pledge to help financially distressed public hospitals
- a promise to reduce unnecessary prescribing of drugs
- efforts to combat substance abuse through prevention and rehabilitation, treatment, and a reduction in the supply of illicit narcotics, as well as the prosecution of drug traffickers
- new job opportunities for seniors
- expanded nutrition programs
- the creation of senior centers and supportive programs for education, recreation, health, and outreach for seniors
- Social Security as a sacred program that was beyond politics
- a greater portability of pension plans and demanded a review of discrimination against women in pension plans

- an overhaul of the "inequitable and archaic" welfare system to promote enhanced dignity and the recipients' return to productivity
- greater coordination among public agencies
- federal assumption of the local government's burden in welfare and a phased-in reduction in the state share
- expansion of child care programs
- low-income energy assistance
- an end to regulations that punish intact families
- homage to veterans with pledges of improved education, training, and other benefits, along with a commitment to study the Agent Orange problem and to initiate construction of a Vietnam War Memorial
- continued federal support for education, full enforcement of Title IX regulations, and backing for compensatory education efforts
- continued aid programs for areas that were affected by the presence of federal installations and military bases
- school desegregation
- bilingual education
- increased support for vocational and technical education
- constitutionally acceptable federal support to low- and moderate-income students in private schools
- full and appropriate public education for handicapped children (in the least restrictive environment)
- an ambitious program of public and private scholarships and grants to aid students (especially low-income, minority, women, and graduate-level students) attending universities and colleges
- adult education, teacher training, and family-centered developmental and educational child care programs
- the school breakfast, milk, and lunch programs
- an extension of child care through new tax credits for families and other means, including opportunities for flexible hours and job sharing for parents
- efforts to acknowledge the problem of juvenile delinquency and to make federal programs more sensitive to the needs of the family
- efforts to increase housing stock, enforce fair housing laws, ease mortgage credit, and promote rehabilitation of housing to address the housing shortage
- mass transit, deregulation of the trucking industry, increased flexibility for railroads, a strong U.S.-flagged ocean transportation system, and a review of the problems confronting the automobile industry
- efforts to revitalize urban areas—a strong jobs policy, public works programs to rebuild city infrastructure, incentives for energy conservation, local government revenue sharing, tax revisions to encourage investment in urban areas, and consolidation of grant programs
- neighborhood development
- stronger small communities and rural areas by protecting prime agricultural land
- the passage of welfare reforms that affected the rural disadvantaged
- the promotion of rural energy self-sufficiency

- improvements in rural housing
- the provision of low-cost electric and telephone service to rural areas
- efforts to attend to the health care needs for rural communities
- increased funding for research and development in science and technology and a pledge to launch the Space Shuttle
- the National Endowment for the Arts and the National Endowment for the Humanities
- full enforcement of civil rights laws, support for desegregation, humanization of immigration laws, and achievement of economic justice
- ratification of the ERA, boycotts of unratified states, and withholding financial and technical support for candidates who do not support the ERA
- the adoption of the District of Columbia Voting Rights Act, passage of the Equal Pay and the Age Discrimination acts, and enforcement of the Fair Housing Act and Voting Rights Act of 1975
- a revision of the Uniform Code of Military Justice
- reforms in the grand jury system
- the enacting of charters for the FBI and intelligence agencies that recognize vital civil liberties
- a constitutionally sensitive criminal code
- the enactment of broad legislation governing financial, insurance, medical, and research records to protect privacy
- reproductive freedom for women
- federal appointments for women and minorities
- the inclusion of handicapped persons in the coverage of the Fair Housing and Civil Rights acts
- greater independence and opportunities for individuals with disabilities, including the right to vote, implementation of section 504 regulations, job training, and accessible federal facilities and transportation
- a national holiday to commemorate Martin Luther King's birthday
- initiatives to combat sexual and domestic violence
- self-determination for American Samoa, Guam, and the Northern Mariana Islands, Puerto Rico, the Virgin Islands
- the recognition of ethnic Americans and their contributions to a pluralist society
- the treaty rights of American Indians and the abandonment of the policy of tribal status termination
- U.S. citizens abroad with promises of tax relief, eligibility for Medicare, and reforms to make it easier for parents to ensure citizenship for their children born overseas
- the deregulation and streamlining of the regulatory process, while reasserting the need for appropriate regulations to protect consumers and providers in the areas of health, safety, and the environment
- fundamental tax reform, including the closure of loopholes

- improvements in the management of the federal government
- more government openness and integrity (e.g., reform in the laws governing lobbyists)
- efforts to curtail the availability of handguns while supporting the right of sportsmen to possess guns for hunting and target shooting
- a revised federal criminal code
- the newly enacted Law Enforcement Assistance Act, the Juvenile Justice and Delinquency Act, and the Runaway Youth Act
- prison reform, federal assistance to the victims of crime, the use of restitution, affirmative action in the recruitment and hiring of police, swift investigation of civil rights complaints, and sanctions against the excessive or illegal use of force by law enforcement personnel
- calls to minimize paperwork and red tape
- the privacy of the mails, which was to be respected by the Postal Service
- public financing of congressional elections
- restrictions on political action committees
- encouragements for voter participation
- "the development of the nation's first comprehensive energy policy" and continued support for energy efficiency and conservation (e.g., residential programs) as the party's highest priority
- a 55-mile-per-hour speed limit
- incentives for the use of cogeneration, solar energy, and renewable energy resources
- an implementation of mandatory building energy-performance standards
- major research efforts to develop synthetic and alternative renewable energy sources
- greater reliance on coal
- cooperative ventures between the federal government and American Indian and Alaskan Native tribes to promote environmentally sound resource development
- accelerated exploration for oil on federal lands
- special energy programs for Hawaii and the U.S. territories and trust territories
- restrictions on offshore oil leases
- research and development of hydrogen- and electric-powered vehicles and alcohol fuels
- the need for a standby gasoline rationing plan and replenishment of the Strategic Petroleum Reserve
- the development of a safe, environmentally sound, toxic and nuclear waste disposal plan and promises to retire nuclear power plants gradually from production
- the use of funds generated by the Windfall Profits Tax to expand mass transit
- the protection of the countryside and coastlines from overdevelopment and mismanagement, while attending to the global problems of deforestation, the loss of irreplaceable species, oil spills, thinning of the ozone shield, growing world population, acid rain, and carbon dioxide buildup

- automobile pollution standards
- mass transit
- recycling
- adequate funding for the Environmental Protection Agency and other environmental agencies
- a study of alternatives to the importation of water into arid and semiarid regions and a national water program
- increased emphasis on desalinization
- continued attention to the expansion of farm exports
- a refusal to impose additional farm embargoes in the future
- an increase in target prices for farm commodities
- low-cost agricultural credit
- increased support for agricultural research
- a strong program of soil and water conservation
- the rebuilding of the agricultural transportation system
- the protection of family farms through mandatory disclosure of foreign farm ownership, estate tax reforms, and modernization of the 1902 Reclamation Act
- more involvement of farmers and ranchers in the development of farm programs
- the enforcement of the laws relating to farm labor organization and bargaining
- retraining programs for farm workers displaced by mechanization
- the Capper-Volstead Act
- multiple-use management of the nation's forests
- speedy resolution of the Roadless Area Review and Evaluation program
- assistance to private, nonindustrial forest owners to improve their management practices
- implementation of a sustained-yield policy on public lands
- a concentration of timber sales in areas of greatest potential
- the development of the U.S. fishing industry, with a phaseout of foreign fishing within the 200-mile offshore limit and increased federal-private research efforts
- fisheries' conservation and management, with a fair share of the costs borne by foreign fishermen using the waters inside the 200-mile limit
- the completion of the Law of the Sea Treaty negotiations
- aquaculture
- sport fishing
- the protection and enhancement of fish habitats
- human rights in the foreign policy arena
- close consultation with allied nations
- improved relations with the Third World
- peace in the Middle East, with special backing for the security of Israel
- the MX missile, cruise missiles, the Trident submarine, rapid-deployment forces, and land-based intercontinental ballistic missiles (ICBMs) as deterrents to Soviet aggression
- arms control efforts, while demanding ratification of the SALT II agreements

- increased wages for military personnel and upgraded combat readiness of the armed forces
- pledges to defend the Persian Gulf against outside forces
- free emigration for Soviet Jewry
- the control of international terrorism
- the ratification of the Genocide Convention
- international efforts to curb illegal immigration (recognizing the special problems associated with Cuban and Haitian immigrants)
- financial backing for the United Nations Children's Fund (UNICEF), the International Red Cross, relief for Kampuchea and the National Cambodian Crisis Committee, Afghan refugees, and the UN High Commissioner for Refugees
- the Camp David Accords with Israel and Egypt
- the recognition of Jerusalem as the capital of Israel (and the promised future site of the U.S. Embassy)
- a denouncement of Iran's hostage taking at the U.S. Embassy in Tehran
- the bargaining over oil prices with the Organization of Petroleum Exporting Countries (OPEC) on the basis of equality
- the North Atlantic Treaty Organization (NATO) and the European Community, along with a negotiated peace in Cyprus and Northern Ireland
- promises to nurture the U.S. relationship with Japan
- pledges to base U.S. export-import policy on the principle of "fair trade," to restrict international "dumping" and to regulate the import of textiles and apparel
- the enforcement of customs laws
- the need for a strong currency
- international energy cooperation
- increased efforts to combat world hunger and the achievement of a new collective worldwide commitment to economic development (including participation by OPEC and the Communist nations)
- greater cooperation with Latin America and Mexico
- the Panama Canal Treaty
- the ratification of Protocol I of the Treaty of Tlatelolco and the American Convention on Human Rights
- a further normalization of relations with the People's Republic of China
- the five-nation Association of Southeast Asian Nations (ASEAN) pact
- the people of East Timor
- further liberalization in the Philippines, Taiwan, and other nations in the Pacific rim
- aid to reconstruct Zimbabwe
- the withdrawal of Soviet and Cuban troops from Africa
- self-determination for Namibia and Southern Africa and an end to apartheid in South Africa, promising to use divestiture to promote its demise
- a normalization of relations with Angola and a negotiated settlement to the conflict in the western Sahara
- the United Nations, while seeking its reform and restructuring

- a reexamination of the "Connally Reservation"
- a new UN high commissioner for human rights
- the creation of a UN Peacekeeping Reserve
- new UN agencies dealing with volunteer service, international trade organizations, higher education, implementation of the Law of the Sea agreement, mediation and conciliation, international disarmament, and international terrorism

OPPOSED:
- a balanced budget amendment
- efforts to weaken occupational health and safety laws
- a sub-minimum wage for youth and other workers, while calling for an increase in the minimum wage

- any constitutional amendment that might restrict a woman's right to an abortion
- all efforts to cut or tax retirement and employment benefits and eliminate mandatory retirement
- the closure of schools serving American Indians and Alaskan Natives without consulting the affected tribes
- redlining
- hate groups like the Ku Klux Klan and American Nazi Party
- "truth tests" in employment
- involuntary sterilization
- the acquisition of coal companies and solar energy companies by major oil corporations

DEMOCRATIC PARTY
VOTE FOR PRESIDENTIAL NOMINATION:

Candidate	Ballot: 1	1a	Candidate	Ballot: 1	1a
Carter	2,123³⁄₁₀₀	2,129³⁄₁₀₀	Tripp	2	2
Kennedy	1,150⁴⁸⁄₁₀₀	1,150⁴⁸⁄₁₀₀	Spannaus	2	2
Brown, E. G., Jr.	11	11	Mondale	1	1
Proxmire	10	10	Muskie	1	1
Matheson	5	5	Carey	1	1
Horbal	5	5	Steed	1	1
Dellums	2½	2½	Brown	1	1
Culver	2	0	Bumpers	1	1
Hance	2	2	uncommitted	10	10
Byrd	2	2	not voting	5	5
Randolph	2	2	absent	2	2

VOTE FOR VICE-PRESIDENTIAL NOMINATION:

Candidate	Ballot: 1	Candidate	Ballot: 1
Mondale	2,428⁷⁄₁₀	Thomas	1
Boozer	49	Wheeler	1
Rendell	28	Shriver	1
Mondragon	19	Nelson	1
Chisholm	12	Kulongoski	1
Simon	11	Moody	1
Daschle	10	Prine	1
Mullen	4	McDermott	1
Harris	3	Aspin	1
Lucey	3	Orwell	1
Jordan	3	Koretz	1
McGovern	2	Peron	1
Winpisinger	2	Gray	1
Tovar	2	Mikulski	1
Udall	2	Biaggi	1
Brown	2	Kuharski	1
Redmond	1	Goldberg	1
Johnson	1	Sikorski	1
Harrington	1		

- irresponsible actions by oil companies
- noise pollution
- the Soviet invasion of Afghanistan and endorsed the boycott of the Olympic Games in Moscow
- the creation of an independent Palestinian state

ALSO:

- noted the accomplishments of the Carter administration and reasserted its commitment to the goals of the Humphrey-Hawkins Full Employment Act

DOWN WITH LAWYERS PARTY

CANDIDATE FOR PRESIDENT:

William Gahres (NJ)

CANDIDATE FOR VICE PRESIDENT:

Joseph F. Loughlin (NJ)

Gahres was a Garnegat (NJ) gadfly involved in local zoning and land use disputes and arguments with the press. He refuted the value of legal notices and the services of lawyers, among other things.

FARMER LABOR PARTY

CANDIDATE FOR PRESIDENT:

Frederick Douglass Kirkpatrick (NY)

PLATFORM HIGHLIGHTS:

Folk singer Kirkpatrick proclaimed his central theme— "We need each other"—through his "Declaration of Interdependence."

SUPPORTED:

- full employment
- health care and insurance for all
- forty acres and a tractor for all African Americans
- the abolition of tax loopholes
- the preservation of nature
- efforts to "take crime out of the suites" (i.e., eliminate white collar crime) and create a nonviolent economy
- a 30-percent cut in the military budget
- the abandonment of the B-1 bomber
- the withdrawal of U.S. troops from the Philippines, the Republic of Korea, and other foreign lands
- the conversion of the educational curricula to teach people how to use their hands and their minds
- a return to an agriculturally dominated society and an educational system that emphasizes "sane and healthy living" and nonviolent work education
- the return of U.S. industry from abroad
- a socialized food program (which would limit food costs to 10 percent of income)
- the preservation of the family farm
- the creation of socialized housing
- an end to the oil monopoly
- the elimination of the oil depletion allowance
- the enforcement of the antitrust laws

- an imposition of heavy fines for price fixing
- "world citizenship"
- a rotating, grassroots world council on basic human needs
- international exchange programs
- reasonable defense measures
- foreign aid based on humanitarian concerns
- basic human rights
- the decentralization of power in the cities
- respect for "seasoned citizens"

OPPOSED:

- bigotry and big business' role in racial discrimination
- white-collar crime
- the criminal abuses of authority by the FBI and the CIA

FREEDOM PARTY

CANDIDATE FOR PRESIDENT:

James Morris Woods (GA)

Claiming he sensed an erosion of constitutional freedoms "by a government that is too large and uncontrollable," Woods entered the 1980 presidential election campaign.

PLATFORM HIGHLIGHTS:

SUPPORTED:

- reductions in government bureaucracy and spending
- the elimination of the federal income tax
- the establishment of a Presidential Youth Committee
- reinvigorated feelings of patriotism
- the formation of a Volunteer Forces of America group under the guidance of senior citizen
- the restoration labor-business harmony
- efforts to elicit the best from teachers, farmers, ministers, and others
- states' rights
- a strong national defense
- a decrease in the country's dependence on foreign oil
- the free enterprise system
- the right for individuals to own gold and silver
- a ratification of the "Liberty Amendment" (which would require privatization of all government business-type activities)

OPPOSED:

- socialism
- high taxes
- treaties that compromise the rights of citizens

INDEPENDENT

CANDIDATES FOR PRESIDENT:

Lord Robert Benedict (NJ)

Earl Edward Black (KS)

Jerry Leon Carroll (CA)

Barton Eugene Chandler (NE)

Jack Cody (TX)

James Wesley Cox (WA)[1]
Charles Wesley De Shon (MO)
Prophet Elijah (NY)[2]
Nell K. Fiola (MN)
Joseph McDermott Graham, Jr. (NJ)
Jeffrey L. Hale (OH)
Richard Rhorer Hill (TX)
Robert Waverly Hobson III (NJ)
Donald Leroy Huffman (OH)
Robert Hulick (KS)
Joseph Jeffers (MO)
Charles Milton Johnson (CA)
Robert Derwood "Buck" Ladner (MS)
Joseph LaMotte (NY)
James Albert Land, Jr. (TX)
Charles Galen McCoy (WA)
William R. Mestice (NJ)
James Robert Montgomery (AL)[3]
Geneva Wilma Mueller (MO)
George Alexander Muzyk (MD)
U. Utah Phillips (UT)[4]
Carl Leon Pickett (TX)
Paul Reed (CA)
Paul Terry Reed (CT)
Charles Norton Reinert (CA)
Arthur P. Sanchez (CA)
K. Core Seaman (CO)
Milton Winfield Showell (MD)
Jimmy Ray Shubert (TX)
Steven Alan Silbiger (KS)
Fred Silverman (NY)
Paul Elmore Somnier, Jr. (AL)
Frank Starr (IN)
Earl Vern "Blackjack" Stevens (MO)
Donald Sullivan (MA)
John Joseph Thomas (DC)
Glen Eldon Totten (WI)
Garrett Brock Trapnell (IL)
Allan Vogel (TX)

[1]Cox campaigned as a "new face," declaring that "the reason and the only one [that I am running for president] is that I want to try and help my fellow Americans." He refused to make "big promises that cannot be kept," but he did indicate he wanted to collect foreign debts and cut foreign aid, promote tax reform and a flat income tax, establish a national health program, and put people back to work.
[2]Prophet Elijah sought the presidency because he was concerned "that many do not have the proper food, clothing, and shelter." He promised jobs for the unemployed, cuts in the military budget, and racial and economic justice. He opposed the death penalty, mandatory celibacy in the priesthood, prayer before saints, and homosexuality. Basing his campaign on the belief that he was "called to prophecy," his political and religious views were closely connected.
[3]Montgomery sought the presidency to right a perceived wrong done to him by the Social Security Administration. His running mate was Leo Frank Suiter of Alabama.
[4]Phillips ran as the "sloth and indolence" candidate and urged voters to vote for themselves. If elected, he promised to take possession of the White House and do nothing. His running mate, Mallard Fillmore, was a fictitious character.

Martin E. Wendelkin (NJ)
James Herbert Wihlborg (AK)

LIBERTARIAN PARTY

CANDIDATE FOR PRESIDENT:
Edward Emerson Clark

CANDIDATE FOR VICE PRESIDENT:
David Koch (NY)

CANDIDATES FOR PRESIDENTIAL NOMINATION:
Edward Emerson Clark (CA)
William H. Hunscher (NH)

PRIMARIES:
MAY 27, 1980 (ID):
Clark 88
uncommitted delegates 39

JUNE 3, 1980 (CA):
no candidates filed

CONVENTION:
September 6–9, 1979, Los Angeles (CA)

PLATFORM HIGHLIGHTS:
The Libertarian platform reiterated the party's Statement of Principles and denied the existence of any conflict between civil order and individual rights. The party's positions were not based on the moral values of specific practices but on a fundamental belief that people's rights must be recognized. Personal responsibility, therefore, was a cardinal tenet. Crime would have been fought through impartial and consistent law enforcement and the decriminalization of "victimless" crimes or those involving drugs, consensual sexual relations, prostitution, gambling, and suicide.

SUPPORTED:
- the repeal of status crimes applied against minors (e.g., curfew laws, runaway laws)
- the government's restitution for wrongful criminal proceedings against an accused person and wrongdoer restitution for victims of crimes
- peremptory challenges to proposed judges by parties in criminal or civil cases
- the notion of a victim's "pardon" for criminals
- an end to the doctrine of state "sovereign immunity"
- an end to the "insanity" or "diminished capacity" defense in criminal cases
- the right to own and use private property while denouncing government restrictions on those rights based on aesthetic values, riskiness, moral standards, cost-benefits estimates, or the promotion of economic growth
- the abolition of both the FBI and the CIA
- the right to privacy and prohibitions against government surveillance of all types, including the information collected by the Census Bureau and other public agencies
- a curtailment of congressional subpoena power

- a dismantling of the internal security committees of Congress
- the unconditional exoneration of persons accused or convicted of draft offenses, desertion, or other acts of resistance to wars and the military
- the right of collective bargaining but also endorsed employers' rights to refuse union recognition
- secondary boycotts
- the removal of all restrictions on immigration, the abolition of the Immigration and Naturalization Service and Border Patrol, full amnesty for illegal aliens, and an end to government restrictions on undocumented noncitizens
- full civil rights for all
- the right of secession from the United States for states and localities
- the extension to children of all rights granted to adults
- total deregulation of the economic sphere, recognizing only a limited public role in protecting property rights
- the repeal of the Sixteenth Amendment (income tax) and the eventual repeal of all involuntary taxes
- amnesty for tax evaders and relieving employers of the "involuntary servitude" of collecting taxes on behalf of the state
- a repeal of legal tender laws
- private ownership of gold
- the elimination of minted coins (with private minting on a competitive basis allowed)
- the use of a free market monetary standard (e.g., gold)
- banking on a free market basis, abolishing the Federal Reserve System, Federal Deposit Insurance Corporation, National Banking System, and other regulatory agencies in the banking and credit fields
- a return to the Jacksonian concept of the government maintaining its own treasury
- a repeal of antitrust laws
- the abolition of the Federal Trade Commission and the Antitrust Division of the Department of Justice
- the right of individuals to form corporations and other types of voluntary association
- the abolition of such federal agencies as the Reconstruction Finance Corporation, Customs Court, and Tariff Commission
- a repeal of the "windfall profits tax"
- nuclear power being subject to the test of the free market
- the abolition of the Department of Energy
- the reform of the nuisance and negligence laws to cover damage done to individuals by air, water, and noise pollution, rather than support government efforts to control pollution
- the abolition of the Environmental Protection Agency
- the abolition of the Consumer Product Safety Commission and the repeal of all laws restricting advertising or requiring individuals to use protective equipment
- the abolition of the Federal Aviation Administration and the Food and Drug Administration
- an end to public education
- an end to compulsory school attendance laws
- tuition tax credits and other tax reforms favorable to private schools
- a reduction of tax support for public schools
- the cessation of forced busing and corporal punishment
- an end to welfare programs and tax-supported services for children
- the elimination of tax discrimination against single persons
- birth control and a woman's right to an abortion
- the abolition of all federal agencies regulating transportation, with public enterprises like Amtrak returned to private ownership
- the privatization of public roads and the national highway system
- the repeal of the 55-mile-per-hour speed limit
- a repeal of minimum wage laws and protective labor legislation for women and children, along with restrictions on day care centers and the National Labor Relations Act
- dollar-for-dollar tax credits for charitable contributions
- the deregulation of health care and the medical insurance industry, including abolition of Medicare, Medicaid, Professional Standards Review organizations, and government health planning boards
- a repeal of land use, zoning, building code, eminent domain, urban renewal, and similar laws, while upholding private, voluntary land use covenants
- the privatization of inland waterways, dam sites, and water systems, while recommending the abolition of the Bureau of Reclamation, Bureau of Land Management, and the Army Corps of Engineers
- the transference of ownership of public lands to the private sector
- a repeal of the Occupational Safety and Health Act and the Social Security Act
- the abolishment of the Postal Service and the Civil Service system
- a repeal of federal campaign finance laws
- the elimination of the Federal Election Commission
- open ballot access to new parties and independent candidates
- a ballot line dedicated to "none of the above" so voters could register their dissent against the listed candidates for a public office
- nonintervention in foreign affairs and limited government engagement beyond national defense
- the elimination of foreign aid
- the abolition of government-sponsored arms sales
- the withdrawal of restrictions on U.S. trade abroad
- the elimination of such agencies as the Export-Import Bank and the Commodity Credit Corporation
- the development of standards to recognize private ownership claims to ocean floors, shellfish beds, broadcast bands, planetary bodies, and other unclaimed property

- calls for the withdrawal of the United States from the World Bank and the International Monetary Fund to bolster the party's arguments against international paper money
- the withdrawal of all U.S. troops stationed abroad (particularly in the Republic of Korea) and reductions in other defense expenditures
- the withdrawal of U.S. participation in NATO and other multilateral and bilateral arrangements
- mutual disarmament of nuclear weapons and missiles among the nuclear powers
- increased limits on the president's power to initiate military action
- the abrogation of all presidential declarations of "states of emergency" and an end to secret executive branch commitments and unilateral acts of military intervention
- a constitutional amendment to clarify the limits of the president's role as commander in chief
- reductions in the size of the diplomatic corps and the immediate withdrawal of the United States from the United Nations (as well as the withdrawal of the United Nations from the United States)
- the right of private citizens to engage in diplomatic negotiations with foreign governments
- calls for condemning all governments for violating human rights, urging that international negotiations be conducted without conceding moral legitimacy to any government or asserting moral superiority by the United States
- a halt to U.S. military and economic interventions in the Middle East and South Africa
- immediate independence for American Samoa, Guam, Micronesia, Puerto Rico, and the Virgin Islands
- an end to the nation's operations in the Panama Canal Zone and the withdrawal of all U.S. forces from Panama

Opposed:
- the use of preventive detention and "no-knock" laws
- "no-fault" insurance
- involuntary mental health treatment or commitment to mental institutions
- mental health "propaganda" and tax-supported mental health centers
- government censorship, including antipornography laws
- the gagging of press coverage
- equal time and "fairness" requirements in broadcasting
- the Federal Communications Act
- efforts to ban cigarette and sugar-coated breakfast food advertising
- prohibitions against the depiction of sex or violence in print, film, or other media
- regulation of "pay TV"
- tax funding for the Corporation for Public Broadcasting
- anticult activities and harassment of unconventional religious groups
- government issuance of identity cards for individual

citizens as well as government secrecy and the widespread use of "classified" information
- terrorism and torture
- any form of gun control
- registration for the draft (or compulsory national service of any kind), military discharges based on sexual preference, and the Uniform Code of Military Justice
- all government interference with bargaining, demanding the repeal of the National Labor Relations Act and all state right to work laws
- protective laws applied to selected groups, urging the repeal of government attempts to regulate private discrimination in employment, housing, and public accommodations
- plans to redistribute wealth or manage trade, deficit budgets, inflationary monetary policies, expansive government spending, impediments to free trade, and public controls on the economy (e.g., wages, prices, rents, profits, production, or interest)
- all personal and corporate taxes, recognizing the right to challenge payment on moral or other grounds
- monopolies as coercive and a natural outgrowth of government regulation
- limits on corporate liability or corporate size, merger restrictions, and the chartering of corporations
- all public subsidies, tariffs, quotas, and public utility franchises
- all government control of the energy field, including pricing, allocation, and production
- government conservation programs
- government support for energy research and the development of energy alternatives
- the need for "strategic storage" of oil, efforts to nationalize energy industries, rationing, and government ownership of energy resources
- fraud and misrepresentation in the marketplace but did not embrace "paternalistic" governmental interventions on behalf of consumers
- the conversion to the metric system
- the fluoridation of water and legal restrictions on what substances a person might ingest
- coercive controls on population growth
- mandatory retirement, occupational licensure, and antipoverty programs
- limits on malpractice suits
- involuntary medical treatment as well as government restrictions on research
- the U.S. government's participation in international cartels
- the U.S. diplomatic approach to People's Republic of China along with the earlier U.S. involvement with Taiwan

Also:
- noted that silence on any other aspect of government should not be construed to imply Libertarian approval

LITTLE PEOPLE'S PARTY

CANDIDATE FOR PRESIDENT:
John Milton Graham (AR)

MIDDLE CLASS PARTY

CANDIDATE FOR PRESIDENT:
Kurt Lynen (NJ)

CANDIDATE FOR VICE PRESIDENT:
Harry Kieve (NJ)

Lynen formed the Middle Class Party because, in his words, he was "angry—angry that the middle class in this country, those that are the backbone of our nation, are the forgotten people, except when it comes to taxes."

PLATFORM HIGHLIGHTS:

SUPPORTED:
- the restoration of power to the middle class
- the nationalization of the oil companies
- the reinstatement of the death penalty
- a constitutionally mandated balanced federal budget
- tax reform to provide relief to the middle class
- the elimination of "political hacks" from government jobs
- an "America first" foreign policy

NATIONAL POLICY REFERENDUM PARTY

CANDIDATE FOR PRESIDENT:
William J. Cox (CA)

NATIONAL STATESMAN PARTY

CANDIDATE FOR PRESIDENT:
Benjamin Calvin Bubar (ME)

CANDIDATE FOR VICE PRESIDENT:
Earl Farwell Dodge (CO)

28TH CONVENTION:
June 18–19, 1979, Motel Birmingham, Birmingham (AL)
Earl Farwell Dodge (CO), temporary chairman
Charles Wesley Ewing (MI), permanent chairman

The National Statesman Party was the name used by the Prohibition Party in the election of 1980.

PLATFORM HIGHLIGHTS:
The platform of the National Statesman Party reaffirmed the party's commitment to the Constitution and its system of checks and balances.

SUPPORTED:
- limits on the power of the federal judiciary by constitutional means
- a return to the gold standard
- a constitutional amendment to require a balanced budget
- limits on the taxing and spending powers of Congress
- reductions in the national debt
- the sale of all government-owned businesses in competition with the private sector
- limits on foreign aid
- the elimination of excessive regulation, control of monopolies, and restrictions on unethical practices by both management and labor
- the enforcement of antitrust laws and laws forbidding strikes by federal government employees
- an end to the government's preference for union shops in awarding contracts
- right-to-work laws
- states' rights and condemned regional governments
- a constitutional amendment to protect life from the moment of conception
- strict enforcement of laws against gambling, narcotics, and commercialized vice
- military preparedness while applauding the concept of the volunteer military
- a reform of the welfare system to remove "undeserving persons," promote self-sufficiency, and stop the distribution of birth control devices to minors without parental consent
- uniform marriage and divorce laws
- nondiscrimination against married people in tax policies and an explicit public policy against extending marriage benefits to unmarried couples
- the separation of church and state but approved of Bible reading and voluntary prayer in public schools or other institutions
- ballot law reforms to extend access to third parties
- revisions in the Social Security laws to make the program voluntary and to establish it on a sound actuarial basis
- the abolition of government controls and subsidies for agriculture
- a long-term prison sentence for the conviction of a criminal act involving a firearm
- the strict enforcement of the immigration laws and deportation of illegal aliens
- the ban on harmful drugs along with efforts to curb tobacco use

OPPOSED:
- communism
- the "giveaway" of the Panama Canal and the "sellout" of Nationalist China
- burdensome restraints on free enterprise
- anarchistic and arbitrary pressure tactics and quota systems
- the ratification of the ERA
- "unnatural lifestyles"
- a guaranteed annual income
- efforts to restrict religious broadcasting and religious schools
- the concept of federal aid to education and demanded

governmental noninterference in the operation of private Christian schools
- socialized medicine, involuntary commitment to mental hospitals, and mass medication programs

Also:
- blamed alcoholic beverages for a host of modern social problems and called for a program of publicity, education, legislation, and administration to eliminate liquor traffic
- promised to repeal all laws that permitted that traffic and to enforce rigorously laws against the manufacture, distribution, and sale of alcoholic beverages

NATIONAL UNITY PARTY

CANDIDATE FOR PRESIDENT:
John Bayard Anderson (IL)

CANDIDATES FOR VICE PRESIDENT:
Milton Stover Eisenhower (MD)
Nancy B. Flint (SD)
J. J. Friedman (IN)
Patrick Joseph Lucey (WI)

The National Unity Party was formed after John Bayard Anderson's quest for the Republican nomination foundered. The party incorporated Anderson's platform as its own.

PLATFORM HIGHLIGHTS:
Supported:
- a gasoline energy conservation tax of fifty cents per gallon to cut consumption and to reduce U.S. dependence on foreign oil
- reductions in the Social Security tax using revenue from the gasoline energy conservation tax
- the development of synthetic fuels, with the private sector providing the leadership
- nuclear power as a future option (especially nuclear fusion) but would halt further expansion pending the development of better safeguards
- a grain embargo on the Soviet Union as a sanction for its invasion of Afghanistan
- the continuation of the "traditionally close relationship" between the United States and Israel
- a strong military and an all-volunteer army
- the vigorous enforcement of affirmative action programs
- an expansion of day care centers
- the passage of a national bottle bill to promote recycling
- initiatives to conserve natural resources and clean up the environment (e.g., through surface mining and reclamation laws, air and water pollution standards, and soil and water conservation programs)
- the Open Housing Act of 1968
- a balanced budget and government spending restraints
- dividend and interest income exemptions and the indexing of personal income tax rates
- a 2 percent reduction in corporate tax rates by 1986
- a reduction in the tax on savings account interest and simplified tax-depreciation allowances
- a new federal manpower policy to upgrade labor
- a 10 percent tax credit for research and development
- an end to mandatory retirement and the Social Security earnings limitation
- the elimination of red tape
- the ERA
- the Alaska National Interest Lands Conservation Act
- a call for "deliberate and judicious" health care reform that would emphasize prevention, the elimination of gaps in coverage, reform of financing mechanisms, and special provisions for the elderly, alcohol and drug abuse, and debilitating diseases
- a dual system of public and private schools, the rights of persons with disabilities, and the Department of Education
- a woman's right to decide for herself whether to have an abortion
- calls for rebuilding the nation's basic industries and aging cities
- meaningful job training
- assistance to unemployed teenagers
- an even-handed and unprejudiced immigration policy

Opposed:
- the proposed constitutional amendment to prohibit school busing
- the B-1 bomber and the MX missile
- the creation of a Palestinian state between Israel and Jordan

NATURAL PEOPLES LEAGUE

CANDIDATE FOR PRESIDENT:
Harley James McLain (ND)

CANDIDATE FOR VICE PRESIDENT:
Jewelie Goeller (ND)

The Natural Peoples League promoted communal living, peace, and organic farming.

PEACE AND FREEDOM PARTY

CANDIDATE FOR PRESIDENT:
Marguerite "Maureen" Smith

CANDIDATE FOR VICE PRESIDENT:
Elizabeth C. Barron (CA)

CANDIDATES FOR PRESIDENTIAL NOMINATION:
Deidre Griswold (NJ)
Gus Hall (NY)
David Ernest McReynolds (NY)
Marguerite "Maureen" Smith (CA)
Benjamin McLain Spock (AR)

PRIMARY:

JUNE 3, 1980 (CA):

Spock 4,071
Hall 2,494
McReynolds 1,596
Griswold 1,330
others 3

PEACE PARTY

CANDIDATE FOR PRESIDENT:
Joseph Thomas Robino, Jr. (AL)

Promising that "the size of a person's pocketbook" and "the color of one's skin, one's sex or religious beliefs matters not to the Peace Party," the platform called for "peace, peace, peace." It sought "peace, brotherhood—right on!" Its final observations noted that "the human tongue is the deadliest of all blunt instruments. The lump in the throat hardest to bear is swallowing your own words. You'll never reap the sheaves of joy from the effects of vice or crime."

RECESS PARTY

CANDIDATE FOR PRESIDENT:
Dottie Kay Hinkle Alt (PA)

REPUBLICAN PARTY

CANDIDATE FOR PRESIDENT:
Ronald Wilson Reagan

CANDIDATE FOR VICE PRESIDENT:
George Herbert Walker Bush (TX)

CANDIDATES FOR PRESIDENTIAL NOMINATION:
John Bayard Anderson (IL)
Anne Legendre Armstrong (TX)
Donald Badgley (NY)
Howard Henry Baker, Jr. (TN)
Nick M. "Nick-Reagan" Belluso (GA)
Ernest William Bost (AZ)
George Herbert Walker Bush (TX)
Ernest Joel Carlson (CO)
William Edward Carlson (FL)
Alvin Glen Carris (KS)
John Bowden Connally (TX)
Philip Miller Crane (IL)
Gerald Thomas DeFelice (CT)
Michael Bernard Denoma (VA)
Robert Joseph Dole (KS)
William J. Dunn (PA)
Benjamin Fernandez (CA)
Gerald Rudolph Ford, Jr. (MI)
Jacob John Gordon (MA)
Alexander Meigs Haig, Jr. (PA)
Samuel Ichiye Hayakawa (CA)
Jesse Alexander Helms, Jr. (NC)
Gerard Andrew Himmelman, Sr. (NJ)

Alvin Joseph Jacobson (PA)
Veldi Arvel Kelley (IL)
John Garfield Kelso (TX)
Charles Thomas "Tommy" Kersey, Jr. (GA)
Norman G. Kurland (VA)
Robert J. Luellen (IN)
Donald Keith MacDonald (CA)
Donald James MacNeil (NH)
Walter James McCloud (MO)
Edison Penrow McDaniels (CA)
Eddie McDowell (NY)
Beatrice Elaine Johnson Mooney (MN)
Tracy Austin Odell, Sr. (CA)
Carl Leon Pickett (TX)
Larry Pressler (SD)
Ronald Wilson Reagan (CA)
Stanley Randolph Ruggierrio (OH)
William Edward Simon (NY)
Harold Edward Stassen (MN)
S. G. Tracy Voigt (NV)
Lowell Palmer Weicker, Jr. (CT)
Weston B. Wetherell (IL)
James Deyerle Whetstone (NC)
Herman B. (Barnes B.) Williams (FL)
Luther James Wilson (KY)
R. W. Yeager (KS)

PRIMARIES:

FEBRUARY 17, 1980 (PR):

Bush 111,940
Baker 68,934
Fernandez 2,097
Connally 1,964
Stassen 672
Dole 483
others 281

FEBRUARY 26, 1980 (NH):

Reagan 72,983
Bush 33,443
Baker 18,943
Anderson 14,458
Crane 2,618
Connally 2,239
Dole 597
others 1,876

MARCH 4, 1980 (MA):

Bush 124,365
Anderson 122,987
Reagan 115,334
Baker 19,366
Connally 4,714
Crane 4,669
Ford 3,398
Dole 577
Fernandez 374
Stassen 218

no preference 2,243
others 2,581

MARCH 4, 1980 (VT):
Reagan 19,720
Anderson 19,030
Bush 14,226
Baker 8,055
Ford 2,300
Crane 1,238
Connally 884
Stassen 105
others 53

MARCH 8, 1980 (SC):
Reagan 79,549
Connally 43,113
Bush 21,569
Baker 773
Fernandez 171
Stassen 150
Dole 117
Belluso 59

MARCH 11, 1980 (AL):
Reagan 147,352
Bush 54,730
Crane 5,099
Baker 1,963
Connally 1,077
Stassen 544
Dole 447
Belluso 141

MARCH 11, 1980 (FL):
Reagan 345,699
Bush 185,996
Anderson 56,636
Crane 12,000
Baker 6,345
Connally 4,958
Stassen 1,377
Dole 1,086
Fernandez 898

MARCH 11, 1980 (GA):
Reagan 146,500
Bush 25,293
Anderson 16,853
Crane 6,308
Connally 2,388
Baker 1,571
Fernandez 809
Dole 249
Stassen 200

MARCH 18, 1980 (IL):
Reagan 547,355
Anderson 415,193
Bush 124,057

Crane 24,865
Baker 7,051
Connally 4,548
Kelley 3,757
Dole 1,843
Ford 1,106
others 306

MARCH 25, 1980 (CT):
Bush 70,367
Reagan 61,735
Anderson 40,354
Baker 2,446
Crane 1,887
Connally 598
Dole 333
Fernandez 308
unpledged delegates 4,256

APRIL 1, 1980 (KS):
Reagan 179,739
Anderson 51,924
Bush 35,838
Baker 3,603
Connally 2,067
Fernandez 1,650
Crane 1,367
Yeager 1,063
Carris 483
Stassen 383
Carlson 311
Badgley 244
none of the names shown. 6,726

APRIL 1, 1980 (WI):
Reagan 364,898
Bush 276,164
Anderson 248,623
Baker 3,298
Crane 2,951
Connally 2,312
Fernandez 1,051
Stassen 1,010
none of the names shown. 2,595
others 4,951

APRIL 5, 1890 (LA)
Reagan 31,212
Bush 7,818
Belluso 155
Stassen 126
Fernandez 84
Pickett 67
none of the names shown. 2,221

APRIL 22, 1980 (PA):
Bush 626,759
Reagan 527,916
Baker 30,846

Anderson 26,890
Connally 10,656
Stassen 6,767
Jacobson 4,357
Fernandez 2,521
others 4,699

MAY 3, 1980 (TX):
Reagan 268,798
Bush 249,819
unpledged delegates 8,152

MAY 6, 1980 (DC):
Bush 4,973
Anderson 2,025
Crane 270
Stassen 201
Fernandez 60

MAY 6, 1980 (IN):
Reagan 419,016
Bush 92,955
Anderson 56,342

MAY 6, 1980 (NC):
Reagan 113,854
Bush 36,631
Anderson 8,542
Baker 2,543
Connally 1,107
Dole 629
Crane 547
no preference 4,538

MAY 6, 1980 (TN):
Reagan 144,625
Bush 35,274
Anderson 8,722
Crane 1,574
Baker 16
Ford 14
Connally 1
unpledged delegates 4,976
others 8

MAY 13, 1980 (MD):
Reagan 80,557
Bush 68,389
Anderson 16,244
Crane 2,113

MAY 13, 1980 (NE):
Reagan 155,995
Bush 31,380
Anderson 11,879
Dole 1,420
Crane 1,062
Stassen 799
Fernandez 400
others 2,268

MAY 20, 1980 (MI):
Bush 341,998
Reagan 189,184
Anderson 48,947
Fernandez 2,248
Stassen 1,938
unpledged delegates 10,265
others 596

MAY 20, 1980 (OR):
Reagan 170,449
Bush 109,210
Anderson 32,118
Crane 2,324
others 1,265

MAY 27, 1980 (ID):
Reagan 111,868
Anderson 13,130
Bush 5,416
Crane 1,024
unpledged delegates 3,441

MAY 27, 1980 (KY):
Reagan 78,072
Bush 6,861
Anderson 4,791
Stassen 1,223
Fernandez 764
unpledged delegates 3,084

MAY 27, 1980 (NV):
Reagan 39,352
Bush 3,078
none of the names shown 4,965

JUNE 3, 1980 (CA):
Reagan 2,057,923
Anderson 349,315
Bush 125,113
Crane 21,465
Fernandez 10,242
others 14

JUNE 3, 1980 (MS):
Reagan 23,028
Bush 2,105
unpledged delegates 618

JUNE 3, 1980 (MT):
Reagan 68,744
Bush 7,665
no preference 3,014

JUNE 3, 1980 (NJ):
Reagan 225,959
Bush 47,447
Stassen 4,571

JUNE 3, 1980 (NM):
Reagan 37,982
Anderson 7,171

Bush 5,892
Crane 4,412
Fernandez 1,795
Stassen 947
unpledged delegates 1,347

JUNE 3, 1980 (OH):
Reagan 692,288
Bush 164,485

JUNE 3, 1980 (RI):
Reagan 3,839
Bush 993
Stassen 107
Fernandez. 48
unpledged delegates. 348

JUNE 3, 1980 (SD):
Reagan 72,861
Bush 3,691
Stassen 987
no preference 5,366

JUNE 3, 1980 (WV):
Reagan 115,407
Bush 19,509
Stassen 3,100

32D CONVENTION:
July 14–17, 1980, Joe Louis Arena, Detroit (MI)
John Jacob Rhodes (AZ), permanent chairman
Guy Adrian Vander Jagt (MI), keynoter

PLATFORM HIGHLIGHTS:
The Republican platform painted a dim picture of the United States under President Carter, describing it as headed on "a continuing downward spiral in economic vitality and international influence." Still, the party challenged the Democrats for their assertion that the nation suffered from "malaise." The Republicans called, instead, for a "new beginning."

SUPPORTED:
- tax reductions and tax indexing
- efforts to improve the welfare system by eliminating fraud, strengthening work incentives, providing educational and vocational incentives, ensuring an adequate living standard for the "truly needy," and enhancing interagency and intergovernmental coordination
- a reform of the food stamp program
- improvements in Veterans Administration (VA) hospitals, "timely and adequate" adjustments in compensation for service disabilities, death benefits, and a preference in federal employment for veterans
- the domestic automobile industry and an accelerated cost-effective effort to improve highway, automobile, and individual driver safety
- a reminder to African Americans that their prosperity was linked to the country's overall economic growth
- enterprise zones, the removal of excessive regulations and disincentives for venture capital, strong enforcement of civil rights laws, and a nondiscriminatory system of federal appointments
- aid to Hispanic Americans in developing a proficiency in English and in reassurances that they would not be barred from educational or employment opportunities because English was not their first language
- the removal of architectural, communications, and transportation barriers for handicapped individuals and the promotion of a healthy and constructive attitude toward handicapped persons
- equal rights and opportunities for women, early career counseling and job training, improvements in the working conditions of women concentrated in low-status and low-paying jobs, easier credit, and adequate child care through private enterprise but departed from previous platforms by not endorsing the ERA
- remedies for discriminatory aspects of Social Security and the tax laws
- vigorous enforcement of civil rights laws in employment, housing, credit, and mortgage access, but rejected quotas and similar mechanisms for ensuring equal rights
- self-determination for American Indians and statehood for Puerto Rico
- the right of U.S. citizens in Guam and the Virgin Islands to vote in national elections
- the adoption of a constitutional amendment to protect the lives of "unborn children" and the denial of tax dollars to fund abortions
- the creation of an educational block grant (with special provisions for the handicapped, disadvantaged, and other needy students)
- the abolishment of the U.S. Department of Education
- the deregulation of public education and prohibitions against compulsory teacher membership in a bargaining unit
- tax credits for tuition paid to private schools
- a halt to the Internal Revenue Service's (IRS) harassment of independent schools
- voluntary, nondenominational prayer in public schools and facilities
- an end to government meddling in U.S. medicine and promises to promote alternatives to institutional care, especially home-based care
- a health care plan emphasizing tax and financial incentives, preventive health care, and innovative health care delivery systems
- Medicare and Medicaid, subject to a detailed reevaluation
- a sub-minimum wage to encourage youth employment
- financial incentives and private sector initiatives to help families care for their older members
- pledges to clean up "the much-abused disability system" and to transfer welfare to the states
- an increase in the availability of noninstitutional child care through local, private organizations

- the elimination of the "marriage tax"
- efforts to enable homemakers to participate in individual retirement accounts
- efforts to "seek every effective means" to help families of "handicapped people" provide for their education and special medical and therapeutic needs through targeted tax relief
- more secure and prosperous neighborhoods through the elimination of urban blight, dangerous streets, and violent crime
- neighborhood self-help through a tax deduction for charitable contributions, whether individuals itemize or not
- the revitalization and preservation of neighborhoods through the creation of a block grant program that would replace categorical grants
- financing and tax incentives for the construction of rental housing to promote housing and home ownership
- a young family initiative
- urban homesteading
- lower tax rates on savings
- the development of innovative alternate mortgage instruments
- the use of mortgage revenue bonds
- a decentralized block grant for housing as a replacement for existing categorical housing grant programs for the elderly, the poor, and the disabled
- local law enforcement agencies and the firm and speedy application of criminal penalties (including the death penalty when authorized by a state)
- mandatory sentences for crimes committed with guns and mandatory sentences for drug pushers and smugglers and a crackdown on the sale and advertisement of drug paraphernalia
- a limited federal role in transportation, arguing for financial and technical support for local authorities through block grants
- a pledge to increase savings and investments through accelerated tax depreciation schedules, limitations on the percentage of the gross national product (GNP) represented by government spending, lower tax rates on savings, and a balanced budget
- promises to give unemployed workers their earned unemployment compensation benefits
- incentives for job retraining and placement
- tax and regulatory changes to revitalize basic U.S. industries
- foreign trade based on reciprocity
- pre-employment, education, apprenticeship, job placement, and retention programs for disadvantaged youth along with a coordinated approach to the use of existing community resources, incentives for the private sector, and the elimination of red tape in all government bureaucracies
- closer relationships between employers and the schools
- efforts to exempt small businesses from onerous regulations

- reductions in business and personal income and estate taxes
- a reform of the patent laws to facilitate innovation
- tax reform legislation to discourage conglomerate takeovers of small businesses
- labor's right to organize and engage in collective bargaining, while rejecting the notion of compulsory union dues and the use of union fees for partisan political purposes
- section 14 (b) of the Taft-Hartley Act
- an enhancement of fair competition and pronouncements that "an informed consumer" is the "best regulator of the free enterprise system"
- the enactment of a temporary moratorium on all new federal regulations and requirements that OSHA concentrate on encouraging voluntary compliance with health and safety regulations by employers
- "profitable farm prices" with "a goal of surpassing parity levels in a market-oriented agricultural economy"
- the use of alcohol and other renewable energy sources, with priority given to agricultural fuel needs
- the expansion of the Food for Peace program
- multiple-use policies that would govern federal lands and assistance for privately owned forests to increase timber production
- an aggressive foreign market expansion program based on fair and effective competition in international trade
- the GATT
- the development of the commercial seafood industry
- protective measures to prevent predatory international commodity "dumping"
- farmer-owned grain reserves but not government-controlled reserves
- the immediate termination of the Carter administration's grain embargo against the Soviet Union and offered to reduce federal regulation of farming
- the development of a "dynamic water policy" and voluntary participation in soil and water conservation programs
- comprehensive labor legislation to create better relations with Canada and Mexico
- revisions and modernization of the nation's food safety laws
- the Capper-Volstead Act
- a desire to return power to state and local governments and to reduce the size and scope of the federal executive branch
- the use of the congressional veto, sunset laws, strict budgetary controls, elimination of the presumption of validity in favor of federal regulations, and the use of restitution to those who have been wronged by federal agencies
- the provision to citizens of the same rights in relation to government agencies as they have in courtrooms
- state and party control over presidential nominating procedures and the repeal of restrictions on campaign

- contributions that impede grassroots participation in federal elections
- broader tax incentives for contributions to charitable and cultural organizations
- a change in the role of government from one of regulation to one of providing incentives for technological and innovative developments
- the stimulation of new energy technology and more efficient energy use
- the restoration of maximum feasible choice and freedom in the energy marketplace
- an elimination of energy shortages to achieve energy self-sufficiency
- the filling of U.S. strategic oil reserves
- a repeal of the windfall profits tax
- decontrols on the prices of all oil and gas products
- the removal of market restrictions on the use of natural gas
- a promotion of the use of coal
- a simplification of the regulations governing mining and coal production and a revision of the Clean Air Act
- the accelerated use of nuclear energy, research and development of the breeder reactor, and rapid development of permanent storage facilities for nuclear wastes
- the domestic gasohol industry but not public support for a synthetic fuel industry
- additional research on renewable energy technologies (i.e., solar, geothermal, wind, nuclear fission, alcohol synthesis, biomass, and other energies)
- the development of the Outer Continental Shelf
- an imperative review of "rigid and narrow" environmental legislation to keep environmental protection from becoming a cover for a "no-growth" policy
- the coordination of immigration and refugee policies, which were considered international in nature, with such global associations of states as the Organization of American States (OAS) and ASEAN
- a balanced budget and a constitutional amendment to achieve it if congressional action was not forthcoming
- the independence of the Federal Reserve System
- an immediate increase in defense spending to offset what was seen as a Soviet advantage
- House Concurrent Resolution 306 as an appropriate strategy for achieving peace through strength
- the deployment of the MX missile and the B-1 bomber
- the development of an air defense system comprised of dedicated modern interceptor aircraft and early warning systems
- an accelerated deployment of cruise missiles in Europe and elsewhere
- the modernization of the military command and control system
- combat readiness among U.S. forces and preparedness in the industrial base
- vigorous research and development of an antiballistic missile system

- the buildup of conventional forces with increases in the serial tanker fleet, naval and marine forces, aircraft carriers and submarines, and the nation's intra- and intertheater airlift capability
- an increase in military pay and benefits indexed to inflation
- the extension of GI Bill benefits to anyone completing two years of active service
- the space program
- reforms of the defense programming and budgeting management system
- improvements in U.S. intelligence capabilities
- U.S. leadership in a multilateral drive to eliminate terrorism
- arms control negotiations based on reciprocity, the security interests of the United States, and linkages to broader political and military behaviors of the parties involved
- a multilateral agreement for the safe management and transfers of nuclear materials in the international market
- a check on the Soviet Union's global ambitions as a goal of foreign policy
- negotiated reductions in strategic weapons but only on terms favorable to U.S. national interests
- Soviet "refuseniks" and their demands for the right to emigrate and the aspirations of the people of Cuba and the captive nations of Eastern Europe to achieve self-determination
- NATO and expectations that NATO allies should assume a greater share of the common defense effort
- Spain's integration into the NATO alliance
- the territorial sovereignty and integrity of Israel
- the constructive roles of Oman and Sudan in Middle East peace negotiations
- the idea that Jerusalem should have remained an undivided city (but did not mention the capital of Israel)
- statehood for Puerto Rico
- stronger relations with Mexico
- a "deep affinity" for Canada
- pledges to keep the Panama Canal "open, secure, and free of hostile control"
- a North American accord designed to foster close cooperation among Canada, Mexico, and the United States
- the mutual interests and special relationships between the United States and Japan
- promises to maintain U.S. ground and air forces in the Republic of Korea
- a continuation of the growing friendship between the United States and the People's Republic of China, while strengthening U.S. relations with Taiwan
- a full accounting of U.S. servicemen still missing in action in Vietnam
- self-determination, economic and political development, and an attitude of friendship with all parties in Africa
- the assertion that "the principal consideration (in giving foreign aid) should be whether or not extending

assistance to a nation or group of nations will advance America's interests and objectives"

- bilateral aid programs and not making military assistance contingent upon "complete approval of a regime's domestic policy"
- the integration of international economic policy with foreign and military policy
- the protection of a strong dollar at home and abroad
- an aggressive export policy
- a reciprocal free trade policy
- reductions in the tax burden felt by U.S. citizens working abroad
- a strengthened merchant marine

OPPOSED:

- the concepts of a guaranteed annual income and federalization of the welfare system
- Washington's invasion of privacy and the dissemination of Social Security, census, and IRS records
- mandatory retirement, the earnings limitation under Social Security, and all attempts to tax Social Security benefits
- socialized medicine
- a national health service or compulsory national health insurance and government meddling in U.S. medicine, promising to promote alternatives to institutional care, especially home-based care
- quotas and similar mechanisms for ensuring equal rights
- forced busing
- gun control
- the use of federal funds for the Legal Services Corporation's defense of persons accused of drug crimes
- withholding taxes on dividends and interest income
- the notion of compulsory union dues and the use of union fees for partisan political purposes
- public financing of congressional elections
- the use of "self-proclaimed advocates to represent consumer interests" in federal agency proceedings
- government-to-government sales of agricultural commodities
- tax advantages for foreign investors in U.S. real estate
- the 55-mile-per-hour speed limit
- post card voter registration
- all wage, price, and credit controls
- a peacetime draft
- the SALT II Treaty and the Democrats' cover-up of Soviet violations of SALT I
- the transfer of high technology to the Soviets and their Eastern European allies
- a unilateral moratorium on the deployment of U.S. and NATO's nuclear weapons
- the establishment of a Palestinian state on the West Bank
- any involvement of the Palestinian Liberation Organization in the Middle East peace process

REPUBLICAN PARTY	
VOTE FOR PRESIDENTIAL NOMINATION:	
Candidate	Ballot: 1
Reagan	1,939
Anderson	37
Bush	13
Armstrong	1
not voting	4
VOTE FOR PRESIDENTIAL NOMINATION:	
Candidate	Ballot: 1
Bush	1,832
others	161

Former president Gerald Ford, Jr., of Michigan was asked to serve on the Republican ticket as the vice-presidential nominee, but he declined. Bush was then nominated for vice president on the first ballot.

- any reimposition of the oil embargo
- Cuban efforts to export revolution to other countries in the Americas
- the Communists' brutality in Cambodia and Laos
- the Sandinistas of Nicaragua and the "subversion" of El Salvador, Guatemala, and Honduras

RIGHT TO LIFE PARTY

CANDIDATE FOR PRESIDENT:
Ellen Cullen McCormack (NY)

CANDIDATE FOR VICE PRESIDENT:
Carroll Driscoll (NJ)

The Right to Life Party was a New York-based antiabortion party. McCormack, its standard-bearer, had previously contested the Democratic presidential nomination in 1976 and qualified for federal matching funds. In the 1980 campaign, she was unable to meet the criteria for matching funds.

SOCIALIST (LIBERTY UNION) PARTY

CANDIDATE FOR PRESIDENT:
David Ernest McReynolds

CANDIDATE FOR VICE PRESIDENT:
Diane Drufenbrock (WI)

CANDIDATES FOR PRESIDENTIAL NOMINATION:
Earl S. Gardner (VT)
Gus Hall (NY)
David Ernest McReynolds (NY)

PRIMARY:

MARCH 4, 1980 (VT):
Gardner 257

McReynolds 165
Hall 76
others 75

CONVENTION:
February 23–24, 1980, Hotel Wisconsin, Milwaukee
   (WI)
Frank Paul Zeidler (WI), temporary chairman
Jim Dubert (IA), chairperson, February 23, 1980,
   morning
Ann Williams Rosenhaft (NY), chairperson, Febru-
   ary 23, 1980, afternoon
Don Busky (PA), chairperson, February 23, 1980,
   evening
R. E. Schlichter (FL), chairperson, February 24,
   1980

Attending this convention were twenty-one delegates
from eleven states, five alternates, and four observers.

PLATFORM HIGHLIGHTS:
The Socialist platform outlined eight "basic aims": (1) an
immediate halt in preparations for war; (2) disarmament
for survival; (3) a crash development of safe energy, focusing on solar power instead of nuclear power; (4) full
employment; (5) increased technical and other aid to
developing nations; (6) an end to racism and sexism; (7) a
shift of power from impersonal, centralized corporations to
neighborhoods and democratic unions; and (8) the social
ownership of basic means of production, with democratic
controls and decentralization.

SUPPORTED:
- a slash in the military budget by 25 percent with the
  funds shifted into civilian production
- a guaranteed right to a meaningful job
- rent control
- a massive public housing initiative
- public ownership and democratic control over all energy resources
- a ban on nuclear power development and the decommissioning of existing plants
- the development of solar energy and mass transit
- the Dellums Health Act
- the imposition of price controls on food, housing, and
  transportation
- the closing of tax loopholes and a shift of the tax burden to those best able to pay
- the enactment of a World Peace Tax Fund Bill to protect conscientious objectors who refuse to pay taxes for
  the military
- the self-employed and small businesses through assistance to cooperatives
- public funding of neighborhood mutual aid societies
  and neighborhood development programs
- the family farmer and the right of farm workers to organize
- 100 percent parity and encouragement for cooperative
  farming

- democratic control of unions together with workers'
  control over industry
- the elimination of the profit motive in areas where it
  had caused environmental destruction
- the belief that human rights include the rights to adequate food and clothing, proper housing, and health care
- the abolition of the CIA
- an extension of employment, parental, legal, and housing rights to lesbians and gays
- affirmative action programs and the struggle against
  racism
- the ratification of the ERA and the elimination of all
  forms of sexism
- the legalization of victimless crimes
- treatment, not punishment, for drug addicts
- the expansion of work-release programs
- the prosecution of white-collar crime
- an eventual achievement of "a society without
  prisons"
- the unilateral decommissioning of nuclear weapons
- the withdrawal of U.S. troops from other lands, the dissolution of military alliances (including NATO and the
  Warsaw Pact), the neutrality of Third World countries,
  and the allocation, through the United Nations, of 1
  percent of U.S. GNP for aid to the Third World
- reconstruction aid to Indochina
- the U.S. government's recognition of the Vietnamese
  government
- the protection of Israel's right to exist
- the creation of a Palestinian state
- the federal government in honoring its treaties with
  Native American nations
- an end to the draft and increased benefits for Vietnam
  War veterans
- an unconditional amnesty for all draft resisters and military deserters

OPPOSED:
- the unilateral U.S. military intervention in foreign nations
- weapon shipments to the Middle East

SOCIALIST (LIBERTY UNION) PARTY
VOTE FOR PRESIDENTIAL NOMINATION:
MCREYNOLDS WAS UNANIMOUSLY NOMINATED FOR
PRESIDENT BY ACCLAMATION.

VOTE FOR VICE-PRESIDENTIAL NOMINATION:
DRUFENBROCK WAS UNANIMOUSLY NOMINATED FOR
VICE PRESIDENT ON THE FIRST BALLOT.

SOCIALIST WORKERS PARTY
CANDIDATES FOR PRESIDENT:
Richard Congress (OH)
Clifton DeBerry (AL, AZ, DC, IL, IN, IA, LA, MA,

MN, MO, NH, NY, NC, ND, PA, RI, TN, UT, VT, VA, WA, WI)[1]

Andrew Pulley (CO, KY, NJ, NM, SD)[1]

CANDIDATE FOR VICE PRESIDENT:
Matilde Zimmerman

The Socialist Workers Party was a proponent of Trotskyite socialism. Its platform condemned militarism and imperialism, promoted the empowerment of women and minorities, and urged greater domestic attention to the needs of the elderly, poor, and persons with disabilities.

THIRD WORLD ASSEMBLY

CANDIDATE FOR PRESIDENT:
John Governor Martin (DC)

CANDIDATE FOR VICE PRESIDENT:
David Kennarth (MD)

The Third World Assembly was formed on January 28, 1979, in Washington, D.C., with forty charter members. Its national convenor was Rogers Gueory. The party focused on the plight of the country's domestic poor, comparing this segment of the population to that of Third World countries.

PLATFORM HIGHLIGHTS:

SUPPORTED:

- calls for the active involvement of Third World people in the local, national, and international political process, including the promotion of candidates and working with the referendum and recall procedures
- a two-pronged attack on economic deprivation, using an overall census formula for some things and a targeted Third World formula for others
- the fostering of Third World businesses and bringing inflation under control in the Third World
- educational reforms to bring schools into the modern age, with curricula stressing morals, etiquette, achievement, and discipline
- affordable housing and rent control, along with full employment
- the promotion of the arts through television and the cinema
- the enhancement of health status for all, along with a 75-percent decrease in the costs of health care
- a government based on the screening and discipline of membership, negotiations, and training
- promises to assist in the resolution of Third World problems and to participate in Third World international conferences
- pledges to guard against satanic influences and to promote brotherhood actively, emphasizing the "liberating theology of Jesus Christ"
- an assertion that the party would "uncover and expose the criminal element of laws in education, employment, housing, land development, and distribution"
- freedom for all "political prisoners"
- the promotion of family life and youth participation in civic affairs
- the protection of full civil rights to be enjoyed by all
- the promotion of public transportation

UNITED INDEPENDENT PARTY

CANDIDATE FOR PRESIDENT:
Royce Huffman (PA)

UNITED NATIONS PARTY

CANDIDATE FOR PRESIDENT:
Emil Matalik (FL)

Matalik created the United Nations Party (also known as the # 1 Party and the United Nations Organization, or 1-U.N.O., Party) in 1964 to promote world peace and the abolition of hunger.

PLATFORM HIGHLIGHTS:

SUPPORTED:

- limits on each family to one child (later increased to two children), one animal, and one tree to counter the world's biggest problem—overpopulation
- the creation of a World presidency, a Universal Congress, and a Global Supreme Court
- the conversion of cities to farm land, thus resolving the urban problems of the world
- the issuance of five usable acres of land to each person for farming
- prohibitions on the public use of tobacco, liquor, and gambling
- free world communications
- the promotion of worldwide free love—"especially for single and virginized people"—and coed nudist camps for prison inmates
- the abolition of the monetary system, replacing it with "volunteerism"

VOTE FOR YOURSELF PARTY

CANDIDATE FOR PRESIDENT:
Owen Frank Balding (IL)

Balding founded the Vote for Yourself Party in 1979, after abandoning his initial creation, the "People's Party." The party urged people to write in their own names for president. It supported abolishing the presidency and creating a five-person governing board in its stead. It also endorsed eliminating the Supreme Court and U.S. Senate and selecting members of the House of Representatives by a daily random drawing in each congressional district.

---

[1]Many states are listed because different states have different filing deadlines. Hence, the Socialist Workers Party filed slates as "placeholders" prior to actual selection of candidates. These place-holders were the names that appeared on the ballots in the states indicated.

WORKERS WORLD PARTY

CANDIDATE FOR PRESIDENT:
Diedre Griswold (NJ)

CANDIDATES FOR VICE PRESIDENT:
Naomi Cohen (NY) (NH, OH)
Larry Holmes (NY)

The Workers World Party was founded as a Marxist party in 1959, but it did not offer candidates for the presidency until 1980.

PLATFORM HIGHLIGHTS:

SUPPORTED:

- jobs for all
- an end to plant closures
- the workers' control of industry
- calls for rebuilding the cities
- a rent rollback
- a channeling of military appropriations into domestic housing, education, and hospital construction
- protections for the jobless and the organization of unorganized workers
- an end to inflation and "pass alongs" to consumers
- the elimination of taxes on incomes under $25,000
- solidarity with workers' struggles abroad
- socialism
- voting rights for poor and working people
- the ratification of the ERA
- the passage of a national gay rights bill and full rights for homosexuals
- amnesty for undocumented workers

- a "people's takeover of the oil industry"
- independence for Puerto Rico
- full implementation of treaties with Native Americans
- the abolition of antilabor laws
- equal opportunity for all disabled and elderly persons
- the protection of the civil rights of prisoners

OPPOSED:

- racism, the Ku Klux Klan, and Nazis
- police brutality
- the military draft, war planning, and nuclear weapons
- sexism
- "all forms of oppression"

WORLD GOVERNMENT PARTY

CANDIDATE FOR PRESIDENT:
John Paul Fritz (HI)

PLATFORM HIGHLIGHTS:

SUPPORTED:

- the relocation of the United Nations to Honolulu (HI)
- the creation of more jobs
- better transportation
- the construction of "flying saucer-type" airships at Pearl Harbor
- a world democracy
- the abolition of the "British caste system"
- a world military establishment
- the irrigation of deserts and a moderation of the world's climate
- the development and population of other planets

GENERAL ELECTION SUMMARY FOR 1980:			
Candidate	*Electoral Votes*	*States*	*Popular Votes*
Reagan (R)	483	43	43,904,153
Carter (D)	49	6 (+ DC)	35,483,883
Anderson (NAT UNITY)	0	0	5,720,060
Clark (LIBRTN)	0	0	921,299
Commoner (CIT)	0	0	234,294
SOC WOR	0	0	49,038
Hall (COM)	0	0	45,023
Rarick (AI)	0	0	41,268
McCormack (RIGHT)	0	0	32,327
Smith (PF)	0	0	18,116
Griswold (W W)	0	0	13,300
Bubar (NAT STA)	0	0	7,212
McReynolds (SOC [LU])	0	0	6,898
Greaves (A)	0	0	6,647
Lynen (MID CL)	0	0	3,694
Gahres (DWL)	0	0	1,718
Shelton (A [KS])	0	0	1,555
Wendelkin (I)	0	0	923
McLain (NAT PEO)	0	0	296
unknown	0	0	23,517

ELECTION OF NOVEMBER 6, 1984

President
RONALD WILSON REAGAN
Vice President
GEORGE HERBERT WALKER BUSH

HIGHLIGHTS

President Ronald Reagan's personal popularity all but ensured his reelection in 1984, and, in fact, he achieved the biggest margin of victory in history in the general election, with 525 electoral votes to former vice president Walter Mondale's 13. Apparently, Americans approved of the president's military buildup and his fiscal conservatism. Despite the predictable win (if not the size of the margin), the 1984 campaign had its interesting aspects. On the Democratic side, Mondale was challenged by Sen. Gary Hart of Colorado, who gave form to what some called "Atari liberalism," a new perspective that combined a rejection of traditional Democratic values with a technocratic form of social consciousness. Mondale's other major challenger was the Reverend Jesse Jackson, a liberal and longtime associate of Martin Luther King, Jr. Jackson put together a rainbow coalition but could not overcome Mondale's organizational strength. When Mondale won the Democratic nomination, he surprised everyone by naming Rep. Geraldine Anne Ferraro of New York as his running mate—the first woman to be so honored by a major party. He also raised eyebrows when he announced in his acceptance speech that he would raise taxes, a statement that would haunt him throughout the campaign. The historic Democratic coalition broke down in this campaign, with southerners, Catholics, and union members moving into the Reagan column. Prosperity and Reagan's refrain of "America was standing tall" in its dealings with other nations carried the day against Mondale's weak campaign themes.

AMERICAN PARTY

CANDIDATE FOR PRESIDENT:
Delmar Daniel Dennis (TN)

CANDIDATE FOR VICE PRESIDENT:
Travis Brownlee (DE)

4TH CONVENTION:
December 1–4, 1983, Charlotte (NC)

PLATFORM HIGHLIGHTS:
SUPPORTED:

- the gradual elimination of agricultural subsidies, production and price controls, and government-owned reserves but also endorsed a protective tariff for agricultural products
- the government's divestment of Amtrak and the Postal Service, abolition of the Interstate Commerce Commission and the Occupational Safety and Health Administration (OSHA), and a hands-off attitude toward business
- the restoration of the death penalty, elimination of plea bargaining, greater use of restitution, and reform of the "over-permissive" parole system
- stiff mandatory state penalties for crimes committed with a gun

- the breaking of relations with the People's Republic of China because it was a major source of illicit drugs
- a repeal of compulsory education laws and initiation of a voucher system
- voluntary, nondenominational school prayer and local control of school systems
- an end to federal financing of elections and abolition of the Federal Election Commission
- the removal of price controls and taxes on the production and distribution of energy
- the abolition of the Department of Energy and the Environmental Protection Agency
- a defeat of efforts to reconsider the Equal Rights Amendment (ERA)
- the control of illegal aliens (i.e., increased efforts to halt illegal immigration and denial of public benefits for aliens not legally residing in the United States)
- congressional limits on the jurisdiction of federal courts and the president's authority to issue executive orders
- freedom of choice in pursuing alternative health treatments, especially for cancer
- a phasing out of federal health care programs and the abolishment of Professional Services Review organizations

- the abolition of the Federal Reserve System
- a return to the gold standard
- a repeal of minimum wage laws and price controls
- restrictions on the political activities of labor unions
- "right-to-work" laws
- a repeal of the National Labor Relations Act and denial of the right of government employees to engage in collective bargaining
- an end to all zoning and land use laws and compulsory federal flood-control insurance
- the relinquishment of federal lands to the states
- the restoration of the House and Senate Internal Security committees and the reestablishment of the Subversive Activities Control Board
- states' rights to legislate on public morality
- the abolition of regional governments and revenue sharing
- the phasing out of Social Security
- a repeal of the Sixteenth Amendment
- a balanced budget
- the creation of a national sales tax
- charities and state and local governments taking over welfare programs
- the severing of diplomatic and trade relations with all Communist countries
- an end to all foreign aid programs
- the Cuban and Nicaraguan anti-communist opposition
- a ban on imports from countries employing slave labor
- the withdrawal of the U.S. presence in the Middle East and pursuing a policy of noninvolvement
- the invasion of Grenada
- the repudiation of the Panama Canal, Strategic Arms Limitations Talks (SALT) I, and SALT II treaties
- the protection of the U.S. offshore resources and fishing rights to a distance of 200 miles
- U.S. sovereignty over the Panama Canal
- a denouncement of secret diplomacy as well as the "scandal-ridden" Department of State
- the ratification of the "Bricker Amendment"
- the withdrawal of the United States from the United Nations
- a requirement that no foreign military action could be pursued for more than seventy-two hours without a declaration of war by Congress

OPPOSED:

- the "bailout" of Chrysler, along with proposals for a national industrial policy
- conversion to the metric system
- abortions vigorously, except when necessary to save the mother's life
- federal initiatives in child care
- gun control efforts
- all federal aid to schools, along with abolishment of the Department of Education

- fluoridation of water
- "socialized medicine" (i.e., national health service or national health insurance)
- the observance of a national holiday in honor of Martin Luther King, Jr.
- open housing laws
- the quota system, which assigned preferential status to a minority based on its numerical percentage of the population
- urban renewal programs
- minimum wage laws and unemployment insurance

BIG DEAL PARTY

CANDIDATE FOR PRESIDENT:
Gerald Baker (IA)

CANDIDATE FOR VICE PRESIDENT:
Ferris Alger (PA)

The Big Deal Party espoused a conservative perspective, urging a reduction in government spending, tax cuts, and curbs on inflationary practices. Claiming to be "incorruptible," Baker stressed the need to fight communism in Africa to protect uranium deposits. He also refused to accept contributions from special interest groups.

CITIZENS (CONSUMERS; PEACE AND FREEDOM) PARTY

CANDIDATE FOR PRESIDENT:
Sonia Johnson

CANDIDATES FOR VICE PRESIDENT:
Bill Thorn (PA)
Richard Walton (RI)
Emma Wong Mar (CA)

CANDIDATES FOR PRESIDENTIAL NOMINATION:
Tom Condit (CA)
Larry Holmes (NY)
Sonia Johnson (VA)
Dennis L. Serrette (NJ)

PRIMARY:

JUNE 5, 1984 (CA):

Johnson	3,171
Condit	1,160
Serrette	731
Holmes	651
others	2

2D CONVENTION:
August 10–12, 1984, Hamline University, St. Paul (MN)
Kathryn Anderson (MN), keynoter
William Ramsey Clark (VA), keynoter
Sonia Johnson (VA), keynoter
Richard Walton (RI), keynoter

More than 125 delegates from thirty states attended the convention.

PLATFORM HIGHLIGHTS:
The platform of the Citizens Party declared that "the rule of men over women is the model for other oppression" and asserted that "feminism is a transformative world view."

SUPPORTED:
- an end to the arms race
- a halt to the production, testing, and deployment of nuclear, chemical, and biological weapons
- a 50 percent reduction in military spending
- a negotiated multilateral troop reduction and cessation of military training exercises abroad
- the conversion of weapon industries to peaceful production
- a declaration of outer space as a weapon-free zone
- a U.S. "no-first-strike" pledge
- the adoption of a noninterventionist foreign policy
- an immediate halt to aid for repressive governments
- peaceful coexistence with other political and economic systems (e.g., Communism)
- a recognition of the principles of self-determination and national liberation
- the abolition of the Central Intelligence Agency (CIA) and other related government entities
- an end to political deportations
- economic planning based on participatory democracy
- the development of democratically controlled sources of investment capital
- the closure of tax loopholes
- the public control of the utility and energy industries
- consumer and worker representation on corporate boards
- restrictions on factory closures (e.g., notice requirements, severance obligations)
- employment programs designed to rebuild the nation's infrastructure and mass transit, to clean up the environment, and to promote conservation and energy alternatives
- a repeal of the Taft-Hartley Act and "right-to-work" laws
- an end to U.S. exploitation of foreign workers in overseas plants
- a moratorium on farm foreclosures and evictions in order to save family farms
- the reversal of the trend toward large agribusiness
- 100 percent parity for crops
- low- or no-interest loans for agricultural debt refinancing
- land use restrictions on the conversion of farm lands
- the promotion of cooperatives to share the purchase of machinery, medical insurance, veterinary services, crop insurance, and other vital farming programs
- crop diversification and ecologically sound farming practices
- an end to the use of chemical insecticides and weed killers

- the ratification of the ERA
- equal pay for comparable work
- an expansion of crime prevention and aid programs for criminal victims
- the expanded availability of low-cost contraception and abortion services
- the elimination of discrimination in employment, housing, education, and medical care
- an inclusion of sexual orientation among the characteristics of "protected classes" in civil rights legislation
- the fulfillment of treaty obligations with Native Americans
- the enforcement of the voting rights act
- services and programs to enable disabled and elderly persons to live independently
- the protection of free speech and personal privacy
- alternatives to punishment for criminals such as restitution, community service, and remedies to victims such as compensation or treatment
- the abolition of capital punishment
- the development of an integrated urban policy
- the decentralization of decision-making authority in all field of society (e.g., education, law enforcement, or health care)
- the establishment of a national health service
- enhanced benefits for the elderly
- improvements in education
- equal opportunity housing programs
- the promotion of clean, safe, and appropriate mass transit
- the strengthening of the Clean Air and Water Act with financial penalties and boycotts until the pollution is ended
- research to deal with the disposal of nuclear waste

CITIZENS (CONSUMERS; PEACE AND FREEDOM) PARTY
VOTE FOR PRESIDENTIAL NOMINATION:

Candidate	Ballot: 1
Johnson	185
abstentions	24

Johnson was nominated without opposition.

VOTE FOR VICE-PRESIDENTIAL NOMINATION:

Candidate	Ballot: 1
Walton	191
abstentions	17

Walton was nominated without opposition. Thorn and Wong Mar did appear on some ballots (e.g., in CA and PA) as the party's vice-presidential candidate.

- prohibitions against "dumping" environmentally unsafe chemicals abroad
- worker education on poisonous substances in the workplace
- a stronger enforcement of OSHA provisions
- the preservation of parks, public lands, wilderness areas, and wildlife habitats
- the protection of mineral resources from unwarranted exploitation
- a public discussion of land use and water pollution policies

COMMUNIST PARTY

CANDIDATE FOR PRESIDENT:
Gus Hall (NY)

CANDIDATE FOR VICE PRESIDENT:
Angela Yvonne Davis (CA)

CONSERVATIVE PARTY

CANDIDATE FOR PRESIDENT:
Noah Gerald Willis (AL)

A southern populist and a former Alabama state representative, Willis preached a conservative program. He called for a balanced budget, a national referendum, monetary reform, and an isolationist foreign policy.

CONSERVATIVE PARTY OF NEW YORK

CANDIDATE FOR PRESIDENT:
Ronald Wilson Reagan (CA)

CANDIDATE FOR VICE PRESIDENT:
George Herbert Walker Bush (TX)

The Conservative Party was a New York State third party that normally endorsed the national ticket of the Republican Party.

CONSTITUTIONAL PARTY

CANDIDATE FOR PRESIDENT:
Owen Frank Balding (IL)

CONSTITUTIONAL PARTY

CANDIDATE FOR PRESIDENT:
Talmadge Martin Warren (VA)

A schoolteacher, Warren sought the presidency as a learning experience for his eighth-grade students.

PLATFORM HIGHLIGHTS:
SUPPORTED:
- equal media space for all candidates in a primary
- a "none of the above" ballot line

- the direct election of Supreme Court justices
- a 20 percent cut in the federal payroll
- restrictions on U.S. investment in Mexico and foreign investments in U.S. businesses
- periodic open bidding for privatized government monopolies such as Amtrak and the Postal Service
- a shift in foreign aid from government to voluntary channels
- the establishment of a national informational network to track and prosecute industrial spying and work for a nuclear-free world
- the deployment of the military to aid the war on drugs
- full government-provided health care for all citizens, who, along with their families, would carefully check all charges
- the monitoring of the possession of semiautomatic and assault weapons and holding criminals responsible for compensating their victims
- a child allowance for married couples with preschool children when the mother does not work outside the home for more than sixteen hours per week

OPPOSED:
- the "borrow and pay" approach to government financing

DEMOCRATIC PARTY

CANDIDATE FOR PRESIDENT:
Walter Frederick Mondale

CANDIDATE FOR VICE PRESIDENT:
Geraldine Anne Ferraro

CANDIDATES FOR PRESIDENTIAL NOMINATION:
Russell Lee Arndt (IL)
Reubin O'Donovan Askew (FL)
Hugh Garland Bagley (CA)
Larry Lee Baker (WA)
Martin James Beckman (MT)
Joseph Robinette Biden (DE)
Jon S. Branning (NY)
Robert L. Brewster (FL)
George Gittion Britt, Jr. (PA)
Gerry Brooks (MI)
Walter Ralph "Buck" Buchanan (CA)
Dale Leon Bumpers (AR)
Carolyn Dorothy Bush (VA)
Lester Francis Byerley, Jr. (NJ)
Raymond Joseph Caplette (CA)
Tom Cardenas (CA)
Anthony Solomon Chavez (TX)
Peggy Ann Childers (GA)
Roy James Clendenan (OH)
Robert Eugene Cotner (OK)
Philip Joseph Covello (NY)
Alan MacGregor Cranston (CA)
Robert F. Cruz (TX)
Susanna Dakin (CA)

Sterling P. Davis, Jr. (MS)
Daniel G. Defosse (IL)
George Robert Diamond (CA)
Jesse Howell Dierlam (AK)
Charles Dieterle (CO)
Marcus Ray Dilworth, Jr. (MS)
Charles Richard Doty (OK)
Willie George Duke (OH)
Thomas Francis Eagleton (MO)
Thomas Niel Garcia (CA)
Gerald M. Gerbig (MI)
John Herschel Glenn, Jr. (OH)
James Irvin Glover (NJ)
Mildred Williams Glover (GA)
Dyke Goodin (GA)
Samuel Lee Graves (NC)
Richard Grayson (FL)
Michael Lee Griffith (KS)
Robert Kennedy Griser (PA)
Irvin James Guenther (KY)
John Dewayne Gullette (FL)
Albert Hamburg (WY)
Frederick Charles Hamre (MA)
Gary Warren Hart (CO)
Sammie Hayes Hart (FL)
Carla Kathryn Schram Hawkinson (MI)
Gerard Andrew "Jerry" Himmelman, Sr. (NJ)
Ernest Frederick "Fritz" Hollings (SC)
J. Harold Huff (TN)
William Henry Hurley (AL)
Jesse Louis Jackson (IL)
William Edward Jahnke (IL)
Richard Broughton Kay (FL)
Joseph Wilber Kelly, Jr. (LA)
Joseph James Kenna (PA)
William E. King (FL)
Claude Roy Kirk, Jr. (FL)
Martha Perry Kirkland (AL)
Stephen Andrew Koczak (DC)
Daniel Francis Christ Kosisky (MD)
William Parker Kreml (SC)
Dale Harbor Kyle (CA)
Lyndon Hermyle LaRouche, Jr. (VA)
Robert Kipley "Kip" Lee (CA)
Ronald Curtis Lewis, Sr. (FL)
Raymond V Liebenberg (CA)
Bobby Locke (TX)
Samuel Marquez (TX)
John Paul Masters, Jr. (IA)
John Martin McCarthy (IL)
George Stanley McGovern (SD)
Walter Frederick Mondale (MN)
Leonard Bernard Murray (UT)
James Arthur Nelson, Jr. (CA)
Grady O'Cummings III (NY)
Edward Thomas O'Donnell, Jr. (DE)

Raphael Ornstein (CA)
Zelma Faye Owens (CA)
Andrew Jeffrey Porter (OK)
George Buchanan Roden (TX)
Ronald Wilson Reagan (CA)
Raymond Allen Peter Rollinson (NJ)
Robert John Roosevelt (MD)
Chester M. Rudnicki (MA)
Vincent J. Sabatini (TX)
Cyril Emil Sagan (PA)
Daniel Ernest Sanderson (CA)
Donald Gene Smith (IN)
Bert Phillip Snyder (NY)
Alphonso Dewitt Steward (NC)
Mrs. Frank Stewart (AL)
Duke Esten Stockton (WA)
Peter Paul Sebastian Swider (MI)
Leonard Dennis Talbow (CO)
Marlin Dale Thacker (AL)
Alfred Timinski (NJ)
Morris King Udall (AZ)
Edward Jesse Vincent (CA)
Betty Jean Williams (IL)
Noah Gerald Willis (AL)
William Joseph Wulforst (NH)

CANDIDATES FOR VICE-PRESIDENTIAL NOMINATION:
Shirley Anita St. Hill Chisholm (NY)
Christina Delzingaro (CA)
Geraldine Anne Ferraro (NY)
Barbara Marx Hubbard (CA)
Gerald Noah Willis (AL)

PRIMARIES:
FEBRUARY 28, 1984 (NH):
Hart 37,702
Mondale 28,173
Glenn 12,088
Jackson 5,311
McGovern 5,217
Reagan 5,058
Hollings 3,583
Cranston 2,136
Askew 1,025
Koczak 155
Buchanan 132
Beckman 127
O'Donnell 74
Willis 50
King 34
Kay 27
Kreml 25
Bagley 24
Kirk 24
Rudnicki 21
Clendenan 20
Sagan 20

Caplette 19
others 5,144

Vice-Presidential Primary:
Noah Gerald Willis (AL) . . . .

MARCH 6, 1984 (VT):
Hart 51,873
Mondale 14,834
Jackson 5,761
Askew 444
others 1,147

MARCH 13, 1984 (AL):
Mondale 148,165
Glenn 89,286
Hart 88,465
Jackson 83,787
Willis 6,153
Hollings 4,759
Askew 1,827
Cranston 1,377
unpledged delegates 4,464

MARCH 13, 1984 (FL):
Hart 463,799
Mondale 394,350
Jackson 144,263
Glenn 128,209
Askew 26,258
McGovern 17,614
Hollings 3,115
Cranston 2,097
Kay 1,328
Koczak 1,157

MARCH 13, 1984 (GA):
Mondale 208,588
Hart 186,903
Jackson 143,730
Glenn 122,744
McGovern 11,321
Hollings 3,800
Willis 1,804
Askew 1,660
Cranston 923
unpledged delegates 3,068

MARCH 13, 1984 (MA):
Hart 245,943
Mondale 160,893
McGovern 134,341
Glenn 45,456
Jackson 31,824
Reagan 3,595
Askew 1,394
Hollings 1,203
Cranston 853
unpledged delegates 5,080
others 380

MARCH 13, 1984 (RI):
Hart 20,011
Mondale 15,338
Jackson 3,875
Glenn 2,249
McGovern 2,146
Cranston 273
Askew 96
Hollings 84
unpledged delegates 439

MARCH 13, 1984, DEMOCRATS ABROAD:
Mondale . . . .
Hart . . . .
Jackson . . . .
McGovern . . . .

MARCH 18, 1984 (PR):
Mondale 141,698
Hart 874
Glenn 436
Davis 31

MARCH 20, 1984 (IL):
Mondale 670,951
Hart 584,579
Jackson 348,843
McGovern 25,336
Glenn 19,800
Williams 4,797
Cranston 2,786
Askew 2,182
others 151

MARCH 27, 1984 (CT):
Hart 116,286
Mondale 64,230
Jackson 26,395
Askew 6,098
McGovern 2,426
Hollings 2,283
Glenn 955
Cranston 196
unpledged delegates 1,973

APRIL 3, 1984 (NY):
Mondale 621,581
Hart 380,564
Jackson 355,541
Glenn 15,941
Cranston 6,815
McGovern 4,547
Askew 2,877
others 84

APRIL 3, 1984 (WI):
Hart 282,435
Mondale 261,374
Jackson 62,524
McGovern 10,166

Glenn 6,398
Cranston 2,984
Hollings 1,650
Askew 683
unpledged delegates 7,036
others 518

APRIL 10, 1984 (PA):

Mondale 747,267
Hart 551,335
Jackson 264,463
Cranston 22,829
Glenn 22,605
LaRouche 19,180
McGovern 13,139
Griser 6,090
Askew 5,071
Hollings 2,972
others 1,343

MAY 1, 1984 (DC):

Jackson 69,106
Mondale 26,320
Hart 7,305

MAY 1, 1984 (TN):

Mondale 132,201
Hart 93,710
Jackson 81,418
Glenn 4,198
McGovern 3,824
unpledged delegates 6,682
others 30

MAY 5, 1984 (LA):

Jackson 136,707
Hart 79,593
Mondale 71,162
LaRouche 4,970
McGovern 3,158
Griser 1,924
Kay 1,344
Koczak 543
unpledged delegates 19,409

MAY 8, 1984 (IN):

Hart 299,491
Mondale 293,413
Jackson 98,190
Glenn 16,046
Brewster 9,815

MAY 8, 1984 (MD):

Mondale 215,222
Jackson 129,387
Hart 123,365
LaRouche 7,836
Glenn 6,238
McGovern 5,796
Cranston 1,768

Hollings 1,467
unpledged delegates 15,807

MAY 8, 1984 (NC):

Mondale 342,324
Hart 289,877
Jackson 243,945
Glenn 17,659
McGovern 10,149
Hollings 8,318
Askew 3,144
Cranston 1,209
unpledged delegates 44,232

MAY 8, 1984 (OH):

Hart 608,528
Mondale 583,595
Jackson 237,133
McGovern 8,991
Cranston 4,653
LaRouche 4,336

MAY 15, 1984 (NE):

Hart 86,582
Mondale 39,635
Jackson 13,495
McGovern 1,561
LaRouche 1,227
Cranston 538
Hollings 450
unpledged delegates 4,631
others 736

MAY 15, 1984 (OR):

Hart 233,638
Mondale 110,374
Jackson 37,106
Glenn 10,831
LaRouche 5,943
Reagan 1,443
others 344

MAY 22, 1984 (ID):

Hart 31,737
Mondale 16,460
Jackson 3,104
LaRouche 1,196
unpledged delegates 2,225

JUNE 5, 1984 (CA):

Hart 1,155,499
Mondale 1,049,342
Jackson 546,693
Glenn 96,770
McGovern 69,926
LaRouche 52,647

JUNE 5, 1984 (MT):

Hart 3,080
Mondale 2,026
Jackson 388

unpledged delegates 28,385
others 335

JUNE 5, 1984 (NJ):
Mondale 305,516
Hart 200,948
Jackson 159,788
LaRouche 10,309

JUNE 5, 1984 (NM):
Hart 87,610
Mondale 67,675
Jackson 22,168
McGovern 5,143
LaRouche 3,330
unpledged delegates 1,477

JUNE 5, 1984 (SD):
Hart 26,641
Mondale 20,495
Jackson 2,738
LaRouche 1,383
unpledged delegates 1,304

JUNE 5, 1984 (WV):
Mondale 198,776
Hart 137,866
Jackson 24,697
LaRouche 7,274
Timinski 632

JUNE 12, 1984 (ND):
Hart 28,603
LaRouche 4,018
Mondale 934
Jackson 51

39TH CONVENTION:
July 16–19, 1984, George R. Moscone Convention
Center, San Francisco (CA)
Charles Taylor Manatt (CA), temporary chairman
Martha Layne Collins (KY), permanent chairman
Mario Matthew Cuomo (NY), keynoter

PLATFORM HIGHLIGHTS:
The 1984 Democratic platform was one of the longest political documents of its type. For its main themes, it promised
economic growth, prosperity, and jobs; justice, dignity, and
opportunity; and peace, security, and freedom.

SUPPORTED:
- a competitive dollar by lowering deficits, reducing interest rates, instituting free savings for private investment, and preventing inflation
- public long-term investments in research, infrastructure, and people, with an emphasis on training, retraining, and education
- efforts to "restore sanity to our fiscal house . . . through
  efficiency and toughness"
- more rational (i.e., lower) defense spending by eliminating waste and requiring allies to shoulder their portion of the burden

- sensible arms control agreements
- progressive tax reform with the closure of loopholes,
  simplification of the tax code, higher rates for corporations, and lower rates for individuals
- higher taxes for the rich and lower taxes for low- and
  moderate-income families
- Social Security
- efforts to control rising health care costs
- efforts to make the Federal Reserve System responsive
  to the growth potential of its monetary policy
- a five-point anti-inflationary program (more noted for
  its lack of specifics than for its content)
- calls for the nation to invest in its people
- a stronger commitment to nutrition programs, child
  care, a reduction in child abuse, efforts to reduce delinquency, runaway assistance programs, surveys of child
  and adolescent health status, suicide prevention initiatives, and motor vehicle safety programs
- improvements in education, including equity in education under Title I
- increased federal funding for schools with an emphasis on
  science, math, communications, and computer literacy
- incentives to enter the teaching professions
- vocational education
- aid to special education programs
- bilingual education and a reduction in the dropout rate
- funding for federal programs for all low- and moderate-
  income pupils, whether in public or private schools
  (except for "segregation" academies, private schools
  whose admissions policies effectively segregate by race)
- a targeted funding for African-American and Hispanic
  colleges, along with programs to develop more scientists
  and engineers without neglecting the arts and humanities
- partnerships with the private sector and initiatives to
  promote adult education
- the arts and humanities and assistance for public television and radio stations
- efforts to address the problems of unemployed minority
  youth and school dropouts, the over-fifty-years-old
  worker, displaced homemakers, and those dislocated by
  changing technologies
- a major comprehensive national job skills development
  policy
- an overhaul of the "antiquated" unemployment compensation system
- job training programs for women on public assistance
- investment in infrastructure and the rebuilding of the
  nation's cities
- the creation of a federal capital budget
- more consultation with local governments
- a commitment to public and government-assisted
  housing
- easier access to mortgage capital and lower interest rates
- the development of a national reconstruction fund and
  the enforcement of fair housing standards to prohibit
  discrimination

- the formulation of a national telecommunications policy and the Fairness Doctrine and Equal Time requirements for the electronic media
- increased competition in the transportation arena
- the promotion of a comprehensive maritime policy
- suggestions that the private sector invest strategically, manage cost and quality, and begin to compete internationally
- cooperation among labor and management, universities, the private sector, and state and local governments as a way of to overcome common economic problems
- the creation of a national Economic Cooperation Council
- employee ownership and participation in the workplace and maintenance of the right to collective bargaining
- federal consumer protection agencies
- individual empowerment, independence, self-respect, and dignity for those who are unable to be completely self-sufficient—the very young, the unskilled, the disabled, and the elderly
- increases in graduate training, research and development funds, and support for the National Science Foundation to promote innovation and small business growth
- the creation of Centers of Excellence
- the promotion of small, minority-, and women-owned businesses
- reduced paperwork and regulation with regard to the business sector and private individuals
- tax code revisions to favor small business development
- stronger seed capital programs
- open world markets, a favorable balance of trade, lowered trade restrictions abroad, and a fair trade policy
- the auto industry
- the modernization and revitalization of "keystone" industries as a quid pro quo for temporary governmental relief
- advance notification of plant closures and large-scale layoffs
- economic coordination with the major industrialized nations
- the liberalization of currency and investment regulations
- a renewed commitment to the family farm and aggressive promotion of farm exports and humanitarian food aid, with a moratorium on farm debt and foreclosures
- soil and water conservation programs
- lower farm credit rates
- adequate support levels for crops being gradually moved toward complete parity
- reductions in excess production of agricultural products
- fair prices for agricultural commodities
- producer-controlled marketing arrangements
- a revitalized commodity reserve system
- an end to land speculation and exorbitant pricing by middlemen
- land use planning
- better management of U.S. natural resources

- increased support for agricultural science and education
- improved rural services (e.g., cooperative electrification and telephone service)
- the accelerated filling of the Strategic Petroleum Reserve
- the promotion of ethanol and other biomass sources of renewable energy, and the development of renewable and alternative energy resources
- aggressive coal exports
- further research and development of solar energy and increased funding for the Solar Energy and Energy Conservation Bank
- a low-income weatherization program
- strong enforcement of health and safety standards for nuclear power plants
- an expanded role for the public in the Nuclear Regulatory Commission
- protection for the public in the transportation of high-level radioactive waste and other hazardous materials
- environmental safeguards for offshore oil and gas exploration
- improvements in (i.e., strengthening of) the Coastal Zone Management Act
- a reevaluation of the Synthetic Fuels Corporation
- the use of environmental protection technologies and standards in synthetic fuels research
- energy conservation measures, lifeline utility rates, recycling, sound resource management, careful planning, strict pollution enforcement, and a strengthened Environmental Protection Agency
- an increase in Superfund resources, enforcement of laws regulating hazardous wastes, expansion of the Resource Conservation and Recovery Act, strengthening of the Clean Air and Clean Water Acts, reduction in sulfur dioxide and nitrogen oxide emissions, and reduction of acid rain
- workplace health and safety enforcement and restrictions on pesticides and herbicides
- management of public lands according to the principles of multiple use and sustainable yield, reclamation, development of a federal water policy, provision of adequate appropriations for the Land and Water Conservation Fund, and protection of wetlands and wildlife
- the protection of the civil rights of all regardless of race, religion, gender, age, national origin, ethnic heritage, sexual orientation, or disability, while condemning the Reagan administration's civil rights record
- a strong, independent Civil Rights Commission
- a renewal of the civil rights commitments of the Departments of Justice and of Labor
- the strengthened enforcement of laws by the Equal Employment Opportunity Commission
- a reversal of the Grove City College case and imposition of a requirement that all institutional recipients of federal funds be required to guarantee equality and equal opportunity in their programs

- the restoration of the historic principles of religious liberty and separation of church and state
- greater authority for the Department of Housing and Urban Development to ensure fair housing
- the continued use of affirmative action programs
- diversity and the elimination of ethnic stereotyping
- assurances of equal access to justice by aiding the Legal Services Corporation
- the ratification of the ERA and attainment of pay, pension, and insurance equity for women
- improvements in child-support collections
- universally available day care
- the political empowerment of minorities and women
- reproductive freedom (including abortion) as a fundamental human right
- a repeal of section 14 (b) of the National Labor Relations Act
- the reform of bankruptcy and labor laws
- the legalization of peaceful picketing by building trades' workers
- the organization of and collective bargaining by public employees and agricultural workers
- prohibitions against the use of polygraphs and "truth tests" in employment
- the enforcement of the Mine Health Safety Act and the Occupational Health and Safety Act and just compensation for injured or disease-affected workers
- full implementation of the Davis-Bacon Act and minimum wage protections under law
- expanded training and apprenticeship opportunities for women and minorities
- the enforcement of the Voting Rights Act, enactment of "same-day" and mail-in registration laws, delayed media projections in national elections, and elimination of all discriminatory barriers to participation in the electoral process
- statehood for "New Columbia" (i.e., the District of Columbia); legislative, judicial, and fiscal autonomy for the District of Columbia; and local control and congressional representation for the District of Columbia
- self-determination for Puerto Rico
- a fair and humane immigration policy
- an end to bracero and guest-worker programs
- the creation of an international body on immigration to address the economic development problems affecting Mexico and Latin America
- efforts to eradicate discrimination against gays and lesbians (including impediments to military service)
- greater efforts to find a cure for AIDS (acquired immunodeficiency syndrome) and to provide effective treatments for people with AIDS
- the resolution of outstanding water and natural resource claims of Native Americans
- a reevaluation of the mission of the Bureau of Indian Affairs
- restitution, reparations, and an apology to Japanese-Americans interned during World War II
- the prosecution of groups (e.g., the Ku Klux Klan and American Nazi Party) responsible for hate crimes
- the elimination of citizenship and tax inequities for U.S. citizens abroad
- self-determination and the right to vote for president for residents of territories of the United States
- comprehensive national health insurance and more effective cost containment
- more basic scientific research and a national policy for the prevention and control of sickle cell disease
- the prevention of cuts in Medicare benefits
- the recognition of non-English-speaking elderly individuals as a neglected population
- an independent Social Security agency
- the rights of disabled persons to employment and independence and the provision of benefits to those who cannot work
- honoring veterans, particularly Vietnam War veterans
- increased efforts to end hunger and homelessness
- honesty in government and an end to official secrecy
- election campaign reforms
- the streamlining of drug control bureaucracies with a comprehensive management plan, along with encouragement for community-based efforts to combat substance abuse
- a comprehensive, community-based anti-drunk-driving program
- criminal justice reforms (e.g., compensation for victims, restitution, and sentencing alternatives)
- control of snub-nosed handguns
- a strong national defense, coupled with efforts to achieve a mutual and verifiable agreement on nuclear arms control
- annual summit meetings with Soviet leaders
- a conditional freeze on the testing, production, and deployment of nuclear weapons
- the resubmission to the Senate of an updated SALT II Treaty for ratification
- the termination of the MX missile and B-1 bomber programs
- economic adjustment programs to retrain defense workers displaced by the cutbacks in weapon programs and other disarmament proposals
- a balance of conventional weapons in Europe as a foreign policy objective
- a revitalized intelligence community and a North Atlantic Treaty Organization (NATO) strengthened by enhanced allied contributions
- greater efficiency in Pentagon procurement programs
- military reforms to ensure combat-ready U.S. troops
- the concept of a Peace Academy
- a stronger Foreign Service
- the appointment of qualified persons as ambassadors
- scholarships for foreign students

- increased educational and cultural exchanges
- an emphasis on bilateral and multilateral diplomacy
- respect for the International Court of Justice and the War Powers Act
- reduced reliance on oil imported from the Persian Gulf
- a settlement of the problems in Cyprus and Ireland
- freedom for Soviet dissidents, refuseniks, and Jews seeking to emigrate to Israel
- a liberalization in domestic affairs for Eastern Europe (especially Poland) and an end to Soviet domination
- the security of Israel and the pursuit of peace in the Middle East
- a transfer of the U.S. Embassy in Israel from Tel Aviv to Jerusalem
- improved relations with countries in Central and Latin America
- stabilized U.S. relations with Cuba and the principle of nonintervention in the internal affairs of nations in the Western Hemisphere
- the Contadora process and the Rio Treaty
- an end to aid for the Nicaraguan Contras, support for the newly elected president of El Salvador, and the encouragement of respect for human rights and military restraint in the Caribbean and Central America
- substantially increased humanitarian aid, economic assistance, and technology transfer for Africa
- self-determination for Namibia
- cooperation and expanded trade with Japan and other Asian countries
- a strengthened security commitment to the Australia-New Zealand-United States (ANZUS) pact
- improved U.S. relations with the People's Republic of China and close cooperation with India
- the democratization process in East Timor, Pakistan, the Philippines, the Republic of Korea, and Taiwan
- a reform of the international monetary system
- the development of a short-term program for reducing the debt service of less-developed countries
- the expansion of the lending capacity of the World Bank and the Export-Import Bank
- reduced international trade barriers
- international population control programs
- efforts to strengthen the United Nations
- the creation of an acceptable international Law of the Sea Treaty
- the ratification of the Genocide Convention, the International Covenants on Human Rights, and the American Convention on Human Rights
- a demand for a full accounting of U.S. servicemen still missing in action (MIA) in Vietnam

OPPOSED:

- a balanced budget amendment to the Constitution or the convening of a constitutional convention

- the failed theory of "Reaganomics" and pointed with alarm to the escalating national debt, rising interest rates, and the recession
- the "sub-minimum wage" and "workfare"
- employment discrimination against seniors
- the feminization of poverty (Most Americans living below the poverty level are women and children, and this was a catch phrase during the campaign.)
- the Strategic Defense Initiative (SDI or "Star Wars") program of the Reagan administration
- a peacetime military draft
- apartheid in South Africa and supported strong sanctions to end it
- Soviet aggression in Afghanistan

DEMOCRATIC PARTY
VOTE FOR PRESIDENTIAL NOMINATION:

Candidate	Ballot: 1
Mondale	2,191
Hart, G. W.	1,200½
Jackson	465½
Eagleton	18
McGovern	4
Glenn	2
Biden	1
Kirkland	1
abstentions	40
absent	10

VOTE FOR VICE-PRESIDENTIAL NOMINATION:

Candidate	Ballot: 1
Ferraro	375
Chisholm	3
Hubbard	(withdrew)
abstentions	1

When Arkansas passed, New York cast its 283 votes for Ferraro and moved that her nomination be made by acclamation. Accordingly, the roll call was never completed, and Ferraro won by acclamation.

INDEPENDENT
CANDIDATES FOR PRESIDENT:
David Randall Adaskin (NY)
Steven Mark Arbit (MI)
Lavern Rommal Arnold (MN)
Hugh Garland Bagley (CA)[1]
Thomas J. Baker (NY)
Robert Charles Banks (VA)

[1]Bagley advocated the annexation of, and statehood for, Mexico as a way of achieving peace, power, oil, and employment. His running mate was Jay Randall Overman of New York.

Thomas Bentley (NY)
Arthur Jay Berman (CT)
Robert B. Binkley (TX)
Earl Edward Black (KS)
Kenneth Myron Bonnell (MS)
Robert Wayne Bradford (MO)
Noah Thomas Bradshaw (GA)
Charles Ayars Breed (MI)
Robert L. Brewster (FL)
Nathan Burdette (IN)
Gilbert Campbell (CO)
Jerry Leon Carroll (CA)
James R. Clauson (TN)
Jack Cody (TX)
Jerome J. Diamond (NJ)
Robert James Dick (CA)
Prophet Elijah (NY)[1]
Maximus T. Englerius (WA)
Clinton-George Essex (MI)
Joseph M. Finerty (VA)
Roger Allen "Jolly Roger" Fleenor (CA)
Michael James Frederichs (IL)
Martha Gorman (CO)
Larry Harmon (DC)[2]
Joseph D. Harrington (MA)
Richard Rhorer Hill (TX)
Thomas Hallowell Hill (NY)
Andrew John (NJ)
Thomas Maundy Joseph Jones (OH)
Frederick Douglass Kirkpatrick (NY)
Rachel Dunn Koch (OR)
Larry Francis Koebel, Jr. (OH)
Christopher Hermann Kreb (IL)
John Patrick Kusumi (CT)
Bobbie Joe Lamb (TX)
Wayne Anthony Lela (IL)
Arthur Blair Lewis (FL)
Henry A. Lewis, Jr. (MS)
Freddie Liggins (TX)
Cesar Lopez-Escapa (FL)
Steven Douglas Mabey (UT)
Isabell Masters (OK)[3]
James Franklin McIntosh III (FL)
John Allen Mitchell (OH)
Kenneth Moore (VA)
George Alexander Muzyk (MD)
Robert Allison Nevers (MA)[4]
David Wesley Peyton (CA)

Harold Lawrence Poland (VA)
James Thomas Poole (IN)
Norman Joseph Pousquet (MA)
Eric Lindsay Price, Sr. (MI)
Windi April Reedy (CO)
Jerome Donald Reitsma (MN)
Merrill Keith Riddick (MT)
Joseph Thomas Robino, Jr. (LA)
Abraham Michael "Abe" Rosenthal (NY)
Robert Garfield Salzgeber
Bobby Saunders (DC)
Susanne Edith Schmidt (MD)
K. Core Seaman (CO)
Ronald Takeo Shigeta, Sr. (HI)
Bobbie Weldon Shofner (NV)
Willis Johnston Stancill (NC)
Robert Gary Stout (MI)
Graham G. Streeter (CA)
J. O. Stroud (OK)
Daniel Stull (FL)
Donald Jerome Sullivan (PA)
Scott Stewart Thomas (AZ)
Garrett Brock Trapnell (IL)
Donald J. Trapp (NJ)
Paul Edward Trent (OK)
Heber J. Trunnell (UT)
Lawrence Douglas Turner (MI)
Sherman Lee Tyler, Jr. (TX)
Steven Kenneth Ury (CA)
Giacomo Valenti (CO)
Milton Vera (NY)
Jon Jay Vinicki (MS)
Lawrence Paul Wagner (CA)
Robert Bryant Winn (AZ)
Victoria Woodhull (satire) (WY)
James Bell Yager (AL)

CANDIDATES FOR VICE PRESIDENT:
Katherine M. Garry (NY)
Daryl Martin Olds (WY)

INDEPENDENT (UNITED CITIZENS; LIBERTY UNION) ALLIANCE

CANDIDATE FOR PRESIDENT:
Dennis L. Serrette (NJ)

CANDIDATES FOR VICE PRESIDENT:
Naomi Azulay (CO)
Dorothy Mars Blancata (PA)
Frances H. Costa (ME)
Nancy Ross (NY)

PRIMARY:
MARCH 6, 1984 (VT):

Serrette 276
others 33

[1]Prophet Elijah sought the presidency because he was concerned "that many do not have the proper food, clothing, and shelter." He promised jobs for the unemployed, cuts in the military budget, and racial and economic justice. He opposed the death penalty, mandatory celibacy in the priesthood, prayer before saints, and homosexuality. Basing his campaign on the belief that he was "called to prophecy," his political and religious views were closely connected.

[2]Harmon's running mate was Milton R. Polland of California.

[3]Masters's running mate was James Russel of Kansas.

[4]Nevers's running mate was Scottie Keillor of Massachusetts.

INDEPENDENT DEMOCRATIC PARTY

CANDIDATE FOR PRESIDENT:

Lyndon Hermyle LaRouche, Jr. (VA)

CANDIDATE FOR VICE PRESIDENT:

Billy M. Davis (MS)

PLATFORM HIGHLIGHTS:

The platform of the Independent Democratic Party was a 447-page document that accused Walter Mondale of being "an agent of Soviet influence," denounced homosexuality, and described the National Education Association as part of "an evil sort of Gnostic cult." Henry Kissinger and Paul Volcker were also denounced. The platform-book outlining the Independent Democratic agenda expressed a desire to win the Democratic Party back from the "radicals" who controlled it. LaRouche and his party saw five "deadly" crises facing the United States in 1984–85: (1) the Soviet drive to establish world domination by 1988, (2) a worldwide financial collapse, (3) a continuing collapse of the agro-industrial output of the West, (4) the eruption of a famine-level worldwide food shortage during 1985–86, and (5) the accelerating erosion of the distinctive features of Judeo-Christian culture.

SUPPORTED:

- the restoration of the gold-reserve basis for U.S. currency and the printing of $500 billion in U.S. currency notes backed by gold
- a declaration of a national economic emergency
- the suspension of the Federal Reserve System's privileges and stronger control over the Federal Reserve System
- limits on the misuse of the Internal Revenue Service's power
- a return of control of the Bureau of the Budget to the Treasury Department
- the reorganization of the executive branch
- negotiations to restructure the debt and foster hemispheric trade
- the creation of cooperative agreements to expand other world trade and an international economic partnership based on the gold-reserve system
- a reorganization of the domestic banking and financial system
- a presidential order that the Federal Reserve loan issues of gold-reserve currency notes at 2 percent to 4 percent rates of interest for categories of designated investments to address the collapse of agro-industry
- an increase in tax exemptions for dependents
- a coordinated effort to rebuild the basic infrastructure of the country
- a revision of the tax code
- crash research and development programs relating to genetic engineering, organized plasmas, coherent radiation of energy, and nonlinear processes of living organisms
- a moratorium on farm foreclosures
- the adoption of a 90 percent parity price structure
- the reorganization of farm debt

- disaster relief for farmers
- the development of freshwater management systems
- better market forecasting systems
- emergency action to relieve the world's food shortage
- a resurrection of national awareness of classical culture and great works of art and literature
- the U.S. system of political-economy and scientific progress
- a commitment to natural law
- a balanced federal budget
- economic expansion as the means to raise new revenues without increasing tax rates
- investment tax credits and a maximum interest rate (with indexing prohibited) to be instituted under the federal criminal code
- large flows of gold-reserve credit to public utilities and government infrastructure programs assisted by long-term credit for construction loans, expanded utility generating capacity, renovation of freight and passenger rail service, expansion of the Army Corps of Engineers
- creation of high-speed cargo vessels, refurbishment of ocean-vessel ports, urgent capital repairs
- reinvigoration of veterans' hospitals, retooling of essential industries
- the establishment of several experimental water desalination stations
- monetary reforms and debt management agreements between the United States and "Ibero-America" (i.e., Spanish-speaking nations of the Western Hemisphere)
- cooperation and famine relief in Africa
- a shift in emphasis in U.S. and Japanese marketing away from excess production of consumer durables into capital-goods production and sales
- joint efforts by Japan and the United States to assist European economic recovery
- SDI (Star Wars), claiming LaRouche first articulated the concept in 1982
- "crash programs" to develop and deploy energy-beam pulse missiles and enhanced radiation effect bombs and a layered ballistic missile defense system
- the removal of all foreign intelligence functions from the Federal Bureau of Investigation (FBI)
- the creation of an academy for the CIA
- calls for military intelligence functions being limited to military professionals, the military general staff having its own intelligence function, and the National Strategic Estimates serving as the interface between the president and the military
- the elimination of the "systems analysis" approach to defense
- high military expenditures and argued that they did not increase the budget deficit because they served to expand the "tax-revenue base"
- the "LaRouche Doctrine" in foreign policy and a disavowal of the distinction between conventional and strategic military capabilities
- a foreign policy based on the principle of strategic con-

flict between the opposing interests of republicanism and oligarchism

ALSO:

- discussed arcane philosophical issues, economic history, John F. Kennedy's assassination, and a host of detailed analyses of water policy, drug trafficking, education, and criminal theory

LIBERAL PARTY OF NEW YORK

CANDIDATE FOR PRESIDENT:
Walter Frederick Mondale (MN)

CANDIDATE FOR VICE PRESIDENT:
Geraldine Anne Ferraro (NY)

The Liberal Party was a New York State third party that normally endorsed the national ticket of the Democratic Party.

LIBERTARIAN PARTY

CANDIDATE FOR PRESIDENT:
David Peter Bergland

CANDIDATE FOR VICE PRESIDENT:
James Arthur Lewis (CT)

CANDIDATES FOR PRESIDENTIAL NOMINATION:
David Peter Bergland (CA)
Eugene Morley Burns (FL) (withdrew)
Theodora "Tonie" Nathan (OR)
James E. Norwood (TX)
Earl Cedric Ravenal (DC)
Mary Jean Ruwart (MI)
Dick Siano (NJ)

CANDIDATES FOR VICE-PRESIDENTIAL NOMINATION:
James Arthur Lewis (CT)
Mary Jean Ruwart (MI)

PRIMARIES:
APRIL 3, 1984 (WI):
Bergland 3,513
   (yes)[1]
Bergland................................ 857
   (no)
others 15

JUNE 5, 1984 (CA):
scattered................................ 34

4TH CONVENTION:
September 1–4, 1983, Sheraton Centre Hotel, New York (NY)

This convention was attended by 735 delegates.

PLATFORM HIGHLIGHTS:
The Libertarians' platform reiterated the party's Statement of Principles and most of the 1980 platform. It denied the

[1]Bergland was the only listed candidate, but was listed with "yes" and "no" choices.

existence of any conflict between civil order and individual rights, claiming the party's positions were not based on the moral values of specific practices but on a fundamental belief that people's rights must be recognized. Personal responsibility was a cardinal tenet. Crime would have been fought through impartial and consistent law enforcement and the decriminalization of "victimless" crimes, that is, those involving drugs, consensual sexual relations, possession or distribution and use of sexually explicit materials, prostitution, gambling, and suicide.

SUPPORTED:

- the trend toward private protection services and voluntary community crime-control groups
- government restitution for wrongful criminal proceedings against an accused person and wrongdoer restitution for victims of crimes
- peremptory challenges to proposed judges by parties in criminal or civil cases
- the notion of a victim's "pardon" for criminals
- the private adjudication of disputes and a change in the rape laws to remove cohabitation as a defense
- the right of juries to decide on the justice of a law (rather than simply the facts of a case)
- an end to the doctrine of state "sovereign immunity"
- a repeal of the Intelligence Identities Protection Act and restrictions on the rights of electronic media and efforts to impose thought control through censorship
- the right of individuals to own and use private property (including their own bodies) and denounced government restrictions on those rights based on aesthetic values, riskiness, moral standards, cost-benefit estimates, or the promotion of economic growth
- restitution for Japanese-Americans whose lands were taken during World War II
- the right to privacy as inviolable and prohibitions against government surveillance of all types, including the information collected by the Census Bureau and other public agencies
- the abolition of the FBI and the CIA
- a curtailment of Congress's subpoena power
- the dismantling of the internal security committees of Congress
- the destruction of all files compiled by the Selective Service
- unconditional exoneration for persons accused or convicted of draft offenses, desertion, or other acts of resistance to wars and the military
- a denial of draft requirements applied to women (on the grounds that the draft should be completely abolished)
- the right of collective bargaining and the rights of employers to not recognize unions
- the legitimacy of secondary boycotts
- the removal of all restrictions on immigration, the abolition of the Immigration and Naturalization Service and Border Patrol, full amnesty for illegal aliens, and an

end to government restrictions on undocumented noncitizens

- a ban on punishing employers who hire undocumented workers
- full civil rights for all, but also a repeal, rather than an extension, of protective laws applied to selected groups and a repeal of government attempts to regulate private discrimination in employment, housing, and public accommodations
- the extension to children of all rights granted to adults
- a repeal of all status offense laws (e.g., laws based on age such as curfew laws and runaway laws)
- the abolition of juvenile courts
- the elimination of laws that treated juvenile offenders as if they were not fully responsible for their crimes
- private adoptions and the right of children to seek non-parental guardians
- the total deregulation of the economic sphere and a limited public role in protecting property rights
- a repeal of the Sixteenth Amendment (income tax) and of all involuntary taxes
- a repeal of federal inheritance taxes
- amnesty for tax evaders and relieving employers of the "involuntary servitude" of collecting taxes on behalf of the state
- a repeal of legal tender laws
- private ownership of gold
- the elimination of minted coins (with private minting on a competitive basis allowed)
- free market banking and the abolition of the Federal Reserve System, Federal Deposit Insurance Corporation, National Banking System, and other regulatory agencies in the banking and credit fields
- the abolition of the Federal Savings and Loan Insurance Corporation, National Credit Union Administration, National Credit Union Central Liquidity Facility, Federal Home Loan Bank, and similar agencies
- a return to the Jacksonian concept of the government maintaining its own treasury
- balanced budget amendments for the federal government and the states
- a repeal of antitrust laws because coercive monopolies were viewed as a natural outgrowth of government regulation
- the abolition of such federal agencies as the Reconstruction Finance Corporation, Customs Court, and Tariff Commission
- the abolition of the Federal Trade Commission and the Antitrust Division of the Department of Justice
- the right of individuals to form corporations and other types of voluntary associations
- a repeal of the windfall profits tax
- the elimination of government support for energy research and the development of energy alternatives
- nuclear power subjected to the test of the free market
- the abolition of the Department of Energy

- a reform of nuisance and negligence laws to cover damage done to individuals by air, water, and noise pollution rather than government efforts to control pollution
- the abolition of the Environmental Protection Agency
- the abolition of the Consumer Product Safety Commission and the repeal of all laws restricting advertising or requiring individuals to use protective equipment (e.g., motorcycle helmets)
- tuition tax credits and other tax reforms favorable to private schools
- an end to compulsory school attendance laws
- the cessation of forced busing and corporal punishment
- a reduction of tax support for public schools
- an end to all subsidies for childbearing (including welfare plans and tax-supported services for children)
- the elimination of special tax burdens on single people
- birth control and a woman's right to an abortion
- midwifery, home births, and women's clinics
- the abolition of all federal agencies regulating transportation and a return to private ownership of such public enterprises as Amtrak
- the privatization of public roads and the national highway system
- the repeal of the 55-mile-per-hour speed limit
- a repeal of minimum wage laws and protective labor legislation for women and children, restrictions on day care centers, and the National Labor Relations Act
- the deregulation of health care and the medical insurance industry, including abolition of Medicare and Medicaid
- the right to pursue unorthodox alternative treatments
- the use of tax credits to promote charity care
- a repeal of land use, zoning, building code, eminent domain, urban renewal, and similar laws, while recognizing private, voluntary land use covenants
- privatization of inland waterways, dam sites, and water systems and the abolition of the civilian functions of the Bureau of Reclamation, Bureau of Land Management, Forest Service, and the Army Corps of Engineers
- the ownership of public lands transferred to the private sector through homesteading
- the abolition of the Department of Agriculture
- the elimination of all government farm programs (including price supports, direct subsidies, and production regulations)
- the deregulation of transportation and the abolition of the Interstate Commerce Commission
- an end to government involvement in pest control (i.e., refers to bans on pesticides)
- a repeal of the Occupational Safety and Health Act and the Social Security Act
- the abolition of the Postal Service and the Civil Service system
- a repeal of federal campaign finance laws
- the elimination of the Federal Election Commission
- open ballot access to new parties and independent candidates

- the addition of a ballot line dedicated to "none of the above" so that voters could register their dissent against the listed candidates for a public office
- nonintervention in foreign affairs and limited government engagement beyond national defense
- the discontinuation of the use of passports
- the elimination of foreign aid
- the abolition of government-sponsored arms sales
- a removal of restrictions on U.S. trade abroad
- the abolition of such agencies as the Export-Import Bank and the Commodity Credit Corporation
- the development of standards to recognize private ownership claims to Antarctica, ocean floors, outer space, and other unowned resources
- an abandonment of all international treaties and agreements (particularly the Law of the Sea Treaty)
- the right of secession of states, territories, and other units of government
- the withdrawal of the United States from the World Bank and the International Monetary Fund, opposing international paper money and any U.S. bailout of foreign governments
- the withdrawal of all U.S. troops stationed abroad (particularly in the Republic of Korea)
- reduced defense expenditures
- the withdrawal of the United States from NATO and other multilateral and bilateral arrangements
- a fostering of mutual disarmament of nuclear weapons and missiles among nuclear powers
- increased limits on the president's power to initiate military action; a constitutional amendment to clarify the limits of the president's role as commander in chief; and the abrogation of all presidential declarations of "states of emergency" and an end to secret executive branch commitments and unilateral acts of military intervention
- a reduction in the size of the diplomatic corps and the immediate withdrawal of the United States from the United Nations (as well as the removal of the United Nations from the United States)
- the right of private citizens to engage in diplomatic negotiations with foreign governments
- a condemnation of all governments for violating human rights, urging that international negotiations be conducted without conceding moral legitimacy to any government or asserting moral superiority by the United States
- a cessation of U.S. military and economic interventions in the Middle East and South Africa
- immediate independence for American Samoa, Guam, Micronesia, and Puerto Rico, and the Virgin Islands
- an end to U.S. operations in the Panama Canal Zone and withdrawal of all U.S. forces from Panama
- the voluntary, peaceful use of outer space
- the abolition of the National Aeronautics and Space Administration, repudiation of the UN Moon Treaty, and privatization of all artificial satellites

OPPOSED:

- government issuance of identity cards for individual citizens, government secrecy, and the widespread use of "classified" information
- the use of preventive detention and "no-knock" laws
- "no-fault" insurance
- forced jury duty
- involuntary mental health treatment or commitment to mental institutions
- mental health "propaganda" and tax-supported mental health centers
- the insanity or "diminished capacity" defenses in criminal cases
- all government censorship, including antipornography laws
- gags on press coverage
- equal time and "fairness" requirements in broadcasting
- the Federal Communications Act
- efforts to ban cigarette and sugar-coated breakfast food advertising
- prohibitions against the depiction of sex or violence in movies, TV, or print media
- the regulation of "pay TV" and tax funding for the Corporation for Public Broadcasting
- anticult activities and harassment of unconventional religious groups on the basis of a strict interpretation of the separation of church and state
- government involvement with the National Ad Council and regulation of political advertising
- the use of eminent domain to municipalize sports teams
- any form of gun control, registration for the draft (or compulsory national service of any kind), military discharges based on sexual preference, and the Uniform Code of Military Justice
- all government interference with bargaining, while demanding the repeal of the National Labor Relations Act and all states' right-to-work laws
- temporary worker plans, including the bracero program
- laws empowering the state to make children "wards of the state" and restrictions on child labor and compulsory education
- statutes outlawing "adults only" apartments
- plans to redistribute wealth or manage trade, deficit budgets, inflationary monetary policies, expansive government spending, impediments to free trade, and public controls on the economy (e.g., wages, prices, rents, profits, production, or interest)
- all personal and corporate taxes and recognized the right to challenge payment on moral or other grounds
- limits on corporate liability, corporate size, merger restrictions, and the chartering of corporations
- all public subsidies, along with tariffs, quotas, and public utility franchises
- all government control of the energy field, including pricing, allocation, and production
- the need for the "strategic storage" of oil, efforts to na-

tionalize energy industries, rationing, and government ownership of energy resources
- government conservation programs
- the Superfund for cleaning up toxic wastes, because it permits responsible parties to escape the full consequences of their actions
- fraud and misrepresentation in the marketplace but did not embrace "paternalistic" governmental interventions on behalf of consumers
- the creation of new national parks or wilderness and recreation areas, instead urging the transfer of such existing areas to private ownership
- conversion to the metric system
- the Federal Aviation Administration and the Food and Drug Administration, seeking to abolish them
- fluoridation of water and legal restrictions on what substances a person might ingest
- public education
- coercive controls on population growth and forced sterilization
- mandatory retirement, occupational licensure, and antipoverty programs but approved "dollar-for-dollar" tax credits for charitable contributions
- medical licensure requirements
- health planning boards
- limits on malpractice suits
- involuntary medical treatment and government restrictions on research
- government-mandated smoking and no-smoking areas in privately owned businesses
- military intervention to protect individual U.S. citizens in foreign lands, with U.S. citizens traveling or investing abroad at their own risk
- incorporation of the Persian Gulf into the U.S. defense perimeter and the stationing of U.S. troops in the Sinai Peninsula
- terrorism and torture
- the expenditure of "billions of American tax dollars" to "buy Israeli and Egyptian participation in the Camp David Accords"
- the U.S. government's diplomatic approach to the Peo-

ple's Republic of China along with its earlier involvement with Taiwan
- the U.S. government's participation in international cartels
- government restrictions on the private exploration, colonization, industrialization, and development of heavenly bodies

ALSO:
- noted that silence on any other aspect of government should not be construed to imply Libertarian approval

NATIONAL UNITY PARTY

CANDIDATE FOR PRESIDENT:
John Bayard Anderson (IL)

CANDIDATE FOR VICE PRESIDENT:
Grace Wagner Pierce (DE)

PAN-AMERICAN PARTY

CANDIDATE FOR PRESIDENT:
William Allen Camps (TX)

PEACE AND FREEDOM PARTY

CANDIDATE FOR PRESIDENT:
Sonia Johnson (VA)

CANDIDATES FOR VICE PRESIDENT:
Tom Condit (CA)
Larry Holmes (NY)
Sonia Johnson (VA)
Emma Wong Mar (CA)
Dennis L. Serrette (NJ)

PRIMARY:
JUNE 5, 1984 (CA):
Johnson 3,171
Condit 1,160
Serrette 731
Holmes 651
others 2

CONVENTION:
August 25–26, 1984, San Luis Obispo (CA)

The Peace and Freedom Party was based in California. It endorsed the Citizens Party's candidate for president but presented its own vice-presidential candidate.

PLATFORM HIGHLIGHTS:
SUPPORTED:
- socialism
- mass organization of public for direct political action
- full employment at union pay levels
- a thirty-hour work week
- the abolition of forced overtime
- unlimited unemployment compensation
- vigorous enforcement of job health and safety laws
- retraining programs

LIBERTARIAN PARTY
VOTE FOR PRESIDENTIAL NOMINATION:

Candidate	Ballot: 1	2	3	4
Bergland				270
Ravenal				242
none of the above				24

VOTE FOR VICE-PRESIDENTIAL NOMINATION: APPROXIMATELY TWENTY INDIVIDUALS WERE CONSIDERED FOR THE VICE-PRESIDENTIAL NOMINATION. LEWIS WAS NOMINATED ON THE THIRD BALLOT.

- a moratorium on layoffs and plant closures
- public disclosure of management's books
- the right to organize and strike
- democratization of unions
- an end to the arms race and the use of nuclear, chemical, and biological weapons
- the immediate withdrawal of all U.S. troops and weapons from abroad
- the dissolution of all military pacts
- a conversion of military production to peaceful purposes
- an end to the draft and restoration of the rights of resisters
- the ratification of the ERA
- equal pay for equal work
- an extension of child care services and paid maternity and paternity leave
- free birth control and abortion services on demand and prohibitions on involuntary abortions and sterilizations
- an end to the physical abuse of women
- the development of free mass transit
- comprehensive environmental planning
- the conservation of natural resources
- the reconstruction of urban areas
- the preservation of open spaces and wilderness regions
- recycling
- the development of a multisource energy system
- gay and lesbian liberation
- full rights for persons with disabilities
- a comfortable, high standard of living for senior citizens
- relief from the fear of deportation for undocumented workers and the enactment of a bill of rights for the undocumented worker
- multilingual and multicultural education
- the integration of schools, except where it promoted cultural disintegration of oppressed minorities
- open admission policies for higher education
- rent control and collective bargaining for tenants
- the mass production of nonprofit, community-controlled housing
- interest-free loans for single-family and cooperative housing
- the abolition of the CIA and the FBI
- proportional representation in legislative bodies
- compensation for crime victims
- the demilitarization and community control of the police
- the abolition of capital punishment
- a repeal of victimless crimes laws
- free legal and court services
- community-release programs and prison reform
- self-organization and mobilization of communities to fight street crime
- the adoption of a Socialist medical system
- an emphasis on preventive medicine and sound nutrition
- the full respect for the human rights of mental patients
- a woman's right to choose birth alternatives
- the restoration of cuts in health funding by the government

- an overhaul of the tax system to make it more responsive to the ability to pay principle

OPPOSED:
- the exploitation of prison labor
- racism
- the teaching of "capitalist propaganda" in schools
- gun control

POPULIST (AMERICAN INDEPENDENT; CONSTITUTION) PARTY

CANDIDATES FOR PRESIDENT:
Paul A. Carroll
Ty Hardin
Jack Metcalf
Robert "Bob" Richards
Noah Gerald Willis

CANDIDATES FOR VICE PRESIDENT:
Charles E. Perry
Maureen Salaman

CANDIDATES FOR PRESIDENTIAL NOMINATION:
William "Bill" Baker (NV)
Paul A. Carroll (OH)
Wayne Cryts (MO)
Raymond Ford (NV)
Charles R. Glenn (PA)
Ty Hardin (AZ) (MA, ME, NJ)
Jim Jeffries (KS)
Charles Thomas "Tommy" Kersey, Jr. (GA)
Judge Richard E. Lee (LA)
Arthur J. "Ajay" Lowery (AR)
Jack Metcalf (WA) (UT)
Gordon Mohr (MS)
John Richard Rarick (LA)
Robert "Bob" Richards (TX)
Noah Gerald Willis (AL) (KS)

CANDIDATES FOR VICE-PRESIDENTIAL NOMINATION:
Charles E. Perry (MD)
Maureen Salaman (CA)

PRIMARIES:
APRIL 3, 1984 (WI):
uncommitted delegates 1,391
others 56

JUNE 5, 1984 (CA):
Glenn 7,374
Lowery 3,567
Mohr 3,052
Willis 2,507
others 4

1ST CONVENTION:
August 18–19, 1984, Civic Hall, Nashville (TN)
William "Bill" Baker (NV), temporary and permanent chairman
John Richard Rarick (LA), keynoter

Attending this convention were 750 delegates. The national committee adopted the Populist's platform on February 29, 1984.

PLATFORM HIGHLIGHTS:

SUPPORTED:

- a repeal of the federal income tax
- the abolition of the Federal Reserve System
- a repudiation of the national debt
- the reactivation of anti-usury laws
- the enactment of fair tariff laws
- the revitalization of the family farm
- the rebuilding of the United States as an international power
- the reclaiming of the free enterprise system with a strong antimonopoly initiative
- a resurrection of "anti-degeneracy" laws and a crackdown on crime
- a rejection of the ERA and gay rights
- restrictions on pornography and illegal drugs
- freedom of choice with regard to public schools and the use of private property
- a reform of welfare laws to get "this vast class of socialist-voting, taxpayer-financed drones off the voting rolls"
- restrictions on judicial review
- reasserting the right to keep and bear arms
- an inventiveness to make the country energy independent
- the freedom of individuals to seek medical help without government interference, including access to health foods, vitamins, and cancer therapies
- a constitutional amendment to permit the direct election of the president after regional primaries and the direct election of federal judges
- the use of proportional representation, the initiative, referendum, and recall at all levels of government
- armed neutrality for foreign policy and restrictions on foreign pressure groups operating in the United States (e.g., the Council on Foreign Relations, the Trilateral Commission, and the Bilderbergers)
- the withdrawal of the United States from the United Nations and the removal of the United Nations from U.S. soil
- a strong national defense, with arms control agreements contingent on appropriate on-site inspections

OPPOSED:

- forced busing and government interference with religious schools
- racial and cultural exploitation and argued against one race forcing another to subsidize it financially or politically
- forced segregation or integration
- immigration from developing countries and supported deportation of illegal aliens
- a peacetime draft

ALSO:

- urged the U.S. government to reward its friends, not its enemies, all the while doubting that either major party would pursued this policy because "the mattoids need communism to scare the people into tolerating massive taxes and a huge war budget, à la George Orwell's 1984"

At the national convention, the Populist Party adopted a statement of critical issues, instead of endorsing the platform approved by the national committee. The statement called for

- the abolition of the Federal Reserve System
- a repudiation of the national debt
- a repeal of the income tax on individuals and the adoption of the Liberty Amendment to the U.S. Constitution
- the imposition of a protective tariff on foreign goods that compete with those of U.S. industries
- restrictions on immigration and a refusal to grant amnesty for illegal aliens
- noninvolvement in foreign wars (including the Middle East)
- the revitalization of the family farm (with parity prices and elimination of foreign-owned farms)
- a moratorium on farm, home, and small business foreclosures
- a greater reliance on alternative fuels
- support for organic farming
- an end to crop production limits
- laws against price-fixing and price-depressing organiza-

POPULIST (AMERICAN INDEPENDENT; CONSTITUTION) PARTY

VOTE FOR PRESIDENTIAL NOMINATION:
SEVERAL STATES HAD BALLOT DEADLINES THAT CAME BEFORE THE POPULIST PARTY'S NOMINATING CONVENTION. ACCORDINGLY, THE FOLLOWING STAND-IN CANDIDATES WERE NOMINATED: METCALF (OF WASHINGTON) WAS NAMED AS THE PRESIDENTIAL CANDIDATE IN UTAH; HARDIN (OF ARIZONA) WAS NAMED IN MAINE, MASSACHUSETTS, AND NEW JERSEY; AND WILLIS (OF ALABAMA) WAS NAMED IN KANSAS. WHEN THE CONVENTION CONVENED, RICHARDS WAS NOMINATED WITH **469** VOTES TO GLENN'S 7 (OTHER CANDIDATES RECEIVED A TOTAL OF 5 VOTES).

VOTE FOR VICE-PRESIDENTIAL NOMINATION:

Candidate	Ballot: 1
Salaman	351
Carroll	80
others	42
abstentions	10

tions such as the Chicago Board of Trade and Chicago Mercantile Exchange

- assistance to farm marketing organizations

PROHIBITION PARTY

CANDIDATE FOR PRESIDENT:
Earl Farwell Dodge (CO)

CANDIDATE FOR VICE PRESIDENT:
Warren Chester Martin

CANDIDATES FOR VICE-PRESIDENTIAL NOMINATION:
Benjamin Calvin Bubar (ME) (declined)
Rayford G. Feather (PA) (declined)
Warren Chester Martin (KS)

29TH CONVENTION:
June 22–24, 1983, Mandan (ND)
Earl Farwell Dodge (CO), temporary chairman
Earle Harold Munn, Sr. (MI), permanent chairman

PLATFORM HIGHLIGHTS:
The platform reaffirmed the Prohibition Party's commitment to the Constitution and its system of checks and balances.

SUPPORTED:

- efforts to limit the power of the federal judiciary by constitutional means
- a return to the gold standard
- a constitutional amendment to require a balanced budget, place limits on Congress's taxing and spending powers, reduce the national debt, and require the sale of all government-owned businesses in competition with the private sector
- limits on foreign aid
- the elimination of excessive regulation of businesses, control of monopolies, and restrictions on unethical practices by both management and labor
- the enforcement of antitrust laws and laws forbidding strikes by federal government employees
- an end to government preference for union shops in awarding contracts
- right-to-work laws
- states' rights and condemned regional governments (e.g., councils of governments)
- resistance to anarchistic and arbitrary pressure tactics and quota systems
- a constitutional amendment to protect life from the moment of conception
- strict enforcement of laws against gambling, narcotics, and commercialized vice
- military preparedness while applauding the concept of the volunteer military
- a reform of the welfare system to remove "undeserving persons," promote self-sufficiency, and stop the distribution of birth control devices to minors without parental consent
- uniform marriage and divorce laws
- nondiscrimination against married people in tax policies

and the adoption of an explicit public policy against extending marriage benefits to unmarried couples

- the separation of church and state but approved a constitutional amendment to permit Bible reading and voluntary prayer in public schools and other institutions
- ballot law reforms to extend access to third parties
- a revision of Social Security laws to make the program voluntary, establish it on a sound actuarial basis, and exempt religious organizations from the payment of Social Security taxes
- the abolition of government controls and subsidies for agriculture
- a ban on harmful drugs and efforts to curb tobacco use
- long-term prison sentences for those convicted of a criminal act involving a firearm
- a strict enforcement of the immigration laws and the deportation of illegal aliens

OPPOSED:

- communism
- the ratification of the ERA
- "unnatural" lifestyles
- a guaranteed annual income
- efforts to restrict religious broadcasting and religious schools
- the concept of federal aid to education and demanded government noninterference in the operation of private Christian schools
- socialized medicine, involuntary commitment to mental hospitals, and mass medication programs
- amnesty for illegal aliens

ALSO:

- blamed alcoholic beverages for a host of modern social problems and called for a program of publicity, education, legislation, and administration to eliminate liquor traffic
- promised to repeal all laws that permitted liquor traffic and to enforce rigorously laws against the manufacture, distribution, and sale of alcoholic beverages

---

PROHIBITION PARTY
VOTE FOR PRESIDENTIAL NOMINATION: DODGE
WAS NOMINATED FOR PRESIDENT BY ACCLAMATION.

VOTE FOR VICE-PRESIDENTIAL NOMINATION:
MARTIN WAS NOMINATED FOR VICE PRESIDENT
BY ACCLAMATION.

PROTEST PARTY

CANDIDATE FOR PRESIDENT:
Theodore Shelby Swanson (IN)

REPUBLICAN PARTY

CANDIDATE FOR PRESIDENT:
Ronald Wilson Reagan

CANDIDATE FOR VICE PRESIDENT:

George Herbert Walker Bush (TX)

CANDIDATES FOR PRESIDENTIAL NOMINATION:

Gary Arnold (MN)
William James Barton (IL)
Shirley Roena Benton (NY)
John Edward Bishop (TX)
Ernest William Bost (AZ)
Henry Paul Cleaver, Jr. (NY)
Clarence Lavern Courton (FL)
Gerald Thomas Defelice (CT)
Mike Eagles (CA)
Charles P. English (FL)
Benjamin Fernandez (CA)
Larry Flynt (CA)
John Herschel Glenn, Jr. (OH)
John Jacob Gordon (MA)
Gary Warren Hart (CO)
Jesse Louis Jackson (IL)
Bedo Istvan Karoly (DC)
David Moore Kelley (TN)
Rick Wilson Knox (MI)
Lyndon Hermyle LaRouche, Jr. (VA)
Steven Dee Livengood (DC)
David Allan MacPherson (PA)
Eddie McDowell (GA)
Alfred J. Mitchell (NY)
Walter Frederick Mondale (MN)
Frederick Eugene Ogin (CA)
Ronald Wilson Reagan (CA)
Benjamin Franklin Schoenfeld (CA)
Harold Edward Stassen (PA)
Herman Eugene Stevens (PA)

PRIMARIES:

FEBRUARY 28, 1984 (NH):

Reagan	65,033
Hart	3,968
Stassen	1,543
Mondale	1,072
Glenn	1,040
Kelley	360
Arnold	252
Fernandez	202
others	2,100

MARCH 6, 1984 (VT):

Reagan	33,218
others	425

MARCH 13, 1984 (FL):

Reagan	344,150

MARCH 13, 1984 (GA):

Reagan	50,793

MARCH 13, 1984 (MA):

Reagan	58,996
unpledged delegates	5,005
others	1,936

MARCH 13, 1984 (RI):

Reagan	2,028
unpledged delegates	207

MARCH 20, 1984 (IL):

Reagan	594,742
others	336

APRIL 3, 1984 (WI):

Reagan	280,608
others	14,205

APRIL 10, 1984 (PA):

Reagan	616,916
others	4,290

MAY 1, 1984 (DC):

Reagan	5,692

MAY 1, 1984 (TN):

Reagan	75,367
unpledged delegates	7,546
others	8

MAY 5, 1984 (LA):

Reagan	14,964
unpledged delegates	1,723

MAY 5, 1984 (TX):

Reagan	308,713
unpledged delegates	11,126

MAY 8, 1984 (IN):

Reagan	428,559

MAY 8, 1984 (MD):

Reagan	73,663

MAY 8, 1984 (OH):

Reagan	658,169

MAY 15, 1984 (NE):

Reagan	145,245
others	1,403

MAY 15, 1984 (OR):

Reagan	238,594
Hart	2,359
Mondale	477
Jackson	412
LaRouche	53
Glenn	51
others	1,399

MAY 15, 1984 (ID):

Reagan	97,450
others	8,237

JUNE 5, 1984 (CA):

Reagan	1,874,897
others	78

JUNE 5, 1984 (MT)

Reagan	66,432
unpledged delegates	5,378
others	77

JUNE 5, 1984 (NJ):

Reagan	240,054

JUNE 5, 1984 (NM):
    Reagan 40,805
    unpledged delegates 2,189

JUNE 5, 1984 (WV):
    Reagan 125,790
    Stassen 11,206

JUNE 12, 1984 (ND):
    Reagan 44,109

33D CONVENTION:
    August 20–23, 1984, Dallas Convention Center,
        Dallas (TX).
    Frank Joseph Fahrenkopf, Jr. (NV), temporary
        chairman
    Robert Henry Michel (IL), permanent chairman
    Katherine Davalos Ortega, keynoter

PLATFORM HIGHLIGHTS:
The Republican platform was a lengthy document based on the theme "America's Future: Free and Secure." Declaring itself the "Party of Hope," the Republicans endorsed the ideas of free enterprise and limited federal government and urged that control over the economy be returned to the people.

SUPPORTED:
- deficit reduction by eliminating wasteful and unnecessary government spending
- calls for expanding incentives for personal savings, reducing the tax on interest income, permitting the indexing of capital assets, and removing the double taxation of dividends
- enterprise zones (i.e., economically depressed areas with special tax breaks for new businesses)
- a flat-rate income tax with lower rates and higher personal exemptions
- a constitutional amendment to require a balanced federal budget
- a line-item veto for the president
- the possible value of reinstituting the gold standard
- the coordination between fiscal and monetary policy (with an end to the Federal Reserve Board's "destablizing actions")
- comprehensive regulatory reform in all areas of government
- the encouragement of innovative competition in telecommunications and financial services
- the establishment of a "youth opportunity wage"
- a repeal of prohibitions on household manufacturing and other work in the home
- tax cuts for family businesses
- lower capital gains taxes
- the extension of incremental research and development tax credits and permission for U.S. firms to cooperate in joint research and development projects
- a repeal of the windfall profits tax
- the decontrol of prices of natural gas

- the encouragement of coal's use as an energy source
- a streamlining of nuclear regulatory procedures
- a redesigned energy policy that would restore public confidence in the fiscal stability of the nuclear industry
- the abolition of the Department of Energy
- a reinvigoration of U.S. agriculture and ranching by fostering a free and competitive economy and promoting a sound agricultural credit policy
- a temporary reduction in interest rates
- a restructuring of commercial farm and ranch debt procedures
- self-employment tax deductions for hospitalization insurance
- the renegotiation of multilateral trade arrangements and an end to embargoes
- a reduction in government regulation of agriculture
- long-term soil, water, and other conservation policies based on volunteer participation and state and local control
- cooperative extension (name of agricultural domestic living program based on agricultural colleges) and maintenance of family farms
- the establishment of regional international research and export trade centers and legislation to protect consumers against agricultural work stoppages
- free trade, with arguments against protectionism but demands for "fair trade" for U.S. products, services, and investments
- the encouragement of debtor nations to lower taxes, follow private investment strategies, and deregulate their markets
- the promotion of home ownership by retaining the mortgage interest deduction, urging states to lower property taxes, promoting "sweat equity" programs, and instituting a voucher system to replace rent subsidies and public housing projects
- the open housing concept, which prohibits discrimination in housing
- the conversion of government housing to private ownership by former tenants
- the need for welfare programs to promote self-sufficiency (particularly for female-headed households)
- welfare as a program that should be state administered and financed through federal block grants
- the food stamp and school lunch programs, but demanded the elimination of fraud and abuse within the programs
- personal tax exemptions to assist young families striving for economic independence and additional incentives to promote foster care and adoption
- Medicare and Medicaid and elimination of excesses and inefficiencies in both programs
- research into yet unconquered diseases, parental rights and responsibilities in relation to the treatment of children, nondiscrimination in the practice of medicine, quicker review and approval of new medicines and

technologies, alcohol and drug abuse prevention and education efforts, and state efforts to increase the legal drinking age

- the restoration and protection of estuaries, wetlands, and beaches
- the control and cleanup of toxic wastes
- the implementation of "meaningful" clean air and water acts
- a reduction in acid rain
- the elimination of the dumping of raw sewage
- assistance in state and local planning for solid and liquid waste disposal
- recycling
- the protection of endangered or threatened plants and wildlife
- the development of renewable and efficient energy sources
- the notion that, quoting Theodore Roosevelt, "conservation means development as much as it does protection"
- the need to develop the U.S. commercial shipping fleet and to restore existing port facilities and shipbuilding and repair capabilities
- the development of a commercial space-transportation industry
- the decentralization of education and getting "back to basics," with a limited federal role of ensuring high standards, protecting civil rights, and promoting family rights
- education reforms (including rewards for exceptional teachers, state support for talented and gifted students, appropriate classroom sizes, appropriate teaching materials, and consistent grading practices) and the right to freedom of religion and speech in the classroom
- students' rights to engage in voluntary prayer in schools
- local financing of education, with federal assistance in the form of a block grant
- the rights of disabled citizens and minorities to equal educational opportunities and aggressive enforcement of the "Protection of Pupil Rights" amendment, which protected the confidentiality of family information
- Title IX rights but sought a reevaluation of sex education programs
- a voucher system in education and conversion from Chapter One (low-income) grants to vouchers
- the use of retirees, businessmen, and scientists as public schoolteachers and an expansion of volunteerism through initiatives such as the "Adopt-a-School" model
- experiments in education such as the Cities-in-Schools project and educational enterprise zones, along with the campaign to abolish illiteracy
- efforts to cut red tape and regulation at the college level
- vocational and technical education
- private support for the arts and humanities

- the National Endowments for the Arts and Humanities (subject to the correction of past abuses)
- a limited federal role in the support and coordination of state and local efforts toward law enforcement and enforcing federal criminal statutes
- the Reagan administration's efforts to interdict narcotics being smuggled across the country's borders and its "aggressive" Marijuana Eradication and Suppression Program
- sentencing reform and secure, adequate prison construction
- states in which capital punishment was used to deter crime
- stiff mandatory sentences for those convicted of armed felonies
- a repeal of the Social Security earnings limitation, elimination of mandatory retirement, encouragement of home-based care, passage of the president's comprehensive crime control package, and removal of barriers that discourage senior citizens from participating in community life
- Civil Rights Act of 1964 but promised to "resist efforts to replace equal rights with discriminatory quota systems and preferential treatment"
- women's rights to full opportunity and advancement but took no position on the ERA
- an elimination of tax discrimination against homemakers
- a reduction in the "marriage penalty" regarding taxes
- the removal of impediments to opportunity for women in business and industry
- equal pay for equal work but refused to back the concept of "comparable worth"
- the elimination of architectural, transportation, communications, and attitudinal barriers against full participation by disabled individuals in education, employment, and recreation
- incentives for family-based care for persons with disabilities, families with children, etc.
- the right of collective bargaining but also the right of states to enact "right-to-work" laws under section 14 (b) of the Taft-Hartley Act
- the right of U.S. citizens in Guam, Puerto Rico, and the Virgin Islands to vote in presidential elections
- the right of American Indian tribes to manage their own affairs and resources
- the designation of Native Hawaiians as Native Americans
- Family Housing Accounts, Family Education Accounts, personal tax exemptions for children (to be doubled), tax credits for child care expenses, and the promotion of private sector initiatives to expand on-site child care facilities in the workplace
- a vigorous enforcement of constitutional laws against obscene materials
- family reunification in immigration policy while encouraging other countries to assume greater refugee re-

sponsibilities so that the United States could regain control of its borders

- restrictions on the jurisdiction of the federal courts and promised that President Reagan would appoint only judges favorable to judicial restraint
- a return of nonessential federal functions to state and local governments
- the expansion of the block grant program
- the encouragement of privatization of government services
- the sale of surplus federal lands
- special attention to reduce the occurrence of illegitimate pregnancies and family breakups
- a constitutional amendment to protect unborn children
- threats to cut funding for the International Development Association, the International Fund for Agricultural Development, and the UN's Educational, Scientific, and Cultural Organization, along with any organization that supported abortion or research on abortion methods
- the abolition of the Federal Election Commission
- a fair and consistent application of campaign financial disclosure laws
- friendship with the people of Canada and Mexico, espousing democratic ideals
- the Organization of American States
- the Nicaraguan Contras
- the "liberation" of Grenada and the Caribbean Basin Initiative
- the special U.S. relationship with Puerto Rico and the Virgin Islands, including the right to statehood for Puerto Rico
- the depiction of the Soviet Union as an aggressive military power and counseled caution in negotiating arms agreements with it
- substantial reductions in nuclear weapons on a fully verifiable basis with suitable sanctions for noncompliance rather than a nuclear "freeze"
- efforts to pressure the Soviet Union to comply with the Helsinki Accords
- an end to human rights violations against Soviet Jews and political activists and the right of free emigration from the Soviet Union
- greater financial and military responsibility by NATO allies for the security of Europe
- NATO's attention to the problems in Cyprus and Northern Ireland and bemoaned the plight of the peoples of Eastern Europe
- relief for Polish nationals seeking asylum
- a refusal to negotiate with the Palestinian Liberation Organization as long as it promoted terrorism and to accept UN Resolutions 242 and 338
- efforts to maintain Israel's military advantage over its adversaries
- the establishment of an Israeli-U.S. free trade area

- Egypt and other moderate Arab governments
- the recognition of Jerusalem as an "undivided city" requiring unimpeded access to all holy places
- the Afghan resistance fighters
- continued aid to or maintenance of defense facilities in the Indian Ocean area, Japan, Pakistan, the Philippines, the Republic of Korea, and Thailand
- Taiwan and efforts to build a long-term relationship with the People's Republic of China
- the economic achievements of the Association of Southeast Asian Nations
- a full accounting of U.S. MIAs in Vietnam and Laos
- friendly nations cooperating on refugee and drug trafficking problems
- a development of the infrastructure of democratic capitalism (e.g., investment in private sector business growth, use of seed capital, and nurturing of product and market development) in Africa
- independence for Namibia
- the expulsion of Cuban troops from Angola
- an end to apartheid through "well-conceived efforts to foster peace, prosperity, and stability" in South Africa
- the decoupling of foreign assistance from the austerity policies of the International Monetary Fund and end to the Carter-Mondale policy of channeling assistance through multinational institutions
- President Reagan's rejection of the UN Convention on the Law of the Sea, promising similar decisive action with regard to Antarctica and outer space
- the U.S. Holocaust Council's plan to erect a museum in Washington, D.C.
- the Peace Corps but demanded that Peace Corps volunteers promote free enterprise development overseas
- the traditional Republican demand for "peace through strength," seeking technological superiority for the U.S. military
- efforts to curb the spread of nuclear weapons and to verify compliance, a willingness for the United States to respond to Soviet violations, and the need "to devote the resources essential to deter a Soviet threat"
- an all-volunteer armed force
- the strengthening of the National Guard and Reserves
- current funding levels for the antisubmarine warfare effort
- reforms in inefficient procurement practices
- homage to veterans and promises of assistance for the "unique readjustment problems" of Vietnam War veterans, including attention to the Agent Orange issue
- aging veterans as a special concern and improvements in their health care (especially for disabled veterans)
- veterans' preference in federal hiring, home ownership programs, and small business assistance
- a stronger national intelligence service and enhanced counterintelligence efforts to halt Soviet commercial espionage and illegal exploitation of U.S. technology

- SDI (Star Wars) as a nonnuclear, space-based defensive system to protect the nation against incoming missiles

OPPOSED:
- the taxation of churches
- the setting of artificially high interest rates and any attempt to increase taxes or withhold dividend and interest income
- wage and price controls
- any rollback of the cuts in estate taxes
- rent controls
- a guaranteed minimum annual income, welfare fraud, and programs that undermined the transition to gainful employment
- compulsory national health insurance
- gun control
- the use of union dues and fees for partisan purposes, along with coercion of workers by violence or intimidation in labor disputes
- "well-intentioned" restrictions on campaign activity
- taxpayer financing of elections
- the use of national identification cards
- public funding for abortions
- the Communist system as "the greatest threat to human rights"
- Fidel Castro's control over Cuba
- Marxist Nicaragua and its threat to Costa Rica, El Salvador, Guatemala, and Honduras
- U.S. assistance to nations with foreign policies contrary to U.S. interests, seeking to eliminate legislative obstacles to international cooperation against terrorism and promising to "lead the free nations" against the "League of Terror"

REPUBLICAN PARTY
VOTES FOR PRESIDENTIAL AND VICE-PRESIDENTIAL NOMINATION: REAGAN AND BUSH WERE RENOMINATED FOR SECOND TERMS IN A SINGLE ROLL CALL VOTE FOR BOTH CANDIDATES, GARNERING 2,233 VOTES (WITH 2 NOT VOTING).

REVOLUTIONARY COMMUNIST PARTY

CANDIDATE FOR PRESIDENT:
Carl Dix (IL)

The Revolutionary Communist Party ran Dix as an "anti-candidate" for president to demonstrate the party's scorn for the electoral process. It claimed, "The right to vote has been won. . . . Now we need the political awareness and sophistication not to use it." The party predicted revolution and urged its followers to join and build the Revolutionary Communist Party as the vanguard of the "coming conflict."

SOCIALIST (LABOR AND FARM) PARTY

PRIMARY:

APRIL 3, 1984 (WI):

William Osborne Hart 13,840
  (yes)
William Osborne Hart 1,769
  (no)
others 67

CONVENTION:
September 3–5, 1983, Seaman's Church Institute, New York (NY)

Approximately sixty delegates attended the convention. They adopted a resolution calling for the party to explore running a joint presidential ticket with the Citizens Party and other interested organizations. Thus, the Socialist Party declined to nominate candidates for the 1984 election. It agreed to a united ticket with the Citizens Party, but when the Socialist Party's membership failed to endorse this action of the Socialist Party National Committee, the Socialist Party withdrew from the election.

SOCIALIST WORKERS PARTY

CANDIDATE FOR PRESIDENT:
Mel Mason (CA)

CANDIDATES FOR VICE PRESIDENT:
Andrea Gonzalez (NJ)
Matilde Zimmerman (NY)

The Socialist Workers Party was a proponent of Trotskyite socialism and supported the rights of minorities, women, and workers. It opposed militarism and imperialism and favored strong state intervention in the economy to redistribute wealth.

THIRD WORLD ASSEMBLY

CANDIDATE FOR PRESIDENT:
John Governor Martin (DC)

The Third World Assembly was formed on January 28, 1979, in Washington, D.C., with forty charter members. Its national convenor was Rogers Gueory.

PLATFORM HIGHLIGHTS:
The party was focused on the plight of the country's domestic poor, comparing this segment of the population to that of Third World countries.

SUPPORTED:
- the people of the Third World being actively involved in the local, national, and international political process, including the promotion of candidates and working with the referendum and the recall procedures

- a two-pronged attack on economic deprivation, using an overall census formula for some things and a targeted formula for others
- a fostering of businesses and bringing inflation under control in the Third World
- educational reforms to bring schools into the modern age, with curricula stressing morals, etiquette, achievement, and discipline
- affordable housing and rent control, along with full employment
- the promotion of the arts through television and the cinema
- the enhancement of the health status of Americans, along with a 75 percent decrease in the costs of health care
- assistance in the resolution of developing nations' problems and participation in international conferences
- an emphasis on the "liberating theology of Jesus Christ" to guard against satanic influences and to promote actively brotherhood
- efforts to "uncover and expose the criminal element of laws in education, employment, housing, land development, and distribution" and sought freedom for all "political prisoners"
- family life and youth participation in civic affairs
- the protection of full civil rights for all
- adult concerns to be addressed by age-appropriate categories
- the promotion of public transportation

UNION PARTY

CANDIDATE FOR PRESIDENT:
Luther James Wilson (DC)

The Union Party promoted a conservative philosophy of government based on the capitalist system.

PLATFORM HIGHLIGHTS:
SUPPORTED:
- the withdrawal of the United States from the International Monetary Fund
- the development of an African-American power structure so that Wilson could "make a contribution to the well-being of my own race—Black Americans"
- stronger controls over nuclear power plants
- new energy sources
- rural development
- Israel
- an end to diplomatic relations with Nationalist China

OPPOSED:
- "creeping" socialism and inflation
- the Helsinki Accords
- the SALT agreements

UNITED NATIONS PARTY

CANDIDATE FOR PRESIDENT:
Emil Matalik (FL)

Matalik created the United Nations Party (also known as the # 1 Party and the United Nations Organization, or 1-U.N.O., Party) in 1964 to promote world peace and the abolition of hunger.

PLATFORM HIGHLIGHTS:
SUPPORTED:
- a view that overpopulation was the world's biggest problem and proposed limiting each family to one child (later increased to two children), one animal, and one tree
- the creation of a World presidency, a Universal Congress, and a Global Supreme Court
- the conversion of cities to farm land, thus resolving the urban problems of the world
- the issuance of five usable acres of land to each person for farming
- prohibitions on the public use of tobacco, liquor, and gambling
- free world communications
- the promotion of worldwide free love—"especially for single and virginized people"—and coed nudist camps for prison inmates
- the abolition of the monetary system and replacing it with "volunteerism"

UNITED SOVEREIGN CITIZENS PARTY

CANDIDATE FOR PRESIDENT:
Arthur J. "Arjay" Lowery (AR)

CANDIDATE FOR VICE PRESIDENT:
Raymond L. Garland (VA)

Claiming to be an "outraged American," Lowery created the United Sovereign Citizens Party to reassert the idea that the supreme political authority in the United States should be in the hands of the people.

PLATFORM HIGHLIGHTS:
SUPPORTED:
- the abolition of the federal income tax
- the establishment of debt-free money based on a bimetallic standard
- stricter regulations on how politicians and bureaucrats spend taxpayer dollars
- an endorsement of the Monroe Doctrine and a cutoff of foreign aid to "America's enemies"
- strict control of immigration under the United Sovereign program
- a "cleanup" of the federal judiciary and protection of the average citizen against criminal elements

OPPOSED:
- the influence of "Big Money" in politics and government

WORKERS LEAGUE

CANDIDATE FOR PRESIDENT:
Ed Winn (NY)

CANDIDATES FOR VICE PRESIDENT:
Helen Betty Halyard (MI)
Jean T. Brust (MN)
Edward Bergonzi (MN)

The Workers League was founded in 1966 as a Trotskyite political party. Its founders were former members of the Socialist Workers Party (SWP) who were expelled for opposing the SWP's "abandonment of Marxism and the strategy of world socialist revolution." The 1984 election marked the party's first presidential campaign.

WORKERS WORLD PARTY

CANDIDATE FOR PRESIDENT:
Larry Holmes (NY)

CANDIDATES FOR VICE PRESIDENT:
Gabrielle Holmes (NY)
Gloria La Riva (CA)
Milton Vera (NY)

PLATFORM HIGHLIGHTS:

SUPPORTED:
- a guaranteed job or income for everyone
- a minimum wage of $10.00 per hour
- increases in Social Security, welfare, disability, and unemployment benefits (in most cases tripled)
- a guarantee of affordable housing
- reductions in rents and mortgage interest rates
- efforts to force landlords to maintain properties
- free health and dental insurance for everyone
- an emphasis on prenatal care, preventive medicine, and special health and nutrition programs for seniors, children, and the disabled
- the provision of sick pay, pensions, maternity and paternity leave, one month's paid vacation, and paid holidays to workers
- the best universities and training schools being open to all, with students paid a stipend to learn
- an end to racism
- the implementation of affirmative action programs
- an end to police brutality
- community control
- bilingual education
- implementation of Native American treaty rights
- independence for Puerto Rico
- full legal and equal rights for undocumented workers
- an increase in day care availability

- equal pay and equal rights for women
- free and unrestricted rights to birth control counseling and services and abortions
- an expansion of programs for youth, offering them incomes, recreational facilities, drug counseling, birth control, affordable housing, AIDS education, and an end to police harassment
- an end to discrimination toward seniors and disabled persons in public facilities, transportation, and employment
- increased funding for AIDS research, treatment, and education, with the excess funds obtained from scrapping the Star Wars program
- an end to U.S. intervention in other areas of the world, particularly in Central America and El Salvador, Grenada, Lebanon, the Middle East, the Persian Gulf, the Philippines, Puerto Rico, and the Republic of Korea
- Palestinian liberation and majority rule in South Africa
- disarmament and an end to the Cold War

OPPOSED:
- layoffs or shutdowns
- evictions, foreclosures, and utility cutoffs
- union-busting, along with harassment, abusive treatment, and hazardous working conditions
- anti-Semitism
- forced sterilization
- the oppression of gays and lesbians and supported abolishing discriminatory laws against them
- freezes or cuts in social programs to reduce the deficit, preferring to cut corporate profits and military appropriations

The Workers World Party initially supported Jesse Jackson's unsuccessful bid for the Democratic presidential nomination.

WORLD CITIZEN PARTY

CANDIDATE FOR PRESIDENT:
Sol Gareth "Garry" Davis (DC)

PLATFORM HIGHLIGHTS:
Davis was a self-designated "world citizen," having renounced his U.S. citizenship in 1948 to protest militarism. The son of band leader Meyer Davis, he urged his followers to "think globally, act locally." The World Citizen Party's platform was "grounded in the Universal Declaration of Human Rights plus ecological rights as outlined in the Stockholm Declaration as well as the rights of ethnic minority groups."

SUPPORTED:
- world citizenship
- the creation of world law and appropriate governmental organs (e.g., World Legislature, World Courts, World Executive, and World Guard Force) essential to guarantee fundamental human rights and freedoms

- the realignment of local and national law to conform to world law
- the recognition and representation of viable ethnic groups
- representation for stateless persons and refugees
- the representation of ecosystems against exploitation

- the mundialization of villages, towns, cities, and universities
- the endorsement of existing national and international organizations and associations promoting world peace, human rights, and world government

GENERAL ELECTION SUMMARY FOR 1984:			
Candidate	Electoral Votes	States	Popular Votes
Reagan (R)	525	49	54,455,075
Mondale (D)	13	1 (+ DC)	37,577,185
Bergland (LIBRTN)	0	0	228,314
Johnson (CIT [CONS; PF])	0	0	72,200
POP (AI; CONST)	0	0	66,336
Serrette (I [UNI CIT; LU] ALL)	0	0	46,868
Hall (COM)	0	0	36,386
Mason (SOC WOR)	0	0	24,706
Holmes (WW)	0	0	17,985
Dennis (A)	0	0	13,161
Winn (WL)	0	0	10,801
Dodge (PROH)	0	0	4,242
Anderson (NAT UNITY)	0	0	1,486
Baker (BIG DEAL)	0	0	892
Lowery (UNI SOV CIT)	0	0	825
unknown	0	0	17,589

ELECTION OF NOVEMBER 8, 1988

President
GEORGE HERBERT WALKER BUSH
Vice President
JAMES DANFORTH QUAYLE

HIGHLIGHTS

The election of 1988 was a nasty affair. To succeed the still popular President Ronald Reagan, Vice President George Bush was the early favorite over his fellow Republicans: Secretary of State Alexander Meigs Haig, Jr., of Virginia; Rep. Jack French Kemp of New York; Sen. Robert Joseph Dole of Kansas; and television evangelist Pat Robertson of Virginia. Ultimately, the contest narrowed to Bush and the conservative alternative, Robertson. The Republican National Convention unanimously nominated Bush after Robertson withdrew. Bush immediately caused a firestorm of criticism by naming James Danforth Quayle, the young senator from Indiana, as his running mate. Quayle had served in the National Guard during the Vietnam War, apparently avoiding the draft through favoritism. While Bush called for a "kinder, gentler nation," his campaign belied the rhetoric, as his negative attack ads cascaded down around the Democrats.

Massachusetts governor Michael Dukakis had obtained the Democratic nod, stressing competence and deft management skills in his quest to head the ticket. His plodding style succeeded because the Democratic race had become an endurance contest, pitting Rep. Richard Andrew Gephardt of Missouri; Sen. Albert Arnold Gore, Jr., of Tennessee; Sen. Paul Simon of Illinois; former governor Bruce Edward Babbitt of Arizona; Sen. Gary Warren Hart of Colorado; and the Reverend Jesse Jackson of Illinois against Dukakis. Gov. Mario Matthew Cuomo of New York, the sentimental favorite of many Democrats, refused to run, preferring to observe from the sidelines. Babbitt, Gephardt, and Simon faltered early. Hart—an early favorite—doomed himself by denying reports of an extramarital affair, only to be discovered flaunting his activities. He dropped out of the race and reentered it after the clamor died down, but the senator never regained his position as a serious contender. Only Jackson survived the primary season, and his fate was sealed by a simple delegate count.

Dukakis the candidate, however, was no match for the Bush juggernaut. The vice president placed strategic ads claiming the governor had "furloughed" a known murderer named Willie Horton, an African American, who apparently committed a rape while on furlough. Crime and racism then became indistinguishable as issues, and the Republicans rode the resulting wave of indignation. Other nonissues rose to prominence in the campaign, as the Republicans pushed a constitutional amendment to punish flag burners and demanded that the Pledge of Allegiance to the flag be recited in public institutions. Put on the defensive, Dukakis never regained the momentum he had immediately after the Democratic Convention. The Bush camp accused him of mismanaging Massachusetts and pointed to Reagan's achievements for examples of what Bush would continue for the nation. In a historic statement that would come back to destroy him in 1992, Bush repeated the theme "Read my lips: No new taxes." Labeled a "tax-and-spend liberal," Dukakis went down in a defeat of landslide proportions.

AMERICAN INDEPENDENT PARTY
CANDIDATE FOR PRESIDENT:
James C. "Jim" Griffin
CANDIDATE FOR VICE PRESIDENT:
Charles J. "Chuck" Morsa (CA)

CANDIDATES FOR PRESIDENTIAL NOMINATION:
James C. "Jim" Griffin (CA)
James Gordon "Bo" Gritz (NV)
Michael James Moore (AZ)
Mitch Standard (IL)

PRIMARY:

JUNE 7, 1988 (CA):

Griffin 9,792

Gritz 5,401

PLATFORM HIGHLIGHTS:

The "mini-platform" of the American Independent Party consisted of seventeen planks.

SUPPORTED:

- the free enterprise system
- a repeal of the personal income tax
- an end to foreign aid
- improvements in Social Security
- tariff protection against foreign competition
- a halt to illegal immigration
- a strong national defense
- the withdrawal of the United States from the United Nations
- an end to U.S. entanglement in "senseless foreign wars"
- the right of labor unions to function without government interference
- the value of local control of schools
- the election of judges
- the abolition of the Federal Reserve System
- a preservation of the right to bear arms

OPPOSED:

- abortion
- excessive government spending
- unconscionable bank foreclosures of family farms

AMERICAN PARTY

CANDIDATE FOR PRESIDENT:
Delmar Dennis (TN)

CANDIDATE FOR VICE PRESIDENT:
Earl Jeppson (UT)

5TH CONVENTION:
June 27, 1987, Salt Lake City (UT)

PLATFORM HIGHLIGHTS:

SUPPORTED:

- a gradual termination of agricultural subsidies, production and price controls, and government-owned reserves but also a protective tariff for agricultural products
- the government's divestment of Amtrak and the Postal Service, abolition of the Interstate Commerce Commission and the Occupational Safety and Health Administration (OSHA), and a hands-off attitude toward business
- the restoration of the death penalty throughout the nation, elimination of plea bargaining, greater use of restitution, and reform of the "over-permissive" parole system
- modest consumer protection laws
- stiff mandatory state penalties for crimes committed with a gun
- the breaking of relations with the People's Republic of China because it was a major source of illicit drugs

- the repeal of compulsory education laws and initiation of a voucher system
- voluntary nondenominational school prayer and local control of school systems
- an end to federal financing of elections and abolition of the Federal Election Commission
- the removal of price controls and taxes on the production and distribution of energy
- the abolition of the Department of Energy and the Environmental Protection Agency
- the adoption of a hands-off policy regarding the nuclear breeder reactor
- the defeat of efforts to reconsider the Equal Rights Amendment (ERA)
- a repeal of the Simpson-Mazzoli Act
- congressional action to constrict the jurisdiction of federal courts and the president's authority to issue executive orders
- a phasing out of federal health care programs and abolition of Professional Services Review organizations
- freedom of choice in pursuing alternative medical treatments but opposed fluoridation of water and "socialized medicine"
- the abolition of the Federal Reserve System, restoration of the gold standard, and a requirement for a balanced budget
- a repeal of minimum wage laws and price controls, restrictions on the political activities of labor unions, right-to-work laws, and the National Labor Relations Act
- an end to all zoning and land use laws and compulsory federal flood-control insurance
- the relinquishment of federal lands to the states
- a repeal of the national holiday in honor of Martin Luther King, Jr.
- the abolition of all administrative courts
- the re-creation of the House and Senate Internal Security committees and the Subversive Activities Control Board
- states' rights to legislate on public morality
- the principle that persons were innocent until proven guilty
- a phasing out of Social Security
- a repeal of the Sixteenth Amendment
- charities and state and local governments assuming responsibility for welfare programs
- the breaking of diplomatic and trade relations with all Communist countries
- an end to all foreign aid programs
- the establishing normal diplomatic relations with Nationalist China
- the Cuban and Nicaraguan anti-communist opposition
- an investigation of U.S. government neglect in locating U.S. servicemen missing in action (MIA) or held as prisoners of war (POWs) in Vietnam

- the removal of the U.S. presence in the Middle East and pursuing a policy of noninvolvement
- the invasion of Grenada
- the High Frontier Program (the Strategic Defense Initiative [SDI], or "Star Wars")
- the protection of the nation's offshore resources and fishing rights to a distance of 200 miles
- U.S. sovereignty over the Panama Canal
- a repeal of the Genocide Convention and ratification of the "Bricker Amendment," along with the withdrawal of the United States from the United Nations
- a requirement that no foreign military action could be pursued for more than seventy-two hours without a declaration of war by Congress

OPPOSED:
- efforts to convene a Federal Constitutional Convention
- the bailout of Chrysler and proposals for a national industrial policy
- conversion to the metric system
- all gun control efforts
- forced busing to achieve school desegregation
- all federal aid to schools and supported abolition of the Department of Education
- open housing laws and the quota system
- regional governments and revenue sharing (i.e., a program to return money to states in the form of unrestricted grants)
- abortions, except when necessary to save the mother's life
- federal initiatives in child care
- urban renewal programs
- minimum wage laws and unemployment insurance
- the right of government employees to engage in collective bargaining
- the Panama Canal, Strategic Arms Limitations Talks (SALT) I, and SALT II treaties
- the concept of mutually assured destruction
- secret diplomacy and the "scandal-ridden" Department of State

ARTISIAN PARTY
CANDIDATE FOR PRESIDENT:
Martin Reuben Bector (NV)

COMMON FOLKS PARTY
CANDIDATE FOR PRESIDENT:
James Donald "Dull" Stewart (NY)

Seeking to raise the potential of the presidency from "boring" to "dull," the Common Folks Party presented a "truly bargain candidate" to the electorate. For all citizens and future generations, its platform called for commitments to quality, peace, honesty and trustworthiness, human rights, a crackdown on crime and criminal elements, better education, integrity, the family, and a better working relationship between the executive and legislative branches of government. Stewart also promised to paint the White House brown.

CONSERVATIVE PARTY OF NEW YORK
CANDIDATE FOR PRESIDENT:
George Herbert Walker Bush (TX)

CANDIDATE FOR VICE PRESIDENT:
James Danforth Quayle (IN)

The Conservative Party was a New York State third party that normally endorsed the national Republican ticket.

CONSTITUTIONAL PARTY
CANDIDATE FOR PRESIDENT:
William Donald Klein (WI)

CONSTITUTIONAL PARTY
CANDIDATE FOR PRESIDENT:
Talmadge Martin Warren (VA)

A schoolteacher, Warren sought the presidency as a learning experience for his eighth-grade students.

PLATFORM HIGHLIGHTS:
SUPPORTED:
- equal media space given to all candidates in a primary
- a "none of the above" ballot line
- the direct election of Supreme Court justices
- a 20 percent cut in the federal payroll
- restrictions on U.S. investment in Mexico and foreign investments in U.S. businesses
- periodic open bidding for privatized government monopolies such as Amtrak and the Postal Service
- a shift in foreign aid from the government to voluntary channels
- the establishment of a U.S. national informational network that would track and prosecute industrial spying and work for a nuclear-free world
- the use of U.S. military forces to aid the war on drugs
- a provision by the federal government of full health care to all citizens, who, along with their families, would closely check all health care charges
- the monitoring of possession of semiautomatic and assault weapons and holding criminals responsible for compensating their victims
- the provision of a child allowance to married couples with preschool children when the mother does not work outside the home for more than sixteen hours per week

OPPOSED:
- the "borrow and pay" approach to government financing

CONSUMER (MINNESOTA PROGRESSIVES) PARTY

CANDIDATE FOR PRESIDENT:
Eugene Joseph McCarthy (MN)

CANDIDATES FOR VICE PRESIDENT:
Florence M. Rice (NY)
Alpha Smaby (MN)
Marguerite "Maureen" Smith (CA)

CONVENTION:
Summer 1988, Philadelphia (PA)

DEMOCRATIC PARTY

CANDIDATE FOR PRESIDENT:
Michael Stanley Dukakis

CANDIDATE FOR VICE PRESIDENT:
Lloyd Millard Bentsen, Jr.

CANDIDATES FOR PRESIDENTIAL NOMINATION:
John Hancock Abbott (CA)
Frank Joseph Ahern (LA)
Tyler Altizer (CO)
Gene P. Alvord (WA)
Douglas Applegate (OH)
Bruce Babbitt (AZ)
Gale Bernell Beery, Sr. (CA)
Joseph Robinette Biden (DE)
David Lyle Boren (OK)
William Warren "Bill" Bradley (NJ)
George Gittion Britt, Jr. (PA)
Larry Joe Buffington (AR) (withdrew)
Peggy Ann Childers (VA)
Billy Joe Clegg (OK)
Roy James Clendenan (OH)
Robert Eugene Cotner (OK)
Gregory Allen Courtney (MO)
Mario Matthew Cuomo (NY)
Blyth William Daylong (WI)
Alan Dechert (CA)
Norbert George Denneril, Jr. (OH)
Maurice Dickey (PA)
Florenzo DiDonato (MA)
Charles Richard Doty (OK)
Michael Stanley Dukakis (MA)
David Ernest Duke (LA)
William Joseph DuPont (IL)
Gloria Jean Ferguson (PA)
John Joseph Daniel Davi Ferrari-Soldo (NY)
Marsha Aileen Lannan Foutch (IL)
Louis Joseph Friedman (CA)
Richard Andrew Gephardt (MO)
James Irvin Glover (NJ)
Mildred Williams Glover (GA)
Willie Odell Goodman (NC)
Albert Arnold Gore, Jr. (TN)
Hosanna Jesse O. Gray (MI)

Gene Autry Griffin (MS)
Dolores Yolanda Gutierrez (CA)
Albert Hamburg (WY)
Michael Lee Hamburg (WY)
Gary Warren Hart (CO)
Carla Kathryn Schram Hawkinson (MI)
Richard Rhorer Hill (TX)
Samuel Boyer Hoff (OH)
Jesse Louis Jackson (IL)
Alfonzo Jones (MI)
Richard Broughton Kay (FL)
John Forbes Kerry (MA)
Caroline P. Killeen (NM)
William E. King (FL)
Claude Roy Kirk, Jr. (FL)
Stephen Andrew Koczak (NJ)
Todd Harris Kornfeld (NY)
Raymond C. Kuehl, Jr. (CA)
Robert Derwood "Buck" Ladner (MS)
Bruce Allen Landy (DC)
Lyndon Hermyle LaRouche, Jr. (VA)
John Leland Lemen (IN)
Nancy Davis Reagan Lite (NC)
Snow Lite (NC)
Vanna Lite (NC)
Stanley Onease Lock (MI)
Bobby Locke (TX)
Eugene Wayne "Billy Martin" Malone, Sr. (CA)
William Anthony Marra (NJ)
Anthony Martin-Trigona (FL)
George Joseph Mauer (FL)
John Henry McCabe (TX)
John Martin McCarthy (IL)
Angus Wheeler McDonald (WV)
James Robert Messenger (NJ)
Grady O'Cummings III (NY)
Edward Thomas O'Donnell, Jr. (DE)
John Joseph Oertel (CA)
Leonard Dietrich Orr (CA)
Daniel Gary Paris (CA)
Eric Lindsay Price (CA)
Johnnie Mae Riley (TX)
George Buchanan Roden (TX)
Ary Dov Rosenbaum (NY)
Conrad W. Roy (NH)
Blanche Rubin (AZ)
Kristopher Paul Rutherford (ME)
Cyril Emil Sagan (PA)
George Santiago (NY)
Patricia Scott Schroeder (CO)
David W. Shepherd (ID)
Paul Simon (IL)
Fred Irvin Sitnick (MD)
Richard H. Stallings (ID)
Richard Pierce Starr (GA)
Mrs. Frank Stewart (AL)

Duke Esten Stockton (WA)
Frank L. Thomas (CA)
Ossie Thorpe (DC)
Reginald Sullivan Voyle Towers (CA)
James A. Traficant, Jr. (OH)
Louis William Treep (FL)
Albert Archer Van Petten (CA)
Alfonso A. "Al" Veloz (CA)
Jim Walden (GA)
Williams (TX)
Thomas L. Woods (CA)
George Wade Paul Zaehringer (WI)
Irwin Zucker (NJ)

CANDIDATES FOR VICE-PRESIDENTIAL NOMINATION:
Lloyd Millard Bentsen, Jr. (TX)
Norris James Dubose (MD)

PRIMARIES:

FEBRUARY 16, 1988 (NH):

Dukakis	44,112
Gephardt	24,428
Simon	21,094
Jackson	9,615
Gore	8,373
Babbitt	5,644
Hart	4,888
LaRouche	188
others	5,018

(including those listed below)

Beery
Denneril
DiDonato
Duke
DuPont
King
Kirk
Koczak
Lock
Marra
Martin-Trigona
O'Donnell
Riley
Roy
Sagan
Thomas
Thorpe
Van Petten
Zucker

FEBRUARY 23, 1988 (SD):

Gephardt	31,226
Dukakis	22,367
Gore	5,990
Simon	4,991
Hart	3,876
Jackson	3,866
others	345

MARCH 1, 1988 (VT):

Dukakis	28,353
Jackson	13,044
Gephardt	3,910
Simon	2,620
Hart	2,055
others	809

MARCH 8, 1988 (AL):

Gore	100,065
Jackson	99,979
Dukakis	19,987
Gephardt	19,324
Hart	4,888
Simon	1,888
Babbitt	1,610
LaRouche	533
unpledged delegates	1,773

MARCH 8, 1988 (AR):

Gore	99,083
Dukakis	50,527
Jackson	46,631
Gephardt	32,464
Hart	10,267
Simon	4,794
Duke	2,745
Babbitt	1,430
LaRouche	1,224
Denneril	237
unpledged delegates	18,839

MARCH 8, 1988 (FL):

Dukakis	342,554
Jackson	185,884
Gephardt	136,339
Gore	135,620
Hart	27,319
Simon	19,462
Babbitt	7,489
undecided	59,906

MARCH 8, 1988 (GA):

Jackson	206,144
Gore	175,160
Dukakis	78,362
Gephardt	36,884
Hart	14,605
Simon	6,434
Babbitt	2,965
unpledged delegates	6,233

MARCH 8, 1988 (KY):

Gore	144,276
Dukakis	58,114
Jackson	48,464
Gephardt	28,636
Hart	11,679
Simon	10,092

Babbitt 1,699
LaRouche. 741
Martin-Trigona 680
Kay 521
unpledged delegates 10,268

MARCH 8, 1988 (LA):
Jackson 183,822
Gore 166,473
Dukakis . . . . . , ... 82,153
Gephardt. 60,787
Hart. 24,260
Duke 19,956
Simon 4,431
Ahern 3,222
Babbitt 2,787
Denneril 2,198
LaRouche 1,529
Kay 893

MARCH 8, 1988 (MD):
Dukakis. 146,709
Jackson 99,047
Gore 30,890
Gephardt. 26,749
Simon 9,727
Hart. 9,384
Babbitt 3,211
LaRouche 1,692
unpledged delegates 9,516

MARCH 8, 1988 (MA):
Dukakis. 281,995
Jackson 93,281
Gephardt. 49,621
Gore 21,311
Simon 17,363
Hart. 7,945
Babbitt 2,871
DiDonato 1,771
LaRouche. 776
no preference 8,159

MARCH 8, 1988 (MS):
Jackson 134,038
Gore 104,924
Dukakis. 27,104
Gephardt. 17,549
Hart. 11,478
Babbitt 1,893
Simon 1,813
LaRouche 1,181
unpledged delegates 8,238

MARCH 8, 1988 (MO):
Gephardt. 229,849
Jackson 53,969
Dukakis. 45,288
Simon 14,357

Gore 11,795
Hart 6,323
Duke 1,553
Babbitt 1,006
LaRouche. 468
Kay 297
Koczak 247
Denneril 179
unpledged delegates 4,998

MARCH 8, 1988 (NC):
Gore 233,832
Jackson 221,305
Dukakis. 136,029
Gephardt. 37,741
Hart. 16,468
Simon 8,398
Babbitt 3,871
no preference 16,105

MARCH 8, 1988 (OK):
Gore 149,881
Gephardt. 75,934
Dukakis. 60,056
Jackson 46,295
Hart. 13,529
Simon 6,119
Duke 2,570
Babbitt 1,480
LaRouche 1,329
Koczak. 1,239
Doty 1,017
Denneril. 558

MARCH 8, 1988 (RI):
Dukakis. 33,668
Jackson 7,255
Gephardt. 1,986
Gore 1,913
Simon 1,370
Hart 728
Babbitt 394
unpledged delegates. 786

MARCH 8, 1988 (TN):
Gore 398,248
Jackson 105,762
Dukakis. 17,949
Gephardt. 8,126
Hart. 4,261
Simon 2,520
Babbitt 1,883
unpledged delegates 2,760

MARCH 8, 1988 (TX):
Dukakis. 233,204
Gore 166,692
Jackson 139,612
Gephardt. 118,127

Hart	39,444
Simon	13,533
Babbitt	5,989
LaRouche	4,897
Duke	4,261
Williams	3,037
Denneril	1,736

MARCH 8, 1988 (VA):

Jackson	151,696
Gore	72,359
Dukakis	60,346
Gephardt	12,873
Hart	5,833
Simon	5,357
Babbitt	2,189
LaRouche	741
unpledged delegates	5,371

MARCH 15, 1988 (IL):

Simon	627,780
Jackson	457,352
Dukakis	242,076
Gore	76,795
Gephardt	31,736
others	23,360

MARCH 20, 1988 (PR):

Jackson	87,757
Dukakis	70,733
Simon	57,639
Gore	45,361
Gephardt	9,159
LaRouche	3,753

MARCH 29, 1988 (CT):

Dukakis	139,968
Jackson	68,193
Gore	18,542
Simon	3,136
others	9,297
uncommitted delegates	1,924

APRIL 5, 1988 (WI):

Dukakis	481,857
Jackson	285,575
Gore	176,009
Simon	48,877
others	18,906
uncommitted delegates	2,473

APRIL 19, 1988 (NY):

Dukakis	784,422
Jackson	573,910
Gore	156,480
Simon	18,529
uncommitted delegates	10,439
others	5,687

APRIL 26, 1988 (PA):

Dukakis	1,002,821

Jackson	408,935
Gore	45,617
Simon	10,115
others	21,246

MAY 3, 1988 (DC):

Jackson	67,812
Dukakis	14,969
Simon	750
Gore	612
others	371

MAY 3, 1988 (IN):

Dukakis	445,485
Jackson	143,089
Gore	22,266
Gephardt	16,665
Simon	12,892

MAY 3, 1988 (OH):

Dukakis	862,273
Jackson	378,354
Traficant	30,070
Gore	29,908
Hart	28,599
Applegate	25,806
Simon	15,464
LaRouche	6,378

MAY 10, 1988 (NE):

Dukakis	105,542
Jackson	43,134
others	14,114
uncommitted delegates	4,701

MAY 10, 1988 (WV):

Dukakis	254,144
Jackson	45,106
Gore	11,560
others	11,338

MAY 17, 1988 (OR):

Dukakis	207,579
Jackson	142,397
others	20,448

MAY 24, 1988 (ID):

Dukakis	37,696
Jackson	8,066
Gore	1,891
Simon	1,409
none of the above	2,308

JUNE 7, 1988 (CA):

Dukakis	1,910,808
Jackson	1,102,093
Gore	56,645
Simon	43,771
LaRouche	25,417

JUNE 7, 1988 (MT):

Dukakis	83,039

Jackson 26,777
others 11,146

JUNE 7, 1988 (NJ):
Dukakis 414,829
Jackson 213,705
Gore 18,062
LaRouche 2,621
Marra 2,594
Duke 2,491

JUNE 7, 1988 (NM):
Dukakis 114,069
Jackson 52,205
others 20,406

40TH CONVENTION:
July 18–21, 1988, Omni Coliseum, Atlanta (GA)
Paul Grattan Kirk, Jr. (MA), temporary chairman
Ann Richards (TX), keynoter
James Claude "Jim" Wright, Jr. (TX), permanent
chairman

Attending this convention were 4,162 delegates and 1,170
alternates.

PLATFORM HIGHLIGHTS:
The 1988 Democratic platform called for "the restoration
of competence and the revival of hope" in the United
States. It endorsed a fundamental right to economic justice, condemned "voodoo economics" and "trickle-down"
policies, and demanded national reinvestment in the people. The platform urged policies promoting lifelong education and training, economic development, a reversal of the
trend toward economic concentration and deregulation,
"fair share" taxation for the rich and large corporations,
deficit reduction, and the retooling of industry.

SUPPORTED:
- family and parental leave legislation
- pay equity
- workplace health and safety enforcement
- accessible child care
- programs to combat child abuse and malnutrition,
  school dropouts, and teenage pregnancy
- aggressive child support enforcement
- quality foster care and family preservation
- strong programs for prenatal care, infant nutrition, and
  preschool education
- fair trade
- notification requirements for plant closures and major
  layoffs
- civilian technological research and the development of
  science, engineering, and mathematics training
- a better balance between fiscal and monetary policy
  and military and civilian research and development
- a significant increase in federal aid to education
- the creation of a National Teacher Corps

- the principle that no one should be denied the opportunity to attend college for financial reasons
- the equalization of educational funding among local
  school districts
- funding for compensatory reading, mathematics, and
  enrichment services to low-income children such as
  Head Start
- expanded support for bilingual education, historically
  African-American and Hispanic-American institutions, special education, the arts and humanities, and
  the campaign against illiteracy
- the appointment of a drug czar to coordinate the nation's effort to halt the international supply of and
  dampen domestic demand for illegal drugs
- drug awareness and education, readily available treatment and counseling, stronger interdiction efforts, a
  summit of nations from the Western Hemisphere to cut
  off the drug supply at its source, and foreign aid to reform drug-based economies, while opposing the legalization of illicit drugs
- increased assistance for local criminal justice agencies
- a ban on "cop killer" bullets
- aid for crime victims
- the multicultural heritage of the United States
- equal access to government services, housing, business
  enterprise, and education
- the ERA
- a revitalization of civil rights enforcement and legal
  services for the poor
- immigration policy reform to make it nondiscriminatory and favorable to family reunification
- affirmative action
- the protection of voting rights
- the fulfillment of treaty obligations with Native
  Americans
- an end to the housing crisis and homelessness
- an increase and renovation of the inventory of public
  and subsidized housing
- the restoration of foreclosed government property to
  productive use
- assistance to first-time home buyers
- the encouragement of employer-assisted housing and development by community-based nonprofit organizations
- infrastructure development as a way to create employment opportunities
- public interest investment of pension funds
- a national health program that would provide federal
  leadership and coordination, guarantee basic health insurance for all, restrain costs, ensure quality, and advance research
- affordable long-term care and health care available to
  all senior and disabled citizens
- reproductive choice regardless of ability to pay
- a declaration of the human immunodeficiency virus/ac-
  quired immunodeficiency syndrome (HIV/AIDS) epi-

demic as a national health emergency, with accelerated research and expedited Food and Drug Administration (FDA) approval of treatments, public health community consensus on voluntary and confidential testing and counseling, and protection of the civil rights of those suffering from AIDS or ARC (AIDS-related complex) or testing HIV-positive

- strong environmental protection measures
- recycling efforts
- the enforcement of toxic waste laws
- the preservation of clean waterways and safe, drinkable water
- the protection of national parks, forests, wildlife refuges, and coastal zones
- an end to offshore oil drilling in environmentally sensitive areas
- efforts to end the threat of the greenhouse effect and depletion of the ozone layer
- the rescue of the tropical rain forests from destruction
- periodic world environmental summits
- family farms with policies governing supply management
- reasonable price supports
- soil conservation and protection of rural water quality
- credit and foreclosure relief for farmers
- the return of federally held foreclosed lands to minority, beginning, and restarting farmers
- research on new uses for farm products
- improved disaster relief
- the development of and federal support for rural health care, housing, education, water supply, and infrastructure
- new sources of capital for rural business
- efforts to fight hunger at home and abroad and pledged to convene an international conference of food-producing nations
- a balanced, coherent energy policy, with special attention to the development of renewable energy resources, international cooperation, and the filling of the Strategic Petroleum Reserve
- the use of natural gas and coal, efforts to combat acid rain, and incentives to promote new oil and gas drilling and development
- reduced reliance on nuclear power, while insisting that such plants be safe and environmentally sound
- easier voter registration and the prevention of election abuses (e.g., through misuse of at-large elections, election day challenges, and registration roll purges)
- the end of discrimination against public employees in civic life
- statehood for the District of Columbia
- self-determination for U.S. territories
- greater autonomy for Puerto Rico
- full and equal access to elective office and party endorsement for women and minorities
- a minimizing of money's influence in the electoral process through campaign financing reform

- a stronger military capable of thwarting terrorist activities
- a stronger economy capable of competing in the global marketplace
- an intellectually stronger nation
- "a spiritually stronger people, steeped in the principles that exemplify the United States to the world"
- the reassertion of U.S. leadership on behalf of democracy, human rights, and a more secure world, while recognizing that the United States cannot be policeman to the world nor retreat from engagement with the world
- an emphasis on military readiness and mobility, with U.S. allies assuming a greater share of the costs and responsibilities of regional defense
- conversion strategies to retrain defense industry workers for space development, communications, and other peacetime growth industries
- the encouragement of a "new, mutually beneficial relationship with the Soviet Union" to promote peace, combat environmental threats, eradicate disease and poverty, and end the arms race
- further progress in disarmament as a follow-up to the Intermediate Nuclear Forces (INF) Treaty
- more aid and debt relief for developing nations
- an end to arms sales to troubled areas of the world
- the "special relationship" between the United States and Israel and urged a return to the Camp David Accords by pursuing peace talks
- security in the Persian Gulf and freedom of navigation
- an end to the Iran-Iraq War through UN peace initiatives
- the peace plan for Central America put forth by President Oscar Arias Sànchez of Costa Rica
- an end to U.S. dealings with drug smugglers in Latin America
- economic cooperation with Mexico
- aid to democratic nations in the Southern Hemisphere
- a commitment to peace and friendship among nations

DEMOCRATIC PARTY
VOTE FOR PRESIDENTIAL NOMINATION:

Candidate	Ballot: 1
Dukakis	2,876¼
Jackson	1,218½
Stallings	3
Biden	2
Gephardt	2
Bentsen	1
Hart	1
abstained	14

VOTE FOR VICE-PRESIDENTIAL NOMINATION:
BENTSEN WAS NOMINATED FOR BY ACCLAMATION, WITH NO OTHER NAMES BEING PRESENTED FOR CONSIDERATION.

- the settlement of the controversies in Cyprus and Northern Ireland by the European allies
- the promotion of pluralism in Eastern Europe and the struggle for human rights in Asia
- independence for Namibia
- an end to the "counterproductive policy" of the United States in Angola
- assistance to Mozambique
- the belief in a United States dedicated to human rights, human dignity, and human opportunity around the world
- a dream of "opportunity for every citizen," a government that was pragmatic and competent, and a nation motivated by ideals and not ideology

OPPOSED:

- irresponsible corporate behavior (e.g., takeovers, monopolistic mergers, insider trading, and golden parachutes)
- waste in the defense establishment
- apartheid in South Africa and urged the imposition of economic sanctions against its government
- hate, violence, negative stereotyping, and English-only pressure groups

GRASSROOTS PARTY

CANDIDATE FOR PRESIDENT:
Jack Herer (MN)

CANDIDATE FOR VICE PRESIDENT:
Dana Beal (MN)

This party supported legalization of the use of marijuana.

INDEPENDENT

CANDIDATES FOR PRESIDENT:
Thomas Jeffery Abramczyk (MI)
R. Jerry Adam (OR)
Charles A. Adams (GA)
Joseph Cockrell Adams, Jr. (LA)
Gordon Hallman Adkins, Sr. (TX)
Gordon Lee Anderson (WA)
Mick Zager Apollo (VA)
Jouett Edgar Arney (KS)[1]
Caesar Serrato Augustine (CA)
Daniel M. Axelrod (NY)
Owen F. Balding (IL)
Nyles Bauer (AZ)
James Mercer Beasley (CA)
Robert Michael Birnberg (CO)
Guy Templeton Black (OH)
Karen-Lee Blauvelt (MA)
Kenneth Myron Bonnell (MS)
John Edwin Boydston (TX)
Robert Wayne Bradford (TN)
Ben Howard Brenneman (VA)
Reed Vance Brown (FL)

James Allen Burner (WV)
Bruce Edward Byers (TX)
Zacoe Patricia Ann Mary Caggiano-Rubin (NY)
Jerry Leon Carroll (CA)[2]
Kevin P. Centanni (LA)
Barry Wayne Childs (LA)
Duane Kerney Cornwall (WA)
Roger Earl Craft (CA)
Matthew J. Cunningham (DC)
Mitchell Jay Davis (NY)
Ralph De Maintenon (CO)
Andrew Samuel Devers (PA)
Don William Dietrich (GA)
James Carter Dorrell (TX)
James George Doyle (CA)
Gary Lee Edge (WI)
Maximus T. Englerius (WA)
Ray Ezell (GA)
Clinton L. Fairchild (MS)
Clarita "Chi Chi" Fazzari (CA)[3]
Kenneth Duane Feeney (IA)
Clinton Ferguson (MS)
Nell K. Fiola (MN)
Mrs. Foggybottom (DC) (satire)
Joel Judson Ford (GA)
Gary Steven Foster (IL)
Michael Joseph Frei (MI)
David Freligh (CA)
George Joseph Gehring, Jr. (CA)
Gregory Iiams Goodwin (HI)
Jason Ralph Green (WI)
Ray Ferrill Green (MA)
Samuel Greenberg (VA)
Irvin James Guenther (KY)
Donald W. Hackett, Jr. (FL)
Thomas Edward Hapka (WI)[4]
Eddie Ray Harris (TX)
Zachary Harris (MI)
John Clayton Harvey (MI)
Robert Bryant Haynes (NC)
John Robert Henry (PR)
Wduan David Hickman (MI)
Margot Sierra Holcomb (NV)
Sebastian Thomas Holms, Jr. (MI)
David Lester Hornberger (CA)
William Henry Hurley (AL)

[1]Arney's running mate was Charles Orval Owens of Kansas.

[2]Carroll's running mate was Marlin Dale Thacker of Alabama. The Carroll-Thacker ticket opposed excessive government spending, inflation, government economic controls, and inadequate assistance for the elderly and disabled. It endorsed equal prices and wages for everyone, increased support for seniors and persons with disabilities, 100 percent parity for farmers, elimination of the 55-mile-per-hour speed limit, adequate fuel for truckers, a balanced federal budget, and personal production of gasohol without red tape.
[3]Fazzari's platform promised to use her management skills as a former Las Vegas mambo dancer to solve the nation's problems. Turned down as a prospective owner of a brothel in Nye County (NV), Fazzari expressed her disgust with politicians during her campaign.
[4]Hapka's running mate was Aaron M. Parker of Wisconsin.

Lido Anthony "Lee" Iacocca (MI)
Arthur Johnson (NY)
Peter Martin Jones (CA)
Henry King (OH)
James John Kendzierski (FL)
Ben Klemens (IL)
James Llewellyn Knowles, Jr. (MN)
Concetta Marie Lamagno (IL)
Bobbie Joe Lamb (TX)
Joseph Landar (NY)
Lawrence Joseph Lang (NJ)
Joyce Padgett Lea (MO)
Stephen Eugene Leach (PA)
William Francis Lee III (VT)
Laurie Legrand (GA)
Max Linovitz (MI)
William Joseph Lira (WA)
Henry Lockwood (WI)
Thomas Macaione
Ronald Ray Mains (IL)
Eddie Bernard Marcus (MN)
Gilbert Leon Marcus (NY)
Hector Marquez (AR)
Isabel Masters (OK)[1]
Trevor Alan McArthur (NE)
James Carver McCandless, Sr. (CA)
Kyle McDaniel, Jr. (MD)
Bobby O'Dell McGee (SC)
Thomas Capitola McKim (OR)
Robert Veto Melfi (FL)
Gary Raymond Mercer (DC)
Jerry Roger Milton (FL)
William Eugene Mitchell (CA)
Myrtle Charlotte Montgomery (CA)
Joseph Westley Newman (MS)
Charles J. Ott (NY)
Auburn Lee Packwood (MO)
Ignatius Page, Jr. (MO)
Samuel Palmer (MS)
Jimmy Pheromone (MD)
Jay Kevin Pokines (NY)
Harold Lawrence Poland (VA)
Robert H. Polk (MA)
Sinisa M. Princevac (IL)
Myron Ralph (NY)
Pretty Bob S. Reams (MI)
Darcy G. Richardson (PA)
James H. Ricketts, Sr. (IN)
Earl A. Roberts, Jr. (CT)
Kenneth George Robichaux (LA)
Nelson Aldrich Rockefeller (DC)
Hassan M. M. Romieh (NY)
Christopher John Rutledge (DC)
Ophelia Candyce Ryals (CA)

Lyle Morris Schlieder (CA)
Vernon Michael Schmucker (CA)
George Michael Senko (CA)
Henry A. Shapiro (NY)
Susan K. Y. Shargal (NH)
Ronald Takeo Shigeta, Sr. (HI)
Rodger D. Smallridge (LA)
Monty Dale Sprague (TN)
Willis Johnston Stancill (NC)
Andrew John Stewart (DC)
Robert Gary Stout (MI)
Donald Jerome Sullivan (MA)
Theodore Shelby Swanson (IN)
Rickey Lynn Swinney (TX)
Glenda Jean Tomosovich (VA)
Justin Alan Torres (VA)
Ralph Preston Townsend (TX)
Robert J. "Bob Tram" Tramutolo (OK)
Donald John Trump (NY)
Sherman Lee Tyler, Jr. (TX)
Greg Autry Wallace (CA)
Sam Wallace (AL)
Frank Ramey Watson, Jr. (OH)
Richard Harold White (AZ)
Oran Richard Wingler (WI)
Robert Bryant Winn (AZ)
Beverly Kathleen Wise (MI)
David Wobser
David Womack (IL)
Robert Bernard Woodson (CA)
James Bell Yager (IN)
Louie Gene Youngkeit (UT)
Ethan R. Zuckerman (NY)

CANDIDATES FOR VICE PRESIDENT:
Michael Owen Childress (VA)
William M. Daguman (CA)
Samuel Dale Darnell (NC)

INTERNATIONALIST WORKERS PARTY

CANDIDATE FOR PRESIDENT:
Herbert George Lewin (PA)

CANDIDATE FOR VICE PRESIDENT:
Emma Wong Mar (CA)

LIBERAL PARTY OF NEW YORK

CANDIDATE FOR PRESIDENT:
Michael Stanley Dukakis (MA)

CANDIDATE FOR VICE PRESIDENT:
Lloyd Millard Bentsen, Jr. (TX)

The Liberal Party was a New York State third party that normally endorsed the national ticket of the Democratic Party.

[1]Masters's running mate was Robert E. Anderson of California.

LIBERTARIAN PARTY

CANDIDATE FOR PRESIDENT:
Ronald E. "Ron" Paul

CANDIDATE FOR VICE PRESIDENT:
Andre Verne Marrou (NV)

CANDIDATES FOR PRESIDENTIAL NOMINATION:
Robert Kipley "Kip" Lee (CA)
Russell Means (SD)
Ronald E. "Ron" Paul (TX)

5TH CONVENTION:
September 1987, Seattle (WA)

PLATFORM HIGHLIGHTS:
The Libertarian platform reiterated the party's Statement of Principles and most of the 1984 platform. It denied the existence of any conflict between civil order and individual rights, claiming the party's positions were not based on the moral values of specific practices but on a fundamental belief that people's rights must be recognized. Personal responsibility was a cardinal tenet. Crime would have been fought through impartial and consistent law enforcement and the decriminalization of such "victimless" crimes as those involving drugs, alcohol, consensual sexual relations, possession or distribution and use of sexually explicit materials, prostitution, gambling, and suicide.

SUPPORTED:

- the trend toward private protection services and voluntary community crime-control groups
- government restitution for wrongful criminal proceedings against an accused person and wrongdoer restitution for victims of crimes
- peremptory challenges to proposed judges by parties in criminal or civil cases
- the notion of a victim's "pardon" for criminals
- the private adjudication of disputes and a change in the rape laws to remove cohabitation as a defense
- the right of juries to decide on the justice of a law (rather than simply the facts of a case) but opposed forced jury duty
- an end to the doctrine of state "sovereign immunity"
- the right to purchase and use radar warning devices and digital audio tape recorders
- a repeal of the Intelligence Identities Protection Act, along with restrictions on the rights of electronic media
- the right of individuals to own and use private property (including their own bodies) and denounced government restrictions on those rights based on aesthetic values, riskiness, moral standards, cost-benefits estimates, or the promotion of economic growth
- restitution for Japanese-Americans whose lands were taken during World War II
- the right to privacy as inviolable and called for prohibitions against government surveillance of all types, including the information collected by the Census Bureau and other public agencies

- the abolition of both the Federal Bureau of Investigation (FBI) and the Central Intelligence Agency (CIA)
- a curtailment of Congress's subpoena power
- the dismantling of the internal security committees of Congress
- the destruction of all files compiled by the Selective Service
- the unconditional exoneration of persons accused or convicted of draft offenses, desertion, or other acts of resistance to wars and the military
- the denial of draft requirements applied to women (on the grounds that the draft should be completely abolished)
- the right of collective bargaining but upheld the rights of employers to not recognize unions
- the legitimacy of secondary boycotts
- the removal of all restrictions on immigration, abolition of the Immigration and Naturalization Service and Border Patrol, full amnesty for illegal aliens, and an end to government restrictions on undocumented noncitizens
- a ban on punishing employers who hire undocumented workers
- full civil rights for all (including the wealthy and persons with different personal habits or political perspectives)
- an extension to children of all the rights granted to adults
- a repeal of all status offense laws
- the abolition of juvenile courts
- the elimination of laws that treated juvenile offenders as if they were not fully responsible for their crimes
- private adoptions and the right of children to seek guardians other than their parents
- American Indian tribes by granting them the authority to select the level of their autonomy (up to absolute sovereignty), with individual American Indians selecting their citizenship while enjoying full property rights
- the establishment of an exchange program to "cash out" remaining federal obligations to Native American tribes
- efforts to hold as fully liable those responsible for damage to American Indian lands through careless disposal of waste materials
- the abolition of the Bureau of Indian Affairs
- a total deregulation of the economic sphere and a limited public role in protecting property rights
- a repeal of the Sixteenth Amendment (income tax) and of all involuntary taxes
- a repeal of federal inheritance taxes
- amnesty for tax evaders and an end to the requirement that employers collect taxes on behalf of the state (i.e., release of employers from "involuntary servitude")
- a repeal of legal tender laws
- the private ownership of gold
- the elimination of minted coins (with private minting on a competitive basis allowed)
- free market banking and the abolition of the Federal Reserve System, Federal Deposit Insurance Corpora-

tion, National Banking System, and other regulatory agencies in the banking and credit fields

- the abolition of the Federal Savings and Loan Insurance Corporation, National Credit Union Administration, National Credit Union Central Liquidity Facility, Federal Home Loan Bank, and similar agencies
- a return to the Jacksonian concept of the government maintaining its own treasury
- the abolition of all regulation of financial and capital markets, including the Securities and Exchange Commission, state "blue sky" laws, and all federal regulation of commodity markets
- balanced budget amendments for the federal government and the states
- a prohibition on the Federal Reserve from acquiring new government securities and the belief that "governments facing fiscal crises should always default in preference to raising taxes"
- a repeal of antitrust laws
- the abolition of the Federal Trade Commission and the Antitrust Division of the Department of Justice
- the right of individuals to form corporations and other types of voluntary association
- the abolition of the Federal Housing Administration (FHA), the Rural Electrification Administration, Federal Home Loan Mortgage Corporation, Federal National Mortgage Association, Farm Credit Administration, Student Loan Marketing Association, and the Small Business Administration
- a repeal of the windfall profits tax
- nuclear power being subjected to the test of the free market
- the abolition of the Department of Energy
- a reform of nuisance and negligence laws of to cover damage done to individuals by air, water, and noise pollution rather than government efforts to control pollution
- the abolition of the Environmental Protection Agency
- the abolition of the Consumer Product Safety Commission and the repeal of all laws restricting advertising or requiring individuals to use protective equipment
- the abolition of the Federal Aviation Administration and the Food and Drug Administration
- an end to public education and, as interim measures, tuition tax credits and other tax reforms favorable to private schools
- an end to compulsory school attendance laws
- the cessation of forced busing and corporal punishment
- a reduction of tax support for public schools
- an end to all subsidies for childbearing (including welfare plans and tax-supported services for children)
- the elimination of special tax burdens on single people
- the abolition of all federal agencies regulating transportation and a return to private ownership of such public enterprises as Amtrak
- the privatization of airports, air traffic control systems, public roads, and the national highway system
- the repeal of the 55-mile-per-hour speed limit
- a repeal of minimum wage laws and protective labor legislation for women and children, restrictions on day care centers, and the National Labor Relations Act
- "dollar-for-dollar" tax credits for charitable contributions and the use of tax credits to promote charity care
- the deregulation of health care and the medical insurance industry including the abolition of Medicare and Medicaid
- the right to pursue unorthodox alternative medical treatments
- midwifery, home births, and women's clinics
- birth control and a woman's right to an abortion
- a repeal of land use, zoning, building code, eminent domain, urban renewal, and similar laws, while recognizing private, voluntary land use covenants
- the privatization of inland waterways, dam sites, and water systems and the abolition of the civilian functions of the Bureau of Reclamation, Bureau of Land Management, Forest Service, and the Army Corps of Engineers
- the ownership of public lands transferred to the private sector through homesteading
- the abolition of the Department of Agriculture
- the elimination of all government farm programs, including price supports, direct subsidies, and production regulations
- the deregulation of transportation and abolition of the Interstate Commerce Commission
- an end to government involvement in pest control
- a repeal of the Occupational Safety and Health Act and the Social Security Act
- the abolition of the Postal Service and the Civil Service system
- an end to government control over political parties, including repeal of the Federal Election Campaign Act and all federal campaign finance laws
- open ballot access to new parties and independent candidates in state elections and the replacement of the ballot system itself with a less restrictive system of tickets or cards printed by candidates
- the addition of a ballot line dedicated to "none of the above" so voters could register their dissent against the listed candidates for a public office
- nonintervention in foreign affairs and limited government engagement beyond national defense
- an end to the use of passports
- the elimination of foreign aid
- the abolition of government-sponsored arms sales
- a withdrawal of restrictions on U.S. trade abroad
- the abolition of such agencies as the Export-Import Bank and the Commodity Credit Corporation
- the development of standards to recognize private ownership claims to Antarctica, ocean floors, outer space and other unowned resources
- the abandonment of all international treaties and agreements (particularly the Law of the Sea Treaty)

- the refusal of the United States to accept the proposed Law of the Sea
- the right of secession for political subdivisions of the United States
- the withdrawal of the United States from the World Bank and the International Monetary Fund, while arguing against international paper money and any U.S. financial bailout of foreign governments
- the withdrawal of all U.S. military personnel stationed abroad (particularly in Central America, Europe, Japan, the Philippines, and the Republic of Korea)
- the abandonment of the Monroe and Reagan doctrines and an end to U.S. participation in the North Atlantic Treaty Organization (NATO) and other multilateral and bilateral arrangements
- a mutual disarmament of nuclear weapons and missiles among nuclear powers
- the withdrawal of U.S. nuclear weapons from Europe
- increased limits on the president's power to initiate military action; a constitutional amendment to clarify the limits of the president's role as commander in chief; and the abrogation of all presidential declarations of "states of emergency" and an end to secret executive branch commitments and unilateral acts of military intervention
- a reduction in the size of the diplomatic corps and the immediate withdrawal of the United States from the United Nations (as well as removal of the United Nations from U.S. soil)
- the right of private citizens to engage in diplomatic negotiations with foreign governments
- a condemnation of all governments for violating human rights and urged that international negotiations be conducted without conceding moral legitimacy to any government or asserting moral superiority by the United States
- immediate independence for American Samoa, Guam, Micronesia, Puerto Rico, and the Virgin Islands
- an end to all U.S. operations in the Canal Zone and the withdrawal of all U.S. forces from Panama
- the voluntary peaceful use of outer space and opposed governmental restrictions on the private exploration, colonization, industrialization, and development of heavenly bodies
- the abolition of the National Aeronautics and Space Administration, repudiation of the UN Moon Treaty, and privatization of all artificial satellites

Opposed:
- laws that imposed a minimum drinking age, that made bartenders and hosts liable for their guests, and that authorized the use of alcohol and drug testing of drivers without probable cause
- government-mandated smoking and no-smoking areas in privately owned businesses
- the use of preventive detention and "no-knock" laws
- involuntary mental health treatment or commitment to mental institutions
- mental health "propaganda" and tax-supported mental health centers
- the use of an insanity or "diminished capacity" defense in criminal cases
- all government censorship, including antipornography laws
- gags on press coverage
- equal time and "fairness" requirements in broadcasting
- the Federal Communications Act
- efforts to ban advertising for cigarettes and sugar-coated breakfast foods
- prohibitions against the depiction of sex or violence in TV, movies, and print media
- the regulation of "pay TV"
- tax funding for the Corporation for Public Broadcasting
- anticult activities and harassment of unconventional religious groups, following a strict interpretation of the separation of church and state
- government involvement with the National Ad Council and regulation of political advertising
- the use of eminent domain to municipalize sports teams
- any form of gun control, registration for the draft (or compulsory national service of any kind), military discharges based on sexual preference, and the Uniform Code of Military Justice
- all government interference with bargaining and demanded the repeal of the National Labor Relations Act and all state right-to-work laws
- temporary worker plans, including the bracero program
- protective laws applied to selected groups and government attempts to regulate private discrimination in employment, housing, and public accommodations
- laws empowering the state to make children "wards of the state" and restrictions on child labor and compulsory education
- statutes outlawing "adults only" apartments
- plans to redistribute wealth or manage trade, deficit budgets, inflationary monetary policies, expansive government spending, impediments to free trade, and public controls on the economy (e.g., wages, prices, rents, profits, production, or interest)
- all personal and corporate taxes and recognized the right to challenge payment on moral or other grounds
- monopolies, which were viewed as coercive and a natural outgrowth of government regulation
- limits on corporate liability and size, merger restrictions, and the chartering of corporations
- all public subsidies along with tariffs, quotas, and public utility franchises
- the Reconstruction Finance Corporation, Federal Financing Bank, Customs Court, Tariff Commission
- plant closure legislation
- government and business alliances to promote "rein-

dustrialization" along with all government guarantees of private loans

- the U.S. government's participation in international cartels
- all government control of the energy field including pricing, allocation, and production
- government conservation programs
- government support for energy research and the development of energy alternatives
- the need for "strategic storage" of oil, efforts to nationalize energy industries, rationing, and government ownership of energy resources
- the Superfund for cleaning up toxic wastes because it permits responsible parties to escape the full consequences of their actions
- fraud and misrepresentation in the marketplace but did not embrace "paternalistic" governmental interventions on behalf of consumers
- coercive conversion to the metric system
- "no-fault" insurance
- fluoridation of water and legal restrictions on what substances a person might ingest
- coercive controls on population growth and forced sterilization
- mandatory retirement, occupational licensure, and antipoverty programs
- medical licensure requirements
- health planning boards
- prescription requirements
- mandatory AIDS testing and contact tracing and FDA restrictions on the availability of treatments for AIDS
- limits on malpractice suits
- involuntary medical treatment and government restrictions on research
- medical education subsidies
- the creation of new national parks or wilderness and recreation areas and instead urged the transfer of such existing areas to private ownership
- the government's issuance of identity cards for individual U.S. citizens as well as government secrecy and the widespread use of "classified" information
- military intervention to protect individual citizens in foreign lands, with U.S. citizens traveling or investing abroad at their own risk
- the Antiballistic Missile (ABM) Treaty and the policy of massive nuclear retaliation known as mutual assured destruction
- terrorism and torture
- U.S. efforts to overthrow the government of Nicaragua and U.S. intervention in El Salvador, Guatemala, and Honduras
- the U.S. invasion of Grenada
- the Neutrality Act of 1794
- U.S. military and economic interventions in the Middle East and South Africa
- the incorporation of the Persian Gulf into the U.S. de-

fense perimeter along with the stationing of U.S. troops in the Sinai Peninsula
- the practice of "re-flagging" foreign ships to bring them under U.S. protection
- the U.S. diplomatic approach to the People's Republic of China and the earlier U.S. involvement with Taiwan

ALSO:

- cautioned that silence on any other aspect of government should not be construed to imply Libertarian approval

NATIONAL ECONOMIC RECOVERY PARTY

CANDIDATE FOR PRESIDENT:
Lyndon Hermyle LaRouche, Jr. (VA)

CANDIDATE FOR VICE PRESIDENT:
Debra Hanania Freeman (MD)

The National Economic Recovery Party backed the personal views of Lyndon LaRouche.

PLATFORM HIGHLIGHTS:

SUPPORTED:

- charges against the Reagan administration of a cover-up in "Irangate"
- a new foreign policy that recognized the inviolability of the established borders in the Middle East region, sought to develop the infrastructure and trade of the region, and guaranteed the national self-defense and internal security of individual nations
- a combination of military containment and irregular warfare to bring Ayatollah Ruhollah Khomeini's regime to an end
- an analysis of the "world economic depression" and identified the causes as U.S. defense expenditures
- an initiation of the recovery by demanding that the percentage of the total labor force employed as operatives in the product of physical output be increased, while simultaneously increasing the average productivity of operatives by high rates of investment in improved technologies
- SDI

OPPOSED:

- "Malthusianism" (i.e., population control) as a liberal fashion with dangerous implications

ALSO:

- focused on the economic collapse of Brazil in significant portions of the party's literature

NEW ALLIANCE (SOLIDARITY; UNITED CITIZENS) PARTY

CANDIDATE FOR PRESIDENT:
Lenora B. Fulani (NY)

CANDIDATE FOR VICE PRESIDENT:
Wynonia Burke (NC) (AK, AZ, NC)

Joyce Dattner (IL) (NY)
B. Kwaku Duren (CA) (CA)
Rafael Mendez (NY) (NM, TX)
Harold Moore (OR) (MS)
Mamie Moore (NJ) (MI)
Barbara R. Taylor (NJ) (NJ)

CONVENTION:
August 20–21, 1988, Roosevelt Hotel, New York
(NY)
Emily Carter (NY), chairperson

Founded in 1979, the New Alliance Party held its first national convention in May 1985 in Chicago (IL). This party was the successor to the Independent Alliance, which fielded a presidential ticket in 1984. Lenora B. Fulani declared her Independent candidacy for president on June 14, 1987, in New York City. A People's Convention was held at the Ramada Hotel Capitol Plaza in Atlanta (GA) from August 21 to August 23, 1987, to confirm her candidacy. The formal nominating convention of the New Alliance Party in 1988 was attended by four hundred delegates and supporters.

PLATFORM HIGHLIGHTS:
The platform insisted on putting "people before profits." It sought nonintervention, disarmament, and peace.

SUPPORTED:

• significant reductions in the military budget
• an end to racism, sexism, anti-Semitism, and antigay bigotry
• full civil rights for lesbians and gay men
• the enactment of a national AIDS bill of rights for persons afficted with the disease
• the enforcement of American Indian treaty rights
• an end to poverty, calling for job opportunities and training, decent welfare benefits, and an end to workfare for all
• the creation of a National Health Service, an end to union busting and givebacks, and restrictions on plant closures
• the need for participatory democracy
• federally subsidized housing
• free quality education from day care through graduate school
• full economic, social, and political equality for women, including abortion on demand
• employment opportunities and accessibility for persons with disabilities
• a high priority for nonnuclear energy resource development and environmental protection, subsidizes for farms, and a moratorium on farm foreclosures
• assurances for the elderly that they would receive adequate social security and pensions
• an amendment of the immigration laws to give full immigration rights and legal protection to all wishing entry into the country

---

NEW ALLIANCE (SOLIDARITY; UNITED CITIZENS) PARTY
VOTE FOR PRESIDENTIAL NOMINATION: FULANI WAS NOMINATED BY ACCLAMATION.

VOTE FOR VICE-PRESIDENTIAL NOMINATION: THE CONVENTION NOMINATED SIX DIFFERENT VICE-PRESIDENTIAL CANDIDATES: BURKE OF NORTH CAROLINA, DATTNER OF NEW YORK, DUREN OF CALIFORNIA, MOORE OF OREGON, MOORE OF NEW JERSEY, AND MENDEZ OF NEW YORK.

NONE OF THE ABOVE

This option was on the ballot in the state of Nevada.

NOUVEAU-CENTURY PARTY OF AMERICA

CANDIDATE FOR PRESIDENT:
Edward Matthew Balcsik (WI)

1 PARTY

CANDIDATE FOR PRESIDENT:
Emil Matalik (NY)

Matalik created the # 1 Party (also known as the United Nations Party and the United Nations Organization, or 1-U.N.O., Party) in 1964 to promote world peace and the abolition of hunger.

PLATFORM HIGHLIGHTS:
SUPPORTED:

• a view that overpopulation was the world's biggest problem and proposed limiting each family to one child (later increased to two children), one animal, and one tree
• the creation of a World presidency, a Universal Congress, and a Global Supreme Court
• the conversion of cities to farm land, thus resolving the urban problems of the world
• the issuance of five usable acres of land to each person for farming
• prohibitions on the public use of tobacco, liquor, and gambling
• free world communications
• the promotion of worldwide free love—"especially for single and virginized people"—and coed nudist camps for prison inmates
• the abolition of the monetary system and replacing it with "volunteerism"

PEACE AND FREEDOM PARTY

CANDIDATE FOR PRESIDENT:
Herbert George Lewin

CANDIDATES FOR VICE PRESIDENT:
Vikki Murdock (NJ, RI)
Emma Wong Mar

CANDIDATES FOR PRESIDENTIAL NOMINATION:
Lenora B. Fulani (NV)
Albert Hamburg (WY)
Larry Holmes (NY)
Shirley Issacson (CA)
Willa Kenoyer (WI)
Herbert George Lewin (CA)

CANDIDATES FOR VICE-PRESIDENTIAL NOMINATION:
Vikki Murdock (CA)
Emma Wong Mar (CA)

PRIMARY:
JUNE 7, 1988 (CA):
Fulani 2,117
Issacson 1,222
Holmes 1,042
Lewin 778
Kenoyer 411
Hamburg 353

POPULIST (CHRISTIAN POPULIST; PATRIOTIC) PARTY

CANDIDATE FOR PRESIDENT:
David Ernest Duke (LA)
[George Vernon Hansen (ID) (declined)]

CANDIDATES FOR VICE PRESIDENT:
James Gordon "Bo" Gritz (NV) (withdrew)
Floyd Cottner Parker (KY)
[Hubert David Patty (TN) (withdrew)]

CANDIDATES FOR PRESIDENTIAL NOMINATION:
David Ernest Duke (LA)
Ralph Forbes (AR)
Warren Freiberg (AR)
James Gordon "Bo" Gritz (NV)
George Vernon Hansen (ID)
Judge Johnson (AR)
Evan Mecham (AZ)
Floyd Cottner Parker, Jr. (KY)
Hubert David Patty (TN)
Marvin Seat (KY)
James A. Traficant (OH)

CANDIDATES FOR VICE-PRESIDENTIAL NOMINATION:
Ralph Forbes (AR)
James Gordon "Bo" Gritz (NV)
Floyd Cottner Parker, Jr. (KY)
Hubert David Patty (TN)
Maureen Salaman (CA)
Everett Sileven (NE)

2D CONVENTION:
September 4–7, 1987, Holiday Inn, St. Louis (MO)
Tom McIntyre (PA), chairman
Bob Weems (MS), keynoter

2D CONVENTION (CONTINUED):
March 11–13, 1988, Holiday Inn Queensgate, Cincinnati (OH)
Tom McIntyre (PA), chairman

PLATFORM HIGHLIGHTS:
The 1988 Populist platform was the same as the 1984 platform.

SUPPORTED:
- a repeal of the federal income tax
- the abolition of the Federal Reserve System
- a repudiation of the national debt
- the reactivation of anti-usury laws
- the enactment of fair tariff laws
- a revitalization of the family farm
- the rebuilding of the United States as an international power
- the reclaiming of the free enterprise system with a strong antimonopoly initiative
- a resurrection of "anti-degeneracy" laws and a crackdown on crime
- a rejection of the ERA and gay rights
- restrictions on pornography and illegal drugs
- freedom of choice with regard to public schools and the use of private property
- the deportation of illegal aliens and an end to immigration from developing countries
- welfare reform to get "this vast class of socialist-voting, taxpayer-financed drones off the voting rolls"
- restrictions on judicial review
- reasserting the right to keep and bear arms
- energy independence for the country
- the freedom of individuals to seek medical help without government interference, including access to health foods, vitamins, and cancer therapies
- a constitutional amendment to permit the direct election of the president after regional primaries and the direct election of federal judges
- the use of proportional representation, the initiative, referendum, and recall at all levels of government
- armed neutrality for foreign policy and restrictions on such foreign pressure groups as the Council on Foreign Relations, the Trilateral Commission, and the Bilderbergers from operating in the United States
- the withdrawal of the United States from the United Nations and removal of the United Nations from U.S. soil
- military and economic aid only to friendly nations
- a strong national defense, with arms control agreements contingent on appropriate on-site inspections

OPPOSED:
- forced busing and government interference with religious schools
- racial and cultural exploitation and argued against one race forcing another to subsidize it financially or politically
- forced segregation or integration
- a peacetime draft

POPULIST (CHRISTIAN POPULIST; PATRIOTIC) PARTY

VOTES FOR PRESIDENTIAL AND VICE-PRESIDENTIAL NOMINATION: RALPH FORBES OF ARKANSAS, WARREN FREIBERG OF ARKANSAS, HANSEN, PATTY, AND MARVIN SEAT OF KENTUCKY WERE NOMINATED FOR PRESIDENT. NOMINATIONS FOR VICE PRESIDENT WERE MADE BEFORE THE PRESIDENTIAL BALLOTING, WITH FORBES, PATTY, MAUREEN SALAMAN OF CALIFORNIA, AND PASTOR EVERETT SILEVEN OF NEBRASKA PLACED IN NOMINATION. SILEVEN AND SALAMAN DECLINED, HOWEVER, AND THE CONVENTION RECESSED. A NOMINATING COMMITTEE MET AND RECOMMENDED FORMER REPUBLICAN REPRESENTATIVE HANSEN FOR PRESIDENT AND PATTY FOR VICE PRESIDENT. HANSEN WAS UNANIMOUSLY NOMINATED. PATTY RECEIVED THE VICE-PRESIDENTIAL NOMINATION OVER RALPH FORBES, 30 VOTES TO 16. ON NOVEMBER 10, 1987, HANSEN DECLINED THE NOMINATION, AND THE TICKET WAS VACATED, PENDING A MEETING OF THE NATIONAL COMMITTEE IN MARCH. MEANWHILE, SPECULATION ON POTENTIAL CANDIDATES CENTERED ON DUKE, JUDGE JOHNSON OF ARKANSAS, EVAN MECHAM OF ARIZONA, AND REP. JAMES A. TRAFICANT OF OHIO.

NEARLY TWO HUNDRED DELEGATES ATTENDED THE MARCH 1988 MEETING OF THE NATIONAL COMMITTEE. TRAFICANT ADDRESSED THE GATHERING. DUKE AND GRITZ WERE NOMINATED FOR PRESIDENT AND VICE PRESIDENT, RESPECTIVELY. GRITZ LATER WITHDREW AS THE VICE-PRESIDENTIAL CANDIDATE, AND PARKER OF KENTUCKY WAS SUBSTITUTED.

ALSO:
- urged the U.S. government to reward its friends, not its enemies, all the while doubting that either major party would pursue this policy because "the mattoids need communism to scare the people into tolerating massive taxes and a huge war budget, à la George Orwell's *1984*"

David Duke had his own platform.

SUPPORTED:
- equal rights for all, including white people
- an end to forced integration and busing
- restrictions on immigration to preserve "our heritage"
- a real crime fighting program, including the right for people to protect themselves
- welfare, "yes"; rip-offs, "no"
- protection for U.S. jobs and industries
- tax reform
- the preservation of the family farm
- a "cleanup" of Wall Street
- the replacement of the Federal Reserve System with a national bank
- free enterprise, not monopoly capital
- a war on AIDS, including counterpressures on the "homosexual lobby"

- the election of all judges
- a strong national defense (with support for Star Wars and the manning of NATO exclusively by European soldiers)
- an adherence to the Monroe Doctrine
- an "America first" policy
- the lifting of sanctions against South Africa

PROHIBITION PARTY

CANDIDATE FOR PRESIDENT:
Earl Farwell Dodge (CO)

CANDIDATE FOR VICE PRESIDENT:
George Ormsby (PA)

30TH CONVENTION:
June 25–26, 1987, Heritage House, Springfield (IL)
Earl Farwell Dodge (CO), keynoter

PLATFORM HIGHLIGHTS:
The Prohibition Party's platform reaffirmed the party's commitment to the Constitution and its system of checks and balances.

SUPPORTED:
- protections for the nation against judicial usurpation of power
- free trade and limits on foreign aid
- a return to the gold standard
- a constitutional amendment to require a balanced budget, place limits on Congress's taxing and spending powers, reduce the national debt, and require the sale of all government-owned businesses in competition with the private sector
- the free enterprise system
- the elimination of excessive regulation on businesses, control of monopolies, and regulation of deceptive business practices
- the abolition of the Federal Reserve System and the withdrawal of the United States from the World Bank
- an enforcement of antitrust laws and laws forbidding strikes by federal government employees
- an end to government preference for union shops in awarding contracts
- right-to-work laws
- states' rights and condemned regional governments
- the adoption of a constitutional amendment to protect life from the moment of conception
- strict enforcement of laws against gambling, narcotics, pornography, and commercialized vice
- military preparedness, while applauding the concept of the all-volunteer military
- a reform of the welfare system to remove "undeserving persons" and promote self-sufficiency
- uniform marriage and divorce laws
- nondiscrimination against married people in tax policies and adoption of an explicit public policy against extending marriage benefits to unmarried couples

- the separation of church and state (and urged cancellation of diplomatic relations with the Vatican), but approved Bible reading and voluntary prayer in public schools or other institutions
- a repeal of the Social Security tax on religious institutions
- ballot law reforms to extend access to third parties
- a revision of the Social Security laws to make the program voluntary, to establish it on a sound actuarial basis, and to place Medicare and Medicaid in separate programs
- the abolition of governmental controls and subsidies for agriculture
- a ban on harmful drugs and efforts to curb tobacco use
- AIDS research and increased efforts to combat the immoral behavior responsible for AIDS
- long-term prison sentences for any conviction of a criminal act involving a firearm
- strict enforcement of the immigration laws and deportation of illegal aliens

OPPOSED:
- communism
- quota systems and sought reversal of the Bakke decision, which reaffirmed racial preference under affirmative action
- efforts to restrict religious broadcasting and religious schools
- socialized medicine and involuntary commitment to mental hospitals
- "unnatural" lifestyles

ALSO:
- blamed alcoholic beverages for a host of modern social problems and called for a program of publicity, education, legislation, and administration leading to prohibition of the manufacture, distribution, and sale of alcoholic beverages

---

PROHIBITION PARTY
VOTES FOR PRESIDENTIAL AND VICE-PRESIDENTIAL NOMINATION: DODGE AND ORMSBY WERE NOMINATED BY UNANIMOUS VOTE FOR THE OFFICES OF PRESIDENT AND VICE PRESIDENT, RESPECTIVELY.

P S PARTY
CANDIDATE FOR PRESIDENT:
Robert Earl Anderson (UT)

REPUBLICAN PARTY
CANDIDATE FOR PRESIDENT:
George Herbert Walker Bush

CANDIDATE FOR VICE PRESIDENT:
James Danforth Quayle

CANDIDATES FOR PRESIDENTIAL NOMINATION:
William Dean Allen, Jr. (TX)
Drew Morris Angel (CA)
Linda Streicher Bieniek (FL)
Patrick Joseph Buchanan (VA)
George Herbert Walker Bush (TX)
Paul Beecher Conley (NY)
Terrence Russell Connors (FL)
Frank Dehart (IA)
John Greene Denison (CA)
Robert Joseph Dole (KS)
Robert Drucker (FL)
Pierre Du Pont (DE)
Charles Ray Evans (DC)
Thomas Stanley Fabish (IL)
Benjamin Fernandez (CA)
Levi Martin Luther Gasking III (TX)
Michele Ann Gess (WI)
Alexander Meigs Haig, Jr. (VA)
Milton Louis Heller (FL)
Kathleen Rebecca Heslop (MS)
William Horrigan, Jr. (CT)
Maurice Horton (IL)
Roger Lee Huddleston (AR)
Dorothy Jean Hulst (MI)
James McAdory Humphreys (NV)
Richard Albert Jackson (DC)
Jessie Alvin Johnson (AR)
Thomas H. Kean (NJ)
Jack French Kemp (NY)
Jeane Kirkpatrick (MD)
Paul Dominique Laxalt (NV)
Michael Stephen Levinson (NY)
Donald Francis MacKay, Jr. (PA)
Isabell Masters (OK)
Mark Alan McDevitt (PA)
Eddie McDowell (GA)
Beatrice Elaine Johnson Mooney (MN)
Pasquale Philip Muccigrosso (NY)
Oliver L. North (VA)
Mark Arthur Oldenburg (IL)
Hubert David Patty (TN)
Mary Jane Rachner (MN)
Marion Gordon "Pat" Robertson (VA)
Michael Wade Rogers (CA)
Donald Edward "Bigfoot" Rouse (CA)
Benjamin Franklin Schoenfeld (CA)
David William Schwehr (WI)
Alice Feggins Sheppard (NY)
"Prince" Robert J. Smith (IL)
Harold Edward Stassen (MN)
Michael Alan Stern (FL)
John Rownald Taylor (IL)
Stephanie Diana Van Vliet (CA)
Roger E. "Catfish" Vogel (OH)
Gordon Held Wharton (TX)
Donald Rose Wright (AK)

PRIMARIES:

FEBRUARY 16, 1988 (NH):

Bush 59,290
Dole. 44,797
Kemp. 20,114
Du Pont. 15,885
Robertson 14,775
Haig 481
Stassen 130
others (including below) 2,153
Drucker . . . .
Horrigan. . . . .
Conley . . . .
Levinson . . . .
Rachner . . . .

FEBRUARY 23, 1988 (SD):

Dole. 51,529
Robertson 18,275
Bush 17,416
Kemp. 4,266
uncommitted delegates 1,220
others 575

MARCH 1, 1988 (VT):

Bush 23,565
Dole. 18,655
Robertson 2,452
Kemp. 1,877
Du Pont 808
Haig 324
others 153

MARCH 8, 1988 (AL):

Bush 87,421
Dole. 22,438
Robertson 19,426
Kemp. 6,296
Haig 301
Du Pont 291

MARCH 8, 1988 (AR):

Bush 21,323
Dole. 11,788
Robertson 7,740
Kemp. 1,931
Haig 301
Du Pont 220

MARCH 8, 1988 (FL):

Bush 391,963
Dole. 132,455
Robertson 73,184
Kemp. 30,240
Du Pont. 4,670
Haig. 3,848

MARCH 8, 1988 (GA):

Bush 172,820
Dole. 74,340

Robertson 53,635
Kemp. 19,712
Du Pont 1,422
Haig. 1,350

MARCH 8, 1988 (KY):

Bush 71,912
Dole. 27,833
Robertson 13,538
Kemp 4,040
Stassen 885
Haig 525
Du Pont 490
unpledged delegates 2,256

MARCH 8, 1988 (LA):

Bush 71,692
Robertson 22,747
Dole. 22,072
Kemp 6,357
Du Pont 899
Haig 548

MARCH 8, 1988 (MD):

Bush 86,770
Dole. 51,710
Kemp 9,787
Robertson 9,738
Du Pont 2,644
Haig. 1,808

MARCH 8, 1988 (MA):

Bush 93,722
Dole. 42,075
Kemp. 11,150
Robertson 7,540
Du Pont. 2,670
Haig. 1,668
no preference 2,383

MARCH 8, 1988 (MS):

Bush 86,976
Dole. 21,693
Robertson 17,144
Kemp 4,744
Haig 308

MARCH 8, 1988 (MO):

Bush 130,128
Dole. 131,367
Robertson 36,378
Kemp. 10,497
Du Pont 1,402
Haig 667
unpledged delegates 4,127

MARCH 8, 1988 (NC):

Bush 123,262
Dole. 109,255
Robertson 26,474
Kemp. 11,313

Du Pont 1,092
Haig 570
no preference 3,803

MARCH 8, 1988 (OK):
Bush 68,950
Dole. 65,278
Robertson 39,364
Kemp. 10,081
Du Pont 855
Haig 681
Masters. 513

MARCH 8, 1988 (RI):
Bush 10,245
Dole. 3,564
Robertson. 905
Kemp 767
Du Pont 83
Haig 48
unpledged delegates. 149

MARCH 8, 1988 (TN):
Bush 138,775
Dole. 50,311
Robertson 28,740
Kemp. 11,312
Haig 871
Du Pont 739
unpledged delegates 1,844

MARCH 8, 1988 (TX):
Bush 191,188
Robertson 48,531
Dole. 42,171
Kemp. 14,816
Du Pont. 1,346
Haig. 1,075
unpledged delegates 4,000

MARCH 8, 1988 (VA):
Bush 105,686
Dole. 49,692
Robertson 29,207
Kemp. 8,604
Du Pont 1,066
Haig 614
unpledged delegates 3,367

MARCH 15, 1988 (IL):
Bush 465,286
Dole. 308,107
Robertson 58,857
others 21,307

MARCH 20, 1988 (PR):
Bush 1,935
Dole. 48

MARCH 29, 1988 (CT):
Bush 72,867
Dole. 20,975

Robertson 3,410
Kemp. 3,360
uncommitted delegates 3,187

APRIL 5, 1988 (WI):
Bush 296,940
Dole. 28,148
Robertson 24,847
uncommitted delegates 2,337

APRIL 26, 1988 (PA):
Bush 687,799
Dole. 105,933
Robertson 79,752

MAY 3, 1988 (DC):
Bush 5,620
Dole 445
Robertson. 262

MAY 3, 1988 (IN):
Bush 350,632
Dole. 42,650
Robertson 28,967

MAY 3, 1988 (OH):
Bush 643,752
Dole. 99,226
Robertson 56,378

MAY 10, 1988 (NE):
Bush 137,229
Dole. 45,376
Robertson 10,273

MAY 10, 1988 (WV):
Bush 109,284
Robertson 10,539
others 2,523

MAY 17, 1988 (OR):
Bush 189,262
Dole. 47,505
Robertson 21,886

MAY 24, 1988 (ID):
Bush 55,464
Robertson 5,876
none of the above. 6,935

JUNE 7, 1988 (CA):
Bush. 1,856,273
Dole. 289,220
Robertson 94,779

JUNE 7, 1988 (MT):
Bush 62,863
others 23,044

JUNE 7, 1988 (NJ):
Bush 241,033
others 14,302

JUNE 7, 1988 (NM):
Bush 68,454
others 19,691

JUNE 14, 1988 (ND):

Bush 36,572
Rachner 2,388

34TH CONVENTION:

August 15–18, 1988, Superdome, New Orleans (LA)
Robert Henry Michel (IL), permanent chairman
Thomas H. Kean (NJ), keynoter

Attending this convention were 2,277 delegates and 2,277 alternates.

PLATFORM HIGHLIGHTS:

The Republican platform was a lengthy document of 103 pages outlining "An American Vision: For Our Children and Our Future." It reaffirmed the theme of the 1984 platform that "freedom works." The Republicans claimed that, under their leadership, the nation led the world—confident of its abilities, proud of its products, sure of its future, and renowned as a pacesetter for all mankind. Their argument, which carried through the entire platform, was based on free enterprise, free markets, and limited government. It was upbeat and embodied a "can-do" attitude, emphasizing the creation of jobs and opportunities.

SUPPORTED:

- incentives for educating, training, and retraining workers through programs such as the Job Training Partnership Act
- a youth training wage (i.e., a sub-minimum wage during training)
- a continuation of the earned income tax credit
- welfare reform to encourage work
- a reform of unemployment insurance
- the elimination of the ban against employment based in the home
- an end to the Social Security earnings limitation
- the creation of enterprise zones
- a 15 percent cut in the capital gains tax
- a reinvigoration of minority business development
- reasonable state and federal product liability standards
- a return to fault-based standards in the civil justice system and an end to frivolous litigation
- tort reform at the state level
- the deductibility of individual retirement account contributions
- punishment for financial manipulators who violate the public trust
- a taxpayers' bill of rights in disputes with government
- the Federal Reserve System's adoption of policies that would achieve long-run price stability
- the federal government returning power to the states
- an elimination of regulations, statutes, and judicial decisions that were unnecessary barriers to productive investment

- the "contracting out" to the private sector of a wide range of federal government activities
- efforts to "defederalize, denationalize, and decentralize government monopolies" and to privatize government assets such as public housing
- the homeowner's mortgage interest deduction
- lower interest rates
- lower property taxes
- urban and rural homesteading by low-income families
- cooperative ventures in construction and rehabilitation
- the FHA mortgage insurance program, Veterans Administration (VA) guarantee program, and Government National Mortgage Association program
- efforts to maintain the strength of savings institutions
- incentives for the private sector to turn foreclosed housing into housing opportunities for low- and moderate-income citizens
- a repeal of rent controls
- resident ownership of public housing units
- the use of housing vouchers
- the creation of a housing block grant program
- open housing
- the return of both the House and Senate to Republican control
- a two-year budget cycle, a supermajority requirement for raising taxes, a legislatively enacted line-item veto, individual transmission of spending bills, and greater rescission authority for the president
- a flexible freeze on current government spending
- the Grace Commission report and a constitutional amendment to require a balanced federal budget
- the use of "all constitutional authority" to control congressional spending
- the General Agreement on Tariffs and Trade but promised to use "free trade," including bilateral agreements, as a weapon against "unfair trade"
- administration efforts to improve the coordination of economic policies among industrialized nations
- the use of U.S. economic aid to promote free market reforms abroad, including "debt-for-equity" swaps
- calls for keeping the family at the center of public policy and establishing a toddler tax credit for preschool children
- an end to discrimination against single-wage-earner families and the erosion of the tax exemption for dependents
- a repeal of the Social Security earnings limitation
- efforts to encourage states to promote child care programs that allow teenage mothers to remain in school
- in-home care
- voluntary child care assistance provided by employers
- other programs to help families with children, including an easier adoption process
- rigorous enforcement of "community standards" against pornography and prohibition on the sale of sexually explicit materials on federal property

- reduced government control of health care while promoting innovation, reform of medical malpractice laws, and hospices
- the private sector's expansion of home health care
- private health insurance policies for acute or long-term care and convertibility of personal funds to pay for long-term care
- employee choice in selecting health plans
- efforts to "work toward" catastrophic health care coverage for children and alternative forms of group health care that foster competition
- special consideration and relief for rural hospitals and health care providers
- continued generous funding for the National Institutes of Health
- state pilot programs to increase the access of low-income persons to health insurance
- wellness promotion
- the acceleration of the FDA's certification of alternatives to animal testing for product safety and efficacy
- the continued provision of experimental drugs to prolong the lives of AIDS victims
- a reform of blood donor laws
- abstinence from drug abuse and sexual activity outside of marriage
- a targeting of federal health programs to help mothers and infants and expressed special concern about fetal alcohol syndrome
- the protection of the fetus in both the workplace and in scientific research
- a human life (i.e., antiabortion) amendment to the Constitution
- the protections of Fourteenth Amendment (citizenship rights) applied to unborn children
- the appointment of federal and state judges who hold a pro-family, pro-life perspective
- a parental consent requirement for minors to receive contraceptives
- the Adolescent Family Life program, which taught sexual abstinence
- efforts to make the entertainment and communications industries more responsible in addressing the youth market
- the development of a model divorce reform law
- improved safety in federally assisted homeless shelters
- greater efforts to provide education for homeless children
- expanded community development block grants
- a recitation of the Pledge of Allegiance in schools
- a vigorous enforcement of antidiscrimination statutes
- a resistance to preferential treatment and discriminatory quota systems
- the rights of students to engage in voluntary prayer in schools
- reductions in the amount of land held by the federal government, particularly in the western states, and de-

clared water rights to be a state issue, not a federal concern
- a removal of the remaining obstacles to equal rights for women but opposed "comparable worth" legislation
- efforts to have more women political candidates at all levels
- the removal of architectural, transportation, communications, and attitudinal barriers for disabled citizens, including full access to the polls, an attack on discrimination in health care, and strong enforcement of statutory prohibitions against discrimination
- the right of individuals with disabilities to participate in the decisions affecting their lives, whether in education or employment
- community-based care under a reformed Medicaid system
- self-determination for American Indian tribes and improvements in the environmental conditions on reservations
- increased participation in federal programs by Native Americans and the preservation of Native Hawaiians' culture
- the right to keep and bear arms but also stiff mandatory penalties for any conviction of a crime committed with a gun
- collective bargaining, state "right-to-work" statutes, and efforts to amend the Hobbs Act to apply it to union officials
- the right to vote in national elections for U.S. citizens in American Samoa, Guam, the Northern Marianas, Puerto Rico, and the Virgin Islands
- statehood for Puerto Rico, if approved by the residents, and the right of Guamanian residents to adopt commonwealth status
- immigration and refugee resettlement as problems for which all democratic nations shared responsibility
- states' rights, along with judicial restraint and statutory limitations on the jurisdiction of federal courts
- an extension of the independent counsel law, civil rights statutes, and health and safety legislation to Congress
- legal protections for congressional "whistle-blowers"
- a constitutional amendment to limit the terms of members of Congress
- home education and educational choice and competition
- family empowerment
- rewards for excellence in learning, teaching, and administration
- prohibitions against public schools providing birth control or information on abortion services or referrals
- efforts to reduce the high school dropout rate
- federal assistance for students at special risk, especially those with physical disabilities
- efforts to encourage talented students
- calls for states to consider the use of educational

- vouchers, performance testing, merit pay, career ladders, volunteerism, and expansions in curricula, particularly in languages and geography
- a campaign against illiteracy, magnet schools, and kindergarten and prekindergarten programs
- Head Start, models of excellence, methods of evaluating teachers, and the development of public-private partnerships in education
- tuition tax credits to assist parents with children in private educational institutions
- federal efforts in higher education focused on low-income students, student loan defaults, the need for greater fiscal responsibility, the creation of a College Savings Bond program, and the preservation of freedom of speech
- stipulations that federal aid to colleges and universities be dependent on maintaining safe and drug-free campuses
- educational benefits for veterans
- vocational-technical education
- prison education
- the Worker Adjustment Program for dislocated workers
- the deductibility of private donations for the arts and humanities, the National Endowments for the Arts and Humanities, and the Institute of Museum Services, while promising to guard against misuse of government grants for the arts
- retooling of science and engineering laboratories at colleges and universities
- the Super Collider project
- tax incentives for private sector engagement in advanced research
- scientific exchanges between government and business
- calls for treating technology flow as part of U.S. trade negotiations
- the strengthening of the Office of the President's Science Adviser and the addition of a Science Advisory Council
- the use of enhanced translation services to expedite the transfer of scientific knowledge from abroad
- greater protection for intellectual property, including allowing private ownership of research products developed under federal sponsorship
- biotechnology
- a stable and secure space environment for all people (including achievement of a manned space station in orbit during the 1990s)
- the development of an antisatellite (ASAT) capability
- a space "comeback" with support for a space station and the National Aerospace Plane
- Project Pathfinder, a replacement shuttle, and the development of alternate launch vehicles
- the Mission to Planet Earth project to advance understanding of earth's environmental and climatic forces and a manned flight to Mars for the year 2000
- an expansion of the private sector's role in space, particularly in the launch of commercial satellites

- the protection of victims' rights
- the reestablishment of the federal death penalty
- a reform of the exclusionary rule and "cumbersome" habeas corpus procedures
- efforts to enact preventive detention laws in the states
- a "drug-free America" and strict accountability for both users and sellers
- the death penalty for major drug traffickers and stiff penalties for drug users
- drug-free workplace requirements for federal contractors and grantees
- the evictions of drug dealers from public housing
- interdiction, seizure, and forfeiture along with efforts to encourage foreign governments to eradicate drug crops
- drug education in the schools along with improved availability of drug rehabilitation and treatment
- income assistance for those who cannot work and work and education as essential components of welfare reform
- the enforcement and strengthening of parental responsibility laws
- welfare programs administered at the state and local levels, permitting pilot programs to encourage reform
- a condemnation of welfare fraud
- calls for giving special attention to urban residents in the national census and waiving the Davis-Bacon Act's wage requirements in cities with severe deterioration of the public infrastructure
- drought relief for farmers and ranchers
- promises to never use food as a weapon against foreign nations
- agricultural trade abroad and an insistence that the European Economic Community phase out its farm subsidies simultaneously with the United States to ensure fair trade between the United States and Europe
- calls for making "free and fair trade" a standard agenda item on every international conference table attended by U.S. delegates
- the Food for Peace program
- continued improvements in the quality standards for grain and other agricultural products
- greater planning flexibility in federal programs
- state supremacy in water laws
- calls for states to review the adequacy of crop irrigation capacity under severe water shortage conditions
- a multiple-use policy on federal lands and forests, including a sustained yield and sound environmental management
- the states assuming farm home exemption and redemption rights
- the creation of rural enterprise zones and assurances that rural communities world receive their fair share of federal assistance
- rural electrification and telephone programs, health care, job training, housing, homesteading, and business and industrial opportunities

- energy self-sufficiency through private initiatives, with a boost from the repeal of the windfall profits tax and the continued filling of the Strategic Petroleum Reserve
- tax incentives and other strategies to promote the exploration and development of oil, natural gas, coal, and new energy resources, including repeal of the Transfer Rule, exploitation of the Arctic, decontrol of prices, flexible use of natural gas to fuel autos and boilers, development of clean coal technologies, and encouragement for coal exports
- research and development in alternative fuels, energy efficiency, conservation, renewables, fusion, and superconductivity, along with improvements in the "national electricity transportation network" and streamlining of the Department of Energy
- further reductions in air and water pollution, particularly against the threat posed by acid rain
- renewed efforts to minimize the release of toxins into the environment, to fight coastal erosion, and to protect the nation's beaches, coral reefs, bodies of water, wetlands, and estuaries
- continued improvement of national parks and wildlife areas
- a public-private partnership to restore declining waterfowl populations
- further protections of endangered species, including efforts to sustain biological diversity
- a revitalization of the environment through scenic easements and the preservation of farmland and open spaces
- restrictions on transfers of public lands in a manner consistent with Reagan-Bush policies
- practices to minimize erosion
- the preservation of architectural, archaeological, and maritime resources
- the cleanup of hazardous waste sites
- resource recovery and recycling
- an end to dumping, including the dumping of medical and hospital waste, in coastal and international waters and other inappropriate places
- the protection of groundwater
- the government's adoption of environmental standards meeting or exceeding those required in the private sector
- the recognition of such problems as the ozone layer's depletion, ocean dumping, climatic change, destruction of tropical forest areas, and earthquakes as environmental concerns deserving international attention
- calls to combine the National Oceanic and Atmospheric Administration with the Environmental Protection Agency
- drug and alcohol testing for persons employed in safety-related positions in the transportation arena
- greater local autonomy in decision making concerning the Highway Trust Fund and the Airport and Airway

Trust Fund (although opposed to diversion of these funds to other than their stated purposes)
- continued growth in the travel and tourism industries
- the timely completion of the National Airspace System plan
- full and fair access to international route authorities for U.S. air carriers
- the development of high-speed rail systems
- reductions in public subsidies for Amtrak
- the contracting out of commuter bus and transit systems for state and local transportation
- the abandonment of the Corporate Average Fuel Economy standards
- an end to foreign protectionism inhibiting U.S.-flagged vessels
- an upgraded U.S. domestic shipbuilding capacity and a stronger merchant marine and Coast Guard
- the Monroe Doctrine and the nation's special relationships with Canada and Mexico
- the governments of Costa Rica, El Salvador, Guatemala, and Honduras and urged U.S. leadership in promoting free market principles throughout Central American and the Southern Hemisphere
- calls for Latin America to "band together to defeat the drug trade"
- efforts to bring international "narco-terrorists" to justice within their own countries or in the U.S. courts
- a greater use of the armed forces in the war on drugs, along with swift extradition of traffickers and more reliance on herbicides to destroy drug crops abroad
- Radio Marti and the creation of a television equivalent
- continued U.S. access to the Panama Canal
- demands for proof of the Soviets' respect for human and religious rights, economic reforms, verifiable compliance with arms control agreements, free emigration, and other changes before believing in the arrival of a new "reality" in Soviet-U.S. relations
- Radio Free Europe, Radio Liberty, and "advanced technologies" like direct broadcast satellites and videotape to articulate U.S. values throughout the world
- NATO and the view that all NATO members should bear "their fair share" of the defense burden
- promises to consult with NATO allies about stopping the proliferation of ballistic missiles, while continuing support for SDI
- peace and justice in Cyprus and Northern Ireland as important to NATO solidarity
- the elimination of trade barriers with Japan as a means of strengthening the U.S.-Japanese relationship
- U.S. mutual defense alliances with the Philippines and the Republic of Korea, along with the commitment to the security of Taiwan
- a closer relationship with the People's Republic of China, while encouraging the Chinese to adopt more free market reforms and to ease political repression
- an end to the Soviets' occupation in Afghanistan and

pledged assistance to the opposition forces, calling for self-determination and the establishment of a representative Afghan government

- continued U.S. friendship with Australia, Pakistan, and Thailand
- pledges of assistance in the refugee problem, especially that related to Amerasian children
- the special relationship with and commitments to Israel
- a demand for the United Nations's recision of Resolution 3379 (equating Zionism with racism) and for the recognition of Jerusalem's role as an undivided city open to people of all faiths
- U.S.-Arab relations, especially those with Egypt and "pro-Western" states, and the territorial integrity of Lebanon
- an end to Marxist imperialism and the development of democracies in Africa, while ensuring humanitarian assistance when necessary (as in the Ethiopian famine)
- Angolan "freedom fighters" while opposing the Communists' influence in Mozambique
- calls for not punishing "innocent black South Africans for the policies of the apartheid government" but did not explicitly state a position on the international boycott
- the Child Survival Program
- preemptive antiterrorist measures involving allied and international cooperation and the creation of a multinational strike force to deal with "narco-terrorists"
- reforms within the State Department to make U.S. diplomatic corps more responsive "to a complex and changing world"
- corrections, through negotiations and force improvements, of an imbalance between U.S. and Soviet conventional forces
- the need to rely on nuclear weapons as the major source of deterrence, while hailing SDI, Civil Defense, and the Ground Wave Emergency Network
- advances in "smart" conventional weapons, modernization of chemical and biological weapons, mutuality in arms reductions, and effective verification of treaty obligations
- superiority on the seas, with calls for fifteen new aircraft carrier battle groups and other enhancements of the nation's naval forces
- defense research and technological development, including initiatives in microminiaturization and superconductivity
- increased efforts to prevent technology transfer to the Soviet Union
- attention to the problems in defense acquisition addressed by the Packard Commission, especially the need to end "revolving door" profiteering
- promises to the nation's military personnel (including the National Guard and Reserves) of "fairness in pay and benefits" and pledges to veterans (especially elderly veterans) of protected health care, education, preferential employment, and housing rights
- special programs for Vietnam War veterans to assist in their readjustment to civilian life
- disabled veterans and those suffering from post-traumatic stress syndrome
- U.S. intelligence and counterintelligence efforts, explicitly endorsing covert activity, the creation of a single joint congressional oversight committee, and the enactment of a law making it a felony for anyone (even a member of Congress) to disclose classified information

OPPOSED:

- any tax increase and a value-added tax
- tax withholdings on savings
- government-mandated professional practice fees
- the earnings test for Social Security recipients
- racism, anti-Semitism, and religious intolerance
- U.S. funding for any foreign or international organizations involved in abortion
- the use of public funds for abortions
- the taxation of churches and religious schools
- the use of compulsory union dues or fees for partisan purposes and wanted to protect workers who choose to work during strikes against labor violence
- public funding of political campaigns
- gerrymandering
- prison furloughs
- the legalization or decriminalization of drug use
- the Democratic Congress for its interference with the president's foreign policy prerogatives
- Daniel Ortega's regime in Nicaragua and applauded the opposition Contras
- the normalization of diplomatic relations with Cuba
- the Vietnamese occupation of Laos and Cambodia and demanded a full accounting of U.S. servicemen MIAs or POWs in Vietnam
- the creation of a Palestinian state
- the Palestinian Liberation Organization (based on its refusal to recognize Israel's right to exist)
- South Africa's apartheid as "morally repugnant," but the platform desired an "effective and coordinated policy" to promote equal rights and a peaceful transition to a truly representative government

---

REPUBLICAN PARTY

VOTE FOR PRESIDENTIAL NOMINATION: BUSH WAS UNANIMOUSLY NOMINATED FOR PRESIDENT.

VOTE FOR VICE-PRESIDENTIAL NOMINATION: QUAYLE WAS NOMINATED FOR VICE PRESIDENT BY ACCLAMATION.

- Libyan terrorism and demanded the release of all U.S. citizens held captive by terrorists anywhere in the world
- a "nuclear freeze"

REVOLUTIONARY COMMUNIST PARTY

CANDIDATE FOR PRESIDENT:
Carl Dix (IL)

The Revolutionary Communist Party ran Dix as an "anticandidate" for president to demonstrate the party's scorn for the electoral process. It claimed, "The right to vote has been won. . . . Now we need the political awareness and sophistication not to use it." The party predicted revolution and urged its followers to join and build the Revolutionary Communist Party as the vanguard of the coming conflict.

RIGHT TO LIFE PARTY

CANDIDATE FOR PRESIDENT:
William Anthony Marra (NJ)

CANDIDATE FOR VICE PRESIDENT:
Joan Andrews (DE)

SOCIALIST (LIBERTY UNION) PARTY

CANDIDATE FOR PRESIDENT:
Willa Kenoyer

CANDIDATE FOR VICE PRESIDENT:
Ron Ehrenreich (NY)

CANDIDATES FOR PRESIDENTIAL NOMINATION:
Willa Kenoyer (MI)
Herbert George Lewin (CA)

PRIMARY:
MARCH 1, 1988 (VT):

Kenoyer	193
Lewin	66
others	26

CONVENTION:
May 23–25, 1987, United Church of Rogers Park, Chicago (IL)
Maggie Feigin, temporary chairperson
Diane Drufenbrock (WI), Ron Ehrenreich (NY), Linda Randolph, Linda Nelson, Stacey Blatt, session chairs

Thirty-five delegates from eight states attended this convention.

PLATFORM HIGHLIGHTS:
SUPPORTED:
- the ratification of the UN Declaration of Human Rights
- an increase in the Aid to Dependent Children and Aid to Families with Dependent Children programs

- municipal ownership of utilities
- no cutoff of utilities to poor people for nonpayment
- a massive program of nonprofit housing, including limited equity cooperatives and neighborhood housing corporations
- the creation of state and cooperative banks for public and pension fund investment in housing
- an emphasis on prevention in health care and an end to profit-making health care corporations
- the creation of health and safety committees in the workplace
- the socialization of medicine, with free and equal access to medical and dental care for all
- the creation of a community-controlled National Health Service
- the passage of the Dellums Health Act
- protection for the right to choose birth alternatives
- patient information rights
- an end to discrimination against people with AIDS and a concerted public health effort to eliminate AIDS
- community-based care for the elderly, developmentally disabled, physically disabled, and persons with mental illness
- a restructuring of the mental health care industry to end reliance on electroshock therapy, drugs, and lobotomies
- "the highest quality professional care for the body and mind as a fundamental right"
- the equitable distribution of educational funds
- appropriate teacher compensation
- functional improvements and integration of schools to end racism, sexism, and class distinctions
- the public ownership of large databases
- the development of alternative and open education opportunities
- the Bill of Rights
- the abolition of the CIA and greater public control over the FBI
- equitable land distribution
- affirmative action
- a repeal of the Simpson-Rodino Act, amnesty for undocumented workers, and the right of undocumented people to unionize
- the abolition of the Immigration and Naturalization Service
- the ERA, massive expansion of day care, Social Security coverage for domestic homemakers, and maternity and paternity leave policies
- free access to contraceptives and abortions for all individuals, including minors, with comprehensive health care provided within the school system
- a ban on involuntary sterilization
- violence-free lives and disapproved of war toys
- a repeal of all sodomy laws and antigay immigration restrictions
- a federal lesbian and gay rights law that would grant

full parental rights (including the right to provide foster care); equal treatment in housing, employment, and social services; and full spousal rights to lesbian and gay couples

- the development of free day care centers from infants through latchkey children
- the rights of young people to be free from abuse at home and exploitation in employment
- an end to discrimination in employment, credit, and housing against seniors
- an expansion of home services and hospice care for older people
- eventual abolishment of prisons
- the demilitarization of police and private security agencies and efforts to subject them to community control
- an end to police crimes against the working class and minority peoples
- the abolition of capital punishment
- an end to victimless crimes
- treatment, rather than punishment, for substance abuse
- the release of political prisoners
- an equally active prosecution of white-collar crimes as that for working-class infractions
- free court services
- an expansion of community-release programs
- an encouragement of neighborhood watch groups
- an emphasis on protections for prisoners against physical abuse and on rehabilitation
- the registration of handguns
- the families of prisoners by treating them with dignity and assisting in their efforts to maintain constructive family ties (including conjugal visits)
- expanded shelters for battered women and children, homeless people, rape victims, and runaways
- treatment instead of punishment for both the victim and the perpetrator of abusive behaviors
- asylum for political and economic refugees
- increased funds for the arts
- unconditional amnesty for all draft resisters and military deserters
- increased benefits and adequate care for veterans
- worker control of all industry through democratic organization of the workplace (e.g., election of supervisors)
- the democratization of unions
- a repeal of the Hatch Act, "right-to-work" laws, and the Taft-Hartley Act
- a thirty-hour work week
- the organization of the "unorganized"—students, housewives, homeless people, part-time workers, prison inmates, the unemployed, and military personnel
- increases in the minimum wage indexed to the cost of living
- a guaranteed right to a job or a livable income
- a punitive tax on runaway industry (i.e., those that go overseas for cheap labor) and restrictions on plant closures
- freedom of information legislation relating to plant safety, hazardous wastes, toxic substances, and the quality of goods and services
- the formation of small business cooperatives to strengthen self-employed workers and small firms
- environmental measures to protect the air, water, soil, and wilderness, along with recycling, a tax on agricultural chemicals, the promotion of corporate responsibility, enactment of a bottle deposit law, and reforestation
- restrictions on billboard advertising
- limits on road building to existing rights-of-way
- a ban on recombinant DNA technology
- the promotion of public funding for neighborhood mutual aid societies as a means of "rehumanizing" the cities
- a decentralized energy industry promoting alternative energy resources (i.e., solar, wind, grain alcohol), municipal control of energy plants, expanded mass transit services and reduced dependence on automobiles, limitations on sulfur emissions from coal burning, decommissioning of nuclear plants, and local declarations of communities as "nuclear-free zones" in the United States and around the world
- a prohibition on corporate farming, thus favoring family farming
- land use planning and limitations on speculation on agricultural lands
- low-cost credits, grants, and technical aid to family farms and agricultural worker cooperatives
- the provision of low-interest loans for ecologically sound, crop-related farm improvements
- cooperatives
- the replacement of nonessential crops with staples
- the organization of farmers and farm workers
- negotiations with canneries
- the purchase of unused meatpacking plants by states or workers to combat monopolization of the industry
- full parity in prices
- a moratorium on farm foreclosures
- the enactment of the Harkins Farm Bill
- rights for farm workers
- efforts to redirect agricultural research away from research that benefits agribusiness in favor of family farms and consumers
- a ban on animal experimentation and the abolition of factory meat farming techniques
- a reestablishment of the "social safety net," protecting workers' pension benefits
- a planned full-employment economy
- social ownership of banks and financial institutions under democratic control
- the international organization of labor
- the cancellation of the debts of developing countries
- progressivity in income taxes
- the closure of tax loopholes

- a cut in the military budget
- tax relief for renters
- a restructuring of the inheritance tax
- the dismantling of Star Wars and the country's first-strike capability
- the destruction of nerve gas and stockpiles of chemical and biological weapons
- unilateral disarmament
- the abidance of treaties with Native American nations
- stronger enforcement of laws against corporations that "dump" dangerous and banned products on markets in developing countries
- the United Nations and the World Court
- the abolition of the National Security Agency
- an end to U.S. military involvement in Central America, including Nicaragua
- the breaking of U.S. relations with South Africa and its "proxy" armies in Angola and Mozambique
- an end to the bombing of civilian populations in such places as El Salvador, Grenada, and Libya
- the recognition of Cuba and Vietnam
- the dismantling of NATO and the Warsaw Pact
- peace negotiations between Israel and the Palestinian Liberation Organization
- self-determination for both Israelis and Palestinians but wanted Israel to withdraw from the occupied territories and make Jerusalem an international city
- an arms embargo in the Middle East and an end to the foreign military presence in the Persian Gulf
- the right of self-defense and the principle of nonviolence in international conflict resolution
- the withdrawal of all nations' troops outside their borders and an end to the support of military dictators abroad
- the provision of 1 percent of the U.S. gross national product to the United Nations to aid underdeveloped countries
- the right of self-determination for Puerto Rico

OPPOSED:
- antiterrorist measures and legislation to restrict dissent
- the privatization of the National Technical Information Service
- racial division
- efforts to make English the official language of the United States
- behavior modification units in prisons and the privatization of prisons
- conscription
- a national sales tax
- foreign interference in Lebanon's internal affairs

ALSO:
- claimed that the Nuremburg principle (i.e., setting standards for crimes against humanity) compelled all individuals to work for peace and "to think globally and act locally for disarmament and against intervention"

SOCIALIST (LIBERTY UNION) PARTY

VOTE FOR PRESIDENTIAL NOMINATION: KENOYER WAS NOMINATED FOR PRESIDENT BY ACCLAMATION.

VOTE FOR VICE-PRESIDENTIAL NOMINATION: EHRENREICH WAS NOMINATED FOR VICE PRESIDENT BY ACCLAMATION.

SOCIALIST WORKERS PARTY

CANDIDATE FOR PRESIDENT:
James Mac Warren (NJ)

CANDIDATE FOR VICE PRESIDENT:
Kathleen Mickells (WV)

The Socialist Workers Party favored Trotskyite socialism, equal rights for women and minorities, and a progressive domestic agenda. It condemned militarism and imperialism. Finally, the party supported black rule in South Africa and Third World liberation movements in general.

SURPRISE PARTY

CANDIDATE FOR PRESIDENT:
Robert L. "Uncle Torvald" Johnson (SD)

Asking voters to "put a Norwegian in the White House," Johnson asserted, "The future ain't what it used to be." He claimed that "any fool can be President. Elect me and I'll prove it." He noted the voters could do worse and usually have.

THIRD PARTY

CANDIDATE FOR PRESIDENT:
Eugene Arthur Hem (WI)

THIRD WORLD ASSEMBLY

CANDIDATE FOR PRESIDENT:
John Governor Martin (DC)

CANDIDATE FOR VICE PRESIDENT:
Cleveland B. Sparrow, Sr. (DC)

The Third World Assembly was formed on January 28, 1979, in Washington, D.C., with forty charter members. Its national convenor was Rogers Gueory. The party was focused on the plight of the country's domestic poor, comparing this segment of the U.S. population to that of Third World countries.

PLATFORM HIGHLIGHTS:
SUPPORTED:
- calls for actively involving Third World people in the local, national, and international political process, including the promotion of candidates and working with the referendum and recall procedures
- a two-pronged attack on economic deprivation, using

an overall census formula for some things and a targeted Third World formula for others

- the fostering of Third World businesses and controls on inflation
- educational reforms to bring schools into the modern age, with the curricula stressing morals, etiquette, achievement, and discipline
- affordable housing, rent control, and full employment
- the promotion of the arts through television and the cinema
- the enhancement of health status for all Americans, along with a 75 percent decrease in the costs of health care
- a Third World Assembly government based on screening and discipline of membership, negotiations, and training
- promises to assist in the resolution of Third World problems and to participate in Third World international conferences
- pledges to guard against satanic influences and to promote brotherhood actively, emphasizing the "liberating theology of Jesus Christ"
- assertions that the party would "uncover and expose the criminal element of laws in education, employment, housing, land development, and distribution" and sought freedom for all "political prisoners"
- family life and youth participation in civic affairs
- the protection of full civil rights for everyone's enjoyment
- adult concerns addressed by age-appropriate categories (e.g., age restrictions on drinking, smoking, access to sexually explicit materials)
- the promotion of public transportation

TRUTH AND FREEDOM PARTY, U.S.A.

CANDIDATE FOR PRESIDENT:
Nick C. Kratsas (OH)

CANDIDATE FOR VICE PRESIDENT:
Judith Hicks Valerio (OH)

WORKERS LEAGUE

CANDIDATE FOR PRESIDENT:
Ed Winn (NY)

CANDIDATE FOR VICE PRESIDENT:
Barry Porster (MI)

PLATFORM HIGHLIGHTS:

The Workers League platform called on all workers, the unemployed, and young people to support its candidates. It ascribed all of the miseries of modern society to capitalism and frankly asserted that "the program of the Workers League is aimed not at reforming the bankrupt profit system, but at its overthrow." The League outlined three fundamental tasks: (1) forging international unity among workers, (2) building an independent labor party, and (3) implementing a Socialist program to abolish the profit system. After a lengthy Marxist analysis of world and domestic events—including references to the evils of multinational corporations and imperialism, unemployment, and homelessness—the platform declared that workers must unite to meet the crisis, reform the nation's unions, and build a Labor Party.

SUPPORTED:

- the nationalization without compensation of basic industries, utilities, closed factories, transportation systems, and the banks—all of which were to be placed under democratic worker control
- a thirty-hour work week at forty hours' pay, with existing work to be divided equally among all in need of work
- a massive public works program as a way of putting millions to work on new housing, hospitals, schools, and transportation facilities
- the immediate restoration of all social benefits lost by workers as a result of layoffs, increases in unemployment benefits, and union coverage for all unemployed workers
- automatic cost-of-living increases in wages and an end to wage discrimination against female employees and minority workers
- free medical care
- expanded training programs for physicians
- a nationalization of hospitals, drug companies, and nursing home chains
- massive increases in funding for education for the elimination of illiteracy, construction of new schools, higher teacher salaries, free higher education, and equalization of resources between school districts
- Social Security payments to guarantee an annual minimum income of $25,000 for retired workers
- pensions protected by federal insurance
- free day care for all working-class families
- the repudiation of the interest paid to bankers on the annual national debt
- a condemnation of all forms of union busting and threatened to nationalize any company that engaged in antilabor practices
- a repeal of the Taft-Hartley, Landrum-Griffin, Taylor, and "right-to-work" laws
- the abolition of the National Labor Relations Board
- prohibitions against the hiring of scabs and corporate "gun-thugs" and promises to rehire the PATCO workers (i.e., the air traffic controllers fired by Reagan) and to free the "framed-up Kentucky coal miners"
- the formation of elected factory committees and workers' defense committees to protect the working class
- such programs for youth as an education system controlled by unions and students, special job training programs, unemployment benefits for youth who cannot

find jobs after finishing school, a minimum wage of $6.00 per hour, full union rights, six weeks' paid vacation, and a public works program to build modern recreation centers in working-class neighborhoods
- a massive housing program, nationalization of real estate monopolies, rent reductions, seizure of vacant housing so that it can be used as emergency shelter for the homeless, and an end to evictions for nonpayment of rent
- the freeing of all political prisoners
- the abolition of the death penalty
- an end to racial, sexual, and sexual preference discrimination in employment, housing, and education
- full rights for Native Americans and the renegotiation of treaties on terms more favorable to their interests
- the protection of the right to abortion on demand
- immigration reform and the abolition of the Immigration and Naturalization Service and Border Patrol
- full legal rights and employment opportunities for undocumented workers
- a ban on discrimination against workers based on language or country of birth
- voluntary English-language instruction through full state subsidies to compensate workers for lost wages
- relief to farmers and small businesses through debt cancellation and easier credit arrangements
- the abolition of the Pentagon, CIA, and other militaristic agencies
- the withdrawal of U.S. troops from abroad
- the nationalization of the military-industrial complex and putting it under worker control
- the cancellation of foreign debts
- the establishment of a Socialist foreign policy
- Palestinians and the repudiation of diplomatic relations with Israel
- an end to the white South African government
- a reunification of Ireland
- independence for Puerto Rico and freedom for all Puerto Rican nationalists held as political prisoners
- Socialist nations under Soviet and Chinese influence, while asserting a need for them to overthrow their "parasitic Stalinist bureaucracies"
- a denouncement of the "fraudulent" campaigns of the Rainbow Coalition, the Communist Party, and the Socialist Workers Party

WORKERS WORLD PARTY

CANDIDATE FOR PRESIDENT:
Larry Holmes (NY)

CANDIDATES FOR VICE PRESIDENT:
Gloria La Riva (CA)
Naomi Cohen (NY)

The candidates of the Workers World Party were announced on September 10, 1987.

PLATFORM HIGHLIGHTS:
SUPPORTED:
- increases in Social Security benefits, unemployment compensation, disability pay, and welfare payments
- the provision of six months of paid maternity and paternity leave
- an end to layoffs and plant or office shutdowns
- the mandatory rehiring of laid-off workers
- pension fund guarantees
- prenotification requirements for factory closures
- promises to ban unsafe and abusive working conditions, to end racist or sexist harassment on the job, and to eliminate union-busting activities
- a rollback of rents and mortgage interest rates
- a prohibition against evictions and foreclosures
- "real homes, not shelters" for the homeless
- strong affirmative action programs and full equality and representation in employment, jobs, housing, education, politics, and other spheres of life for African Americans, Hispanic Americans, Asians, Native (i.e., indigenous) and Arab peoples, and women
- assurances to oppressed peoples of their rights of self-determination, the use of their own languages, and the unrestricted practice of their culture
- the rights of undocumented workers and a halt to deportations
- equal pay for equal work for women
- an end to the oppression of lesbians and gays, young people, the elderly, and disabled persons
- easy access for the disabled to all public facilities
- the abolition of the death penalty and preventive detention
- human rights
- free and accessible college, technical, and professional education for all
- the construction of more schools, libraries, and day care centers
- incentives for more people to become teachers
- free, quality health care for everyone, from the cradle to the grave
- protection for the reproductive rights of women, including access to birth control and abortion
- an end to forced sterilization
- an immediate provision of free and nutritious food for the hungry
- declaring AIDS a major public health crisis but opposed mandatory testing or quarantines
- the use of Star Wars money to fund a full-scale research program to find a cure and provide treatment for AIDS
- a diversion of the "Pentagon budget" to projects to protect the environment, to provide jobs and housing, and to create senior centers and youth programs
- an end to U.S. interventions abroad, the withdrawal of U.S. troops from bases around the world, and the building of "a foreign policy of peace and friendship, not exploitation and intimidation"

OPPOSED:
- racism, anti-Semitism, and attacks on women, lesbians, and gays
- police brutality
- the oppression of the poor, workers, prisoners, political activists, and undocumented aliens
- military aid for the Contras, the arms race, and preparations for war

WORLD CITIZEN PARTY
CANDIDATE FOR PRESIDENT:
Sol Gareth "Garry" Davis (DC)

Davis was a self-designated "world citizen," having renounced his U.S. citizenship in 1948 to protest militarism. The son of band leader Meyer Davis, he urged his followers to "think globally, act locally."

PLATFORM HIGHLIGHTS:
The platform of the World Citizen Party was "grounded in the Universal Declaration of Human Rights plus ecological rights as outlined in the Stockholm Declaration as well as the rights of ethnic minority groups."

SUPPORTED:
- world citizenship
- the creation of world law and appropriate government organs (e.g., World Legislature, World Courts, World Executive, and World Guard Force) essential to guarantee fundamental human rights and freedoms
- the realignment of local and national law to conform to world law
- the recognition and representation of viable ethnic groups
- representation for stateless persons and refugees
- the representation of ecosystems against exploitation
- the mundialization of villages, towns, cities, and universities
- the endorsement of existing national and international organizations and associations promoting world peace, human rights, and world government

GENERAL ELECTION SUMMARY FOR 1988:			
Candidate	*Electoral Votes*	*States*	*Popular Votes*
Bush (R)	426	40	48,886,097
Dukakis (D)	111	10 (+DC)[1]	41,809,074
Paul (LIBRTN)	0	0	432,179
Fulani (NEW ALL)	0	0	217,219
Duke (POP)	0	0	47,047
McCarthy (CONSUM)	0	0	30,905
Griffin (AI)	0	0	27,818
LaRouche (NAT EC REC)	0	0	25,562
Write-in	0	0	21,041
Marra (RTL)	0	0	20,504
Winn (WL)	0	0	18,693
Warren (SOC WOR)	0	0	15,604
Lewin (PF)	0	0	10,370
Dodge (PROH)	0	0	8,002
Holmes (W W)	0	0	7,846
Kenoyer (SOC [LU])	0	0	3,882
Dennis (A)	0	0	3,475
Herer (GRASS)	0	0	1,949
Youngkeit (I)	0	0	372
Martin (TW)	0	0	236
King (I)	0	0	157
Macaione (I)	0	0	93
Wobser (I)	0	0	59
McDaniel (I)	0	0	39
Masters (I)	0	0	13
Adam (I)	0	0	1
none of the above	0	0	6,934

[1]Lloyd Bentsen (D, TX) received 1 electoral vote from West Virginia.

ELECTION OF NOVEMBER 3, 1992

President
WILLIAM JEFFERSON "BILL" CLINTON
Vice President
ALBERT ARNOLD GORE, JR.

HIGHLIGHTS

Gov. William Jefferson "Bill" Clinton of Arkansas won a three-way race for the presidency in 1992 in one of the most personalized campaigns of the twentieth century. Clinton began his quest in a crowded Democratic field that included Sen. J. Robert "Bob" Kerrey of Nebraska; Gov. Lawrence Douglas Wilder, Jr., of Virginia; former senator Paul Efthemios Tsongas of Massachusetts; Sen. Thomas R. "Tom" Harkin of Iowa; and former governor Edmund Gerald "Jerry" Brown, Jr., of California. In the wings, Gov. Mario Matthew Cuomo again played coy before eventually bowing out as a prospective candidate. Clinton's march to the nomination suffered a number of reversals: tabloids claimed he had had a twelve-year affair with a woman, it was revealed he had smoked marijuana in college, and veterans decried his avoidance of the draft and his protests against the Vietnam War. Clinton, however, kept hammering at his themes of reviving the faltering economy and restoring faith in government. By the time of the convention, only Brown remained to wage a symbolic opposition to the victorious Clinton.

Meanwhile, the Republicans seemed in disarray. Normally, the incumbent president would easily be renominated, and Bush, flush from victory in the Gulf War, had expected to ride into another term as a war hero and statesman. Instead, an economic downturn forced people's attention on neglected domestic issues, and Bush's popularity plummeted. Conservative commentator Patrick Joseph Buchanan waged an embarrassing challenge for the nomination and split the party along doctrinal lines. When Clinton selected Sen. Al Gore of Tennessee as his running mate, President Bush found he could no longer count on the South as a base of his strength. Further confounding the campaign, Henry Ross Perot of Texas entered the contest as an independent candidate and drew support away from both parties. Once again, negative ads dominated the airwaves, with Bush continually stressing the "character" issue and Clinton attacking the "trickle down" theory of Republican economics and blaming Bush for the recession. In the end, Clinton emerged as the first president since 1968 to win office with less than half of the popular vote, or 43 percent.

AFRICAN AMERICAN EVOLUTIONARY ARMY

CANDIDATE FOR PRESIDENT:
Dennis Barker Carey (MI)

PLATFORM HIGHLIGHTS:

SUPPORTED:

- efforts to enhance prosperity for everyone
- free and equal time requirements in broadcasts and other media for all political candidates
- the direct election of Supreme Court justices
- the military superiority of the United States
- job preference for U.S. citizens
- limits on imports
- restrictions on foreigners studying at U.S. universities and colleges
- at least minimal health care access for all U.S. citizens

- "common language" legislation
- an end to the presidential library "pyramids" program
- prohibitions against foreign banks assisting in the buyout of U.S. businesses
- the development of alternative energy sources
- a ban on the export of products banned for domestic sale
- improved benefits for veterans
- ways to help other nations outside of government channels

OPPOSED:

- corruption, oppression, and suppression

AMERICAN CONSTITUTIONAL PARTY

CANDIDATE FOR PRESIDENT:
Talmadge Martin Warren (VA)

A schoolteacher, Warren sought the presidency as a learning experience for his eighth-grade students.

PLATFORM HIGHLIGHTS:

SUPPORTED:

- equal media space for all candidates in a primary
- a "none of the above" ballot line
- the direct election of Supreme Court justices
- a 20 percent cut in the federal payroll
- restrictions on U.S. investment in Mexico and on foreign investments in U.S. businesses
- periodic open bidding for such privatized government monopolies as Amtrak and the Postal Service
- a shift in foreign aid from government to voluntary channels
- the establishment of a national informational network to track and prosecute industrial spying and to work for a nuclear-free world
- the deployment of the military to aid the war on drugs
- government-provided full health care for all citizens, who, along with their families, would closely monitor all health care charges
- the monitoring of the possession of semiautomatic and assault weapons and holding criminals responsible for compensating their victims
- a child allowance for married couples with preschool children when the mother does not work outside the home for more than sixteen hours per week

OPPOSED:

- the "borrow and pay" approach to government financing

AMERICAN INDEPENDENT PARTY

CANDIDATE FOR PRESIDENT:
Howard Phillips

CANDIDATE FOR VICE PRESIDENT:
Albion Williamson Knight, Jr. (MD)

CANDIDATES FOR PRESIDENTIAL NOMINATION:
James Gordon "Bo" Gritz (NV)
Howard Phillips (VA)
Barbara S. Scott-Davenport (CA) (write in)

PRIMARY:
JUNE 2, 1992 (CA):
Phillips 15,456
Scott-Davenport 13

CONVENTION:
August 29, 1992, Sacramento (CA)
Merino D. Short, chairman

The day after the convention, the party's central committee voted to affiliate with the U.S. Taxpayers Party. For the platform, see the U.S. Taxpayers Party, as the AIP adopted the U.S. Taxpayers Party platform.

AMERICAN INDEPENDENT PARTY VOTE FOR PRESIDENTIAL NOMINATION	
Candidate	Ballot: 1
Phillips	40
Gritz	8

VOTE FOR VICE-PRESIDENTIAL NOMINATION:
KNIGHT WAS NOMINATED FOR VICE PRESIDENT
BY ACCLAMATION.

AMERICAN PARTY

CANDIDATE FOR PRESIDENT:
Robert Junior Smith (UT)

CANDIDATE FOR VICE PRESIDENT:
Doris Feimer (ND)

PLATFORM HIGHLIGHTS:
The permanent platform of the American Party urged a prohibition against secret negotiations and treaties by the government.

SUPPORTED:

- efforts to cut off trade to any nation that denied its citizens the right to emigrate and to take their property with them
- an invincible military posture
- a requirement of a declaration of war for any U.S. military intervention longer than seventy-two hours
- the withdrawal of the federal government from all charitable, welfare, public works, and educational activities
- the elimination of any subsidies or public enterprises to produce, sell, transport, of distribute any good or perform any service not authorized by the Constitution
- calls to restrict the government to a limited agency of the several states, living within an annual budget adopted by Congress
- the death penalty
- local law enforcement
- the right of citizens to exchange goods, services, and real property by any mutually agreed upon media of exchange
- the right to mine, own, trade, and use precious metals

OPPOSED:

- world government and foreign aid
- gun control
- abortion and euthanasia

AMERICAN PARTY

CANDIDATE FOR PRESIDENT:
Robert Edward Kern (NY)

The American Party's platform condemned the misrepresentation of the U.S. people by their leaders, claiming that education had been neglected, that the Constitution had been "sabotaged," and that it was time to "throw the rascals out." It urged faith in the people.

AMERICAN POLITICAL PARTY

CANDIDATE FOR PRESIDENT:
George L. Berish (HI)

CANDIDATE FOR VICE PRESIDENT:
Linda L. Smith (HI)

PLATFORM HIGHLIGHTS:
The platform of the American Political Party declared that the government's proper role was to "act reliably and impartially" and to guarantee each citizen equal participation in the process of obtaining consensus. While equity and justice were stressed, the party reminded voters that minority rights needed to be respected and that parties should be held accountable for their platform promises.

SUPPORTED:
- a uniform national sales tax on property, goods, and services—without exceptions—to finance government
- the direct funneling of educational funds to parents and more testing
- the inclusion of logic, ethics, mastery of a common language, history, and productive knowledge in school curricula
- environmental protection as a national obligation
- a woman's decision to have children as a matter exclusively within her control
- an end to discrimination against minorities and outspoken public condemnation against injustices
- children's right of citizenship from birth and of not being considered the property of their parents
- the requirement that couples could not be considered as potential parents until they had had a "loving relationship" for at least four years and met other qualifications
- term limits for members of Congress and a pay raise to attract people to public office who are interested in more than just power
- absolute separation of church and state, with no taxes on religious functions
- tests to separate true churches from commercial organizations posing as churches
- the reinstatement of the death penalty and the admission of testimony by crime victims
- a revision of the "exclusionary rule" in evidentiary proceedings

AMERICAN POLITICAL PARTY

CANDIDATE FOR PRESIDENT:
Roger T. Davis (IL)

APATHY PARTY

CANDIDATE FOR PRESIDENT:
James Harlan Boren (VA)

CANDIDATES FOR VICE PRESIDENT:
Wild Bill Weldon (OK)
Bill Wiedman

Billed as a "dark, dark horse," Boren launched his campaign with the motto "When in doubt, mumble." Instead of busing students to school, Boren advocated busing schools to the students. Claiming that bureaucracy is the highest and most beautiful form of self expression, Boren articulated the virtues of red tape and advocated "dynamic inaction" as a way of life.

PLATFORM HIGHLIGHTS:
SUPPORTED:
- efforts to put people to work studying the problem of unemployment
- the switching of the objectives of the Defense Department and the Postal Service, with the Defense Department delivering the mail and the Post Office delivering munitions
- government leaks that promoted memos and "orbital dialogue"
- an international Bureaucrats' Olympics, featuring an executive shot put competition over lunchtime
- the resolution of the population problem by lengthening the gestation period
- the regulation of the economy "to meet the proliferation of standards of wage-price harmonics and monetary proficiency within the spectral contingencies of the corporate linkage with the anticipatory disparity of domestic portfolios"

OPPOSED:
- paper shredding

APATHY PARTY

CANDIDATE FOR PRESIDENT:
Hugh A. Slacker (ME)

PLATFORM HIGHLIGHTS:
The Apathy Party presented its platform as "the 10 percent solution."

SUPPORTED:
- limits on employers to prevent them from making ten times more than their employees
- limits on taxpayers from paying more or less than 10 percent of their gross pay in federal taxes
- caps on inheritances to 10 percent of the benefactor's wealth
- caps on capital gains to 10 percent
- requirements that welfare recipients contribute 10 percent of their time to community activity
- a release of 10 percent of all government secrets each year for the next ten years

- the adoption of term limits of five two-year terms for representatives and two five-year terms for senators
- restrictions on departing elected officials from leaving office with more than 10 percent of their incoming portfolio
- a 10 percent ceiling on business profit and loss

ALSO:
- concluded with the cryptic plank of "Ten by ten by ten"

BLOCK PARTY
CANDIDATE FOR PRESIDENT:
Susan Marilyn Block (CA)

PLATFORM HIGHLIGHTS:
SUPPORTED:
- "free orgasms for everyone!"
- individual control of "our lives as creative individuals"
- the gradual dismantling of the federal government
- a check-off system for individual taxpayers to direct how they want their taxes to be spent
- limits on the federal government's role to protect the United States against foreign invaders and dangerous toxins
- the Bill of Rights
- self-governing and self-policing communities
- an end to "vice crimes" through legalization of drug use and prostitution
- an effort to "stop all the bloviating about 'family values'"
- the pursuit of happiness as long as that pursuit did not hurt anyone else

BULL MOOSE PARTY
CANDIDATE FOR PRESIDENT:
Paul Charles Daugherty (SC)

Daugherty's platform was "Debt, Depression, Done Deal! . . . before 1999!" He claimed he was a "boring, middle class, hard-working, God-fearing, patriotic S.O.B."

COMMUNIST PARTY
CANDIDATE FOR PRESIDENT:
Benjamin Franklin Schoenfeld (CA)

This party was not associated with the Communist Party U.S.A. The Communist Party, USA, did not run candidates for national office in 1992. It split up after its convention in Cleveland in December 1991. Remnants formed Committees of Correspondence and held a conference in Berkeley (CA) from July 17 to July 19, 1992, but no nominations for public office were made.

DEMOCRATIC-FARMER LABOR PARTY
CANDIDATE FOR PRESIDENT:
Robert Fritchoff Hanson (NJ)

DEMOCRATIC PARTY
CANDIDATE FOR PRESIDENT:
William Jefferson "Bill" Clinton

CANDIDATE FOR VICE PRESIDENT:
Albert Arnold Gore, Jr.

CANDIDATES FOR PRESIDENTIAL NOMINATION:
John Hancock Abbott (CA)
Lawrence A. "Larry" Agran (CA)
Nathan J. Averick (IL)
Larry Lee Baker (WA)
George H. Ballard III (PA)
John A. "Jack" Barnes (KS)
Donald M. Baumgartner (MT)
Donald Innes Beamgard (KS)
George William Benns (MD)
Lloyd Millard Bentsen, Jr. (TX)
Frank Joseph Bona (FL)
James Harlan Boren (VA)
Thomas Joseph Bradley, Jr. (NC)
James Robert Bridges (TX)
Edmund Gerald "Jerry" Brown, Jr. (CA)
Stephen Burke (NY)
Ulysses Burnett (IN)
Lester Francis Byerley, Jr. (NJ)
John Patrick Cahill (NY)
Raymond Joseph Caplette (CA)
Willie Felix Carter (TX)
Charles Caussey (UT)
Aaron Brian Clarkson (KY)
Roy James Clendenan (OH)
William Jefferson "Bill" Clinton (AR)
Frank A. Clough, Jr. (OR) (withdrew)
Ruth Coleman (WA)
James Robert Cooper (TX)
Bob Cunningham (SC)
Mario Matthew Cuomo (NY)
Dean Adams Curtis (CA)
Barry J. Deutsch (NY)
Norris James Dubose, Jr. (MD)
Barry Alan Ellsworth (UT)
Robert C. Emerson (AL)
Ernest E. English, Jr. (NY)
Clinton Ferguson (MS)
Jerome P. Fetiak (NY)
Susan Carole Fey (IL)
Fernando Rivera Figueroa (PA)
Paul Cary Fisher (IL)
Richard Francis Flynn (NY)
Marsha Aileen Foutch (IL)
Moshe Friedman (NY)
Lenora B. Fulani (NY)
James Bryant Gay, Jr. (TX)
Richard Andrew Gephardt (MO) (declined)
Albert Arnold Gore, Jr. (TN) (declined)
Karen Lee Gratto-Irwin (CA)
Albert Hamburg (WY)

Robert Fritchoff Hanson (NJ)
Thomas R. "Tom" Harkin (IA)
Paul Harper (CA)
Calvin D. Harris (AZ)
Eddie Ray Harris (TX)
Gary Hauptli (KS)
Carla Kathryn Schram Hawkinson (MI)
Tod Howard Hawks (KS)
James Leon Hayes (CO)
Karl J. Hegger (IL)
Rufus Taylor Higginbotham (TX)
Russell Munoz Batiste Hirshon (DC)
Joseph E. Holcomb (NV)
Margot Sierra Holcomb (NV)
Gilbert H. Holmes (DC)
William Horrigan, Jr. (CT)
William Henry Hurley (AL)
Alfonzo Jones (MI)
Alan M. Kaplan
Alan Craig Kazdoy (TX)
J. Robert "Bob" Kerrey (NE)
Caroline P. Killeen (AZ)
Kenneth Ellis Klammer (NY)
Ron Kovic (CA)
William Parker Kreml (SC)
Joseph Lamotte (NY)
Lyndon Hermyle LaRouche, Jr. (VA)
Thomas Robert "Tom" Laughlin (CA)
James Meyward Livingstone (GA)
Stanly Onease Lock (MI)
Jerome John Maher (MI)
Patrick J. Mahoney, Jr. (FL)
Steven P. Malloy (CA)
Jeffrey Flake Marsh (IA)
Ronald Eugene Maynard (OR)
Johnnie Louis McAlpine (OK)
Eugene Joseph McCarthy (VA)
James D. McCracken (CA)
Angus Wheeler McDonald (WV)
Sherry Ann Meadows (TX)
Messiah (Fred Irwin Sitnick) (MD)
George John Mitchell (ME)
Fanny Rose Zeidwerg Monyek (NJ)
Charles Leroy Moore, Jr. (NC)
David John Morascini (CT)
Ralph Nader (DC)
Christopher B. "Chris" Norton (NY)
Grady O'Cummings III (NY)
Edward Thomas O'Donnell, Jr. (DE)
Andy Olson (CA)
William Douglas Pawley, Jr. (FL)
Billie Delle Payne (CA)
Laton Pendleton (MI)
Henry Ross Perot (TX)
John Phillips (DC)
Harold Lawrence Poland (VA)
Mary Jane Rachner (MN)

John Donald Rigazio (NH)
Johnnie Mae Riley (TX)
Charles Robb (VA)
John David "Jay" Rockefeller IV (WV)
    (declined)
Raymond Rollinson (MD)
Blanche Rubin (AZ)
Red Ryder (CA)
Roger A. Sack (WA)
Cyril Emil Sagan (PA)
Charles Sano (CA)
Virginia Justine Schaefer (AZ)
Stephen H. Schwartz (NY)
Barbara S. Scott-Davenport (CA)
Mary Ann Tomkins Segal (DC)
Tom Shiekman (FL)
Joseph Simonetti (PA)
Fred Irwin "Messiah" Sitnick (MD)
Henry Michael Sligh (SC)
Eugene R. "Gene" Smith (CA)
Oscar Smith, Jr. (NY)
Ralph Eugene Spelbring (IN)
John Joseph Staradumsky (RI)
Stuart Marc Starky (IL)
Wilhelm Friedrich Steiner (CA)
Mrs. Frank Stewart (AL)
Peter Paul Sebastian Swider (FL)
Leonard Dennis Talbow (CO)
John Rownald Taylor (TX)
Marlin Dale Thacker (AL)
Curly Thornton (MT)
Reginald Sullivan Voyle Towers (CA)
Paul Efthemios Tsongas (MA)
Raymond John Van Skiver (KS)
Charles Gordon Vick (TN)
Vera Watts (MI)
Robert Gene Webb (CA)
Lawrence Douglas Wilder, Jr. (VA)
    (withdrew)
Robert Ormand Williams (AZ)
Charles Woods (NV)

CANDIDATES FOR VICE-PRESIDENTIAL NOMINATION:
    William Warren "Bill" Bradley (NJ)
    Mario Matthew Cuomo (NY)
    Albert Arnold Gore, Jr. (TN)
    Lee Herbert Hamilton (IN)
    J. Robert "Bob" Kerrey (NE)
    Endicott Peabody (NH)
    John David "Jay" Rockefeller IV (WV)
    Susan K. Y. Shargal (NH)
    Dudley A. Whitman (FL)
    Harris Llewellyn Wofford (PA)

PRIMARIES:
FEBRUARY 18, 1992 (NH):
    Tsongas 55,638
    Clinton 41,522

Kerrey 18,575
Harkin. 17,057
Brown 13,654
Cuomo 6,577
   (write in)
Laughlin 3,251
Nader 3,054
   (write in)
Woods 2,862
Agran 298
Fulani 286
McCarthy. 88
LaRouche 60
Kovic 25
others 4,872

Vice-Presidential Primary, February 18, 1992:
Peabody. 34,533
Shargal 20,347
Nader 1,097
   (write in)
Cuomo 739
   (write in)
Tsongas. 649
   (write in)
Kerrey. 502
   (write in)
others 2,956

FEBRUARY 25, 1992 (SD):
Kerrey 23,892
Harkin. 15,023
Clinton 11,375
Tsongas 5,729
Brown 2,300
Agran 606
LaRouche. 441
Wilder 137
Burke . . . .
Emerson . . . .
Friedman . . . .
Hamburg . . . .
Hawks. . . . .
Laughlin. . . . .
McAlpine . . . .
McCarthy. . . . .
Thornton . . . .
Woods . . . .

MARCH 2, 1992 (CO):
Brown 69,073
Clinton 64,470
Tsongas 61,360
Kerrey 29,572
Harkin. 5,866
Woods 1,051
Agran 672

Burke 532
McCarthy. 488
LaRouche 328
Hayes 279
Talbow 202
Hawks. 165
Shiekman 76
Marsh 59
McAlpine. 48
Rollinson 46
Wilder . . . .
uncommitted 5,356

MARCH 3, 1992 (GA):
Clinton 259,907
Tsongas 109,148
Brown 36,808
Kerrey 22,095
Harkin. 9,893
uncommitted 17,256

MARCH 3, 1992 (MD):
Tsongas 230,490
Clinton 189,906
Brown 46,480
Harkin. 32,899
Kerrey 27,035
LaRouche 4,259
uncommitted 36,155

MARCH 3, 1992 (UT) (UNOFFICIAL):
Tsongas 10,582
Brown 8,971
Clinton 5,780
Kerrey 3,447
Harkin. 1,274
Woods 153
Agran 55
Caussey. 45
Pawley 13
uncommitted 720
others 598

MARCH 7, 1992 (SC):
Clinton 73,221
Tsongas 21,338
Harkin. 7,657
Brown 6,961
Cunningham. 1,369
Woods 854
Kerrey. 566
Kreml 336
McDonald 268
LaRouche 204
uncommitted 3,640

MARCH 10, 1992 (FL):
Clinton 570,566
Tsongas 388,124

Brown 139,569
Harkin 13,587
Kerrey 12,011

MARCH 10, 1992 (LA):
Clinton 267,002
Tsongas 42,508
Brown 25,480
McCarthy 15,129
Woods 8,989
Burke 4,294
Harkin 4,033
Agran 3,511
LaRouche 3,082
Kerrey 2,984
Marsh 2,120
Laughlin 1,867
Hawks 1,469
Rollinson 1,089
McAlpine 870

MARCH 10, 1992 (MA):
Tsongas 526,297
Brown 115,746
Clinton 86,817
Nader 32,881
Kerrey 5,409
   (withdrew)
Harkin 3,764
   (withdrew)
McCarthy 3,127
Agran 2,224
LaRouche 2,167
uncommitted 12,198
others 2,255

MARCH 10, 1992 (MS):
Clinton 140,013
Brown 18,408
Kerrey 16,000
Tsongas 15,425
LaRouche 13,087
Harkin 2,466
uncommitted 11,984

MARCH 10, 1992 (OK):
Clinton 293,266
Brown 69,624
Woods 16,828
Harkin 14,015
Kerrey 13,252
LaRouche 6,474
McAlpine 2,670

MARCH 10, 1992 (RI):
Tsongas 26,825
Clinton 10,762
Brown 9,541
Kerrey 469

Woods 408
Harkin 319
Fey 308
LaRouche 300
McCarthy 235
Staradumsky 168
Laughlin 94
Rollinson 91
Agran 79
Burke 53
Thornton 52
uncommitted 703

MARCH 10, 1992 (TN):
Clinton 214,485
Tsongas 61,717
Brown 25,560
Harkin 2,099
Kerrey 1,638
others 432
uncommitted 12,551

MARCH 10, 1992 (TX):
Clinton 972,151
Tsongas 285,192
Brown 118,923
Woods 30,092
Kerrey 20,298
Harkin 19,617
LaRouche 12,220
Benns 7,876
Higginbotham 7,674
Hawks 4,924
McAlpine 4,009
uncommitted 12,217

MARCH 17, 1992 (IL):
Clinton 776,829
Tsongas 387,891
Brown 220,346
Harkin 30,710
Kerrey 10,916
LaRouche 6,599
Agran 3,227
uncommitted 67,612

MARCH 17, 1992 (MI):
Clinton 297,280
Brown 151,400
Tsongas 97,017
Harkin 6,265
Kerrey 3,219
LaRouche 2,049
uncommitted 27,836
others/write ins 906

MARCH 24, 1992 (CT):
Brown 64,472
Clinton 61,698

Tsongas 33,811
Agran 2,688
Harkin. 1,919
Kerrey 1,169
McCarthy 1,036
LaRouche. 896
uncommitted 5,430

April 5, 1992 (PR):
Clinton 62,273
Brown. 921
Kerrey. 930
Boren 357
Tsongas. 59
Woods 78
Harkin 31
LaRouche. 27
Agran 17
McAlpine. 13
Shiekman. 10
others 359
uncommitted 204

April 7, 1992 (KS):
Clinton 82,145
Tsongas 24,413
Brown 20,811
Kerrey 2,215
Hauptli 1,303
Woods 1,119
Beamgard 1,009
Harkin 940
Barnes 892
Hawks. 765
LaRouche. 631
Spelbring 537
Van Skiver 510
Pawley 364
Marsh 160
Agran 147
McAlpine. 131
none of the above. 22,159

April 7, 1992 (MN):
Clinton 63,584
Brown 62,706
Tsongas 43,588
Perot 4,250
  (write in)
Harkin. 4,077
McCarthy 3,704
Kerrey 1,191
Agran 1,042
Woods 990
Rachner 620
LaRouche. 532
Burke 348
McAlpine. 183

Hawks. 111
Marsh. 106
Averick. 105
uncommitted 11,366
write in/others 5,667

April 7, 1992 (NY):
Clinton 412,349
Tsongas 288,330
Brown 264,278
Harkin. 11,535
Kerrey 11,147
Agran 10,733
McCarthy 9,354

April 7, 1992 (WI):
Clinton 287,356
Brown 266,207
Tsongas 168,619
McCarthy 6,525
Harkin. 5,395
Agran 3,193
LaRouche 3,120
Kerrey 3,044
uncommitted 15,487

April 28, 1992 (PA):
Clinton 715,031
Brown 325,543
Tsongas 161,572
LaRouche 21,534
Harkin. 21,013
Kerrey 20,802

May 5, 1992 (DC):
Clinton 45,716
Tsongas 6,452
Brown 4,444
uncommitted 5,292

May 5, 1992 (IN):
Clinton 301,905
Brown 102,379
Tsongas 58,215
Kerrey 14,350

May 5, 1992 (NC):
Clinton 443,498
Brown 71,984
Tsongas 57,589
Kerrey 6,216
Harkin. 5,891
no preference 106,697

May 12, 1992 (NE):
Clinton 68,562
Brown 31,673
Tsongas 10,707
Harkin 4,239
McCarthy 1,520
LaRouche 1,148

Woods 485
Agran 280
uncommitted 24,714

MAY 12, 1992 (WV):
Clinton 225,130
Brown 36,102
Tsongas 21,101
McDonald 10,092
Kerrey 3,166
LaRouche 3,118
Harkin 2,771
Woods 1,459
Spelbring 1,080

MAY 19, 1992 (OR):
Clinton 147,204
Brown 103,142
Tsongas 33,606
McCarthy 6,213
LaRouche 2,925
Woods 1,743
Agran 1,479
Clough . . . .

MAY 19, 1992 (WA):
Clinton 62,171
Brown 34,111
Perot 28,311
  (write in)
Tsongas 18,981
Harkin 1,858
Kerrey 1,489
LaRouche 1,060

MAY 26, 1992 (AR):
Clinton 338,700
Brown 55,013
LaRouche 14,008
uncommitted 89,725

MAY 26, 1992 (ID):
Clinton 27,034
Brown 9,241
LaRouche 1,980
Agran 991
none of the above 15,569

MAY 26, 1992 (KY):
Clinton 207,569
Brown 30,675
Tsongas 18,072
Harkin 7,135
Kerrey 3,237
uncommitted 103,440

JUNE 2, 1992 (AL):
Clinton 296,786
Brown 29,506
uncommitted 88,651

JUNE 2, 1992 (CA):
Clinton 1,359,112
Brown 1,150,460
Tsongas 212,522
McCarthy 60,635
Kerrey 33,935
Agran 24,784
LaRouche 21,971
Scott-Davenport 66
  (write in)
McDonald 62
  (write in)
Ryder 38
  (write in)
Harper 7
  (write in)
Killeen 5
  (write in)
Payne 5
  (write in)
Kaplan 4
  (write in)
Olson 3
  (write in)
Sano 0
  (write in)

JUNE 2, 1992 (MT):
Clinton 54,785
Brown 21,626
Tsongas 12,574
uncommitted 27,914

JUNE 2, 1992 (NJ):
Clinton 221,429
Brown 71,584
Tsongas 41,884
LaRouche 6,283
Ballard 1,996
Hanson 1,397
uncommitted 29,322

JUNE 2, 1992 (NM):
Clinton 95,446
Brown 30,462
Tsongas 11,428
uncommitted 35,090

JUNE 2, 1992 (OH):
Clinton 631,993
Brown 195,893
Tsongas 109,467

JUNE 9, 1992 (ND):
LaRouche 7,072
Woods 6,686
Perot 5,866
  (write in)
Shiekman 4,952

Clinton 2,946
Brown 14
Tsongas 6

41ST CONVENTION:
July 13–16, 1992, Madison Square Garden, New York (NY)
Thomas Stephen Foley (WA), honorary cochair
Ann Richards (TX), permanent chairman
Barbara Charlene Jordan (TX), keynoter
Zell Miller (GA), keynoter
William Warren "Bill" Bradley (NJ), keynoter

Attending this convention were 4,288 delegates.

PLATFORM HIGHLIGHTS:
The Democratic platform called for a "revolution in government" to restore basic values and the country's economic greatness and to put people first. It promised "tough choices" and "results-oriented government" under a "New Covenant" of opportunity, responsibility, community, and national security. The party rejected both the Republicans' "do-nothing" philosophy and the "Big Government" theories of the past.

SUPPORTED:
• infrastructure development
• defense conversion to peacetime uses
• development of a national information network
• investment tax credits for investment in new technologies
• deficit reduction
• revitalization of cities through community development programs, targeted fiscal assistance, public works, use of enterprise zones, and summer jobs and youth employment initiatives
• family farmers
• investment in agricultural research and rural business development
• expansion of earned income tax credit
• reform of occupational safety laws to hold employers more accountable
• right of collective bargaining
• public school choice and site-based educational decision-making
• programs to reduce school dropout rate
• standards for core school curriculums, coupled with competency testing
• apprenticeship programs
• domestic GI bill providing college loans to be paid back by community service
• affordable health care
• improved rate of childhood immunization
• elimination of preexisting condition exclusions in health care insurance coverage
• expanded access to mental health treatment
• nutrition education

• reproductive choice, including the right to a safe and legal abortion
• increased efforts to combat breast and cervical cancer
• a war on AIDS and HIV disease
• full funding for the Ryan White Act
• expanded clinical trials for treatments and vaccines
• streamlining the FDA drug approval process
• tax relief for middle class families with children
• a coordinated transportation policy, with a commitment to mass transit
• alternative-fueled vehicles and greater reliance on natural gas
• stronger air and water pollution standards
• investment in development of renewable energy sources
• conservation and recycling
• ratification of the Equal Rights Amendment
• affirmative action
• legal services for the poor
• civil rights protection for gay men and lesbians
• full enforcement of the Americans with Disabilities Act
• efforts to meet trustee obligations to Native Hawaiians and other Native Americans
• aggressive prosecution of those who commit hate crimes
• right of self-determination for Puerto Rico, American Samoa, Guam, Northern Mariana Islands, Virgin Islands, and Palau
• a crackdown on deadbeat parents and a national child support enforcement system
• pay equity between genders
• family and medical leave
• increased efforts to prevent child and spousal abuse
• expanded and affordable child care programs
• prenatal and well-baby care initiatives
• nutrition, income, transportation, and abuse protection services for senior citizens
• public investment in education and job training for welfare recipients
• a limit on welfare benefits to two years for able-bodied persons who can work in private sector or community service jobs
• enhanced flexibility for states and local governments in achieving federal mandates
• campaign finance reform
• efforts to increase voter participation through universal same-day registration
• statehood for the District of Columbia

OPPOSED:
• private school vouchers
• anti-Semitism, racism, homophobia, bigotry, and negative stereotyping
• the forcible return of anyone (e.g., Haitian boat people) fleeing political repression as "a betrayal of American values"

DEMOCRATIC PARTY
VOTE FOR PRESIDENTIAL NOMINATION:

Candidate	Ballot: 1
Clinton	3,372
Brown	596
Tsongas	209
Casey	10
Schroeder	8
Agran	3
Gore	1
Daniels	1
Simonetti	1
abstentions/absent	53
other (unspecified)	2
uncommitted	1

On the first ballot, the rules were suspended, and Clinton's nomination was made by acclamation.

VOTE FOR VICE-PRESIDENTIAL NOMINATION:
GORE WAS NOMINATED FOR VICE PRESIDENT BY ACCLAMATION.

EXPANSIONIST PARTY
CANDIDATE FOR PRESIDENT:
L. Craig Schoonmaker (NY)

The Expansionist Party billed itself as a "Let's-Do-Something" party for people "who have lost patience with passivity, cynical alienation, and negativism." It asserted the existence of a single morality applicable to all people on all continents and suggested that power should be used to ensure its defense and advancement.

PLATFORM HIGHLIGHTS:
SUPPORTED:
- the promotion of a world union between the United States and those nations that shared its fundamental, "pro-human" values, and the overthrow of those nations that did not share "pro-human" values
- efforts to rid the world of dictatorships and tyrants, with the failure to do so seen as a "gutless and morally lazy" response
- calls for the wealth and power of the United States to be used to liberate the world and bring it under one universal government based on the U.S. Constitution
- statehood for Australia, New Zealand, Puerto Rico, the Virgin Islands, and the English-speaking Canadian provinces
- American Samoa, Guam, and the Trust Territory of the Pacific in joining the United States as a single state
- a Western Hemisphere Common Market of Quebec, the United States, and other nations
- the establishment of the West Indies and Oceania as commonwealths associated with the United States

- a proposal for the United States to join the European Common Market in order to forge a North Atlantic Common Market
- the integration of all North Atlantic Treaty Organization (NATO) forces into a single military
- the establishment of English as the co-language of Western Europe
- the abolishment of travel and work restrictions

OPPOSED:
- injustice, exploitation, and poverty

FEDERALIST PARTY
CANDIDATE FOR PRESIDENT:
Robert Allen Mark Selwa (MI)

FREEDOM FOR LAROUCHE (ECONOMIC RECOVERY; INDEPENDENT; INDEPENDENTS FOR LAROUCHE; JUSTICE, INDUSTRY, AND AGRICULTURE; JUSTICE, INDUSTRY, AND OPPORTUNITY) PARTY
CANDIDATE FOR PRESIDENT:
Lyndon Hermyle LaRouche, Jr. (VA)

CANDIDATES FOR VICE PRESIDENT:
James Luther Bevel (PA)
Debra Hanania Freeman (MD)
Elliott Greenspan (NJ)

Since 1989 and throughout the 1992 campaign, LaRouche languished in federal prison, having been convicted of charges that his organization and he bilked their followers of funds through illegal credit card manipulations. His party's platform focused on the theme "LaRouche was Right." For example, LaRouche predicted the continuation of the recession and the collapse of the banking system.

PLATFORM HIGHLIGHTS:
SUPPORTED:
- "federalization" of the Federal Reserve System and the issuance of $500 billion worth of gold-reserve currency notes
- a return to the American System of economics
- the development of high-speed rail systems, using maglev technology
- nuclear fission and, ultimately, nuclear fusion, as the answer to the energy crisis
- nuclear desalinization and the North American Water and Power Alliance
- measures to deal with a potential "biological holocaust" resulting from the nation's failure to prevent the spread of the acquired immunodeficiency syndrome (AIDS) and other diseases: expanding the health care system by rebuilding the nation's hospitals, adding hundreds of

thousands of new beds, reopening closed emergency wards and trauma centers, and initiating a new Hill-Burton Commission

- an "Apollo-style, crash research program" to fight degenerative diseases and the use of optical biophysics to find a cure for AIDS
- the regulation of health insurance companies in addition to a new catastrophic health insurance plan, Medicare, and Medicaid
- a massive public works program aided by support from a National Bank
- a major war on drugs
- the development of classical educational curricula (e.g, classical language, plastic arts, physical science, and classical music)
- the eradication of poverty across the globe
- the colonization of the Moon, Mars, and the Solar System beyond
- the establishment of a durable peace among nations
- LaRouche's concept of building and strengthening a "productive triangle" running from Paris to Berlin to Vienna, and investments within that triangle to help "jump-start" other economies (including the U.S. economy)
- the need for the United States to engage in "great projects" to develop the nation and the world

OPPOSED:
- the North American Free Trade Agreement (NAFTA)
- the Trilateral Commission
- the deregulation of air traffic, the railroads, highways, and waterways
- "environmentalism"

FREEDOM OF CHOICE PARTY

CANDIDATE FOR PRESIDENT:
Jouett Edgar Arney (KS)

CANDIDATE FOR VICE PRESIDENT:
Carl L. Kemp (KS)

PLATFORM HIGHLIGHTS:
SUPPORTED:
- a balanced economy based on need and demand rather than on dollar earnings for some corporations
- the elimination of the most-favored trade status for such nations as the People's Republic of China
- the elimination of aid for nations engaged in or supporting war
- the principle of trade parity and reciprocity
- incentives for business investment instead of foreign aid to develop the infrastructure of emerging nations in the Third World
- the termination of farm price supports
- housing assistance for students and pay increases for teachers
- equal, quality health care available to all
- the abolition of parole in favor of educational programs for inmates

- the prosecution of persons involved in the Iran-Contra "matter" for murder
- congressional term limits, voting rights for prisoners, and criminal sanctions for public officials' receipt of honoraria

GRASSROOTS PARTY

CANDIDATE FOR PRESIDENT:
Jack Herer (CA)

CANDIDATE FOR VICE PRESIDENT:
Derrick P. Grimmer (MO)

The Grassroots Party supported the legalization of marijuana.

ILLINOIS TAXPAYERS PARTY

CANDIDATE FOR PRESIDENT:
Howard Phillips (VA)

CANDIDATE FOR VICE PRESIDENT:
Alexander B. Magnus, Jr. (IL)

For the platform, see the U.S. Taxpayers Party, as the Illinois Taxpayers Party adopted the platform of the U.S. Taxpayers Party

INDEPENDENT

CANDIDATES FOR PRESIDENT:
Frank Ahern (LA)[1]
Stanley Franklin Allen (CA)[2]

[1]Ahern's platform indicated he was for a balanced economy, enforcement of social responsibility on businesses, an end to the overly permissive society and political expediency, greater concern for our fellow citizens, a campaign against organized and unorganized crime, campaign disclosure and disclosure of public contracts, a career diplomatic service at the ambassadorial level, an open meetings law, ethics legislation, public financing of political campaigns, an end to lobbying, open access to government records, environmental and beautification "workfare" for welfare recipients, elimination of speed traps, improved status for the elderly, creation of new industries (e.g., fish farming, dirigibles, solar energy), national educational television, creation of medical computer banks, elimination of the electoral college, full enforcement of antitrust laws, universal military training, a cut in the defense budget, travel restrictions on Congress and work attendance requirements for all political officeholders, greater discipline in schools, an end to the congressional seniority system, election of three or more vice presidents, procedural reforms in Congress, relocation of commercial and industrial headquarters from New York, creation of a Federal Department of Recreation, a complete overhaul of the nation's justice system and penal institutions, and greater use of semiprofessional medical services at reasonable cost.
[2]Allen's platform called for an Educational Economical Resource Program and a nonpolluting transportation system (using a prefabricated transportation lane). It urged roll call votes in Congress, separate election of the vice president (or abolition of the office), elimination of presidential libraries, expanded energy research efforts, abolition of the Central Intelligence Agency (CIA), competitive bidding for privatized government monopolies (e.g., Postal Service and Amtrak), open access to government records (including loans and repayments), increased pay for the workforce, creation of a new industrial base, tax reductions and cuts in public expenditures, cutbacks in military spending, an end to the deregulation of financial institutions, victim compensation, crash programs to aid inner-city areas, improvements in air and water quality and waste management, foreign aid and population control, nutrition support for families with preschool children, workfare alternatives to welfare, a long-term foreign policy, a "domestic content" requirement for all defense production, and an end to unequal trade relations.

Don Allensworth (MD)
George Washington America (NY)[1]
Gordon Lee Anderson (WA)[2]
Thomas William Bailey (PA)
Harold James Baker, Jr. (OR)[3]
Lester Dale Begin (CA)[4]
Anthony T. "Tony" Bellizzi (NY)[5]
Guy Templeton Black (OH)[6]
Abraham Washington Bognuda (CA)
James George Borden (HI)[7]

[1]America's platform called for a restoration of the country's moral values and future by rebuilding the United States on all fronts for peace, prosperity, and freedom. He urged democratic capitalism with a human face; low interest rates; women's right to privacy; federal home and education loan guarantees; elimination of homelessness; universal health care; credible solutions for the budget deficit, national debt, and savings and loan crisis; creation of a presidential office for citizen suggestions; and a more personalized approach to creating a bond between the president and the people.

[2]Anderson's platform favored elimination of national conventions, campaign funding, campaign contributions, and other influence peddling. It sought equal time on television and radio for all candidates; simplification and greater fairness of federal tax procedures; elimination of the presidential war powers (à la Grenada, Panama, Kuwait); and domestic wars on poverty, stupidity, bigotry, racism, sexism, child abuse, continued damage to Native Americans, tobacco, poor education, the absence of adequate health care, neglect of the homeless and jobless, and other wastes of human potential. A cartoonist, Anderson claimed, "We need a cartoonist in the White House; that is where the jokes are."

[3]Baker described himself as an isolationist and a nationalist, asserting that "charity begins at home." He was opposed to abortion except in cases of forcible rape.

[4]Begin advocated the industrialization of the United States to give the nation control of the world market. He wanted the country's power to rest with the corporations and businesses.

[5]Bellizzi's platform favored returning the government to the people by cutting back the bureaucracy and outlawing lobbyists. He opposed a taxpayer bailout of the savings and loan industry, supported an end to deficit spending, urged a job for every citizen, called for the closure of tax loopholes, advocated a new international economic order, promoted environmental cleanup (including international agreements and enforcement), demanded a reduction in fossil fuel dependence and stricter standards for pollution controls, sought a phaseout of nuclear power, and encouraged solar power and alternative energy resources. His platform gave priority to peacemaking, racial harmony and equality, the promotion of human rights, strengthening the United Nations, demilitarization of the planet, and respect for life. It urged increases in mental health assistance, more AIDS research and treatment, universal health care, and an end to deprivation, starvation, and homelessness domestically and internationally. Bellizzi wanted to empower people, convey a new spirit of volunteerism and involvement, promote the arts, emphasize education, be an advocate for youth, establish a national service corps, and provide national vision, faith, and strength.

[6]Black's platform urged an end to nuclear power, foreclosure of homes and farms, and research experiments on other species (including some human experiments). He wanted to promote the use of Seeing Eye, hearing ear, and mobility dog guides; encourage the use of manufactured housing; support the use of natural, organic foods; and develop each student's best abilities in public, private, or home schooling.

[7]Borden's platform declared "overtaxation" was the "greatest threat to the stability of the American people" and demanded a cut in federal expenditures and the adoption of the line-item veto. It sought national health insurance, a closer free enterprise partnership between government and business, creation of an Industrial Governmental cabinet position, uniform application of the criminal statutes for white-collar and other crimes, an increase in solar energy tax breaks, adoption of a national energy plan to promote self-sufficiency, a consistent foreign policy based on human rights values, an end to tariffs and restrictions on international free trade, top priority for rebuilding the nation's infrastructure, development of an economic plan (without advocating a "planned economy"), international cooperation to eradicate terrorism "with the barrel of a weapon," increased investment in education, and protection of the environment's rain forests, endangered species, and the ozone layer.

David Marshall Borkenhagen (OR)
Chadwick Lynn Bradford (IL)
Drew Bradford (NJ)
James Robert Bridges (TX)[8]
Karen E. Brown-Gerdine (CO)
G. P. Buck (NJ)[9]
Scott Allan Burritt (IL)
William Michael Bryk (NY)
James Michael "Mike" Carroll (MS)
Jerry Leon Carroll (CA)[10]
Willie Felix Carter (TX)[11]
Eyan V. Chang (CA)
Thomas L. Chapman (FL)
Barry Wayne Childs (FL)[12]
Frank Clough (MO)
Bryant Sears Condit (WY)
Teresa Ann Conway (VA)
Blanche Marie Cox (FL)[13]
James C. Cox (FL)
Rhonda Lee Coyle (FL)
Linda Joan Carter Cramer (CA)[14]
Maureen Gayle Dawson (Canada)
Gerald Thomas Defelice (CT)
Primero Henry Deherrera (CO)
Raymond Freed Detweiler (PA)[15]
Edwin Donnelly (OH)

[8]Bridges supported cuts in the military budget to fund social needs. He advocated a policy of nuclear deterrence, subject to strict moral conditions; viewed foreign aid as essential to create a real international system based on the equality of peoples; and pledged support for the people of Eastern and central Europe.

[9]According to Buck, "You got to go with the people" to be president. The candidate urged listening to people at the 7-Eleven, giving them "good weed," low taxes, and lots of money. The platform sought to "go with the flow," with "no pigs busting in." Buck promised to go to Lithuania if elected.

[10]Carroll's running mate was Marlin Dale Thacker of Alabama. On the one hand, their ticket opposed excessive government spending, inflation, government economic controls, and inadequate assistance for the elderly and disabled. On the other, it endorsed equal prices and wages for everyone, increased support for seniors and persons with disabilities, 100 percent parity for farmers, elimination of the 55-mile-per-hour speed limit, adequate fuel for truckers, a balanced federal budget, and personal production of gasohol without red tape.

[11]Carter claimed his candidacy was "God's will," as revealed to Carter in a vision.

[12]In his platform Childs promised to "bring America back to a country of people who: 1. own businesses of their own in their homes or townships; [and] 2. are elected to office without a salary, thereby causing a different attitude and saving a large sum of money."

[13]Cox favored a strong military, strong drug enforcement, and strong law enforcement. She wanted to end school overcrowding, eliminate educational red tape, and pay vital jobs—for example, police, military, teachers, and firefighters—salaries commensurate with their value. Her platform called for an end to agricultural crop controls, encouragement for domestic products, sale of surplus crops abroad, universal employment, an end to slums, housing and national health care for all, promotion of adoption as an alternative to abortion, and the creation of a balance of trade.

[14]Cramer promised to make the United States a "paradise" if elected, adding, "And I can do it, single-handed."

[15]Detweiler wanted to stop wasteful government spending, restrict corporate raiders, impose a protective tariff on imports, encourage long-term investments through tax reforms, improve the health care system, act more responsibly in the consumption of energy, and utilize wastes (including hazardous wastes) to improve the environment.

Robert Jack Downey (CA)
Barbara S. Eastman (CA)
Delbert L. Ehlers (IA)[1]
Stephen M. Falcone (ID)
Clarita "Chi Chi" Fazzari (CA)[2]
Jerome P. Fetiak (NY)
Christopher C. Fox (NC)
George Joseph Gehring, Jr. (CA)
Russell Bryan Gill (IN)[3]
Jim Ronald Glover (FL)[4]
Fernando Gomez (NC)[5]
Ray Ferrill Green (MA)[6]

William Bruce Greenwood, Jr. (CA)
Irvin James Guenther (KY)[7]
Tracy Allen "Hollywood" Hall (MD)
Albert Hamburg (WY)[8]
Zachary Harris (MI)
Earl John Hartje (IL)
Lee Wayne Haynes (NV)
Samuel Boyer Hoff (DE)[9]
David Lester Hornberger (CA)[10]
Mildred T. "Millie" Howard (OH)[11]
Donna Marie Hylton (VA)
Richard Albert Jackson (DC)
William H. Jenkins (NC)
Arthur Gleason Johnson (NY)
Alan M. Kaplan (FL)
Henry King (OH)
Roberta J. King (WA)
Dmitri A. "Pete" Kubbs (IL)
Americus Hector Liberator (NE)
Bobby Locke (TX)
Leslie Lummis (Guam)[12]
Steven Douglas Mabey (UT)
Rupert Lewis "Bob" Mercer (GA)
Ms. Merepeace (ID)

[1]Ehlers's running mate was Rick Wendt of Iowa.

[2]Fazzari promised to use her management skills as a former Las Vegas mambo dancer to solve the nation's problems. Turned down as a prospective owner of a brothel in Nye County (NV), Fazzari expressed her disgust with politicians during her campaign. She ultimately endorsed the candidacy of Ross Perot of Texas.

[3]Gill's platform advocated the conversion of defense expenditures to such peaceful uses as job creation and assistance for homeless persons. It suggested salary increases for senators and representatives in Congress, supported a woman's right to an abortion, and urged an annual referendum on foreign aid, defense spending, and federal salaries.

[4]Glover's running mate was Jan Peter Christensen of New York, who was nominated after the first two potential candidates—Sis Cunningham and Dave Van Ronk—declined. Glover's campaign condemned the "power elite" responsible for the decline in constitutional rights, education, medical care, the environment, and the economy. He saw social control being achieved by the "fat cats" through dividing the population along gender, racial, religious, socioeconomic, or lifestyle lines. He argued that the "drug war" was ruining the economy by making drugs more expensive and more profitable for suppliers. The government was accused of covering up its involvement in the assassinations of John F. Kennedy; Martin Luther King, Jr.; Robert F. Kennedy; and John Lennon. Foreign affairs were to be resolved through cooperative efforts among the president, Congress, and international courts.

[5]Gomez chose Harold Pope of North Carolina as his running mate. Gomez put forth a platform demanding that Congress should conduct all votes by roll call and should send to every voter a copy of congressional members' voting records and the president's action on legislation at the close of each session. It favored a "none of the above" ballot line, public funding for the National Endowment for the Arts, a thirty-year ban on lobbying by former federal officials, simplified and reduced federal laws, and open access to federal records regarding loans and repayments. The platform also proposed rebuilding the nation's infrastructure with domestic labor, requiring businesses sold to foreign interests to remain operative in the United States, limiting U.S. investment in Mexico and other countries, requiring businesses (including agriculture) to hire unemployed U.S. citizens first, giving foreign nationals only temporary work permits, charging royalties payable to the government for all mining and other extractive industries, having the government take over failed defense industries, encouraging privatization wherever possible, establishing a barter system for oil imports and a domestic oil distribution system subject to price controls, prohibiting exports abroad of any product banned in the United States, and eliminating all direct foreign aid, favoring instead international foundations and charities for public aid. He encouraged civilian uses of defense technology, assistance for veterans, U.S.-based military production, and base closures abroad when the host countries required rental payments. Finally, Gomez also called for curtailing criminal and terrorist elements in international banking within U.S. borders, promoting state-chartered banks, limiting federal bond sales to raising funds to meet war expenses, using community clinics to maintain a government-sponsored minimal health care plan for the poor, and providing government-salaried doctors to medically underserved areas.

[6]Green's platform demanded a complete reevaluation of the American people's priorities. It condemned the national debt, taxation without representation, foreign aid, foreign intervention, the savings and loan crisis, and environmental pollution. At the same time, it called for a guaranteed minimum standard of national health care; educational standards based on work force needs; a national job opportunity listing; a recognition that all U.S. citizens are racially and ethnically mixed; equal justice, protection, and representation for all; and a guaranteed drug-free environment.

[7]Guenther's platform demanded that "God's Holy Commandments" be allowed back in the public schools, promised higher education for those who could not afford it, urged creation of a Civilian Conservation Corps for unemployed youth, assured coverage of plastic surgery's costs for those who could not afford it, offered assistance to the hungry, recognized those wanting to be heard, and supported those "wanting to live, but denied the right."

[8]Campaigning as a "war veteran against nuclear weapons," Hamburg argued that politicians lavished raises on themselves and lived in luxury, peddling favors to enrich special interests. He sought support for speaking out against such "bipartisan corruption."

[9]Describing himself as a moderate on foreign policy and domestic economic issues and a liberal on social policy, Hoff declared his opposition to the death penalty and his support for abortion rights. He also favored the repeal of the Twenty-second Amendment to the Constitution.

[10]Hornberger's platform condemned both the Republicans and the Democrats for wasting the natural resources of the United States, particularly its old growth forests. It advocated a fine of $25,000 per linear foot and one year in jail for cutting any tree in a national forest or park. It also proposed a constitutional amendment to restrict the ownership of U.S. land, businesses, banks, homes, farms, and natural resources to U.S. citizens only.

[11]Howard's platform saw government's role as a limited one. She wanted to freeze government spending; simplify taxation through a flat tax; abolish real estate, excise, sales, and personal property taxes; fund transportation infrastructures and energy development through a gasoline tax; restrict the national government to defense, foreign policy, and oversight of state equity issues; limit government salaries; create individual employee health care funds with employer contributions; and end busing. The platform advocated the use of public school uniforms, prohibitions against the sale of defense systems to foreign countries, an end to the Security Council veto in the United Nations, use of the National Guard to assist local law enforcement in the drug war, and cutting off welfare for illegitimate pregnancies. It denounced the Gulf War and the invasion of Panama and questioned the need for aid to the former Soviet Union. Howard sought constitutional amendments to ban abortions, balance the federal budget, and abolish references to race, creed, origin, religion, gender, and so forth from census forms, job and grant applications, and school records.

[12]Lummis wanted to eliminate the Federal Reserve System and replace it with an Association of State Treasurers. Payments on loans would be used to balance the budget and wipe out the deficit.

Cullen Meyer (OH)[1]
William Christopher Meyer (WA)[2]
Kelsie Carter Miller (NM)
Jerry Roger Miller (FL)
Julian P. Miller (AL)
Burton L. Mooney (FL)[3]
Julie Ann Moyer (IL)[4]
George Alexander Muzyk (MD)
Jean Joie de'Vivre Nate (FL)
Elijah Anderson Omega (CA)[5]
Kim Peterson (GA)
Calvin E. Phillips, Sr. (OH)
Philip Andrew Pirtle (IL)
I Pulleverdown (AZ)[6]
Darcy G. Richardson (PA)
Ophelia Candyce Ryals (CA)[7]
Robert Lee "Bobby" Saunders (MD)
Terrance R. Scott (CO)[8]
Barbara S. Scott-Davenport (CA)
Mary Ann Elizabeth Shechan (CA)
Rickey D. Simmons (AR)

Keith Harold Slinker (PA)
Alphonso Dewitt Steward (NC)
Michael Ross Tunick Strauss (MA)[9]
Paul Leslie Stuck (TX)
Carl W. Taylor (WA)
Eric McBride Thompson (MN)[10]
William Ray Thompson, Jr. (TX)
Robert L. Tobin (NY)
Paul Edward Trent (OK)
Roy Wayne Tyree (IL)
Charlotte Uhler (MD) (withdrew)
Nan C. Weatter (MI)
Walter Henry Williams, Jr. (TX)
Vernon Leroy Wilmington (FL)[11]
Winton Danley Worswick (NV)[12]
Howard Worthy (MI)[13]
James W. "Jim" Wright (OR)
Stephen Thomas Zammuto (FL)

[1]C. Meyer proposed a special tax on labor hired by and farm products bought by businesses. The proceeds would be used to give a "living wage" to low-paid workers and family farmers. He urged the Democratic Party to nominate Bill Clinton for vice president under a Meyer presidency as a way of tutoring a future Clinton presidency.

[2]W. C. Meyer promised to "be honest" and work on the crime problem, on balancing the budget, reducing the national debt, reforming the tax system, and establishing equal rights for all, without quotas or early retirement.

[3]Mooney supported a flat tax, a two-term limit on serving as president, a balanced budget, Civilian Conservation Corps camps for the homeless, greater accountability for the CIA, an end to welfare, restoration of the U.S. park system, restitution for families of U.S. servicemen missing in action (MIAs) or held as prisoners of war (POWs), creation of a national health policy for all, an end to capital punishment, creation of tent cities in the desert to house aliens awaiting deportation, an end to foreign aid, increased support for teachers' salaries, establishment of centers for abused women and victims of crime, greater accountability for Congress, maintenance of the nation's nuclear arsenal, and a national recycling program for the United States.

[4]Moyer's running mate was Marlee Anderson of Illinois.

[5]Omega's platform defended flag burning as social protest, opposed gun control, supported mandatory prison terms for public officials convicted of wrong doing, endorsed criminal penalties for waving the Confederate flag, urged jailing or exiling hate groups, demanded life in prison for wrongful police shootings or killings, and suggested jail for those caught begging and sleeping on the streets. It advocated socialized medicine, an end to the Internal Revenue Service's (IRS) harassment of citizens, a link between taxation and voters' permission to spend public funds, a steeply graduated income tax, an end to foreign aid, a national initiative and referendum, a requirement of at least 50 percent of the popular vote to win election for president, and uniform election hours.

[6]I Pulleverdown (probably a fictitious name) issued a "final warning" to voters to obey God's Ten Commandments "or perish in Hell forever." He claimed that he was the "new, true leader" who was "the Chosen One." He stated, "Jesus is the answer to all of our problems, and I know all of the solutions to all of our problems."

[7]Ryals promised, if elected president, to use her salary to help homeless individuals. She advocated a drug-free United States, restraints on the Federal Bureau of Investigation (FBI), more personal contact between the president and the people, a national referendum on questions of war, and the elimination of the electoral college.

[8]Scott questioned the Gulf War, advocated home ownership through equity projects, opposed the General Agreement on Tariffs and Trade (GATT), promised to make the Small Business Administration a cabinet-level department, blamed the arms race for the deficit and pledged to bring it under control, and urged the closing of tax loopholes.

[9]In his platform, Strauss expressed his dissatisfaction with the nation's current leadership and his desire to do something that "looked good" on his résumé. Claiming that "literally tens of people have volunteered their support" for his candidacy, he urged a grassroots campaign in which supporters could each give two cents ("Your Two Cents' Worth") to his campaign fund. He advocated nonmilitary solutions to political problems; promised to create a Department of Peace; sought to enhance education by decreasing classroom size, promoting continuing teacher education, preserving local control of schools, and improving instructional aids; suggested that the federal government's proper roles in combating homelessness were to act as a clearinghouse of information and to set up, run, and evaluate programs; demanded development of new products and technologies to ensure a benign environment; supported decriminalization of drug use and increased emphasis on education and rehabilitation; urged diversity in energy policy through research and development of many different technologies; endorsed aid to the former Eastern Bloc nations; and called for the declassification of secret government documents.

[10]Thompson's platform opposed nuclear testing, focusing instead on peace, justice, and the empowerment of people. It promised a unilateral moratorium on the design, production, testing, and deployment of nuclear weapons; reductions in defense expenditures by $150 billion; an end to the Strategic Defense Initiative (SDI, or Star Wars); economic conversion programs; taxes on pollution and fuels; the installation of photovoltaic panels and a retrofit of energy conservation devices on all federal buildings; and an end to the subsidization of logging and grazing on federal land, road construction, tobacco production, and destructive farming techniques. Thompson also proposed limiting the CIA to intelligence gathering only, honoring treaties with Native Americans and international agencies, doubling the taxes on alcohol and tobacco to fund substance abuse education and treatment, decriminalizing marijuana, establishing a Peace Fund tax, reforming Social Security, and convening a constitutional convention to address a balanced budget, equal rights for women, gun control, abortion, term limits, and a ban on war.

[11]Wilmington ran his campaign through a chain letter. His only platform pledge was to establish a balanced budget.

[12]Worswick declared his candidacy because he believed "the Democratic and Republican tickets have become Stalinist monopolies." He described himself as a "hard-line Constitutionalist" who saw only five functions for the federal government: to house the Senate, House of Representatives, and Supreme Court; to man an army; and to handle interstate and international trade. He promised to eliminate the national debt in eighteen to twenty-four months, disband the IRS, create a flat tax, enforce the law against usury, stockpile gold and silver, make Cuba the fifty-first state, and encourage Mexico to become the next five states in the Union.

[13]Worthy demanded an end to deficit financing in government. He promised to eliminate the federal government, abolish the income tax, rescind property taxes, and reestablish the "Commonwealth of Independent United States."

Curtis Zar (FL)
Daniel Ian Zwillinger (MA)[1]

CANDIDATES FOR VICE PRESIDENT:
John Aschenbach (IL)
Bill Jarvis (WA)

INDEPENDENT (CAMPAIGN FOR A NEW TOMORROW; PEACE AND FREEDOM) PARTY

CANDIDATE FOR PRESIDENT:
Ron Daniels (OH)

CANDIDATE FOR VICE PRESIDENT:
Asiba Tupahache (NY)

PLATFORM HIGHLIGHTS:

SUPPORTED:

- free abortion on demand
- the elimination of all forms of discrimination
- adequate, free, community-controlled child care facilities
- a free, quality, equal education for all (based on a curricula of inclusion) from preschool to graduate school
- an enactment of a housing bill of rights
- a free universal system of national health care
- pay equity
- paid parental leave
- the ratification of the Equal Rights Amendment (ERA)
- statehood for the District of Columbia
- a domestic Marshall Plan to revitalize devastated rural and urban areas
- a demilitarization of the economy and its conversion to civilian production
- respect for the sovereignty and treaty rights of Native Americans
- reparations for African Americans
- a socially responsible economy with sustainable development, environmental justice, and progressive taxation
- the withdrawal of all U.S. troops from foreign soil
- complete nuclear disarmament
- respect for human rights and democracy

[1]Zwillinger's platform endorsed a balanced budget; suggested that federal environmental standards and occupational safety and health regulations be applied to any company (and its suppliers) selling products or services in the United States (even overseas firms) on a phased-in basis; demanded pro bono work by physicians, hospitals, and health clinics; supported universal childhood immunizations; advocated alternative national service in a modified Civilian Conservation Corps (as a means of rebuilding the nation's infrastructure) or hospices and child care; urged creation of a Department of Peace; called for broader access (electronically and through other means) of nonclassified government information; and recommended restrictions on the movement of large sums of money in pension fund investments. He favored denial of early parole or release for prisoners who cannot read or write as a means of encouraging literacy; sought taxation of the commercial income of religious groups; advocated adoption of the "English Rule," which requires the loser in lawsuits to pay all costs; and opposed lawyer and "expert witness" contingency fee cases.

- the right of self-determination for all peoples
- the economic development of Third World nations

The Peace and Freedom Party held its nominating convention in San Diego (CA) from August 15 through August 17, 1992. The party endorsed the independent nominations of Daniels and Tupahache.

INDEPENDENT TICKET

CANDIDATE FOR PRESIDENT:
Henry Ross Perot (TX)

CANDIDATE FOR VICE PRESIDENT:
James Bond Stockdale (CA)

Perot's campaign for the presidency was quite unconventional. He did not adopt a formal platform but instead published a book—United We Stand: How We Can Take Back Our Country—to outline his views. Sold in supermarkets and bookstores around the country, the book became a best-seller. In it, Perot warned against the mounting national debt and argued that professional politicians (an elite and bipartisan group in Perot's view) had created "a government that comes at us instead of a government that comes from us." He urged people to reassert their "ownership" of the country and to end government gridlock.

BOOK HIGHLIGHTS:

SUPPORTED:

- a $1,000 limit on campaign contributions
- restrictions on political action committees
- a stronger Federal Election Commission
- a shorter campaign season
- Saturday and Sunday elections as a means to increase voter participation
- free and equal access to the airwaves for all candidates
- easier voter registration
- the elimination of the electoral college
- tighter restrictions on foreign lobbyists
- a tough ethics law for politicians and lobbyists
- prohibitions on lobbying by former government officials
- an end to the use of government-owned civilian aircraft and the 89th Wing of the Air Force (used by top officials for travel) to cut off the "pampered royalty" of professional politicians
- a requirement that cabinet officials spend most of their time outside of Washington
- the fostering of a new perspective among public employees that citizens are the owners of the nation
- the elimination of restrictions on public employees that stifle initiative
- drastic cuts in White House and executive branch staff
- a slash in the congressional budget and the elimination of perks
- the reorganization and streamlining of congressional procedures

- reforms in the congressional retirement system
- the notion of an "Electronic Town Hall" to increase citizen participation in government
- the notion that in order to "repair our economic engine" the country had to "fix the system first"
- demands that federal agencies cut their discretionary spending by 15 percent
- the line-item veto
- a "real" deficit reduction law
- a simplified tax system and stronger collection efforts
- the elimination of "special tax favors," farm subsidies, protective tariffs, and business meal deductions
- a leaner defense budget
- an end to public subsidies for the rich
- controls on entitlement costs by making those who could afford to do so pay more and imposing higher premiums for users
- an increase in tobacco and gasoline taxes
- greater defense burden sharing by U.S. allies
- the stimulation of investment and an end to the capital gains tax for small business investment
- the creation of mentor programs
- the restructuring of credit markets to make credit more accessible to small businesses
- incentives for growth industries
- efforts to put "government on the side of jobs and growth"
- incentives for savings and strategies for encouraging investment (e.g., investment tax credits, research and development tax credits, and tax breaks for long-term capital gains)
- environmental protection because "conservation makes basic economic sense"
- a long-term energy policy to reduce U.S. dependence on foreign oil, including a "safe standard modular reactor," better waste disposal technologies, and more use of natural gas and coal
- research of all kinds
- educational reform
- preschool educational programs
- replication of successful school programs
- empowerment of parents (including school "choice")
- the restoration of local school district autonomy with accountability
- the creation of national standards and testing
- an increase in instructional hours during the school day
- a reform of the teacher certification process
- a better use of school buildings during nonschool hours (e.g., for day care, community activities, medical clinics)
- increased treatment and rehabilitation services for drug addicts, along with mandatory drug testing for prisoners
- the centralization of all federal drug interdiction and enforcement activities
- mandatory life sentences without parole for persons convicted of three violent crimes, regardless of the perpetrators' ages at the time their crimes were committed
- marketable skills and literacy requirements as conditions of release from prison for criminals convicted of violent crimes
- the conversion of former military bases into rehabilitation centers for youth convicted of drug or violent crime charges
- vigorous prosecution of gangs
- public and private experiments to divert gangs into legitimate profit-making enterprises
- a long-term health care strategy with a national health board to oversee cost containment and to set a national health policy
- a basic benefit package for universal coverage and "appropriate" tax treatment for benefits
- flexibility for the states in health care reform and the promotion of discussions that he hoped would lead to a consensus perspective
- stronger child support enforcement
- a national compromise on abortion (although Perot was personally in favor of a woman's right to an abortion)
- a national commitment to eliminate racial prejudice
- international free and fair trade as a basis for foreign policy, with special attention being given to the opportunities in the Pacific rim, while seeking "an America that leads"
- NATO's replacement by another mechanism that would reflect the new realities of Europe

---

INDEPENDENT TICKET

VOTE FOR PRESIDENTIAL NOMINATION: PEROT'S SUPPORTERS ENCOURAGED HIM TO BECOME A CANDIDATE AFTER HE APPEARED ON "LARRY KING LIVE," A TELEVISION TALK SHOW. HE INDICATED HE WOULD ENTER THE RACE IF "AVERAGE AMERICANS" GOT HIM ON THE BALLOT IN EVERY STATE. JUST AS THAT POSSIBILITY WAS REALIZED IN JULY 1992, PEROT UNEXPECTEDLY DECLINED TO RUN. THEN, AFTER A PERIOD OF UNFAVORABLE PUBLICITY, HE CHANGED HIS MIND AND FORMALLY ENTERED THE CONTEST ON OCTOBER 1, 1992.

VOTE FOR VICE-PRESIDENTIAL NOMINATION: WHILE NO NATIONAL CONVENTION WAS HELD, WILHELM FRIEDRICH STEINER OF CALIFORNIA OFFERED HIMSELF AS AN UNSOLICITED RUNNING MATE FOR PEROT. PEROT HAD ANNOUNCED HIS SUPPORT FOR HIS LONGTIME FRIEND, STOCKDALE, A FORMER NAVY OFFICER AND POW IN VIETNAM, WHEN PEROT'S INDEPENDENT CANDIDACY WAS FIRST DISCUSSED. ACCORDINGLY, STOCKDALE'S NAME WAS ON THE BALLOT IN ALL FIFTY STATES AND THE DISTRICT OF COLUMBIA AS PEROT'S VICE-PRESIDENTIAL NOMINEE.

- aid to the former Soviet Union
- continued isolation of Fidel Castro's Cuba
- the promotion of market capitalism in Latin America
- democratization in South Africa
- continued military and economic assistance to Israel
- a "new vision" for the role of the United States in the world

Opposed:

- government funds for the space station and Rural Electrification Administration
- "over-regulation"

Also:

- preached that the nation was a "team," the solution to its problems required "teamwork," and "only the people can remake our country"

INDEPENDENT VOTER PARTY

CANDIDATES FOR PRESIDENTIAL NOMINATION:
John Quinn Brisben (IL)
Earl Farwell Dodge (CO)
James Gordon "Bo" Gritz (PA)
Michael Stephen Levinson (NY)
Howard Phillips (VA)
Darcy G. Richardson (PA)
Robert Junior Smith (IL)
Erick McBride Thompson (MN)

PRIMARY:
March 10, 1992 (MA)

Phillips 352
Gritz 177
Smith 54
Richardson 36
Thompson 35
Dodge 26
Brisben 24
Levinson 21
others 391
none of the above 269

LIBERTARIAN PARTY

CANDIDATE FOR PRESIDENT:
Andre Verne Marrou

CANDIDATE FOR VICE PRESIDENT:
Nancy Lord

CANDIDATES FOR PRESIDENTIAL NOMINATION:
Richard Benjamin "Dick" Boddie (CA)
Craig Franklin
Robert Kipley "Kip" Lee (CA)
Nancy Lord (DC)
Andre Verne Marrou (NV)
Rita Sue Ontiveros (FL)
David Raaflaub (MI)
Mary Jane Ruwart (MI)

Hans Schroeder (PA)
Barbara S. Scott-Davenport (CA)

CANDIDATES FOR VICE-PRESIDENTIAL NOMINATION:
Richard Benjamin "Dick" Boddie (CA)
Craig Franklin
Nancy Lord (DC)
Mary Jane Ruwart (MI)
Calvin Warburton (NH)

PRIMARIES:
February 18, 1992 (NH):
Marrou

May 12, 1992 (NE):
Marrou 5

June 2, 1992 (CA):
Marrou 15,002
Scott-Davenport 8
Lee 4

6TH CONVENTION:
August 29–31, 1991, Chicago (IL)
David F. Nolan (CO), keynoter
Dave Walter, permanent chairman

At the convention, 449 delegates were admitted to vote for the presidential candidate.

PLATFORM HIGHLIGHTS:
The Libertarian platform reiterated the party's Statement of Principles and most of the 1988 platform. It denied the existence of any conflict between civil order and individual rights, claiming the party's positions were not based on the moral values of specific practices but on a fundamental belief that people's rights must be recognized. Personal responsibility was a cardinal tenet. Crime would have been fought through impartial and consistent law enforcement and the decriminalization of such "victimless" crimes as those involving drugs, alcohol, consensual sexual relations, possession or distribution and use of sexually explicit materials, prostitution, gambling, and suicide.

Supported:

- a repeal of antiracketeering statutes used to punish insider trading, sale of sexually explicit material, and nonviolent antiabortion protests
- a trend toward private protection services and voluntary community crime-control groups
- government restitution for wrongful criminal proceedings against an accused person and wrongdoer restitution for victims of crimes
- peremptory challenges to proposed judges by parties in criminal or civil cases
- the notion of a victim's "pardon" for criminals
- the private adjudication of disputes and a change in the rape laws to remove cohabitation as a defense
- the right of juries to decide on the justice of a law (rather than simply the facts of a case)

- an end to the doctrine of state "sovereign immunity"
- an end to involuntary mental health treatment or commitment to mental institutions
- the elimination of funding for mental health research
- an end to the insanity or "diminished capacity" defense in criminal cases
- the right to purchase and use radar warning devices and digital audio tape recorders
- the right of individuals to own and use private property (including their own bodies) and denounced government restrictions on those rights based on aesthetic values, riskiness, moral standards, cost-benefits estimates, or the promotion of economic growth
- restitution for Japanese-Americans whose lands were taken during World War II
- the right to privacy as inviolable and prohibitions against government surveillance of all types, including the information collected by the Census Bureau and other public agencies
- the right of employers to require AIDS testing as a condition of employment
- the abolition of both the FBI and the CIA
- a curtailment of Congress's subpoena power
- the dismantling of the internal security committees of Congress
- the destruction of all files compiled by the Selective Service
- unconditional exoneration for persons accused or convicted of draft offenses, desertion, or other acts of resistance to wars and the military
- the denial of draft requirements applied to women (on the grounds that the draft should be completely abolished)
- the right of collective bargaining and employers' rights to not recognize unions
- the repeal of the National Labor Relations Act and all state right-to-work laws, denouncing all government interference with bargaining
- the legitimacy of secondary boycotts
- the removal of all restrictions on immigration, the abolition of the Immigration and Naturalization Service and Border Patrol, full amnesty for illegal aliens, and an end to government restrictions on undocumented noncitizens
- a ban on punishing employers who hire undocumented workers
- all refugees
- full civil rights for all (including the wealthy and persons with different personal habits or political perspectives)
- accusations against the government of undermining family life and designing welfare laws to destroy families and households
- the extension to children of all rights granted to adults
- a repeal of all status offense laws
- the abolition of juvenile courts

- the elimination of laws that treated juvenile offenders as if they were not fully responsible for their crimes
- private adoptions along with the right of children to seek guardians other than their parents
- the authority of American Indian tribes to select the level of their autonomy (up to absolute sovereignty), with individual American Indians selecting their citizenship while enjoying full property rights
- an exchange program to "cash out" remaining federal obligations to Native American tribes
- efforts to hold as fully liable those responsible for damage to American Indian lands through careless disposal of waste materials
- the abolition of the Bureau of Indian Affairs
- the condemnation of the "war on drugs" as a threat to individual liberty and the repeal of all laws establishing civil or criminal penalties for the use of drugs or limiting the right to keep and bear arms
- total deregulation of the economic sphere, with only a limited public role in protecting property rights
- the repeal of the Sixteenth Amendment (income tax) and all involuntary taxes
- a repeal of federal inheritance taxes
- amnesty for tax evaders and relieving employers of the "involuntary servitude" of collecting taxes on behalf of the state
- a repeal of legal tender laws
- private ownership of gold
- the elimination of minted coins (with private minting on a competitive basis allowed)
- free market banking and the abolition of the Federal Reserve System, Federal Deposit Insurance Corporation, National Banking System, and other regulatory agencies in the banking and credit fields
- the abolition of the Federal Savings and Loan Insurance Corporation, National Credit Union Administration, National Credit Union Central Liquidity Facility, Federal Home Loan Bank, and similar agencies
- the abolition of such federal agencies as the Reconstruction Finance Corporation, Federal Financing Bank, Customs Court, Tariff Commission
- a return to the Jacksonian concept of the government maintaining its own treasury
- the abolition of all regulation of financial and capital markets, including the Securities and Exchange Commission, state "blue sky" laws, and all federal regulation of commodity markets
- balanced budget amendments for all federal and state governments
- a prohibition on the Federal Reserve System from acquiring new government securities
- the belief that "governments facing fiscal crises should always default in preference to raising taxes"
- any condemnation of monopolies as coercive and a natural outgrowth of government regulation
- a repeal of antitrust laws

- the abolition of the Federal Trade Commission and the Antitrust Division of the Department of Justice
- the right of individuals to form corporations and other types of voluntary association
- a condemnation of government and business alliances to promote "reindustrialization" along with all government guarantees of private loans
- the abolition of the Federal Housing Administration (FHA) , the Rural Electrification Administration, Federal Home Loan Mortgage Corporation, Federal National Mortgage Association, Farm Credit Administration, Student Loan Marketing Association, and the Small Business Administration
- a repeal of the windfall profits tax
- a rejection of government support for energy research and the development of energy alternatives
- the abolition of the Nuclear Regulatory Commission and the Department of Energy and nuclear power being subjected to the test of the free market
- reform of nuisance and negligence laws to cover damage done to individuals by air, water, and noise pollution, rather than government-supported efforts to control pollution
- the abolition of the Environmental Protection Agency
- the abolition of the Consumer Product Safety Commission and the repeal of all laws restricting advertising or requiring individuals to use protective equipment
- the abolition of the Federal Aviation Administration
- the abolition of the Food and Drug Administration
- an end to public education and urged states to repeal their constitutional provisions guaranteeing a public education
- tuition tax credits and other tax reforms favorable to private schools as interim measures
- an end to compulsory school attendance laws
- the cessation of forced busing and corporal punishment
- a reduction of tax support for public schools
- an end to all subsidies for childbearing (including welfare plans and tax-supported services for children)
- child care tax credits
- the elimination of special tax burdens on single people
- the abolition of all federal agencies regulating transportation and a return to private ownership of such public enterprises as Amtrak
- the privatization of airports, air traffic control systems, public roads, and the national highway system
- a repeal of federal speed limits
- a repeal of minimum wage laws and protective labor legislation for women and children, along with restrictions on day care centers and the National Labor Relations Act
- the deregulation of health care and the medical insurance industry, including the abolition of Medicare and Medicaid
- the right to pursue unorthodox alternative medical treatments

- midwifery, home births, and women's clinics
- birth control and a woman's right to an abortion
- "dollar for dollar" tax credits for charitable contributions and the use of tax credits to promote charity care
- a repeal of laws restricting the commercial sale of human body parts
- the right of hopelessly ill persons to terminate their lives
- a repeal of land use, zoning, building code, eminent domain, urban renewal, and similar laws, while recognizing private, voluntary land use covenants
- the privatization of inland waterways, dam sites, and water systems
- the abolition of the civilian functions of the Bureau of Reclamation, Bureau of Land Management, Forest Service, and the Army Corps of Engineers
- all ownership of public lands transferred to the private sector through homesteading
- the abolition of the Department of Agriculture
- the elimination of all government farm programs (including price supports, direct subsidies, and production regulations)
- a repeal of federal inheritance taxes
- the deregulation of transportation and abolition of the Interstate Commerce Commission
- an end to government involvement in pest control
- a repeal of the Occupational Safety and Health Act and the Social Security Act
- the abolition of the Postal Service and the Civil Service system
- an end to government control over political parties, including repeal of the Federal Election Campaign Act and all federal campaign finance laws
- open ballot access to new parties and independent candidates in state elections and the replacement of the ballot system itself in favor of a less restrictive system of tickets or cards printed by candidates
- a ballot line dedicated to "none of the above" to enable voters to register their dissent against the listed candidates for a public office
- nonintervention in foreign affairs and limited government engagement beyond national defense
- an end to the use of passports
- the elimination of foreign aid
- the abolition of government-sponsored arms sales
- the withdrawal of restrictions on U.S. trade abroad
- the abolition of such agencies as the Export-Import Bank and the Commodity Credit Corporation
- the development of standards to recognize private ownership claims to Antarctica, ocean floors, outer space, and other unowned resources
- the abandonment of all international treaties and agreements (particularly the Law of the Sea Treaty)
- the right of secession for states and other governmental entities
- calls for the withdrawal of the United States from the

World Bank and the International Monetary Fund, while arguing against international paper money and any U.S. financial bailout of foreign governments

- efforts to withdraw all U.S. military personnel stationed abroad (particularly in Central America, Europe, Japan, the Philippines, and the Republic of Korea), to abandon the Monroe and Reagan doctrines, to withdraw from participation in NATO and other multilateral and bilateral arrangements, and to foster mutual disarmament of nuclear weapons and missiles
- the abrogation of the Antiballistic Missile (ABM) Treaty and the policy of massive nuclear retaliation known as mutual assured destruction
- the withdrawal of U.S. nuclear weapons from Europe
- increased limits on the president's power to initiate military action
- the abrogation of all presidential declarations of "states of emergency"
- an end to secret executive branch commitments and unilateral acts of military intervention
- a constitutional amendment to clarify the limits of the president's role as commander in chief
- reductions in the size of the diplomatic corps
- an end to foreign aid
- the immediate withdrawal of the United States from the United Nations (as well as the removal of the United Nations from U.S. soil)
- the right of private citizens to engage in diplomatic negotiations with foreign governments
- a condemnation of all governments for violating human rights and urged that international negotiations be conducted without conceding moral legitimacy to any government or asserting moral superiority by the United States
- a repeal of the Neutrality Act of 1794
- immediate independence for American Samoa, Guam, Micronesia, Puerto Rico, and the Virgin Islands
- the voluntary peaceful use of outer space
- the abolition of the National Aeronautics and Space Administration, repudiation of the UN Moon Treaty, and privatization of all artificial satellites

OPPOSED:
- laws imposing a minimum drinking age or making bartenders and hosts liable for their guests, along with laws authorizing the alcohol and drug testing of drivers without probable cause
- government-mandated smoking and no-smoking areas in privately owned businesses
- the wholesale confiscation of alleged criminals' property prior to their conviction
- the labeling of cases as "civil" cases to avoid due process of law, excessive use of police force, use of preventive detention, and "no-knock" laws
- "no-fault" insurance
- forced jury duty

- school speech codes and all government censorship, including antipornography laws
- gags on press coverage
- restrictions on electronic bulletin boards and newspapers
- the Federal Communications Act
- efforts to limit commercial speech and advertising
- the government's involvement with the National Ad Council as well as the regulation of political advertising
- anticult activities and harassment of unconventional religious groups, following a strict interpretation of the separation of church and state
- the use of eminent domain to municipalize sports teams
- the use of search warrants against innocent third parties, random roadblocks, and random police searches of passengers on mass transit
- government restrictions on private research relating to encryption and deciphering
- the government's issuance of identity cards (especially the Social Security card) for individual citizens
- government secrecy and the widespread use of "classified" information
- any form of gun control, registration for the draft (or compulsory national service of any kind), military discharges based on sexual preference, and the Uniform Code of Military Justice
- terrorism and torture
- plant closure legislation
- preferential treatment such as affirmative action and the repeal, rather than extension, of protective laws applied to selected groups and of government attempts to regulate private discrimination in employment, housing, and public accommodations
- laws empowering the state to make children "wards of the state"
- restrictions on child labor and compulsory education
- statutes outlawing "adults only" apartments
- plans to redistribute wealth or manage trade, deficit budgets, inflationary monetary policies, expansive government spending, impediments to free trade, and public controls on the economy (e.g., wages, prices, rents, profits, production, or interest)
- all personal and corporate taxes and recognized the right to challenge payment on moral or other grounds
- all tax increases
- limits on corporate liability and on corporate size, merger restrictions, and the chartering of corporations
- all public subsidies, along with tariffs, quotas, and public utility franchises
- all government control of the energy field, including pricing, allocation, and production
- government conservation programs
- the need for "strategic storage" of oil, efforts to nationalize energy industries, rationing, and government ownership of energy resources

- the Superfund for cleaning up toxic wastes because it permitted responsible parties to escape the full consequences of their actions
- fraud and misrepresentation in the marketplace, along with "paternalistic" governmental interventions on behalf of consumers
- conversion to the metric system, deemed as coercive
- fluoridation of water and legal restrictions on what substances a person might ingest
- the denial of tax-exempt status for private schools on the basis of discrimination
- coercive controls on population growth and forced sterilization
- public funding for abortions
- mandatory retirement, occupational licensure, and antipoverty programs
- medical licensure requirements
- health planning boards
- prescription requirements
- mandatory AIDS testing and contact tracing, as were FDA restrictions on the availability of AIDS treatments
- limits on malpractice suits
- involuntary medical treatment and government restrictions on research
- medical education subsidies
- military intervention to protect individual U.S. citizens in foreign lands, advising U.S. citizens traveling or investing abroad that they did so at their own risk
- U.S. government participation in international cartels
- U.S. military and economic interventions and diplomatic meddling anywhere in the world

- the incorporation of other nations into the U.S. defense perimeter
- government restrictions on the private exploration, colonization, industrialization, and development of heavenly bodies
- the creation of new national parks or wilderness and recreation areas and urging transfer of such existing areas to private ownership

ALSO:
- noted that silence on any other aspect of government should not be construed to imply Libertarian approval

LIBERTY UNION PARTY

CANDIDATE FOR PRESIDENT:
Lenora B. Fulani (NY)

CANDIDATES FOR VICE PRESIDENT:
Barbara Garson (CA) (declined)
Carole Mulholland

CANDIDATES FOR PRESIDENTIAL NOMINATION:
John Quinn Brisben (IL) (Socialist Party)
Lenora B. Fulani (NY) (New Alliance Party)
Ron Daniels (IL) (Independent)

CONVENTION:
June 28, 1992

The Liberty Union Party was a left-wing Vermont-based party. Also see the New Alliance Party and Socialist Party.

LOOKING BACK PARTY

CANDIDATE FOR PRESIDENT:
Isabell Masters (OK)

CANDIDATE FOR VICE PRESIDENT:
Walter Ray Masters (KS)

The Looking Back Party expressed concern about "our bread and meat table," farmers, the trade deficit, health care, and "life on this planet." It proposed a jail sentence of six months for anyone who discriminated against minorities, equal pay for equal work, a minimal foreign relations role for the country, education for the disadvantaged, and "integrated biscuits on all tables."

NATIONAL SEA SONG PARTY

CANDIDATE FOR PRESIDENT:
Jan Peter Christensen (NY) (withdrew)

The platform of the National Sea Song Party called for resupplying the garrison at Fort Sumter and preserving the Union. Christensen's slogan was "A candidate so weird, his own wife wouldn't vote for him." Christensen, however, dropped out of the presidential race to accept the vice-presidential candidacy on an Independent ticket with Jim Ron Glover.

LIBERTARIAN PARTY
VOTE FOR PRESIDENTIAL NOMINATION:

Candidate	Ballot: 1
Marrou	257
Boddie	155
Schroeder	7
Raaflaub	6
Ruwart	2
Franklin	1
Lord	1
none of the above	20

VOTE FOR VICE-PRESIDENTIAL NOMINATION:

Candidate	Ballot: 1	2	3
Ruwart	129	64	0
Franklin	10	0	0
Warburton	19	20	0
Lord	98	180	240
Boddie	179	160	180

NATURAL LAW PARTY

CANDIDATE FOR PRESIDENT:
John Hagelin (IA)

CANDIDATE FOR VICE PRESIDENT:
Vinton Michael Tompkins

The Natural Law Party was formed on April 20, 1992, in Fairfield (IA). Its membership consists largely of followers of Maharishi Mahesh Yogi.

PLATFORM HIGHLIGHTS:
The platform of the Natural Law Party offered "Proven Solutions to America's Problems." It envisioned a national economy in which no citizen suffered from unemployment, recession, inflation, or economic hardship; in which America's businesses were highly competitive; and in which the national debt was reduced and the tax burden decreased.

SUPPORTED:
- significant tax cuts
- reduced government spending
- a balanced budget
- the improved health and productivity of workers
- the development of human resources
- a stabilized economy to increase the standard of living
- tax incentives to corporations using scientifically validated stress reduction programs (such as transcendental meditation, or TM)
- TM practice to decrease health care costs and absenteeism and to increase productivity and job performance; estimates of $1.2 trillion in savings by applying TM throughout society
- prevention and natural medicines (including Maharishi Ayur-Ved, an ancient Hindu medical practice) as the keys to saving health care costs
- a nationally subsidized health care system for lower-income families (replacing Medicaid) and private sector health insurance incorporating its principles within two to three years
- the teaching of "consciousness" in schools by building TM into the curricula
- full funding for Head Start
- government loans for college-bound students
- tax incentives for parents to keep their children in school until age twenty-one
- the creation of national standards for major subject areas in high school
- a longer school year
- the creation of a National Commission on Multicultural Education
- the addition of computer support to the National Literacy Act
- upgraded teacher skills
- the establishment of model schools
- improvements in the nutritional value of school lunches
- the establishment of community centers of knowledge
- the creation of a National Apprenticeship Program
- crime-fighting programs such as the school dropout programs and life-relevant education
- urban revitalization
- reductions in social stress
- rehabilitation for criminals
- commitments to energy efficiency and the use of renewable, safe, and nonpolluting energy sources through support for research, the creation of financial incentives, and the use of performance standards
- a de-emphasis on fossil fuels and a halt to nuclear energy development
- a timber moratorium on cutting in the national parks, national forests, and national monuments until sustainable management was achieved
- crop diversification, conservation tillage, and low-cost, integrated pest management systems
- local farmers' markets, organic crops, and the family farm
- a smaller, more flexible military force
- research and high technology rather than massive conventional weaponry
- the development of human resources
- reductions in SDI
- a halt to nuclear testing
- decreases in U.S. nuclear arsenals
- reductions in U.S. military troops stationed abroad
- the incorporation of a group of 7,000 TM-Sidhi experts into the military to add proven peace-creating programs to existing military resources
- the conversion of defense personnel and resources to peacetime domestic tasks
- a foreign policy based on the exportation of knowledge, not military aid
- the diversity of cultures, religions, and economic systems in the world and promised to promote programs of conflict resolution through TM
- the abolition of the electoral college
- calls for all U.S. citizens to vote
- measures to ensure ballot access
- campaign fairness for incumbents and challengers
- public funding for campaigns and the elimination of political action committees and "soft" political money
- a shortened campaign season
- restrictions on lobbying
- the need to make public servants more accountable (reserving to the public the right to raise salaries of elected officials directly)
- the recommendations of the Grace Commission and demanded elimination of waste and fraud (which it said accounted for 80 percent of the federal budget)
- privatization wherever possible
- job training programs and other initiatives to strengthen the economy and create new jobs, so that labor would be at a premium and workers could command better pay and working conditions

- drug rehabilitation, education, and interdiction programs, along with enlightened city planning—all founded on TM principles
- TM as a way of reducing social stresses that cause bigotry and discrimination
- the creation of a special federal department to deal solely with women's issues and another for the concerns of minorities
- efforts to strengthen family values such as asserting that primary-care parents should not be forced to work and recognizing senior citizens as the source of social wisdom
- jobs and an improved economy for Native Americans, respect for treaty rights and American Indian sovereignty, and respect for sacred sites and burial grounds
- the protection of environmentally sound subsistence rights and cultural integrity
- efforts to reduce the number of abortions through education and prevention programs, and the denial of the government's right to regulate matters relating to reproduction
- a national referendum on capital punishment "once violent crime has been significantly reduced"
- a national referendum on gun control being presented to the electorate "once a more coherent national consciousness has been created" that is less stressed than the current environment

OPPOSED:
- Defense Department procurement procedures, claiming that "government waste was out of control"
- the absence of performance standards in government
- multiple pension "double-dipping"
- inadequate debt collection
- pork-barrel spending
- the chaotic budgeting process

NATURAL LAW PARTY
VOTES FOR PRESIDENTIAL AND VICE-PRESIDENTIAL NOMINATION: THE NATIONAL CANDIDATES WERE SELECTED BY THE PARTY'S EXECUTIVE COMMITTEE.

NEW ALLIANCE PARTY

CANDIDATE FOR PRESIDENT:
Lenora B. Fulani (NY)

CANDIDATE FOR VICE PRESIDENT:
Maria Elizabeth Munoz (CA)

PLATFORM HIGHLIGHTS:
SUPPORTED:
- an open and more democratic election process
- full civil rights for minorities, gays and lesbians, and workers
- a free and comprehensive health care system
- an AIDS bill of rights and increased funding for AIDS treatment and research

- a reform of the mental health system to decrease treatment reliance on drugs and electroshock therapy
- the restoration of democracy in Haiti and Zaire
- the recognition of the rights of Palestinians
- an end to the undeclared war against Libya
- free education from day care through graduate school
- the federal assumption of the burden of financing education
- adult education and literacy programs
- a multicultural curricula that recognized the rights of women and gay people
- the adoption of a constitutional amendment guaranteeing the right to decent housing
- prohibitions against evictions for failure to pay rent
- the elimination of emergency housing in barracks-style "shelters" and a greater use of existing housing stock, with support services for persons with AIDS
- the elimination of residency requirements for voting
- African-American political solidarity
- affirmative action to foster the employment and education of Latinos
- free migration of Latino workers to the United States along with the extension of federal labor law protections to migrant workers
- bilingual education and denouncements of the "English-only" movement
- the development of programs to curtail Latino school dropouts and to expand college aid for Latino students
- self-determination for Puerto Rico (along with the withdrawal of all U.S. troops from the island)
- the release of all Puerto Rican political prisoners and the right of Latin American political refugees to obtain asylum
- full reinstitution of all Native American treaty rights and the payment of reparations for wrongful takings of lands in violation of treaty obligations
- independent civilian review boards to investigate complaints against the police along with the repeal of mandatory sentencing laws, expansion of education and job training for prisoners, fair compensation for inmate labor, more humane parole review procedures, and the extension of political rights to prisoners
- the right to abortion on demand
- no condemnation of pornography
- promises of a decent standard of living for everyone, regardless of employment status
- an increase in the welfare budget
- the right of welfare recipients to engage in collective bargaining
- an end to the harassment of welfare recipients
- gay and lesbian rights, including the rights to become foster parents and to form domestic partnerships
- a decriminalization of drugs
- an end to capital punishment
- the abolition of the Taft-Hartley Act and right-to-work laws

- the right to picket
- requirements that all companies with government contracts have union contracts
- an extension of labor rights under the Wagner Labor Relations Act to agricultural workers
- the free migration of workers, coupled with a requirement that U.S. firms opening factories abroad must employ unionized workers
- an increase in the minimum wage
- the abolition of the National Labor Relations Board
- guaranteed employment at union wage
- an indefinite extension of unemployment insurance
- more democracy as the answer to pollution and to prevent profiteers from dividing and conquering "by pitting poor people desperate for employment and progressive-minded middle class people—environmentalists—against one another"
- the National Endowment for the Arts
- animal rights, opposing killing for furs, mutilation for testing cosmetics, and the performance of redundant experiments for "educational" purposes

OPPOSED:
- workfare requirements
- anti-Semitism but the party also asserted that it was not Zionist
- all censorship
- gun control, deeming guns as essential for personal protection in poor communities wracked by violence

NEW PARADIGM PARTY
CANDIDATE FOR PRESIDENT:
Barry Alan Ellsworth (UT)

NEW WORLD ORDER PARTY
CANDIDATE FOR PRESIDENT:
Sol Gareth "Garry" Davis (DC)

Davis was a self-designated "world citizen," having renounced his U.S. citizenship in 1948 to protest militarism. The son of band leader Meyer Davis, he urged his followers to "think globally, act locally."

PLATFORM HIGHLIGHTS:
The platform of the New World Order Party (formerly the World Citizen Party) was "grounded in the Universal Declaration of Human Rights plus ecological rights as outlined in the Stockholm Declaration as well as the rights of ethnic minority groups."

SUPPORTED:
- world citizenship
- the creation of world law and appropriate government organs (e.g., World Legislature, World Courts, World Executive, and World Guard Force) essential to guarantee fundamental human rights and freedoms

- the realignment of local and national law to conform to world law
- the recognition and representation of viable ethnic groups
- representation for stateless persons and refugees
- the representation of ecosystems against exploitation
- the mundialization of villages, towns, cities, and universities
- the endorsement of existing national and international organizations and associations promoting world peace, human rights, and world government

PEACE AND FREEDOM PARTY
CANDIDATE FOR PRESIDENT:
Ron Daniels

CANDIDATE FOR VICE PRESIDENT:
Asiba Tupahache (NY)

CANDIDATES FOR PRESIDENTIAL NOMINATION:
Ron Daniels (OH)
Lenora B. Fulani (NY)
Leon C. Paulos (CA) (write in)
Barbara S. Scott-Davenport (CA) (write in)
R. Alison Star-Martinez (CA)

PRIMARY:
JUNE 2, 1992 (CA):
Fulani 4,586
Daniels 2,686
Star-Martinez 1,434
Scott-Davenport 3
Paulos 3

CONVENTION:
August 15–16, 1992, San Diego (CA)

The convention ratified the independent candidacies of Daniels and Tupahache for president and vice president, respectively.

PEACE AND JUSTICE PARTY
CANDIDATE FOR PRESIDENT:
Erik McBride Thompson (MN)

PLANET PARTY
CANDIDATE FOR PRESIDENT:
Robert Adgate "Bob" Congdon (MN)

PLATFORM HIGHLIGHTS:
SUPPORTED:
- calls for General Electric to clean up the planet
- promises to balance the budget and reduce the deficit
- cuts in the federal bureaucracy by 30.76 percent
- a national day care proposal
- efforts to detect "at risk" youth in advance
- affirmative action
- accessibility to state governors

- the creation of at least one new tax bracket of 53 percent on gross income over $82,150
- requirements for everyone to learn about the Myers-Briggs Type Indicator for Students (the short form)

OPPOSED:
- child abuse

POPULIST (AMERICA FIRST) PARTY
CANDIDATE FOR PRESIDENT:
James Gordon "Bo" Gritz (PA)

CANDIDATE FOR VICE PRESIDENT:
Cy Minett (TX)

3D CONVENTION:
May 2–3, 1992, Clark (NJ)

PLATFORM HIGHLIGHTS:
The 1992 Populist platform was identical to the platforms adopted in 1984 and 1988.

SUPPORTED:
- a repeal of the federal income tax
- the abolition of the Federal Reserve System
- a repudiation of the national debt
- the reactivation of anti-usury laws
- the enactment of fair tariff laws
- a revitalization of the family farm
- the rebuilding of the United States internationally
- efforts to reclaim the free enterprise system with a strong antimonopoly initiative
- a resurrection of "anti-degeneracy" laws and a crackdown on crime
- restrictions on pornography and illegal drugs
- freedom of choice with regard to public schools and the use of private property
- efforts to repulse immigration from Third World countries and to deport illegal aliens
- welfare reform to get "this vast class of socialist-voting, taxpayer-financed drones off the voting rolls"
- restrictions on judicial review
- the right to keep and bear arms
- inventiveness to make the country energy independent
- the freedom of individuals to seek medical help without government interference, including access to health foods, vitamins, and alternative cancer therapies
- a constitutional amendment to permit the direct election of the president after regional primaries and the direct election of federal judges
- the use of proportional representation and the initiative, referendum, and recall at all levels of government
- armed neutrality, with restrictions on foreign pressure groups operative in the United States (e.g., the Council on Foreign Relations, the Trilateral Commission, and the Bilderbergers)
- demands for the withdrawal of the United States from

the United Nations and the removal of the United Nations from U.S. soil
- a strong national defense, with arms control agreements contingent on appropriate on-site inspections
- military and economic aid only to friendly nations, not enemies, but doubted that either major party would pursue this policy because "the mattoids need communism to scare the people into tolerating massive taxes and a huge war budget, à la George Orwell's 1984"

OPPOSED:
- the ERA and gay rights
- forced busing and government interference with religious schools
- racial and cultural exploitation and argued against one race forcing another to subsidize it financially or politically
- forced segregation or integration
- a peacetime draft

Gritz also had his own platform.

SUPPORTED:
- reduced taxes
- an end to the foreign buyout of the United States
- a return to government basics
- an end to all illegal immigration
- welfare reform (including workfare)
- reductions in foreign aid
- an end to affirmative action
- a return to high moral standards and decency

OPPOSED:
- the "New World Order"

> **POPULIST (AMERICA FIRST) PARTY**
> VOTES FOR PRESIDENTIAL AND VICE-PRESIDENTIAL NOMINATIONS: GRITZ AND MINETTE WERE UNANIMOUSLY NOMINATED FOR PRESIDENT AND VICE PRESIDENT, RESPECTIVELY.

PROHIBITION PARTY
CANDIDATE FOR PRESIDENT:
Earl Farwell Dodge (CO)

CANDIDATE FOR VICE PRESIDENT:
George Ormsby (PA)

CONVENTION:
June 24–26, 1991, Minneapolis (MN)
Earl Farwell Dodge (CO), keynoter and permanent and temporary chairman

PLATFORM HIGHLIGHTS:
SUPPORTED:
- a commitment to the Constitution and its system of checks and balances

- protections against judicial usurpation of power
- free trade and limits on foreign aid
- a return to the gold standard
- a constitutional amendment to require a balanced budget, place limits on congressional taxing and spending powers, reduce the national debt, and require the sale of all government-owned businesses in competition with the private sector
- the free enterprise system
- the elimination of excessive regulation on businesses, control of monopolies, and regulation of deceptive business practices
- the abolition of the Federal Reserve System and withdrawal from the World Bank
- enforcement of antitrust laws and laws forbidding strikes by federal government employees
- an end to government preference for union shops in awarding contracts
- right-to-work laws
- states' rights and condemned regional governments
- a constitutional amendment to protect life from the moment of conception
- strict enforcement of laws against gambling, narcotics, pornography, and commercialized vice
- military preparedness, while applauding the concept of the all-volunteer military
- a reform of the welfare system to remove "undeserving persons" and to promote self-sufficiency
- uniform marriage and divorce laws
- nondiscrimination against married people in tax policies and an explicit public policy against extending marriage benefits to unmarried couples
- the separation of church and state (and urged cancellation of diplomatic relations with the Vatican) but approved Bible reading and voluntary prayer in public schools or other institutions
- a repeal of the Social Security tax on religious institutions
- ballot law reforms to extend access to third parties
- the revision of the Social Security laws to make the program voluntary, establish it on a sound actuarial basis, and place Medicare and Medicaid in separate programs
- the abolition of government controls and subsidies for agriculture
- the ban on harmful drugs and efforts to curb tobacco use
- AIDS research and increased efforts to combat the immoral behavior responsible for AIDS
- a long-term prison sentence for the conviction of a criminal act involving a firearm and strict enforcement of the immigration laws and deportation of illegal aliens

OPPOSED:
- communism

- quota systems and a reversal of the Bakke decision
- "unnatural" lifestyles
- efforts to restrict religious broadcasting and religious schools
- socialized medicine and involuntary commitment to mental hospitals

ALSO:
- blamed alcoholic beverages for a host of modern social problems and called for a program of publicity, education, legislation, and administration leading to prohibition of the manufacture, distribution, and sale of alcoholic beverages

---

PROHIBITION PARTY

VOTE FOR PRESIDENTIAL NOMINATION: DODGE WAS NOMINATED FOR PRESIDENT BY ACCLAMATION.

VOTE FOR VICE-PRESIDENTIAL NOMINATION: ORMSBY WAS ALSO NOMINATED FOR VICE PRESIDENT BY ACCLAMATION.

READERS OF THE NEW AMERICAN PARTY

CANDIDATE FOR PRESIDENT:
Paul Leslie Stuck (TX)

REPUBLICAN PARTY

CANDIDATE FOR PRESIDENT:
George Herbert Walker Bush

CANDIDATE FOR VICE PRESIDENT:
James Danforth Quayle

CANDIDATES FOR PRESIDENTIAL NOMINATION:
Sharon Scarrella Anderson (MN)
Frank Barella III (AZ)
Jack J. H. Beemont (KS)
Norman Walter Bertasavage (PA)
Richard P. Bosa (NH)
Emmanuel L. Branch (WI)
Patrick Joseph Buchanan (VA)
George Herbert Walker Bush (TX)
Gavin Clark-Davis (CA)
Billie Joe Clegg (MS)
Paul Beecher Conley (NY)
Paul Charles Daugherty (SC)
Doil Eskine Dean (MI)
Georgiana H. Doerschuck (FL)
Charles Richard Doty (OK)
David Ernest Duke (LA)
Roger Durrett (NC)
James Eaquinta (CA)
Oscar Adolph Erickson, Jr. (CA)
Thomas Stanley Fabish (CA)
Lowell Jackson Fellure (WV)

Michele Ann Gess (WI)
William Bruce Greenwood, Jr. (CA)
Maurice Horton (IL)
Paul Jensen (MI)
F. Dean Johnson (CA)
Alan Keyes (MD)
Stephen Arthur Chaim Kingstone (NY)
Stephen Andrew Koczak (DC)
Vincent A. Latchford (NJ)
James Patrick Lennane (FL)
Michael Stephen Levinson (NY)
Isabell Masters (OK)
Eddie McDowell (FL)
John David Merwin (NH)
Steven D. Michael (WA)
Amatul-Mannan Q. Katherine Bengalee Miller
    (VA)
Beatrice Elaine Johnson Mooney (MN)
David Naster (KS)
Jean Joie De'Vivre Nate (FL)
Joel Gary Neuberg (CA)
Frederick Eugene Ogin (CA)
Carl August Paleveda (FL)
Hubert David Patty (TN)
Patrick Layton Paulsen (CA)
Howard Phillips (VA)
David Sherman Ramsey (AZ)
Margaret S. Range (AL)
Pretty Bob S. Reams (MI)
Richard Frederick Reber, Jr. (GA)
Tennie Beatrice Rogers (CA)
Norman A. Russ (CT)
Conrad A. Ryden (NC)
Edward William Ryng (CA)
Aaron Wayne Sartain (KS)
Barbara S. Scott-Davenport (CA)
Terrance R. Scott (CO)
Gary Lee Sinkola (AK)
Philip P. Skow (KS)
Charles Thomas Smit (MN)
Brian C. Smith (RI)
Crawford Smith (SC)
Milton J. Southerland
Harold Edward Stassen (MN)
Wilhelm Friedrich Steiner (CA)
Alphonso Dewitt Stewart (MO)
Jack Trinsey (PA)
Marion Knitter Ziehlke (MI)
George A. Zimmermann (TX)

CANDIDATES FOR VICE-PRESIDENTIAL NOMINATION:
Herbert Porter Clark, Jr. (NH)
William G. Hare (CT)
Bruce Allen Landy (DC)
James Danforth Quayle (IN)
Wilhelm Friedrich Steiner (CA)

PRIMARIES:
FEBRUARY 18, 1992 (NH):
Bush 92,233
Buchanan 65,087
Tsongas 3,677
Nader 3,257
Clinton 1,696
Lennane 1,684
Paulsen 657
others 5,874

Vice-Presidential Primary, February 18, 1992:
Clark 26,179
Quayle 6,613
    (write in)
Hare 5,110
Peabody 181
    (write in)
Shargal 5
    (write in)
others 4,428
FEBRUARY 25, 1992 (SD):
Bush 30,964
uncommitted 13,707

MARCH 2, 1992 (CO):
Bush 132,000
Buchanan 58,753
Zimmerman 1,592
Jensen 1,332
Scott 719
Koczak 659
Rogers 535

MARCH 3, 1992 (GA):
Bush 291,905
Buchanan 162,082

MARCH 3, 1992 (MD):
Bush 168,374
Buchanan 71,647

MARCH 7, 1992 (SC):
Bush 99,558
Buchanan 38,247
Duke 10,553
Daugherty 482

MARCH 10, 1992 (FL):
Bush 608,077
Buchanan 285,386

MARCH 10, 1992 (LA):
Bush 83,744
Buchanan 36,525
Duke 11,955
Paulsen 1,186
Rogers 1,111
Zimmerman 474
Fabish 114

MARCH 10, 1992 (MA):

Bush 176,927
Buchanan 75,004
Duke 5,587
uncommitted 10,130
others 2,347

MARCH 10, 1992 (MS):

Bush 111,200
Buchanan 25,988
Duke 16,325
Clegg 407
Rogers 252

MARCH 10, 1992 (OK):

Bush 151,612
Buchanan 57,933
Duke 5,672
Masters 1,830
Rogers 674

MARCH 10, 1992 (RI):

Bush 9,911
Buchanan 5,012
Duke... 327
uncommitted 440

MARCH 10, 1992 (TN):

Bush 178,219
Buchanan 54,585
Duke 7,709
uncommitted 5,022
others 118

MARCH 10, 1992 (TX):

Bush 556,280
Buchanan 190,572
Duke 20,255
Zimmerman 1,349
Rogers 754
uncommitted 27,936

MARCH 17, 1992 (IL):

Bush 634,588
Buchanan 186,915
Horton 9,937

MARCH 17, 1992 (MI):

Bush 296,301
Buchanan 111,491
Duke 11,124
uncommitted 23,531
others 135

MARCH 24, 1992 (CT):

Bush 66,356
Buchanan 21,815
Duke 2,294
uncommitted 9,008

APRIL 5, 1992 (PR):

Bush 260,200

Buchanan 1,031
Duke 827
blank 499
others 368

APRIL 7, 1992 (KS):

Bush 132,131
Buchanan 31,494
Paulsen 5,105
Duke 3,837
Masters 1,303
Skow 1,105
Zimmerman 766
Beemont..................................... 735
Doty 417
Koczak 262
Daugherty 236
Fellure 164
Rogers....................................... 85
Patty 62
Fabish 44
Naster .... (withdrew)
none of the above....................... 35,450

APRIL 7, 1992 (MN):

Bush 84,841
Buchanan 32,094
Stassen 4,074
Perot 3,558
  (write in)
Anderson 300
Mooney 196
Zimmerman 135
Rogers....................................... 61
uncommitted 4,098
write ins 3,399

APRIL 7, 1992 (NY):

Bush.............................. (unopposed)
(Primary was not held because Bush was unopposed.)

APRIL 7, 1992 (WI):

Bush 364,507
Buchanan 78,516
Duke 12,867
Stassen 3,819
Branch...................................... 1,013
others 26,451
uncommitted 8,725

APRIL 28, 1992 (PA):

Bush 774,865
Buchanan 233,912

MAY 5, 1992 (DC):

Bush 4,265
Buchanan.................................... 970

MAY 5, 1992 (IN):

Bush 374,666
Buchanan 92,949

MAY 5, 1992 (NC):
Bush 200,387
Buchanan 55,420
no preference 27,764

MAY 12, 1992 (NE):
Bush 156,346
Buchanan 25,847
Duke 2,808
Zimmerman 1,313
Rogers 751

MAY 12, 1992 (WV):
Bush 99,232
Buchanan 17,873
Fellure 6,023

MAY 19, 1992 (OR):
Bush 187,786
Buchanan 53,519
Duke 6,331

MAY 19, 1992 (WA):
Bush 86,839
Perot 25,423
   (write in)
Buchanan 13,273
Michael 2,612
Duke 1,501

MAY 26, 1992 (AR):
Bush 45,392
Buchanan 6,503

MAY 26, 1992 (ID):
Bush 73,299
Buchanan 15,184
Duke . . . . (withdrew)
none of the above 26,566

MAY 26, 1992 (KY):
Bush 75,240
uncommitted 26,779

JUNE 2, 1992 (AL):
Bush 113,808
Buchanan 11,492
uncommitted 27,664

JUNE 2, 1992 (CA):
Bush 1,537,544
Buchanan 553,336
Scott-Davenport 153
   (write in)
Neuberg 21
   (write in)
Conley 15
   (write in)
Doty 8
   (write in)
Southerland 6

JUNE 2, 1992 (MT):
Bush 64,818
Buchanan 10,725
uncommitted 14,928

JUNE 2, 1992 (NJ):
Bush 226,920
Buchanan 45,585

JUNE 2, 1992 (NM):
Bush 54,498
Buchanan 7,699
uncommitted 23,372

JUNE 2, 1992 (OH):
Bush 769,245
Buchanan 155,327

JUNE 9, 1992 (ND):
Bush 39,512
Paulsen 4,110
Perot 2,265
   (write in)

35TH CONVENTION:
August 17–20, 1992, Astrodome, Houston (TX)
Robert Henry Michel (IL), permanent chairman
Phil Gramm (TX), keynoter

PLATFORM HIGHLIGHTS:
The 1992 Republican platform announced a "Vision Shared: Uniting Our Family, Our Country, Our World." It recited the accomplishments of the Bush administration and lauded family values and personal responsibility.

SUPPORTED:
• a reform of adoption and foster care laws and calls for states to explore ways to promote marital stability
• job sharing, telecommuting, compressed work weeks, private sector parental leave policies, and flextime as ways of allowing parents to spend more time with their children
• tax reforms, including restoring the value of the dependent deduction, eliminating the marriage penalty, and streamlining requirements for in-home care
• home-based schools and youth apprenticeship programs that include a year of college
• choice in education through a voucher system
• the use of "distance learning"
• the use of technology in schools
• reforms of the teacher certification system
• abstinence education
• competency testing and merit pay for teachers
• voluntary school prayer and recitation of the Pledge of Allegiance in public places
• a uniform claim and data system
• rehabilitation and long-term care, better prenatal and other preventive care, extension of the Good Samaritan law, regulatory reforms, modification of the an-

titrust laws in medicine and greater use of technology in the practice of medicine (particularly in rural areas)

- government funds for research at the National Institutes of Health (e.g., to combat breast and cervical cancer)
- the search for a cure for AIDS, which was seen as being like "any other communicable or sexually transmitted disease"
- efforts to protect the fetus in both the workplace and in scientific research
- efforts to help the homeless
- Social Security and the elimination of the earnings limitation
- long-term care and research to combat Alzheimer's disease
- the Boy Scouts of America
- a national crusade against pornography and a national computerized registry to trace persons convicted of molesting children
- the abolition of the "outdated ban on home work" (i.e., work based in the home) and the "antiquated Davis-Bacon Act"
- stronger enforcement of child support laws along with tough penalties against welfare fraud
- the establishment of welfare requirements: work for those capable of working, school attendance for recipients' children, and education or training programs for young adult heads of households
- increased rights for the victims of crime and restitution
- local law enforcement officials and incentives provided to personnel leaving the armed forces to enter the law enforcement profession
- women's rights and the "right to life," endorsing a constitutional amendment prohibiting abortions and denying the use of public revenues for abortions
- the appointment of judges based on their respect for "traditional family values and the sanctity of innocent human life"
- the full implementation of the Americans with Disabilities Act
- reductions in the amount of federal land holdings, especially in the western states
- stiff mandatory sentences for crimes committed with firearms
- collective bargaining along with the right of states to enact right-to-work laws
- an amendment to the Hobbs Act to make it apply to unions and greater legal protection from violence for workers who stay on the job during strikes
- self-determination for American Indian tribes, including easier eligibility for federal programs (e.g., enterprise zone designation)
- Native American and Hawaiian cultures
- a commitment to keeping the economy of the United States "first in the world," which meant keeping infla-

tion and interest rates low and stable through a sound monetary policy

- no attempts to increase taxes and "ultimate" repeal of the 1990 tax increases, with cuts in the tax rates and caps on the growth of non-Social Security entitlements
- a reduction in the capital gains tax
- an investment tax allowance
- a $5,000 tax credit for first-time home buyers
- a modification of the "passive loss rule" (i.e., a tax code provision)
- a $500 increase in the personal income tax exemption
- calls to make permanent the research and development tax credit
- the passage of federal enterprise zone legislation
- a deduction for individual retirement accounts
- simplified taxes
- religious and ethnic fraternal benefit societies not being subject to taxation
- efforts to make pensions more portable
- a freeze on new regulations, calling government regulation a "hidden tax on American families"
- state efforts to lower property taxes
- a repeal of rent control laws
- the FHA mortgage insurance program, the National Mortgage Association, and the Veterans Administration (VA) guarantee program
- open housing laws
- tax incentives for home owners
- small businesses and technology, which were seen as the key to the country's future
- funds for basic research, investment in emerging technologies, improved education in science and engineering, enhanced tax credits for research and development, elimination of unnecessary regulation, protections for intellectual property, and accelerated pace of technology transfer from the government to the private sector
- the completion of Space Station Freedom, the National Aerospace Plane, and single-stage-to-orbit rockets and lowering the cost of access to space by the private sector
- the People's Republic of China's accession to GATT, the NAFTA, and the Enterprise for the Americas Initiative with Latin America
- the notion that U.S. aid, whether bilateral or through international organizations, should promote market reforms, limit regulation, and encourage free trade
- foreign privatization of state-owned industries as an opportunity for U.S. companies to purchase some of the assets
- the withholding of funds from international organizations involved in abortion
- a "leaner, more effective government," with decentralized authority, the free enterprise system, and empowerment rather than dependency

- a constitutional amendment to limit the number of terms members of Congress could serve
- demands that Congress cover itself in the laws it applies to the nation
- calls for Congress to slash its own bureaucracy and to enact laws to protect Capitol Hill whistle-blowers
- proposals for a constitutional amendment to balance the budget, the line-item veto for the president, sunset laws, zero-based budgeting in Congress, and other reforms intended to demonstrate the need for a change to Republican majorities in the House and Senate
- the greater use of states' nonpartisan redistricting commissions to end gerrymandering and campaign finance reforms that target political action committees, arbitrary spending limits, and public financing proposals
- the creation of "Quality Workers for a Quality America" coalition to promote customer-friendly government and to manage government in the public interest
- the privatization of public facilities (including state and local facilities built with federal aid), with particular support for the private sector's assumption of airport operation and management
- the Tenth Amendment's perspective on states' rights
- reforms in the legal system, including use of the "Fairness Rule," elimination of frivolous lawsuits, banning of "junk scientists" posing as expert witnesses, and automatic disclosure during discovery
- product liability reforms and an end to "defensive medicine"
- self-determination and full rights for resident U.S. citizens in other territories, statehood for Puerto Rico, and the establishment of commonwealth status for Guam
- humane treatment of animals but denounced animal rights extremists
- increased exports, new products, and new markets as the most viable way to expand U.S. agriculture
- pledges to fight unfair international competition and protectionism in the Uruguay Round, NAFTA, and bilateral agreements
- increased research and development for ethanol
- easier access to farm credit
- improvements in the maritime industry as a way of decreasing the cost of shipping agricultural products
- the Conservation Reserve
- voluntary erosion control undertakings
- the opening of the coastal plain of the Arctic National Wildlife Refuge and selected areas of the outer continental shelf to oil and gas exploration and development
- decontrols on wellhead prices for clean natural gas
- the restoration of the original intent of the Mining Law of 1872
- the development of clean coal technologies
- the underwriting of the Super Conducting Super Collider
- the development of the next generation of nuclear power plants

- the siting and licensing of a permanent waste depository and a monitored retrievable storage facility
- the development of renewable energy sources and research
- the multiple use of federal lands
- the total deregulation of the trucking industry and abolition of the Interstate Commerce Commission
- fair access to international routes for U.S. air carriers
- the development of high-speed rail systems through private investment
- short-haul aircraft with vertical take-off and landing capability, intelligent highways (i.e., with built-in electronic directional devices), an efficient battery for electric cars, perfected natural gas vehicles, greater private investment in space travel, and removal of regulatory impediments to intermodal transport
- President Bush's confrontation at the 1992 Rio Conference, as the party asserted its intent to use "scientifically respectable risk-benefit assessments to settle environmental controversies"
- an overhaul of the Superfund program to speed cleanup of hazardous waste and develop more greenways in urban areas
- the fall of communism abroad, giving much of the credit to President Bush and urging voters to trust him with the "awesome responsibility" of leading the nation into an uncertain future
- the Gulf War under the leadership of President Bush as a great victory for the United States and the free world
- the NATO alliance and asserted that "the United States must remain a European power"
- a UN peacekeeping effort and immediate cease-fire in Yugoslavia, condemning the violence there
- peaceful solutions to the problems in Cyprus and Northern Ireland
- the country's special relationship with Israel, promising continued military assistance and expressing a willingness to negotiate and limit arms sales to the Middle East
- the direct talks between Israel and its Arab neighbors, giving President Bush credit for them but shying away from suggesting that the United States impose a solution on the parties
- the "legitimate rights of the Palestinian people"
- Jerusalem as an undivided city, with free access to all holy places
- unrestricted emigration to Israel
- Egypt, recognizing it as the leader of the Arab world and promising it generous aid
- an end to the Arab boycott of Israel and restoration of a strong central government in Lebanon
- the defeat of drug lords in the Western Hemisphere (and praised the end of Manuel Noriega's government in Panama)
- lower barriers to trade and investment
- open access to U.S. shipping through the Panama Canal

- the restoration of democracy to Haiti
- an end to Fidel Castro's regime in Cuba
- Radio and TV Marti and the spirit of Cuba Libre
- continued cooperation with Japan and greater Japanese responsibility for self-defense and worldwide prosperity
- the U.S. commitment to Taiwan
- improved relations with the People's Republic of China, contingent on democratic reforms
- the special U.S. ties to the Philippines and the Republic of Korea
- Cambodia's movement toward peace and democracy and demanded a full accounting of U.S. POWs and MIAs in Southeast Asia before normal relations could resume with Vietnam
- the international effort to end anarchy in Somalia
- peaceful change in South Africa through constructive engagement with the South African government and continued opposition to apartheid
- calls for the international burden for peacekeeping and foreign aid to be shared among all democracies
- the role of private voluntary agencies in meeting the needs of the newly liberated countries in Eastern Europe and the former Soviet Union
- continued cooperation with the Russian and other former Soviet governments in dismantling conventional and nuclear weapons, as the Republicans urged movement beyond the terms of the ABM Treaty toward a stronger Nuclear Nonproliferation Treaty
- the idea that the Soviet bloc's demise was cause for celebration but not for relaxing defenses
- cuts in the U.S. armed forces but "not a free fall"
- a triad of land-, sea-, and air-based strategic forces, with continued testing of nuclear weapons
- the need to maintain U.S. military technological superiority, the nation's readiness to combat terrorism, continued development of SDI, development of the country's industrial base, and "robust levels of investment" in research and development
- the continuation of arms reductions, an end to the micromanagement of defense programs, and reductions in the number of oversight committees
- the all-volunteer military
- a preference for veterans in federal employment, education, and retraining programs
- a halt to the sale of sexually explicit materials in military facilities
- sufficient funding to maintain the integrity of the veterans hospitals and medical care system and to assist unemployed veterans
- the U.S. intelligence community and its operations, including covert action

OPPOSED:

- public school programs related to birth control or abortion
- government control over health care, preferring less

global reforms such as new tax credits and deductions (perhaps in the form of vouchers), elimination of pre-existing condition exclusions, authorization of health insurance purchasing pools for small businesses, overrides of state mandates, use of risk pools, malpractice reforms, and 100 percent deductibility of health insurance premiums for the self-employed
- clean needle and condom distribution programs, asserting that prevention was a personal responsibility
- the inclusion of gays and lesbians among the protected classes in the civil rights laws, same-sex marriages, and adoptions by gay couples
- the use of public funds to subsidize obscenity and blasphemy in the guise of art
- euthanasia, assisted suicide, and nonconsensual rationing of health care to persons with disabilities
- gun control
- taxes on savings and dividends
- the value-added tax
- union dues being used for partisan purposes against the wishes of individual union members
- the "blatant political bias" of the Corporation for Public Broadcasting and demanded greater accountability
- statehood for the District of Columbia and demanded greater congressional scrutiny of its law enforcement, courts, and expenditures
- agricultural price controls, commodity programs, and restrictions on production
- bureaucratic harassment of farmers, ranchers, and timber families regarding endangered species and wetlands but expressed an appreciation of wetlands and biological diversity
- the use of Legal Service Corporation funds to attack U.S. agricultural practices
- a carbon tax
- any actions that would undermine U.S. sovereignty in either political or economic matters
- the creation of an independent Palestinian state
- compulsory domestic service as a backdoor method of reinstituting the draft

REPUBLICAN PARTY VOTE FOR PRESIDENTIAL NOMINATION:	
Candidate	Ballot: 1
Bush	2,166
Buchanan	18
Phillips	2
Keyes	1

VOTE FOR VICE-PRESIDENTIAL NOMINATION: THE CONVENTION HALL WAS NEARLY EMPTY WHEN QUAYLE'S NAME WAS PLACED IN NOMINATION, AND HE WON BY ACCLAMATION.

- combat positions for women and the continued exclusion of homosexuals from the military

SAVE AMERICA PROGRESSIVE PARTY

CANDIDATE FOR PRESIDENT:
Billy Joe Clegg (FL)

The platform of the Save America Progressive Party demanded the deportation of "flag-burning traitors," the elimination of the IRS, full benefits for veterans, an increase in the minimum wage, the elimination of the capital gains tax, and the promotion of the word of Jesus Christ. It opposed most-favored-nation status for the People's Republic of China, homosexuality (advocating compulsory quarantine of gays and lesbians to prevent AIDS), abortion, and obscenity parading as "art."

SOCIALIST PARTY

CANDIDATE FOR PRESIDENT:
John Quinn Brisben (IL)

CANDIDATES FOR VICE PRESIDENT:
Barbara Garson (MA) (William Davis Edwards [CA] deceased)

CONVENTION:
September 1, 1991, Chicago (IL)
David Ernest McReynolds (NY), cochairman
Karl Fisher (IL), cochairman

PLATFORM HIGHLIGHTS:
The Socialist Party's platform sought to restore high, progressive tax rates on wealthy individuals and corporations.

SUPPORTED:
- socialized banking and credit industries
- the restructuring of the housing industry to provide affordable homes for all (including a provision for sweat equity)
- the restoration of democratic labor's right to organize
- centralized pension funds under a democratically controlled National Pension Authority
- the allocation of jobs and capital according to a national economic development plan
- family allowances and adequate day care
- the creation of a complete, publicly funded and administered health care system for all
- sex education, contraceptives, and abortion services
- the protection of individuals from involuntary medical or surgical procedures
- the elimination of domestic and sexual violence
- increased research on AIDS and disease such as cancer
- maternity and paternity leave
- expanded benefits for seniors
- equal educational and retraining opportunities
- amnesty and full civil rights for undocumented workers

- ratification of the ERA and the UN Declaration of Human Rights and the enactment of a lesbian and gay rights law
- equal rights, including economic justice, regardless of gender, age, race, ethnicity, physical disability, sexual orientation, or lifestyle
- the decriminalization of victimless crimes (including substance abuse)
- the abolition of behavior modification units in prisons
- a halt to police brutality
- neighborhood watch groups
- expanded community control and oversight of police
- a repeal of Taft-Hartley and "right-to-work" laws, along with plant closure legislation, an increased minimum wage, union democracy, and a call for a thirty-hour work week
- a progressive income tax and tax relief for renters
- universal nuclear disarmament and renunciation of the first-strike capability of the United States
- the dismantling of NATO
- an end to wars fought to protect corporate profits
- continued sanctions against South Africa
- recognition for Vietnam and Cuba
- the fulfillment of treaty obligations with Native American nations
- the withdrawal of U.S. troops stationed abroad
- the cancellation of Third World debt
- the abolition of the CIA, National Security Agency, and other covert organizations attempting to overthrow foreign governments
- the creation of a cabinet-level Department of Peace
- the destruction of the stockpiles of nerve gas and chemical and biological weapons
- a halt to public spending on useless weapon systems and troop deployments
- the notion that greed was endangering the planet
- renewable, decentralized energy sources
- public ownership of utilities and energy plants and a ceiling on household utility charges
- expanded foot and bicycle paths, mass transit systems, and interurban railways
- land reform and the replacement of corporate farming with family-centered, ecologically sound food production
- low-cost loans, grants, and technical help for family farmers and cooperatives
- the right of farmers and farm workers to organize and bargain collectively
- promises to farmers of parity for their crops
- recycling
- the conservation of natural resources

OPPOSED:
- the designation of English as the only official language
- factory meat farming
- research on recombinant DNA

SOCIALIST PARTY

VOTE FOR PRESIDENTIAL NOMINATION:
BRISBEN WAS NOMINATED FOR PRESIDENT.

VOTE FOR VICE-PRESIDENTIAL NOMINATION:
EDWARDS WAS NOMINATED FOR VICE PRESIDENT, BUT
HE DIED ON AUGUST 5, 1992. THE NATIONAL
COMMITTEE NAMED GARSON AS HIS REPLACEMENT.
SHE WAS ALSO NAMED AS THE VICE-PRESIDENTIAL
CANDIDATE FOR THE LIBERTY UNION PARTY IN
VERMONT, BUT SHE DECLINED ITS NOMINATION.

SOCIALIST WORKERS PARTY

CANDIDATE FOR PRESIDENT:
James Mac Warren (IL)

CANDIDATES FOR VICE PRESIDENT:
Estelle DeBates (NY)
Willie Mae Reid (IL) (IL, IA, LA, NM, TN, UT, WI)

The Socialist Workers Party favored Trotskyite socialism, equality for women and minorities, an end to apartheid in South Africa, a Palestinian homeland, Third World liberation movements, and a progressive domestic agenda. It also opposed militarism and imperialism.

STATESMEN PARTY

CANDIDATE FOR PRESIDENT:
Earl A. Roberts, Jr. (CT)

The Statesmen Party promised to donate 20 percent of the president's salary to nongovernmental organizations.

PLATFORM HIGHLIGHTS:
SUPPORTED:
- a streamlined government
- a line-item veto
- the removal of the prevailing wage in government contracts and a review of contracts for overcharges
- an energy conservation and recycling program throughout the government
- reductions and closure of overseas bases
- a strengthened National Guard and requirements of one years' military service for every youth under twenty-one
- an end to farm subsidies for agribusinesses
- the development of ocean farming
- an elimination of the production and export of nationally banned agricultural products
- organic and integrated pest management farming
- mass weatherization programs and recycling
- stronger parent-teacher relationships
- a longer school year
- increased encouragement for mechanically and intellectually gifted students
- competency testing for students and teachers
- longer court hours
- the reinstitution of the death penalty in the United States
- boot camps and community service for juvenile offenders
- a "common language" law
- stiffer penalties for white-collar crimes
- the enforcement of the 200-mile limit for offshore fishing
- the removal of longlines in fishing
- the rebuilding of fishing stocks
- fathom limits for trawler activity
- restrictions on wetland filling and coastal development
- international space exploration
- boycotts for political and environmental upheavals
- nonmilitary foreign aid
- promises to seek quality instead of quantity in humanity, promoting family planning and permitting abortion as a private and personal matter
- the retraining and retooling of strategic nonmilitary economies
- an emphasis on decentralization, conservation, efficiency, and long-term growth
- the interaction between manufacturing and educational training

OPPOSED:
- new taxes

SURPRISE PARTY

CANDIDATE FOR PRESIDENT:
Robert L. "Uncle Torvald" Johnson (SD)

Asking voters to "put a Norwegian in the White House," Johnson asserted, "The future ain't what it used to be." He claimed that "any fool can be President. Elect me and I'll prove it." He noted the voters could do worse and usually have.

TAKE BACK AMERICA PARTY

CANDIDATE FOR PRESIDENT:
John Andrew Yiamouyiannis (OH)

CANDIDATE FOR VICE PRESIDENT:
Allen C. McCone (MO)

PLATFORM HIGHLIGHTS:
SUPPORTED:
- protective tariffs
- restrictions on foreign ownership of real estate
- an end to bailouts of the banking system
- the government's issuance of enough money to pay back the national debt
- the abolition of the federal individual income tax
- economy in government
- the imposition of an "excessive charges" tax on licensed professionals

- a pollution tax
- a resource consumption tax
- a graduated corporate tax on salaries and perks
- the creation of a national health service rather than national health insurance
- a restoration of confidence in the integrity of public officials
- the creation of opportunities for individual success and the building of self-esteem
- the nuclear family
- economic growth to permit a voluntary return to one-income families
- a reawakening of moral awareness
- parity for agricultural prices

THIRD PARTY

CANDIDATE FOR PRESIDENT:
Eugene Arthur Hem (WI)

CANDIDATE FOR VICE PRESIDENT:
Joanne Rolland (WI)

TISCH INDEPENDENT CITIZENS PARTY

CANDIDATE FOR PRESIDENT:
Howard Phillips (VA)

CANDIDATE FOR VICE PRESIDENT:
Robert Emmanuel "Bob" Tisch (MI)

For the platform, see the U.S. Taxpayers Party.

TRUTH AND FREEDOM PARTY, U.S.A.

CANDIDATE FOR PRESIDENT:
Nick C. Kratsas (OH)

CANDIDATE FOR VICE PRESIDENT:
Judith Hicks Valerio (OH)

The 1992 platform for the Truth and Freedom Party urged the enactment of the Notch Baby Reform Act of 1991, sought the revitalization of Volunteers in Service to America (VISTA) to build barracks-type shelters for the homeless and nonviolent jail inmates, condemned the Gulf War, and demanded the right to jobs, health care, and freedom from wars for all U.S. citizens.

TWENTY-FIRST CENTURY PARTY

The Twenty-first Century Party was formed under the leadership of the National Organization for Women. It organized in a convention at the Capital Hilton Hotel in Washington, D.C., from August 29 to August 30, 1992. No nominations were made for public office.

U.S. FELLOWSHIP PARTY

CANDIDATE FOR PRESIDENT:
Lloyd Osborne "Alamo" Scott (TX)

U.S. TAXPAYERS PARTY

CANDIDATE FOR PRESIDENT:
Howard Phillips (VA)

CANDIDATES FOR VICE PRESIDENT:
Stephen Carey Graves (AR) (LA, WY)
Albion Williamson Knight, Jr. (MD)
Robert Emmanuel "Bob" Tisch (MI) (MI)

CONVENTION:
September 4–5, 1992, New Orleans (LA)
William K. Shearer (CA), temporary chairman
Ted Adams (SC), permanent chairman
Otto Scott (CA), keynoter

Delegates from thirty-two states and the District of Columbia attended the convention. Rep. William Dannemeyer of California, Ambassador David Funderbunk of North Carolina, and the Libertarian Party's former standard-bearer, Ronald E. "Ron" Paul of Texas, addressed the convention.

PLATFORM HIGHLIGHTS:
Supported:

- political reform
- more jobs for Americans
- parental control of education
- home schooling
- an end to federal funding for education
- the end of technology transfers to enemies of the United States
- the preservation of U.S. defense capabilities
- the deployment of SDI
- the abolition of congressional pensions
- the elimination of congressional pay beyond a per diem
- the abolition of the franking privilege
- reduced congressional staffs
- liberalized ballot access
- the abolition of the 1974 federal election law
- equal rights to access the media
- term limits on members of Congress
- efforts to balance the budget
- the withdrawal of the United States from the United Nations and from other international bodies
- the right of self-defense against criminals
- the right to bear arms
- the restoration of the death penalty and requirements for victim restitution
- a repeal of the Seventeenth Amendment (the direct election of senators)
- a halt to federal funding of special interest groups (including farm subsidies)
- restrictions on the ability of Congress to "buy votes" from the federal Treasury

- an expansion of the House of Representatives by doubling, tripling, or even quadrupling it
- judicial accountability
- an end to the income tax
- the abolition of the IRS
- a change in the day taxes were payable
- an end to fiat money
- a rejection of environmental extremism
- an end to the Social Security tax
- the abolition of federal regulatory commissions
- a reduction of federal ownership of public lands
- the promotion of private charities

OPPOSED:
- the "New World Order"
- foreign aid
- funding for the National Endowment for the Arts
- socialized medicine
- excessive government spending
- burdensome regulation
- racial quotas of any kind
- condom distribution in schools
- abortion
- gay rights

U.S. TAXPAYERS PARTY

VOTE FOR PRESIDENTIAL NOMINATION: PHILLIPS WAS NOMINATED ON THE FIRST BALLOT, RECEIVING 264 OF THE 270 VOTES CAST.

VOTE FOR VICE-PRESIDENTIAL NOMINATION: THE CANDIDACIES OF ALL THREE VICE-PRESIDENTIAL NOMINEES—KNIGHT, TISCH, AND GRAVES—WERE APPROVED BY ACCLAMATION.

WORKERS LEAGUE

CANDIDATE FOR PRESIDENT:
   Helen Betty Halyard (MI)

CANDIDATE FOR VICE PRESIDENT:
   Fred Mazelis (NY)

PLATFORM HIGHLIGHTS:

The 1992 platform of the Workers League articulated four "basic truths:" (1) capitalism was responsible for the economic and social crisis confronting the world, (2) the depression of 1990 had assumed global dimensions, (3) the two major parties served the interests of big business, and (4) mobilization of the working class to establish socialism was the only solution to the crisis.

SUPPORTED:
- jobs for all and a reduced work week of thirty hours
- an increase in the minimum wage to $10 per hour, indexed to inflation
- the abolition of wage discrimination
- cost-of-living adjustments in benefits and wages
- an end to the Savings and Loan bailout and a $500 billion public works program in its place
- full income and benefits protection for unemployed workers
- a ban on evictions, foreclosures, and utility cutoffs
- restoration of all social welfare cuts and extension of jobless and welfare benefits, subject to a minimum weekly stipend of $300
- the provision of food to the hungry through the Food Stamp, congregate meals for seniors, and school lunch programs
- the provision of housing for the homeless
- lower rents
- guarantees of basic services such as heat, electricity, and water
- the creation of a state-run universal medical system to provide free health care for everyone
- the establishment of a crash program to assist drug addicts, especially pregnant women and newborn babies
- a massive program for research and treatment of AIDS, cancer, and sickle cell anemia
- a program to train new doctors
- the elimination of illiteracy
- the construction of new schools and supplies
- the elimination of public subsidies for private and parochial schools
- increased funding for Head Start and expanded preschool and child care programs
- higher teachers' salaries
- equalized educational expenditures
- free college and university education for all
- job training programs and unemployment benefits for young workers
- full union rights for youth
- a reduced work week for workers under twenty years of age to permit more recreation
- a prohibition against night work and unhealthy tasks for youth
- a ban on corporal punishment and an end to a police presence and the use of metal detectors in schools
- a guaranteed minimum annual income of $25,000 for Social Security beneficiaries
- a protected right to retire at age sixty after thirty years of work
- improvements in nursing home care and services
- supplemental allowances for related caregivers in the home
- secured pension benefits
- the creation of workers' committees to enforce health and safety regulations
- guarantees of full-wage benefits for disabled workers
- the removal of toxic chemicals and substances from the workplace
- workers' control of work sites in medical facilities

- early retirement for workers in hazardous occupations
- guaranteed vacations of six weeks per year
- prohibitions against the hiring of scabs and corporate "gun thugs"
- a repeal of the antiunion Taft-Hartley, Landrum-Griffin, Taylor, and "right-to-work" laws
- the closure of such union-busting businesses as Nuckols and Vance International
- the abolition of the National Labor Relations Board
- calls for freeing "framed" strikers and rehiring PATCO air traffic controllers
- union democracy and solidarity with workers around the world in opposition to multinational corporations
- immigration reforms with undocumented workers granted full legal rights
- a ban on discrimination against linguistic and cultural minorities
- a requirement for bilingual instruction in the schools
- English-language instruction provided on a voluntary basis to immigrant workers and their families, with workers being paid full compensation for lost wages
- the restoration of all cuts in funding for libraries, museums, and the arts
- workers' and young people's access to music, dance, opera, and drama programs at a nominal fee
- artists, musicians, and scientists having control over funding for the arts and sciences
- a shift in the tax burden to the rich, with reduced taxes on incomes below $40,000 per year and progressive tax rates climbing to 100 percent for everything over $150,000 per year
- steeply progressive inheritance taxes
- the abolition of business secrets
- the establishment of worker control over production
- the nationalization of banks, automobile companies, the health care and pharmaceutical industries, large real estate and construction firms, supermarket chains, mass media, and basic industries
- the cancellation of government debts to banks
- the abolition of the stock, bond, and commodity markets
- the abolition of the death penalty
- freedom for political prisoners
- an end to racial, gender-based, and sexual preference discrimination
- abortion on demand
- the abolition of police forces and creation of workers' self-defense organizations to replace them
- the protection of the citizenship and treaty rights of Native Americans
- a public referendum to declare war
- the abolition of the Pentagon and the CIA
- the withdrawal of U.S. troops from overseas
- the nationalization of the military-industrial complex and its conversion to peacetime uses
- independence for Puerto Rico
- an end to the blockade of Cuba and reparations paid to Cuba, Grenada, Iraq, Libya, Nicaragua, Panama, and Vietnam
- an end to colonialist imperialism
- the defense of the remaining gains of the October 1917 Russian Revolution against any capitalist restorationist program in the former Soviet Union and Eastern Europe

ALSO:

- urged creation of the Fourth International to build worker solidarity throughout the world
- asserted the need for a Labor Party under revolutionary leadership to bring the vision of a Workers Government to reality

WORKERS WORLD PARTY

CANDIDATE FOR PRESIDENT:
Gloria Estella La Riva (CA)

CANDIDATE FOR VICE PRESIDENT:
Larry Holmes (NY)

PLATFORM HIGHLIGHTS:

SUPPORTED:

- the ten-point "Fighting Program" of the Workers World Party that sought jobs for all at good pay, through a tripling of the minimum wage
- promises to ban unsafe and abusive working conditions, to end racist or sexist harassment on the job, and to eliminate union-busting activities
- increases in Social Security benefits, unemployment compensation, disability pay, and welfare payments
- a provision of six-months' paid maternity and paternity leave
- an end to layoffs and plant or office shutdowns
- the mandatory rehiring of laid-off workers
- pension fund guarantees
- prenotification requirements for factory closures
- a rollback of rents and mortgage interest rates
- a prohibition against evictions and foreclosures
- "real homes, not shelters" for the homeless
- pledges to provide jobs and housing
- the creation of senior centers and youth programs
- strong affirmative action programs and full equality and representation in employment, jobs, housing, education, politics, and other spheres of life for African Americans, Latinos, Native Americans, Asians and Arab peoples, and women
- the rights of oppressed peoples to self-determination, to use their own languages, and to the unrestricted practice of their culture
- rights for undocumented workers and a halt to deportations
- equal pay for equal work for women
- unimpeded access to all public facilities for the disabled
- the abolition of the death penalty and preventive detention

- human rights
- free and accessible college, technical, and professional education for all
- the construction of more schools, libraries, and day care centers
- incentives for people to become teachers
- free, quality health care for everyone from the cradle to the grave
- the protection of the reproductive rights of women, including access to birth control and abortion
- an end to forced sterilization
- the immediate provision of free and nutritious food for the hungry
- the view that AIDS was a major public health crisis but opposed mandatory testing or quarantine, and the use of Star Wars money to fund a full-scale research program to find a cure and provide treatment for AIDS

- an end to U.S. intervention abroad
- the diversion of the "Pentagon budget" to projects seeking to protect the environment
- the withdrawal of U.S. troops from bases abroad to "build a foreign policy of peace and friendship, not exploitation and intimidation"

OPPOSED:

- racism
- anti-Semitism
- attacks on women, lesbians, and gays
- police brutality
- the oppression of lesbians and gays, young people, the elderly, disabled persons, the poor, workers, prisoners, political activists, and the undocumented
- the arms race and preparations for war

GENERAL ELECTION SUMMARY FOR 1992:			
Candidate	*Electoral Votes*	*States*	*Popular Votes*
Clinton (D)	370	32 (+DC)	44,908,233
Bush (R)	168	18	39,102,282
Perot (IT)	0	0	19,221,433
Marrou (LIBRTN)	0	0	291,612
Gritz (POP [AM FIR])	0	0	98,918
Fulani (NEW ALL)	0	0	73,248
Phillips (US TAX)[1]	0	0	42,960
Hagelin (NAT LAW)	0	0	37,137
Daniels (I [CNT; PF])	0	0	27,396
LaRouche (FFL)	0	0	25,863
James Mac Warren (SOC WOR)	0	0	22,883
Bradford (I)	0	0	4,749
Herer (GRASS)	0	0	3,875
Halyard (WL)	0	0	3,050
Brisben (SOC)	0	0	2,909
Yiamouyiannis (TBA)	0	0	2,199
Ehlers (I)	0	0	1,149
Boren (APATHY)	0	0	956
Dodge (PROH)	0	0	935
Hem (THIRD)	0	0	405
Masters (LB)	0	0	327
Smith (A)	0	0	292
La Riva (W W)	0	0	181
Moyer (I)	0	0	2
Carter (I)	0	0	1
Tyree (I)	0	0	1

[1]US TAX votes include those for the American Independent Party, the Illinois Taxpayers Party, and the Tisch Independent Citizens Party

BIBLIOGRAPHY

Autobiographies, Biographies, Memoirs

Aldred, Guy Alfred. *Convict 9653: America's Vision Maker: [The] Story of Eugene Victor Debs, the United States' Great Socialist Anti-Militarist.* Glasgow, Scotland: Strickland Press, 1942.

Arnold, Stanley Norman. *I Ran Against Jimmy Carter.* New York: Manor Books, 1979.

Ashmore, Lewis. *The Modesto Messiah: The Famous Mail-Order Minister.* Bakersfield, Calif.: Universal Press, 1977.

Asinof, Eliot. *Fox is Crazy Too: The True Story of Garret Trapnell, Adventurer, Skyjacker, Bank Robber, Con Man, Lover.* New York: Morrow, 1976.

Barnes, Jack, et al. *James P. Cannon: A Political Tribute.* New York: Pathfinder Press, n.d.

Barton, A. C. *Life of Col. Jesse Harper of Danville, Ills.: Farm-boy, Lawyer, Editor, Author, Orator, Scholar, and Reformer. Presented in a Brief Biography, to Which is Added Choice Selections from His Speeches and Writings. . . .* Chicago: M. A. Donohue, 1904.

Blackorby, Edward C. *Prairie Rebel: The Public Life of William Lemke.* Lincoln: U. of Nebraska Press, 1963.

Brief Sketches of the Life of Victoria Woodhull (Mrs. John Biddulph Martin). N.p.: 1893.

Brough, James. *The Vixens: A Biography of Victoria and Tennessee Claflin.* New York: Simon and Schuster, 1980.

Brown, Maria Ward. *The Life of Dan Rice.* Long Branch, N. J.: self-published, 1901.

Browne, William E. *The Presidential Candidates: Sketches and Portraits of the Nominees of All Parties: Presidential Season of 1888.* Providence, R.I.: J. A. and R. A. Reid, 1888.

Campbell, Reverend William W. *Life and Character of Jacob Broom.* Wilmington: Historical Society of Delaware, 1909.

Dunnahoo, Terry. *Before the Supreme Court: The Story of Belva Ann Lockwood.* Boston: Houghton Mifflin, 1974.

Duram, James C. *Norman Thomas.* New York: Twayne, 1974.

Eisele, Albert. *Almost to the Presidency: A Biography of Two American Politicians.* Blue Earth, Minn.: Piper, 1972.

Eisenman, Abram. *Why I Should Be President.* 2 vols. Savannah, Ga.: Savannah Sun, 1963–1969.

Ellsworth, William Ledyard. *The Life and Personal History of Captain Ellsworth, Candidate of the American Alliance for President of the United States.* N.p.: 1884?

Engdahl, John Louis. *Debs and O'Hare in Prison.* Chicago: National Office, Socialist Party, 1919.

Eugene V. Debs (1855–1955): The Centennial Year. New York: Debs Centennial Committee, Socialist Society, USA, 1956.

Fabos, Julius Gy. *Frederick Law Olmsted, Sr.: Founder of Landscape Architecture in America.* Amherst: U. of Massachusetts Press, 1968.

Faubus, Orval Eugene. *In This Faraway Land.* Conway, Ark.: River Road Press, 1971.

Fay, Bernard. *The Two Franklins: Fathers of American Democracy.* New York: AMS Press, 1969.

Finke, Blythe Foote. *Angela Davis: Traitor or Martyr of the Freedom of Expression.* Charlottesville, N.Y.: SamHar Press, 1972.

Fladeland, Betty Lorraine. *James Gillespie Birney: Exponent of Political Action Against Slavery.* Ann Arbor, Mich.: U. Microfilms, 1952.

———. *James Gillespie Birney: Slaveholder to Abolitionist.* Ithaca, N.Y.: Cornell U. Press, 1955.

Fleischman, Harry. *Norman Thomas, A Biography: 1884–1968.* Syracuse, N.Y.: W. W. Norton, 1969.

Foner, Philip Sheldon. *Black Socialist Preacher: The Teachings of Reverend George Washington Woodbey and His Disciple, Reverend G. W. Slater, Jr.,* San Francisco: Synthesis Publications, 1983.

Foster, William Zebulon. *More Pages from a Worker's Life.* New York: American Institute for Marxist Studies, 1977.

———. *Pages from a Worker's Life.* New York: International, 1939.

Fox, Mary Virginia. *Lady for the Defense: A Biography of Belva Lockwood.* New York: Harcourt Brace Jovanovich, 1975.

Frady, Marshall. *Wallace.* New York: World, 1968.

Frothingham, Octavius Brooks. *Gerrit Smith: A Biography.* New York: G. P. Putnam's Sons, 1878. Reprint, New York: Negro Universities Press, 1969.

Fry, Daniel William. *Atoms, Galaxies, and Understanding: Cosmology in Its Simplest Form.* El Monte, Calif.: Understanding, 1960.

Garraty, John Arthur, ed. *Silas Wright.* New York: Columbia U. Press, 1949.

George Francis Train and the Pennsylvanians. New York: "Printed for the Publisher," 1864.

Gillette, Don Carle. *He Made Lincoln Laugh: The Story of Dan Rice.* New York: Exposition Press, 1967.

Ginger, Ray. *The Bending Cross: A Biography of Eugene Victor Debs.* New Brunswick, N.J.: Rutgers U. Press, 1949.

Gitlow, Benjamin. *I Confess: The Truth About American Communism.* New York: E. P. Dutton, 1940. Reprint, Westport, Conn.: Hyperion Press, 1975.

———. *The Whole of Their Lives: Communism in America, A Personal History and Intimate Portrayal of Its Leaders.* New York: Charles Scribner's Sons, 1948. Reprint, Freeport, N.Y.: Books for Libraries Press, 1971.

Glad, Paul W. *The Trumpet Soundeth: William Jennings Bryan and His Democracy, 1896–1912.* Lincoln: U. of Nebraska Press, 1960.

———. *William Jennings Bryan: A Profile.* New York: Hill and Wang, 1968.

Goldwater, Barry Morris. *With No Apologies: The Personal and Political Memoirs of United States Senator Barry M. Goldwater.* New York: Morrow, 1979.

Gorham, Charles Orson. *Leader at Large: The Long and Fighting Life of Norman Thomas.* New York: Farrar, Straus and Giroux, 1970.

Green, Gabriel (with Warren Smith). *Let's Face the Facts About Flying Saucers.* New York: Popular Library, 1967.

Green, Samuel Worcester. *Beriah Green.* New York: self-published, 1875.

Greenbaum, Fred. *Robert Marion La Follette.* Boston: Twayne, 1975.

Gregory, Dick. *Write Me In!* New York: Bantam Books, 1968.

Gurko, Miriam. *The Lives and Times of Peter Cooper.* New York: Crowell, 1959.

Hale, William Harlan. *Horace Greeley: Voice of the People.* New York: Harper, 1950.

Hall, Benjamin Franklin. *The Republican Party and Its Presidential Candidates . . . With Sketches . . . of Fremont and Dayton.* New York: Orton and Mulligan, 1856.

Hallinan, Vincent. *A Lion in Court.* New York: Putnam, 1963.

Hallinan, Vivian Moore. *My Wild Irish Rogues.* Garden City, N.Y.: Doubleday, 1952.

Halstead, Fred *Out Now: A Participant's Account of the American Movement Against the Vietnam War.* New York: Monad Press, 1978.

Hammond, Charles Addison. *Gerrit Smith: The Story of a Noble Man's Life.* Geneva, N.Y.: Press of W. F. Humphrey, 1900.

Harden, Edward Jenkins. *The Life of George Michael Troup.* Savannah, Ga.: E. J. Purse, 1859.

Harlow, Ralph Volney. *Gerrit Smith: Philanthropist and Reformer.* New York: Holt, 1939. Reprint, New York: Russell and Russell, 1972.

Hay, John. *Fifty Years of the Republican Party.* Jackson, Mich.: self-published, 1904.

Hayes, John Lord. *A Reminiscence of the Free-Soil Movement in New Hampshire, 1845.* Cambridge, Mass.: J. Wilson and Son, 1885.   .

Hayes, Melvin L. *Mr. Lincoln Runs for President.* New York: Citadel Press, 1960.

Haynes, Frederick Emory. *James Baird Weaver.* Iowa City: State Historical Society of Iowa, 1919. Reprint, New York: Arno Press, 1975.

Haywood, William Dudley. *Bill Haywood's Book: The Autobiography of William Haywood.* New York: International, 1929.

Heck, Frank Hopkins. *Proud Kentuckian: John C. Breckinridge, 1821–1875.* Lexington: U. Press of Kentucky, 1976.

Hendrick, Burton Jesse. *Statesmen of the Lost Cause: Jefferson Davis and His Cabinet.* Boston: Little, Brown, 1939.

Hendrickson, James E. *Joe Lane of Oregon: Machine Politics and the Sectional Crisis, 1849–1861.* New Haven, Conn.: Yale U. Press, 1967.

Hibben, Paxton. *The Peerless Leader: William Jennings Bryan.* New York: Russell and Russell, 1967.

Hicks, Obediah. *Life of Richard F. Trevellick: The Labor Orator.* New York: Arno and the New York Times, 1971.

Hill, Donna. *Joseph Smith: The First Mormon.* Garden City, N.Y.: Doubleday, 1977.

Hillquit, Morris. *Loose Leaves from a Busy Life.* New York: Macmillan, 1934.

Holbrook, Stewart Hall. *Dreamers of the American Dream.* Garden City, N.Y.: Doubleday, 1957.

____. *Lost Men of American History.* New York: Macmillan, 1946.

Hopkins, Alphonso Alva. *The Life: Clinton Bowen Fisk, with a Brief Sketch of John A. Brooks.* New York: Funk and Wagnalls, 1888. Reprint, New York: Negro Universities Press, 1969.

Howard, Cecil Hampden Cutts. *Life and Public Service of Gen. John Wolcott Phelps.* Brattleboro, Vt.: Frank E. Housh, 1887.

Howe, Edgar F. *Biographical Sketches of General John Bidwell, Prohibition Nominee for President, and Dr. James B. Cranfill, Prohibition Nominee for Vice-President, with Nominating Speeches, National Platform, and Bidwell's Letter of Acceptance.* Redlands, Calif.: The Facts, 1892.

Hughes, Thomas. *Life and Times of Peter Cooper.* London: Macmillan, 1886.

Hunt, Rockwell Dennis. *John Bidwell: Prince of California Pioneers.* Caldwell, Idaho: Caxton Printers, 1942.

Huntley, Theodore A., ed. *The Life of John W. Davis.* New York: Duffield, 1924.

Hutchinson, William T. *Lowden of Illinois: The Life of Frank O. Lowden.* 2 vols. Chicago: U. of Chicago Press, 1957.

Hyde, George E. *Spotted Tail's Folk: A History of the Brule Sioux.* Norman: U. of Oklahoma Press, 1961.

Isely, Jeter Alan. *Horace Greeley and the Republican Party, 1853–1861: A Study of the New York Tribune.* Princeton: Princeton U. Press, 1947. Reprint, New York: Octagon Books, 1965.

James P. Cannon As We Knew Him. New York: Pathfinder Press, 1976.

Johnpoll, Bernard K. *Norman Thomas on War: An Anthology.* New York: Garland, 1974.

____. *Pacifist's Progress: Norman Thomas and the Decline of American Socialism.* Chicago: Quadrangle Books, 1970.

Johnson, Roger T. *Robert M. La Follette, Jr. and the Decline of the Progressive Party in Wisconsin.* Hamden, Conn.: Archon Books, 1970.

Johnson, Sonia. *From Housewife to Heretic.* Garden City, N.Y.: Doubleday, 1981.

Johnston, Johanna. *Mrs. Satan.* New York: Popular Library, 1967.

Jones, Bill. *The Wallace Story.* Northport, Ala.: American Southern, 1966.

Jones, James Pickett. *Black Jack: John A. Logan and Southern Illinois in the Civil War Era.* Tallahassee: Florida State U. Press, 1967.

Julian, George Washington. *Political Recollections, 1840 to 1872.* Chicago: Jansen, McClurg, 1884. Reprint, New York: Negro Universities Press, 1970.

Karsner, David. *Debs Goes to Prison.* New York: I. K. Davis, 1919.

____. *Debs: His Authorized Life and Letters from Woodstock Prison to Atlanta.* New York: Boni and Liveright, 1919.

____. *Talks with Debs in Terre Haute (and Letters from Lindlahr).* New York: New York Call, 1922.

Kasper, John. *Segregation or Death.* Washington, D.C.: Seaboard White Citizens Council, 1958.

Kelly, Margaret Jean. *The Career of Joseph Lane: Frontier Politician.* Washington, D.C.: Catholic U. of America, 1942.

Kennedy, John Pendleton. *Discourse on the Life and Character of William Wirt, Late Attorney General of the United States. . . .* Baltimore: W. and J. Neal, 1834.

Kerr, Laura Nowak. *The Girl Who Ran for President.* New York: T. Nelson, 1947.

King, Willard L. *Lincoln's Manager: David Davis.* Cambridge, Mass.: Harvard U. Press, 1960.

Kingdon, Frank. *An Uncommon Man: Henry Wallace and 60 Million Jobs.* New York: Readers Press, 1945.

Kisner, Arlene, comp. *Woodhull & Claflin's Weekly: The Lives and Writings of Notorious Victoria Woodhull and Her Sister Tennessee Claflin.* Washington, N.J.: Times Change Press, 1972.

Knox, Thomas Wallace. *The Lives of James G. Blaine and John A. Logan: Republican Presidential Candidates of 1884. . . .* Hartford, Conn.: Hartford, 1884.

Kunzog, John C. *One Horse Show: The Life and Times of Dan Rice: Circus Jester and Philanthropist.* Jamestown, N.Y.: self-published, 1962.

Lachicotte, Alberta Morel. *Rebel Senator: Strom Thurmond of South Carolina.* New York: Devin-Adair, 1966.

La Follette, Belle Chase, and Fola La Follette. *Robert M. La Follette, June 14, 1855–June 18, 1925.* 2 vols. New York: Hafner, 1953, 1971.

La Follette, Robert Marion. *La Follette's Autobiography: A Personal Narrative of Political Experiences.* Madison, Wis.: Robert M. La Follette, 1913. Reprint, Madison, Wis.: U. of Wisconsin Press, 1960.

Legge, Madeleine. *Two Noble Women, Nobly Planned: Victoria C. Woodhull Martin; Tennessee Claflin, Lady Cook.* Walham Green, South Wales, U.K.: Phelps Brothers, 1893.

Le Prade, Ruth. *Debs and the Poets.* Pasadena, Calif.: published privately by Upton Sinclair, 1920.

Lester, Charles Edwards. *Life and Character of Peter Cooper.* New York: J. B. Alden, 1883.

MacDonald, Dwight. *Henry Wallace: The Man and the Myth.* New York: Vanguard Press, 1948.

Mack, Edward Clarence. *Peter Cooper: Citizen of New York.* New York: Duell, Sloan and Pearce, 1949.

Maddox, Lester Garfield. *Speaking Out: The Autobiography of Lester Garfield Maddox.* Garden City, N.Y.: Doubleday, 1975.

Maney, Patrick J. *"Young Bob" La Follette: A Biography of Robert M. La Follette, Jr., 1895–1953.* Columbia: U. of Missouri Press, 1978.

Marberry, M. M. *Vicky.* New York: Funk and Wagnalls, 1967.

Marsh, John. *The Napoleon of Temperance: Sketches of the Life and Character of the Hon. Neal Dow, Mayor of Portland and Author of the Maine Law.* New York: American Temperance Union, 1852.

Mason, Mel. *The Making of a Revolutionary.* New York: Pathfinder Press, 1982.

Maurer, James Hudson. *It Can Be Done: The Autobiography of James Hudson Maurer.* New York: Rand School Press, 1938.

Maxwell, Robert S. *La Follette.* Englewood Cliffs, N.J.: Prentice Hall, 1969.

____. *La Follette and the Rise of the Progressives in Wisconsin.* Madison: State Historical Society of Wisconsin, 1956. Reprint, New York: Russell and Russell, 1973.

McCoy, Donald R. *Calvin Coolidge: The Quiet President.* New York: Macmillan, 1967.

____. *Landon of Kansas.* Lincoln: U. of Nebraska Press, 1966.

McCulloch, Margaret Callender. *Fearless Advocate of the Right: The Life of Francis Julius Le Moyne, M.D., 1798–1879.* Boston: Christopher Publishing House, 1941.

McDevitt, John Jay. *A Millionaire for a Day.* Philadelphia: Dando, 1914.

McDonald, Frank V. *Notes Preparatory to a Biography of Richard Hayes McDonald.* Vol. 1. Cambridge, Mass.: U. Press, 1881.

McDowell, Edwin. *Barry Goldwater: Portrait of an Arizonan.* Chicago: Henry Regnery, 1964.

McElhiney, Thomas. *Life of Martin Van Buren.* Pittsburgh, Pa.: J. T. Shryock, 1853.

McElroy, Robert. *Jefferson Davis: The Real and the Unreal.* New York: Harper and Brothers, 1937.

McFee, Inez Nellie Canfield. *The Story of Peter Cooper: A Tale of a Noble Purpose.* Instructor Literature Series, no. 218. Chicago: Hall and McCreary, 1912.

McIlhany, William H., II. *Klandestine: The Untold Story of Delmar Dennis and His Role in the F.B.I.'s War Against the Ku Klux Klan.* New York: Arlington House, 1975.

McKay, Seth Shepard. *W. Lee O'Daniel and Texas Politics, 1938–1942.* Lubbock: Texas Technological College, 1944.

Meade, Marion. *Free Woman: The Life and Times of Victoria C. Woodhull.* New York: Knopf, 1976.

Meador, Edward Kirby. *The Meadors and the Meadows.* Boston: Meador, 1941.

"Meet Kent Courtney." Conservative Society of America Pamphlet Number 2, n.d.

"Meet Your Vote" Supplement for 1992 Presidential Elections: All Are Applying. Who Will You Hire for President?. DeKalb, Ill.: Better Yet Publications, 1992.

Mehling, Mary Bryant Alverson. *Cowdrey-Cowdary-Cowdray Genealogy.* N.p.: Frank Allaben Genealogical, 1911.

Memoir of James Buchanan of Pennsylvania. Philadelphia: C. Sherman and Son, 1856.

Merrill, Louis Taylor. "General Benjamin F. Butler and the Campaign of 1868." Ph.D. thesis, U. of Chicago, 1939.

Moley, Raymond. *The American Century of John C. Lincoln.* New York: Duell, Sloan and Pearce, 1962.

Moos, Malcolm Charles. *Dwight D. Eisenhower.* New York: Random House, 1964.

Morais, Herbert Montfort, and William Cahn. *Gene Debs: The Story of a Fighting American.* New York: International, 1948.

Morgan, Howard Wayne. *Eugene V. Debs: Socialist for President.* Syracuse, N.Y.: Syracuse U. Press, 1962.

Morris, Benjamin Franklin. *The Life of Thomas Morris: Pioneer and Long a Legislator of Ohio and U.S. Senator from 1833 to 1839.* Cincinnati, Ohio: Moore, Wilstach, Keys and Overend, 1856.

Morris, Charles E. *Progressive Democracy of James M. Cox.* Indianapolis, Ind.: Bobbs-Merrill, 1920.

Morris, Joe A. *Nelson Rockefeller: A Biography.* New York: Harper, 1956.

Mowry, George Edwin. *Theodore Roosevelt and the Progressive Movement.* Madison: U. of Wisconsin Press, 1946.

Nadelson, Regina. *Who is Angela Davis? The Biography of a Revolutionary.* New York: P. H. Wyden, 1972.

Nalle, Ouida Wallace Ferguson. *The Fergusons of Texas; or, 'Two Governors for the Price of One:' A Biography of James Edward Ferguson and His Wife, Miriam Amanda Ferguson, Ex-Governors of the State of Texas. . . .* San Antonio, Tex.: Naylor, 1946.

Nash, Howard Pervear. *Stormy Petrel: The Life and Times of General Benjamin F. Butler, 1818–1893.* Rutherford, N.J.: Fairleigh Dickinson U. Press, 1969.

National Portrait Gallery Staff. *If Elected . . . Unsuccessful Candidates for the Presidency, 1796–1968.* Washington, D.C.: Smithsonian Institution Press, 1972.

Neal, Nevin Emil. *A Biography of Joseph T. Robinson.* Ann Arbor, Mich.: U. Microfilms, 1959.

Nearing, Scott. *The Debs Decision.* New York: Rand School of Social Science, 1919.

Nevins, Allan. *Abram S. Hewitt: With Some Account of Peter Cooper.* New York: Octagon Books, 1967.

Newcombe, Alfred W. "Alson J. Streeter: An Agrarian Liberal." *Journal of the Illinois State Historical Society* 39, no. 1 (March 1946): 74.

Nichols, Roy Franklin. *Franklin Pierce: Young Hickory of the Granite Hills.* Philadelphia: U. of Pennsylvania Press, 1931.

Noble, Iris. *Labor's Advocate: Eugene V. Debs.* New York: Messner, 1966.

Noblin, Stuart. *Leonidas Lafayette Polk, Agrarian Crusader.* Chapel Hill: U. of North Carolina Press, 1949.

Oliver, John A. *Eldridge Cleaver Reborn.* Plainfield, N.J.: Logos International, 1977.

Painter, Floy Ruth. *That Man Debs and His Life Work.* Bloomington: Indiana U. Graduate Council, 1929.

Palmer, Frederick. *This Man Landon: The Record and Career of Governor Alfred M. Landon of Kansas.* New York: Dodd, Meade, 1936.

Palmer, George Thomas. *A Conscientious Turncoat: The Story of John A. Palmer, 1817–1900.* New Haven: Yale U. Press, 1941.

Palmer, John McAuley. *Personal Recollections of John M. Palmer: The Story of an Earnest Life.* Cincinnati, Ohio: R. Clarke, 1901.

Palmer, Loomis T. *The Life of General U.S. Grant.* Chicago: Fairbanks and Palmer, 1887.

Parker, P. A. *Angela Davis: The Making of a Revolutionary.* New Rochelle, N.Y.: Arlington House, 1973.

Parks, Joseph Howard. *John Bell of Tennessee.* Baton Rouge: Louisiana State U. Press, 1950.

Parks, Norman Lexington. *The Career of John Bell as Congressman from Tennessee, 1827–1841.* Nashville, Tenn.: self-published, 1942.

Parrish, William Earl. *David Rice Atchison of Missouri.* Jefferson City: U. of Missouri Press, 1961.

Parton, James. *The Presidency of Andrew Jackson.* New York: Harper and Row, 1967.

Perkins, Jonathan Ellsworth. *The Biggest Hypocrite in America: Gerald L. K. Smith Unmasked.* Los Angeles: American Foundation, 1949.

Peter Cooper: A Tribute in Commemoration of the Hundredth Anniversary of His Birth. New York: Alumni Association of the Cooper Union, 1891.

Petersen, Arnold. *Daniel De Leon: Internationalist.* New York: New York Labor News, 1944.

____. *Daniel De Leon: Social Architect*. New York: New York Labor News, 1941.

____. *Daniel De Leon: Social Scientist*. New York: New York Labor News, 1945.

____. *De Leon the Uncompromising*. New York: New York Labor News, 1939.

Peterson, Frank Ross. *Prophet Without Honor: Glen H. Taylor and the Fight for American Liberalism*. Lexington: U. Press of Kentucky, 1974.

Peterson, Norma L. *Freedom and Franchise: The Political Career of B. Gratz Brown*. Columbia: U. of Missouri Press, 1965.

Pomeroy, Marcus Mills. *The Life and Public Services of Benjamin F. Butler, Major-General in the Army and Leader of the Republican Party*. New York: self-published, 1868.

Potterf, Rex M. *William Jennings Bryan: The Great Commoner*. Fort Wayne, Ind.: Allen County-Fort Wayne Historical Society, 1961.

Pringle, Henry Fowler. *The Life and Times of William Howard Taft*. 2 vols. New York: Farrar and Rinehart, 1939.

____. *Theodore Roosevelt: A Biography*. New York: Harcourt, Brace, 1931.

Proctor, John Clagett. "Belva Ann Lockwood: Only Woman Candidate for President of the United States." *Columbia Historical Society Records* (1935): 192–204.

Pulley, Andrew. *How I Became a Socialist*. New York: Pathfinder Press, n.d.

Pusey, Merlo John. *Charles Evans Hughes*. 2 vols. New York: Macmillan, 1951.

____. *Eisenhower, the President*. New York: Macmillan, 1956.

Raisky, L. G. *Daniel De Leon: The Struggle Against Opportunism in the American Labor Movement*. New York: New York Labor News, 1932.

Rayback, Joseph G. *Martin Van Buren*. New York: Eastern Acorn Press, 1982.

Rayback, Robert J. *Millard Fillmore: Biography of a President*. Buffalo, N.Y.: H. Stewart, 1959.

Raymond, Rossiter Worthington. *Peter Cooper*. Freeport, N.Y.: Books for Libraries Press, 1972.

Reeve, Carl. *The Life and Times of Daniel De Leon*. New York: Humanities Press, 1972.

Reid, Whitelaw. *Horace Greeley*. New York: Charles Scribner's Sons, 1879.

Remini, Robert Vincent, ed. *Andrew Jackson*. New York: Twayne, 1966.

____. *Martin Van Buren and the Making of the Democratic Party*. New York: Columbia U. Press, 1959.

Richards, Bob. *The Heart of a Champion*. Westwood, N.J.: F. H. Revell, 1959.

Riddleberger, Patrick W. *George Washington Julian: Radical Republican—A Study in Nineteenth Century Politics and Reform*. Indianapolis: Indiana Historical Bureau, 1966.

Ridge, Martin. *Ignatius Donnelly: The Portrait of a Politician*. Chicago: U. of Chicago Press, 1962.

Rinzler, Carol E., ed. *Frankly McCarthy*. Washington, D.C.: Public Affairs Press, 1969.

Robinson, Edgar Eugene, and Vaughn Davis Bornet. *Herbert Hoover, President of the United States*. Stanford, Calif.: Hoover Institution Press, 1975.

Rogers, Earl M., ed. *The Wallace Papers: An Index to the Microfilm Editions of the Henry A. Wallace Papers in the U. of Iowa Libraries, the Library of Congress, and the Franklin Delano Roosevelt Library*. Iowa City: U. of Iowa Libraries, 1975.

Rosser, Charles McDaniel. *The Crusading Commoner: A Close-Up of William Jennings Bryan and His Times*. Dallas, Tex.: Mathis, Van Nort, 1937.

Royce, Charles C. *John Bidwell: Pioneer, Statesman, Philanthropist—A Biography*. Chico, Calif.: self-published, 1906.

Russell, Francis. *The Shadow of Blooming Grove: Warren G. Harding in His Times*. New York: McGraw-Hill Book, 1968.

Russell, George B. *J. Bracken Lee*. New York: R. Speller, 1961.

Russell, Thomas, and Elias Nason. *The Life and Public Services of Hon. Henry Wilson*. Boston: B. B. Russell, 1872.

Sachs, Emanie. *The Terrible Siren*. New York: Harper and Brothers, 1928.

Sanders, Bernard. *Eugene V. Debs: Trade Unionist, Socialist, Revolutionary, 1855–1926: An Historical Narrative*. Folkways Records, FH 5571, 1979. (sound recording)

Sanders, Lon. *Notable Democrats*. St. Louis, Mo.: Sanders Engraving, 1916.

Savell, Richard H. *John P. Hale and the Politics of Abolition*. Cambridge: Harvard U. Press, 1965.

Sayre, Ralph Mills. *Albert Baird Cummins and the Progressive Movement in Iowa*. Ann Arbor, Mich.: U. Microfilms, 1958.

Scarry, Robert J. *Millard Fillmore: The Man and the Cabin*. Moravia, N.Y.: self-published, 1965.

Schapsmeier, Edward L. *Prophet in Politics: Henry A. Wallace and the War Years, 1940–1965*. Ames: Iowa State U. Press, 1970.

Schapsmeier, Edward L., and Frederick H. Schapsmeier. *Henry A. Wallace of Iowa: The Agrarian Years, 1910–1940*. Ames: Iowa State U. Press, 1968.

Scheer, Robert, ed. *Eldridge Cleaver: Post-Prison Writings and Speeches*. New York: Random House, 1969.

Schmidt, Karl M. *Henry A. Wallace: Quixotic Crusade, 1948*. Syracuse, N.Y.: Syracuse U. Press, 1960.

Schmitz, John G. *Stranger in the Arena*. Santa Ana, Calif.: Rayline Printing, 1974.

Schnittkind, Henry Thomas. *The Story of Eugene Debs*. Boston: Independent Workmens Circle, 1929.

Schriftgiesser, Karl. *The Gentleman from Massachusetts: Henry Cabot Lodge*. Boston: Little, Brown, 1944.

Schuckers, Jacob W. *The Life and Public Services of Salmon Portland Chase*. New York: D. Appleton, 1874.

Scott, Walter. *Peter Cooper: The Good Citizen*. New York: Church and Home, 1888.

Sears, Stephen W. *George B. McClellan: The Young Napoleon*. New York: Ticknor and Fields, 1988.

Seidler, Murray. *Norman Thomas: Respectable Rebel*. Syracuse, N.Y.: Syracuse U. Press, 1967.

Seitz, Don C. *Horace Greeley, Founder of the New York Tribune*. Indianapolis, Ind.: Bobbs-Merrill, 1926.

Selvin, David F. *Eugene Debs: Rebel, Labor Leader, Prophet—A Biography*. New York: Lothrop, Lee and Shepard, 1966.

Shadegg, Stephen C. *Barry Goldwater: Freedom is His Flight Plan*. New York: Fleet, 1961.

Shaw, Esmond. *Peter Cooper and the Wrought Iron Beam*. New York: Cooper Union Art School, 1960.

Shepard, Edward Morse. *Martin Van Buren*. Boston: Houghton, Mifflin, 1899. Reprint, New York: Chelsea House, 1980.

Sherwin, Oscar. *Prophet of Liberty: The Life and Times of Wendell Phillips*. New York: Bookman Associates, 1958.

Sherwood, George W. *Eulogy on the Life and Character of William Wirt. . . .* Baltimore, Md.: J. Lucas and E. K. Deaver, 1834.

Shirey, Keith Faires. *Barry Goldwater: His Political Philosphy*. Los Angeles: Brewster Publications, 1963.

Shumway, Harry Irving. *Good Man Gone Wrong? Roger Babson and the Church*. Richmond, Va.: Central, 1940.

Silverstein, Peter, ed. *Eugene McCarthy: A Man of Courage*. New York: Maco, 1968.

Skarda, Charles M. Robinson. *The Late Senator: Notes on the Life of Joe T. Robinson of Arkansas, 1872–1937*. Little Rock, Ark.: self-published, 1959.

____. *A Short Pedigree of the Late Senator from Arkansas, Joseph Taylor Robinson, a Descendant of English Families, Descendant of Edward I*. Little Rock, Ark.: self-published, 1956.

Sketches from the Life of Dan Rice: The Shakespearian Jester and Original Clown. Albany, N.Y.: E. James, 1849.

Smiley, David L. *Lion of White Hall*. Madison: U. of Wisconsin Press, 1962.

Smith, Earl L. *Yankee Genius: A Biography of Roger W. Babson, Pioneer in Investment Counseling and Business Forecasting Who Capitalized on Investment Patience*. New York: Harper, 1954.

Smith, Elbert B. *Francis Preston Blair*. New York: Free Press, 1980.

Smith, James Wesley. *Goldwater and the Republic That Was*. New York: Carlton Press, 1965.

Smith, John Corson. *Our Comrade General John A. Logan . . . October 13, 1904*. Chicago: Rogers and Smith, 1904.

Smith, Willard H. *Schuyler Colfax: The Changing Fortunes of a Political Idol*. Indianapolis: Indiana Historical Bureau, 1952.

Smith, William Ernest. "The Blairs and Fremont." Columbia, Missouri Ph.D. thesis, U. of Wisconsin, 1927.

____. *The Francis Preston Blair Family in Politics*. New York: Da Capo Press, 1969.

Southard, Samuel Lewis. *A Discourse on the Professional Character and Virtues of the Late William Wirt*. Washington, D.C.: Gales and Seaton, 1834.

Southwick, Leslie. *Presidential Also Rans and Running Mates, 1788–1980*. Jefferson, N.C.: McFarland, 1984.

Spalding, Charles Sumner. *Peter Cooper: A Critical Bibliography of His Life and Works*. New York: New York Public Library, 1941.

Spalding, George Burley. *A Discourse Commemorative of the Character and Career of Hon. John Parker Hale*. Concord, N.H.: Republican Press Association, 1874.

Sparkman, Ivo Hall. *Journeys with the Senator*. Huntsville, Ala.: Strode, 1977.

Stalvey, James Benjamin. "Daniel De Leon: A Study of Marxian Orthodoxy in the United States." Ph.D. thesis, U. of Illinois, 1946.

Stanwood, Edward. *James Gillespie Blaine*. Boston: Houghton Mifflin, 1905.

Stavis, Benedict. *We Were the Campaign: New Hampshire to Chicago for McCarthy*. Boston: Beacon Press, 1969.

Steinhaeuser, Walter Philip. *Biographical Sketch of Dr. Reynell Coates, Founder of the Patriotic Order of Sons of America*. Asbury Park, N.J.: C. W. Clayton, Printer, 1913.

Stern, Madeleine B., ed. *The Victoria Woodhull Reader*. Weston, Mass.: M & S Press, 1974.

Stevenson, Marietta. "William Jennings Bryan as a Political Leader." Ph.D. thesis, U. of Chicago, 1926.

Stewart, Dwight. *Mr. Socialism: Being an Account of Norman Thomas and His Labors to Keep America Safe From Socialism*. Secaucus, N.J.: L. Stuart, 1974.

Stewart, Justin. *Wayne Wheeler: Dry Boss—An Uncensored Biography of Wayne B. Wheeler*. Westport, Conn.: Greenwood Press, 1970. Reprint of 1928 edition.

Stickles, Arndt Mathias. *Simon Bolivar Buckner: Borderland Knight*. Chapel Hill: U. of North Carolina Press, 1940.

Stillwell, Lucille. *John Cabell Breckinridge*. Caldwell, Idaho: Caxton Printers, 1936.

Stoddard, Henry Luther. *Horace Greeley: Printer, Editor, Crusader*. New York: G. P. Putnam's Sons, 1946.

Stoddard, William Osborn. *Andrew Jackson and Martin Van Buren*. New York: F. A. Stokes, 1887.

____. *Zachary Taylor, Millard Fillmore, Franklin Pierce and James Buchanan*. New York: F. A. Stokes and Brother, 1888.

Stone, Irving. *They Also Ran: The Story of the Men Who Were Defeated for the Presidency*. New York: Doubleday, 1966.

Swallow, Silas Comfort. *Four Score, and More: An Omnium Gatherum and Multum in Parvo*. Harrisburg, Pa.: United Evangelical Publishing House, 1922.

____. *Then and Now, or Some Reminiscences of an Octogenarian*. Harrisburg, Pa.: self-published, 1920.

____. *III Score and X: Or, Selections, Collections, Recollections of Seventy Busy Years*. Harrisburg, Pa.: United Evangelical Publishing House, 1909.

Swanberg, W. A. *Norman Thomas: The Last Idealist*. New York: Charles Scribners, 1976.

Taylor, Glen Hearst. *The Way It Was With Me*. Secaucus, N.J.: L. Stuart, 1979.

Thelen, David Paul. *The Early Life of Robert M. La Follette, 1855–1884*. Chicago: Loyola U. Press, 1966.

____. *Robert M. La Follette and the Insurgent Spirit*. Boston: Little, Brown, 1976.

Thompson, Donald E., compiler. *Indiana Authors and Their Books*, vol. 2: *1917–1966*. Crawfordsville, Ind.: Wabash College, 1974.

Thomas, Frederick William. *John Randolph, of Roanoke, and Other Sketches of Character, Including William Wirt*. Philadelphia: A. Hart, 1853.

Thornton, Willis. *The Life of Alfred M. Landon*. New York: Grosset and Dunlap, 1936.

____. *The Nine Lives of Citizen Train*. New York: Greenberg Publisher, 1948.

Thwing, Eugene. *The Life and Meaning of Theodore Roosevelt*. New York: Current Literature, 1919.

Tilton, Theodore. *Victoria C. Woodhull: A Biographical Sketch*. New York: Golden Age, 1871.

Timothy, Mary. *Jury Woman: The Story of the Trial of Angela Y. Davis*. San Francisco: Glide Publications, 1975.

Tinkcom, Harry Marlin. *John White Geary: Soldier-Statesman, 1819–1873*. Philadelphia: U. of Pennsylvania Press, 1940.

Tipton, Thomas Weston. *Forty Years of Nebraska: At Home and In Congress*. Lincoln: Nebraska State Historical Society, 1902.

Trachtenberg, Alexander L. *The Heritage of Gene Debs: Selections*. New York: International, 1955.

Train, George Francis. *My Life in Many States and in Foreign Lands, Dictated in My Seventy-Fourth Year*. New York: D. Appleton, 1902.

Trefousse, Hans Louis. *Ben Butler: The South Called Him Beast!* New York: Twayne, 1957.

____. *Benjamin Franklin Wade: Radical Republican from Ohio*. New York: Twayne, 1963.

A Tribute to James G. Birney. Detroit, Mich.: J. Warren's Book and Job Office, 1863.

A Tribute to the Memory of John A. Logan from the Home of Lincoln. Springfield, Ill.: O. H. Oldroyd, 1887.

Tuckerman, Bayard. *William Jay and the Constitutional Movement for the Abolition of Slavery*. New York: Burt Franklin, 1969.

Turnbull, Clive. *Bonanza: The Story of George Francis Train*. Melbourne, Australia: Hawthorne Press, 1946.

Tussey, Jean Y., ed. *Eugene V. Debs Speaks*. New York: Pathfinder Press, 1970.

U.S. Congress, Senate Committee on Finance. *Hearings . . . on the Nomination of T. Coleman Andrews, Commissioner of Internal Revenue-Designate, 26 January 1952*. Washington, D.C.: Government Printing Office, 1953.

U.S. Congress, Senate Committee on the Judiciary. *Communist Leadership: "Tough Guy" Takes Charge, (Gus Hall), Hearings, Subcommittee on the Internal Security Act and Other Internal Security Laws*. 86th

Cong., 2d sess., 2–3 February 1960. Washington, D.C., Government Printing Office, 1960.

U.S. Congress. *Memorial Addresses on the Life and Character of John Alexander Logan (A Senator from Illinois). . . .* 49th Cong., 2d sess. Washington, D.C.: Government Printing Office, 1887.

U.S. Congress. *Memorial Services Held in the House of Representatives and Senate of the United States . . . in Eulogy of James B. Utt, Late a Representative from California.* 91st Cong., 2d sess. Washington, D.C.: Government Printing Office, 1970.

United States Senator Eugene J. McCarthy: One of Those Uncommon Men Who Puts His Courage in the Service of His Country. Minneapolis, Minn.: Gilbert, 1964.

Ursul, R. Gordon. *Sieg Heil Yawl: The Wallace Years and Uncivil Rights.* Chesapeake, Va.: Collective Writers Library, 1976.

Van Deusen, Glyndon G. *Horace Greeley: Nineteenth Century Crusader.* Philadelphia: U. of Pennsylvania Press, 1953.

Vaughan, Curtis M. *Faubus' Folly: The Story of Segregation.* New York: Vantage Press, 1959.

Vinson, John Chalmers. *William E. Borah and the Outlawry of War.* Athens: U. of Georgia Press, 1957.

Wack, Henry Wellington. *Personal Recollections of a Great Baconian, Hon. Ignatius Donnelly.* New York: Bacon Society of America, n.d.

Walker, J. Samuel. *Henry A. Wallace and American Foreign Policy.* Westport, Conn.: Greenwood Press, 1976.

Wall, Samuel W. *Round the World with Train: A Typhoon. . . .* Boston: Round the World, 1893.

Wallace, Cornelia. *C'nelia.* Philadelphia: A. J. Holman, 1976.

Wallace, George Corley, Jr. *The Wallaces of Alabama.* Chicago: Follett, 1975.

Walsh, J. C. *Charles O'Conor.* New York: American Irish Historical Society, 1928.

Walsh, Robert. *Biographical Sketch of Andrew Jackson.* Albany, N.Y.: self-published, 1828.

Warden, Robert B. *An Account of the Private Life and Public Services of Salmon Portland Chase.* Cincinnati, Ohio: Wilstach, Baldwin, 1874.

Warren, Harris Gaylord. *Herbert Hoover and the Great Depression.* New York: Oxford U. Press, 1959. Reprint, Westport, Conn.: Greenwood Press, 1980.

Watson, James Eli. *As I Knew Them: Memoirs of James E. Watson.* New York: Bobbs-Merrill, 1936.

Watson, Thomas Edward. *The Life and Times of Andrew Jackson.* Thomson, Ga.: Press of the Jeffersonian Publishing Company, 1912.

____. *The Life and Times of Thomas Jefferson.* New York: D. Appleton, 1903.

Werlich, Robert. *"Beast" Butler: The Incredible Career of Major General Benjamin Franklin Butler.* Washington, D.C.: Quaker Press, 1962.

Werner, Morris Robert. *Bryan.* New York: Harcourt, Brace, 1929.

West, Richard Sedgewick, Jr. *Lincoln's Scapegoat General: A Life of Benjamin F. Butler, 1818–1893.* Boston: Houghton Mifflin, 1965.

Western [pseud.]. *Biography of Joseph Lane.* Washington, D.C.: Congressional Globe, 1852.

Wheeler, Burton K., with Paul F. Healy. *Yankee from the West.* Garden City, N.Y.: Doubleday, 1962.

Whicher, George Frisbie. *William Jennings Bryan and the Campaign of 1896.* Boston: Heath, 1953.

White, Helen M., ed. *Ignatius Donnelly Papers, 1812–1943.* St. Paul: Minnesota Historical Society, 1966.

White, Horace. *The Life of Lyman Trumbull.* Boston: Houghton Mifflin, 1913.

Wilkinson, J. Harvie, III. *Harry Byrd and the Changing Face of Virginia Politics, 1945–1966.* Charlottesville: U. Press of Virginia, 1968.

Willey, Malcolm MacDonald. *William Jennings Bryan as a Social Force.* Chapel Hill: U. of North Carolina Press, 1924.

Williams, Wayne Cullen. *William Jennings Bryan.* New York: G. P. Putnam's Sons, 1936.

____. *William Jennings Bryan: A Study in Political Vindication.* New York: Fleming H. Revell, 1923.

Wilson, Charles Morrow. *The Commoner: William Jennings Bryan.* Garden City, N.Y.: Doubleday, 1970.

Wilson, Forrest. *Crusader in Crinoline.* Philadelphia: Lippincott, 1941.

Wilson, Henry. *The Position of John Bell and His Supporters.* Boston: Bee Printing, 1860.

Wilson, James Grant. *Meet General Grant.* New York: Fawcett World Library, 1957.

Wilson, Major L. *The Presidency of Martin Van Buren.* Lawrence: U. Press of Kansas, 1984.

Wise, James Waterman. *Meet Henry Wallace.* New York: Boni and Gaer, 1948.

Wise, W. Harvey, Jr. *A Bibliography of Andrew Jackson and Martin Van Buren.* New York: B. Franklin, 1970.

Wise, W. Harvey, Jr., and John W. Cronin, comps. *A Bibliography of Zachary Taylor, Millard Fillmore, Franklin Pierce, James Buchanan.* Washington, D.C.: Riverford, 1935.

Woodward, Comer Vann. *Tom Watson: Agrarian Rebel.* New York: Macmillan, 1938.

Woodward, W. E. *Meet General Grant.* New York: Fawcett World Library, 1957.

Writings and Speeches of Eugene V. Debs. New York: Hermitage Press, 1948.

Zabriskie, Frances Nicoll. *Horace Greeley: Editor.* New York: Funk and Wagnalls, 1890.

Zachos, John Celiveros, ed. *The Political and Financial Opinions of Peter Cooper.* New York: Trow's Printing and Bookbinding, 1877.

Zahnd, John. *The Long Trail.* Indianapolis, Ind.: self-published, 1945.

Zipser, Arthur. *Working Class Giant.* New York: International, 1981.

CAMPAIGN LITERATURE AND TRACTS

After Thirty Years: The Weekly People and the Socialist Labor Party Through a Generation. New York: National Executive Committee, Socialist Labor Party, 1921.

Allen, Emory Adams. *The Life and Public Services of James Baird Weaver . . . to Which is Added the Life and Public Services of James G. Field. . . .* N.p.: People's Party, 1892.

Bittleman, Alexander. *Milestones in the History of the Communist Party.* New York: Workers Library, 1937.

Black, James. *Brief History of Prohibition and of the Prohibition Reform Party.* New York: National Committee of the Prohibition Reform Party, 1880.

Campbell, Gil. *Everybody for President.* New York: Workman, 1984.

Cannon, James Patrick. *The First Ten Years of American Communism.* New York: Pathfinder Press, 1974.

Facts for Those Who Will Understand Them: Gen. Cass's Position on the Slavery Question Defined by Himself and His Friends. Also a Brief Notice of Southern Objections to Millard Fillmore, the Whig Vice Presidential Candidate. Washington, D.C.: J. and G. S. Gideon, Printers, 1848.

The Facts: La Follette-Wheeler Campaign Textbook. Chicago: La Follette-Wheeler Campaign Headquarters, 1924.

Ferguson, George W. *The Old Standards and the New Party.* New York: Fortuny's, 1940.

Finch, Mary Baird. *Silver Party Songbook.* Pueblo, Col.: self-published, 1896.

Foster, John Onesimus. *Our Standard Bearer: Life Sketches and Speeches of Gen. Clinton Bowen Fisk.* Chicago: Woman's Temperance Publication Association, 1888.

Gleed, Charles Sumner. *A Bird's Eye View of the Political Situation in Kansas, With Especial Reference to the People's Party*. Topeka, Kans.: Republican State Headquarters, 1893.

Golden Jubilee of De Leonism, 1890–1940: Commemorating the Fiftieth Anniversary of the Founding of the Socialist Labor Party. New York: Socialist Labor Party of America, 1940.

Goldman, Albert. *The Question of Unity Between the Workers Party and the Socialist Workers Party*, Long Island City, N.Y.: Workers Party Publications, 1947.

Greene, Charles Gordon, and B.F. Hallett. *Whigery is Federalism*. Boston: self-published, 1840.

Greenhaw, Wayne. *Watch Out for George Wallace*. Englewood Cliffs, N.J.: Prentice-Hall, 1976.

Haaland, Jasper. *Farmers and the War*. New York: Workers Library, 1940.

Hale, Annie Riley. *Bull Moose Trails: Supplement to 'Rooseveltian Fact and Fable'*. New York: self-published, 1912.

Hillson, Jon, et al. *A Socialist View of the Chicago Elections: Forging a Black-Latino-Labor Alliance*. New York: Pathfinder Press, n.d.

Hinshaw, David, ed. *Landon: What He Stands For. . . .* New York: Mail and Express, 1936.

Hodgson, James Goodwin, comp. *A Labor Party for the United States*. New York: H. W. Wilson, 1925.

Hogg, Will Clifford. *His Own Words to Discover His Motives: The Ferguson Idea of University Control*. Austin, Tex.: self-published, 1917.

Independent Black Political Action, 1954–1978. New York: Pathfinder Press, 1978.

The Independent Democrats' 1984 Platform. New York: Independent Democrats for La Rouche, 1984.

The Intelligent Voter's Guide: Official 1928 Campaign Handbook of the Socialist Party. New York: Socialist National Campaign Committee, 1928.

John Bell: His "Past History Connected with the Public Service." Nashville, Tenn.: Union and American Office, 1860.

Kelly, Walt. *The Pogo Candidature*. Kansas City, Kans.: Sheed Andrews and McMeel, 1976.

Knox, Thomas Wallace. *The Republican Party and Its Leaders: A History of the Party from Its Beginning to the Present Time . . . Lives of Harrison and Reid*. New York: P. F. Collier, 1892.

Le Fevre, Benjamin. *Campaign of '84. Biographies of S. Grover Cleveland, the Democratic Candidate for President, and Thomas A. Hendricks, the Democratic Candidate for Vice-President. . . .* Philadelphia: Fireside, 1884.

Let Us Have Peace: A Complete History of the Republican Party, Its Past Achievements and Present Aims, by "Fair Play." Pittsburgh: Barr and Myers, 1868.

Levinson, Edward, and Maynard C. Krueger, eds. *A Plan for America: Official 1932 Campaign Handbook of the Socialist Party*. Chicago: Socialist Party of America, 1932.

Lewis, Jim, with Jim Peron. *Liberty Reclaimed*. Self-published, 1984.

The Life, Speeches, and Public Services of John Bell, Together with a Sketch of the Life of Edward Everett, Union Candidates for the Offices of President and Vice-President of the United States. New York: Rudd and Carleton, 1860.

The Lives of Horatio Seymour and Frank P. Blair, Jr. Philadelphia: T. B. Peterson and Brothers, 1868.

Livingstone, William E. *Livingstone's History of the Republican Party . . . From Its Foundation to the Close of the Campaign of 1900. . . .* Detroit, Mich.: self-published, 1900.

Lloyd, William Bross. *The Socialist Party and Its Purposes*. Chicago: Goodspeed Press, 1918.

Lovestone, Jay. *The La Follette Illusion. . . .* Chicago: Workers Party of America, 1924.

MacBride, Roger Lea. *A New Dawn for America: The Libertarian Challenge*. Ottawa, Ill.: Green Hill, 1976.

Mann, Jonathan B. *An Appeal to the Loco Focos, Drawn From Their Own Documents*. Boston: Whig Republican, 1840.

Mason, John Mitchell. *A Voice of Warning to Christians on the Ensuing Election of a President of the United States*. New York: G. F. Hopkins, 1800.

Mayo, Robert. *A Word in Season: Or, Review of the Political Life and Opinions of Martin Van Buren*. Washington, D.C.: W. M. Morrison, 1840.

McCabe, James Dabney. *The Life and Public Services of Horatio Seymour; Together with a Complete and Authentic Life of Francis P. Blair, Jr.* New York: United States, 1868.

Medill, Joseph, comp. *Socialist Campaign Book*. Chicago: National Headquarters, Socialist Party, 1908.

Messaros, Waldo. *Life of Gen. Benjamin Harrison . . . With a Sketch of the Life and Public Services of Whitelaw Reid. . . .* Philadelphia: Political Publishing, 1892.

Metcalfe, Prichard Lee. *Victorious Democracy: Embracing Life and Patriotic Services of Hon. William J. Bryan*. Chicago: Dominion, 1900.

Michels, Nicholas. *The Rise and Fall of Prohibition in Illinois, 1839–1855: A Crushing Defeat Concealed by Prohibitionists. . . .* Chicago: self-published, 1912.

Mizner, Thomas W. *Bryan the Brave, the Light of Silver Freedom, by a White Slave*. Detroit, Mich.: Seaside Press, 1896.

Morgan, Edwin Barber. *Fillmore's Political History and Position. George Law and Chauncey Shaffer's Reasons for Repudiating Fillmore and Donelson. . . .* New York: Office of the *New York Tribune*, 1856.

Nichols, John Wesley. *The People's Candidate for President, 1872, George Francis Train. The Coming President. The Man of Destiny. First Campaign Gun. . . .* New York: self-published, 1872.

1944 Platform: For President, Edward A. Teichert; For Vice-President, Arla A. Albaugh. New York: Socialist Labor Party, 1944.

The 1960 Democratic Fact Book: The Issues and Record. Washington, D.C.: Democratic National Committee, 1960.

Oldroyd, Osborn Hamiline. *The March to Victory: The Great Republican Campaigns of 1860 and 1896. . . .* Chicago: Laird and Lee, 1896.

Panghorn, J. G. *The B. & O. Red Book for the National Democratic Convention of 1884*. Chicago: Knight and Leonard, 1884.

The People's Life of General Zachary Taylor, the Hero of Palo Alto, Monterey, and Buena Vista, With Numerous Illustrative Anecdotes. Also, A Biography of Millard Fillmore. Philadelphia: Lindsay and Blakiston, 1848.

Pickett, Leander Lycurgus. *Uncle Sam or the Pope, Which?* Louisville, Ky.: Pentecostal, 1916.

The Pilgrims of Hope: An Oratorio for the Clintonian Celebration of the New Year. Republished from "The American" of January 1, 1820 . . . Occasioned by the Nomination of De Witt Clinton as a Candidate for the Office of President of the United States, in the Year 1812. . . . Albany, N.Y.: Packard and Van Benthuysen, 1820.

The Political Prohibitionist for 1887. New York: Funk and Wagnalls, 1887.

The Political Reformation of 1884: A Democratic Campaign Book. New York: Democratic National Committee, 1884.

Portraits of Republican and Democratic Candidates, With Nominating Speeches, and Sketches of the Lives of the Candidates. Chicago: Vandercook, 1884.

President II: Being Observations on the Late Official Address of George Washington: Designed to Promote the Interest of a Certain Candidate for the Executive, and to Explode the Pretensions of Others. Newark, N.J.: n.p., 1796.

The Public Record and Past History of John Bell & Edw'd Everett. Washington, D.C.: National Democratic Executive Committee, 1860.

Ramsdell, Henry J. *Life and Public Services of Hon. James G. Blaine, the Brilliant Orator and Sagacious Statesman. The Bosom Friend of the*

Lamented Garfield, and Now Choice of the Nation for President of the United States . . . Also the Life of the Courageous Soldier, Distinguished Senator and Nominee for the Vice-Presidency, Gen. John A. Logan, by Ben Perley Poore. Philadelphia: Hubbard Brothers, 1884.

"Read Then Vote for 'Six With Added Six' for President." Montclair, N.J.: Arabula, 1920.

Read! Read! Thou Hypocrite . . . Being a Reply to 'A Statement Proving Millard Fillmore . . . to Be an Abolitionist'. . . . Washington, D.C.: Towers, 1848.

"The Record—Frank R. Beckwith." (campaign literature). Indianapolis, Ind.: N.p., ca. 1960.

Republican National Committee. *History of the Republican Party.* Washington, D.C.: Republican National Committee, 1962.

Riker, Carroll L. *On to Washington: The National Party and Its Platform.* Chicago: National Political Review Association, 1894.

Rosenthal, Alter. *The Difference Between the Socialist Party and the Socialist Labor Party. . . .* Brooklyn, N.Y.: Grayzel, 1908.

Russell, J. J. *The Next Battle: How and Why Col. W. J. Bryan Was Defeated for the Presidency in 1896. . . .* New York: L. A. Skinner, 1898.

Sanial, Lucien. *The Socialist Almanac and Treasury of Facts.* New York: Socialistic Cooperative Publishing Association, 1898.

Satterlee, W. W. *The Political Prohibition Textbook.* Minneapolis, Minn.: self-published, 1883.

Seidman, Joel Isaac. *A Labor Party for America?* Katonah, N.Y.: Brookwood Labor Publications, 1936.

Shibley, George Henry. *The Financial Plank of the Allied Reform Parties for 1900.* New York: Humboldt Library, 1900.

Sketches of the Lives of Franklin Pierce and William R. King, Candidates of the Democratic-Republican Party for the Presidency and Vice Presidency of the United States. N.p.: Democratic National Committee, 1852.

Small, Samuel White. *Pleas for Prohibition.* Atlanta, Ga.: self-published, 1890.

Smalley, Eugene Virgil. *The Republican Manual: History, Principles, Early Leaders, Achievements, of the Republican Party, with Biographical Sketches of James A. Garfield and Chester A. Arthur.* New York: American Book Exchange, 1880.

Smith, C. W. *The Democratic Party: Its Origin, History and Political Tendency in the United States, from 1793 to 1888, by a "Hidden Hand."* Washington, D.C.: J. H. Wheeler, 1888.

Smith, Roderick Henry. *Proposed Platform of the American Party.* New York: self-published, 1907.

Socialist Hand Book: For President Allen (!) L. Benson; For Vice-President George R. Kirkpatrick: The Workers Candidates, Not Backed by Wall Street or the War Trust. Chicago: Socialist Party, 1916.

Socialist Party Campaign Leaflets, 1912. Washington, D.C.: Library of Congress, HX 89 .S74.

The Socialist Trade and Labor Alliance versus the 'Pure and Simple' Trade Union: A Debate . . . Between Daniel De Leon . . . and Job Harriman. . . . New York: New York Labor News, 1900.

The Socialist Workers Party: An Obituary. New York: Spartacist, 1984.

"Sonia Johnson, Citizen for President," Campaign Update, undated (1984).

Speeches of Eugene V. Debs, With a Critical Introduction. New York: International, 1928.

Speeches of Millard Fillmore, at New York, Newburgh, Albany, Rochester, Buffalo, &. Also Evidences of Fremont's Romanism. Washington, D.C.: American Party, 1856.

The Standard Pocket Cyclopedia and Campaign Manual, 1912. . . . Chicago: Laird and Lee, 1912.

A Statement Proving Millard Fillmore, the Candidate of the Whig Party for the Office of Vice President, to be an Abolitionist. . . . N.p., 1848.

Stedman, Seymour. *Socialism and Peace.* Chicago: National Office, Socialist Party, 1917.

Stewart, Gideon Tabor. *Broken Reeds: The Republican Party Tried by Its Record—Address at Westerville, Ohio, August 25, 1875: The Crime of Crimes.* New York: self-published, 1875.

Struble, Wallace R. *A Jab at the Devil: An Argument for a Christian Political Party.* Colon, Mich.: Express, 1895.

The Tariff: Martin Van Buren, the People's Friend and Candidate . . . Henry Clay, the Candidate of Politicans and Speculators . . . Whiggery Exposed. Columbus: Ohio Statesman, 1844.

Taylor and Fillmore: Life and Public Services of Major-Gen. Zachary Taylor. Also, the Life and Services of the Hon. Millard Fillmore. Hartford, Conn.: Belknap and Hamersley, 1848.

Taylor and Fillmore: Life of Major-General Zachary Taylor, With Characteristic Anecdotes and Incidents. Also, Life of the Honorable Millard Fillmore. Philadelphia: T. K. and P. G. Collins, 1848.

Thompson, Carl Dean. *Socialist Campaign Book.* Chicago: National Headquarters, Socialist Party, 1912.

Tinelli, L. W. *Fremont, Buchanan and Fillmore: Or, the Parties Called to Order.* New York: Livermore and Rudd, 1856.

Tinney, Calvin. *Is It True What They Say About Landon? A Non-Partisan Portrait.* New York: Wise-Parslow, 1936.

Tomlinson, Homer Aubrey. *It Came to Pass in Those Days: The Shout of a King.* Queens Village, N.Y.: Church of God, USA, Headquarters, 1968.

Trachtenberg, Alexander L. *A Political Guide for the Workers: Socialist Party Campaign Book, 1920.* Chicago: Socialist Party of the United States, 1920.

A True Account of the Singular Sufferings of John Fillmore, and Others, on Board a Noted Pirate Ship . . . To Which is Added a Brief Biography of Hon. Millard Fillmore. Utica, N.Y.: R. Potter, 1851.

Upshaw, William David. *Bombshells for Wets and Reds: The Twin Devils of America.* Cincinnati, Ohio: God's Bible School, 1936.

Vail, Walter S., ed. *The Words of James G. Blaine on the Issues of the Day . . . With a Biographical Sketch, Together with the Life and Public Service of John A. Logan.* Boston: D. L. Guernsey, 1884.

The Van Buren Platform: Or, Facts for the Present Supporters of Martin Van Buren. Washington, D.C.: J. and G. S. Gideon, Printers, 1848.

Watkins, Aaron Sherman. *Why I am a Prohibitionist.* Self-published, 1912.

Watson, Thomas Edward. *The People's Party Campaign Book, 1892: Not a Revolt; It Is a Revolution.* Washington, D.C.: National Watchman, 1892.

Watson, William Robinson. *The Whig Party: Its Objects, Its Principles, Its Candidates, Its Duties, and Its Prospects. . . .* Providence, R.I.: Knowles and Vose, 1844.

Weaver, James Baird. *A Call to Action: An Interpretation of the Great Uprising, Its Source and Causes.* Des Moines: Iowa Printing, 1892.

Weik, Jesse M. *History of the Republican Party and National Convention, 1908.* Chicago: Sidney M. Weil, 1908.

Wells, John G. *Wells' Illustrated National Campaign Handbook for 1860.* New York: self-published, 1860.

Wells, John Whitson. *Meet Mr. Landon.* Kansas City, Mo.: Alexander Printing, 1936.

Wheeler, Leslie. *Jimmy Who? An Examination of Presidential Candidate Jimmy Carter: The Man, His Career, His Stands on the Issues.* Woodbury, N.Y.: Barron's Educational Series, 1976.

The Whig Banner Songster . . . to Which is Added a Condensed Life of the Hon. Henry Clay and Many New Songs. Baltimore, Md.: T. Horton, 1844.

Whig Falsehoods Exposed. General Pierce and the Religious Test. Gen. Scott's Insult to the Catholic Church. N.p.: 1852.

The Whig Portrait Gallery. New York: American Review, 1848.

Williams, C. R. *Lives of Blaine and Logan: The People's Edition—Book of Reference*. Philadelphia: E. T. Haines, 1884.

Williams, Edwin. *The Life and Personal Administration of Ex-President Fillmore (From Walker's Statesman's Manual) To Which are Added, Reasons for His Election to the Presidency, Extracts From His Recent Speeches, and a Sketch of the Life of Andrew Jackson Donelson, of Tennessee*. New York: E. Walker, 1856.

Wilson, Alonzo E. *Prohibition Hand-book and Voter's Manual, 1900*. Chicago: self-published, 1900.

Wortman, Tunis. *A Solemn Address to Christians and Patriots, Upon the Approaching Election of a President of the United States. . . .* New York: David Denniston, 1800.

Wyeth, Newton. *Republican Principles and Policies: A Brief History of the Republican National Party*. Chicago: Republic Press, 1916.

Yarrington, J. T. *The Temperance-Political Question: Shall We Sustain the National Prohibition Party?* 4th ed. Carbondale, Pa.: self-published, 1873.

GENERAL HISTORIES

Ballman, John William, ed. *The Presidential Campaign . . . of 1896*. Cincinnati: W. J. Berg, 1896.

The Battle of 1900: An Official Handbook for Every American Citizen. Chicago: Monarch Book, 1900.

Billington, Ray Allen. *The Protestant Crusade, 1800–1860: A Study of the Origins of American Nativism*. New York: Rinehart, 1938, 1952 (2d ed.).

Blood, F. G. *Handbook and History of the National Farmers' Alliance and Industrial Union*. Washington, D.C.: National Farmers' Alliance and Industrial Union, 1893.

Boyd, James Penny. *Men and Issues of '92*. Philadelphia: Publishers' Union, 1892.

____. *Parties, Problems and Leaders of 1896*. Philadelphia: Publishers' Union, 1896.

Buenker, John D. and Edward R. Kantowicz, eds. *Historical Dictionary of the Progressive Era, 1890–1920*. New York: Greenwood Press, 1988.

Cannon, James Patrick. *From Left Opposition Toward New Revolutionary Party, 1932–1934*. New York: Monad Press, 1985.

____. *History of American Trotskyism from Its Origin (1928) to the Founding of the Socialist Workers Party (1938)*, 2d ed. New York: Pathfinder Press, 1972.

Chamberlin, Everett. *The Struggle of '72*. Chicago: Union, 1872.

Cooper, Thomas Valentine, and Hector T. Fenton. *American Politics (Non-Partisan) from the Beginning to Date: Embodying a History of All the Political Parties. . . .* Philadelphia: Fireside, 1892.

The Criterion: Which Exhibits Portraits of the Three Candidates, Facts in the Lives of Each, the Platforms of the Three Parties, and the Constitution of the United States. New York: J. C. Buttre, 1856.

Darling, Edgar S. *National Contest, Containing Portraits and Biographies of Our National Favorites. . . .* Detroit, Mich.: Darling Brothers, 1888.

Draper, Theodore. *American Communism and Soviet Russia*. New York: Viking Press, 1960.

Eaton, Herbert. *Presidential Timber: A History of Nominating Conventions, 1868–1960*. New York: Free Press of Chicago, 1964.

Ekirch, Arthur Alphonse. *Progressivism in America: A Study of the Era from Theodore Roosevelt to Woodrow Wilson*. New York: New Viewpoints, 1974.

Election 1972. New York: Encyclopedia Americana, 1972.

Ellis, Edward Sylvester. *Great Leaders and National Issues of 1896. . . .* Philadelphia: self-published, 1896.

Ewing, Cortez Arthur Milton. *Presidential Elections from Abraham Lincoln to Franklin D. Roosevelt*. Norman: U. of Oklahoma Press, 1940.

Extracts from Leading Publications in Vindication of the Universal Peace Union and Its President. Philadelphia: Universal Peace Union, 1898.

Fallows, Rt. Rev. Samuel. *The American Manual and Patriots' Handbook*. Chicago: Century Book and Paper, 1889.

Flanders, Joseph R. *A Sketch of Political Parties and Their Principles. . . .* Springfield, Ill.: Springfield Printing, 1881.

Foner, Philip Sheldon. *American Socialism and Black Americans*. Westport, Conn.: Greenwood Press, 1977.

____. *History of the Labor Movement in the United States*. 6 vols. New York: International, 1947.

Ford, Henry Jones. *The Rise and Growth of American Politics*. New York: Macmillan, 1898.

Fox, Dorus Morton. *History of Political Parties, National Reminiscences and the Tippecanoe Movement*. Des Moines: Iowa Printing, 1875.

Frederick, James Mack Henry. *National Party Platforms of the United States: Presidential Candidates, Electoral and Popular Votes*. Akron, Ohio: Werner, 1896.

Gabriel, Richard A. *The Political Machine in Rhode Island*. Kingston: Bureau of Government Research, U. of Rhode Island, 1970.

Ganley, Albert C. *The Progressive Movement: Traditional Reform*. New York: Macmillan, 1964.

Gardiner, Oliver Cromwell. *The Great Issue: or, The Three Presidential Candidates. . . .* Westport, Conn.: Negro Universities Press, 1970. Reprint of 1848 edition.

Goodspeed's Biographical and Historical Memoirs of Central Arkansas (Pulaski, Jefferson, Lonoke, Faulkner, Grant, Saline, Perry, Garland, and Hot Springs Counties). Chicago: Goodspeed, 1889.

Goodspeed's Biographical and Historical Memoirs of Mississippi. Chicago: Goodspeed, 1891.

Gould, Lewis L. *The Progressive Era*. Syracuse, N.Y.: Syracuse U. Press, 1974.

____. *Reform and Regulation: American Politics, 1900–1916*. New York: Wiley, 1978.

Great Political Issues and Leaders of the Campaign of 1900. . . . Chicago: W. B. Conkey, 1900.

Green, James R. *Grass Roots Socialism: Radical Movements in the Southwest, 1895–1943*. Baton Rouge: Louisiana U. Press, 1978.

Hanson, John Wesley, Jr., and Stanley Waterloo, eds. *The Parties and the Men; Or, Political Issues of 1896*. Chicago: W. B. Conkey, 1896.

Harrison, Edwin I. *A Booklet of National Political Platforms: Of All Parties*. Le Roy, Ill.: self-published, 1896.

Hart, William Octave. *The Democratic Conventions of 1908–1912–1916, Republican Conventions of 1912–1916, and Progressive Convention of 1912*. New Orleans, La.: self-published, 1916.

Henry, W. H. F. *The Voice of the People: Or, The History of Political Issues in the United States. . . .* Indianapolis: J. E. Sherrill, 1884.

Higham, John. *Strangers in the Land: Patterns of American Nativism, 1860–1924*. New York: Atheneum, 1963.

Hillquit, Morris. *Recent Progress of the Socialist and Labor Movements in the United States*. Chicago: C. H. Kerr, 1907.

Hillquit, Morris, Samuel Gompers, and Max S. Hayes. *The Double Edge of Labor's Sword*. New York: Arno Press, 1971. Reprint of 1914 edition.

Hofstadter, Richard. *The Progressive Movement, 1900–1915*. Englewood Cliffs, N.J.: Prentice-Hall, 1963.

Honegger, Ruth, and Marino Pascal. *Beyond the Politics of Exclusion Towards an Art of Inclusion: Presidential Candidates: 1992*. Catalog of an art exhibit at the Armory Center for the Arts, Pasadena, Calif., October 11–December 23, 1992.

Hooper, Osman Castle. "The Coxey Movement in Ohio." *Ohio Archaeological and Historical Quarterly* 9 (1900): 155–176.

Hopkins, James Herron. *History of Political Parties in the United States*. New York: G. P. Putman's Sons, 1900.

Hornstein, Leon. *The Campaign of '88: A Handy Volume Containing the Lives of the Democratic and Republican Candidates. . . .* Chicago: Hornstein Brothers, 1888.

Houghton, Walter Raleigh. *Conspectus of the History of Political Parties and the Federal Government.* Indianapolis, Ind.: Granger and Davis, 1880.

____. *History of American Politics (Non-Partisan) . . . from 1607 to 1882.* Indianapolis, Ind.: F. T. Neely, 1883.

Howe, Daniel Walker, comp. *The American Whigs: An Anthology.* New York: Wiley, 1973.

____. *The Political Culture of the American Whigs.* Chicago: U. of Chicago Press, 1979.

Hubbell, John. "The National Free Soil Convention of '48." *Buffalo Historical Society Publications* 4 (1896): 147–162.

Hutchins, Stilson. *Political Manual for 1880.* N.p., 1880.

Isaac, Paul E. *Prohibition and Politics: Turbulent Decades in Tennessee, 1885–1920.* Knoxville: U. of Tennessee Press, 1965.

Jackson, William Rufus. *Missouri Democracy: A History of the Party and Its Representative Members—Past and Present, With a Vast Amount of Informative Data.* Chicago: S. J. Clarke, 1935.

Jay, John. *The Presidential Election.* New York: A. S. Barnes, 1880.

Johnston, Alexander. *American Political History, 1763–1876.* New York: G. P. Putnam's Sons, 1905.

____. "The History of Political Parties, 1789–1850." In *Narrative and Critical History of America,* vol. 7, edited by Winsor Justin, 267–356. Boston: N.p.

Jones, J. Levering. *A Brief Survey of the Principles and Achievements of the Republican Party.* Philadelphia: W. F. Fell, 1888.

Jordan, William, George. *The Five National Platforms Dissected, Classified, Indexed. . . .* New York: Jordan, 1912.

Kipnis, Ira. *The American Socialist Movement, 1897–1912.* New York: Columbia U. Press, 1952. Reprint, Westport, Conn.: Greenwood Press, 1968.

Knappman, Edward W., ed. *Presidential Election, 1968.* New York: Facts on File, 1970.

Knoles, George Harmon. *The Presidential Campaign and Election of 1892.* New York: AMS Press, 1971.

Laidler, Harry Wellington. *The Socialism of Our Times.* New York: Da Capo Press, 1976. Reprint of 1929 edition.

____. *Toward a Farmer-Labor Party.* New York: League for Industrial Democracy, 1938.

Lambert, Oscar D. *Presidential Politics in the United States, 1841–1844.* Durham, N.C.: N.p., 1936.

Larner, Jeremy. *Nobody Knows: Reflections on the McCarthy Campaign of 1968.* New York: Macmillan, 1970.

Larson, Arthur. *A Republican Looks at His Party.* New York: Harper and Brothers, 1956.

Leonard, Ira M., and Robert D. Parmet. *American Nativism, 1830–1860.* New York: Van Nostrand Reinhold, 1971.

Le Sueur, Maridel. *Crusaders.* New York: Blue Heron Press, 1955.

Lokos, Lionel. *Hysteria 1964: The Fear Campaign Against Barry Goldwater.* New Rochelle, N.Y.: Arlington House, 1967.

Lorant, Stefan. *The Glorious Burden: A History of the Presidency and Presidential Elections, from George Washington to James Earl Carter, Jr.* Lenox, Mass.: Authors Editions, 1976.

Luckey, George J. *The American Voters, Vade Mecum: Containing . . . Proceedings of the Republican and Democratic National Conventions of 1884, and Lives . . . of Blaine and Logan, Cleveland and Hendricks.* Philadelphia: W. H. Thompson, 1884.

Mahoney, J. Daniel. *Actions Speak Louder: The Story of the New York Conservative Party.* New Rochelle, N.Y. Arlington House, 1968.

Marcus, Robert D. *Grand Old Party: Political Structure in the Gilded Age, 1880–1896.* New York: Oxford U. Press, 1971.

Martin, John Bartlow. *The Deep South Says Never.* New York: Ballantine Books, 1957.

McCarthy, Eugene Joseph. *The Year of the People.* Garden City, N.Y.: Doubleday, 1969.

McConnell, George Murray. *Presidential Campaigns from Washington to Roosevelt.* Chicago: Rand McNally, 1908.

McCurry, Dan C., comp. *The Farmer-Labor Party: History, Platform, and Programs.* New York: Arno Press, 1975.

McKee, Thomas Hudson. *The National Conventions and Platforms of All Political Parties.* Baltimore, Md.: Friedenwald, 1906.

McKenna, George, comp. *American Populism.* New York: Putnam, 1974.

McMath, Robert C. *Populist Vanguard, A History of the Southern Farmers Alliance.* Chapel Hill: U. of North Carolina Press, 1975.

McMurray, Donald Le Crone. *Coxey's Army: A Study of the Industrial Army Movement of 1894.* Seattle: U. of Washington Press, 1968.

McNeill, George E. *The Labor Movement: The Problem of Today.* Boston: A. M. Bridgman, 1887.

McPherson, Edward. *A Handbook of Politics.* 14 vols. Washington, D.C.: J. J. Chapman, 1868–1894.

Merriam, Charles Edward, and Louis Overacker. *Primary Elections.* Chicago: U. of Chicago Press, 1928.

Miller, James Martin. *Leaders and Issues of the Campaign of 1904: Containing Biographies of All the Presidential Candidates. . . .* Philadelphia: self-published, 1904.

Minnigerode, Meade. *Presidential Years, 1787–1860.* New York: G. P. Putnam's Sons, 1928, 1938 (rev. ed.).

Mirkin, Stanford M., ed. *1964 Guide to Conventions and Elections.* New York: CBS News Election Unit, Dell, 1964.

Moore, Edmund Arthur. *A Catholic Runs for President: The Campaign of 1928.* New York: Ronald Press, 1956.

Moore, Rolland Bryant, comp. *1900 Campaign Manual. . . .* New Britain, Conn.: self-published, 1900.

Moos, Malcolm Charles. *Politics, Presidents, and Coattails.* Baltimore, Md.: Johns Hopkins Press, 1952.

Moos, Malcolm Charles, and Stephen Hess. *Hats in the Ring.* New York: Random House, 1960.

Morgan, Howard Wayne. *American Socialism: 1900–1960.* Englewood Cliffs, N.J.: Prentice-Hall, 1964.

Morin, Relman. *The Associated Press Story of Election 1968.* New York: Pocket Books, 1969.

Morris, Charles, ed. *Men and Issues of 1904: Containing Intimate Biographies of the Presidential Candidates. . . .* Philadelphia: J. C. Winston, 1904.

____. *A Voter's Guide for the Campaign of 1900: Great Issues and National Leaders. . . .* Philadelphia: John C. Winston, 1900.

Murray, Robert K. *The 103rd Ballot: Democrats and the Disaster in Madison Square Garden.* New York: Harper and Row, 1976.

Myers, Chesterfield W. *Coxey's Warning: A Vindication of Coxeyism.* N.p.: self-published, 1894.

Nash, Howard Pervear. *Third Parties in American Politics.* Washington, D.C.: Public Affairs Press, 1959.

The National Parties; Their Platforms and the Speeches of Acceptance of Their Presidential Candidates. . . . Brooklyn, N.Y.: Brooklyn Daily Eagle, 1908.

National Platforms of the Republican, Democratic, Fusion Populist or People's, Mid-Road Populist or People's, and Prohibition Parties. . . . 2d ed. Omaha, Nebr.: Union Pacific Railway, 1900.

National Political Campaign of 1944. Washington, D.C.: United States News Service, 1944.

Nicoll, Charles H. *Our Presidents, from 1788 to 1892, with Portrait and Biography of Each, Also Portraits and Sketches of the Lives of the Present Candidates.* New York: Nicholl and Roy, 1892.

1964 Presidential Election Guide. New York: Whitney Communications Corporation, Book Division, 1964.

Norton, Anthony Banning. *The Great Revolution of 1840: Reminiscences of the Log Cabin and Hard Cider Campaign.* Mount Vernon, Ohio: A. B. Norton, 1888.

Nugent, Walter T. K. *The Tolerant Populists; Kansas, Populism and Nativism.* Chicago: U. of Chicago Press, 1963.

Ogden, Daniel, and Arthur Peterson. *Electing the President, 1964.* San Francisco, Calif.: Chandler, 1964.

Oneal, James, and B. A. Werner. *American Communism, A Critical Analysis of Its Origins, Development, and Programs.* New York: E. P. Dutton, 1947. Reprint, Westport, Conn.: Greenwood Press, 1972.

Ostrander, Gilman Marston. *The Prohibition Movement in California, 1848–1933.* Berkeley: U. of California Press, 1957.

Oulahan, Richard. *The Man Who . . . : The Story of the 1932 Democratic National Convention.* New York: Dial Press, 1971.

Overacker, Louis. *The Presidential Primary.* New York: Macmillan, 1926. Reprint, New York: Arno Press, 1974.

Patton, Jacob Harris. *Political Parties in the United States: Their History and Influence, From the Adoption of the Constitution to the Accession of Theodore Roosevelt to the Presidency. . . .* New York: New Amsterdam Book, 1902.

Penicks, Thomas B. *Presidential Campaign 1884.* Washington, D.C.: self-published, 1883.

The People's Edition of the Lives of the Candidates for President and Vice-President of the United States. . . . Albany, N.Y.: R. Duncan, 1888.

Petersen, Svend. *A Statistical History of the American Presidential Elections.* New York: Frederick Ungar, 1963.

Platt, George Washington. *A History of the Republican Party.* Cincinnati, Ohio: C. J. Krehbiel, 1904.

Pocket Manual of 1896 Politics. Minneapolis, Minn.: Calderwood and Heffron, 1896.

Political Party Platforms in Presidential Campaigns, 1840 to 1904. Washington, D.C.: Globe Printing, 1904.

Political United States . . . Lives of the Candidates for President and Vice President for the Campaign of 1900. . . . Washington, D.C.: R. A. Dinsmore, 1900.

Pollack, Norman. *The Populist Mind.* Indianapolis, Ind.: Bobbs-Merrill, 1967.

_____. *The Populist Response to Industrial America.* Cambridge: Harvard U. Press, 1962.

Popov, Milorad I. *The American Extreme Left: A Decade of Conflict.* London, England: Institute for the Study of Conflict, 1972.

Portraits and Sketches of the Lives of All of the Candidates for the Presidency and Vice Presidency, for 1860. New York: J. C. Buttre, 1860.

Potter, David Morris, ed. *Party Politics and Public Action, 1877–1917.* New York: Henry Holt, 1960.

Potterf, Rex M. *Presidential Election of 1860.* Fort Wayne, Ind.: Public Library of Fort Wayne and Allen County, 1960.

Prescott, Lawrence F. *Living Issues of the Campaign of 1900: Its Men and Principles . . . Including the Platforms of All Parties and Biographies of the Presidential Candidates. . . .* Philadelphia: National, 1900.

The Presidential Candidates and Platforms, Biographies, and Nominating Speeches. Brooklyn, N.Y.: Brooklyn Daily Eagle, 1896.

Prufer, Julius Fielding. *American Political Parties and Presidential Elections, Containing a Chart Showing the Development of Political Parties, 1679–1932. . . .* Philadelphia: McKinley, 1932.

Quint, Howard H. *The Forging of American Socialism: Origins of the Modern Movement.* Columbia: U. of South Carolina Press, 1953.

Rand McNally Political Atlas: A Compendium of Facts and Figures, Platforms, Biographies and Portraits—The Men and the Issues of the Presidential Campaign of 1920. Chicago: Rand, McNally, 1920.

Ranney, Austin, ed. *The American Elections of 1980.* Washington, D.C., American Enterprise Institute, 1981.

Ratner, Lormer. *Antimasonry: The Crusade and the Party.* Englewood Cliffs, N.J.: Prentice Hall, 1969.

Rayback, Joseph G. *Free Soil: The Election of 1848.* Lexington: U. Press of Kentucky, 1971.

Raynolds, L. D. *National Platforms and Political History of the United States.* Chicago: W. L. Raynolds, 1896.

Record, Wilson. *The Negro and the Communist Party.* Chapel Hill: U. of North Carolina Press, 1951. Reprint, New York: Atheneum Press, 1971.

Remini, Robert Vincent, ed. *The Age of Jackson.* New York: Harper and Row, 1972.

The Republican Party: Its History in Brief, 1854–1954. Washington, D.C.: Republican Centennial Committee, 1954.

Reunion of the Free Soilers of 1848–1852, at the Parker House, Boston, Massachusetts, June 28, 1888. Cambridge, Mass.: J. Wilson and Son, 1888.

Robinson, Edgar Eugene. *The Roosevelt Leadership, 1933–1945.* Philadelphia: Lippincott, 1955.

Robinson, William Alexander. *Jeffersonian Democracy in New England.* New Haven: Yale U. Press, 1916. Reprint, New York: AMS Press, 1968.

Rochester, Anna. *The Populist Movement in the United States.* New York: International, 1944.

Rozwenc, Edwin Charles, and John C. Matlon. *Myth and Reality in the Populist Revolt.* Boston: Heath, 1966.

Saloutos, Theodore. *Farmer Movements in the South, 1865–1933.* Berkeley: U. of California Press, 1960.

_____. *Populism: Reaction or Reform?* New York: Holt, Rinehart and Winston, 1968.

Salt, Mark H., ed. *Candidates and the Issues: An Official Handbook for Every American Citizen; Policies and Platforms of All Parties. . . .* N.p.: self-published, 1908.

Saposs, David Joseph. *Communism in American Politics.* Washington, D.C.: Public Affairs Press, 1960.

Schlesinger, Arthur Meier, Jr. *The Age of Jackson.* Boston: Little, Brown, 1945.

_____. *The Age of Roosevelt.* Boston: Houghton Mifflin, 1957.

_____, ed. *The Coming to Power: Critical Presidential Elections in American History.* New York: Chelsea House, 1972.

Schoenebaum, Eleanore W., ed. *Political Profiles: The Eisenhower Years.* New York: Facts on File, 1977.

Schwantes, Carlos A. *Coxey's Army: An American Odyssey.* Lincoln: U. of Nebraska Press, 1986.

Seitz, Don C. *The Dreadful Decade.* Indianapolis, Ind.: Bobbs-Merrill, 1926.

Sellers, James Benson. *The Prohibition Movement in Alabama, 1902–1943.* Chapel Hill: U. of North Carolina Press, 1943.

Shannon, David A. *Progressivism and Post War Disillusionment, 1898–1928.* New York: McGraw-Hill, 1966.

Shaplen, Robert. *Free Love and Heavenly Sinners.* New York: Alfred A. Knopf, 1954.

Sheldon, William Du Bose. *Populism in the Old Dominion: Virginia Farm Politics, 1885–1900.* Gloucester, Mass.: P. Smith, 1967.

Shibley, George Henry. *Initiative and Referendum: A Republican Form of Government. . . .* Forest Grove: Oregon State Grange, 1909.

Sinclair, Andrew. *Prohibition: The Era of Excess.* Boston: Little, Brown, 1962.

Sindler, Allan P. *Political Parties in the United States.* New York: St. Martin's Press, 1966.

Sipes, William B. *Our Presidential Elections, Party Platforms, Biographies of All the Presidents, Election Returns, Statistics, Etc., Etc. . . . .* New York: F. B. Miller, 1888.

Smith, Chester Alan. *The American Comedy.* Boston: R. G. Badger, 1913.

Smith, Denys Harrison Herbert. *Polls Apart: Background to American Presidential Elections.* London: Cohen and West, 1960.

Stanwood, Edward. *A History of Presidential Elections.* 4th ed. Boston: Houghton, Mifflin, 1896.

____. *A History of the Presidency.* New ed. rev. by Charles Knowles Bolton. 2 vols. Clifton, N.J.: A. M. Kelley, 1928. Reprint, New York: Houghton Mifflin, 1975.

Starobin, Joseph Robert. *American Communism in Crisis, 1943–1957.* Berkeley: U. of California Press, 1972.

Stinnett, Ronald F. *Democrats, Dinners and Dollars: A History of the Democratic Party, Its Dinners, Its Ritual.* Ames: Iowa State U. Press, 1967.

Stoddard, Henry Luther. *Presidential Sweepstakes: The Story of Political Conventions and Campaigns.* New York: G. P. Putnam's Sons, 1948.

Tenney, Jack Breckinridge. *Red Fascism: Boring From Within . . . by the Subversive Forces of Communism.* Los Angeles: Federal Printing, 1947.

____. *The Tenney Committee: The American Record.* Tujunga, Calif.: Standard Publications, 1952.

____. *Zionist Network: A Tenney Report.* Tujunga, Calif.: Standard Publications, 1953.

Terkel, Studs. *American Dreams, Lost and Found.* New York: Pantheon Books, 1980.

____. *The Great Divide: Second Thoughts on the American Dream.* New York: Avon Books, 1989.

____. *"The Good War:" An Oral History of World War Two.* New York: Ballantine Books, 1984.

____. *Hard Times: An Oral History of the Great Depression.* New York: Pantheon Books, 1970.

____. *Working: People Talk About What They Do All Day and How They Feel About What They Do.* New York: Pantheon Books, 1974.

Timberlake, James H. *Prohibition and the Progressive Movement, 1900–1920.* Cambridge: Harvard U. Press, 1963.

Tindall, George Brown. *A Populist Reader.* New York: Harper and Row, 1966.

Towne, Charles Arnette. *Universal Peace Movement.* Washington, D.C.: Government Printing Office, 1912.

Tragle, Henry I., comp. *Coxey's Army.* New York: Grossman, 1974.

Trefousse, Hans Louis. *The Radical Republicans: Lincoln's Vanguard for Racial Justice.* New York: Knopf, 1969.

Tucker, Ray Thomas. *Mirrors of 1932.* New York: Brewer, Warren and Putnam, 1931.

Turner, Henry A., ed. *Politics in the United States: Readings in Political Parties and Pressure Groups.* New York: McGraw-Hill, 1955.

Unger, Irwin. *The Greenback Era: A Social and Political History of American Farmers, 1865–1879.* Princeton: Princeton U. Press, 1964.

____. *Populism: Nostalgic or Progressive?* Chicago: Rand McNally, 1964.

U.S. Congress, House Committee on Un-American Activities. *Organized Communism in the United States.* Washington, D.C.: Government Printing Office, 1953.

Vincent, Cuthbert. *The Political Textbook: Containing the Declaration of Independence, the Constitution of the United States, and all the Platforms of All Parties.* Omaha, Nebr.: Vincent, 1900.

Wallace, Irving. *The Nympho and Other Maniacs.* New York: Pocket Books, 1972.

Wallace, Irving. *The Square Pegs: Some Americans Who Dared to Be Different.* New York: Berkley, 1957.

Walton, Richard J. *Henry Wallace, Harry Truman, and the Cold War.* New York: Viking Press, 1976.

Warner, Hoyt Landon. *Progressivism in Ohio, 1897–1917.* Columbus: Ohio State U. Press, 1964.

Warren, Sidney. *The Battle for the Presidency.* Philadelphia: Lippincott, 1968.

Waters, Agnes. *The White Papers.* Washington, D.C.: self-published, 1940.

Watkins, William. *American Rank and File Labor Delegation to Soviet Russia.* New York: International, 1928.

Wells, John F., ed. *Time Bomb (The Faubus Revolt).* Little Rock, Ark.: General, 1962.

Wheeler, Edward Jewitt. *Prohibition: The Principle, The Policy, and the Party. . . .* New York: J. R. Anderson, 1889.

Whitener, Daniel Jay. *Prohibition in North Carolina, 1715–1945.* Chapel Hill: U. of North Carolina Press, 1945.

Whitman, Alden. *Labor Parties, 1827–1834.* New York: International, 1943.

Yearley, Clifton K. *Britons in American Labor: A History of the Influence of the United Kingdom Immigrants on American Labor, 1820–1914.* Baltimore, Md.: Johns Hopkins Press, 1957.

Yearns, Wilfred Buck. *The Confederate Congress.* Athens: U. of Georgia Press, 1960.

Young, Donald. *American Roulette: The History and Dilemma of the Vice Presidency.* New York: Holt, Rinehart and Winston, 1972.

General References

Adams, Oscar Fay. *A Dictionary of American Authors,* 5th ed. New York: Houghton Mifflin, 1904. Reprint, Detroit, Mich.: Gale Research, 1969.

American Annual Cyclopedia and Register of Important Events. . . . 14 vols. New York: D. Appleton, 1862–1875.

The Annual Obituary. New York: St. Martin's Press, 1981, 1982, 1983.

Appleton's Annual Cyclopaedia and Register of Important Events of the Year. New York: D. Appleton, various years. 1883–1902.

Banta, R. E., compiler. *Indiana Authors and Their Books,* vol. 1: *1816–1819.* Crawfordsville, Ind.: Wabash College, 1949.

Biographical Directory of the American Congress, 1774–1971. Washington, D.C.: U.S. Government Printing Office, 1971.

Bland, Thomas A. *The Spartan Band: Biographical Sketches of . . . Representatives in Congress of the National Greenback Party.* Washington, D.C.: R. H. Darby, 1879.

Bliss, William D. P., ed. *Encyclopedia of Social Reform.* New York: Funk and Wagnalls, 1908.

Cherrington, Ernest Hurst, ed. *Standard Encyclopedia of the Alcohol Problem.* Westerville, Ohio: American Issue, 1925.

Clymer, Ernest Fletcher. *Historical Abstract of Presidential Conventions and Elections. . . .* New York: W. E. Rudge, 1924.

Congressional Quarterly. *Presidential Elections Since 1789.* 2d ed. Washington, D.C.: Congressional Quarterly, 1979.

Cox, Norman W., et al., eds. *Encyclopedia of Pennsylvania Biography.* 20 vols. New York: Lewis Historical, 1914.

Day, Glenn. *Minor Presidential Candidates and Parties of 1988.* Jefferson, N.C.: McFarland, 1988.

____. *Minor Presidential Candidates and Parties of 1992.* Jefferson, N.C.: McFarland, 1992.

De Leon, Solon, Irma C. Hayssen, and Grace Poole. *The American Labor Who's Who.* New York: Hanford Press, 1925.

Destler, Chester McArthur. *American Radicalism, 1865–1901.* New York: Octagon Books, 1963.

Diggins, John P. *The American Left in the Twentieth Century.* New York: Harcourt Brace Jovanovich, 1973.

Dilling, Elizabeth. *The Red Network: A "Who's Who" and Handbook of Radicalism for Patriots.* Kenilworth, Ill.: self-published, 1934.

Drake, Francis S. *Dictionary of American Biography including Men of the Time*. Boston: James R. Osgood, 1872. Reprint, Detroit, Mich.: Gale Research, 1974.

Editors of Who's Who in America. *The Celebrity Who's Who*. New York: World Almanac, 1986.

Ehrenhalt, Alan, ed., *Politics in America*. Washington, D.C.: Congressional Quarterly, 1983–.

Encyclopedia of American History. Rev. ed. Guilford, Conn.: DPG Reference, 1981.

Encyclopedia of Biography of Connecticut. Chicago: Century Publishing and Engraving, 1892.

Encyclopedia of Biography of Illinois. 3 vols. Chicago: Century Publishing and Engraving, 1892–1902.

Encyclopedia of Contemporary Biography of New York. 3 vols. New York: Atlantic Publishing and Engraving, 1877.

Encyclopedia of Contemporary Biography of Pennsylvania. 3 vols. New York: Atlantic Publishing and Engraving, 1889–1893.

Encyclopedia of Southern Baptists. 2 vols and supplement. Nashville, Tenn: Broadman Press, 1958, 1971.

Extremism on the Right: A Handbook. New York: New York Anti-Defamation League of B'nai B'rith, 1983.

Ferguson's War on the U. of Texas: A Chronological Outline, January 12, 1915 to July 31, 1917, Inclusive. Austin, Tex.: Ex-Students Association of the U. of Texas, 1917.

Filler, Louis. *Dictionary of American Conservatism*. Secaucus, N.J.: Citadel Press, 1988.

____. *A Dictionary of American Social Reform*. New York: Philosophical Library, 1963.

____. *From Populism to Progressivism: Representative Selections*. Huntington, N.Y.: R. E. Krieger, 1978.

Fink, Gary M. *Biographical Dictionary of American Labor*. Westport, Conn.: Greenwood Press, 1984.

____. *Biographical Dictionary of American Labor Leaders*. Westport, Conn.: Greenwood Press, 1974.

Fitch, Charles Elliott. *Encyclopedia of Biography of New York*. 3 vols. Boston: American Historical Society, 1916.

Fogarty, Robert S. *Dictionary of American Communal and Utopian History*. Westport, Conn.: Greenwood Press, 1980.

Forster, Arnold, and Benjamin R. Epstein. *Danger on the Right*. New York: Random House, 1964.

____. *The Troublemakers*. Garden City, N.Y.: Doubleday, 1952.

Fox, C. J. *Centennial Record of Presidential Nominations, Campaigns and Elections, 1789–1889*. Baltimore: American Book and Job Printing Office, 1889.

Friedman, Leon, and Fred L. Israel, eds. *The Justices of the United States Supreme Court, 1789–1969*. 4 vols. and supplement (1969–1978). New York: Chelsea House, in association with R. R. Bowker, 1969.

Gannon, Francis X. *Biographical Dictionary of the Left*. 4 vols. Belmont, Mass.: Western Island, 1971.

Garraty, John Arthur, ed. *Encyclopedia of American Biography*. New York: Harper and Row, 1974.

George, John, and Laird Wilcox. *Nazis, Communists, Klansmen, and Others on the Fringe*. Buffalo, N.Y.: Prometheus Books, 1992.

Gibson, Arrell, ed. *Encyclopedia of Missouri*. St. Clair Shores, Mich.: Somerset, 1985.

Giddings, Edward J. *American Christian Rulers, or Religion and Men of Government*. New York: Bromfield, 1890.

Gille, Frank H., ed. *The Encyclopedia of New York*. St. Clair Shores, Mich.: Somerset Press, 1982.

Glashan, Roy R. *American Governors and Gubernatorial Elections, 1775–1978*. Westport, Conn.: Meckler Books, 1979.

Goodman, Robert A., ed. *Biographical Dictionary of Marxism*. Westport, Conn.: Greenwood Press, 1986.

Gorman, Robert A., ed. *Biographical Dictionary of Neo-Marxism*. Westport, Conn.: Greenwood Press, 1985.

Graves, John Temple, Clark Howell, and Walter Williams. *Eloquent Sons of the South: A Handbook of Southern Oratory*. Boston: Chapple, 1909.

Guide to U.S. Elections. Washington, D.C.: Congressional Quarterly, 1975, 1985.

Hatch, Louis Clint. *A History of the Vice Presidency of the United States*. Revised by Earl L. Shoup. Westport, Conn.: Greenwood Press, 1970. Reprint of 1934 edition.

Hate Groups in America: A Record of Bigotry and Violence. New York: Anti-Defamation League of B'nai B'rith, 1983.

Haynes, Frederick Emory. *Social Politics in the United States*. Boston: Houghton Mifflin, 1924.

Headley, P. C. *Public Men of Today*. Marshalltown, Iowa: Barnes and Ballou, 1883.

Henry, William Wirt, and Ainsworth R. Spofford. *Eminent and Representative Men of Virginia and the District of Columbia in the Nineteenth Century*. Madison, Wis.: Brant and Fuller, 1893.

Herringshaw, Thomas William. *Herringshaw's American Blue-Book of Biography*. Chicago: American Publishers' Association, 1914.

____. *Herringshaw's Encyclopedia of American Biography of the Nineteenth Century*. Chicago: American Publishers' Association, 1901.

Hine, Robert V. *California's Utopian Colonies*. New Haven, Conn.: Yale U. Press, 1966.

Hofstadter, Richard. *The Paranoid Style in American Politics*. Chicago: U. of Chicago Press, 1979.

Hoke, Henry. *It's A Secret*. New York: Reynel and Hitchcock, 1946.

Holcombe, Arthur Norman, Edward B. Logan, and J. T. Salter, et al. *The American Political Scene*. New York: Harper and Brothers, 1936.

Holli, Melvin G., and Peter d'A. Jones, eds. *Biographical Dictionary of American Mayors, 1820–1980*. Westport, Conn.: Greenwood Press, 1982.

Hospers, John. *Libertarianism: A Political Philosophy for Tomorrow*. Los Angeles: Nash, 1971.

Hugo, George B., and James F. Carey. *Socialism, the Creed of Despair: A Debate in Faneuil Hall, March 22, 1909. . . .* Boston: N.p., 1909.

Ingham, John N. *Biographical Dictionary of American Business Leaders*. 4 vols. Westport, Conn.: Greenwood Press, 1983.

James, Edward T., Janet Wilson James, and Paul S. Boyer, eds. *Notable American Women, 1607–1950*. 3 vols. and supplement (Modern Period). Cambridge, Mass.: Belknap Press of Harvard U., 1971.

Johnpoll, Bernard K., and Harvey Klehr. *Biographical Dictionary of the American Left*. New York: Greenwood Press, 1986.

Johnson, Allen, and Dumas Malone, eds. *Dictionary of American Biography*. 20 vols. and 7 supplements. New York: Charles Scribner's Sons, 1928.

Johnson, Ingrid E., ed. *Encyclopedia of the United States: Indiana*. St. Clair Shores, Mich.: Somerset, 1984.

Johnson, Rossiter, ed. *The Twentieth Century Biographical Dictionary of Notable Americans*. 10 vols. Boston: Biographical Society, 1904. Reprint, Detroit, Mich.: Gale Research, 1968.

Kane, Joseph Nathan. *Facts About the Presidents*. New York: Ace Books, 1976.

Kunstmann, ed. *Encyclopedia of Ohio*. St. Clair Shores, Mich.: Somerset, 1982.

Lanman, Charles. *Biographical Annals of the Civil Government of the United States, During Its First Century*. Washington, D.C.: James Anglim, Publisher, 1876. Reprint, Detroit, Mich.: Gale Research, 1976.

Lawrence, David. *Stumbling into Socialism and the Future of Our Political Parties*. New York: D. Appleton-Century, 1935.

Lender, Mark Edward. *Dictionary of American Temperance Biography: From Temperance Reform to Alcohol Research, the 1600s to the 1980s.* Westport, Conn.: Greenwood Press, 1984.

Logan, Rayford W., and Michael R. Winston. *Dictionary of American Negro Biography.* New York: W. W. Norton, 1982.

Lossing, Benson John. *Harper's Encyclopedia of United States History: From 458 A. D. to 1905.* 10 vols. New York: Harper and Brothers, 1905, 1915. Reprint of 1915 edition, Detroit, Mich.: Gale Research, 1974.

Mandelbaum, Seymour J. *The Social Setting of Intolerance: The Know-Nothings, the Red Scare, and McCarthyism.* Chicago: Scott, Foresman, 1964.

Marquis, Albert Nelson. *The Book of Chicagoans.* Chicago: A. N. Marquis, 1905.

____. *The Book of Minnesotans.* Chicago: A. N. Marquis, 1907.

Martin, Michael, and Leonard Gelber, eds. *Dictionary of American History.* Totowa, N.J.: Rowman and Littlefield, 1978.

McCloskey, Burr. *He Will Stay Till You Come: The Rise and Fall of Skinny Walker.* Durham, N.C.: Moore, 1978.

McConville, Mary St. Patrick. *Political Nativism in the State of Maryland, 1830–1860.* Washington, D.C.: Catholic U. of America, 1928.

McCoy, Donald R. *Angry Voices: Left-of-Center Politics in the New Deal Era.* Lawrence, Kans.: U. of Kansas Press, 1958.

McHenry, Robert. *Liberty's Women.* Springfield, Mass.: G. and C. Merriam, 1980.

McMullin, Thomas A., and David Walker. *Biographical Directory of American Territorial Governors.* Westport, Conn.: Meckler, 1984.

McReynolds, David. *We Have Been Invaded by the 21st Century.* New York: Praeger, 1970.

Medal of Honor Recipients, 1863–1978. U.S. Senate Committee on Veterans Affairs, 96th Cong., 1st sess., Senate Committee Print No. 3, 14 February 1979. Washington, D.C.: U.S. Government Printing Office, 1979.

Melton, J. Gordon. *Biographical Dictionary of American Cult and Sect Leaders.* New York: Garland, 1986.

Men of Minnesota. St. Paul, Minn.: R. L. Polk, 1915.

Men of Progress. . . . Detroit, Mich.: Evening News Association, 1900.

Michigan Biographies. Lansing, Mich.: Thorpe and Godfrey, 1888.

Michigan Biographies, Volume 2. Lansing, Mich.: Historical Commission, 1924.

Morris, Dan, and Inez Morris. *Who Was Who in American Politics.* New York: Hawthorn Books, 1974.

Morris, Richard B. *400 Notable Americans.* New York: Harper and Row, 1965.

Myers, Gustavus. *History of Bigotry in the United States.* New York: Random House, 1943.

Naison, Mark. *Communists in Harlem During the Depression.* Urbana: U. of Illinois Press, 1983.

Nash, Jay Robert. *Zanies: The World's Greatest Eccentrics.* Piscataway, N.J.: New Century, 1982.

National Cyclopaedia of American Biography. 63 vols. and 13 supps. New York: James T. White, 1893–.

Notable Men of the West. Chicago: Inter Ocean Newspaper, 1902.

Nowinson, Richard, ed. *Who's Who in United States Politics and American Political Almanac.* Chicago: Capitol House, 1950.

Oldfield, Reuben Bertram. *Ben Field's (Comic) Political Dictionary and History of the Great Political Parties.* Bath, N.Y.: Steuben Courier Press, 1920.

Owen, Thomas McAdory. *History of Alabama and Dictionary of Alabama Biography.* Spartanburg, S.C.: The Reprint. Westport, Conn.: Greenwood Press, 1978.

Paulsen, Pat. *How to Wage a Successful Campaign for the Presidency.* Los Angeles: Nash, 1972.

Peterson, Bettina, and Anastasia Toufexis, eds. *What Are the Answers? Norman Thomas Speaks to Youth.* New York: Washburn, 1970.

Porter, Kirk H., and Donald Bruce Johnson, comps. *National Party Platforms, 1840–1968.* Urbana: U. of Illinois Press, 1970.

Press, Jaques Cattell, ed. *Who's Who in American Politics.* New York: R. R. Bowker, various years.

Preston, Wheeler. *American Biographies.* New York: Harper and Brothers, 1940. Reprint, Detroit, Mich.: Gale Research, 1974.

Raimo, John. *Biographical Directory of American Colonial and Revolutionary Governors, 1607–1789.* Westport, Conn.: Meckler Books, 1980.

Ribuffo, Leo P. *The Old Christian Right.* Philadelphia: Temple U. Press, 1983.

Rice, Stewart A. *Farmers and Workers in American Politics.* New York: Columbia U. Press, 1924.

Ripley, George, and Charles Dana, eds. *The New American Cyclopaedia.* New York: D. Appleton, 1858–1863. Known as *The American Cyclopaedia* in subsequent editions, 1873–1876, 1883–1884 (16 vols.).

Robinson, Edgar Eugene. *The Presidential Vote, 1896–1932.* New York: Octagon Books, 1970.

Roche, John P., and Leonard W. Levy. *Parties and Pressure Groups.* New York: Harcourt, Brace and World, 1964.

Rossiter, Clinton. *The American Presidency.* 2d ed. New York: Harcourt, Brace and World, 1960.

____. *Parties and Politics in America.* Ithaca, N.Y.: Cornell U. Press, 1960.

Sait, Edward McChesney. *Sait's American Parties and Elections.* New York: Appleton-Century-Crofts, 1952.

Salter, John Thomas. *Public Men In and Out of Office.* Chapel Hill: U. of North Carolina, 1946.

Sanders, Lloyd C., ed. *Celebrities of the Century.* 2 vols. London: Cassell, 1887. Reprint, Ann Arbor, Mich.: Gryphon Books, 1971.

Schapsmeier, Edward L., and Frederick H. Schapsmeier. *Encyclopedia of American Agricultural History.* Westport, Conn.: Greenwood Press, 1975.

Schauinger, Joseph Herman. *Profiles in Action: American Catholics in Public Life.* Milwaukee, Wis.: Bruce, 1966.

Schlesinger, Stephen C. *The New Reformers: Forces for Change in American Politics.* Boston: Houghton, Mifflin, 1975.

Schoenebaum, Eleonore W., ed. *Political Profiles: The Nixon/Ford Years.* New York: Facts on File, 1979.

____. *Political Profiles: The Truman Years.* New York: Facts on File, 1978.

Scott, Henry W. *Distinguished American Lawyers.* New York: Charles L. Webster, 1891.

Seidle, Thomas C. *Thomas C. Seidle's Photographs of the Most Eminent Modern Statesmen and Politicians of the United States of America.* Reading, Pa.: Thomas C. Seidle, 1894.

Seitz, Don C. *Uncommon Americans.* Indianapolis, Ind.: Bobbs-Merrill, 1925.

Shepard, Leslie, d. *Encyclopedia of Occultism and Parapsychology.* 2 vols. and supp. Detroit, Mich.: Gale Research, 1978.

Shutter, Marion D., and J.S. McLain. *Progressive Men of Minnesota.* Minneapolis, Minn.: Minneapolis Journal, 1897.

Sikes, J. R. *Pen Pictures of Prohibition and Prohibitionists.* Loudonville, Ohio: P. H. Stauffer, 1887.

Simmons, William J. *Men of Mark.* Cleveland, Ohio: G. M. Rewell, 1887. Reprint, Chicago: Johnson, 1970.

Smith, William Albert. *A History of the Anti-Saloon League of Illinois.* Chicago: Anti-Saloon League of Illinois, 1925.

Sobel, Robert, and John Raimo, eds. *Biographical Directory of the Governors of the United States, 1789–1978.* Westport, Conn.: Microfilm Review, Meckler Books, 1978.

Sobel, Robert, ed. *Biographical Directory of the United States Executive Branch, 1774–1977.* Westport, Conn.: Greenwood Press, 1977.

Spiller, Roger J., ed. *Dictionary of American Military Biography*. 3 vols. Westport, Conn.: Greenwood Press, 1984.

Stedman, Seymour. *Eugene V. Debs, Plaintiff in Error, vs. the United States of America, Defendant in Error: In Error to District Court of the United States for the Northern District of Ohio. Petition for Rehearing*. Chicago: Champlin Law Printing, 1919.

____. *Rose Pastor Stokes, Plaintiff in Error, vs. United States of America, Defendant in Error. Brief for Plaintiff in Error . . . In Error to the District Court of the United States for the Western District of Missouri*. Chicago: Champlin Law Printing, 1918.

Stineman, Esther. *American Political Women: Contemporary and Historical Profiles*. Littleton, Colo.: Libraries Unlimited, 1980.

Strong, Donald. *Organized Anti-Semitism in America*. Washington, D.C.: American Council on Public Affairs, 1941.

Suall, Irwin. *The American Ultras: The Extreme Right and the Military-Industrial Complex*. New York: New America, 1962.

Suran, Bernard G. *Oddballs: The Social Maverick and the Dynamics of Individuality*. Chicago: Nelson-Hall, 1978.

Taylor, Tim. *The Book of the Presidents*. New York: Arno Press, 1972.

Temple, Oliver P. *Notable Men of Tennessee from 1833 to 1875*. New York: Cosmopolitan Press, 1912.

Thwing, Eugene. *The Literary Digest Political Cyclopedia*. New York: Funk and Wagnalls, 1932.

Van Doren, Charles, ed. *Webster's American Biographies*. Springfield, Mass.: G. and C. Merriam, 1974.

Van Norman, Louis E., ed. *An Album of Representative Prohibitionists*. New York: Funk and Wagnalls, 1895.

Vexler, Robert I. *The Vice Presidents and Cabinet Members*. 2 vols. Dobbs Ferry, N.Y.: Oceana Publications, 1975.

Villard, Oswald Garrison. *Prophets True and False*. New York: Alfred A. Knopf, 1928.

Wakelyn, Jon L. *Biographical Dictionary of the Confederacy*. Westport, Conn.: Greenwood Press, 1977.

Warner, Ezra J. *Generals in Blue*. Baton Rouge: Louisiana State U. Press, 1964.

____. *Generals in Gray*. Baton Rouge: Louisiana State U. Press, 1959.

Warner, Ezra J., and W. Buck Yearns. *Biographical Register of the Confederate Congress*. Baton Rouge: Louisiana State U. Press, 1975.

Webster's American Military Biographies. Springfield, Mass.: G. and C. Merriam, 1978.

Webster's Biographical Dictionary. Springfield, Mass.: G. and C. Merriam, 1969.

Whitman, Alden. *American Reformers*. New York: H. W. Wilson, 1985.

Who Was Who in America. 7 vols. Chicago: Marquis Who's Who, various years.

Who's Who in Government. Chicago: Marquis Who's Who, 1972, 1975, 1977.

Who's Who in Labor. New York: Arno Press, 1976.

Willard, Frances E., and Mary A. Livermore. *American Women*. 2 vols. New York: Mast, Crowell and Kirkpatrick, 1897. A revised edition of *Woman of the Century*. Buffalo, N.Y.: Charles Wells Moulton, 1893. Reprint, Detroit, Mich.: Gale Research, 1973.

Williams, Michael. *The Shadow of the Pope*. New York: Whittlesey House, 1932.

Wilson, James Grant, and John Fiske, eds. *Appleton's Cyclopedia of American Biography*. New York: D. Appleton, 1888–1889.

Wolfson, Abraham. *Spinoza: A Life of Reason*. New York: Modern Classics, 1932.

Periodicals

The McCarthy Advance. Chicago: Official newspaper of McCarthy for President, 1968.

The Militant. Official newspaper of the Socialist Workers Party, 1939–.

The National Prohibitionist. Official newspaper of the National Prohibition Party, to 1911 (Succeeded by National Statesman, q.v.).

National Statesman. Official newsletter of the National Prohibition Party.

New Militant. New York: 1934–1936. Official organ of the Workers Party of the United States.

New York (New York) *Times*. 1851–.

The Presidential Convention Newsletter. Libertarian Party, August, 1975.

Weekly People. Palo Alto, California, 1891–. Official newspaper of the Socialist Labor Party; formerly published in New York.

The Whig Banner. Vol. 1. Palatka, Fla.: 1846.

Whig Banner Melodist. Philadelphia: Published for the Whigs of the Union, 1844.

Workers World. New York: Official newspaper of the Workers World Party.

Studies and Histories of Political Parties and Elections

Ader, Emile Bertrand. *The Dixiecrat Movement: Its Role in Third Party Politics*. Washington, D.C.: Public Affairs Press, 1955.

Ahern, M. L. *The Great Revolution: A History of the Rise and Progress of the People's Party in the City of Chicago and County of Cook, With Sketches of the Elect in Office*. Chicago: Lakeside Publishing and Printing, 1874.

Anspach, Frederick Rinehart. *The Sons of the Sires: A History of the Rise, Progress, and Destiny of the American Party, and Its Probable Influence on the Next Presidential Election*. Philadelphia: Lippincott, Grambo, 1855.

Argersinger, Peter H. *Populism and Politics: William Alfred Peffer and the People's Party*. Lexington: U. Press of Kentucky, 1974.

Arnett, Alex Mathews. *The Populist Movement in Georgia*. New York: Columbia U. Press, 1922.

Babin, Gregory, and Leonard Babin. *Presidential Candidates, 1789–1944*. Rochester, N.Y.: self-published, 1946.

Bagby, Wesley Marvin. *Progressivism's Debacle: The Election of 1920*. Ann Arbor, Mich.: U. Microfilms, 1954.

____. *The Road to Normalcy: The Presidential Campaign and Election of 1920*. Baltimore: Johns Hopkins U. Press, 1962.

Bain, Richard C. and Judith H. Parris. *Convention Decisions and Voting Records*. Washington, D.C.: Brookings Institution, 1973.

Baker, Peter John. "The Presidential Election of 1928." Master's thesis, Georgetown U., 1950.

Bart, Philip, ed. *Highlights of a Fighting History: 60 Years of the Communist Party, USA*. New York: International, 1979.

Bell, Daniel. *Marxian Socialism in the United States*. Princeton, N.J.: Princeton U. Press, 1967.

Bennett, David Harry. *Demagogues in the Depression: American Radicals and the Union Party, 1932–1936*. New Brunswick, N.J.: Rutgers U. Press, 1969.

Blanchard, Rufus. *Rise and Fall of Political Parties in the United States*. Chicago: National School Furnishing, 1884.

Blocker, Jack S. *Retreat from Reform: The Prohibition Movement in the United States, 1890–1913*. Westport, Conn.: Greenwood Press, 1976.

Blue, Frederick J. *The Free Soilers: Third Party Politics, 1848–1854*. Urbana: U. of Illinois Press, 1973.

Burdette, Franklin L. *The Republican Party: A Short History*. New York: Van Nostrand, 1972.

Burr, John Green. "The Age of Antiformalism in American Politics, 1790–1800: A Preamble to a History of the American Whig Party." Master's thesis, Georgetown U., 1951.

Byrne, Gary C. and Paul Marx. *The Great American Convention: A Political History of Presidential Elections*. Palo Alto, Calif.: Pacific Books, 1976.

Carlson, Jody. *George C. Wallace and the Politics of Powerlessness: The Wallace Campaigns for the Presidency, 1964–1976*. New Brunswick, N.J.: Transaction Books, 1981.

Chambers, William Nisbet. *The Democrats, 1789–1964: A Short History of a Popular Party*. Princeton, N.J.: Van Nostrand, 1964.

Chester, Lewis, Godfrey Hodgson, and Bruce Page. *An American Melodrama: The Presidential Campaign of 1968*. New York: Viking Press, 1969.

Clancy, Herbert John. *The Presidential Election of 1880*. Chicago: Loyola U. Press, 1958.

Cohn, David Lewis. *The Fabulous Democrats: A History of the Democratic Party in Text and Pictures*. New York: Putnam, 1956.

Coleman, Charles Herbert. *The Election of 1868: The Democratic Effort to Regain Control*. New York: Columbia U. Press, 1933.

Colvin, David Leigh. *Prohibition in the United States*. New York: George H. Doran, 1926.

Crandall, Andrew Wallace. *The Early History of the Republican Party, 1854–1856*. Boston: R. G. Badger, 1930. Reprint, Gloucester, Mass.: P. Smith, 1960.

Cummings, Milton C., Jr., ed. *The National Election of 1964*. Washington, D.C.: Brookings Institution, 1966.

Curtis, Francis. *The Republican Party: A History of Its Fifty Years' Existence and a Record of Its Measures and Leaders, 1854–1904*. 2 vols. New York: G. P. Putnam's Sons, 1904.

David, Paul T., Ralph M. Goldman, and Richard C. Bain. *The Politics of National Party Conventions*. Washington, D.C.: Brookings Institution, 1960.

Diamond, Martin. *Socialism and the Decline of the American Socialist Party*. Chicago: U. of Chicago Press, 1956.

Dobbs, Farrell. *Revolutionary Continuity: Birth of the Communist Movement, 1918–1922*. New York: Pathfinder Press, n.d.

____. *Revolutionary Continuity: Marxist Leadership in the U.S.—The Early Years, 1848–1917*. New York: Monad Press, 1981.

Draper, Theodore. *The Roots of American Communism*. New York: Viking Press, 1957.

Dyson, Lowell K. *Red Harvest: The Communist Party and American Farmers*. Lincoln: U. of Nebraska Press, 1982.

Eldersveld, Samuel James. *Political Parties: A Behavioral Analysis*. Chicago: Rand McNally, 1964.

Ernst, Harry. *The Primary That Made a President: West Virginia, 1960*. New York: McGraw-Hill Book, 1962.

Ershkowitz, Herbert. *The Origin of the Whig and Democratic Parties: New Jersey Politics, 1820–1837*. Washington, D.C.: U. Press of America, 1982.

Feigert, Frank B. *Parties and Politics in America*. Boston: Allyn and Bacon, 1976.

Fenton, John H. *People and Parties in Politics: Unofficial Makers of Public Policy*. Glenview, Ill.: Scott, Foresman, 1966.

Ferguson, Paul H. *The American Party Drama*. New York: Vantage Press, 1966.

Fess, Simeon Davidson. *The History of Political Theory and Party Organization*. Boston: Ginn, 1910.

Fifty Years of American Marxism, 1891–1941. . . . New York: Socialist Labor Party of America, 1941.

Fine, Nathan. *Labor and Farmer Parties in the United States, 1828–1928*. New York: Rand School of Social Science, 1928.

Fischer, David H. *The Revolution of American Conservatism: The Federalist Party in the Era of Jeffersonian Democracy*. New York: Harper and Row, 1965.

Fite, Emerson David. *The Presidential Campaign of 1860*. Port Washington, N.Y.: Kennikat Press, 1967.

Flower, Frank Abial. *History of the Republican Party, Embracing Its Origin, Growth and Mission. . . .* Grand Rapids, Mich.: Union Book, 1884.

Foley, John, Dennis A. Britton, and Eugene B. Everett, Jr., eds. *Nominating a President: The Process and the Press*. New York: Praeger, 1980.

Foner, Eric. *Free Soil, Free Labor, Free Men: The Ideology of the Republican Party Before the Civil War*. New York: Oxford U. Press, 1970.

Foster, William Zebulon. *History of the Communist Party of the United States*. New York: International, 1952.

Gammon, Samuel Rhea. *The Presidential Campaign of 1832*. Baltimore: Johns Hopkins Press, 1922. Reprint, New York: Da Capo Press, 1967.

Gardner, C. *Acts of the Republican Party as Seen by History*. Winchester, Va.: Eddy Press Corporation, 1906.

Garson, Robert A. *The Democratic Party and the Politics of Sectionalism, 1941–1948*. Baton Rouge: Louisiana State U. Press, 1974.

Gieske, Millard L. *Minnesota Farmer-Laborism: The Third Party Alternative*. Minneapolis: U. of Minnesota Press, 1979.

Gilder, George, and Bruce K. Chapman. *The Party That Lost Its Head*. New York: A. A. Knopf, 1966.

Glad, Paul W. *McKinley Bryan and the People*. Philadelphia: Lippincott, 1964.

Goldman, Ralph Morris. *The Democratic Party in American Politics*. New York: Macmillan, 1966.

____. *Search for Consensus: The Story of the Democratic Party*. Philadelphia: Temple U. Press, 1979.

Goldwin, Robert A., ed. *Political Parties in the United States: Four Essays*. Chicago: U. of Chicago Press, 1961.

____. *Political Parties in the Eighties*. Washington, D.C.: American Enterprise Institute for Public Policy Research and Kenyon College, 1980.

____. *Political Parties USA*. Chicago: Rand McNally, 1964.

Good, Josephine L. *The History of Women in Republican National Conventions and Women in the Republican National Committee*. Washington, D.C.: Republican National Committee, 1963.

Goodman, William. *The Party System in America*. Englewood Cliffs, N.J.: Prentice-Hall, 1980.

____. *The Two-Party System in the United States*. Princeton, N.J.: Van Nostrand, 1964.

Goodwyn, Lawrence. *Democratic Promise: The Populist Movement in America*. New York: Oxford U. Press, 1976.

____. *The Populist Moment: A Short History of the Agrarian Revolt in America*. New York: Oxford U. Press, 1978.

Gordy, John Pancoast. *A History of Political Parties in the United States in Three Volumes*. 3 vols. Athens: Ohio, 1895.

Gould, Lewis L. *Progressives and Prohibitionists: Texas Democrats in the Wilson Era*. Austin: U. of Texas Press, 1973.

Greenstein, Fred. *The American Party System and the American People*. Englewood Cliffs, N.J.: Prentice-Hall, 1963.

Hackney, Sheldon. *Populism: The Critical Issues*. Boston: Little, Brown, 1971.

____. *Populism to Progressivism in Alabama*. Princeton, N.J.: Princeton U. Press, 1969.

Haworth, P. L. *The Hayes-Tilden Disputed Presidential Election of 1876*. Cleveland, Ohio: n.p., 1906.

Haynes, Frederick Emory. *Third Party Movements Since the Civil War*. Iowa City: State Historical Society of Iowa, 1916. Reprint, New York: Russell and Russell, 1966.

Hecker, Eugene Arthur. *Political Parties in the United States, 1789–1949: From George Washington to Harry Truman—A Summary*. St. Louis, Mo.: Commercial Color Press, 1952.

Henderson, Gordon Grant. *An Introduction to Political Parties*. New York: Harper and Row, 1976.

Herzog, Arthur. *McCarthy for President*. New York: Viking Press, 1969.

Hesseltine, William Best. *The Rise and Fall of Third Parties, From Anti-Masonry to Wallace*. Washington, D.C.: Public Affairs Press, 1948.

____. *Third Party Movements in the United States*. Princeton, N.J.: Van Nostrand, 1962.

Hicks, John Donald. *The Populist Revolt: A History of the Farmers, Alliance and the People's Party*. Lincoln: U. of Nebraska Press, 1961.

Hillquit, Morris. *History of Socialism in the United States*. 5th ed. New York: Funk and Wagnalls, 1910.

Hinshaw, David. *Political Party Platforms*. New York: Institute of Public Relations, 1944.

Hofstadter, Richard. *The Idea of a Party System: The Rise of Legitimate Opposition in the United States, 1780–1840*. Berkeley: U. of California Press, 1969.

Holcombe, Arthur Norman. *The New Party Politics*. New York: W. W. Norton, 1933.

____. *The Political Parties of Today*. New York: Harper, 1924. Reprint, New York: Arno Press, 1974.

Holmes, Arthur. *Parties and Their Principles: A Manual of Political Intelligence, Exhibiting the Origin, Growth, and Character of National Parties. . . .* New York: D. Appleton, 1859.

Hornig, Edgar Albert. *The Presidential Election of 1908*. Ann Arbor, Mich.: U. Microfilms, 1955.

Howe, Irving, and Lewis Coser. *The American Communist Party: A Critical History, 1919–1957*. Boston: Beacon Press, 1957.

Huckshorn, Robert Jack. *Political Parties in America*. North Scituate, Mass.: Duxbury Press, 1978.

Hurt, Peyton. *The Rise and Fall of the "Know Nothings" in California*. San Francisco: California Historical Society, 1930.

Ippolito, Dennis S., and Thomas G. Walker. *Political Parties, Interest Groups and Public Policy: Group Influence in American Politics*. Englewood Cliffs, N.J.: Prentice-Hall, 1980.

Isaacs, William. *Contemporary Marxian Political Movements in the United States, 1917–1939*. New York: U. Press, 1942.

James, Judson L. *American Political Parties in Transition*. New York: Harper and Row, 1974.

____. *American Political Parties: Potential and Performance*. New York: Pegasus, 1969.

Johnson, Donald B. *The Republican Party and Wendell Willkie*. Urbana: U. of Illinois Press, 1960.

Johnson, Samuel A. *Essentials of Political Parties: Their Relation to American Government*. Woodbury, N.Y.: Barron's Educational Series, 1974.

Jones, Charles, O. *The Republican Party in American Politics*. New York: Macmillan, 1965.

Jones, Chester Lloyd, comp. *Readings on Parties and Elections in the United States*. Westport, Conn.: Negro Universities Press, 1970. Reprint of 1912 edition.

Jones, Stanley Llewellyn. *The Presidential Election of 1896*. Madison: U. of Wisconsin Press, 1964.

Keefe, William J. *Parties, Politics and Public Policy in America*. 2d ed. Hinsdale, Ill.: Dryden Press, 1976.

Keller, David R. *Nativism or Sectionalism: A History of the Know Nothing Party in Lancaster County, Pennsylvania*. Lancaster: Lancaster County Historical Society, 1971.

Kelsey, Rayner Wickersham. *Political Parties in the United States*. Philadelphia: McKinley, 1930.

Kent, Frank Richardson. *The Democratic Party: A History*. New York: Century, 1928. Reprint, New York: Johnson Reprint, 1968.

Key, Valdimer Orlando, Jr. *Politics, Parties, and Pressure Groups*. 5th ed. New York: Thomas Y. Crowell, 1964.

King, Josephine Yager. *The Concept of a Two-Party System in American Political Thought, 1789–1888*. Ann Arbor, Mich.: U. Microfilms, 1950.

Kleeberg, Gordon S. *The Formation of the Republican Party as a National Political Organization*. New York: Moods, 1911.

Kuhn, Henry, and Olive M. Johnson. *The Socialist Labor Party During Four Decades, 1890–1930*. New York: New York Labor News, 1931.

Ladd, Everett Carl. *Transformations of the American Party System: Political Coalitions from the New Deal to the 1970's*. New York: W. W. Norton, 1975.

Libby, Orin Grant. "A Study of the Greenback Movement, 1876–1884." *Transactions of the Wisconsin Academy of Science, Arts and Letters* (1900): 530–543.

A List of Recent References on a Farmer-Labor Party. Mena, Ark.: Commonwealth College, 1936.

Livermore, Shaw. *The Twilight of Federalism: The Disintegration of the Federalist Party, 1815–1830*. Princeton, N.J.: 1862.

Long, John D., ed. *The Republican Party: Its History, Principles, and Policies*. New York: M. W. Hazen, 1888.

Lowe, David E. "NSRP: A Sordid Tale." *Anti-Defamation League Bulletin* 42 (March 1985): 3–6.

MacDougall, Curtis Daniel. *Gideon's Army*. 3 vols. New York: Marzani and Munsell, 1965.

MacKay, Kenneth Campbell. *The Progressive Movement of 1924*. New York: Columbia U. Press, 1947.

Macy, Jesse. *Political Parties in the United States, 1846–1861*. New York: Macmillan, 1900. Reprint, New York: Arno Press, 1974.

Madron, Thomas William, and Carl P. Chelf. *Political Parties in the United States*. Boston: Holbrook Press, 1974.

Manly, Chesly. *The Twenty Year Revolution: From Roosevelt to Eisenhower*. Chicago: Henry Regnery, 1954.

Mann, Arthur. *The Progressive Era: Liberal Renaissance or Liberal Failure?* New York: Holt, Rinehart and Winston, 1963.

Manning, Joseph Columbus. *Fadeout of Populism: Presenting, in Connection, the Political Combat Between the Pot and the Kettle*. New York: T. A. Hebbons, 1928.

Margulies, Herbert F. *The Decline of the Progressive Movement in Wisconsin*. Madison: State Historical Society of Wisconsin, 1968.

Markowitz, Norman D. *The Rise and Fall of the People's Century: Henry A. Wallace and American Liberalism, 1941–1948*. New York: Free Press, 1973.

Martin, Roscoe Coleman. *The People's Party in Texas: A Study in Third Party Politics*. Austin: U. of Texas Press, 1970.

Mayer, George H. *The Republican Party, 1854–1964*. New York: Oxford U. Press, 1964, 1967.

Mayfield, John. *Rehearsal for Republicanism: Free Soil and the Politics of Antislavery*. Port Washington, N.Y.: Kennikat Press, 1980.

Mayo, Charles G., and Beryl L. Crowe, comps. *American Political Parties: A Systematic Perspective*. New York: Harper and Row, 1967.

Mazmanian, Daniel A. *Third Parties in Presidential Elections*. Washington, D.C.: Brookings Institution, 1974.

McCarthy, Charles. *The Anti-Masonic Party: A Study of Political Antimasonry in the United States, 1827–1840*. American Historical Association Report, 1902, I. Washington, D.C.: Government Printing Office, 1903.

McCormick, Richard Patrick. *The Second American Party System: Party Formation in the Jacksonian Era*. Chapel Hill: U. of North Carolina Press, 1966.

McDonald, Neil A. *The Study of Political Parties*. New York: Random House, 1955.

McDonald, William P., and Jerry G. Smoke. *The Peasants' Revolt: McCarthy 1968*. Mt. Vernon, Ohio: Noe-Bixby Publications, 1969.

McGuire, James K. *The Democratic Party of the State of New York: A History of the Origin, Growth and Achievements. . . .* New York: United States History, 1905.

McKay, Kenneth Campbell. *The Progressive Movement of 1924.* New York: Octagon Books, 1947.

McNeal, John Edward. *The Antimasonic Party of Lancaster County, 1828–1843.* Lancaster, Pa.: Lancaster County Historical Society, 1965.

Meredith, Milo R. *Practical Politics and Democracy: An Exposition of the Political Phase of Our Democracy—How the Political Party System of Government Operates in the United States of America.* Boston: Meador, 1945.

Mering, John Vollmer. *The Whig Party in Missouri.* Columbia: U. of Missouri Press, 1967.

Michelet, Simon. *Women Delegates at National Conventions.* Washington, D.C.: National Get-Out-The-Vote Club, 1928.

Miller, Raymond Curtis. "The Populist Party in Kansas." Ph.D. thesis, U. of Chicago, 1928.

Minor, Henry Augustine. *The Story of the Democratic Party.* New York: Macmillan, 1928.

Minor, Robert. *The Heritage of the Communist Political Association.* New York: Workers Library, 1944.

Moos, Malcolm Charles. *The Republicans: A History of Their Party.* New York: Random House, 1956.

Munger, Daniel. *Political Landmarks: Or, History of the Parties, From the Organization of the General Government to the Present Day.* Detroit, Mich.: Fox and Eastman, 1851.

Murphrey, Elizabeth H., ed. *Socialist Party of America Papers, 1897 to 1964: Guide to the Microfilm Edition.* Glen Rock, New Jersey, Microfilming Corporation of America, 1975. Reprint, Glen Rock, N.J.: Addendum, 1977.

Myers, Constance A. *The Prophet's Army: Trotskyists in America, 1928–1941.* Westport, Conn.: Greenwood Press, 1976.

Myers, William Starr. *The Republican Party: A History.* Rev. ed. New York: Century, 1931. Reprint, New York: Johnson Reprint, 1968.

Myrus, Donald, ed. *Law and Disorder: The Chicago Convention and Its Aftermath.* Chicago: self-published, 1968.

Nichols, Ray Franklin. *The Invention of American Political Parties.* New York: Macmillan, 1967.

Olin, Spencer C. *California's Prodigal Sons: Hiram Johnson and the Progressives, 1911–1917.* Berkeley: U. of California Press, 1968.

Oliphant, Laurence. *On the Present State of Political Parties in America.* Edinburgh, Scotland: W. Blackwood and Sons, 1866.

Ormsby, Robert McKinley. *A History of the Whig Party: Or, Some of Its Main Features. . . .* 2d ed. Boston: Crosby, Nichols, 1860.

Ostrogorskii, Moisei Iakovlevich. *Democracy and the Organization of Political Parties.* New York: Haskell House, 1970.

Overdyke, William Darrell. *The Know-Nothing Party in the South.* Baton Rouge: Louisiana State U. Press, 1950. Reprint, Gloucester, Mass.: Peter Smith, 1968.

Owens, John Robert, and P. J. Staudenraus. *The American Party System: A Book of Readings.* New York: Macmillan, 1965.

Parmet, Herbert S., and Marie B. Hecht. *Never Again: A President Runs for a Third Term.* New York: Macmillan, 1968.

The Party Battle. New York: Arno Press, 1974.

Peel, Roy V., and Thomas Claude Donnelly. *The 1932 Campaign: An Analysis.* New York: Farrar and Rinehart, 1935.

____. *The 1928 Campaign: An Analysis.* New York: R. R. Smith, 1931. Reprint, New York: Arno Press, 1974.

Penniman, Howard R. *The American Political Process.* Princeton, N.J.: Van Nostrand, 1962.

____. *Sait's American Parties and Elections.* New York: Appleton-Century-Crofts, 1948.

Peterson, Walfred Hugo. *The Foreign Policy and Foreign Policy Theory of the American Socialist Party, 1901–1920.* Ann Arbor, Mich.: U. Microfilms, 1958.

Pinchot, Amos Richards Eno. *History of the Progressive Party, 1912–1916.* New York: New York U. Press, 1958.

Plunkett, Margaret Louise. "A History of the Liberty Party with Emphasis Upon Its Activities in the Northeastern States." Ph.D. diss., Cornell U., 1930.

Polakoff, Keith Ian. *Political Parties in American History.* New York: Wiley, 1981.

Polenberg, Richard, ed. *Radicalism and Reform in the New Deal.* Menlo Park, Calif.: Addison-Wesley, 1972.

Pomper, Gerald. *Nominating the President: The Politics of Convention Choice.* Evanston, Ill.: Northwestern U. Press, 1963.

Ranney, Austin, ed. *The Doctine of Responsible Party Government: Its Origins and Present State.* Urbana: U. of Illinois Press, 1954.

Ranney, Austin, and Willmoore Kendall. *Democracy and the American Party System.* New York: Harcourt, Brace and World, 1956.

Remini, Robert Vincent, ed. *The Election of Andrew Jackson.* Philadelphia: Lippincott, 1963.

Ricker, Ralph Ross. *The Greenback-Labor Movement in Pennsylvania.* Bellefonte, Pa.: Pennsylvania Heritage, 1966.

Ring, Elizabeth. *The Progressive Movement of 1912 and the Third Party Movement of 1924 in Maine.* Orono: U. of Maine Press, 1933.

Roberts, Edwin A. *Elections 1964.* Silver Spring, Md.: National Observer, 1964.

Robinson, Edgar Eugene. *The Evolution of American Political Parties; A Sketch of Party Development.* New York: Harcourt, Brace, 1924.

____. *They Voted for Roosevelt: The Presidential Vote, 1932–1944.* New York: Octagon Books, 1970.

Robinson, Lloyd. *The Hopefuls: Ten Presidential Campaigns.* Garden City, N.Y.: Doubleday, 1966.

Rockwood, D. Stephen, Cecilia Brown, Kenneth Eshleman, and Deborah Shaffer. *American Third Parties Since the Civil War: An Annotated Bibliography.* New York: Garland, 1985.

Rohlfing, Charles C., and James C. Charlesworth. *Parties and Politics: 1948.* Philadelphia: American Academy of Political and Social Science, 1948.

Roseboom, Eugene Holloway. *A Short History of Presidential Elections.* New York: Collier Books, 1967.

Roseboom, Eugene Holloway, and Alfred E. Eckes, Jr. *A History of Presidential Elections from George Washington to Jimmy Carter.* 4th ed. New York: Macmillan, 1979.

Rosenstone, Steven J., Roy L. Behr, and Edward H. Lazarus. *Third Parties in America: Citizen Response to Major Party Failure.* Princeton, N.J.: Princeton U. Press, 1984.

Rosewater, Victor. *Backstage in 1912: The Inside Story of the Split Republican Convention.* Philadelphia: Dorrance, 1932.

Ross, Earle D. *The Liberal Republican Movement.* Seattle: U. of Washington Press, 1970.

Ross, Irwin. *The Loneliest Campaign: The Truman Victory of 1948.* New York: New American Library, 1968.

Runyon, John H., Jennefer Verdini, and Sally S. Runyon. *Source Book of American Presidential Campaign and Election Statistics, 1948–1968.* New York: Frederick Ungar, 1971.

Scammon, Richard M., and Alice V. McGillivray. *America Votes.* Washington, D.C.: Congressional Quarterly, various years.

Schattschneider, Elmer Eric. *Party Government.* New York: Farrar and Rinehart, 1942.

____. *Political Parties and Democracy.* New York: Holt, Rinehart and Winston, 1964.

____. *The Struggle for Party Government.* College Park: U. of Maryland, 1948.

Schlesinger, Arthur Meier, Jr., ed. *History of U.S. Political Parties.* 4 vols. New York: Chelsea House, 1973.

____, ed. *History of American Presidential Elections, 1789–1968.* 4 vols. New York: Chelsea House, 1971.

Schmeckebier, Laurence Frederick. *History of the Know Nothing Party in Maryland.* Baltimore, Md.: Johns Hopkins U. Press, 1899.

Schnapper, Morris Bartel. *Grand Old Party: The First Hundred Years of the Republican Party, A Pictorial History.* Washington, D.C.: Public Affairs Press, 1955.

Schrank, Alice DeGanton. *Political Parties: Promise and Performance.* Bay City, Mich.: Rich-Errington, 1975.

Seasholes, Bradbury. *Voting, Interest Groups, and Parties.* Glenview, Ill.: Scott, Foresman, 1967.

Seilhamer, George Overcash. *History of the Republican Party.* New York: Judge, 1899.

Selby, Paul. *Genesis of the Republican Party in Illinois.* Decatur: Illinois Republican Editorial Association, 1904.

Shadegg, Stephen C. *What Happened to Goldwater? The Inside Story of the 1964 Republican Campaign.* New York: Holt, Rinehart and Winston, 1965.

Shadgett, Olive Hall. *The Republican Party in Georgia, From Reconstruction Through 1900.* Athens: U. of Georgia Press, 1964.

Shannon, David A. *The Decline of American Communism: A History of the Communist Party of the United States Since 1945.* New York: Harcourt, 1959.

____. *The Socialist Party of America.* Chicago: Quadrangle Books, 1967.

____. *The Socialist Party of America: A History.* New York: Macmillan, 1955.

Shaw, Barton C. *The Wool-Hat Boys: Georgia's Populist Party.* Baton Rouge: Louisiana U. Press, 1984.

Shenk, Hiram Herr. *The Know-Nothing Party in Lebanon County.* Lebanon, Pa.: Lebanon County Historical Society, 1907.

Sherman, Richard B. *The Republican Party and Black America from McKinley to Hoover, 1896–1933.* Charlottesville: U. Press of Virginia, 1973.

Silbey, Joel H. *A Respectable Minority: The Democratic Party in the Civil War Era, 1860–1868.* New York: Norton, 1977.

Simms, Henry Harrison. *The Rise of the Whigs in Virginia, 1824–1840.* Richmond, Va.: William Boyd Press, 1929.

Sloane, William Milligan. *Party Government in the United States of America.* New York: Harper and Brothers, 1914.

Smalley, Eugene Virgil. *A Brief History of the Republican Party from Its Organization to the Presidential Campaign of 1888.* 3d ed. New York: J. B. Alden, 1888.

Smallwood, Frank. *The Other Candidates.* Hanover, N.H.: U. Press of New England, 1983.

Smith, Florence Emeline. "The Populist Movement and Its Influence in North Carolina." Ph.D. thesis, U. of Chicago, 1929.

Smith, Joseph P. *History of the Republican Party in Ohio.* Chicago: Lewis, 1898.

Smith, Theodore Clarke. *The Free Soil Party in Wisconsin.* Madison: State Historical Society of Wisconsin, 1895.

____. *The Liberty and Free Soil Parties in the Northwest.* New York: Russell and Russell, 1967.

Socialist Labor Party and the U.S.S.R. New York: New York Labor News, 1978.

Sorauf, Frank Joseph. *Party Politics in America.* Boston: Little, Brown, 1968.

____. *Political Parties in the American System.* Boston: Little, Brown, 1964.

Soule, Leon Cyprian. *The Know Nothing Party in New Orleans: A Reappraisal.* Baton Rouge: Louisiana Historical Association, 1962.

Spooner, Walter W. *The Democratic Party: A History.* New York: Liberty History, 1920.

Stabler, John Burgess. *A History of the Constitutional Union Party: A Tragic Failure.* Ann Arbor, Mich.: U. Microfilms, 1954.

Stanley, Frederic Arthur. *The Third Party.* New York: Macaulay, 1915.

Stedman, Murray Salisbury, and Susan W. Stedman. *Discontent at the Polls: A Study of Farmer and Labor Parties, 1827–1948.* New York: Russell and Russell, 1950, 1967.

Stern, Clarence Ames. *Golden Republicanism: The Crusade for Hard Money.* Ann Arbor: U. of Michigan, 1964.

Stevens, Harry Robert. *The Early Jackson Party in Ohio.* Durham, N.C.: Duke U. Press, 1957.

Stickney, Charles. *Know-Nothingism in Rhode Island.* Providence: Rhode Island Historical Society, 1894.

Stolen, Mildred Clara. "Influence of the Democratic Element in the Republican Party of Illinois and Indiana, 1854–1860." Ph.D. diss., Indiana U., 1938.

Storms, Roger C. *Partisan Prophets: A History of the Prohibition Party.* Denver, Colo.: National Prohibition Foundation, 1972.

Stout, Richard T. *People!* New York: Harper and Row, 1970.

Sundquist, James L. *Dynamics of the Party System: Alignment and Realignment of Political Parties in the United States.* Washington, D.C.: Brookings Institution, 1973.

Supple, Robert Vincent. *The Political Rise of William Jennings Bryan from 1888 to the Nomination for the Presidency by the Democratic Party in 1896.* Ann Arbor, Mich.: U. Microfilms, 1952.

Tamiment Library. *A Guide to Daniel Bell's Files on the Communist Party (U.S.A.), Socialist Party, and Labor Unions.* New York: Tamiment Library, 1970.

Thayer, George. *The Farther Shores of Politics.* New York: Simon and Schuster, 1967.

Thomas, G. Scott. *The Pursuit of the White House: A Handbook of Presidential Election Statistics and History.* New York: Greenwood Press, 1987.

Thomas, Evangeline. *Nativism in the Old Northwest, 1850–1860.* Washington, D.C.: Catholic U. of America, 1936.

Thomas, Harrison Cook. "The Return of the Democratic Party to Power in 1884." Ph.D. diss., Columbia U., 1919.

Thompson, Charles Manfred. *Attitude of the Western Whigs Toward the Convention System.* Cedar Rapids, Iowa: Torch Press, 1912.

____. *The Genesis of the Whig Party in Illinois.* Springfield, Ill.: State Journal, 1913.

____. *The Illinois Whigs Before 1846.* Ph.D. diss., U. of Illinois, 1915.

Thomson, Charles Alexander Holmes, and Francis M. Shattuck. *The 1956 Presidential Campaign.* Washington, D.C.: Brookings Institution, 1960.

Tillett, Paul, ed. *Inside Politics: The National Conventions, 1960.* Dobbs Ferry, N.Y.: Oceana, 1962.

Townsend, Walter A. *Illinois Democracy: A History of the Party and Its Representative Members—Past and Present.* Springfield, Ill.: Democratic Historical Association, 1935.

Trachtenberg, Alexander L., et al., eds. *The American Socialists and the War Board, with Socialists and the Problems of War.* New York: Garland, 1973. Reprint of 1917 edition.

Tucker, Ray Thomas, and Frederick R. Barkley. *Sons of the Wild Jackass.* Boston: L. C. Page, 1932.

Turner, Andrew Jackson. *The Genesis of the Republican Party.* Portage, Wis.: self-published, 1898.

Tweedy, John. *A History of the Republican National Conventions from 1856 to 1908.* Danbury, Conn.: self-published, 1910.

U.S. Congress, House Committee on Internal Security. *Communists in the Trotsky Mold: A Report on the Socialist Workers Party and the Young Socialist Alliance.* Washington, D.C.: Government Printing Office, 1971.

U.S. Congress, House Committee on Internal Security. *The Workers World Party and Its Front Organizations: A Study.* Washington, D.C.: Government Printing Office, 1974.

U.S. Congress, House Committee on Un-American Activities. *Un-American Propaganda Activities in the United States (Gerald L. K. Smith)*, Hearings, 30 January 1946. Washington, D.C.: Government Printing Office, 1946.

Usher, Ellis Baker. *The Greenback Movement of 1876–1884 and Wisconsin's Part in It*. Milwaukee, Wis.: E. B. Usher, 1911.

Van Buren, Martin. *Inquiry into the Origin and Course of Political Parties in the United States*. New York: Hurd and Houghton, 1867.

Viorst, Milton. *Fall From Grace: The Republican Party and the Puritan Ethic*. New York: Simon and Schuster, 1971.

Vorees, Edith. *Political Parties in the United States*. New York: Pageant Press, 1960.

Wachman, Marvin. *History of the Social-Democratic Party of Milwaukee, 1897–1910*. Urbana: U. of Illinois Press, 1945.

Walton, Haines, Jr. *Black Political Parties*. New York: Free Press, 1972.

____. *Black Republicans: The Politics of the Black and Tans*. Metuchen, N.J.: Scarecrow Press, 1975.

____. *The Negro in Third Party Politics*. Philadelphia: Dorrance, 1969.

Warren, Frank A. *An Alternative Vision: The Socialist Party in the 1930's*. Bloomington: Indiana U. Press, 1974.

Watson, Dick, John Elliott, and Dick Strome. *Zacherly for President*. New York: Macaulay, 1960.

Weinstein, James. *The Decline of American Socialism, 1912–1925*. New York: Monthly Review Press, 1967.

Weston, Florence. *The Presidential Election of 1828*. Washington, D.C.: Ruddick Press, 1938. Reprint, Philadelphia: Porcupine Press, 1974.

Wharton, O. P. *Lincoln and the Beginning of the Republican Party in Illinois*. Springfield: Illinois State Journal, 1912.

White, Charles M. *The Socialist Labor Party, 1890–1903*. Ann Arbor, Mich.: U. Microfilms, 1959.

White, F. Clifton, and William J. Gill. *Suite 3505: The Story of the Draft Goldwater Movement*. New Rochelle, N.Y.: Arlington House, 1967.

White, William Allen. *What It's All About: Being a Reporter's Story of the Early Campaign of 1936*. New York: Macmillan, 1936.

Whitehurst, Alto Lee. "Martin Van Buren and the Free Soil Movement." Ph.D. thesis, U. of Chicago, 1932.

Williams, R. Hal. *The Democratic Party and California Politics, 1880–1896*. Stanford, Calif.: Stanford U. Press, 1973.

Witcover, Jules. *Marathon: The Pursuit of the Presidency, 1972–1976*. New York: Viking Press, 1977.

Woodard, Douglas Dutro. *The Presidential Election of 1896*. Master's thesis, Georgetown U., 1949.

Woodburn, James Albert. *American Politics: Political Parties and Party Problems in the United States—A Sketch of American Party History . . .*, New York: G. P. Putnam's Sons, 1924.

Wynar, Lubomyr Roman. *American Political Parties: A Selective Guide to Parties and Movements of the 20th Century*. Littleton, Colo.: Libraries Unlimited, 1969.

Young, Alfred Fabian. *The Democratic-Republican Movement in New York State, 1788–1797*. Ann Arbor, Mich.: U. Microfilms, 1958.

Youngdale, James M., ed. *Third Party Footprints*. Minneapolis, Minn.: Ross and Haines, 1966.

Proceedings and Minutes/Convention Records Democratic Party

Official Proceedings of the Democratic National Convention, Held in Cincinnati, June 2–6, 1856. Cincinnati, Ohio: Enquirer Steam Printing Establishment, 1856.

Official Proceedings of the Democratic National Convention, Held in 1860, at Charleston and Baltimore. . . . Cleveland, Ohio: Nevins' Print, 1860.

Official Proceedings of the Democratic National Convention, Held in 1864 at Chicago. Chicago: Times Steam Book and Job Printing House, 1864.

Official Proceedings of the Democratic National Convention, Held at New York, July 4–9, 1868. Boston: Rockwell and Rollins, Printers, 1868.

Official Proceedings of the Democratic National Convention, Held at Baltimore, July 9, 1872. Boston: Rockwell and Churchill, Printers, 1872.

Official Proceedings of the Democratic National Convention, Held at St. Louis, Missouri, June 27th, 28th and 29th, 1876. St. Louis, Mo.: Woodward, Tiernan and Hale, 1876.

Official Proceedings of the Democratic National Convention, Held in Cincinnati, Ohio, June 22d, 23d, and 24th, 1880. . . . Dayton, Ohio: Daily Journal Book and Job Rooms, 1882.

Official Proceedings of the Democratic National Convention, Held in Chicago, Illinois, July 8th, 9th, 10th and 11th, 1884. New York: D. Taylor's Democratic Printing House, 1884.

Official Proceedings of the Democratic National Convention, Held in St. Louis, Missouri, June 5th, 6th, and 7th, 1888. St. Louis, Mo.: Woodward and Tiernan Printing, 1888.

Official Proceedings of the Democratic National Convention, Held in Chicago, Illinois, June 21st, 22d, and 23d, 1892. Chicago: Cameron Amberg, 1892.

Official Proceedings of the Democratic National Convention, Held in Chicago, Illinois, July 7th, 8th, 9th, 10th and 11th, 1896. Logansport, Ind.: Wilson, Humphreys, 1896.

Official Proceedings of the Democratic National Convention, Held at Kansas City, Missouri, July 4th, 5th, and 6th, 1900. Chicago: McLellan Printing, 1900.

Official Proceedings of the Democratic National Convention, Held in St. Louis, Missouri, July 6, 7, 8, 9, 1904. . . . New York: Publishers' Printing, 1904.

Official Proceedings of the Democratic National Convention, Held at Denver, Colorado, July 7, 8, 9, and 10, 1908. . . . Chicago: Western Newspaper Union, 1908.

Official Proceedings of the Democratic National Convention, Held at Baltimore, Maryland, June 25, 26, 27, 28, 29 and July 1 and 2, 1912. . . . Chicago: Peterson Linotyping, 1912.

Official Proceedings of the Democratic National Convention, Held at St. Louis, Missouri, June 14, 15, and 16th, 1916. Chicago: Democratic National Committee, 1916.

Official Proceedings of the Democratic National Convention, Held at San Francisco, California, June 28, 29, 30, July 1, 2, 3, 5, and 6, 1920. Indianapolis, Ind.: Bookwalter-Ball Printing, 1920.

Official Proceedings of the Democratic National Convention, Held in Madison Square Garden, New York City, June 24, 25, 26, 27, 28, 30, July 1, 2, 3, 4, 5, 7, 8, and 9, 1924. Indianapolis, Ind.: Bookwalter-Ball-Greathouse Printing, 1924.

Official Proceedings of the Democratic National Convention, Held in Houston, Texas, June 26, 27, 28 and 29, 1928. Indianapolis, Ind.: Bookwalter-Ball-Greathouse Printing, 1929.

Official Proceedings of the Democratic National Convention, 1972. Washington, D.C.: Democratic National Committee, 1972.

Official Proceedings of the Democratic National Convention, New York City, July, 1976. Washington, D.C.: Democratic National Committee, 1976.

Official Report of the Proceedings of the Democratic National Convention held at Chicago, Illinois, June 27th to July 2nd, Inclusive, 1932, Resulting in the Nomination of Franklin D. Roosevelt (of New York) for President and John N. Garner (of Texas) for Vice-President. Washington, D.C.: Democratic National Committee, 1932.

Official Report of the Proceedings of the Democratic National Convention held at Philadelphia, Pennsylvania, June 23rd to June 27th, Inclusive, 1936, Resulting in the Re-Nomination of Franklin D. Roosevelt (of New York) for President and John N. Garner (of Texas) for Vice-President. Washington, D.C.: Democratic National Committee, 1936.

Official Report of the Proceedings of the Democratic National Convention held at Chicago, Illinois, July 15th to July 18th, Inclusive, 1940, Resulting in the Re-Nomination for Franklin D. Roosevelt of New York for President and the Nomination of Henry A. Wallace of Iowa for Vice President. Washington, D.C.: Democratic National Committee, 1940.

Official Report of the Proceedings of the Democratic National Convention, Chicago, Illinois, July 19th to July 21st, Inclusive, 1944, Resulting in the Re-Nomination of Franklin D. Roosevelt of New York for President and the Nomination of Harry S. Truman of Missouri for Vice President. Chicago: Democratic National Committee, 1944.

Official Report of the Proceedings of the Democratic National Convention held at Chicago, Illinois, July 21 to July 26, Inclusive, 1952, Resulting in the Nomination of Adlai E. Stevenson of Illinois for President and the Nomination of John J. Sparkman of Alabama for Vice President. Washington, D.C.: Democratic National Committee, 1955.

Official Report of the Proceedings of the Democratic National Convention, August 13 Through August 17, 1956, Resulting in the Re-Nomination of Adlai E. Stevenson of Illinois for President and in the Nomination of Estes Kefauver of Tennessee for Vice President. Washington, D.C.: Democratic National Committee, 1960.

Official Report of the Proceedings of the Democratic National Convention and Committee, 1960. Washington, D.C.: National Document, 1965.

Official Report of the Proceedings of the Democratic National Convention held August 24–27, 1964, Resulting in the Nomination of Lyndon B. Johnson of Texas for President, and in the Nomination of Hubert H. Humphrey of Minnesota for Vice President. Washington, D.C.: Democratic National Committee, 1968.

Proceedings of the National Democratic Convention, Held in Baltimore, on the 5th of May, 1840. . . . Baltimore, Md.: Republican, 1840.

Proceedings of the Democratic National Convention, Held at Baltimore, May 22, 1848. Washington, D.C.: Blair and Reeves, 1848.

Proceedings of the Democratic National Convention, Held at Baltimore, June 1–5, 1852. Washington, D.C.: R. Armstrong, 1852.

Report of the Proceedings of the 35th Quadrennial Convention of the Democratic National Committee, August 26–30, 1968, Resulting in the Nomination of Hubert H. Humphrey of Minnesota for President and in the Nomination of Edmund S. Muskie of Maine for Vice President. Chicago: Democratic National Committee, 1968.

Republican Party

Harvey, Charles Mitchell. *Republican National Convention, St. Louis, June 16th to 18th, 1896: With a History of the Republican Party. . . .* St. Louis, Mo.: I. Haas Publishing and Engraving, 1896.

Official Proceedings of the Eleventh Republican National Convention, Held in the City of St. Louis, Mo., June 16, 17, and 18, 1896. . . . Minneapolis, Minn.: Harrison and Smith, Printers, 1896.

Official Proceedings of the Republican Convention Convened in the City of Pittsburgh, Pennsylvania, on the 22d of February, 1856. Washington, D.C.: Republican Association of Washington, 1856.

Official Proceedings of the Republican National Convention, Held at Chicago, June 3, 4, 5 and 6, 1884. . . . Minneapolis, Minn.: C. W. Johnson, 1903.

Official Proceedings of the Thirteenth Republican National Convention, Held in the City of Chicago, June 21, 22, 23, 1904. . . . Minneapolis, Minn.: Harrison and Smith, 1904.

Official Proceedings of the Twelfth Republican National Convention, Held in . . . Philadelphia, June 19, 20 and 21, 1900. Philadelphia: Dunlap Printing, 1900.

Official Report of the Proceedings of the Eighteenth Republican National Convention, Held in Cleveland, Ohio, June 10, 11 and 12, 1924. . . . New York: Tenny Press, 1924.

Official Report of the Proceedings of the Fifteenth Republican National Convention, Held in Chicago, Illinois, June 18, 19, 20, 21 and 22, 1912. . . . New York: Tenny Press, 1912.

Official Report of the Proceedings of the Fourteenth Republican National Convention, Held in Chicago, Illinois, June 16, 17, 18 and 19, 1908. . . . Columbus, Ohio: Republican National Convention, 1908.

Official Report of the Proceedings of the Nineteenth Republican National Convention, Held in Kansas City, Missouri, June 12, 13, 14 and 15, 1928. . . . New York: Tenny Press, 1928.

Official Report of the Proceedings of the Seventeenth Republican National Convention, Held in Chicago, Illinois, June 8, 9, 10, 11 and 12, 1920. . . . New York: Tenny Press, 1920.

Official Report of the Proceedings of the Sixteenth Republican National Convention, Held in Chicago, Illinois, June 7, 8, 9 and 10, 1916, Resulting in the Nomination of Charles Evans Hughes, of New York, for President, and the Nomination of Charles Warren Fairbanks, of Indiana, for Vice-President. New York: Tenny Press, 1916.

Official Report of the Proceedings of the Twentieth Republican National Convention, Held in Chicago, Illinois, June 14, 15 and 16, 1932. . . . New York: Tenny Press, 1932.

Official Report of the Proceedings of the Twenty-Eighth Republican National Convention. . . . Washington, D.C.: Republican National Committee, 1966.

Official Report of the Proceedings of the Twenty-First Republican National Convention, Held in Cleveland, Ohio, June 9, 10, 11 and 12, 1936. . . . New York: Tenny Press, 1936.

Official Report of the Proceedings of the Twenty-Fourth Republican National Convention, Held in Philadelphia, Pennsylvania, June 21, 22, 23, 24 and 25, 1948. . . . Washington, D.C.: Judd and Detweiler, 1948.

Official Report of the Proceedings of the Twenty-Second Republican National Convention, Held in Philadelphia, Pennsylvania, June 24, 25, 26, 27 and 28, 1940. . . . Washington, D.C.: Judd and Detweiler, 1940.

Official Report of the Proceedings of the Twenty-Third Republican National Convention, Held in Chicago, Illinois, June 26, 27 and 28, 1944. . . . Washington, D.C.: Judd and Detweiler, 1944.

Official Report of the Proceedings . . . Resulting in the Nomination of Dwight D. Eisenhower, of New York, for President and the Nomination of Richard M. Nixon, of California, for Vice President. Washington, D.C.: Republican National Committee, 1952.

Official Report of the Proceedings . . . Resulting in the Nomination of Dwight D. Eisenhower, of Pennsylvania, for President and the Nomination of Richard M. Nixon, of California, for Vice President. Washington, D.C.: Republican National Committee, 1956.

Official Report of the Proceedings . . . Resulting in the Nomination of Richard M. Nixon, of California, for President, and the Nomination of Henry Cabot Lodge, of Massachusetts, for Vice President. Washington, D.C.: Republican National Committee, 1960.

Proceedings of a Convention of Republican Delegates from the Several States in the Union, for the Purpose of Nominating a Candidate for the Office of Vice-President of the United States. Baltimore, Md.: S. Hacker, 1831.

Proceedings of the National Union Convention, Held in Baltimore, Maryland, June 7th and 8th, 1864. New York: Baker and Godwin, Printers, 1864.

Proceedings of the National Union Republican Convention, Held at Chicago, May 20 and 21, 1868. Chicago: Evening Journal Printing, 1868.

Proceedings of the National Union Republican Convention, Held at Philadelphia, June 5 and 6, 1872. . . . Washington, D.C.: Gibson Brothers, Printers, 1872.

Proceedings of the Ninth Republican National Convention, Held at Chicago, Illinois, June 19, 20, 21, 22, 23 and 25, 1888. . . . Chicago: Republican National Committee, 1888.

Proceedings of the Republican National Convention, Held at Chicago, May 16, 17, and 18, 1860. Albany, N.Y.: Weed, Parsons, Printers, 1860.

Proceedings of the Republican National Convention, Held at Cincinnati, Ohio . . . June 14, 15, and 16, 1876. . . . Concord, N.H.: Republican Press Association, 1876.

Proceedings of the Republican National Convention, Held at Chicago, Illinois . . . June 2d, 3d, 4th, 5th, 7th and 8th, 1880. . . . Chicago: J. B. Jeffrey Printing and Publishing House, 1881.

Proceedings of the Tenth Republican National Convention, Held in the City of Minneapolis, Minnesota, June 7, 8, 9 and 10, 1892. . . . Minneapolis, Minn.: Harrison and Smith, Printers, 1892.

Republican National Convention Proceedings. Washington, D.C.: Republican National Committee, various years.

Smith, Henry Harrison. All the Republican National Conventions from Philadelphia, June 17, 1856: Proceedings, Platforms, and Candidates. . . . Washington, D.C.: R. Beall, 1896.

OTHER PARTIES

Breitman, George, ed. The Founding of the Socialist Workers Party: Minutes and Resolutions, 1938–1939. New York: Monad Press, 1982.

The Eighteenth Convention of the Socialist Party of America, Detroit, Michigan, May 30th–June 3rd, 1934. Chicago: National Executive Committee, Socialist Party, 1934.

The Founding of the Socialist Workers Party: Minutes and Resolutions, 1938–1939. New York: Monad Press, n.d.

Mailly, William, ed. National Convention of the Socialist Party, Held at Chicago, Illinois, May 1 to 6, 1904. Chicago: National Committee, Socialist Party, 1904.

The March of Socialism, 1928–1932: Journal of the Seventeenth National Convention, Socialist Party, Milwaukee, Wisconsin, May 20–24, 1932. Chicago: Socialist Party, 1932.

Massachusetts Liberty Convention, and Speech of Hon. John P. Hale, Together with His Letter Accepting His Nomination for the Presidency. Boston: Massachusetts Liberty Party, 1848.

Minutes of the Prohibition Party National Convention. N.p.: Prohibition Party, 1920.

National Convention of the Workers (Communist) Party of America: Report of the Central Executive Committee. Chicago: Daily Worker, 1925.

Nineteenth National Convention, Socialist Labor Party, April 25–April 28, 1936. New York: National Executive Committee, Socialist Labor Party, 1938.

Official Minutes of the Nominating Convention of the Peace and Freedom Party of the State of Washington. Seattle, Washington, Peace and Freedom Party, 17 September 1968.

Oliver Dyer's Phonographic Report of the Proceedings of the National Free Soil Convention at Buffalo, New York, August 9th and 10th, 1848. Buffalo, N.Y.: G. H. Derby, 1848.

Platform of the Prohibition Party, 1916. Chicago: Prohibition National Campaign Committee, 1916.

Proceedings of the Democratic Whig National Convention, Which Assembled at Harrisburg, Pennsylvania, on the Fourth of December, 1839, for the Purpose of Nominating Candidates for President and Vice-President of the United States. Harrisburg, Pa.: R. S. Elliott, 1839.

Proceedings of the National Convention of the Socialist Labor Party, 9th–10th. New York: Socialist Labor Party, 1896–1901.

Proceedings of the National Liberty Convention, Held at Buffalo, New York, June 14th and 15th, 1848: Including the Resolutions and Addresses Adopted by That Body, and Speeches of Beriah Green and Gerrit Smith on That Occasion. Utica, N.Y.: S. W. Green, 1848.

Proceedings of New Jersey Socialist Unity Conference. Jersey City, N.J.: Socialist Party-Socialist Labor Party, 1906.

Proceedings of the Ninth Annual Convention of the Socialist Labor Party, July 4th to July 10th, 1896. New York: I. Goldman, Steam Printer, 1896.

Proceedings of the 17th National Convention of the Socialist Labor Party, May 12–14, 1928. N.p.: 1928.

Proceedings of the Socialist Labor Party National Convention. N.p.: 1900.

Proceedings of the Socialist Labor Party National Convention. N.p.: 1904.

Proceedings of the Socialist Labor Party National Convention. N.p.: 1936.

Records of the Socialist Labor Party of America. 39 reels. Madison, Wisconsin, Division of Archives and Manuscripts, State Historical Society of Wisconsin, 1970. Microfilm.

Resolutions Adopted by the Antimasonic Members of the Legislature of Massachusetts, and Other Citizens of Boston and Vacinity, Opposed to the Nomination of Martin Van Buren and Richard M. Johnson . . . , (In Favor of D. Webster and F. Granger for President and Vice President). Boston: D. Hooton, Printer, 1836.

Socialist Labor Party Collected Pamphlets. Washington, D.C.: Library of Congress, HX 81 .S55.

Socialist Labor Party File. Washington, D.C.: Library of Congress, XJK 2391 .S63.

Socialist Labor Party Convention Proceedings. Proceedings of the Ninth Annual Convention of the Socialist Labor Party, July 4th to July 10th, 1896. New York: I. Goldman, Steam Printer, 1896.

Socialist Labor Party Convention Proceedings, various years.

Socialist Party National Convention Minutes. N.p.: Socialist Party, 1900–.

Socialist Party, 1975 Convention Report. Milwaukee: Socialist Party, U.S.A., 1975.

Socialist Party Papers, in Duke U. Library, Durham, N.C.

Socialist Workers Party File. Washington, D.C.: Library of Congress, XJK 2391 .S64.

Spargo, John, ed. National Convention of the Socialist Party, Held at Indianapolis, Indiana, May 12 to 18, 1912. Chicago: M. A. Donohue, 1912.

Work, John M., ed. National Convention of the Socialist Party, Held at Chicago, Illinois, May 10 to 17, 1908. Chicago: Allied Printing Trades Council, 1908.